AF488301

SCHOLIA PUGILLĀTŌRIA
VOLUME I · 2022–2023

SCHOLIA PUGILLĀTŌRIA
VOLUME I · 2022–2023

SCHOLIA PUGILLĀTŌRIA
A Journal of Personal Combat
VOLUME I · 2022–2023

The Development of Boxing: The Ancient World

Castor Dioscurus & Pollux Dioscurus

0x1768.47fe.f30e.6db6.d82a.ee7c.3bef.a921.3f7a.8c68.ee18.1a60.462d.7938.46a7.e063
0x4699.1d93.d126.1fb0.6302.ffc8.376a.996f.f015.1377.40a8.6aa1.8b6c.3c27.f112.2617

First paperback edition November 2023.

ISBN 979-8-218-32551-0

WWW.PUGILISM.CC

Published by West Martian Limited Company, Cheyenne, Wyoming.

WWW.WESTMARTIAN.COM

TABLE OF CONTENTS

The Development of Boxing: Origins in Biomechanics and Social Mechanics; The Ancient World (Prehistory)

Castor Dioscurus; Pollux Dioscurus

Contents

Abstract

We survey the prehistorical and historical development of boxing as a tradition of upright hand-to-hand combat. The sociological origin of conspecific violence in primates and hominids is discussed, and comparison with precedents in other animal species is made. Boxing is defined as a family of related orthograde agonistics. We speculate on the motivation behind boxing's perennial popularity among humans, and lay the groundwork for a thorough historical examination.

Scholia Pugillātōria 1 (2022): 1–22.

Address author correspondence to scholia@protonmail.com.

1 Introduction

Modern sport boxing (in both its combat-performative and exercise-oriented forms) descends from a rich tradition of unarmed upright hand-to-hand combat. Contemporary boxing has solidified a number of conventions and technologies of interpersonal combat articulated during two active periods of development in the West: a long childhood in the ancient world and an adolescence from the seventeenth through twentieth centuries. Many of the features we associate indelibly with boxing are modern innovations: time-limited rounds, the neutral corner, the hook, the count, the seconds. Others are ancient when not aboriginal: gloves, the ring, the referee, the cutman. Ancient boxing and early modern boxing as preserved in the received and discovered record also present many features no longer present due to the evolution of rules, safety protocols, and perhaps spectator taste: for example, injurious strikes, kicks, chancery, weaponized gloves, and throws. In this article, we survey the prehistorical and historical development of boxing as a tradition of upright hand-to-hand combat. The sociological origins of conspecific violence in primates and hominids is discussed, and comparison with precedents in other animal species is made. We ask why boxing remains perennially popular among humans, and lay the groundwork for a thorough historical examination.

We begin by identifying the unique elements that are present in boxing and review the criteria by which ancient accounts and depictions of boxing have been identified. We proceed through a prehistorical and historical recapitulation of boxing's development, including a biomechanical consideration of several features. As rules and conventions evolve, the practiced sport itself changes in response.

1.1 Separating the modern from the ancient

In the ancient world, boxing was a mimetic practice adopted by a variety of cultures, but its earliest recorded origins are found in third millennium Mesopotamia, extending as far north as the Black Sea region. There is little unambiguous textual evidence for boxing before the Hellenistic era, when literary depictions of boxing became relatively commonplace. Visual representations of boxing are often in the eye of the beholder. However, we believe that the unique mechanics of unarmed orthograde combat can help disambiguate these examples. Graphic representations of boxing are remarkably similar over thousands of years: fighters step towards one another with their legs in profile, their bared chests twisted towards the viewer; each raises one hand in a fist and their forearms cross. The hand closest to the viewer (the back hand) is lowered, with the elbow bent. This is the "stock" illustration of boxing attested all the way from Mesopotamia in the third millennium BC to Bœotia and Northern Italy in the early first. Interesting variations occur, but the stability of this form is remarkable (Festuccia 2016, p. 108). It is tempting to find in this depiction some echo of modern boxing praxis, to gaze across four thousand years and witness the same scene taking place at a local recreational center or boxing gym. But in this we may be misleading ourselves.

Observing these ancient images, we are naturally inclined to reflect on the modern preoccupations of boxing, that is, of its participants, spectators, and critics. However, we might do well to approach these forms as if they were utterly alien to us. Consider for instance the *Boxing Boys* of Akrotiri. If we take for granted some of the published hypotheses about this fresco (Dioscurus and Dioscurus 2022), we then encounter a truly curious spectacle taking place on Bronze Age Thera. It depicts an orthograde, paired combat in which pre-adolescent boys devel each other with a gloved hand while grasping each other's long locks of hair with the other, the fingers of their ungloved hands free to inflict even more punishment (Immerwahr 1990). One boy wears jewelry; both are naked but for a ceremonial girdle, possibly linked to a sea goddess (Parke 1987). The encounter arguably results in concussion and lasting injury to the spine (Davis 1977, Ferrence and Bendersky 2005). We wonder who might sanction such a duel, and for what purpose? Is this boxing, or something entirely different? Was this an elite sport of princes, a coming-of-age ceremony anticipated by parents eager to see the young fighters as the embodiment of their family's strength and vitality (Marinatos 1984, Morgan 2000)? Or perhaps these were ritual reënactors of a sacred story whose details were only half-remembered by the organizers of the combat. Or was it all merely a dance? The images simply do not tell us all we would like to know. Unfortunately, with no textual descriptions to accompany such images, with only the context of surrounding artefacts and the location where they were found as our guides, we are left to make our best guesses on limited information. Still, we argue that diverse types of Bronze Age boxing attested in the ancient Mediterranean and Near East form a coherent practice.

After a little more than a century of recorded boxing in England, Fewtrell (1790) commented on what he called "pitched battles." He described such an encounter in this way: "Two men free from enmity are matched in fight, without any cause for passion, without any motive for vengeance, nay immediately after having mutually given the most known marks of good will, they assault each other with all appearance of deadly hatred and determined revenge. The ties of humanity are broken, and Nature revolts at the fight" (pp. 10–11). Is he praising or criticizing the encounter? The perplexity with which boxing is viewed by moderns likely gripped the ancients, as well. Despite its brutality, boxing is by no means nonsensical violence; to characterize it as such is to miss a fundamental aspect of masculinity in ancient, early modern, and modern western culture. Using the earliest visual records of boxing and ancient textual sources, we argue that boxing has always been laden with value and virtue.

1.2 Definitions: Hand-to-hand combat and boxing

Conspecific violence is ubiquitous in the animal kingdom, with struggles over living environment, food and water, mates, and status being continually contested by members of most species. If we include survival in the face of attack by a predator, we can reason that all nonsessile creatures engage in something we could term "combat". Humans, primates, and presumably early hominids all engage(d) in warfare and hand-to-hand combat, whether armed or unarmed. Recent theories about the evolution of the hominin fist propose that our species became fit for closed-fist (boxing-style) combat, presumably due to pressures of sexual selection. Forms of "play-fighting" are frequently observed in immature mammals, including primates, where hand/forelimb strikes are involved. This suggests a role for ontogeny in the development of pugilistic behavior and may even have implications for the development of human fighting abilities across the lifespan.

Is boxing a practical fighting technique? Is it "merely" performative? What selective pressures have shaped it to mirror the æsthetic tastes and sensibilities of societies that boxed? What is the elemental, unchangeable core of boxing? We recognize boxing (synonymous with pugilism) as a family of orthograde combat techniques between two combatants.[1] We also consider boxing to be a sport practiced by those convention deems "boxers" (such as Roman boxers employing the *cæstus* or Greek boxers engaging in kicking). Much like the Germanic language family, swaths of mutually intelligible traditions span a dazzling variety of practices, and little can be said in common other than "orthograde combat": variations include kicking, grappling to the ground, use of hand-augmenting weapons, and helmets. In the modern era, boxing has become symbolically linked with the iconic padded boxing glove, which is arguably ancillary to the kinetic aspects at the core of boxing praxis. Boxing is differentiated from several East Asian martial arts such as Okinawan karate by a relative absence of formalism (e.g. *kata*) and the general (but not universal) absence of kicking and kneeing. Certain criteria have been used by previous authors in distinguishing boxers from other combatants; we examine the validity of these suppositions incidentally below and in subsequent articles.

2 Hominin combat and the biomechanics of violence

The ætiology of violence in humans and hominins is by no means a settled matter. To best understand the origins of ancient boxing, we will concern ourselves in this section with what is known about violence between male primates—and to a far more limited extent, other vertebrates—at different stages of their lifespan. We examine two lines of evidence: hominin aggression and biomechanical considerations.

2.1 Animal aggression

Male intrasexual competition is widely distributed throughout the animal kingdom. Fighting ability and performance in combat have been recognized as a determining factor in female mate selection since Darwin (1859). "Agonistic behaviors help to ensure survival, provide advantage in competition, and communicate social status" (Fortes et al. 2017, p. 98).

Multiple studies have shown that aggressive behavior against conspecifics is rewarding, that positive outcomes can lead to more aggression, and that aggressive behavior can be a source of pleasure (Kudryavtseva 2020). It is also evident that "positive fighting experience" in mice can lead to a kind of "addiction" to aggressive behavior (ibid.). This takes place due to a neurochemical imbalance whereby inhibitory processes are dominated by excitation processes. These processes are themselves enhanced by the release of dopamine accompanying repeated experiences of victory over a conspecific. What inferences can we draw from this research about combat between humans?

Punching performance in hand-to-hand combat serves as a signal for sexual selection; skill at fighting likely translated into fitness at survival in the ancestral environment. Fighting to terms other than death not only reduces the devastating consequences of losing, it preserves necessary resources by strictly limiting and agreeing on the stakes of particular contests. We thus observe a spectrum from fighting, to ritual fighting, to play fighting.

---

[1] According to a second century AD inscription, at least one Greek community in Asia Minor designated a version of pankration that allowed only "upright hitting", a technique called ορτθοπαιία (from 'upright' and 'hit' or 'play') (Gardiner 1930, p. 221).

In species that exhibit ritualized fighting, the phenomenon is proposed to develop from injurious fighting in three stages (Lorenz 1969, pp. 108–109):

- Increase in time between threatening movements and assault;
- Exaggeration, repetition, and colorfulness of threatening movements;
- Inhibition against devastating injury.

Groos (1898) argues that play-fighting behavior in animals is "preparation for the later struggle for the female" (Groos 1898, p. 135). He provides detailed observations of "tussling" in a wide variety of animals, particularly during their youth. This includes dogs, cats, hyenas, bears, badgers, and so forth. His description of seals is particularly charming, if a little on the anthropomorphic side:

> [Y]oung sea bears also play and quarrel like puppies. The father stands by and watches them, and if a quarrel begins in earnest he urges them on with growls, and kisses and licks the victor, then pushes him to the ground, and is pleased if he resists (Groos 1898, p. 144).

Because this "tussling" behavior is observed in non-carnivorous animals, Groos (1898) reasons that it must be largely due to the instinct to compete with rival conspecifics to gain sexual advantage, not as training to hunt, *vel sim*. However, Groos also admits that some animals, like dogs, may continue play-fighting well into adulthood. Tautologically, perhaps, he ascribes this merely to "playful" behavior (Groos 1898, p. 149). Play-fighting "furnish[es] practice for the contest of courtship, without being in any sense satisfying to the sexual instinct. Among many animals that play in this way the female yields to the victor of the males without resistance" (Groos 1898, p. 136).

Chimpanzee aggression sometimes results in reconciliation ("affiliative postconflict reunion"). Reconciliation as a social feature of combat includes spontaneous invitation and preferential contact with former opponents (Preuschoft et al. 2002, Suchak et al. 2016, Suchak and de Waal 2016).

2.2 Hominin aggression

Mankind engages in social violence of a kind distinct from that of any other known species. Some of this is norm-enforcing (such as parental or military discipline or some forms of bullying) while other violence may be ritual (such as human sacrifice or entertainment). These forms of violence are distinct from dominance displays due to the additional broader social substrate which enables them and lends them meaning. There are several competing (and complementary) theories about the utility of violence which seek to explain why it persists in ritualized form: a game-theoretic analysis, a naturalist account, a theory of civilizational preparedness, and a theory of play.

2.2.1 Evolutionary Game Theory

It has been argued by primatologists that "uncontrolled aggression is certainly disastrous to primate societies, but the complete absence of aggression may be equally disastrous" (Bernstein and Gordon 1974, p. 311). They maintain that ritualized aggression among primates enhances social cohesion. Of primates Bernstein (1984, p. 302) writes: "Many responses in an agonistic exchange probably serve primarily to assess the ability and willingness of an opponent to escalate and continue the encounter."

Compare Lazar's (2016) ethical observation that "individual human beings enjoy fundamental rights to life and liberty, which prohibit others from harming them in certain ways." If aggression (in both expression and release) is a necessary component of stable human civilization and coexistence, then we need to understand—as a descriptive rather than prescriptive ethics—why modern *Homo sapiens* continues to fight.

Per Wilson (1978, p. 100): "Human beings have a marked hereditary predisposition to aggressive behavior." Freud understood aggression as a drive that seeks release. Lorenz elaborated on the similarity between aggression in humans and other animal species. Like Freud, Lorenz agreed that aggression required release, which can be sought in competitive sport. In *The Anatomy of Human Destructiveness*, Fromm (1973) argued that humans have a death instinct unique to our species, which propels us to forms of violence unknown in the animal world. Wilson disagreed with all of this. He argued for at least seven different types of aggression, all with different ætiologies:

1. Defense and conquest of territory
2. Assertion of dominance within well-organized groups
3. Sexual aggression
4. (Acts of aggression by which weaning is terminated)
5. Aggression against prey
6. Defensive counterattacks against predators
7. Moralistic and disciplinary aggression used to enforce the rules of a society

Which of these might apply to the development of pugilism? We remove only one from the list (item four, given in parentheses above). All of the others are candidate possibilities that shaped *Urboxen*. (We further add an eighth option: scapegoating or sacrifice, as distinct from items 2 and 7.) Wilson argues that aggression in animal species is density-dependent and is exhibited in relation to the scarcity of essential resources. The natural outcome of aggression is that organisms move away from each other, die faster, and give birth less (Wilson 1978, p. 101).

One argument against Freud and Lorenz' drive–discharge model is the observation that war does not seem to release enough steam, as it were, to displace aspects of lesser violence.[2] In fact, minor forms of personal violence like combat sports are perhaps even more prominent in warlike societies.

"The channels of formalized aggression are deep; culture is likely to turn into one or the other but not to avoid them completely. These channels are shaped by genetic predisposition to learn aggressive responses and the physical properties of the home range that favor particular forms of the responses" (Wilson 1978, pp. 114–115). According to this hypothesis, there are many ways that a stereotypical violence pattern, such as boxing, might develop. Consider a society in which male reproduction is limited by a relatively small female population. In such a case, pugilism between males might be used to determine which male is more fit to reproduce. This convention would help avoid excessive and potentially lethal competition

---

[2] Wilson includes among these: "combative sports, malevolent witchcraft, tattooing and other ritualized forms of body mutilation, and the harsh treatment of deviates" (Wilson 1978, p. 105).

that could affect activities like hunting and warfare where a large number of males is desirable and, in any event, bears less direct relation to the number of females. The specific conditions of boxing would be affected by material culture and adaptable traditions already present in the group. These might include a particular attitude towards blood, materials available for weaponizing the hands, and existing rites of passage for young men. It would be helpful to recognize how pugilism varied across ancient cultures and what elements remained the same, to better understand how the aggressive nature of humans is expressed in formalized ways. As with many other aspects of ancient culture, it may be impossible to determine whether boxing developed independently in a variety of Mediterranean and Near Eastern societies or whether it developed once and spread. In either case, boxing clearly scratched an itch among ancient people. The transcendence of boxing across space and time, when so many other human activities have disappeared or transmogrified, is truly impressive.

According to Wilson (1978), "[H]uman aggression cannot be explained as a dark-angelic flaw or a bestial instinct.... Human beings are strongly predisposed to respond with unreasoning hatred to external threats and to escalate their hostility sufficiently to overwhelm the source of the threat by a respectably wide margin of safety" (p. 119). The author goes on to admit that, "our brains do appear to be programmed to the following extent: we are inclined to partition other people into friends and aliens.... We tend to fear deeply the actions of strangers and to solve conflict by aggression" (ibid.).

In *The Selfish Gene*, Dawkins sets out to explain Lorenz' observation that animals fight in such a way that they do minimal damage to one another. "To a survival machine, another survival machine (which is not its own child or another close relative) is a part of its environment.... It differs from a rock or a river in one important respect: it is inclined to hit back" (Dawkins 1976, p. 71). However, Dawkins reasons, "[T]here is no obvious merit in indiscriminately trying to kill rivals" (ibid., p. 73). He declares, "There are costs as well as benefits resulting from outright pugnacity" (ibid.). Dawkins then goes on to outline an "evolutionarily stable strategy" for intraspecific competition. Consistent with his thesis against group selection and based on the work of John Maynard Smith and George Price (a paper entitled "The Logic of animal conflict"), Dawkins argues that a population composed of genetically-predisposed 'hawks' and 'doves' (or fighters and lovers, if you will), naturally settles on a stable ratio where 'doves' outnumber 'hawks'. Given the naïve assumptions of such a model, it has been elaborated to include 'retaliators,' which behave like doves until attacked; and 'prober-retaliators' which do the same, but experiment with unprovoked attack on occasion. Simulations show that 'retaliator' is the most stable strategy, followed closely by 'prober-retaliator' (ibid., p. 80). In a population of retaliators, no other population is able to invade and succeed. According to Dawkins, this explains the 'gloved fist' aspect of animal aggression without resorting to arguments based on "the good of the species". It may be of interest to us, as well.

If early humans behaved as organisms with the dispositions available in the modified dove–hawk contest, they, too, would naturally settle on an equilibrium with a preponderance of retaliators in the gene pool. The retaliation strategy looks a lot like a boxing match: "a retaliator behaves like a hawk when he is attacked by a hawk, and like a dove when he meets a dove" (ibid., pp. 79–80). A successful boxer, arguably, will employ some combination of the retaliator and prober-retaliator strategies to maximize potential for success in the ring (and minimize potential for injury when confronted by a 'hawk').[3] The stability of the (prober-)retaliator strategy may be what makes boxing such a ubiquitous form of male–male competition across human societies.

2.2.2 Naturalist origins

Although "nature red in tooth and claw" (a phrase due to Alfred Lord Tennyson) was a position notoriously attributed to the first advocates of the theory of evolution, thinkers earlier than the evolutionary biologists have also recognized upon naturalist grounds the origins and necessity or inevitability of personal violence. Political philosopher Joseph de Maistre wrote (in the mouth of a character), "In the immense sphere of living things, the obvious rule is violence, a kind of inevitable frenzy which arms all things *in mutua funera*. ... Once you enter the animal kingdom, the law suddenly becomes frighteningly obvious. A power at once hidden and palpable appears constantly occupied in bringing to light the principle of life by violent means. In each great division of the animal world, it has chosen a certain number of animals charged with devouring the others .... There is not an instant of time when some living creature is not devoured by another" (de Maistre 1821). Notwithstanding his picturesque phrasing, de Maistre recognizes the self-evident fact that nature exists in a churn of competitive violence. Any naturalist account must grapple with the observable facts that violence is endemic to the activities of life at all stages of development.

2.2.3 Naturalism and preparedness

Another theorist of mass violence (war) rather than personal combat, German World War I officer Ernst Jünger proposed that violence is, or early became, innate to the human experience of the world: "War has raised us to fight, and we will remain fighters as long as we live" (Jünger 1922). Jünger (1951) further elaborates that civility is but veneer over an iconic figure fulfilling the Latin maxim *se vis pacem, para bellum*: "Long periods of peace foster certain optical illusions: one is the conviction that the inviolability of the home is grounded in the constitution, which should guarantee it. In reality, it is grounded in the family father, who, sons at his side, fills the doorway with an axe in his hand" (Jünger 1951, p. 78). Together, these present a way to sociologically understand combat sports, including boxing, as a call for the men of a community to be always vigilant and prepared for combat at need.

2.2.4 Play and sport

As mentioned above, play-fighting is frequently observed throughout the animal kingdom and serves as a proxy for genetic fitness in nature. Play encourages physical development and preparation against an eventual need for future combat. Play serves a key role in psychological development (e.g. hand-eye coordination), social development, and physical development. J. S. Russell considered the value of "dangerous sport" for the normal developmental behavior of adults and children: "Dangerous sport with its higher level of danger can provide a venue

---

[3] The classic division in boxing styles between boxers and brawlers may at first blush seem roughly equivalent to the distinction btween doves and hawks. The comparison is not entirely apt, however, since doves must run away when attacked and a boxer does not do so (at least not in any kind of terminative sense). On the other hand, if dove-like behavior in the boxing ring is considered periodic rather than terminal retreat, then the application of Maynard Smith and Price's work may still be relevant.

for participants not only to test themselves against danger to see what they are capable of, but it also creates the possibility of realizing an important fact in human life that leads to living more fully and meaningfully, that is, the fact that we are mortal beings" (Russell 2005; cf. Russell 2007). (Russell hints at a deep psychological point as well: at some stage in the conscious awakening of mankind, our ancestors recognized their own mortality in a way that differed from animal instinct.) Play affords developing children the opportunity to observe and internalize the importance of rules, honor, status, and sportsmanship; in short, play as social activity socializes its participants.

2.3   The biomechanics of orthograde combat

Orthograde combat is not unique to humans, but in other species it frequently represents a departure from the norm, such as two dogs standing on their hind legs to gambol or kill, or two bears standing to claw and swat each other. Only kangaroos seem to mimic the otherwise hominid behavior of striking with the forelimbs, as "boxing kangaroos" will use their short forearms to hold opponents still while they kick at them.

In an anthropological attempt to understand the uprightness of human combat, we invoke the theory of "spinal catastrophism" (Moynihan 2019). Spinal catastrophism draws attention to the spine's literal embodiment of the history of evolutionary trauma, including the cervical spine's role in the final erection of the skull and face in hominid evolution. The spine facilitates reflex arcs which allow hair-trigger reactions to an antagonist's movements. The orthograde spine embodies the distinctly human nature of boxing as two opponents confront one another, able to look each other in the face and present the entire forward surface of their bodies in personal combat. This mutual upright facing paradoxically demonstrates disarmament and engagement simultaneously, as the vulnerable belly and organs are forward and protected only by the guard and reaction of the fighter's skill and chance.

A number of researchers have recently proposed and studied the theory that hominin hand evolution occurred along a line highly compatible with hand-to-hand striking-based combat (Carrier 2011, Morgan and Carrier 2013, Horns et al. 2015). According to the pugilism hypothesis of hominin hand evolution, humans can strike with 55% more force using a "fully buttressed" fist than an unbuttressed fist, and with twice as much force as an open-handed slap. "The evolutionary significance of the proportions of the hominin hand…[made] it possible to use the hand as a club during fighting" (Horns et al. 2015, p. 3215).[4] Altogether, the ontogeny of the hominin fist, with a high thumb-to-digit length ratio in hominins versus the last common ancestor of humans and chimps, exhibits the hallmarks of an evolutionarily selected feature.

2.4   Biomechanics of striking

We refer to all hand-based blows, punches, and elbows as "strikes" and all leg-based kicks and knees as "kicks". These include many kinds of contact (such as eye gouges, eye rakes, and "fibbing") which are so illegal in modern sport boxing as to be almost forgotten, as well as

---

[4]Gloved versus ungloved combat does not seem to affect the biomechanics of striking: "Few differences were evident when comparing the kinematics of gloved versus bare-handed punches" (Whiting et al. 1988, p. 130). See also Dinu and Louis (2020).

common but modern innovations (such as the hook). We denote chancery, clinching, and to-the-ground wrestling (as in pankration) as "grappling".

How does an archetypal untrained, inexperienced human strike under duress in combat? The joints which administer strikes using the arms are the shoulder and elbow. The elbow tends to naïvely favor the biomechanics of a hammer blow, that is, a hit along the plane of the arm striking with the little finger muscles (the meat at the edge of the hand opposite the thumb). The shoulder is farther away and conditions the motion less, providing a fulcrum around which the hammer blow occurs.

A developmentally primitive fighter will also be fighting bare-fisted ("bare-knuckle"), which tends to expose the fine bones of the fist to damage and limits the power and targets of blows. For these and related striking angles, even glancing blows can break the fifth and fourth metacarpals, a condition known eponymously as "boxer's fracture" (Soong et al. 2010). Between damage to the fingers, fist, wrist, and forearm, the hammer strike is often abandoned in an experienced or reflective fighting strategy. The canonical "karate chop," however, retains something of its flavor.

The next ontogenetic development after the hammer strike is the direct punch, which has a variety of nuanced forms, all of which entail that the strike occurs in line with the forearm and is delivered and absorbed by the fist, primarily in the second and third metacarpals. (These bones are harder and the knuckles tend to be more calloused than the fourth and fifth metacarpals.) A buttressed fist can deliver kinetic energy effectively into another's body, while remaining capable of quick reconfiguration to grapple, grab, or rake with an open hand.

A more sophisticated catalogue of strikes, including uppercuts, hooks, and technical nuances of grappling, cannot be recovered from the ancient record. We must defer a more complete discussion of advanced strikes.

2.5 Duel vs mêlée

Boxing characteristically distinguishes itself as a duel rather than a brawl or mêlée of many combatants. Generalized battle of one group against another, as observed among chimpanzees, is a pragmatic tactic in warfare but likely results in generalized injury and destruction. Limitation of combat to a pair of competent warriors allows each side to put forward a "strong horse" who can demonstrate before the gods the worthiness of their claim. However, as boxing clearly occurs for reasons besides the open or covert warfare of two groups, dueling combat persists for reasons other than the limitation of damage and injury.

Monomachy is incentivized by the higher payoff in terms of status, access to mates, and so forth, while entailing typically commensurable risks. (One of the highest risks is that the opponent defects and allows into the combat space other allied combatants, but we elide this eventuality for now.) Winning and losing leads to direct hormonal and physiological effects, notably increased testosterone for the winner and increased cortisol for the loser (Slimani et al. 2018). (The evidence for decreased testosterone in the loser is contestable, cf. Oliveira et al. 2014.) Personal combat demands a high level of performance from each combatant in terms of reaction speed, striking power, situational awareness, and ability to remain within mutually agreed parameters of combat (rules and conventions).

3 Paleolithic/Neolithic combat

Philostratus of Athens, a chronicler of boxing who wrote in the early Roman Imperial period, gave us his best guess as to the *fons et origo* of the sport. However, no one in that era could have possibly unearthed the prehistoric origins of boxing. Even the Sumerians, who grant us the first glimpse of pugilism in the historic record, could not have captured in stone or clay the details of the first boxing match. This is not merely because of the great time depth at which the first boxing encounter likely took place, but because boxing represents something so elemental to our natures that it is hard to imagine it ever being invented at all.

Given that it is impossible for us to observe boxing *in statu nascendi*, the inferences we make about combat between early humans must remain speculative. We know of no representation of upright, single combat predating the reliefs and plaques made by Mesopotamian artisans and their Caucasian counterparts in the third millennium BC (Dioscurus and Dioscurus 2022). While we might learn something about the agonistics practiced by our earliest hominin ancestors by studying fighting behaviors in chimpanzees (see Section 2), we have few options for filling in the enormous gap between the dawn of humanity and the rise of Sumer.

Perhaps the only way to reasonably speculate about this vast developmental period is to study spontaneous fighting between untrained, unarmed *Homo sapientes*. One early observation of young children fighting one another has it thus: "[V]ery small boys seldom stand for their combats...[T]hey fight, rolling over on the floor, and each seek[s] to keep the upper hand" (Groos 1901, p. 175). The same author continues his description of contests among children: "In playful fighting...the blow with the fist is not much used" (Groos 1901, p. 179). We speculate from anecdotal evidence that such encounters may be initiated with a few standing punches but quickly resolve into 'horizontal' fighting—something akin to the Greek pankration, or an instigated fight between two fourteen-year-old boys. The impulse to push an opponent to the ground is strong. This downward trajectory is likely a functional primitive of single combat between humans. The combatant who goes to the ground first is at a manifest disadvantage, since strikes will be more effective from above and his mobility for defense is limited. Of course, many tactics can be learned and subsequently employed to shift the balance in favor of the fallen, overwhelmed combatant; and a fallen, armed opponent is still in good shape with respect to a standing, unarmed one. However, if both combatants are untrained and unarmed, we take it as a functional primitive that the one on the ground first is more likely to suffer injury and defeat.

Moreover, spontaneous agonistic encounters between young humans are typically brief, and may involve only a few strikes with the hands or feet. This is typically followed by submission or retreat of one combatant. In one study, hitting and pushing/pulling serve as the most common instigation of fights between children.

All of this is to argue in favor of our position that boxing is not natural. That is, prolonged agonistic encounters where combatants remain on their feet for the duration of the fight are unlikely to be observed among the untrained and the unarmed, just as they are rare among the very young. If the natural course of fighting (when it continues) is to fall and wrestle, as we suppose, then we are presented with a riddle. Why remain standing in a fight? Indeed, why box at all?

3.1 Boxing ritual in the earliest human societies

It is a *locus communis* to claim that sport is ritual. The validity of the claim depends, however, on the contested and pliable definition of both the subject and predicate across an anfractuous literature. Despite this, it is relatively uncontroversial to claim that sport is a type of play. So what are play and ritual? A foundational argument has been made that play and ritual are the same thing. Or, at least, they are both aspects of the same process, one by which humans channel "rhythm, harmony, change, alternation, contrast and climax" into a coherent practice (Huizinga 1955, p. 75). Huizinga argues that, "[P]lay is older and more original than civilization" (ibid.). This is an appealing lens through which to speculate on the development of pre-civilizational boxing.

In its ritual context, (modern) sport, including boxing, has been confirmed as "a social situation during which individuals engaged in problematic and consequential action communicate to one another that they understand the ideal demands their roles place on them, agree with the values assumed by those ideals, and are capable of fulfilling role expectations" (Birrell 1981, p. 355–356). At the same time, sport may be considered "a social ceremony structurally capable of fulfilling social functions comparable to those of religious ceremonies, specifically as an arena for the creation of symbolic leaders and the display of heroic action." In this sense, sport-as-ritual "reaffirm[s] the values of the social order" (Birrell 1981, p. 356). Thus sport presumes some form of social order and so, too, must the most primordial form of boxing. We imagine that at some early stage of social development, humans transduced the elemental energies of rough-and-tumble, largely 'horizontal', fighting into a form of upright, unarmed combat that was both a projection and a reinforcement of an emerging social order. Such an order likely invested value in qualities associated with success in hunting animals, defending the community from outsiders, and subduing rivals. Such qualities probably included competitive and aggressive behavior, resistance to pain, courage, strength, perseverance, agility, and, not least of all, spunk. All are associated with successful modern sport boxers, whose tradition ultimately devolves from Mesopotamia. In Mexico, the same qualities seem to be prized among traditional *Tigre* boxers, who practice a sport with a distinct, American lineage (Saunders 1984, Zorich 2008).

One definition of a game is "a voluntary attempt to overcome unnecessary obstacles"; the addition of physical exertion, to the point of exhaustion, makes the activity a 'sport' (Connor 2012). Perhaps related to notions of play, we also tentatively connect boxing to Neolithic dancing: it has been argued that the "significance of dancing is related to the Neolithic revolution ... [T]he beginnings of agriculture involved a cognitive revolution concerning the relationships between work investment and its final product, referring to the agricultural cycle. Through dancing at scheduled agricultural ceremonies and festivals communities transmitted messages to themselves with regard to the task at hand" (Verhoeven 2011, p. 805). "The high supernatural powers also became involved in the process, as the circle of dance is the actual place where contact is made between this and the other world" (Garfinkel 2003, p. 82).

Because sustained pugilistic combat is unlikely to occur spontaneously among unarmed, untrained combatants, boxing is a good candidate for an emergent ritualistic behavior. Fistfighting is arguably such a basic ritual that we can imagine it accompanying humans in their greatest and earliest migrations. Thus, we find positive evidence for boxing in both the pre-Columbian Americas and southwest Asia at early dates. Another possibility is that boxing is not passed on culturally but that it emerges over and over again as a basic ritual behavior—a response to any number of bio-social primitives including sexual selection, aggression, and hierarchy.

Rituals "are not in themselves immediately and functionally productive in the material world" (Renfrew 2018, p. 13). This characterization is apt for boxing insofar as boxing does not accomplish the same real-world objectives as fighting. In other words, *any* regulation of fighting removes fighting from its essential evolutionary functions and makes it a product of culture. In boxing, one's opponent is permitted to stand; indeed, he is compelled to stand, thus forcing both fighters to contend with each other on equal ground throughout the duration of the encounter. It is this neutralization of advantage, which is most elemental to boxing, that suggests to us ritual behavior.

The following basic attributes of ritual have been proposed and subsequently debated (Bell 1997, pp. 138–69), as summarized by Renfrew (2018, p. 12):

1. Formalism of expression and gesture
2. Traditionalism, [in] conformity with earlier cultural practices
3. Disciplined invariance, involving repetition and physical control
4. Rule governance, restricting human action and interaction
5. Sacral symbolism, with the use of sacred symbols
6. Performance, involving actions undertaken in public

As to all of these, with the possible exception of number five (see below), there is no question that all modern sport boxing fits the bill. As for our hypothetical, prehistoric proto-boxing, there is of course no way to assess formalism or traditionalism. However, we will indulge in shameless speculation regarding the other points. By limiting fighting to an upright posture, regardless of the many other rules that accresced to the sport over time, it is arguable that even 'vertical' proto-boxing achieved a level of physical control and restricted human action far more than its evolutionary antecedent, rough-and-tumble. In addition, we can assume some form of public performance if the earliest forms of boxing were related to sexual selection, and this is a strong possibility, as we argue in Section 2. Together, we find some evidence that proto-boxing at its inception had some ritualistic elements. To these, other formal characteristics were added. We find it relatively easy to argue in favor of boxing-as-ritual in any tradition for which graphic or textual evidence exists.[5]

One of the most controversial points in Bell (1997)'s schematization of ritual is the fifth, since it inevitably draws the litigant into the question of what, exactly, is sacred. "Sacral symbolism" need not be associated with a particular religious tradition. Can a boxing ring become a sacred space that represents, symbolically, a field of battle or a lek? Do boxing gloves stand in symbolically for some more lethal form of violence? Are the accoutrements of the boxing ring (the gloves, the headgear, the mouthpiece) sacralized through use, if not by prayer and offerings, cf. the *cascos* of the *Tigre* boxer (Saunders 1984, Zorich 2008)? The sacred may be ever in the eye of the beholder, so we leave it for now, as many students of ritual have also chosen to do (Rappaport 1999), only to return when we present more palpable evidence from the historical civilizations that have, in one way or another, entered the squared circle.

---

[5] As noted earlier, equating sport and ritual in any case is hardly controversial. We will later attempt to examine more specific ritual aspects of boxing in post-neolithic cultures, based on evidence rather than mere speculation, as is regrettably our only recourse in the current section.

Are all sports rituals? All games? All play? What made boxing special? Perhaps some are uncomfortable citing chimpanzees' playful rough-and-tumble as a ritual (despite indications that this activity includes formalized gesture). On the other hand, it may be difficult to accept a repentine transformation from play to ritual that uniquely characterizes our species. Now we find ourselves wading into debates about what constitutes ritualized behavior among humans, as opposed to other species—another world into which we choose not to venture. In any event, the boundary between play and ritual is, upon reflection, a vexation to our discernment. We leave this argument to be taken up by others, but we do assert that the *Urboxen*—a hypothetical, upright, pugilistic combat that took place when the city-states of Sumer were yet dust—must have met the standards of ritual on a number of criteria.

One critic claims, "Boxing and wrestling clearly emerge from the 'rough-and-tumble' play of animals and children" (Renfrew 2018, p. 17). At least for boxing, this is hardly as clear as it may seem at first glance, as we have attempted to show. Boxing could just as easily have emerged from the sacralization of earnest fighting with the fists, nails, legs, and so forth. When under duress, and in an authentically aggressive stance, children seem just as unlikely to naturally engage in 'vertical' pugilism as their adult counterparts. The same question that bedevils our analysis also vexes Renfrew's: how exactly did horizontal rough-and-tumble become vertical boxing? Renfrew's claim provides no additional light on that particular matter. Perhaps upright fighting is in fact more playful in some sense, but we are aware of no reports, and find no anecdotal evidence of our own, to suggest that very young children engage in standing fisticuffs or do so as a form of spontaneous play (absent the influence of modern sport boxing). We are confident that the ritual patrons of proto-boxing were grown combatants who chose to go about their usual rough-and-tumble while standing up, thus severely limiting their options. By restricting themselves it is possible that they were paying reverence to some now long-forgotten god.

As we point out elsewhere, the norms of modern sport boxing appear to limit the amount of wrestling that can go on in the ring. Ancient depictions reflect a standing posture, as well. Indeed, we define boxing as an upright activity; when it ceases to be vertical, it ceases to be boxing. Agreements, pacts, covenants, codes, etc., are necessary to keep the fighters from tackling each other and otherwise doing whatever else is necessary to claim victory. Two solitary fighters engaged in a contest are unlikely to hold themselves to such a standard, absent a highly-internalized code of morality.[6] More likely, in the earliest boxing matches, a participative audience or one or more referees were necessary to keep the fighters vertical. In the oldest representations of boxers we find a 'third man in the ring', whose staff-wielding job was as likely to impose order on the fighters as it was to perform ritual blessings on them before or after the encounter.

It is notoriously difficult to detect play and ritual in early human societies. Speculation can run wild when we consider the 'lives' of artefacts and imagine the lives of those who created them. However, the association between ritual behavior and boxing is pervasive across human cultures in time and space. We believe that is suggestive of a deep-time connection between boxing and ritual. Ritual behavior is still evident in the conventions and traditions of modern sport boxing, including the procession of fighters to the ring (the 'ring walk'); sounding the time-keeping bell in honor of the recently deceased; and the way fighters 'touch

---

[6]In modern sport boxing, sparring has a richly-elaborated, if sometimes tacit, set of rules relating to personal conduct during the simulated bout. In a local boxing gym, a sign posted near the ring presents sparring partners with the brief, paradoxical reminder: "This is NOT a fight!"

gloves', primarily, to signal mutual respect.[7] *Tigre* boxing in Guerrero, Mexico, is explicitly ritualistic in its imbriferous pretensions (Saunders 1984, Zorich 2008). Many analyses of the *Boxing Boys* fresco rely on ritual to explain the strange scene that unfolds before us at Akrotiri (Dioscurus and Dioscurus 2022). To be clear, we do not argue that all of these ritualistic elements are relics of boxing's past, or that any of them can be used to reconstruct the character of our hypothetical *Urboxen*. Instead, we believe that boxing naturally attracts ritualistic behaviors: its participants extend the practice into new zones of meaning. The core elements of boxing (stay standing; use only the hands; fight in the presence of witnesses) may be elaborated in countless ways, depending on the sacramental proclivities of the fighters and the spectators.

There is a common apothegm among boxing enthusiasts that one does not "play" boxing,[8] therefore (they reason) it is more than a game and different from other sports. While it may seem infelicitous to think of boxing (or wrestling) as a 'game' like backgammon, croquet, or basketball, boxing is indisputably recognized as an Olympic 'game' and has other characteristics of games, as well. According to one commentator on the Greek games:

> Certain sports, such as boxing, clearly appear to be substitutions for what Huizinga would call "original violence":[9] that is, they are 'restrained' and relatively 'safe' versions of contests that might otherwise lead to serious injury or death (Spivey 2018).

Boxing, however, is not merely a simulation of violence; it *is* violence. Anyone who has boxed competitively will affirm this, fully aware of the fact that all offensive techniques in boxing are designed to maximize injury as quickly as possible, regardless of context. Even routine sparring matches are hardly 'safe' and frequently result in injuries, non-devastating though these may be. There is no path to victory in a competitive boxing match other than by beating one's opponent into submission.[10] In a lek or even a local bar, by contrast, a symbolic gesture—including a low-pitched growl—may scare off an opponent and thereby win the day. Rather than a "substitution" for violence or a "safe" form of violence, boxing is in fact hyper-violence. To argue that boxing substitutes for violence among men is as absurd as arguing that cockfighting substitutes for violence among roosters. By adhering to a strict code, boxers are compelled by other men to attack each other in a confined space. They must remain on their feet while doing so. Moreover, while one depends on social sanction and explicit commitment to remain within the rules, violence above and beyond that permitted

---

[7] While commanded by the referee to 'touch gloves' at the beginning of a bout, it is increasingly common to see fighters 'touch gloves' without an authority compelling them to do so, e.g., at the beginning of each round when the fighters emerge from their corners (including the first round, redundantly, mere seconds from the last time they 'touched 'em up'); after a foul, perhaps to indicate that the infraction was not intentional and as a mutual recommitment to the rules; other instances are less explicable but may even be intended, in some cases no doubt haplessly, to reduce the aggression of a rival. This behavior is less common in professional boxing.

[8] The saying has been attributed to Sugar Ray Leonard (b. 1956).

[9] Huizinga invokes this concept when discussing the breakdown of international law, i.e., what results when "one member...of a community of states...proclaims the interests and power of its own group...as the sole norm of its political behavior...Society then sinks down to the level of the barbaric, and *original violence* retakes its ancient rights" (Huizinga 1955, p. 101, emphasis added). Huizinga views original violence (one cannot help but think of Cain and Abel) as the contradiction of the "immemorial play-spirit" (ibid.).

[10] The introduction of timed rounds allows a fighter to stay on the defensive a good part of the time, but even the most effective defensive tactics cannot lead to a clear victory without some convincing aggression.

does take place on occasion in the ring. Violence in the boxing ring is not optional—it is inevitable. To remove the violence from boxing (wrestling, pankration, etc.) would be to change it into something else entirely. The most primordial conventions make it so.

The boxing ring itself serves as an ideal incubator for what Lorenz (1969) called 'critical reaction' fighting. In the boxing ring, fighters are completely hemmed in by the ropes and can seek no exit but victory or defeat; flight is not among their options. In more traditional settings, pugilists are kept in place by the encircling crowd of spectators. Circumcluded by the bodies of men who prevent their escape, the fighters feel a a dual obligation not only to suppress their flight instinct but to measure up to the cultural expectations of the peers who corporally surround them. In such a situation "the fighter stakes his all, because he cannot escape and can expect no mercy. The most violent form of fighting behavior is motivated by fear, by the most intense flight impulses whose natural outlet is prevented by the fact that the danger is too near; so the animal, not daring to turn its back on it, fights with the prover-bial courage of desperation" (Lorenz 1969, p. 25). It is little wonder that western culture has so readily adopted the construct of fighting for sport in a cage, e.g., in mixed martial arts competitions that also sometimes feature boxing and kickboxing.[11]

Boxing is a ritual designed to commit combatants to concentrated, unrelenting violence.[12] We agree with Spivey that the rules of boxing restrain the fighters, but we differ with him when it comes to how this changes the outcome. For us, the primordial restraints (stay stand-ing; use only the hands; fight in the presence of witnesses) make boxing a more dangerous, protracted, and social form of violence than a typical encounter between, e.g., two inebriated rivals who clash briefly in an alleyway. We believe that understanding this dynamic is crucial to understanding how and why boxing arose. Ancient rules of boxing matches, so far as we can discern them, were unconcerned with the safety of fighters. Instead, these codes poten-tialized human aggression and turned it into an offering worthy of the supernatural patrons that governed the contexts in which it occurred. Boxing was (and remains) a transpersonal experience, typical of other forms of ancient ritual. Boxing dissolves the egos of the combat-ants. By fighting each other in a sacralized context, with all natural options for flight and ne-gotiation removed, boxers are united in purpose. While each fighter directs violence against his rival, it is precisely the same form of violence for each, ideally matched in intensity. Only

---

[11]Perhaps more effectively than the boxing ring, the cage communicates to a modern audience the desper-ate nature of the battle: both fighters are trapped and only one can emerge victorious. The reluctance of box-ing promotions to adopt the cage may be an element of traditionalism. It may also be functional, since, de-spite its metaphorical power, the cage also obstructs the audience's view. More recent promotions have toyed with the shape and depth of the fighting area. As mentioned, Ultimate Fighting matches occur in a UFC-octagon™, effectively eliminating corners, and surrounded by material resembling chain-link fencing which varies in height; the Bare Knuckle Fighting Championship uses a circular fighting area, circumscribed by traditional ropes wound through eight (!) posts, a fighting area which it has patented as the "Squared Circle"; BYB Ex-treme Bare Knuckle Fighting touts a three-sided ring "affectionately known as 'The Trigon'"; the Valor Bare Knuckle promotion introduced the Bout Circle™ (or more colloquially, the 'pit'), a circular, flat ring sur-rounded by an octagonal area of inclined mats with no ropes or caging; this intellectual property was pioneered, but apparently not legally protected, by Big Knockout Boxing, which from 2013 to 2015 staged matches in a similar fighting area also christened 'the pit' (https://www.ufc.com/octagon; https://www.bareknuckle.tv/about; https://www.youtube.com/c/BYBExtreme/about; https://valorbk.com/about-valor-bare-knuckle/; Keefer (2014). accessed November 25, 2021).

[12]A spare number of innovations have been introduced to conceal the true nature of boxing from its Victorian, Edwardian, and modern critics, but the safety of fighters remains illusory, as indeed it must: Purged of risk, boxing ceases to be recognizable. By far, the most consequential of modern innovations to promote safety in boxing is time-keeping, including limiting the number of rounds.

Figure 1: Huizinga regarded "original violence" as the antithesis of the "immemorial play-spirit". "Cain Killing Abel", woodcut by Albrecht Dürer (1511).

when we recognize the concentrated violence at the heart of boxing do we begin to glimpse the terrible rationale behind its most brutal variations. For example, if we persist in regarding boxing as mock violence, we will never understand why fighters in northern Italy and the Eastern Alps hammered each other with weights clutched in their hands; why the Lucanians gloried in sprays of blood from a boxer's bursting nose; or why the Romans strapped sharp objects to a boxer's hands in order to make fatal trauma inevitable. Rules define an ambit of acceptable violence, making escalation legible.

Like other games, boxing is rule-governed and it involves risk. The outcome is not predetermined. If the first rule of boxing is 'thou shalt stand up', then from the moment of this declaration, it became a game. But why not a ritual, instead? Indeed, the murky boundaries between play, games, and rituals are contested. In the earliest days, we speculate that divination by ritual, hence (in one form) religious divination by single-champion combat, became a "game" by the introduction of non-religious divination, i.e. gambling.

4 Boxing in History

Tales and depictions of boxing are almost as old as written history. We see boxing or close analogues presented in many ancient cultures from Mesopotamia to the Orient. While the foregoing analysis of human sociality, ritual and play, and biomechanics places real limits on the development of pugilism, at only a few points are we able to identify the speculative first introduction of an innovation by a civilization.

Consider, for instance, the ring. In prehistory, two fighters would have faced off without the expedient of a confined space of encounter. Yet at some point before the modern age, the ring became *de rigueur*. Each of the elements of boxing was invented and introduced; in some cases, we have evidence of early usage, and in others, none. We identify the following elements of boxing, all of which are associated with the tradition at some point. Some are primeval to the sport; others are as late as the twentieth century.

- Strikes (*sine qua non*) (and particular strikes: from hooks to haymakers to eye rakes)
- Stance (upright as *sine qua non*; squared-off, orthodox, southpaw, etc.)
- Paired combatants/unarmed single-champion combat (*sine qua non*)
- Bloodshed
- Ring/definite boundary
- Ring walk
- Rounds (timed or otherwise delimited breaks)
- Clinching/chancery/fibbing
- Swatting/blocking
- Grabbing/grappling
- Slipping
- Throws
- Kicks/knees
- Trading blows
- Tapping out/yielding
- Termination conditions
- Pre-fight devotions, including a face-off
- Musical accompaniment
- Gambling/fixing fights
- Gloves/*sphairai*/*cæstus*
- Wraps/*himantes*
- Glovedness: dual vs single (sinistral, dextral, enantiomorphic)
- Handheld "dumbbells"
- Kilt/skirt/shorts
- Helmet/headgear
- Belt or girdle (for title or devotion; see also the Muay Thai *Pra Jiad* armband)
- Groin protection (incl. the κυνοδέσμη *kunodesmē*)
- Mouth guard
- Motivation (ceremonial, funerary, entertainment)
- Amateur versus professional designation
- Training/training camp/*palaistra*
- Weight classes
- Punching bag/speed bag
- Shadow boxing
- Adjutants: judges, referee, coaches, seconds
- Corporal correction

- Seasonal competition
- Disqualification/fouling/forbidden strikes or moves

As our subsequent articles review the history of boxing in various ancient cultures, we will highlight the earliest known occurrences of many of these features, as well as situate interesting forms, such as glove development. We will also consider the ramifications which different rule sets had for the fighters and the sport as a whole.

References

C. Bell. *Ritual: Perspectives and Dimensions.* Oxford University Press, Oxford, 1997.

Irwin S. Bernstein. The adaptive value of maladaptive behavior, or you've got to be stupid in order to be smart. *Ethology and Sociobiology,* 5(4):297–303, 1984. doi: https://doi.org/10.1016/0162-3095(84)90008-6.

Irwin S. Bernstein and T. P. Gordon. The function of aggression in primate societies. *American Scientist,* 62:304–311, 1974.

Susan Birrell. Sport as ritual: Interpretations from Durkheim to Goffman. *Social Forces,* 60 (2):354–76, 1981. doi: 10.2307/2578440.

David R. Carrier. The advantage of standing up to fight and the evolution of habitual bipedalism in hominins. *PLoS ONE,* 6(5), 2011.

S. Connor. *A Philosopy of Sport.* Reaktion, London, 2012.

Charles Darwin. *On the Origin of Species by Means of Natural Selection, or the Preservation of Favoured Races in the Struggle for Life.* John Murray, London, 1859.

E. N. Davis. *The Vapheio Cups and Aegean Gold and Silver Ware.* Garland, New York, 1977.

Richard Dawkins. *The Selfish Gene.* Oxford University Press, Oxford, 1976.

Joseph de Maistre. *Les soirées de Saint-Pétersbourg,.* Librairie Ecclésiastique de Rusand, Paris, 1821.

Daniel Dinu and Julien Louis. Biomechanical analysis of the cross, hook, and uppercut in junior vs. elite boxers: Implications for training and talent identification. *Frontiers in Sports and Active Living,* 2:1–10, 2020. doi: 10.3389/fspor.2020.598861.

Castor Dioscurus and Pollux Dioscurus. The development of boxing: The ancient world (Western Asia and Egypt). *Scholia Pugillātōria,* 1:23–71, 2022.

S. C. Ferrence and G. Bendersky. Deformity in the 'boxing boys'. *Perspectives in Biology and Medicine,* 48(1):105–123, 2005.

Silvia Festuccia. Sport representation: Transfer images of agonistic contests. In Rolf A. Stucky, Oskar Kaelin, and Hans-Peter Mathys, editors, *Proceedings of the 9th International Congress on the Archaeology of the Ancient Near East,* volume 1, pages 99–110. Harrassowitz Verlag, 2016.

Thomas Fewtrell. *Boxing reviewed; or, the science of manual defence, displayed on rational principles*. Scratcherd and Whitaker, London, 1790.

P. M. Fortes, L. Albrechet-Souza, M. Vasconcelos, B. M. Ascoli, A. P. Menegolla, and R. M. M. de Almeida. Social instigation and repeated aggressive confrontations in male swiss mice: Analysis of plasma corticosterone, CRF and BDNF levels in limbic brain areas. *Trends in Psychiatry and Psychotherapy*, 39(2):98–105, 2017. doi: 10.1590/2237-6089-2016-0075.

Erich Fromm. *The Anatomy of Human Destructiveness*. Holt, Rinehart and Winston, New York, 1973.

Norman E. Gardiner. *Athletics of the Ancient World*. Clarendon, Oxford, 1930.

Y. Garfinkel. *Dancing at the Dawn of Agriculture*. University of Texas Press, Austin, 2003.

Karl Groos. *The Play of Animals*. D. Appleton, New York, 1898. Trans. by Elizabeth L. Baldwin.

Karl Groos. *The Play of Man*. D. Appleton and Co., New York, 1901. Trans. by Elizabeth L. Baldwin.

Joshua Horns, Rebekah Jung, and David R. Carrier. *In vitro* strain in human metacarpal bones during striking: Testing the pugilism hypothesis of hominin hand evolution. *Journal of Experimental Biology*, 218:3215–3221, 2015.

Johann Huizinga. *Homo Ludens:*. Beacon Press, Boston, MA, 1955.

S. A. Immerwahr. *Aegean Painting in the Bronze Age*. Pennsylvania State University Press, University Park, PA, 1990.

Ernst Jünger. Der Kampf als inneres erlebnis. In *Sämtliche Werke, Vol. 5*, pages 11–108. Klett, Stuttgart, 1922.

Ernst Jünger. *Der Waldgang*. Klostermann, Frankfurt, 1951.

Case Keefer. Big Knockout Boxing takes shot as alternative combat sport this weekend. *Las Vegas Sun*, 2014. August 13, https://lasvegassun.com/news/2014/aug/13/big-knockout-boxing-takes-shot-alternative-combat-/, accessed 25 November 2021.

Natalia N. Kudryavtseva. Positive fighting experience, addiction-like state, and relapse: Retrospective analysis of experimental studies. *Aggression and Violent Behavior*, 52:1–11, 2020.

Seth Lazar. War (stanford encyclopedia of philosophy), 2016. URL `https://plato.stanford.edu/entries/war/`. Accessed 6 May 2022.

Konrad Lorenz. *On Aggression*. Bantam, New York, 1969.

Nanno Marinatos. *Art and Religion in Thera: Reconstructing a Bronze Age Society*. D. & I. Mathioulakis, Athens, 1984.

Lyvia Morgan. Form and meaning in figurative painting. In Susan Sherrat, editor, *The Wall Paintings of Thera: Proceedings of the First International Symposium*, pages 925–946. Hidryma Theras, Athens, 2000.

Michael H. Morgan and David R. Carrier. Protective buttressing of the human fist and the evolution of hominin hands. *The Journal of Experimental Biology*, 216:236–244, 2013.

Thomas Moynihan. *Spinal Catastrophism: A Secret History*. Urbanomic, Falmouth, 2019.

Gonçalo A. Oliveira, Sara Uceda, Tânia F. Oliveira, Alexandre C. Fernandes, Teresa Garcia-Marques, and Rui F. Oliveira. Testosterone response to competition in males is unrelated to opponent familiarity or threat appraisal. *Frontiers in Psychology*, 5(1):1240, 2014.

H. W. Parke. A Note on the fresco of the 'Boxing Boys' at Akrotiri. *Journal of Prehistoric Religion*, 1:35–38, 1987.

Signe Preuschoft, Xin Wang, Filippo Aureli, and Frans B. M. de Waal. Reconciliation in captive chimpanzees: A reevaluation with controlled methods. *International Journal of Primatology*, 23:29–50, 2002.

Roy Rappaport. *Ritual and Religion in the Making of Humanity*. Cambridge University Press, Cambridge, 1999.

Colin Renfrew. Introduction: Play as the precursor of ritual in early human societies. In Colin Renfrew, Iain Morley, and Michael Boyd, editors, *Ritual Play and Belief in Evolution and Early Human Societies*, pages 9–19. Cambridge University Press, Cambridge, 2018.

J. S. Russell. The Value of Dangerous Sport. *Journal of the Philosophy of Sport*, 32(1):1–19, 2005.

J. S. Russell. Children and dangerous sport and recreation. *Journal of the Philosophy of Sport*, 34(1):176–193, 2007.

Nick Saunders. Jaguars, rain and blood: Religious symbolism in Acatlán, Guerrero, Mexico. *Cambridge Journal of Anthropology*, 9(1):77–81, 1984.

Maamer Slimani, Armin Huso Paravlic, Helmi Chaabene, Philip Davis, Karim Chamari, and Foued Cheour. Hormonal responses to striking combat sports competition: a systematic review and meta-analysis. *Biology of Sport*, 35(2):121–136, 2018.

M. Soong, C. Got, and J. Katarincic. Ring and little finger metacarpal fractures: mechanisms, locations, and radiographic parameters. *The Journal of Hand Surgery*, 35(8):1256–9, 2010.

Nigel Spivey. Epic games. In Colin Renfrew, Iain Morley, and Michael Boyd, editors, *Ritual Play and Belief in Evolution and Early Human Societies*, pages 250–263. Cambridge University Press, Cambridge, 2018.

Malini Suchak and Frans B. M. de Waal. Reply to schmidt and tomasello: Chimpanzees as natural team-players. *Proceedings of the National Academy of Sciences*, 113(44):E6730–E6730, 2016. doi: 10.1073/pnas.1614598113. URL https://www.pnas.org/doi/abs/10.1073/pnas.1614598113.

Malini Suchak, Timothy M. Eppley, Matthew W. Campbell, Rebecca A. Feldman, Luke F. Quarles, and Frans B. M. de Waal. How chimpanzees cooperate in a competitive world. *Proceedings of the National Academy of Sciences*, 113(36):10215–10220, 2016. doi: 10.1073/pnas.1611826113. URL https://www.pnas.org/doi/abs/10.1073/pnas.1611826113.

Marc Verhoeven. Retrieving the supernatural: Ritual and religion in the prehistoric Levant. In Timothy Insoll, editor, *The Oxford Handbook of the Archaeology of Ritual and Religion*, pages 795–810. Oxford University Press, Oxford, 2011.

William C. Whiting, Robert J. Gregor, and Gerald A. Finerman. Kinematic analysis of human upper extremity movements in boxing. *The American Journal of Sports Medicine*, 16 (2):130–136, 1988. doi: 10.1177/036354658801600207.

Edward Osborne Wilson. *On Human Nature*. Harvard University Press, Cambridge, MA, 1978.

Zach Zorich. Fighting with jaguars, bleeding for rain. *Archaeology*, 61(6):46–52, 2008.

Changelog

- ~2022.5.6. First public release.
- ~2022.7.25. Minor proofreading changes.
- ~2022.10.29. Correct error in carpal numbering.
- ~2023.9.27. Add comments on chimpanzee postcombat reconciliation; minor proofreading changes.
- ~2023.9.27. Minor proofreading changes.

The Development of Boxing: The Ancient World (Western Asia and Egypt)

Castor Dioscurus; Pollux Dioscurus

Contents

Abstract

The earliest written and visual records of boxing occur in Western Asia, from the Crimea to Mesopotamia. Particular styles of boxing can be identified from related artifacts, and various motives for the practice are revealed. We contest the translation of certain ancient terms as "wrestling", suggesting that boxing is far more prevalent in Mesopotamian literature than earlier scholars have proposed. We offer tentative identification of previously overlooked works of visual art as "boxing" images.

1   Introduction

The ancient world displayed an astonishing variety of forms which are nonetheless recognizable as part of a single tradition of upright combat we denominate "boxing". Polygenesis seems likely, and as we outline the historical record we draw attention to the probable *terminus ad quem* of many innovations, as well as—to the extent possible—their motivation and ramifications.

Scholia Pugillātōria 1 (2022): 23–71.

Address author correspondence to scholia@protonmail.com.

2   Western Asia

The earliest extant evidence for a sport in the boxing tradition comes from Western Asia. Archæologists can generally do little more than assign broadly estimated dates to the artifacts we will discuss. For this reason, these dates alone cannot confirm whether boxing images first appeared in the Caucasus or in Mesopotamia. However, it is relatively uncontroversial to claim that images of pugilistic behavior first appeared in Western Asia (including the Caucasus and the Crimea) in the third millennium before Christ.

At this stage, we identify depictions of boxing primarily by raised fists and often a squared stance, with fighters occasionally reflecting the "confronted animals" motif in a symmetrical pose. It is clear that strikes, upright stance, and so forth exist, and have likely have existed for a long time prior (Dioscurus and Dioscurus 2022a). As far as attire is concerned (and when detail is sufficient), we note that boxers from this early period are universally depicted with bare chests and wear a kind of kilt.[1] Other elements of the sport are as yet undocumented in the historic record.

2.1   The Caucasus and Crimea

The oldest known visual representation of a boxing match is a decorated flesh-hook produced in the north Caucasus sometime in the early Bronze Age. Participants in the Maykop culture raised massive kurgans to mark the burials of their esteemed dead and built dolmens (single-chambered megalithic structures) that functioned as abditories for their hoards. One such dolmen, located near Tsarskaya (modern Novosvobodnaya, Adyghe Republic), contained a bronze flesh-hook adorned with two boxers. Radiocarbon dating of surrounding material suggests that the hook was created no later than 2900 BC, and perhaps as early as 3200 BC. Given the proposed date of its manufacture, the flesh-hook has been described as "the earliest sculptural image of a fist fight in the world" (Trifonov et al. 2021, p. 26).[2]

The boxers confront one another while standing on a representation of the down-turned horns of an animal, probably a bull.[3] An orthogonal projection, in the shape of a hook (also pointing downward) was used to retrieve flesh or hide from a boiling cauldron. Users of the instrument would have mounted it on a pole projecting into the hollow base of the hook (Figure 1).

The figures on the Tsarskaya flesh-hook are poorly preserved, but the essential features identifying them as pugilists are unmistakable (Figure 2). The fighters extend their arms towards one another with clenched fists.[4] The arms of one figure are bent with elbows raised to the level of the shoulders, just as a modern boxer delivers a proper hook to the head. The other combatant appears to throw a jab to the chin of his adversary while holding his right arm lower, bending it at the elbow and drawing it close to his chest. The similarity between the postures of these figures and various Mesopotamian depictions—not to mention modern fighters—is remarkable.

---

[1]Admittedly, this style of dress is common in depictions of Mesopotamian men engaged in a variety of other activities, as well. However, the bare-chested character of boxing is a ubiquarian element of the activity in virtually all ancient contexts where visual information is available.

[2]"[С]амым ранним в мире скульптурным изображеннем кулачного поединка"

[3]This is arguably the first of many representations, literary and visual, that link bulls and pugilism.

[4]An early interpretation suggested that the figures represent adorants, with their hands raised in prayer.

Figure 1: The Tsarskaya flesh-hook with figures of boxers positioned on a representation of down-turned bull horns.

Below the groin and buttocks, the legs of the flesh-hook boxers are rendered rather amorphously, so the fighters' stance cannot be evaluated precisely. The figures are entirely naked, but for a belt. They may bear some kind of protection over their genitals, but the artist has not indicated how this is secured, i.e., no part of the loincloth appears to stretch ventrocaudally. It has been argued that the artist intended for the boxers to appear ithyphallic (Trifonov 2015, p. 87). One of the figures wears a beard.

If the boxers on the Tsarskaya flesh-hook were rendered in relief, it has been argued, they would look much like depictions of two figures known as "fighting twins" found on several other objects discovered in the nearby Caucasus and as far away as the Crimea (Rezepkin 2000). Dated perhaps only a few hundred years after the manufacture of the Tsarskaya flesh-hook, these figures appear to have constituted a cultural theme celebrated by the early Bronze Age inhabitants of the region.[5]

The anthropomorphic Kazanki Stele (Figure 3),[6] discovered in the Crimea, depicts a pair of these "boxing twins". They assume a significantly different posture compared to fighting figures in Mesopotamian art. Their lead hands are in contact while their back arms are raised to shoulder level and retroflex, arcing down and forward. This gives the impression of a different kind of fight, perhaps one where the front arm is immobilized by grasping the opponent while only the back hand is free to do injury.

The "boxing twins" on the similar Akchokrak stele (Figure 4) are not so convincingly engaged in combat, were it not for explicit comparison with the Kazanki stele. On the Akchorak stele, also discovered in the Crimea, the twins seem to bend slightly backwards at the hips with one arm high and another low, as if they are jointly reaching for some unseen object.

An exceptionally well-preserved dolmen on the northern coast of the Black Sea contains a primitive depiction of boxing, etched into the gigantic outward-facing foundation

---

[5] These Crimean and Caucasian boxers bring to mind the mythopoeic twins of much later Greek myth. The Dioscuri, associated strongly with boxing, are even connected to the Black Sea littoral, having sailed around it with Jason and the other Argonauts in search of the Golden Fleece. Pollux/Polydeuces boxed the king of the Bebrycians in Bithynia, on the Turkish coast of the Black Sea.

[6] Anthropomorphic stele of this design (similar face, arms, belt, etc.) have been documented widely in the Black Sea region, as far south as Risqueh, near the Red Sea, as far east as Sahryeri, near the Caspian, and as far south as northern Iraq (Tell Billa), near the Tigris (Jeunesse 2015, Kodaş 2015).

Figure 2: Boxers positioned on the Tsarskaya flesh-hook. Dated to 2900 BC at the latest, this artifact is perhaps the oldest sculptural representation of a boxing match.

stones (Trifonov 2015). Dated between 2480 and 2200 BC, the Džubga Dolmen stands on the Taman Peninsula, near Krasnodar, in Southern Russia. The appearance of a boxing petroglyph on the dolmen's face (Figure 6) suggests that its builders partook in the same culture as those who created the various boxing artifacts found just across the Kerch Strait, in the Crimea.

The motif of the "boxing twins" also appears on the Verkhorichchya Stele (Figure 5). The identification of the figures on these heavily eroded artifacts is admittedly tenuous, but a number of archæologists, including A. A. Formozov and Viktor Trifonov agree that they are engaged in some form of unarmed ritual combat. The juxtaposition of the bodies in the Verkhorichchya stele is particularly suggestive of the close quarters at which boxers spar with one another. While the figures on the Džubga Dolmen are separated, their outstretched front arms effectively communicate a mutually-directed aggressive stance. In both sets of twins, the back arm extends backward and curls under. This could be a naive representation of the guard hand or perhaps a rough copy of the boxing iconography seen in votive plaques like the one found at Tell es-Senkereh, in modern Iraq (Figure 12).

These objects naturally lead us to wonder, did boxing on the northern coast of the Black Sea develop auturgically? On the basis of the shared elements in Mesopotamian and Caucasian–Crimean depictions, Trifonov et al. (2021) argue that boxing as a cultural practice emanated from Sumer to the headwaters of the Euphrates and beyond (see Section 2.2 for a full review of boxing in Mesopotamia). This of course privileges the narrative of cultural transmission from Mesopotamia to surrounding regions, which may not be accurate, particularly in the context of fist-fighting. As a ubiquitous practice among humans, there is little reason to presume that boxing was not already a native practice on the northern coast of the

Figure 3: "Boxing twins" on an anthropomorphic stele found at Kazanki, Crimea.

Figure 4: "Boxing twins" on an anthropomorphic stele found at Akchokrak, Crimea.

Figure 5: Detail of "boxing twins" on the Verkhorichchya Stele.

Figure 6: Detail of "boxing twins" on the Džubga Dolmen, in Krasnodarsk Krai, Russia. The Dolmen is dated 2480–2200 BC.

Black Sea when its inhabitants first came in contact with, e.g., the metallurgical techniques of Mesopotamia.

2.2 Mesopotamia

The first artifacts that indisputably depict boxers and boxing matches were produced in the city states of Sumer. As civilization grew up between the Tigris and Euphrates, writers and artists produced more and more evidence of boxing taking root and spreading. While the record is primarily visual, some literary evidence of boxing survives. In both cases, the evidence is contested and depends on our interpretation of sometimes ambiguous words and gestures.

According to one authority, boxing matches were organized in ancient Mesopotamia, though "we know little more than that they were part of festivals and took place in the area of the sanctuary [*Heiligtum*]" (Sallaberger 1983, p. 178). We cannot fully understand the inclusion of boxing iconography at temple sites without some delibation of the Mesopotamian temple cultus, which we provide in the present section. However, it is well beyond the scope of our work to give a full account of Mesopotamian religion.

2.2.1 Visual representations

Three gray limestone figurines, two housed at the Louvre and one at the University of Zürich (No. 1942; see Figure 7), may be the oldest representations of boxers in Mesopotamia. Crafted in the Late Uruk period, ca. 3300 BC, the figures are naked; they wear beards with no mustaches, shaved around the mouth; and they appear to wear caps. Critically for their interpretation as pugilists, their elbows are bent at the waist and their hands form fists (Trifonov et al. 2021, p. 35). Human figures from this period are typically depicted with their hands clasped, as in prayer. A bearded figure of similar date, though carved from alabaster with more sophisticated portrayal of the musculature, also clenches the fists at the level just below the chest (Iraq Museum, No. 61986). We admit that the designation of these figures as boxers is tenuous; they are more typically referred to as "priest-kings," e.g., by Aruz (2003, pp. 25, 38).

The link between pugilism and these figurines is based primarily on their nudity and the fact that their hands are not clasped in prayer, like the ubiquarian orant figures of the (later) Early Dynastic period (Trifonov et al. 2021, p. 35). Aruz (2003, p. 38) argues that the figures' nakedness "is probably connected with a ritual activity." This is not out of line with the potential ritual function of boxing in Mesopotamian religion (see below). In coetaneous (Late Uruk) cylinder seals, nude figures are depicted carrying assorted objects, including agricultural produce, "toward an elaborate temple facade" (ibid.). Late Uruk sculpture in the round does not appear to admit the possibility of disengaging the figure's extremities from the block of the body. Perhaps lacking the technical expertise to render extended arms and separated legs to effectively communicate the dynamism of boxers, the limestone figures merely incorporate the static iconography of Mesopotamian pugilists. Features like nudity, beards, well-developed pectorals, shoulders, and biceps may have been included for this purpose, though of course non-pugilists may bear the same features. The arms of all the relevant figures are bent at the elbow, with the fists clenched against the abdomen and the thumbs on top.

A limestone plaque from the Sin Temple at Khafājah, ca. 2500 BC (Iraq Museum, No.

Figure 7: A limestone figure from the Late Uruk Period (3300–3000 BC), kept at the University of Zürich (No. 1942). It has been claimed that the figure represents a boxer (Trifonov et al. 2021, p. 35).

9012), depicts boxers and a few surrounding figures including a referee or trainer (holding a staff) and a musician (far left) (Pelzel 1973, pp. 61–62). No definitive translation of the inscription that appears between the boxers has been offered, but one scholar tentatively claims that it means "son of..." (Aruz 2003, p. 73). The plaque has two other registers above the one shown in Figure 8, with a perforation in the center. These depict seated figures and their attendants, along with men and women who bear various vessels and esculents, including a goat. The "heavy belt and codpiece" worn by the boxers may be an early indication of groin protection (Aruz 2003, op. cit.) It has been conjectured that the plaque was donated by individuals who sponsored or participated in a festival like the one depicted, which was probably "a celebration associated with the fertility of the plant world" (ibid.). Thus, in one of the earliest depictions of boxing, we find it most likely connected to a sacred rite of spring. Sin, the divine patron of the temple, was a lunar deity of considerable importance in the Sumero-Akkadian pantheon. He was associated with bulls probably because of the visual resemblance between a pair of horns and the crescent moon (cf. Figure 21).

The perforation in the center of the plaque gives us a good indication of its purpose. It was probably used as decorative reinforcement for a door-locking mechanism in the temple (Hansen 1963, Zettler 1987). The plaque was fixed in the doorjamb and a peg, securely slotted into the doorjamb, went through the perforation in the plaque. This peg served as an anchor for a cord or hook attached to the door. Once fastened, the peg and adjoining portion of the cord or hook were covered with clay and impressed with a seal. To open the door, the seal would have to be broken, indicating that an unauthorized person had accessed the room on the other side. This suggests that the contents of the locked room were of considerable cultic importance. Anyone accessing that sacred space would first encounter a depiction of a temple ceremony that included boxing. This can leave little doubt as to the sacral nature of pugilism at this time in Khafājah, and perhaps of its particular importance to the cult of Sin, i.e., the moon.

But what, exactly, was the purpose of Mesopotamian rituals that included boxing? Deciphering the religion of ancient Mesopotamian cultures has proven much more difficult than one might first imagine. One prominent scholar has despaired that it simply cannot be accomplished. Due to the fragmentary nature of available evidence, spread across several millennia, languages, and cultures, Oppenheim argued: "[A] Mesopotamian religion should not be written" (1964, p. 172). Nevertheless, a broad view has since emerged that ritual duels were held during "temple holidays and funeral games" and that they were "closely associated with the cult of heroes and the development of ideas about death and immortality" (Trifonov et al. 2021, p. 35). Some neo-Sumerian texts, which refer to the provisioning of athletes, suggest that boxers may have been maintained by the state or the temple (Sjöberg 1985, p. 9). Elsewhere, it is suggested that "Sumerian boxing" constituted part of the "Hieros Gamos", i.e., a sacred marriage between a god and goddess (Maṭḥaf al-'Irāqī 1942, p. 66). A poem called "The Marriage of Martu" (discussed below) may "point to an old custom of arranging fistfights and trials of strength as a part of preparations for a wedding" (Sjöberg 1985, p. 8). Hierurgical boxing clearly took place in the temple courtyard. Visual representations of these holy fights were displayed in the innermost cellæ of the god's dwelling, indicating that boxing was regarded as far more than an entertainment. Nevertheless, the precise cultic role of boxing in Mesopotamian religion may never be fully understood.

A terracotta plaque similar to the Sin plaque, also divided into registers, depicts boxers in the same location, i.e., at the bottom right (Maṭḥaf al-'Irāqī 1942, p. 67, fig. 33). This item was

Figure 8: Two pieces of limestone plaque from the Early Dynastic IIIA period, spliced together. The piece on the left is from Level IX of the Sin Temple at Khafājah. The fragment on the right was held in the Iraq Museum (No. 9012) but its location after the looting of the museum in 2003 has not been verified (Mathaf al-ʾIrāqī 1942, p. 67, fig. 32). The piece on the left is the lower left of a larger plaque housed at the Oriental Institute of the University of Chicago (No. A-12147).

found at the Temple of Nintu, a mother goddess, and presumably served the same purpose as the plaque found in the Temple of Sin. According to one critic, the "naturalistic" boxers depicted in both the Nintu and Sin plaques are "surprisingly coherent and believable in their movement... The slightly plump flesh is emphasized at the expense of the bony structure so that the figures takes on a somewhat bouncy, rubbery appearance" (Pelzel 1973, p. 69).

It has been suggested that the combatants depicted on the Nintu plaque are engaged in a new year's celebration (Akītu) associated with the victory of Marduk over Tiamat (Offner 1962, pp. 34, 38). A ritual fight may have been only loosely associated with the mythic story itself, i.e., the fighters did not themselves represent the gods. Instead, the fighters may have contended merely to dramatize the ongoing struggle between the forces of order and chaos that lay at the heart of Mesopotamian religion (Lambert 1963).

Because the lower register of the Nintu plaque depicts two pairs of wrestlers at left, some commentators have argued that the combatants on the right (the ones we have been discussing) are also wrestlers, though they are depicted as having "just made contact" (Pelzel 1973, p. 68). While we appreciate the elegance of this interpretation (viz., only wrestlers are presented), we find it more compelling to interpret the figures in the lower right as boxers, based on their posture and the position of their arms, which appears to us more pugilistic in character. Moreover, the appearance of boxers in the lower right of both the Nintu and Sin plaques provides another kind of hermeneutic elegance. It may be that boxers were presented at this location in votive plaques to suit the artists' iconographic sensibilities or to fulfill some ritual purpose associated with sacred geometry. One plaque may have even inspired the other. Indeed, the figures on the Nintu plaque are "so close as to be almost duplicates [of the Sin boxers], save for the fact that they beardless and at least one is also bald" (ibid., p. 69).

A stela from Tell Aqar (near modern Badra, Iraq) preserves a depiction of combatants in an attitude highly similar to that of the figures on the Nintu and Sin plaques. Reportedly housed at the Iraq Museum (no number provided), the heads of the low-relief boxers are

Figure 9: A plaque found at the Temple of Nintu, depicting two boxers with their arms extended towards one another, at right (Frankfort 1943, p. 313, pl. 62–b).

missing. They are naked except for loincloths that resemble those worn by the boxers in the Sin plaque. The fighters' front feet cross slightly and their back hands meet at the level of the torso (Sjöberg 1985, p. 8). Like their heads, the raised front arms of the fighters cannot be distinguished. According to Sjöberg, who dates the Tell Aqar stela to around 2900 BC, this is the "earliest representation of wrestlers" (ibid.). As the posture is almost identical to the boxers on the Nintu and Sin plaques, we argue that the Tell Aqar figures are, in fact, pugilists.

A boxer may also be visible on a fragment of an alabaster votive plaque (Iraq Museum No. 42494) found at the Nintu Temple in Khafājah and dated to around 2600 BC (Pelzel 1973, pp. 71–71). A seated deity with a beard and long hair, wielding a mace and a scimitar in one hand and a frond in the other, looks on while a barely visible figure strides away from him.[7] The figure is arguably nude. It is relatively uncommon for figures to face away from divinities in these kinds of depictions (attendants typically fix their gaze on the deity), so it has been argued that the individual depicted is a boxer or wrestler facing off with his opponent while the god looks on, doubtless amused by the spectacle (ibid., p. 71). The scene occurs in the lower register of the plaque, consistent with the placement of boxers in the Sin and (terracotta) Nintu artifacts discussed earlier.

An Old Babylonian (2000–1750 BC) terracotta plaque from Tell as-Senkereh (Larsa, an important city-state of Sumer) has been described as a scene depicting two boxers, with musical accompaniment, i.e., clappers and a drum (Figure 12).[8] One boxer throws a left while the other throws a right, crossing in the air without making contact. The other fist of each fighter is lowered to the waist with the elbow bent. The boxers may be wearing caps (*Kalot-*

---

[7] In the heavily eroded piece, the best indication of the figure's direction is the presence of a clearly defined foot that crosses behind the front-most foot of the seated divinity.

[8] The drum has been identified as the 'ala' instrument and its presence at boxing/wrestling events is noted throughout Sumero-Akkadian literature (Mirelman 2014).

Figure 10: Detail of a stela from Tell Aqar (Badra), Iraq depicts boxers on the right. The rightmost figure wears a loincloth like those of the Sin boxers (Figure 8) (Iraq Museum, no inventory number available).

Figure 11: The seated deity in this fragment of an alabaster votive plaque, found at the Nintu Temple at Khafājah and dated to around 2600 BC, may be watching a boxing match. Only the leftmost contestant is preserved, and only partially. While most of his features are heavily eroded, the boxer's foot can be seen between those of the god (Iraq Museum No. 4294).

tenmütze) and appear barefisted (Opificus 1961, p. 169). Their chests are uncovered and their loins are girt with kilts (British Museum, No. 91906). A fragmentary terracotta plaque from Kiš (Tell al-Uhaymir), arguably based on this one, is conserved in the Ashmolean Museum at Oxford (Opificus 1961, p. 169).

Figure 12: Terracotta plaque of boxers and musicians from Larsa (Tell es-Senkereh), Iraq. Old Babylonian (2000–1750 BC). British Museum No. 91906.

A terracotta plaque from Eshnunna (Figure 13), probably from Tell Asmar, in the Diyala region of modern Iraq, portrays two bearded pugilists wearing beaded necklaces.[9] Their waists are wrapped in fringed kilts and they may be sporting caps (though curly hair is also suggested). Each projects one foot towards his opponent, with a slight bend in the knees. The opponents' feet cross. If this were a representation of a modern boxing match, we could say the figure on the right boxes southpaw, using his right hand as his lead, his jab, or his "one". By contrast, the fighter on the right is in orthodox stance, putting his left hand to this use. Both fighters disobey the modern convention of raising their "two" hand to their face for protection. Instead, this arm is bent at a near ninety-degree angle at the waist, leaving the fist at the level of the abdomen. In the Eshnunna plaque, the pectoral muscles are emphasized, as are the calf muscles of the boxers' lead legs. The Louvre tentatively dates the plaque to the first half of the second millennium BC. This is perhaps the most proleptic of Mesopotamian representations of boxing. Its features are to be found in depictions of boxers throughout the Mediterranean Basin for at least two millennia. Indeed, its influence is still palpable in the ubiquitous iconography of modern boxing posters and in the "face-off" that precedes well-publicized fights.

Another terracotta plaque (see Figure 14),[10] now held at the Louvre and similar to the Es-

---

[9]The other prominent example of ancient boxers wearing jewelry comes from the boxing boys of Akrotiri.

[10]An inventory number for this item has not been identified, despite an extensive search of the Louvre's online

Figure 13: Terracotta plaque of boxers from Eshnunna (Tell Asmar?), located at the Louvre (No. AO-12447) and dated to around 2000 BC.

Figure 14: This terracotta plaque, which is kept at the Louvre, has an unfortunately non-specific provenance: "Babylonia, beginning of [the] second millennium" (Amiet 1980, p. 386, pl. 437; p. 450). It is similar to the Eshnunna plaque, also held at the Louvre (Figure 13).

hnunna artifact, is said to originate in "Babylonia", ca. 2000 BC (Amiet 1980, p. 386, pl. 437; p. 450). The figures are most likely bearded. Because the fingers were not clearly delineated by the artist or have eroded, it is hard to rule out the possibility that the boxers are gloved. They certainly wear kilts similar to their counterparts in the Eshnunna plaque. The figure on the left may we wearing a necklace, but only a few beads are visible. The composition of the two boxer plaques at the Louvre is similar but by no means identical. We believe both portray telestic boxing matches between adult males that were widely known in Mesopotamia throughout the Bronze Age.

A relief depicting boxers with wristbands, identified by Iraq Museum no. 10039, has been observed (Poliakoff 1987, p. 172, fn. 3) but this item is perhaps now lost and, in any event, a photograph cannot be located.[11] Another Old Babylonian terracotta plaque from Girsu (Tell Telloh) is described by Parrot (1948, p. 286) as "une scéne de pugilat."[12] It appears to show a

<hr>

collections, accessed April 1, 2022.

[11] Item 10039 could not be identified in the Iraq Museum database of the Oriental Institute of Chicago, http://oi-archive.uchicago.edu/OI/IRAQ/dbfiles/im_nos.htm, accessed May 22, 2021.

[12] Just a few sentences later, Parrot (1948, p. 286) calls the same scene one of "lutte á main plate". Unfortunately, the author's ambivalence towards boxing and wrestling is consistent with that of many other interpreters of Mesopotamian art.

bearded man, naked to the waist, menacing a fallen opponent by gesturing with his arm.

Extant depictions of boxing in Mesopotamia have been dated no later than the early second millennium BC. No depictions of boxing have been discovered in Mesopotamian art of the Assyrian or neo-Babylonian periods. This may reasonably be interpreted as a decline in the cultic importance of boxing in the lands between the Tigris and Euphrates well before the end of the Bronze Age. By then, however, indications of boxing were appearing throughout the Mesopotamian periphery, viz., in Iran, the Levant, and Anatolia.

2.2.2 Literary representations: The oldest written word for 'boxing'

The oldest written word for 'boxing' was impressed in clay tablets in Mesopotamia five thousand years ago. There are three Romanized transliterations for the word 'boxing' in Sumerian: gešpú, ĝeš(b/p)a, and ŋešba; they can also mean 'fist', maybe in a *pars pro toto* sense. While discussing Sumeria, we will use the term GEŠPÚ (in small caps) to cover all three of the transliterations that appear in the Sumerological literature, except when greater specificity is required. In such instances the transliteration will appear in lower case.[13]

There are three cuneiform spellings of GEŠPÚ in Sumerian, combining a variety of Sumerian cuneiform signs (see Figure 15). The most common is a compound of šu 'hand' and BULÙG (also known as DIM4), which may mean 'malt', 'approach', 'bow', or 'beg'. BULÙG may also be written as PAP.PAP; PAP may mean 'prudence', 'protection', 'father', 'brother', 'man', or 'leader'.[14] The third attested form is ŠU.BULÙG plus the sign BA, a symbol which on its own may mean 'allot', a type of vessel, a type of tool, or a type of garment. In this case, Sumerologists render the spelling ĝeš(b/p)a or ŋešba.

Owing to the polysemy of these signs, a great many compositional meanings present themselves as potential etymologies of Sumerian GEŠPÚ. The combination 'hand'+'protection' is well-suited to the context of boxing, but 'hand'+'brother', 'approach', 'bow', or 'beg' may all be appropriate, as well. As we will argue elsewhere, boxing itself is polysemous, so perhaps it is no wonder that the first word used to refer to the practice should also be vegete with meaning.[15]

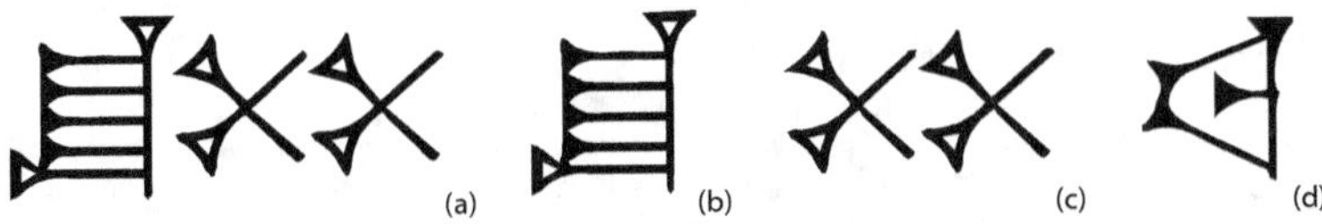

Figure 15: (a) Cuneiform signs for the most commonly occurring form of GEŠPÚ; and various components in this and other forms of the word: (b) šu; (c) BULÙG / DIM4 / PAP.PAP; and (d) BA.

Sumerian GEŠPÚ appears to be equivalent to Akkadian *(ḫ)umāšu* (Sjöberg et al. 2021).

---

[13] For consistency with the Hittitological literature, we will exclusively use the term GEŠPÚ (in small caps) in Section 2.5.

[14] It is not obvious why ŠU.BULÙG and ŠU.PAP.PAP are considered different forms in the *Pennsylvania Sumerian Dictionary*, since their cuneiform spellings are identical.

[15] Some may even wish to advance the proposition that Sumerian boxing had chrematitic origins, with the victor securing, e.g., a handful of malt for his pains.

Unfortunately, the meaning of the Akkadian equivalent is not well-established. In addition to 'boxing', it has been translated as 'strength', 'wrestle', 'wrestling', 'wrestling match' (*Ringkampf*), and 'link in a chain' (*maillon*). GEŠPÚ is found in a number of Akkadian dictionaries, where it is variously translated as 'strength', 'wrestling', 'wrestling hook',[16] 'wrestler', and 'athlete'.[17] One scholar who argues *ḫumāšu* is related to wrestling, and to the wrestler's belt in particular, concludes with a prevarication: "The language in which these proposals are advanced is consciously hypothetical. To do otherwise would, doubtless, be too daring" (Sasson 1974, p. 410). The transliterations gešpú and geš(p/b)a are together attested a total of seven times in the *Pennsylvania Sumerian Dictionary*.[18] All attestations are from the fourth and third millennia BC.

The transliteration ŋešba, written with the same cuneiform signs as the GEŠPÚ variants, occurs 58 times in the Sumerian corpus.[19] It is most frequently translated as 'boxer', but also as 'fist', 'boxing', and 'fist fight'. While the cuneiform spellings associated with this transliteration are identical to those noted earlier for GEŠPÚ, three instances of ŋešba are preceded by the determiner LÚ, designating a male profession; this reinforces the translation 'boxer'. The transliteration ŋešba is posited in cuneiform inscriptions from the Early Dynastic IIIa to the post-Old Babylonian periods, i.e., roughly from the third to the second millennium BC.

An untranslated tablet from Tell Jokha (Umma) dated to the Ur III period (2100–2000 BC) appears to refer to a 'glorious boxer' (transliterated KÙ GEŠBÁ[BA])[20] followed by a mention of the deity Ningišzida,[21] sometimes associated with vegetation and the underworld, sometimes associated with victory.[22] The former quality seems to be referenced in this particular text, which may identify the god as a pugilist (Stone 2016).

Hill and Jacobsen (1990, p. 71, fn. 88) describe the courtyard of the Kitîtum temple, near modern-day Baghdad, by referring to the enactment, in the temple courtyard, of an activity called GEŠPÚ LIRÙM. LIRUM can be spelled ŠU.KAL in cuneiform and LIRÚM is spelled AŠ; both are glossed as 'strength'.[23] The Akkadian equivalent is *(ḫ)umāšu ú ubāru* and the phrase is frequently rendered merely as 'wrestling' though it clearly consists of two activities separated by the conjunction *ú* 'and'. Hill and Jacobsen point out that the phrase regularly coöccurs with the Sumerian verb RA (Akkadian *maḫāṣu*) 'hit', implying that striking was a component of GEŠPÚ LIRUM.[24] Another authority has no trouble accepting that GEŠPÚ

---

[16]Sallaberger refers disparagingly to the "phantom" hook proposal, which he claims arises from a misinterpretation of the loincloth that dangles between the legs of the Khafājah pugilists (see Figure 8): ...*mit einem zwischen den beinen hindurchführenden Schurz belkeidet sind* (1983, p. 17, fn. 838).

[17]Citations include Labat and Malbran-Labat (1988, p. 165), Black et al. (1999, p. 421), and Borger (2004, p. 370).

[18]'ĝešba', http://psd.museum.upenn.edu/epsd/epsd/e2071.html, accessed June 5, 2021.

[19]'[ŋešba]' http://oracc.museum.upenn.edu/epsd2/00029322, accessed June 5, 2021.

[20]This appears to be yet another transliteration, not attested in the *Pennsylvania Sumerian Dictionary*. However, the inscription itself manifests one of the standard cuneiform spellings of GEŠPÚ discussed earlier, viz., ŠU.BULÙG.BA.

[21]This divinity is depicted, in some instances, with serpents emerging from his shoulders.

[22]Princeton Theological Seminary #1446, https://cdli.ucla.edu/search/search_results.php?SearchMode=Text&ObjectID=P127212, accessed March 12, 2022.

[23]http://oracc.museum.upenn.edu/dcclt/signlists/00033186; http://oracc.iaas.upenn.edu/dcclt/nineveh/P397287/html; accessed online August 6, 2021.

[24]In another translation, GEŠPÚ is rendered 'tricks', presumably some kind of tactic or set of tactics associated with wrestling. Hardly secure in this translation, however, the author points out that "[t]his practice of wrestling needs further investigation" (Vermaak 1993, p. 17, fn. 42).

means 'boxing', noting that gešba can be confidently rendered as "fist" in Sumerian sentences such as, "Before that, he hit me with his fist" (Sallaberger 1983, p. 178, fn. 838).

We now undertake a closer examination of a document that mentions GEŠPÚ. A thirteenth-century text (VAT 10610) found at Assur but believed to be an importation from Babylon, describes the proceedings when the cultic image of a god was brought into the Ešumeša temple at Nippur (Lambert 1960, pp. 118–120). In this context, "athletic young men" engage in GEŠPÚ "for [the deity]", most likely Ninurta (ibid., p. 120). Here, GEŠPÚ LIRUM is associated with the verb RA. Since it is a bilingual text, the equivalencies in Sumerian and Akkadian are easily established: Sumerian GEŠPÚ is Akkadian *úmaši* while LIRUM is *abari*. The relevant passage reads:

> Drum and cymbal [...] sing out to you,
> Fat oxen and [fat] sheep are slaughtered for you as the king's offering,
> Athletic young men fight for you with physique and might...
> When you enter Ešumeša, the house which stretches to heaven and the under-
> world... (ibid.).

This "Hymn to Ninurta" is undoubtedly related to the visual depictions discussed in the previous section, which frequently link music and sacrifice to pugilism, e.g., the limestone plaque excavated at The Sin Temple of Khafājah (Figure 8). Worshiped as the patron of both healing and warfare, Ninurta's association with the bruising art seems appropriate.

A thousand years older than the *Iliad* and the *Odyssey*, a short poem called "The Marriage of Martu" (Kramer 1990) offers a Bronze Age account of boxing. GEŠPÚ is mentioned in this work, first written down in the Old Babylonian period, between 1900 and 1600 BC. According to the narrative, an Amorite mountain,[25] storm, and/or warrior god named Martu seeks a wife. He goes to the city of Inab and fights in a competition. Martu comes to a place called the É GEŠPÚ, which likely refers to a location where boxing matches took place (lit. 'the house of boxing') or perhaps the school in which boxers trained (cf. É DUB.BA 'the house of the tablet' for scribes) (Rollinger 1994, p. 18–22). At the Temple of Inab, Martu engages in an activity that involves hitting his opponents, causing many to require bandages and others to die (Bernhardt and Kramer 1956–57). Given the action of hitting and outcomes including bleeding wounds and death,[26] GEŠPÚ in this context is not likely to mean 'wrestling'.[27] Despite this, GEŠPÚ is typically translated as 'wrestling' in English versions of "The Marriage of Martu".[28] We correct this error by following the suggestion of Hill and Jacobsen, noting the presence of the verb RA 'hit', not to mention the serious, even fatal, injuries that Martu inflicts on his opponents. Accordingly, we conclude that the Martu episode is best understood as a boxing tournament.

---

[25] "The most frequently attested epithet of the god Martu in all hymnic sources is his characterization as 'the man/one of the hills/mountains'" (Klein 1997, p. 102).

[26] According to one translation, "In the main courtyard he [sc., Martu] lifts dead bodies" (Klein 1997, p. 107).

[27] Deaths in wrestling were not unknown in the (much later) Greco-Roman world but they were more rare than in boxing (Brophy and Brophy 1985). Indeed, unlike boxing, "[W]restling was never...meant to be a 'victory or death' contest" (ibid., p. 175). The level of danger involved in wrestling depends on what tactics were allowed in the Mesopotamian variety. There is no positive evidence that it was more dangerous than the wrestling practiced by later ancient peoples.

[28] For example, the translation of Vanstiphout (1998) is used as the basis for the English version available at https://etcsl.orinst.ox.ac.uk/cgi-bin/etcsl.cgi?text=t.1.7.1#. Reflecting the ambiguity of the term, Mirelman (2014) translates GEŠPÚ as 'boxing/wrestling'. Klein (1997, p. 107) calls it "an athletic wrestling or fighting contest."

In "The Marriage of Martu", the pugilistic encounters were held in honor of Numušda, a god of wild nature associated with storms. He was depicted as having a violent nature, which speaks to his association with boxing in the poem. As a prize for his victory in the boxing ring, Martu is offered silver and jewels but he chooses to marry the daughter of Numušda instead. The playing of drums is explicitly mentioned in the poem. In this respect, the scene is reminiscent of the boxing festivities depicted in the Tell as-Senkereh plaque (Figure 12).

One objection that could be raised to our interpretation of GEŠPÚ in "The Marriage of Martu" is that the fighters wear íB.LÁ, translated by Vanstiphout as 'belt' (1998). While belts are indeed associated with wrestling in a variety of ancient (and modern) cultures, there are many ancient examples of fighters girding themselves for boxing matches, as well, including graphic depictions of boxers on Thera and Crete (Dioscurus and Dioscurus 2022b), along with textual evidence in the *Odyssey,* in which combatants don the ζῶμα. Much has been made of the belts worn by the Boxing Boys of Akrotiri, which may be associated with a protective sea goddess (Parke 1987). In addition, the gloss of 'belt' versus 'loincloth' in the Martu narrative also seems uncertain. íB is glossed as 'hips' and LÁ or LAL can be glossed as 'hang', 'hold', 'lift', or 'carry', as well as 'stretch', 'reach' and 'extend'. Elsewhere, íB-LAL is glossed tentatively as 'underwear' (Halloran 1996–2020). Thus, if one starts from the premise that GEŠPÚ refers to boxing in the "The Marriage of Martu", then the 'belt' that is worn by the combatants need not supply counterevidence in favor of a wrestling scenario. As we have demonstrated, this 'belt' could just as easily refer to a boxing loincloth (see Figure 8) or kilt, such as the garment depicted in the Tell as-Senkereh plaque (see Figure 12).

A hymn of Šulgi (C) refers to the king's prowess as a sportsman. He proclaims himself "the strong man of GEŠPÚ and LIRÙM" and boasts, "In GEŠPÚ I was indeed the strong one" (Vermaak 1993, pp. 16–17). While Vermaak prefers the gloss 'tricks', he notes that the meaning of GEŠPÚ is "still open to discussion." In this case, we again propose 'boxing' as the best alternative, following Hill and Jacobsen (1990), particularly because Šulgi himself seems to differentiate GEŠPÚ and LIRÙM as separate activities. Šulgi might be recognized as the first non-mythic, named boxer in history.

For mythic boxers, we turn to the Epic of Gilgameš and related Sumero-Akkadian literature. The violent encounter between Gilgameš and his rival-turned-best-friend Enkidu does not use the term GEŠPÚ or its Akkadian equivalent *úmaši.* The only two verbs used in the relevant passage are Akkadian *ṣabātu* 'seize' and *lâdum* 'crouch'. Seizing or clinching one's opponent is a common technique in modern boxing and may have played an even more important part in the ancient Mesopotamian variety, as it does in modern Muay Thai. We will see the verb 'crouch' later, connected to Hittite boxers resting between rounds (Section 2.5).

Translations differ in ways that lead to different mental images of the bout. In one reading, Gilgameš and the wild man smash into the doorjamb; in another they demolish it (Akk. *abātu*) (George 2003, Gelb et al. 1964). Where terms are not specific, much is inferred from the consequences of the battling brothers' activity: the walls quake. The passage sometimes translated to mean that the combatants fought like oxen (indicating to some the low center-of-gravity typical of wrestlers) might instead simply mean they fought like experts, including trained pugilists (George 2003, pp. 180–181, 191). When it comes to the fight, the text describes a rowdy altercation that takes place in the doorway of a wedding house—and not much more. The composer may have been more interested in the significance of the location (see our earlier discussion on the positioning of votive boxing plaques in temples) rather than the activity itself, which perhaps required no elaboration for a contemporary listener familiar with Mesopotamian personal combat.

The fifth month of the Babylonian year, Abu, was sacred to Gilgameš.[29] During this month, a festival occurred in which "young men fight in their doorways in wrestling matches [GEŠPÚ LIRUM] and trials of strength." A Late Babylonian menology (the Nippur Compendium) explains that Abu is the month of warfare, wrestling (*úmaši*), and trials of strength (*abari*) (George 2003, p. 126).[30] A Sumero-Akkadian menology known as Astrolabe B functioned as a kind of *Farmer's Almanac* in ancient Mesopotamia, drawing relationships between the month and the stars on one hand and agricultural and social activities on the other. Significant portions of the text can be dated to between 1400 and 1000 BC. The bilingual entry for the month of Gilgameš has been translated: "For nine days the young men contest in wrestling and athletics in their city quarters" (Çağırgan 1984, pp. 405, 411).[31] Sumerian GEŠPÚ LIRUM is translated as Akkadian *úmáš úbari* in this text. It has been speculated that GEŠPÚ LIRUM was practiced by young men to commemorate the fight between Gilgameš and Enkidu.

In the Sumerian poem, the "Death of Gilgameš", the ritual combat of Abu is described: "[T]he warriors, the young men and the onlookers shall make a semi-circle around a doorway,[32] and in front of it, wrestling matches [GEŠPÚ LIRUM] and trials of strength will occur." The ritual fight takes place in front of funerary figurines and includes a torchlit ceremony commemorating the dead (including Gilgameš himself) (ibid., pp. 126–127).

The ritual combat also may be closely bound to a vaguely described Mesopotamian tradition involving single combat between the king and a challenger. The ritual could have toppled the king or confirmed his authority (George 2003, pp. 169–170). "[T]he king of the gods had to confirm his position by a display of physical supremacy at regular intervals" (ibid., p. 170). During the Akītu festival at Babylon, the earthly representative of Marduk was slapped in the face before being reinstalled as king. Perhaps these rituals, linked to the epic conflict between Gilgameš and Enkidu, were mythopoeic vestiges of a long-discontinued rite of kingship. Indeed, there is reason to believe that such a tradition informed the composer of the Epic of Gilgameš. Before their encounter, Enkidu is proclaimed by the people as a champion, counterpart, or rival (Akk. *meḫrum*) to the king and they opine on how well the two are matched physically (ibid., p. 190). The people seem to goad the two heroes to fight, surrounded by a festival atmosphere at Uruk.

Finally, we encounter the earliest reports of prizefighting in Sumerian literature. Besides "The Marriage of Martu", where the victor is offered a monetary prize before requesting a wife instead, Sallaberger mentions two other instances of chrematitic boxing; these may or may not be associated with the Sumerian temple cultus (1983, p. 16, fn. 53). In one, the boxer (the son of a musician named Alla) receives a silver ring worth ten shekels for mixing it up with his opponent. In the other, a second boxer identified by his patronymic receives an unidentified gift for 'beating up' (Sum. TAG.TAG) his adversary. The verbs are not specific enough to indicate the outcomes of the matches precisely, but since only one boxer is paid

---

[29] The Gregorian equivalent of this month comprises the end of July and the beginning of August.

[30] The latter term may be the Akkadian cognate of the verb *abaq* used to describe the conflict between Jacob and a divine being in Genesis (see Section 2.4).

[31] Astrolabe B indicates that the month sacred to Gilgamesh was also associated with the star Sirius and the warrior god Ninurta. During this month, the Annunaki or fate deities were celebrated with the lighting of torches, which evidently provoked a rivalry between Girra, the god of fire and Šamaš, the solar god.

[32] Literally, "form a doorway like a crescent".

and his activity is described in positive terms, we can only imagine that the victor was the one who took home the prize.

It appears that boxing was not commonly represented in Assyrian art,[33] though a few texts found at Assur refer to organized athletic events including wrestling and, arguably, boxing (Sjöberg 1985). Some of these texts may have been imported from other locations and were perhaps substantially older than Assyrian culture itself. One text is associated with Gilgameš celebrations (Reiner and Pingree 1981, p. 81, lines 13–15). An incantation text from the first millennium BC admonishes the sorcerer to "place (two) figurines of bitumen (representing) two grappling wrestlers." This translation, provided by Sjöberg, is based on the transliteration of the original cuneiform text (Nies and Keiser 1920, No. 22, lines 172-173). Nies and Keiser, who unfortunately do not provide their own translation of the two relevant, fragmentary lines, descry the critical Akkadian word *úmaši* for what is rendered by Sjöberg as 'grappling wrestlers'. As we note elsewhere, this term is equivalent to GEŠPÚ in Sumero-Akkadian bilingual texts and thus the incantation may in fact refer to pugilists made of bitumen. Another text uncovered at Assur is published in Lambert (1960, p. 116), *ut supra*. Finally, Sjöberg refers to a text from Tell Kuyunjiq (Nineveh) that mentions athletes performing at a festival of a goddess. Unfortunately, no citation was provided and so we have been unable to verify the Akkadian term(s) used to describe these hierurgical athletes. We suspect a word like *úmaši* appears in this as-yet unidentified text.

Thus, we see that a variety of textual sources in ancient Mesopotamia refer to boxing, though there has been a tendency to render the term GEŠPÚ and its equivalents as 'wrestling' in some English[34] translations of Sumerian and Akkadian literature. Given the tentative nature of most of these translations, we have argued for the translation 'boxing' as a more convincing alternative in many of them. This, in turn, serves as a complement to the intriguing (and generally incontestable) graphic evidence of Mesopotamian fist fighting.

2.3   Iran

We are aware of only one ancient object suggestive of boxing in the region that is today circumscribed by the borders of Iran. The golden bowl of Hasanlu (Tehran Museum No. 10712) was discovered by archæologists working in the extreme northwest, near the border with Iraq (Porada 1959, Winter 1989). The culture that made the bowl has not yet been identified but it was clearly influenced by the neighboring Assyrians, Urartians, and Hurrians. The settlement at Hasanlu was destroyed by fire around 800 BC (most likely by fighters from Urartu) and the bowl was discovered among the remains of individuals who may have been looting or attempting to preserve it (Danti 2014). Because of the unique circumstances of its deposition, it is difficult to date the production of the bowl, which was perhaps already three hundred years old at the time of Hasanlu's cataclysmic demise.

The figures of interest on the Hasanlu bowl include what appear to be a hero and a mountain deity, engaged in fistic combat. The hero wears "ribbed shields which seem to have the function of boxing gloves" (Porada 1959, p. 20). He is dressed in a kilt, with bare chest, in the manner of Mesopotamian fighters. His hair is held back in a fillet, perhaps ad-

---

[33] One potential counterexample is a cylinder seal used by Assyrian merchants at Kaneš, in Anatolia, discussed in Section 2.5. In addition, the provenance of many of the cylinder seals discussed in Section 2.4 is unknown; based on their iconography, some of the seals could be of Assyrian origin.

[34] As we have remarked elsewhere, German scholars seem more open to regarding this activity as a fistfight.

Figure 16: Detail of repoussé boxers on the golden bowl of Hasanlu (Tehran Museum No. 10712). Deposited around 800 BC, there is no consensus as to its age. The figure on the left represents a a hero battling a mountain deity, right. Note the corded boxing gloves covering the fists of the heroic figure.

dressing the same problem experienced by criniferous boxers down to the present age, viz., hair occluding one's vision. The hero engages with a figure emerging from a depiction of a mountain, identified by a great number of arches (as in Hittite art). Similarly bare-chested, the mountain deity's hands look like the paws of an animal. Both hands are stretched out and the torso and head lean backward. The same is true of the heroic figure, who bends dramatically retrograde at the waist.

With both arms outstretched and with the body leaning backward, we notice at once that this is a unique depiction of a boxing match in the ancient world. It suggests a variety of boxing where the head was the primary target, and so had to be held as far away from one's adversary as possible.[35] As for the boxing gloves, if the execution of the bowl can be placed at the beginnings of Iron Age Hasanlu, then the repoussé boxer wears one of the early depictions of boxing gloves in ancient art. This artifact is, however, most likely antedated by Minoan depictions of boxing (which also feature gloves) produced much earlier in the second millennium BC. We believe the Hasanlu boxing gloves represent an older version of the Greek ἱμάντες or boxing thongs. Like the Greek version, the Hasanlu gloves may be composed of leather strips, or perhaps they were made of rope (a proposed etymon of ἱμάς).

The duel between a man and a mountain deity is particularly interesting, given the strong association between boxing and mountain worship among the Hittites. The Hittites of course predated the ill-starred Iron Age residents of Hasanlu by hundreds of years, but successors of the Bronze Age Anatolian kingdom may have influenced the myths of Hasanlu, most likely by way of the Hurrians. Indeed, a connection has been posited between Hurrian mythology and the boxers on the Hasanlu gold bowl (Porada 1959). The heroic figure may represent the weather god Tešub, come to fight his archrival (and by some accounts, his brother), the rock monster Ulikummi (Güterbock 1951; 1952). This story was found, written in Hurrian, among the trove of Hittite documents discovered in central Anatolia. We turn to Hittite boxing in Section 2.5.

There are only two literary references to boxing in classical Iran; both are indirect and both come from Greek commentators. Strabo indicated that Parthian boys were trained in the athletic competitions of the pentathlon, which was known to include javelin-throwing or boxing—but not both (*Strab.* XV.iii 18). Thucydides suggested that boxers from this region donned belts: "To this day among some foreign peoples, especially in Asia, when prizes for boxing and wrestling are offered, belts are worn by the combatants" (*Thuc.* I.vi, 5, trans. Livingstone 1951). Writing during the fifth century BC, Thucydides may have been referring to the Achæmenians, but the statement is of course far too general to be conclusive. One scholar notes, "[T]here is little indication that boxing was of any great significance as a recreational activity in Iran" (Spier 1975, p. 155).

2.4 The Levant

The account of Jacob's 'wrestling' match with 'Ēl, YHWH, or one of his divine emissaries (Genesis 32:22–32) uses the Hebrew verb *abaq*, meaning 'to become dusty' to describe the struggle, which lasted until dawn. It is derived from the triliteral root *abq*, meaning 'dust'. The verb occurs only twice in the Hebrew Bible, both times in the story of Jacob's encounter

---

[35] We note, however, that this is a losing proposition for any boxer who wants to land a punch and defend himself at the same time. The awkward position depicted on the Hasanlu bowl puts the boxer at too great a distance from his opponent to strike with much force.

46

with divinity at Peniel. While generations of scholars have concluded that Genesis 32 describes a wrestling bout between Jacob and the divine being, the text itself is ambiguous, merely suggesting that the combatants got themselves dirty. It is clear from the context that this was an epic battle (the prolonged length of the match recalls the encounter between Gilgameš and Enkidu), but there is no way of knowing from the words of the text whether it was constituted of orthograde or pronograde combat (both of which are well attested in the ancient Near East). When examined closely, *abaq* is as difficult to translate as Sumerian GEŠPÚ or Akkadian *ḫumāšu*, though it is confidently and consistently rendered in English translation as 'wrestle' (KJV, NAS, INT). We are hesitant to suggest that YHWH and Jacob boxed at the stream Jabbok, but there is nothing in the text that rules it out—as long as they got dirty in the process. The two combatants most likely engaged in a sort of rough-and-tumble that involved strikes. We surmise as much because the struggle ended with a blow: the divine being 'touched' the socket of Jacob's hip. In Job 1:19, the same verb is rendered 'smite' (KJV).

Hip displacement, whereby the ball head of the femur becomes removed from its seat in the acetabulum (the 'socket'), typically occurs due to traumatic injury. In the modern world, it is most frequently observed as a result of motor vehicle collisions, where the patient's thigh strikes the dashboard of the car, "sending a posteriorly directed force to the joint" (Dawson-Amoah et al. 2018, p. 242). According to one review, "among elite wrestlers, the hip is rarely even noted as a source of problems" (Byrd et al. 2017, p. 334). In the ancient world, hip displacement may have occurred most often when individuals fell or were struck in the leg by animals or heavy objects. While it is plausible that Jacob suffered this injury in the course of a wrestling encounter, the text may well indicate that the injury came about due to contact between Jacob's hip and the divinity's fist.

The wrestling motif is perhaps more unambiguously suggested in the next passage: the divine being asks Jacob to "let me go"—a verb rendered in I Kings and elsewhere in Genesis more generically as "send away" (KJV). While one may reasonably wonder what—besides a particularly effective wrestling hold—could have dissuaded a deity from taking his leave at his own pleasure, there is still no explicit verb of grasping or grappling found anywhere in the text. Given the ancient Near Eastern traditions of boxing we discuss in this article, as well as the fact that Jacob's hip was traumatically 'smitten' by the divinity's fist during the bout, it seems entirely plausible that Jacob's struggle with the divine being involved some form of boxing, most likely in addition to wrestling. Thus, the account in Genesis 32 may have its closest Near Eastern analogs in the "Marriage of Martu" and the Epic of Gilgameš.

Aside from our admittedly tenuous identification of a boxing battle in the Hebrew Bible, there is substantial evidence of pugilism in the glyptic art of the ancient Levant. Cylinder seals were used widely as a security device throughout Mesopotamia and its neighboring regions during the Bronze and Iron Ages. Rolled across a clay tablet, the carved cylinder left the impression of a scene associated with the authority who had made the impression, thus authenticating the authorship of the tablet for its intended reader. While the cylinder seals depict a variety of scenes, the combat or contest scene is one of the most common (Thompson 2013, p. 11). We argue that a good number of these combat scenes depict ancient forms of boxing.

For example, the seal illustrated in Figure 17 dates from sometime between 1850 and 1620 BC and was collected in Syria, though no more specific provenance is available (Teissier 1984, pp. 87–88, 326). The figures on the left are engaged in boxing or wrestling while the figures on the right confront one another with knives in hand. Thompson argues that the

Figure 17: Impression of a Syrian cylinder seal (a more precise provenance is not available). Boxers appear on the left, knife fighters on the right. One of the boxers wear's a top knot, a fashion frequently attested in much later Roman depictions of boxers and pankratiasts. 1850–1620 BC. Marcopoli Collection, Summa Galleries (?), Seal No. 547 (Teissier 1984).

figures on the left are grasping each other's wrists, suggestive of wrestling. However, the open character of the hands does not convey to us the same interpretation. We believe it is just as likely that they are boxing. The fighters wear a split skirt or paneled loincloth and appear to be belted. Their arms furthest from the viewer cross in the fashion well attested from the earliest depictions of boxing found in lower Mesopotamia (see Section 2.2). The 'ball-staff' that appears in the field between the two pairs of fighters is likely a fertility symbol associated with the goddess Ištar (Thompson 2013, p. 21), strongly suggesting that pugilism in this context related to sexual success. The hand (which appears to the far left and right in Figure 17, is thought to represent the tradition of severing a prisoner's hands, perhaps associated with Ištar's dual role as a war deity (ibid.). One remarkable aspect of this glyptic is the topknot worn by the leftmost boxer. This hairstyle is observed in depictions of boxers well into late Antiquity, most likely because it served the purpose of keeping the hair out of the face and away from the grasp of an adversary.

Another seal (British Museum No. 130651) was excavated at Level VII (Middle Bronze Age) of the Alalakh Palace in far southern Turkey (Figure 18). In the Middle Bronze Age, Alalakh passed between the hands of Mari and Yamhad. It was destroyed by the Hittite king Hattušili I at the end of that period. The seal is made of black chlorite and, we argue, depicts a pair of boxers in combat with each other, urged on by a third figure, standing to their right.

The Alalakh boxers "seem to be aiming, or even grasping, at each other's faces" (Collon 2000, p. 287). Collon sees in this a similarity to the boys in the Akrotiri Boxer Fresco; we will address Minoan boxing, and this fresco in particular, extensively in Dioscurus and Dioscurus (2022b). Collon notes further: "There is no evidence, however, for the single boxing glove

Figure 18: Impression of a chlorite cylinder seal (British Museum No. 130651) depicting boxers and animal-fighting. Middle Bronze Age, 2100–1500 BC.

that the [Akrotiri] boxers wear." We disagree. Based on the differential size of the boxers' back hands (also, the size of these hands compared to the hands of the figure to their right, including one which is clearly clenched), we conclude the figures are each wearing only one boxing glove. Moreover, the glyptic represents an example of enantiomorphic boxing, given that the enlarged striking hands are on the arms of the opposed figures furthest from the viewer. Collon notes that the seal is "extremely coarsely engraved" (p. 287). For this reason, in part, we disagree with Thompson's (2013) claim that the fighters hold daggers in the hands closest to the viewer (p. 21). We also agree with Collon in rejecting the possibility that the Alalakh figures are wrestlers. Besides the fact that the contestants aim for each other's faces, as Collon puts it, British Museum curators note that their attitude is dissimilar to that of the wrestlers adorning the walls of the Chapel of Khety at Beni Hasan (XIth Dynasty Egypt) and is in fact more similar to the posture of the boxing boys of Akrotiri.[36]

A significant figure stands to the right of the boxers in the Alalakh seal. He appears to wear a headdress and a calf-length skirt (the boxer's kilts barely reach their upper thigh). The right hand of this figure is clenched and the left hand is open. His posture seems to indicate that he is encouraging the fighters and perhaps even mimicking their blows with his clenched fist. Looking at this glyptic figure, one naturally recalls a spectator at a modern boxing match, muscles tensed and hands balled into fists in eager anticipation of a desired outcome in the ring. A third figure in pugilistic scenes would later become much more common, especially in Greek vase painting. In these cases, the third figure usually wields an implement suggesting his authority as a referee or trainer. In the Alalakh seal, the role of this figure is more ambiguous but his presence recalls both the figure in the limestone plaque from the Sin Temple of Khafājah (Figure 8) and foreshadows the ubiquitous "third man in the ring" found in many later depictions.

In the seal's terminal we observe a quadruped, perhaps a dog, sitting on its haunches and

---

[36] https://www.britishmuseum.org/collection/object/W_1939-0613-119

turning its head towards a lion jumping on its back. The appearance of these animals combatant are perhaps intended to parallel the boxers in the scene. Given the close relationship between animal fighting (cynomachy, alectryomachy, and bear-baiting, in particular) and pugilism in the early modern era, the animals may be tautegorical, i.e., depictions of theriomachy that actually accompanied boxing matches at Alalakh.[37] The two birds flying above the fighting animals may be representations of a Syrian goddess (Thompson 2013, p. 21). According to Thompson, "[T]his seal may portray a type of ritual combat involving two warriors/heroes in the presence of an official and the gods" (p. 21).

Boxing matches are represented in two or three cylinder seals found at Ugarit (Ras Shamra, northern Syria), dated to the early second millennium BC (Schaeffer-Forrer 1983, pp. 50, 55–56). In the older of the two (Figure 19), one of the boxers is occluded by damage to the cylinder, but his arm is visible, crossing that of his adversary, in the confrontation pose typical of Mesopotamian boxers of roughly the same era (see Figures 12, 13, 14).[38] The boxer wears a horizontally-striated loincloth or kilt and a double-necklace. The boxers appear to wear bracelets on one or both wrists. An entatic column or "portable altar" (ibid., p. 55) with flat extremities stands between the boxers at about the height of the knees. A third figure, probably the referee, views the action, dressed in an embroidered robe draped from one shoulder. He appears to make a formal ring gesture with his right hand. A feline and a bird are partially visible behind him.

Figure 19: Impression of a fragmented Ugaritic hematite cylinder seal showing a boxer crossing arms with another (partially visible) boxer and separated by an altar. An official stands nearby, making a ring gesture (National Museum of Damascus). The object is dated to the eighteenth century BC.

In a cylinder of perhaps slightly less antiquity (Figure 20), the boxers have not yet begun their duel. The fingers of the hands facing one another, pointing upward, are disproportionately elongated in the same manner observed in much later Etruscan tomb paintings (e.g., in

---

[37] We will remark on a similar juxtaposition of human and animal fighting among the Hittites (Section 2.5).

[38] A third Ugaritic cylinder seal, in stone rather than hematite, is mentioned by Schaeffer-Forrer (1983, p. 50) as including athletes, presumably boxers, making the same gesture. The item is identified as RS 25.180 but no photograph of the seal has been located.

the Tomba della Scimmia at Chiusi, early fifth century BC). Their other arms are lowered behind their backs, not bent at the elbow, with their hands open. Between the boxers is a column or altar; above it and between the fighters' raised hands glows an eight-pointed star. The fighters are bare-headed and they wear necklaces and short striated loincloths or kilts. Identified as a referee by Schaeffer-Forrer (1983, p. 56), the individual to the right is nonetheless dressed in the same fashion as the boxers (cf. Figure 19, where the third party is more richly robed). He is separated from the fighters by another, smaller column or altar, and is accompanied by the image of a whale (*un cétacé* ibid.) floating over his back shoulder. If we extend Thompson's (2014) interpretation of the Alalakh cylinder seal, we might argue that the whale represents a deity in whose honor the combatants fight each other.

Figure 20: Impression of a Ugaritic hematite cylinder seal showing two boxers saluting one another before the initiation of combat; an official or a third boxer stands nearby (National Museum of Aleppo). The object is dated between 1750 and 1650 BC.

The cylinder seal impression shown in Figure 20 is similar in many ways to another one presented by Thompson (2013, p. 8, fig. 1.1). While no provenance is given, the seal is dated to between 1850 and 1720 BC and is almost certainly Syrian in origin. It features two figures in a pose similar to the one assumed by the boxers in the Ugaritic hematite cylinder seal *ut supra*: one hand is raised in salute and the other is lowered to a neutral (non-defensive) position. The third figure in the scene holds a dagger in each hand. The dagger in his left hand points downward to an ankh symbol, suggesting Egyptian influence. In the terminal, a griffin rampant soars above a guilloche; below the guilloche, an ibex couchant. Both animals face the fighters. In the "prize" position between the fighters, a table is laden with objects; this table is a common feature of boxing depictions well into late antiquity, including in a mosaic at the Villa Selene on the Libyan coast. A seven- or eight-pointed star blazes above the fighters; along with the animals, this is likely a representation of a divinity whose numinous presence sacralizes the combat (Thompson 2013).

A Hematite cylinder seal, probably from Cyprus, depicts bull-headed demons or men wearing bull masks engaging in a boxing match (British Museum No. 89320). The position between the fighters, reserved for a prize in later Greek depictions, is occupied by the head of a stag (Figure 21). A cross-disc and crescent hover above and between them. We speculate that the men wearing bull masks represent the close connection between animal fighting and boxing best established by the practice of *tarpa* among the Hittites.

Figure 21: Detail of boanthropic pugilists from an impression of a hematite cylinder seal that was probably found on Cyprus (British Museum No. 89320). The object is undated.

2.5　Anatolia

Remarkably, our acquaintance with boxing in Bronze Age Anatolia comes to us almost exclusively by way of textual, not visual, sources. These can be dated securely to no later than the thirteenth century BC (Carter 1988, p. 185). By comparison, it took the Greeks 500 more years to write about boxing (if we discount speculation about boxing-related matter on the Phaistos disk).

The Hittites, an Indo-European group who inhabited central Anatolia throughout most of the second millennium BC, recorded many elements of their unique cultus on clay tablets. These were buried in the ruins of their capital, Ḫattuša (modern Boğazköy), from the fall of the Hittite empire until the first decade of the twentieth century. Inscribed in an adapted version of Old Assyrian cuneiform, the writing on the tablets borrows heavily from the Sumerian and Akkadian languages, among others. Accordingly, we once more encounter the Sumerogram GEŠPÚ, now scattered across the tablets excavated at Ḫattuša.[39]

Unlike the Sumerian and Akkadian forms mentioned earlier, GEŠPÚ is spelled uniformly in Hittite texts. It is rendered as ŠU.PAP.PAP, with the innovation of shifting the second PAP to the left and shortening its strokes, so that it partially overlaps with the first (see Figure 22). Early on, German scholars translated the Sumerogram GEŠPÚ as *Faust* 'fist', *Faustschlag* 'punch', and *Offensivkraft* 'offensive power' in Hittite texts (Sommer 1932, p. 181–183). The term is now generally rendered as 'boxing' in English translations of Hittite literature.

In five different Hittite texts,[40] GEŠPÚ appears seven times in contexts where it can be translated confidently as 'boxing'.[41] In several additional cases, it has been argued that GEŠPÚ

---

[39]The hieroglyphic form of Luwian, a close linguistic relative of Hittite, may have had a sign for 'boxing', as well. PUGNUS (a fist, thumb up, palm-side forward, pointing rightward, with almost half the forearm showing and wearing a bracelet) represents a verb with a highly uncertain meaning (Hawkins 1975, p. 128). It has been claimed that PUGNUS means 'to fight' (Hawkins 1995, p. 119). Other contend that it can mean 'to hold', 'to serve', 'to conquer', and 'to live' (Goedegebuure 2012, p.177).

[40]CTH 526.14, 526.31, 526.34, 528.106, 648; GEŠPÚ appears three times in CTH 526.14.

[41]At least one Hittitologist prefers the translation 'wrestling', but we find this unacceptable, given the secure etymology of the Hittite word *ḫulḫuliya* 'wrestling' (a reduplicated form of the verb 'wind' or 'twist'), with which

Figure 22: The cuneiform sign for GEŠPÚ 'boxing' as it appears in Hittite texts. As in Sumerian, the sign is a composite of ŠU+PAP.PAP. However, the two PAP signs overlap, with the strokes of the second PAP shortened (cf. Figure 15a).

denotes a representation of a fist, a work of art which, in turn, may have been associated with boxing (Güterbock and Kendall 1995).[42] As with a number of other Sumerograms that appear in Hittite texts, we do not know how Hittite speakers pronounced GEŠPÚ. Unfortunately, this means we cannot infer from Hittite anything about the roots of the word 'boxing' in other Indo-European languages.

Around the thirteenth century BC, the Hittite royal house began to gather information about autochthonous cults within its realm. This resulted in so-called "cult inventories" describing the religious festivals observed in provincial cities across the empire. According to one authority, "Hittite religious festivals were characterized by a variety of types of activity, including processions, sacrifices, offerings, prayers, purification ceremonies, ritual meals, and occasionally, athletic contests or tests of physical prowess" (Carter 1988, p. 185). Another scholar writes that Hittite festivals "constitute those rituals where the symbolic power of action is most strongly perceived" (Cammarosano 2018, p. 103). The cult inventories contain the majority of references to GEŠPÚ and they generally present boxing in a similar way across different texts.

One inventory, known as the "Cults of Ḫakmiš"[43] (CTH 526.14.), contains three references to boxing as part of various festivals. We read, for example:

PANI DINGIR-*lim* GEŠPÚ *ḫulḫuliya tieškanzi duškiškanzi*

Before the god, they step into the ring to box and wrestle. They rejoice (KUB 25.23 i 21'–22').

This formula is found in numerous Hittite texts, referencing boxing in front of a god, i.e., a cultic image, usually one that has been brought out of its sanctuary to a remote location. In a related text (CTH 526.18), which mentions only wrestling, designated women place a garland on the deity, and on the officiating priest. From the texts, an adumbrant vision emerges of boxing as a sacred activity, carried out as the consummation of a joyful, much-anticipated event. The word *ḫulḫuliya*, sometimes coöccurring with GEŠPÚ in the festival texts, has been firmly reconstructed as 'wrestling'. In the text above, the phrase lacks a conjunction between GEŠPÚ and *ḫulḫuliya*, so it is not clear whether boxing and wrestling are described asyndetically, or whether the practice mentioned is a kind of boxing–wrestling, like the later Greek *pankration* (Puhvel 1988, p. 29).

the Sumerogram in question frequently coöccurs (Carter 1988, p. 186).

[42] CTH 527; see below for an extended discussion of one such artifact in the shape of a fist.

[43] The city of Ḫakmiš was most likely located in or near modern Amasya, in the mountains above the Black Sea coast (Cammarosano 2018, p. xxv)

Much hinges on the translation of the verb *dušk-*, which is nearly ubiquitous in mentions of Hittite boxing. Some translators have rendered the verb phrase as 'they entertain (the deity)' (Hazenbos 2003, p. 36) or 'they rejoice over (the god)' (Cammarosano 2018, p. 365) with no firm resolution as to whether the exuberance associated with the verb *dušk-* has an external object or not. It is likely that the god himself was the most significant spectator of the Hittite boxing matches. The object of veneration in the text quoted above is a mountain god named Ḫalwannaš. In another text, CTH 526.34, telestic boxing takes place in honor of the mountain god Paḫušanuwaš (Hazenbos 2003, pp. 91–93). Elsewhere, a tutelary god, known only by the Sumerian designation ᵈLAMMA[44] and an otherwise unknown deity, Kurḫazuššaraš, are mentioned (Hazenbos 2003, p. 127). In "The Cults of Ḫakmiš", gods from the towns of Urišta and perhaps Parduwata were honored by the fisticuffs, the former being the origin of the mountain god Ḫalwannaš previously mentioned.[45] The god of Parduwata is unnamed.

Why did Hittite boxing take place in association with mountain worship? According to one scholar, "[T]he numinous nature of mountains, which after all constituted the most impressive features of the topography of the Hittite homeland, rendered them an appropriate location—that is, sacred space—for making contact with para-human elements of the cosmos beyond Storm-gods and the mounts themselves" (Beckman 2013, p. 155). That boxing was carried out in this setting reaffirms the sacral nature of pugilism among the Hittites. Mountain deities were often associated with hunting, due presumably to the availability of wild game in these remote, formidable locations. Perhaps boxing served as a rite of passage for young men before they were allowed to hunt. In any case, there is plenty of evidence that boxing in Hittite culture was strongly associated with sacred festivity, as was the case in Egypt and Sumer, and much later in Etruria.

The seasonal timing of Hittite pugilism is also relevant. Boxing festivities in Anatolia appear to have taken place in the spring (Cammarosano 2018, pp. 363, 367, 369); one such account is preceded by the words, "When in spring it thunders..." (KUB 25.34 i 8'). This is the first clear indication we have of a seasonal component to boxing.[46] We note elsewhere that traditional boxing in Russia typically occurred from late winter through spring and that folk boxing matches in the Americas still occur in the spring. Given the inter-hemispheric nature of this pattern, it is tempting to reason that male–male aggression (perhaps as a form of competition for mates) occurs around the Vernal Equinox. However, there is no clear evidence that male testosterone levels, which may lead to increased aggression, change seasonally (Smith et al. 2013) and (modern) monthly birthrates do not support such a hypothesis, either. Nevertheless, dramatic increases in temperatures, accompanied by renewal and growth in the animal and vegetal worlds, seem to have a deep spiritual and æsthetic resonance among humans. For the Hittites, too, spring was a special time associated, in particular, with the return of unstable weather. The katabatic weather god Telipinu was ritually evoked from the dark earth to again unleash storms and life-sustaining rainwater on Ḫatti-land. Exactly what connection the Hittites drew between the natural changes of springtime and boxing is unclear. Boxing in some American traditions is explicitly associated with rainfall—the pugilist's

---

[44] For the Hittites, many deities were referenced by the Sumerogram ᵈLAMMA. They were commonly worshiped as protectors of objects, locations, and of both mortal and divine beings (McMahon 1991).

[45] It has been speculated that Urišta and Parduwata had been occupied by enemies of the Hittites so that their gods were revered in neighboring Ḫakmiš (Cammarosano 2018, p. 359).

[46] In Section 2.2, we remarked on the possibility that the boxing plaque from the Sin Temple at Khafâjah depicts a springtime festival.

dripping blood functions analogically as precipitation. Whether such an association existed among the Bronze Age Hittites is worthy of consideration.

Finally, it may be instructive to look closely at the verbs used in these texts, as they provide us with extra information about Hittite boxing praxis. The verb *tiya-* is inflected in the third person plural, as in the quote above. This verb is translated in other contexts as 'go', 'walk', 'go on' or even 'stay'. According to some scholars, this verb indicates motion *into* a space. In the Hittite boxing texts, no preposition is provided nor is GEŠPÚ inflected for case. Moreover, the verb often (though not exclusively) occurs with the infix *-ške-* (as in the quote above). The infix is sometimes translated as an imperfective marker and sometimes as a marker of incipient action, e.g., "They start to step in". The verb is often rendered 'step into' in the Hittite boxing texts, e.g., Cammarosano (2018, p. 365). Into what are the fighters stepping, or beginning to step? Cammarosano takes the liberty of translating the goal of the action as 'a fight', i.e., "they step into a fight". In our own translation, we suggest the pugilists are stepping into a designated location for combat, i.e., a 'ring'. We emphasize, however, that there is no explicit goal of the verb *tiya-* in the original texts and so the 'ring' can only be inferred (tenuously) from the semantics of the verb itself.

In a festival text (KBO 23.55), domesticated ungulates participate in a bloodsport closely associated with the activity of boxers. In fact, it can be reasoned that the Hittite text refers to the agon of both boxers and beasts by the same word, *tarpa*. According to the text, after the pugilists step into *tarpa*, four rams step into *tarpa*, followed by several bulls which do the same.

The word *tarpa* is unfortunately little understood, though recognized by most authorities as a bit of "fight game terminology" (Soysal 2003, p. 105). One scholar has argued that *tarpa* is a ceremony for the victorious boxers (as in the Patroclan games of the *Iliad*), where rams and bulls are the prizes (Puhvel 1988, p. 30). Despite some potential links between *tarpa* and the Greek and Sanskrit words for 'delight' and 'satisfaction', we prefer the interpretation in which animals are compelled to fight one another, mirroring the actions of the boxers. Indeed, we might posit an etymological association of our own, linking Hittite *tarpa* to Proto-Slavic *tъrpěti* 'to suffer, endure'.

In the festival text, after the men box, several bulls enter the *tarpa*. The verb *tiya-* 'enter, step into' is the same one used for humans who 'enter' GEŠPÚ in this scene, as well as in the "Cults of Ḫakmiš". For this reason, and in line with Soysal's claim that *tarpa tiya-* is a "reciprocal aggressive behavior or violent act" (op. cit.) we conjecture that *tarpa* is a bloodsport for animals.[47]

That the *tarpa* bloodsport accompanies boxing is consistent with numerous visual parallels between the agonistics of men and animals, witnessed, for example, on the cylinder seal of Alalakh and in the greater context of the Boxing Boys fresco at Akrotiri, both of which are likely contemporaneous with the late Bronze Age festival texts found at Ḫattuša.[48] It is not hard to imagine that Hittite festivals involved both types of bloodsport—human and

---

[47] We are not the first to offer this hermeneutic of *tarpa*, though we are moved to more explicit argumentation. One authority has hypothesized that the *tarpa tiya-* act may be translated as "ram- and bull-wrestling (?)" (Hoffner 1978, p. 247). Another explicitly states that the animals fight (Gurney 1977, p. 207)

[48] We will take up the connection between animal bloodsport and its relation to boxing elsewhere. For now, we note that there is no doubt that the revival of boxing in early modern England was closely associated with alectryomachy, and adopted many of its conventions for, *inter alia*, weighing and 'setting-to' the adversaries, as well as counting them out.

animal—in tandem. Given the choice of animals for *tarpa*, we are inclined to believe that the Hittites perceived similarities in the way boxers engage with their fists and the way rams and bulls engage with their horns.[49]

Bulls are still set against each other in many parts of the world, including Turkey, where the sport is known as *boğa güreşi* 'bull wrestling'; in the Balkans it is called *borbe bikova*, 'fight of bulls'. Bull wrestling also takes place in the Ajara province of Georgia (Shamiladze 1967). Though lesser known, bloodsport between rams was documented in Georgia (relatively close to the Hittite homelands) as late as the nineteenth century (Roskoschny 1884). A common practice in and around the Georgian capital at the time, *q'ochebis brdzola* 'ram wrestling' is well-described by the poet Ioseb Grishashvili (Grishasvhili 1927, pp. 20–21). Three-year old rams, called *erk'emali* or *q'ochi*,[50] were kept on a leash to prevent them from butting heads with any other animal before the fight; this was believed to make them angrier. They were fed only bread. Moreover, their horns were filed to irritate them and thus stimulate aggression. Finally, on the day of the fight the rams were adorned with a collar studded with colorful stones and they were drugged with liquid barley. On the way to the arena, the rams were paraded through the streets in a four-wheeled cart, to the cheers of the pedissequous crowd. After his discussion of ram-wrestling, Grishashvili immediately turns to native Georgian boxing, called *k'rivi*, recognizing the inherent parallel between the two activities.[51] He writes, "The idle citizen of Tbilisi likes a fight, whether the rivals meet in front of an indifferent beauty or they release fighting cocks or *erk'emali* rams into a ring" (ibid., p. 20).[52]

The festival text that mentions *tarpa* also contains what may be the earliest commentary on a boxing match—predating Homer by as much as half a millennium. While the language is somewhat cryptic (most Hittite texts are), it nonetheless presents compelling evidence regarding the behavior of Hittite boxers in the ring (Gilan 2001, pp. 116–118). Immediately before the passage regarding *tarpa*, we read the following:

> *maḫḫan anzel laknuzi na=at palwanzi apaša* ANA DINGIR[LIM] UŠKEN *nu anzel paršana-*[x]*-aizi*

> When our [man] lays him out, [the crowd] cheers and he bows down before the deity, and our [man] squats (KBO 23.55 21'–23').

It does not take much imagination to fill in the blanks: the crowd favorite (*anzel* 'our' [man]) defeats his opponent with a devastating blow (*laknu-* 'cause to fall'). The crowd cheers (*palwa-*) 'our' man's victory. The defeated boxer is compelled to bow (UŠKEN) before the cultic image of the deity. Meanwhile, 'our' man, the champion, crouches (*paršnāi-*), resting while he awaits his next opponent.[53]

The textual sources support an interpretation of Hittite boxing consistent with observations we made in our earlier study of the Sumerian variety. The Hittites boxed at holy mountain sites; the Sumerians did so in temple courtyards. The sacred setting of pugilism in the

---

[49] This is evidently true of the Minoans, as well, who juxtaposed the famous 'Boxing Boys' with antelope engaged in a sylvestrian tussle.

[50] The term *q'ochi* can also be used to describe a man who is able to fight well.

[51] Both forms of bloodsport are described in a single section, entitled *k'rivi* 'boxing'.

[52] "Истому тбилисцу нравится бой—сходятся ли соперники на глазах у равнодушной красавицы, выпускают лн в круг бойцовых петухов или баранов-эркемалн."

[53] It is our experience that a crouching posture is readily adopted by exhausted boxers who do not benefit from a stool to sit on between rounds.

ancient Near East betokens the transcendent power boxing had over fighters and audiences in the ancient world. Supernatural beings associated with boxing in both cultures were storm and mountain gods (Numušda and Martu in "The Marriage of Martu" and Ḫalwannaš and Paḫušanuwaš, intera alia, in the Hittite cult inventories). As personifications of the destructive forces of nature, these gods were aptly associated with brutal monomachy.[54]

Two pieces of artwork are suggestive of boxing in ancient Anatolia. The first is a cylinder seal, most likely executed by an Assyrian artisan and used by a merchant at Kaneš, the early capital of the Hittite kingdom (Figure 23). The merchant community was largely, if not exclusively, made up of Assyrian traders and so the object is not necessarily reflective of Hittite boxing. It probably has more to do with boxing traditions in Mesopotamia (Section 2.2) and the Levant (Section 2.4). Nonetheless, the seal may be a clue as to the introduction of boxing to the Hittites.

The boxers stride towards one another with their arms crossed. The arm closest to the viewer is bent at the elbow but points to the ground rather than towards the adversary. The boxer at left is naked while the boxer at right wears a belt. Both wear caps. The boxer on the right is bearded. A lamb or goat occupies the "prize" position between them. Two figures stand to the left; one holds a lamb or kid. The figure closest to the fighters is kilted and gestures towards them. This figure is most likely the official by now familiar from glyptic representations of boxing in the Levant (Section 2.4). In the terminal of the seal we find a personage with his foot resting on the head of a slaughtered bull and his arms lifting up the animal's hindquarters. The figure is probably intended to represent a divine being like Gilgameš—or perhaps Enkidu—slaughtering the bull of heaven. The head of the divine being is eroded beyond recognition. Thus, the seal may be a depiction of the boxing matches that took place (though at considerable remove of time and space) in the holy month of Gilgameš (described in Section 2.2).

Figure 23: Impression of a cylinder seal from Kaneš, in Anatolia, ca. 2000 BC. The seal is almost certainly of Assyrian origin (Teissier 1984, Seal No. 386).

The other artifact associated with pugilism in ancient Anatolia is of Hittite origin, though its connection to boxing is more speculative. Perhaps one of the most famous pieces of Hittite material culture, a 14th-century silver drinking vessel in the shape of a fist (Boston Mu-

---

[54] Traditional Slavic fistfighting was analogously associated with the storm god Perun.

seum of Fine Arts, No. 2004.2230), is a remarkable piece in its own right (Figure 2.5). Here we emphasize its potential relationship to Hittite pugilism. The realistically-rendered fist includes a "bar[-]like object with rounded edges... decorated with palmettes" that protrudes slightly beyond the little finger (Pilavci 2017, p. 167). We believe that this object is a fist-load weapon—a smaller, lighter version of the curious weapons used extensively in early Iron Age boxing matches of northern Italy and the eastern Alps.[55] Carrying the weapon in the fist, just as it is represented in the Hittite artifact, would allow a boxer to deliver significantly heavier blows (Lazar 2011).

If the Hittite drinking vessel is intended to represent a boxer's fist, then it is necessary to discuss the intricately carved cuff or bracelet that the boxer wears. Wrist adornment among ancient pugilists is well attested, including among Ugaritic boxers (Figure 19) and in representations of boxers on a relief (No. 10039) held in the Iraq Museum (Poliakoff 1987, p. 172, fn. 3). The Eshnunna boxers wear bracelets (Figure 13), as do the boxers on another terracotta plaque housed at the Louvre (Figure 14). In Dioscurus and Dioscurus (2022b), we will observe the use of bracelets among Minoan boxers. The rich detail of the Hittite artifact allows us to see what might have been inscribed on this fairly ubiquitous piece of boxing attire.

The bracelet on the Hittite fist is not illustrated with a pugilistic scene, as we might expect. Instead, it is decorated with a repoussé procession of musicians and others bearing a variety of potulents and esculents. They all advance towards a divine being, most likely the weather god (Pilavci 2017, p. 182). At the far right of the procession, another deity, perhaps a vegetation god, stands. Surrounded by flora, the god's presence may indicate that the scene depicts a springtime festival—like those in which boxing occurred. At the head of the procession, nearest the main deity and before an altar, another figure, identified by a hieroglyph as Hittite king Tudḫaliya IV, performs a libation using a pitcher. According to Pilavci (2017), the libation is "the central act of worship to encounter the divine" (p. 183). While we find little on the bracelet to suggest a direct link to pugilism, it was not uncommon for Hittite artisans to fashion drinking vessels in the form of fists and for these to be used in ceremonial settings (Güterbock and Kendall 1995). These vessels, known as GEŠPÚ in numerous textual sources and made of a variety of materials, were likely synecdochical for boxing itself and further suggest the high esteem in which the Hittites held sacred pugilism.[56] The band around the boxer's wrist reinforces the ties between Hittite boxing and the worship activities described in the documents reviewed above.

3 Egypt

As we have demonstrated, the visual and textual corpus of boxing in ancient Western Asia is of considerable magnitude and complexity. Egypt, on the other hand, presents us with comparatively few examples of boxing as a deeply-ingrained cultural practice.[57]

---

[55] Representations of these implements, which are often described as 'barbells', will be discussed at length in Dioscurus and Dioscurus (2023).

[56] A raised fist is frequently attested in Hittite iconography, where it has traditionally been interpreted as a signal of reverence (Güterbock and Kendall 1995, p. 55), or perhaps as a salutation. We find it equally if not more plausible that the fist expressed power and strength, and hearkened directly to the sacred pugilistic encounters which, as we have demonstrated, were of considerable significance to the Hittites.

[57] Wrestling and stick-fighting, on the other hand, are amply attested. It is possible, though few boxing artifacts remain in Egypt, that Egyptian pugilism was in fact highly influential for other cultures, including those of the

Figure 24: A Bronze Age drinking vessel in the shape of a fist (Boston Museum of Fine Arts, No. 2004.2230). The object was created in the Hittite kingdom around 1300 BC and bears a hieroglyphic identifying one of its rulers. The fingers curl around a bar with rounded edges, embossed with a palmette on the end. It protrudes slightly beyond the *digitus auriculāris*. This bar is likely a fist-load weapon.

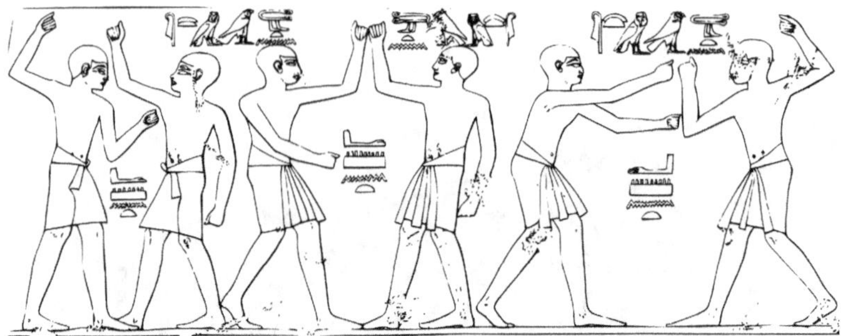

Figure 25: Three pairs of boxers from the Tomb of Kheruef. At waist level between fighters are the hieroglyphs for 'boxing'; above them are three instances of the phrase, "Horus 'Appearing in Truth' has prevailed".

The Tomb of Kheruef (Tomb 192 at Western Thebes) holds the most information we have about boxing in Ancient Egypt. The boxing scenes depicted in the lower register of the west portico of the north wing of the Tomb of Kheruef are associated with the raising of the *djed* column at the Festival of Sed during the reign of Amenhotep III. Six pairs of boxers are represented in a variety of poses (see Figures 25 and 26). The boxers in two registers (three pairs of boxers in each register) strike similar postures and bear similar, though not identical, hieroglyphic inscriptions.

Fakhry (1943) states that the boxers depicted in the Tomb of Kheruef are priests, based on their apparel. Indeed, a functionary designated as ⸻ *ʿḥꜣw-ʿ* 'fighter priest' had some role to play in the Apophis/Apep ritual. This specialized priest was the ritual opponent of Apophis, who appears in art as a giant serpent or crocodile. The nature of the fight is unknown; it may have involved the desecration of a figure associated with Apophis. However, a fight between priests reenacting the conflict of Ra and Apophis is not out of the question, given the use of a derivative of the verb *ʿḥꜣ* 'fight' as the primary designation of the priest in the Apophis ritual. The priest's job was to fight for a petitioner against his or her Apophis (Ritner 1993, p. 221, fns. 1028–1029).[58] The religious nature of the boxing depicted at the Tomb of Kheruef is undisputed (De Vries 1960, p. 235). However, most of the details remain speculative.

According to one authority, "[A]thletic competitions or demonstrations were conducted as part of the ceremonies of certain Egyptian religious festivals, as is illustrated by the inclusion of pugilistic exercises...in the ceremony of the raising of the Djed-column, as portrayed in the tomb of Kheruef at Thebes" (De Vries 1960, p. 156). The Kheruef reliefs have also been described as "jubilee rites" that had "a proper part to play in the general theme of joy and re-

---

ancient Mediterranean. For example, in Section 2.4, we mentioned a Levantine cylinder seal with boxers and an Egyptian ankh symbol. Boxing among the Minoans may have been influenced by Egyptian practice, as well, though there is still little conclusive evidence on the matter.

[58] According to available interpretations of the scenes at the Tomb of Kheruef, the fighter priests are participating in a different ritual, unrelated to Apophis/Apep.

Figure 26: Three more pairs of boxers from the Tomb of Kheruef. In addition to slightly modified hieroglyphic inscriptions found in similar positions in Figure 25, the verb 'hit', accompanied by the ditto sign, appears at far right.

lease from anxiety at the accession or rejuvenation of the monarch" (Aldred 1957, p. 116).

Given the natural expectation that the hieroglyphic writing in these registers might help us interpret the significance of the scene, we turn to the hieroglyphs that accompany these eighteenth-dynasty boxers. In Figure 25, between the individual fighters in each pair, we find the same hieroglyphic inscription, ⸗⸗ transliterated as ῾*mnt* and translated as 'boxing' (Epigraphic Survey 1980, p. 63). The same term is found between the fighters in each pair in Figure 26; between the rightmost boxers, we find this term followed by the iteration mark, ⸗. This may indicate that the scene in Figure 25 is a duplicate of the scene in Figure 26 (De Vries 1960, p. 226). Over each pair of boxers in Figure 25 we find the inscription ⸗⸗⸗, translated as "Horus 'Appearing in Truth' has prevailed" (Epigraphic Survey 1980, p. 64). This appears in variant forms (with additional hieroglyphs, sometimes split up, and rearranged).[59] The rather cryptic statement has been interpreted to mean that "these ceremonial games were performed in honor of the king" (De Vries 1960, p. 228). It is also possible that the sequence of hieroglyphs "states the purpose of the contests," although not even a tentative explanation along these lines is provided (ibid.). Above and between the two leftmost pairs of boxers in Figure 26 we find an abbreviated version of this statement. Elsewhere we find the verb ⸗⸗ *ndr* 'hit'.[60]

The meaning of the boxing match is still elusive. Beyond controversy is the fact that the larger scene in the Tomb of Kheruef, of which the boxers clearly take part, depicts the raising of the *Djed*-pillar. Egyptologists agree that the captions of the boxing matches indicate that 'Horus' is the winner. The role of "fighter priests" who perform ritual combat, perhaps against figurines representing gods or malign forces, has been suggested (Ritner 1993, p. 221, fn. 1029) and may bear some connection to the ritual battle depicted at Kheruef. The raising of the *Djed* is understood to be a reaffirmation of the divine leadership of the pharaoh. It is also strongly linked to the Osirian myth and, more specifically, to the contest

---

[59] The invariant transliteration used to cover all five instances is *iṯ n Ḥr ḫ῾ m mȝ῾t* (De Vries 1960, p. 225).

[60] These inscriptions occur to the left of the leftmost boxer in Figure 25 (not pictured); and to the right of the rightmost boxer in Figure 26, where it is followed by the iteration mark ⸗.

between Set and Horus for the crown. However, the rite, "does not illustrate or re-enact the myth" or "present a logically developing story in a modern sense" (van der Vliet 1989, p. 407).

Osiris was murdered by his brother Set, which naturally led to conflict between the latter and Osiris' son, Horus. The fate of the cosmos hung in the balance, as would the polity during a microcosmic succession crisis. The spectre of widespread violence could be averted through a contest between the rivals (or, in the case of the Tomb of Kheruef, perhaps, their sacralized proxies). Indeed, zany contests between Set and Horus are something of a subgenre in Ancient Egyptian literature (no extant versions depict a boxing match, however). Set and Horus were such illustrious bruisers that they are referred to simply as "the two fighters" (*āḥawi*) in the Theban recension of the Book of the Dead (Budge 1911, p. 87). In one popular version of the myth, Set issues a challenge: "Let [Horus] come outside with me, then I shall show you that my hands are stronger than his" (Frankfort 1948, p. 128).

Given the argument that the Djed rite was not a literal reënactment of the Osirian myth, it is still possible that the boxing represented a more abstract version of the fight between Set and Horus in which the winner, whoever it turned out to be, became a kind of theophoric version of Horus, as announced by the hieroglyphic caption.[61] According to van der Vliet, "[T]he rite of raising the [D]jed plunges us into the 'creative darkness of liminality', out of which a new and stabilized state of political or individual existence is to arise" (1989, p. 411). The fisticuffs that accompany the raising of the Djed arguably represent the resolution of Girard's "sacrificial crisis": a violent rivalry is subdued through a no-less violent but nonetheless circumscribed pugilistic encounter, averting the disaster of a succession war (1977, pp. 39–67). While many of the details are yet umbratilous, the representations of boxing at Kheruef may be the clearest extant visual renderings of Bronze Age boxing as a ritual activity.

We also note the posture of the fighters and the techniques they appear to use. Stark differences from the Mesopotamian tradition, observed in the previous sections, are immediately evident. Absent are the crossed arms (even though the feet interrupt one another in the leftmost pairs of each register and legs cross between non-combatants at the far right of Figure 26). No prizes appear between the fighters, only hieroglyphs describing the action. Manifestations of the divine are absent or indirect, perhaps signaled by the hieroglyphic inscriptions. Likewise absent are bracelets, belts, and any suggestion of nudity in the encounter. All the fighters are kilted, as in many West Asian depictions.[62]

Depsite persistent claims that Egyptian renderings of human activity are static and stiff, these boxers move in a variety of ways suggestive of uppercuts or shovel-punches, overhand rights, and hammer-blows from above. In two registers, the Kheruef reliefs arguably provide more information about punching technique than any artifact in the ancient corpus we have discussed so far.

The Kheruef boxers' foot position is also remarkably realistic, a detail ignored in the visual depictions uncovered in Mesopotamia and its satellites. Fighters lift the back foot so that the heel is off the ground, providing maneuverability and extra "reach" to more effectively strike the adversary. The leftmost pair of boxers in Figure 25, by contrast, are notably flat-footed. To the trained modern eye, the most whimsical technique is that of the left-hand

---

[61] Another, less dramatic interpretation, is that Horus merely invested his power in the victorious boxer and thereby himself prevailed.

[62] There are only a few Mesopotamian portrayals in which the fighters are naked. Opificus (1961, p. 169) reports an unpublished terracotta plaque from Assur, conserved in Istanbul, where the boxers, or perhaps wrestlers, are nude. One figure grabs the raised left foot of his opponent (Photo No. 18923, Vorderasiatischen Museum, Berlin).

fighter in the rightmost pair of each register. This boxer casts both arms forward in an offensive maneuver observed only among the most untrained modern fighters. It would never be tolerated in a contemporary boxing gym, where the classic boxing stance allows for only one hand to strike while the other "guards" in defense. Assuming that the image is a realistic depiction, it is probable that the boxer who adopted this technique would suffer from the many sharp blows he was unable to block. But he might land a few good ones, too.

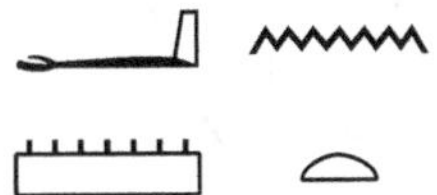

Figure 27: Hieroglyphs for ʿmnt 'boxing' found in the Tomb of Kheruef, associated with scenes of pugilism (De Vries 1960, p. 224).

Figure 28: Hieroglyphs for the formula it̠ n Ḥr ḫʿm mꜣʿt 'Horus "appearing in truth" has prevailed' found in the Tomb of Kheruef, associated with scenes of pugilism (De Vries 1960, p. 224).

Figure 29: Hieroglyphs for nd̠rʿ'strike' found in the Tomb of Kheruef, associated with scenes of pugilism (De Vries 1960, p. 224).

In the Tomb of Meryra II (ca. 13th century BC), two figures in the "Tribute of the South" (East Wall) are engaged in barefisted boxing. Nearby spectators cheer. Wrestlers are located close at hand, as in Mesopotamian reliefs (Davies 1905, Pl. 38). The boxers' hands do not appear wrapped or gloved; both arms are raised in a confused jumble of offensive and defensive maneuver, with the figure on the right raising an open hand, perhaps to ward off his opponent. The figure on the left lands a right to the jaw of the figure on the right, whose head rocks backward from the impact.

The Meryra II scene is regarded as an entertainment for the pharaoh Akhenaten or Amenhotep IV (De Vries 1960, p. 239, fn. 1). According to De Vries, the scene resembles "a mixture of punching, pushing, and semi-clinch that one sees even in modern boxing bouts" (ibid.).

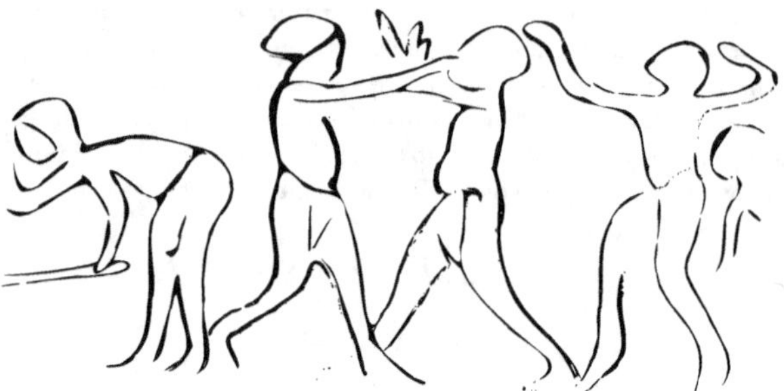

Figure 30: Boxing figures from "Tribute of the South" (East Wall), Tomb of Meryra II.

The raucous joy of the spectator to the right of the combatants is suggestive of the entertainment aspect of this match (and reminiscent of an analogous figure in the Alalakh cylinder seal, Figure 18), as opposed to the more formal, ritual aspects of pugilism emphasized in the Tomb of Kheruef.

A painting at the Tomb of Khons (Western Thebes tomb 31) depicts two figures standing atop a boat. Although not a boxing scene, as the fighters or dancers wield sticks in their hands (the Egyptian stick-fighting tradition of *nabbût*), Decker (2001) points out that the site of the contest creates an effect similar to that of a modern boxing ring, but with a notable and unprecedented consequence: the loser surely falls from the roof into the river! This is one of the earliest depictions of a fighting match between two combatants which is clearly constrained by a physical feature of the space.

4   Conclusion

Boxing's long childhood in early history reveals the distinctive features of orthograde dual fistfighting we can recognize as the earliest traditions in the boxing family. Whether or not boxing was polygenetically discovered by different civilizations, it exhibited both surprising fecundity and stability throughout the Middle Eastern cultures who adopted it for ritual, entertainment, or sacral purposes.

References

Cyril Aldred. Year twelve at El-Amarna. *Journal of Egyptian Archaeology*, 43:114–117, 1957.

Pierre Amiet. *Art of the Ancient Near East*. Harry N. Abrams, New York, 1980. Trans. by John Shepley and Claude Choquet.

Joan Aruz, editor. *Art of the First Cities: The Third Millennium BC from the Mediterranean to the Indus*. Metropolitan Museum of Art, New York, 2003.

Figure 31: Boat scene from the Tomb of Khons with two stick-wielding figures standing on the roof of the boat cabin.

Gary Beckman. Intrinsic and constructed sacred space in Hittite Anatolia. In Deena Ragavan, editor, *Heaven on Earth: Temples, Ritual, and Cosmic Symbolism in the Ancient World*, number 9 in Oriental Institute Seminars, pages 153–174. University of Chicago, Chicago, IL, 2013.

Inez Bernhardt and Samuel Noah Kramer. Götter-Hymnen und Kult-Gesänge der Sumerer auf zwei Keilschrift-'Katalogen' in der Hilprecht-Sammlung. *Wissenschaftliche Zeitschrift der Friedrich-Schiller-Universität Jena*, 6:389–395, 1956–57.

Jeremy Black, Andrew George, and Nicholas Postgate. *A Concise Dictionary of Akkadian*. Harrassowitz, Wiesbaden, 1999.

Rykle Borger. *Mesopotamisches Zeichenlexikon*. Ugarit Verlag, Münster, 2004.

Robert Brophy and Mary Brophy. Deaths in the Pan-Hellenic Games ii: All combative sports. *The American Journal of Philology*, 106:171–198, 1985.

E. A. Wallis Budge. *Hieroglyphic Vocabulary to the Theban Recension of the Book of the Dead*. Kegan Paul, Trench, Trübner and Co., London, 1911.

J. W. T. Byrd, J. C. Clohisy, Y. J. Kim, F. W. Gwathmey, K. S. Jones, and M. B. Millis. Hip dysplasia in wrestlers: three lessons learned. *Journal of Hip Preservation Surgery*, 4(4): 332–336, 2017.

Michele Cammarosano. *Hittite Local Cults*. Society of Biblical Literature, Atlanta, GA, 2018.

Charles Carter. Athletic contests in Hittite religious festivals. *Journal of Near Eastern Studies*, 47:185–187, 1988.

G. Çağırgan. Three more duplicates to Astrolabe B. *Belleten*, 48:399–416, 1984.

D. Collon. Syrian glyptic and the Thera wall paintings. In S. Sherratt, editor, *The Wall Paintings of Thera: Proceedings of the First International Symposium*, pages 283–294. Thera Foundation, Athens, 2000.

Michael D. Danti. The Hasanlu (Iran) gold bowl in context: All that glitters... *Antiquity*, 88:791–804, 2014.

Norman de Garis Davies. *The Rock Tombs of El Amarna: The Tombs of Panehesy and Meryra II*, volume 2. Egypt Exploration Fund, London, 1905.

K. Dawson-Amoah, J. Raszewski, N. Duplantier, and B. S. Waddell. Dislocation of the hip: A review of types, causes, and treatment. *The Ochsner Journal*, 18(3):242–252, 2018.

Carl E. De Vries. *Attitudes of the Ancient Egyptians toward physical-recreative activities*. PhD thesis, University of Chicago, 1960.

Wolfgang Decker. Sports. In Ronald B. Redford, editor, *The Oxford Encyclopedia of Ancient Egypt*, volume 3, pages 310–314. Oxford University Press, Oxford, 2001. Trans. Elizabeth Schwaiger.

Castor Dioscurus and Pollux Dioscurus. The development of boxing: Origins in biomechanics and social mechanics; The ancient world (Prehistory). *Scholia Pugillātōria*, 1: 1–22, 2022a.

Castor Dioscurus and Pollux Dioscurus. The development of boxing: The ancient world (The Ægean). *Scholia Pugillātōria*, 1:73–111, 2022b.

Castor Dioscurus and Pollux Dioscurus. The development of boxing: The ancient world (The Eastern Alps, Pre-Roman Italia, and Sardinia). *Scholia Pugillātōria*, 1:191–247, 2023.

Epigraphic Survey. *The Tomb of Kheruef: Theban Tomb 192.* Oriental Institute of Chicago, Chicago, IL, 1980.

Ahmed Fakhry. A Note on the Tomb of Kheruef at Thebes. *Annales du Service des Antiquités de l'Égypte*, 62:449–508, 1943.

Henri Frankfort. *More sculpture from the Diyala region*, volume 60 of *University of Chicago Oriental Institute Publications*. University of Chicago Press, Chicago, 1943.

Henri Frankfort. *Ancient Egyptian Religion: An Interpretation*. Harper and Row, New York, 1948.

Ignace J. Gelb, Benno Landsberger, A. Leo Oppenheim, and Erica Reiner. *The Assyrian Dictionary of the Oriental Institute of the University of Chicago*. The Oriental Institute, Chicago, 1964.

A. R. George. *The Babylonian Gilgamesh Epic: Introduction, Critical Edition, and Cuneiform Texts*, volume 1. Oxford University Press, Oxford, 2003.

Amir Gilan. Kampfspiele in hethitischen festritualen: eine interpretation. In Thomas Richter, Doris Prechel, and Jörg Klinger, editors, *Kulturgeschichten. Altorientalistische Studien für Volkert Haas zum 65. Geburtstag*, pages 113–124. Saarbrücker Druckerei und Verlag, Saarbücken, 2001.

René Girard. *Violence and the Sacred*. Johns Hopkins University Press, Baltimore, MD, 1977. Trans. by Patrick Gregory.

Petra Goedegebuure. Book review of: "Iron Age Hieroglyphic Luwian Inscriptions" by Annick Payne. *Journal of Near Eastern Studies*, 76:175–180, 2012.

Ioseb Grishasvhili. *Dzveli Tbilisis lit'erat'uruli bohema*. Sakhelgami, Tbilisi, 1927.

O. R. Gurney. Review of Keilschrifttexte aus Boghazköi, 23. Heft, by H. Otten and C. Rüster. *Journal of the Royal Asiatic Society of Great Britain and Ireland*, 109(2):207, 1977.

Hans Gustav Güterbock. The Song of Ullikummi: Revised text of the Hittite version of a Hurrian myth. *Journal of Cuneiform Studies*, 5(4):135–161, 1951.

Hans Gustav Güterbock. The Song of Ullikummi: Revised text of the Hittite version of a Hurrian myth. *Journal of Cuneiform Studies*, 6(1):8–42, 1952.

Hans Gustav Güterbock and Timothy Kendall. A Hittite silver vessel in the form of a fist. In J. B. Carter and S. P Morris, editors, *The Ages of Homer: A Tribute to Emily Townsend Vermeule*, pages 45–60. University of Texas Press, Austin, TX, 1995.

John A. Halloran. Sumerian lexicon, version 3.0, 1996–2020. https://www.sumerian.org/sumerlex.htm. Accessed 4 June 2021.

Donald P. Hansen. New votive plaques from Nippur. *Journal of Near Eastern Studies*, 22: 145–166, 1963.

J. D. Hawkins. The negatives in Hieroglyphic Luwian. *Anatolian Studies*, 25:119–156, 1975.

J. David Hawkins. Harrassowitz, Wiesbaden, 1995.

Joost Hazenbos. *The Organization of the Anatolian Local Cults During the Thirteenth Century BC*, volume 21 of *Cuneiform Monographs*. Brill-Styx, Leiden, 2003.

Harold D. Hill and Thorkild Jacobsen. The Kitîtum complex at Ishchali. In Harold D. Hill and Thorkild Jacobsen, editors, *Old Babylonian Public Buildings in the Diyala Region*, volume 98 of *Oriental Institute Publications*, pages 7–66. The Oriental Institute, Chicago, 1990.

Harry A. Hoffner, Jr. Review of *Keilschrifttexte aus Boghazköy*, Heft XXIII by H. Otten and C. Rüster. *Bibliotheca Orientalis*, 35:246–48, 1978.

Christian Jeunesse. Les statues-menhir de Méditerranée occidentale et les steppes. Nouvelles perspectives. In Gabriel Rodriquez and Henri Marchesi, editors, *Statues-menhirs et pierres-levées du Néolithique à aujourd'hui: Actes du 3e colloque international sur la statuaire mégalithique*, pages 123–138. Maraval, Saint-Pons-de-Thomières, 2015.

Jacob Klein. The god Martu in Sumerian literature. In I. L. Finkel and M. J. Geller, editors, *Sumerian Gods and their Representations*, pages 99–116. Styx, Groningen, 1997.

Ergül Kodaş. Les stèles d'Hakkâri 5 (nord du Proche-Orient): nouvelles réflexions sur leur identification chrono-culturelle. In Gabriel Rodriquez and Henri Marchesi, editors, *Statues-menhirs et pierres-levées du Néolithique à aujourd'hui: Actes du 3e colloque international sur la statuaire mégalithique*, pages 115–122. Maraval, Saint-Pons-de-Thomières, 2015.

Samuel Noah Kramer. The Marriage of Martu. In Jacob Klein and Aaron Jacob Skaist, editors, *Bar-Ilan Studies in Assyriology dedicated to Pinḥas Artzi*, pages 11–25. Bar-Ilan University Press, Ramat Gan, 1990.

Rene Labat and Florence Malbran-Labat. *Manual d'Epigraphie Akkadienne: Signes, Syllabaire, Ideogrammes*. Librairie orientaliste P. Geuthner, Paris, 6th edition, 1988.

W. G. Lambert. *Babylonian Wisdom Literature*. Clarendon Press, Oxford, 1960.

W. G. Lambert. The great battle of the Mesopotamian religious year: The conflict in the akītu house (a summary). *Iraq*, 25(2):189–190, 1963.

Tomaž Lazar. The Fighting techniques of the Hallstatt period boxers: An attempt at reinterpretation of the situla art. *Arheološki vestnik*, 62:261–288, 2011.

Matḥaf al-'Irāqī. *A Guide to the 'Iraq Museum Collections*. Government Press, Baghdad, 1942. Government of 'Iraq. Directorate General of Antiquities.

Gregory McMahon. *The Hittite State Cult of the Tutelary Deities*. Oriental Institute, Chicago, 1991.

Sam Mirelman. The Ala-instrument: Its identification and role. *Yuval: Studies of the Jewish Music Research Centre*, 8:148–171, 2014.

James Buchanan Nies and Clarence Elwood Keiser. *Historical, Religious and Economic Texts and Antiquities*, volume 2 of *Babylonian Inscriptions in the Collection of James B. Nies*. Yale University Press, New Haven, CT, 1920.

Gratianne Offner. Jeux corporels en Sumer: Documents relatifs a la compétition athlétique. *Revue d'Assyriologie et d'archéologie orientale*, 56(1):31–38, 1962.

Ruth Opificus. *Das Altbabylonische Terrakottarelief*, volume 2 of *Untersuchungen zur Assyrologie und Vorderasiatishcen Archäologie*. Walter de Gruyter and Co., Berlin, 1961.

A. L. Oppenheim. *Ancient Mesopotamia: Portrait of a Dead Civilization*. University of Chicago Press, Chicago, 1964.

H. W. Parke. A Note on the fresco of the 'Boxing Boys' at Akrotiri. *Journal of Prehistoric Religion*, 1:35–38, 1987.

André Parrot. *Tello: Vingt campagnes de fouilles (1877–1933)*. Albin Michel, Paris, 1948.

Suzanne Meek Pelzel. *Perforated Sumerian votive plaques*. PhD thesis, New York University, 1973.

Turkan Pilavci. *Drinking a god and sacrificing a drink: Agency of the Hittite libation vessels*. PhD thesis, Columbia University, 2017.

Michael Baron Poliakoff. *Combat Sports in the Ancient World*. Yale University Press, New Haven, CT, 1987.

Edith Porada. The Hasanlu Bowl. *Expedition Magazine*, 1(3):18–22, 1959.

Jaan Puhvel. Hittite athletics as prefigurations of Ancient Greek games. In Wendy J. Raschke, editor, *The Archaeology of the Olympics: The Olympics and other festivals in Antiquity*, pages 26–31. University of Wisconsin Press, Madison, WI, 1988.

Erica Reiner and David Pingree. *Babylonian Planetary Omens: Enūma Anu Enlil, Tablets 50–51*, volume 2 of *Bibliotheca Mesopotamica*. Undena Publications, Malibu, CA, 1981.

Alexej D. Rezepkin. *Das frühbronzezeitliche Gräberfeld von Klady und die Majkop-Kultur in Nordwestkaukasien*. Verlag Marie Leidorf, Rahden, 2000.

Robert Kriech Ritner. *The Mechanics of Ancient Egyptian Magical Practice*. Oriental Institute of Chicago, Chicago, IL, 1993.

Robert Rollinger. Aspekte des Sports im alten Sumer: Sportliche Betätigung und Herrschaftsideologie im Wechselspiel. *Nikephoros*, 7:7–64, 1994.

Hermann Roskoschny. *Das asiatische Russland*. Gressner and Schramm, Leipzig, 1884.

Walther Sallaberger. *Der kultische Kalender der Ur III–Zeit*, volume 7/1 of *Untersuchungen zur Assyriologie und Vorderasiatischen Archaologie*. Walter de Gruyter, Berlin, 1983.

Jack M. Sasson. Reflections on an unusual practice reported in ARM X:4. *Orientalia*, 43: 404–410, 1974.

Claude F.-A. Schaeffer-Forrer. *Corpus des Cylindres-Sceaux de Ras Shamra-Ugarit et d'Enkomi-Alasia*. Éditions Recherche sur les civilisations, Paris, 1983.

Vakhtang M. Shamiladze. *Voprosy byta i kul'tury naselenija Adžarii*. Mecniereba, Tbilisi, 1967.

Åke Waldemar Sjöberg. Trials of strength: Athletics in Mesopotamia. *Expedition Magazine*, 27(2):7–9, 1985.

Åke Waldemar Sjöberg, Erle Leichty, and Steve Tinney. ŋešba. In *Pennsylvania Sumerian Dictionary (ePSD2)*. Pennsylvania Sumerian Dictionary Project, 2nd edition, 2021. URL http://oracc.org/epsd2/o0029322. Version 2.4. Accessed 5 August 2021.

Ryan P. Smith, Robert M. Coward, Jason R. Kovac, and Larry I. Lipshultz. The evidence for seasonal variations of testosterone in men. *Maturitas*, 74(3):208–212, 2013.

Ferdinand Sommer. *Die Aḫḫijava-Urkunden*. Abhandlungen der Bayerischen Akademie der Wissenschaften, Philosophisch-historische Abteilung, München, 1932. Neue Folge 6.

Oğuz Soysal. Did a Hittite acrobat perform a bull-leaping? *Nouvelles Assyriologiques Brèves et Utilitaires*, pages 105–107, 2003.

David L. Spier. *The influences of warfare on the recreational activities of the ancient Assyrians and Iranians*. PhD thesis, University of Alberta, 1975.

Adam Stone. Ningišzida (god). In *Ancient Mesopotamian Gods and Goddesses*. The Open Richly Annotated Cuneiform Corpus and the UK Higher Education Academy, 2016. URL http://oracc.museum.upenn.edu/amgg/listofdeities/ningizida/. Accessed 5 August 2021.

Beatrice Teissier. *Ancient Near Eastern Cylinder Seals from the Marcopoli Collection*. University of California Press, Berkeley, 1984.

Gail D. Thompson. *A comparative study of Near Eastern and Ægean glyptic art, 2000–1400 BC: Combat, hunt, chariot, boar, goat, bird, and bull scenes*. PhD thesis, State University of New York at Buffalo, 2013.

V. A. Trifonov, N. I. Shishlina, A. Y. Loboda, and V. A. Khvostikov. The flesh-hook featuring a scene of fist fighting from a Maikop culture dolmen near the village of Tsarskaya in the northwest caucasus. *Kratkiye Soobshcheniya Instituta Arkheologii*, (251):25–42, 2021.

Viktor Trifonov. Représentation, par similitude, de l'art mégalithique dans le Caucase occidental, en Crimée, et en Europe occidental. In Gabriel Rodriquez and Henri Marchesi, editors, *Statues-menhirs et pierres-levées du Néolithique à aujourd'hui: Actes du 3e colloque international sur la statuaire mégalithique*, pages 81–88. Maraval, Saint-Pons-de-Thomières, 2015.

J. van der Vliet. Raising the djed: A Rite de marge. In S. Schoske, editor, *Akten des vierten Internationalen Ägyptologen Kongresses: München 1985*, pages 405–411. Buske, Hamburg, 1989.

Herman L. J. Vanstiphout. The Marriage of Martu, 1998. Unpublished manuscript.

P. S. Vermaak. Šulgi as sportsman in the Sumerian self-laudatory royal hymns. *Nikephoros*, 6:7–21, 1993.

I. J. Winter. The Hasanlu Gold Bowl: Thirty years later. *Expedition Magazine*, 31(2):87–106, 1989.

Richard L. Zettler. Sealings as artifacts of institutional administration in ancient Mesopotamia. *Journal of Cuneiform Studies*, 39:210–214, 1987.

Changelog

- ~2022.6.2. First public release.
- ~2022.6.3. Minor edits.
- ~2022.6.5. Minor additions to Sections 2.2 and 3.
- ~2022.6.6. Minor edits; `mxedruli` for Georgian text fixed.
- ~2022.8.14 Pagination fixed.
- ~2022.10.27 Full proofread; minor edits.
- ~2022.10.29 Minor edit.
- ~2022.11.25 Brophy and Brophy (1985) citation added with note.
- ~2023.09.28 References and notes on the "Marriage of Martu"; `mxedruli` removed; minor proofreading.

The Development of Boxing: The Ancient World (The Ægean)

Castor Dioscurus; Pollux Dioscurus

Contents

Abstract

Boxing in the ancient Ægean (Crete and the Cyclades) developed a unique visual vocabulary strongly suggestive of ritual and magic. A variety of artifacts depict boxers engaged in an anagogical praxis unobserved in the ancient Near East. The unusual attire of Ægean pugilists indicates that, like contemporary muay Thai and dambe boxers, Ægean boxers of the Bronze Age sought mystical protection in the ring. Deposition of boxer figurines at peak sanctuaries leads us to believe that Minoan boxing was linked to chthonic deities. We note the variety of pugilistic styles attested in the *disjecta membra* of boxing art deposited by the inhabitants of the Bronze Age Ægean.

1 Introduction

The evidence for boxing on the islands of the Bronze Age Ægean is fragmentary but convincing and abundant nonetheless. While only the barest inferences regarding pugilism can be made from Ægean writing, the rich pictorial testimonia of Bronze Age boxing on Crete,

Scholia Pugillātōria 1 (2022): 73–111.

Address author correspondence to scholia@protonmail.com.

Thera, and Naxos lead us to believe that boxing enjoyed a significant efflorescence there. During a period of perhaps a thousand years, practitioners experimented with a variety of parameters including boxing gloves *sensu lato*, participants, and striking. We will organize our discussion of these and other features by artistic medium. It is beyond the scope of this article to introduce the Minoan and Cycladic civilizations in all but the broadest terms. Moreover, we defer the mountain of evidence regarding boxing on mainland Greece (and Cyprus) to a future article.

The civilizations of the Bronze Age Ægean Sea thrived on the islands of Crete and the Cyclades from the third millennium until late in the second millennium BC. Boxing is among the Ægean cultural practices that have fascinated scholars for decades. The activity is amply attested in Minoan and Cycladic art across multiple sites and media. Minoan boxing, in particular, is remarkable for its wide variety of forms, including unique hand covering and attire. There should be no question that in the realm of Minos and across the 'wine dark sea' in the neighboring Cyclades, boxing was a meticulously elaborated practice, though its meaning to the ancient Ægeans eludes us. The relationship between Minoan pugilism and forms of boxing in Western Asia and Egypt offers intriguing insights into the development of orthograde, unarmed combat in the Mediterranean basin (Dioscurus and Dioscurus 2022).

Minoan and Theran boxers are represented in the context of a unique visual vocabulary that emphasizes the fitness of the male boxer, his elite status, and his hierurgical activity. As we have explained elsewhere, 'sacred boxing' was not unknown in Egypt, Mesopotamia, Anatolia, and the Levant. Ægean boxing may well be related to those forms in this sense, but it clearly distinguishes itself in many others.

2 Visual Evidence

2.1 Plaques

A marble plaque found on the Cycladic œ of Naxos and dated to sometime in the third millennium is suggestive of a boxing match (Figure 1). The plaque shows three male figures "crudely pocked in silhouette, not outlined with incision" (Hood 1978, p. 94). The two figures at left confront one another, one with an unnaturally elongated arm that he waves over the head of his adversary. The role of the third figure is ambiguous; he may be joining in the fight or he may represent a spectator or referee. All the figures raise their arms. The boxing plaque, along with two similar pieces—one showing men hunting and another depicting men in a boat—may have originally formed a frieze illustrating various aspects of male endeavor.

The simplistic figurative rendering suggests the plaque was executed during the earliest phases of Cycladic civilization. Naxos, which is set in the Ægean Sea north of Thera, assumed a central role in the Cycladic culture of the Bronze Age, so its residents were presumably involved in seafaring commerce. Given the early date of the plaque, however, it is unlikely that the artist was influenced by Near Eastern depictions of boxing, which were not that common in the third millennium (Dioscurus and Dioscurus 2022). Thus, the Naxos plaque may be the first evidence of autochthonous pugilism in the Ægean. We acknowledge, however, that the plaque does not unambiguously represent a boxing match, or even fist fighting. Later Ægean depictions do so much more clearly.

Figure 1: Detail of a marble plaque with male figures engaged in unarmed combat, from Korfi t'Aroniou, Naxos, and dated before 2000 BC (Naxos Archæological Museum, no inventory number). The somewhat smaller figure at right may be a spectator or referee.

In addition, an unpublished ivory plaque found at Poros, on Crete, is said to depict paired boxers in the manner of the Boxer Rhyton (Rethemiotakis 2014, p. 151).

2.2 Figures and figurines

Minoan worshipers on Bronze Age Crete were drawn to holy sites on the summits of mountains, called peak sanctuaries [Ger. *Gipfelheiligtümer*], where they engaged in as yet poorly understood hierurgical activity.[1] In their peak sanctuaries, the Minoans deposited anthropo- and zoömorphic figurines, often in the clefts of rocks or in deep chasms, if available.[2] Unforunately, the publication of peak sanctuary finds is still "very limited" (Morris 2009, p. 185) and critical approaches that emphasize the "stereotypical" or "crude" nature of the figurines tend to suggest a uniform peak sanctuary cult across Minoan Crete, when a theory of "local preferences and needs" may be more appropriate (ibid., p. 186).

A sanctuary could be marked by an enclosing wall with an altar in the center where sacrifices and votive offerings were made. The Minoan peak sanctuaries of Crete were constructed in the late third millennium and some were in continuous use for more than a thousand years. Looting and erosion have resulted in the extensive fragmentation of the figurines that survive.

We will emphasize the deposition of anthropomorphic figurines that represent boxers. These finds, which include fragmented representations of arms and boxing gloves, have been

---

[1]Peatfield (2009, p. 253) catalogs the most common attributes of the sanctuaries: position on or near the summit of a prominent mountain, with an altitude range of between 700 and 4,000 feet above sea level; visible to nearby settlements; accessible; close to nearby settlements; close to "areas of human activity and exploitation"; and intervisible with other peak sanctuaries.

[2]A deep chasm associated with the Kophinas sanctuary is called Trypa tou Kofinou. While it has yet to be excavated, it "allegedly contains Minoan artifacts and bones" and therefore may contain even more evidence of Minoan boxing (Soetens 2009, p. 262).

discovered primarily at Kophinas,[3] the highest summit in the Asterousia mountains on the south-central coast of Crete (Rethemiotakis 2014). The Kophinas sanctuary has a deposition record extending from as early as 3500 BC to as late as 1500 BC (Soetens 2009, p. 266).[4] The holy site is located in the vicinity of nearly fifty natural effluxes from the local aquifer (Soetens 2009, p. 264).[5] On this basis, it has been argued, "A sequence of ritual actions that involved throwing offerings and libations into chasms, other crevices, or even human-made receptacles may have been conceived as the means to request that water penetrate the mountain and find its way to the numerous springs around [it]... A strong interest in fertility was expressed at the peak sanctuaries by the dedication of representative figurines of flocks and humans" (Soetens 2009, p. 265).

The clearest example of a boxing figure comes (most likely) from the Kophinas sanctuary (Rethemiotakis 2001, p. 128). It is now housed in the British Museum (No. 1970,1107.1; Figure 2). This terracotta figure, complete with its original legs, probably stood about thirteen inches tall.

Dated to the seventeenth century BC, it undoubtedly represents a boxer.[6] He wears a single enlarged glove on his left hand (the right arm is missing). From the frontal view, the Kophinas Boxer's glove appears remarkably modern in its shape and proportions; it resembles nothing so much as a standard sixteen-ounce boxing glove of the twentieth century. However, closer examination reveals that, it is "shaped like a semi-spherical cup, hollow underneath with a ledge around the 'rim'" (Rethemiotakis 2014, p. 150).[7] Together with other Minoan artifacts, including fragments found at Kophinas (Rethemiotakis 2014), we note that there was some variation in the size, shape, and constitution of Minoan boxing gloves (see Figures 3 and 4). We may even observe a descendant of the Kophinas Boxer's glove in Greek art of the seventh century BC (e.g., a pedestaled krater, National Archeological Museum of Athens, No. 12896). The curious boxing glove worn by the Kophinas Boxer is also attested in a splendid Minoan artifact known as the Boxer Rhyton (Sec. 2.5.1).

Perched precariously atop the pugilist's head, the distinctive conical hat was most likely donned in ceremonies that took place before combat. According to one commentator, the hat is an "insignium of official, sacerdotal or even divine status" (Rethemiotakis 2001, p. 126). It taxes credulity to imagine a scenario in which a hat serves any practical purpose in the boxing ring. The closest parallel may be found in the *mongkon*, a braided headgear worn by fighters during the rite of *wai khru* that precedes muay Thai bouts. After the initiatory *wai khru* is performed, the headgear is removed before the first bell rings and the boxers commence their agonistics.[8] Rethemiotakis (2014, p. 150) suggests that the Kophinas Boxer may be at prayer (due to the placement of his hand), congruent with our interpretation of the hat's ceremonial

---

[3] Another figurine, most likely a boxer, was discovered at Palaikastro (Figure 5).

[4] According to Soetens (2009, p. 266), the "remarkable longevitiy" of the Kophinas sanctuary attests to its importance in Minoan religious practice.

[5] There was likely a processional path from nearby Phaistos to Kophinas, a distance of about 15 miles by modern roads (Soetens 2009, p. 267).

[6] Figurines of this type were "usually modeled from several pieces of clay that were joined through the use of shaped clay pegs, for example at the neck or at the join between torso and skirt" (Morris 2009, p. 181). In the case of the Kophinas Boxer, the head positioning has been restored so that the original ligature between head and body is unknown.

[7] Elsewhere, Rethemiotakis describes the glove more succinctly as having a "perimetric rim" (2001, p. 128).

[8] Dambe boxers in Nigeria (discussed further in Section 2.6.1) also wear hats on occasion, though none so pavonine as that of the Kophinas Boxer.

Figure 2: Restored fragment of a terracotta boxer figure (British Museum No. 1970,1107.1) found at a hypæthral peak sanctuary at Kophinas, Crete, and dated to 1700–1600 BC. The "pad" or patch is visible in the lower image, as well as another view of the glove.

nature. Based on evidence from Minoan/Mycenæan seals and signet rings, Rethemiotakis argues that "a conical hat or tiara" may have been used as an "insignia of power or hieratic office" (ibid.). If this is correct, then it puts the Kophinas boxer squarely in the realm of the hierurgical boxers we observed throughout Mesopotamia and its satellites (Dioscurus and Dioscurus 2022).

Another curious detail of the Kophinas Boxer is a patch that covers his left shoulder. It has been described as a "pad" by curators at the British Museum, though this may suggest a thickness which the object does not itself possess.[9] It is hard to imagine that this bit of material conferred safety from blows in any practical sense. Instead, it is more likely a protective amulet worn on the boxer's body during or immediately before combat. The patch bears a double cross, similar in form to the *Croix de Lorraine*. We are unaware of this symbol appearing elsewhere in Minoan or Cycladic art. Like the small looped object in the belt of one of the Boxing Boys of Akrotiri (Section 2.6.1), the purpose of the shoulder patch is most likely telesmatic.

As we will elaborate in the sections below, there is mounting evidence that, as in contemporary muay Thai and dambe boxing, Bronze Age boxing of the Ægean was marked by ritual activity: fighters sought protection by wearing magical objects during or immediately before their fights. In the case of the Kophinas Boxer, another possibility is that only the representation of the boxer was adorned in this way, perhaps to protect a particular fighter from harm through a kind of *participation mystique*, i.e., by the fighter or his ritual patron forming an identity with the enchanted figure.

This leads us to further speculation on the significance of the votive boxer figurines deposited at Cretan peak sanctuaries. It has been argued that they were intentionally simplified in order to represent "only selected aspects of the human form" (Morris 2009, p. 180). The Kophinas Boxer was most likely designed to accentuate his attire (the hat, the patch, and the boxing glove) and his broad chest. The meaning of these elements to the Minoan observer remains elusive. One commentator has argued, however, that figures like the Kophinas Boxer were intended to project "the exercised, athletic body of coteries of male worshipers" as an "ideal value" (Rethemiotakis 2001, p. 126).[10]

Most scholars believe that the figurines represent participants who actually took part in the peak sanctuary rituals. Perhaps boxers commissioned their own images to be made, then offered them at the sanctuary in an attempt to gain some divine favor. Given the brutal nature of boxing among the Minoans, it is reasonable to assume that such a ritual participant would request protection in future bouts or healing from injuries previously sustained.

More generally, it has been hypothesized that "the main purpose of the peak sanctuaries was the ritual supplication for water, which was essential to fertility" (Soetens 2009, p. 268). In a later article, we will take up the subject of how contemporary 'folk boxing' in Mexico still serves this imbriferous function. It is possible that the Minoans viewed the spilling of blood during fist fights as a prefiguration of rainfall, as their New World counterparts do to this day (Zorich 2008).

Along with the Iuktas sanctuary, Kophinas had a "strong spiritual attraction" owing to its katabatic chasms (Soetens 2009, p. 268). The prevalence of boxing iconography at Kophinas suggests that pugilism, too, was associated with chthonic powers. Minoan boxing

---

[9] https://www.britishmuseum.org/collection/object/G_1970-1107-1

[10] We cannot help but think of the Mattel sword-and-planet-themed media franchise "Masters of the Universe", with muscle-bound action figures created for the *participation mystique* of young boys in the 1980s.

was brutal, as indicated by such artifacts as the Boxer Rhyton (Section 2.5.1). The Minoans nurtured a love of gladiatorial combat which, like boxing, must have routinely sent souls to the underworld, accessed through the chasms associated with Minoan peak sanctuaries (Evans 1921–1935, vol. 3, pp. 500, 502). The Kophinas sanctuary may have even served as a memorial for boxers who expired in combat. We find support in this speculation from Morris (2009), who argues that the figures deposited at Kophinas and elsewhere "should be read not as undifferentiated worshipers, but as individuals operating within a complex social reality" (p. 187). Rethemiotakis (2001) finds support for the claim that boxers belonged to a specialized guild capable of commissioning these *ex-voto* offerings "charged with ideological meaning" (p. 128–129).

It is unclear whether the gestures assumed by the figurines should all be subsumed into simple categories like supplication. With the boxer figurines, in particular, one might wonder whether or not they were represented in the act of combat. Because the arms of figurines with an open gesture are more likely to be broken (Morris 2009, p. 186), we may not expect to find surviving boxer figurines *in flagrante pugnā*, as observed in the Minoan glyptic arts. This, of course, does not mean that such sculptures did not exist.

Among the "elite artifact[s]" (Soetens 2009, p. 267) deposited at Kophinas are at least three arms terminating in boxing gloves (Figure 3) and at least three more boxing gloves *sans bras* (Figure 4).

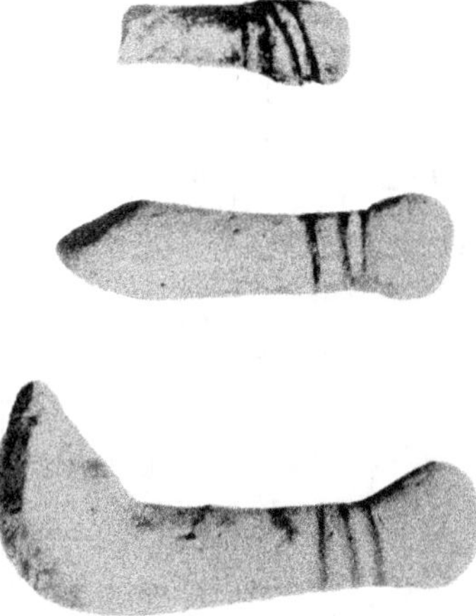

Figure 3: Three arms of boxers found at the Kophinas peak sanctuary (Heraklion Archæological Museum).

The arms are described as having a "hemispherical finial with perimetric rim and incised band" (Rethemiotakis 2001, p. 126). These undoubtedly once belonged to figurines of boxers and offer an illuminating analog to depictions on rhyta (see Section 2.5.1) and frescoes

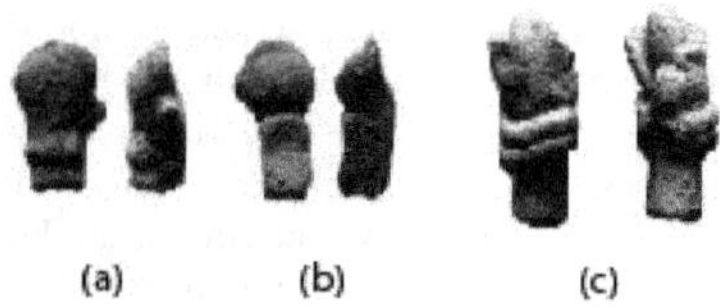

Figure 4: Three sets of gloves found at the Kophinas peak sanctuary (Heraklion Archæological Museum?). Gloves (a–b) have the 'perimetric rim' of the Kophinas boxer (Figure 2).

(see Sec. 2.6.1). Additional pieces of legs have been discovered which the excavator asserts "probably belong to figurine groups of boxers in action" (Rethemiotakis 2001, p. 128). Any such figurines were most likely intended for display and bespoke the high social status of their dedicators, associated as they were with the pugilistic activities of the palace culture.

The gloves, which we will see again in the Boxer Rhyton (Sec. 2.5.1), deserve special comment. As shown in Figure 4 (a–b), they have the appearance of a cup covering the knuckles. This is obscured when the rounded base of the cup faces the viewer. When the viewer sees the cup from the side, however, it is clear that its rim could be sharp (Figure 4 (b), right). Similar forms are immediately visible to the careful observer of the Boxer Rhyton. The boxing glove in Figure 4 (c) is anomalous. It appears to have three prongs—perhaps a preview of some version of the late Roman *cæstus*. The sanguigenous nature of Minoan boxing can be inferred from these instruments of punishment.

Another sculptural representation of a boxer was found at a peak sanctuary near Palaikastro (perhaps Mt. Petsofas?) in eastern Crete (Figure 5). Unlike the Kophinas boxer, the Palaikastro Boxer's hands are not enlarged to suggest boxing gloves, nor do we detect a perimetric rim on the palm side of the gloves.[11] The figure is athletic in build and does not raise his hands in the supplication gesture typical of Cretan orant figurines. Instead, he bends his arms at the elbow and pushes his knuckles against each other.[12] Most important for our interpretation, the Palaikastro Boxer wears a loincloth identical to the pugilist depicted in the Tylissos fresco (Figure 20). This wide, leaf-like apron covers both front and back, secured with a wide belt, leaving the upper thighs exposed. His locks of hair are reminiscent of those worn by the young boxers of Thera (Figure 16).

The existence of figures like the Kophinas and Palaiakastro Boxers suggest a "strong message of social emulation" (Rethemiotakis 2014, p. 152). As members of a distinguished male group, Minoan boxers may have sought "effective ways to consolidate and set off their ideological identity within a broader frame of competitive behaviors and practices of the elite class" (ibid.). Moreover, the figurines "project the perception of a hardy, manly body, a diachronic ideal" intended for Minoan society more generally (ibid., p. 155).

A fragmentary boxer scene, executed in the round, is described by Rethemiotakis (2014, p. 151) but unfortunately photographs of the sculpture are unavailable. It apparently includes a male figurine acquired by the Heraklion Archæological Museum in the 1960s, in addition

---

[11] We will observe various examples of bare-knuckle boxers elsewhere in the Minoan corpus, including on the Boxer Rhyton.

[12] It has been observed that bringing the hands in front of the chest is "the commonest gesture of the Minoan clay figurines in all periods" (Rethemiotakis 2001, p. 80).

Figure 5: Figurine of a boxer found at Palaikastro (Heraklion Archæological Museum No. 3904). The boxer, which stands about 7.25 inches tall, wears a loincloth similar to the one worn by a boxer depicted at Tylissos (Figure 20).

Figure 6: Ivory arm with a clenched fist, found near the Royal Road at Knossos and dated to between 1500 and 1450 BC (Heraklion Archæological Museum, no inventory number). It can be inferred that the complete figure would have been approximately 1.3 feet tall (Hood 1978, p. 120).

to other fragments from Kophinas "confiscated by the police" (ibid.). The original scene probably depicted two boxers in a tableau similar to those on the Boxer Rhyton.

Finally, another disembodied arm has been found, the structure of which has brought at least one commentator to the conclusion that it belonged to a boxer (Hood 1978, p. 120). The arm, which has a bare, clenched fist, is associated with the palace culture of Knossos (Figure 6). It must have originally belonged to a representation of a pugilist a little over one foot tall.

2.3   Seal impressions

Seals, together with the impressions they left in clay and other media, functioned as a kind of cryptographic device in the Bronze Age Mediterranean and Near East.[13] Boxing appears to have been a favored subject to inscribe on Ægean seals, a fact we infer from the remains of two seal impressions. These offer further insights into the boxing culture of Minoan Crete.

The first seal impression (Figure 7), found in a repository at the palace complex in Knossos, shows a boxer assuming a classic pose we will observe repeatedly on drinking vessels (Sec. 2.5). In the drinking-vessel scenes, the boxer always faces right, with his fallen opponent before him and his chest towards the viewer. Also, on the drinking vessels, the boxer's left arm is raised and slightly arched, his right arm bent more acutely and lowered. The seal that produced the impression under consideration (Figure 7) was evidently not intended as a copy of these drinking-vessel scenes, because here the boxer's back faces the viewer. This is the only piece of Minoan boxing art where the boxer moves in this direction.[14] The skillful artisan was toying with his audience's expectations. We see the shoulder, back, and gluteal muscles

---

[13] We review several Levantine seal impressions related to pugilism in Dioscurus and Dioscurus (2022).

[14] On the original seal (which does not survive) the boxer would have faced right but his back, of course, would have faced the viewer.

rippling across the boxer's body, as well as a column of doubtful interpretation (see Sec. 2.5). We expect to find a fallen boxer to the figure's left, but insufficient detail remains to consider this subject in depth. The figure wears a band around his right wrist, suggestive of a boxing glove.

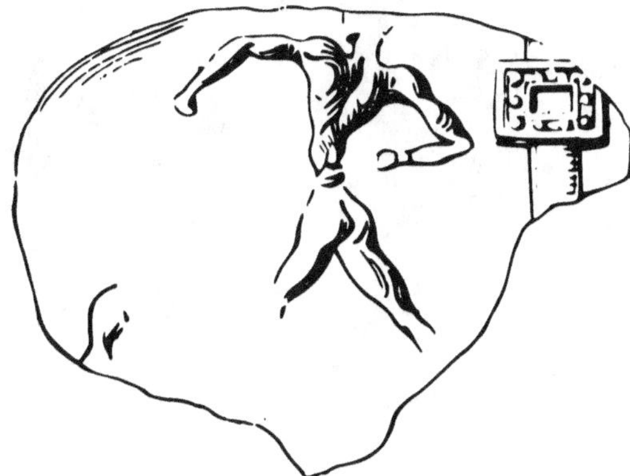

Figure 7: Boxing scene on a repository sealing from Knossos. Unconventionally for Minoan boxing art, the boxer shows the viewer his back.

In another seal impression, this one from the Little Palace at Knossos (Evans 1921–1935, vol. IV, p. 600, Fig. 594), we watch as a boxer tumbles to the ground head first, his arms splayed out to brace his fall (Figure 8). The opponent's legs appear at left, so that the two boxers' bodies overlap dramatically. The boxer is apparently bald but little detail is visible in the impression, which is only a fragment of the original. In truth, the boxer appears to dive to the ground. It is not clear what sequence of boxing and wrestling moves might have brought this about, but it seems plausible that the boxer has been thrown into this unenviable position by his doughty adversary.

2.4   Relief sculpture

Evans catalogs three arm fragments from high reliefs that may have belonged to boxers (1921, vol. III, pp. 497–503). Unfortunately, in none of these cases is there evidence of a boxing glove to provide us greater certainty. Evans' ingenious interpretation is based on a close examination of the musculature represented in the fragments, flexed, in one case (p. 501, Fig. 345), to support the weight of a fallen boxer (as we will see in numerous instances on the Boxer Rhyton, Sec. 2.5.1).

A stucco fragment corresponding to a closed fist and forearm (Figure 9) is considered by at least one author to belong to an otherwise unknown bas-relief sculpture of a boxer, *le boxeur au bracelet* (Coulomb 1981, p. 37). The fist is closed with the enlarged thumb parallel to the forefinger. The wrist is adorned with a five-ringed bracelet. The outside rings are brown and the inner three rings are cream in color. The bracelet may have been intended to protect

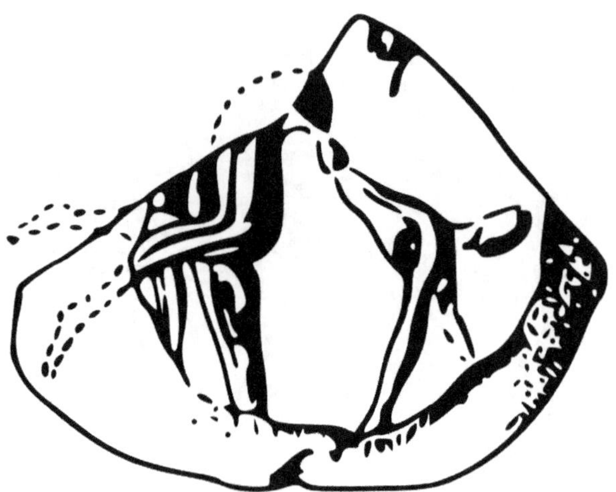

Figure 8: Seal impression of an overthrown champion, from Little Palace, Knossos, 3rd Millennium.

against wrist injuries as in modern boxing (Coulomb 1981, p. 39, n. 42). The *pouce énorme* 'enormous thumb' of the hand may suggest encasement of the thumb, as well. Coulomb suggests that in Minoan bare-knuckle bouts, boxers would have used "a large wrist strap extended by a type of fingerguard" (1981, p. 39).[15] Perhaps the wrist and thumb were wrapped with a continuous band to provide support and protection to the exposed thumb.

2.5 Rhyta

The rhyton is a conically shaped drinking vessel that cannot be laid on a flat surface without spilling its contents. Perhaps originally designed as skeuomorphs of drinking horns, rhyta were used at elite tables throughout the ancient world. Over time their decoration became more and more elaborate and the vessels assumed a variety of spectacular shapes, including a Hittite rhyton shaped as a fist (Güterbock and Kendall 1995, Dioscurus and Dioscurus 2022). Some rhyta were perforated at the bottom and could only hold liquid when plugged, suggesting ceremonial use (McInerney 2011). At least three rhyta in the Minoan realms were closely associated with boxing.

2.5.1 The Boxer Rhyton

Among the remains of a Minoan settlement near Phaistos, now called Hagia Triada, a black steatite (soapstone) rhyton was discovered in the early twentieth century.[16] Dated to between

---

[15] *un large bracelet de maintien du poignet prolongé par une sorte de doigtier protecteur.*

[16] The soft stone allowed the artisan to carve rich details, which in turn permit the modern observer to access the adumbrant world of Minoan boxing.

Figure 9: A fragment from a lost bas-relief sculpture known as *le boxeur au bracelet*, this fist and forearm suggest that a variety of boxing gloves were used at Knosssos (Heraklion Archæological Museum, no inventory number).

1550 and 1500 BC and now housed in the Heraklion Archæological Museum (No. 342 + 498 + 676), the vessel is elaborately carved with images of men boxing each other and leaping bulls,[17] two athletic activities cultivated among the upper echelons of Minoan palace culture (Rethemiotakis 2001, p. 128). Though fragmented and now heavily reconstructed, many of the key details of the rhyton's carvings have survived the forces of weather and pillage. The rhyton is perforated at the bottom. It has been argued that it was meant to contain sacrificial blood from a bull (N. Marinatos, cited by McInerney, 2011). Though troubling to modern Western sensibilities, it is just as likely that the rhyton was intended to hold the blood of human victims shed during the activity depicted on its surface.[18]

Four registers (Figures 10 and 11) arranged vertically on the rhyton show boxers in plumed helmets (register I); bull-leapers (register II); boxers with helmets (no plumes; register III); and bare-headed boxers (register IV). The Minoans, who sedulously accounted for hairstyle and headdress in their rendering of the human form, used these distinguishing characteristics in the Boxer Rhyton, as well (Davis 1986, Rethemiotakis 2001). We are still unsure what the various hairstyles represent, though age, social status, and hieratic disposition have all been suggested. In the context of a boxing match, the role of the helmets, at least, seems relatively accessible to us.

In registers I and III, the boxing takes place in front of a kind of colonnade, with capped pillars. According to one commentator this is "undoubtedly a synoptic rendering of the palatial architectural environment" (Rethemiotakis 2001, p. 128). According to another, it is evidence that Minoan pugilism took place in religious shrines (Hood 1978, p. 146). In a similar scene from a repository sealing found at Knossos (Figure 7), Evans saw in the column an indication of the "'Grand Stands' [that] enabled crowds of spectators to look on at agonistic contests" (Evans 1921–1935, vol. I, p. 689). Yet another critic saw in them flagpoles draped with banners (Graham, p. 231). These theories may not be mutually exclusive, as it seems that the Minoan attraction to boxing was cultic even as it accresced to the aristocratic culture of the Bronze Age Ægean. Boxing in the palatial context must have attracted wide attention. Minoan pugilists most likely battled at sites like the so-called theatral areas of Knossos and

---

[17] The danger of these athletic contests may be what unites them thematically.

[18] This possibility seems less remote when we consider the sanguinary nature of pugilism in the ancient as well as contemporary New World (Zorich 2008, Saunders 1984).

Figure 10: Detail of the two upper registers of the Boxer Rhyton: Plumed boxers in register I and bull-leaping in register II (Heraklion Archæological Museum No. 342 + 498 + 676).

Figure 11: Detail of the two lower registers of the Boxer Ryhton: Helmeted boxers in register III and unhelmeted boxers in register IV (Heraklion Archæological Musem No. 342 + 498 + 676).

Phaistos, where the bloodletting could be exhibited to a large crowd (Baikie 1913, p. 101).

While we can infer much about Minoan boxing from the activity of the figures on the rhyton (notably their posture and the dynamism of their limbs), their gauntlets are most puzzling. Almost all of the fighters wear one or more cup-shaped coverings over the back of their fists, secured at the wrists by straps. There can be no doubt that these gloves have the same formal characteristics as those found at the Kophinas peak santcuary (Sec. 2.2).

Poliakoff (1987) suggests that the helmeted fighters on the boxer rhyton wear "devices that cover the whole hand with what seems to be a stiff plate" (p. 68). He argues that "a wrist strap secures the plate under the boxer's fist" and notes that gloves capable of such damage explain the helmets (ibid., p. 659, Fig. 68). However, it is not only the helmeted boxers that wear this distinctive gauntlet. In register IV of the Boxer Rhyton, bare-headed boxers also wear a similar, if not identical, glove (see Figures 11 and 12 IIb and IIh). Only one boxer has an unambiguously ungloved hand; this is one of the defeated, bare-headed boxers (see Figure 12 IIi). It is possible that all of the fallen bare-headed boxers are also bare-handed—unlike their fallen, helmeted counterparts.

The left- and right-hand gloves are rendered somewhat differently for the bare-headed (standing) boxers in register IV (see Figure 12 II). The left-hand (apparently striking) glove conforms to Poliakoff's description (though it is arguable that the plate curves around the back of the fist only and extends beyond it, to a sharp point). This is in contradistinction to the right (apparently non-striking) hand, the depiction of which suggests a shorter, more pointed, perhaps cultrate glove.

The lead hand of the fighters in register III and IV appears gloved in most cases. There is almost always some indication of a wristband and never any indication of fingers on this hand, which also happens to be the hand most strongly implicated in the knockout punch delivered. For one figure in register IV (the rightmost in Figure 11) the left glove looks almost modern, with a large thumb. In register IV, the lowered (right) hand of all pugilists is narrow and pointed, suggesting that it is not gloved, although, in any case, the hand is hardly naturalistic. The artist is capable of including fingers on the hand: the downed opponent with both legs in the air, in register IV, has a curved finger and thumb. If this was a fair fight, then it suggests one-gloved boxing of an enantiomorphic variety: the fallen pugilist would presumably have a glove on his right hand (not shown), while the victorious boxer wears a glove on his left. In many cases, the gloves seem sharply pointed, or at least almond-shaped.

It is also possible that these apparent differences in form come from the variable angle from which the gloves are presented to the viewer. In any event, the artisan has paid exquisite attention to these details, once more suggesting their profound significance to the culture that commissioned and produced the artifact, which is only about 18 inches tall and carved in relatively unforgiving stone.

While the helmeted boxers have the cup-shaped glove on both hands, the bare-headed boxers (register IV) seem to wear a different glove on their forward and back hands. Given the fact that the bear-headed boxers wear the cup-shaped glove, it is less likely that they represent boxers in training. Indeed, if the modern analogy holds, then it is even possible that the helmeted boxers, who are more protected from the injurious blows, are the ones in training. If, as we hypothesize, the bare-headed fallen boxers are not wearing gloves, then register IV may depict a kind of pugilistic human sacrifice rather than a 'fair' match between equally-

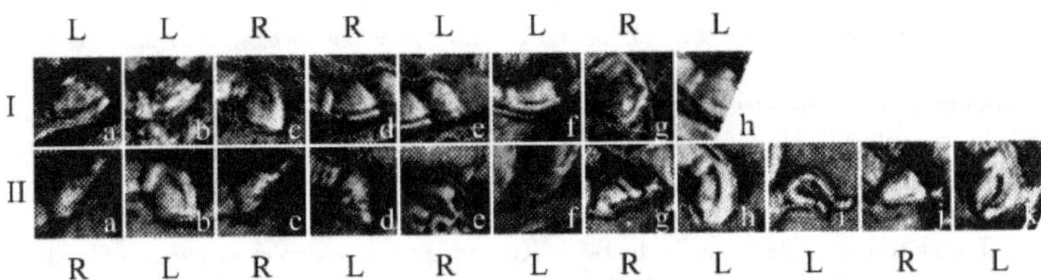

Figure 12: Detail of all boxers' hands from registers III and IV of the Boxer Rhyton (see Figure 11). The left (L) and right (R) hands of helmeted boxers appear on the top row (I, corresponding to the upper register in Figure 11); the hands of bare-headed boxers appear on the bottom row (II, corresponding to the lower register in Figure 11).

equipped adversaries.[19][20]

The artist who executed the Boxer Rhyton made some puzzling iconographic choices. "Instead of depicting the fighters in actual conflict, [he] has represented the individual combats a moment before or a moment after they are won and thereby has avoided any contact between the figures" (Davis 1977, pp. 30–31).[21] This is not true of the combatants in register I of the Boxer Rhyton, who seem to be punching and maybe even kicking each other. When describing the lack of contact between fighters, Davis seems to describe registers III and IV only. It is difficult to discern whether the overwelt boxers depicted on the rhyton are utterly vanquished or presume to continue their fight. Having delivered a stunning recumbentibus, the gesture of the standing boxer is also ambiguous: does he intend to strike even more blows?

Because the combatants in register III wear helmets, it can be assumed that a boxer in such a contest intended to inflict considerable injury on his opponent and/or that some degree of safety was to be maintained during the bout.[22] A blow with such a 'glove' could easily blind or otherwise mutilate the face of an adversary.[23] If strikes to the body were allowed, the result would be no less sanguinary, though perhaps more easily remedied after the encounter.

It is possible that the half-fallen boxer in register I may be kneed in the chest by a heavily eroded figure standing behind him. This, and the fact that the boxers in register I wear a kind

---

[19] We are not the first to suggest that the Minoans sacrificed human beings. In a Late Minoan IB house near Knossos, excavation revealed the bones of "several children that appear to have been defleshed deliberately" (Younger and Rehak 2008, p. 170). South of Knossos, on the route to Mount Iuktas, the skeleton of a young male was found "lying on a platform next to a lance blade"; the excavator concluded that he was a victim of ritual sacrifice (ibid.).

[20] A student observed to us that the Boxer Rhyton furthermore appears to exhibit the earliest instance of foot wraps for boxers.

[21] A useful comparison can be made to the 'Boxing Boys' fresco of Akrotiri, where the artist positions the gloved hand of one boxer *behind* the face of his opponent, suggesting the blow may not have landed at all (see Sec. 2.6.1).

[22] Modern boxing headgear offer a revealing, if somewhat ambiguous, parallel. While headgear are considered by many to offer greater protection, at least to amateur boxers, it is well known, among boxers at least, that they limit peripheral vision and thereby increase the chance of being struck from the side. Since the International Boxing Association banned headgear (for men's competition only) within the past decade, the accuracy of claims that they serve as an unequivocal protection to fighters appears to be in considerable doubt (Wang 2013).

[23] Mayan boxers, who carried a type of fist-load weapon, are also represented wearing heavy helmets (Taube and Zender 2009, Taube 2018). Boxers represented in the situla art of northern Italy and the Eastern Alps use fist-load weapons, but have completely bare (and shaven) heads (Lazar 2011).

of puttee, may suggest a form of kickboxing. However, the "kickboxing" attitude observed in register IV and confirmed by Koehl (2006) may be more akin to a defensive technique seen in modern mixed martial arts, when one combatant has fallen and the other remains standing and able to strike. The best choice for the boxer on the ground may be to strike out with his legs. Owing to the artist's penchant for acrobatic movement, however, the flailing legs of the boxer may simply suggest his dramatic downfall.

Though to the modern viewer the Boxer Rhyton appears to depict a pastiche of boxing, wrestling, and kickboxing styles, the fights on the rhyton almost certainly formed a coherent praxis for the Minoan spectator/participant—one that was linked to an elaborate male cultus. It has been proposed that the rhyton "may have been used in communal elite male rituals" which probably also included "dining, drinking, and anointing" (Koehl 2006, p. 336). Indeed, it has lately become fashionable to interpret the Boxer Rhyton in terms of "male initiation rituals" (ibid., p. 165). We imagine a scene in which the boxers drank from the rhyton before the bouts to calm their nerves and reinforce their sense of common feeling before pummeling each other before gods and other witnesses.

2.5.2 Other rhyton fragments

An additional steatite fragment, with a figure closely resembling the bare-headed pugilists in register IV of the Boxer Rhyton (Figure 11), was first published in the 1960s. It was initially thought to be a sherd of the celebrated rhyton found at Hagia triada (Warren 1969, p. 177, fn. 1). However, a later consensus emerged that the object, referred to as the "High Mowing" fragment,[24] in fact comes from another, albeit highly similar, steatite vessel (Davis 1977, p. 31, fn. 71). While we do not agree with the claim that the boxers on the High Mowing Fragment and in register IV of the Boxer Rhyton wear "caps", we concur with the assessment that they are "dressed only in a kind of jockey strap with a roll around the waist and a tail hanging down the back" (Benson 1966, p. 36). The scene suggests a powerful blow has been landed, though which hand did the dirty work is unclear to us (*pace* Benson, who believes it was the left). The artist presents the boxer to us in the moment when the hands are being withdrawn back into a guard stance. The awkward cantilevering of the boxer's limbs is probably meant to suggest the rotation of his torso and the recoil from the delivery of a "three–four" (hook) combination—in the terms of modern pugilism.

An unhelmed boxer in a pose similar to the boxers on the High Mowing and Hagia Triada rhyta is found on another fragment of dark steatite (Evans 1921–1935, vol. 1, p. 689, Fig. 510). The only identified remains of a rhyton (or perhaps a pyxis), the fragment was excavated in a chamber at Knossos that also housed a representation of tauromachy. In the sherd we see what must have been a 'stock' pose for boxers as depicted in this medium: arms extended downwards, the right arm bent at a greater angle than the left, which is only slightly *cambré*. We cannot agree with Evans that the left arm is held out for defense and the right is ready to strike a blow (ibid., p. 690). Instead, we think that the scene represents the retraction of the arms after the knockout has been delivered. Brawny and dynamic, the energetic pugilist revels in his triumph; a subtle tumescence below his waistline betokens his confidence and swagger (Figure 14). The mound at his feet has been described as the bent knee of his fallen opponent, whose broken frame lies just beyond the fragment's edge. The scene bears such a

---

[24] The fragment was in the private collection of Beulah Emmet, headmistress of High Mowing School at Wilton, New Hampshire (Benson 1966, p. 36).

Figure 13: Shown here is the High Mowing fragment, once considered a piece of the Boxer Rhyton, now considered more likely from a duplicate rhyton (private collection of Beulah Emmet).

strong resemblance to register IV of the Boxer Rhyton that it may have come from another copy of that masterpiece.

Figure 14: Victorious boxer, with the knee of fallen opponent at bottom. From a fragment of a dark steatite rhyton or pyxis found at Knossos.

Evans sees in the fragment delicate traces of a *cæstus* "bound round the wrist" (ibid., pp. 690–691). In fact, it may extend to the bicep, presaging much later Greek and Roman developments in boxing glove structure. Elsewhere, Evans notes the "beautiful modeling" of the legs, which emphasizes the muscular thighs, a prerequisite for successful modern boxers, as well (1900–1901, p. 96). The narrow waist, circumscribed by a tight belt, is a hallmark of Minoan art; we have observed it, though without comment, in other depictions of Minoan pugilists.

Finally Evans (1921–1935, vol. IV, p. 600, Fig. 595) illustrates a fragment of another steatite vessel, probably a rhyton, from Stà Hellenikà, Knossos (our Figure 15). In his lively description, the master writes: "The winner of the bout throws his adversary—who seems to have leaped upon him—backwards by a powerful uppercut" (p. 600). Warren (1969, p. 85) notes that this relief scene was a chance find above the Little Palace in 1933. Evans (op. cit., p. 600) imagines that such a scene should precede a representation of the defeated pugilist falling on his back, e.g., in the seal impression he illustrates elsewhere (our Figure 8). Perhaps the most fanciful image in the Minoan boxing repertoire, we cannot help but smile at the force conveyed through the arm of the assailing pugilist, despite the absence of virtually any visible muscular exertion on his part. This proleptic image delightfully foreshadows the pugilism of comic books and cartoon cinema—the dream of every little boy who ever threw an uppercut at a rival's chin.

Figure 15: Detail from a fragment of a steatite vessel from Knossos (Heraklion Archæological Museum No. 2329). What an uppercut!

2.6 Frescoes

2.6.1 The Boxing Boys

Sometime in the Late Bronze Age, a strong earthquake prompted the residents of Akrotiri on the Cycladic isle of Thera[25] to flee *à la débandade* (Marinatos 1999, vol. 3, pp. 64–66).[26]

---

[25]Some do not consider Bronze Age artifacts on Thera to represent Minoan culture *per se* although there can be little doubt that Bronze Age residents of Akrotiri, including the artist who painted the 'Boxing Boys', were strongly influenced by Minoan culture (Koehl 1986, p. 101, fn. 13). Accordingly, we treat the 'Boxing Boys' as Minoan.

[26]To date, no human remains have been found in the volcanic layers that whelved Thera.

Figure 16: The 'Boxing Boys' of Akrotiri: 'Alpha' (L) and 'Beta' (R). About half the fresco has been inpainted. Some details, like the shape of the boxing glove, are conjectural.

Later, a massive volcanic eruption on the island filled many of Akrotiri's buildings with ash and pumice.[27] An edifice today known as Building B was among the doomed structures. Later a stream of water swept through the ruins of Building B, causing further damage to the precious artwork that had been abandoned there (Doumas 1992, p. 109).

On August 10, 1970, the excavators who had been laboring in and around Building B for several years found "[a] piece of fresco lying face upwards on the floor [that] depicts the head of a youth... wearing a necklace and bracelet of amethyst" (Marinatos 1971, p. 31). This piece of plaster, fallen from an interior wall of Room 1 (hence B1), was the first recognized bit of the the 'Boxing Boys' fresco, a masterpiece of Minoan art today conserved in the National Archaeological Museum at Athens (Figure 16).

Unlike some other frescoes at Akrotiri, much of the 'Boxing Boys' fresco could not be recovered (Figure 17). Modern inpainting offers a glimpse of what the fresco may have looked like when it was first composed, but the results of this technique, regardless of the discretion with which it is applied, must be regarded critically. The restored fresco is frequently cited as a primary example of ancient boxing, even though approximately 47% of it has been inpainted by twentieth-century artists who were forced to make a number of critical guesses as to what the original looked like.[28]

We can profit from understanding the conditions in which the 'Boxing Boys' fresco was discovered. About half of the fresco was presumably crushed, weathered to dust, or swept away long before archæologists arrived. The deposition of the bits still extant at the time of the excavation provided no incontestable evidence as to their original position on the wall. In fact, the primary account of the fresco's excavation does not refer to any piece of the fresco being found *in situ*. The fresco was originally painted on plaster that covered a partition wall of unfired bricks. Luckily, pieces of the 'Boxing Boys' fresco "had mostly fallen together with the bricks without getting detached" (Marinatos 1971, p. 32). The earthquake that first toppled the partition wall in B1 left the bricks in a confused jumble before the coming of the even more destructive *nuées ardentes*, followed later by at least one torrent of rainwater. It does not appear that the bricks of the partition wall were themselves fitted back together during the fresco's reconstruction. Instead, the bits of fresco were removed—most easily from bricks that had fallen face-up, but also from bricks that had fallen face-down. In the case of the latter, excavators scratched away the brick to reveal the stucco beneath (Marinatos 1971, p. 32). Bits of fresco were removed and reassembled some time later with the assistance of "infrared rays and specific photographs," during a period of recueillement in Athens (Marinatos 1971, pp. 47, 49)

Given the much-deprecated state of the 'Boxing Boys' as we have it, we will begin our analysis, *faute de mieux*, by examining the surviving fresco without inpainting (Figure 17) and proceed from what is clear to what is conjectural. To ease discussion, we will call the boxer on the left 'Alpha' and the boxer on the right 'Beta'.

Both boys have a fairly impassive countenance despite the punches they deliver to each other's head. Alpha, whose facial coloring is somewhat paler than Beta's, attacks his opponent with an outstretched left arm.[29] Alpha's left hand, though damaged, is likely in contact

---

[27] The initial eruption, along with subsequent pyroclastic clouds and tsunamis, were likely implicated in the general decline of Minoan civilization across the Ægean.

[28] Our calculation is based on the figures we present here. We have excluded the decorative border below the boys' feet, as well as the ivy-leaf garland above them.

[29] Determining the left and right arms of Alpha is not as easy at it may at first appear. The best clue is the beaded

Figure 17: The 'Boxing Boys' of Akrotiri (Thera) with modern inpainting removed. Only original bits of the fresco are included in this image.

with Beta's face. Alpha's left arm is adorned with a blue-beaded bracelet about the bicep.[30] Alpha's right arm is lower and inflects upward from a bent elbow. His lower forearm and wrist reveal a black gauntlet with a bright blue cuff and a gold band, perhaps another bracelet. A tiny portion of the glove's terminus is visible, but not enough survives to define the glove's shape.[31] Alpha's stance is wide; both his feet are partially visible but detail in the region of the upper thigh is absent, so the left and right legs cannot be identified with certainty. The longer extension of his left arm may suggest Alpha is an orthodox fighter delivering a left-hand jab to his opponent. If we presume the biomechanics of a modern boxing technique, then it is Alpha's left foot that projects closest to Beta.

Both boxers wear belts at the level of the omphalos.[32] There is no evidence of a ventral–caudal extension of these belts, suggesting they are just that, and not loincloths.[33] Both Alpha and Beta have shaved heads except for a few locks that dangle in the front and back. The pendulous posterior tresses reach below shoulder level and suggest that these locks were spared the razor from the boys' infancy.[34] The scalp is blue in color.[35] In addition to the beads on his right arm, Alpha wears similar jewelry around his neck (draping onto his chest) and on both ankles.

Owing to severe damage to the fresco's right side, much less evidence is available regarding Beta. Despite the lacuna, Marinatos (1971) still concluded that Beta is "more vivid and more aggressive" than his sparring partner (p. 49). He seems somewhat shorter than Alpha, and some (e.g., Marinatos 1971) consider him to be younger. Beta wears a dark purple belt with a slender loop tucked in at his hip.[36] Beta's right hand extends behind Alpha's face. The angle of his legs and the placement of his feet are barely discernible. Evidence for the position of his left arm is questionable. Beta appears to project his belly somewhat more than Alpha, giving rise to speculation that Beta is disfigured by spondyolysis, perhaps by routine fighting (Ferrence and Bendersky 2005, p. 109). While Alpha stands in simple profile, Beta's posture is more complex. His head and belly are in profile while his shoulders are in frontal or three-quarter view (recall that Beta's legs and feet are almost entirely absent). It could be that Beta is turning his torso (starting at the shoulders), thereby delivering a right hook to the left side

---

necklace that Alpha wears. The artist has carefully rendered the necklace so that it is interrupted by his right shoulder (Immerwahr 1990, p. 52). Faint outlines of the right shoulder against the chest and the chest against the left bicep also provide a layered perspective.

[30] Marinatos (1971, p. 31) regarded it as a "bracelet of amethyst".

[31] This dark speck may instead be a part of Beta's hypothetical left-hand glove, supposing his elbow is bent.

[32] Immerwahr (1990) asserts that the belts are "probably of leather" (p. 52).

[33] According to one commentator, the boys wear "a belt with a knot and a loincloth" common to Cretan "adorants as well as people engaged in sports" (Marinatos 1984, p. 109). It is possible that the artist chose to render no trace of the genital covering of this hypothetical loincloth because that portion was invisible in profile, but we are unconvinced. Alpha's belt, for example, extends slightly beyond his belly, but there is no evidence of material below that point. A strict reading of the image—all relevant portions of which are preserved—tells us it is a belt and not a loincloth. Belts worn by otherwise nude boxers are well attested in toreutic situla art of northern Italy and the Eastern Alps (Lazar 2011).

[34] The consensus seems to be that that the boys, with their still adipescent torsos and lack of musculature (Immerwahr 1990, p. 52), are between six and ten years old; Marinatos (1971, p. 47) estimates they are 7–8.

[35] Marinatos (1971, p. 32) originally considered this to be a "lapis-lazuli head-cover," with the hair presumably appearing through its openings. In the same volume (pp. 47–48), he claimed it was "a kind of wig" and cites Homeric verses referring to blue hair as support. Others argue that the blue coloring merely indicates shaved skin. Its pallor may be due to the fact that it was only recently exposed to the sun.

[36] This may be the "knot" referred to by Marinatos (1984, p. 109) but its size and structure are not consistent with a knot made of the same wide material that extends around the boys' waists.

of Alpha's jaw.

Some have noted that Alpha wears jewelry while Beta does not, perhaps indicating their relative status (Immerwahr 1990, Ferrence and Bendersky 2005). However, many relevant portions of Beta's legs, feet, and left arm are missing, so the total absence of jewelry on his body cannot be confirmed. Certainly, Beta does not wear an earring in his left ear or a necklace and his (right) glove does not bear the blue cuff or bracelet of Alpha. However, Beta could be wearing a single earring on his right side, invisible because he stands in left profile. A boxing glove on his missing left arm could have been equipped with a cuff and bracelet just like Alpha's.

Another feature, remarkable for its inclusion in the inpainted fresco, is the distal portion of Alpha's boxing glove. We can guess as to the gauntlet's length, based on the orientation of the arm, but the glove's shape is simply unavailable to the viewer.[37] It may be scalloped or pointed like the Minoan boxing gloves of the Boxer Rhyton or of the fragments found at Kophinas (Rethemiotakis 2014, p. 160, Figs. 7–10). The inpainter chose to render Alpha's glove as a blunt, club-like object, reminiscent of at least some Cretan boxing gloves (Figure 2). This (modern) rendering of the glove may also owe something to later Greek depictions, e.g., on the Enkomi krater (British Museum No. 1897,0401.1287). In the context of the fresco alone, however, the shape of the boxing glove is entirely conjectural.

While oft-repeated, the claim that the boys each wear a single boxing glove is based on the slimmest of primary evidence and reinforced by the suppositions of the inpainting. While a solid case can be made that single-gloving is true of Alpha, Beta's left arm is mostly dislimned; his left wrist and hand are entirely absent.[38] In addition to the glove on his right hand, Beta may have worn a glove on his left hand, too. This claim depends crucially on the reconstruction of his left arm, which disappears at exactly the position on his forearm where the boxing glove should manifest. Marinatos (1971, p. 49) indicates that "the position of the hands cannot be accepted with absolute certainty for it was possible that the boxers [including Beta] held one elbow bent against the adversary." Indeed, there is not much to recommend the position of Beta's left arm. The relevant stucco bits could just as easily belong to one of his or Alpha's legs. Single-gloved and two-to-one-gloved combat is not unknown in later Greek depictions of pugilism (see, e.g., a kantharos, Dresden Staatliche Kunstsammlungen, No. 865499; and an oinochoe, Cleveland Museum of Art, No. 1916.1062) and Minoan depictions (e.g., the Boxer Rhyton) suggest dual-gloving as well as ungloved fights.

There are at least two restored versions of the 'Boxing Boys' fresco that merit discussion. The fresco as we know it today, and which has been the object of our contemplation thus far, was first published in Marinatos (1971, Color Plates E–F; Plates 57b, 117, 119–120). A photograph of this version appeared in *Time* magazine in 1972. It is described in a caption that reads "Two princes: playful boys in a boxing pose were imaginatively reconstructed from hundreds of fragments."[39]

Curiously, in the same volume as the color plates mentioned above, Marinatos presents

---

[37] This seems no great deterrent to most commentators, who tend to follow the lead of the inpainter rather uncritically. Immerwahr (1990), for example, calls the glove "mitt-shaped" (p. 52) and Ferrence and Bendersky (2005) call it "spherical" (p. 109) without commenting on its hypothetical nature.

[38] More secure evidence of one-gloved boxing is found in early Greek vase painting.

[39] "The Lost Atlantis", Feb. 28, 1972, vol. 99(9), pp. 56–57. Another article ("Light on Lost Epochs", April 16, 1973, vol. 101(16), pp. 46–48) mentions "two boys playfully boxing"; no photograph is included. By the 1980s, it had been concluded that the boxing match depicted at Akrotiri was "of a ritual nature [and] not merely a children's game" (Marinatos 1984, p. 109).

Figure 18: An alternative reconstruction of the 'Boxing Boys' fresco (cf. Figures 16 and 17) with novel sartorial features unattested in the original, including the curious extensions of the boxers' belts and a nimiety of gold bands on Alpha's (L) arms and ankles (Marinatos 1968, back cover). Its disuse in later publications suggests that this version has been discredited and perhaps even disavowed by the scholars and artists who produced it.

a drawing of the the fresco with a number of features not found in the canonical reconstruction and without any comment (1971, Fig. 3, p. 48). This version (Figure 18) persisted in print until at least 1976, when a reprint of Marinatos' first volume (1968) included a color graphic of the novel reconstruction on its back cover. In the novel reconstruction, Alpha bears the same curious loop in his belt as his adversary, even though there is no extant plaster in this position. The boys wear a kind of net or mail across their haunches, hanging from their belts. An animal hide (?), spotted in Alpha's case, drapes from each boy's belt and dangles over the hypogastric region.[40] We find no evidence for these graphic accretions in the surviving fragments of the fresco. Except for some dark splotches on Alpha's hindquarters (these are rendered as an unidentifiable accessory—perhaps they are weights holding the netting in place), there is no primary evidence for any other clothing besides his belt. Scholars and staff at the National Archæological Museum of Athens excluded these fanciful elements from the reconstruction that captivates visitors today (Figure 16). The existence of an alternative version of the fresco highlights the differences of opinion that apparently arose between scholars as it was being restored. This is worth our attention because it emphasizes the doxastic nature of the inpainted 'Boxing Boys' fresco and leads us to question how we evaluate its meaning.

Next we turn to the fresco's *mise-en-scène* for clues as to its interpretation. As mentioned above, the fresco was discovered in Room B1. Building B was two-storied and some have argued it was a domestic unit, though in his initial description Marinatos (1971, pp. 29–33) suggests that the site was associated with hierurgy. The fresco was found on the south wall of Room B1, on the second story, across from a window on the north wall. It has been argued that this window made the fresco visible to passersby on the street below (Doumas 2005). This reinforces the possibility that boxing was a public, rather than private, activity on Thera. In fact, the fresco may have functioned as a kind of Bronze Age billboard, proclaiming that boxing matches regularly took place in Building B.

The fresco was situated between two doors, one leading south to Room B1-α and the other leading west to B1-β. Anyone entering these rooms would have seen the 'Boxing Boys'. Room B1-α has been described as "a sacred apartment" or a congeries of "sacral repositories" due to the presence of "two tables of offerings" found *in situ*, as well as vessels for "holy oil" (Marinatos 1971, p. 31; Plates 54–55). Room B1-β is of a "still unknown nature" (ibid.). Intriguingly, the beaten clay floor of B1-β shows the talon marks of a domesticated bird larger than a hen, as well as the prints of other unidentified animals. We believe this could suggest the presence of fighting animals—like gamecocks—in proximity to the fresco.

The walls adjacent to the 'Boxing Boys' fresco bear some evidence that fighting animals were associated with the fighting boys. A procession of cavorting antelopes (*Oryx beisa*), a species unknown on the modern island, leads the viewer from the north window to the agon depicted on the south wall. It has been argued that the iconography of Room B1 would lead the viewer to contemplate the juxtaposition between the natural world and the world of human activity, specifically when it comes to conflict. According to Marinatos (1984, p. 112), "The boxing contest is perceived in relation to nature" (Marinatos 1984, p. 112). Citing Morgan (1995), Georma (2019, p. 37) argues, "[I]t is widely acknowledged that human activities are rendered in Theran and Minoan art as part of and in total harmony with the natural world." Georma continues: "On the whole, the young boys participate in an initiation rite effectuated through boxing and are at the same time symbolically associated with the male

---

[40] Was this suggestion of a loincloth an attempt to bowdlerize the nudity suggested in the original?

animals, the antelopes, which exhibit vigour and strength through their posture. What the painter evidently aimed for was the harmonious integration of the compositions in the eyes of the residents or visitors from all viewpoints in the room" (ibid.). Why integrate animals into the scene? Like the Hittites, the Minoans may have linked human and animal blood-sport (Soysal 2003, Dioscurus and Dioscurus 2022). The claw marks and hoof prints on the second story of Building B suggest that animals were kept there. Perhaps Room B1 was used to hold divinatory fights between animals and youths like the ones depicted on the walls. It may be that the curious 'antelope' are in fact a kind of Bronze Age livestock that was kept for its fighting ability, like the rams of the Hittite bloodsport, *tarpa*.

As we have already suggested, modern critics tend to view Minoan boxing as a ritualistic activity: "[B]oxing was probably a popular sport in the life of the people of that era. We presume that it was held in the context of initiation rites and perhaps other rituals..." (Georma 2019, p. 36). Various ritual elements in the fresco have been identified, including the boys' hair and attire. For example, one critics writes: "[T]he hairlocks left unshaved in the Thera frescoes, in conjunction with other pictorial features, reveal a developed set of artistic and social conventions for indicating the specific stages of life from youth to maturity to old age" (Davis 1986, p. 399). However, it seems that consensus has not emerged on the interpretation of Minoan coiffure.[41] In any event, the locks would have presented a tantalizing functional opportunity during combat—particularly among small boys—with one hand freed up for mischief. These tresses were likely grasped and pulled to antagonize, taunt, and subdue (Ferrence and Bendersky 2005, p. 109).

Some writers seem to take the impractical wearing of jewelry (by Alpha) and the boys' age to suggest it is only a playful match (e.g., *Time* 1972). Others conclude that the adversaries are deadly serious. For example, Alpha's eye rolls up in his head after Beta delivers a shocking blow (Davis 1977, p. 31). Still another commentator takes the jewelry and the relatively static, relatively non-overlapping poses, to indicate that this is "no childish game but a rituali[z]ed sport" (Morgan 2000, p. 930). The boxers wear only belts, which do not constrict their stomachs (as in other Minoan representations, most notably the Boxer Rhyton of Hagia Triada). There is no indication of a breechcloth or codpiece as in the Boxer Rhyton. We agree with Morgan that the attitude of the boys is not at all playful. The boys stand "firmly and with confidence on a solid level rendered by a black band" (Georma 2019, p. 35). In other words, they mean business.

The adornment of a fighter's limbs, like Alpha's, is not unknown in modern muay Thai boxing. Thai boxers routinely wear armbands, necklaces, and garlands into the ring; with the occasional exception of armbands (*pra jiad* in Thai), these are removed at the initiation of combat.[42] These accoutrements are worn for good luck and as signs of rank in the fight game. Alpha may have worn them for similar reasons; perhaps they distinguished him as the champion.[43] The slender looped object tucked into Beta's belt may be a protective amulet. The use of telesms is also a common feature of dambe (introduced below).

The Akrotiri boys wear belts of different colors; Alpha wears blue while Beta wears dark

---

[41] Girls depicted at Xeste 3, another Akrotiri site, wear their hair this way, as well (Immerwahr 1990, p. 52).

[42] Western boxers occasionally wear necklaces during the in-ring preliminaries, always removing them—sometimes with an osculation and other signs of devotion—before setting-to.

[43] It is possible that, by convention (as in the Hagia Triada duos), the victor appears on the left. Though an opposing viewpoint (Immerwahr 1990, p. 52) argues that in the Akrotiri contest the boxer on the right (Beta) is winning, having just delivered an aggressive blow (Ferrence and Bendersky 2005, p. 110).

purple. Differentiating the color of a boxer's attire from that of his opponent is still practiced in modern sport boxing, with red/blue the typical color scheme in the amateur and Olympic varieties. This is presumably designed to help judges accurately register a fighter's merits and demerits despite fast action in the ring.[44] The color-based differentiation of the boys may suggest betting on the outcome of the agon; it would be easier for the audience to bet on "blue" or "purple" if they were otherwise unfamiliar with the boys names or families.[45]

The belts—which seem to lack the genital-protective function of loincloths worn by adult men—have been the subject of comment by numerous observers including Parke (1987). He interprets the belt as the headdress of a poorly-attested sea goddess worn about the waist to rescue sailors from naufrage. According to him, the boys—residents of an island where marine commerce was paramount to survival—wear the belt to indicate their supplication of this protective deity. In a marvelous flight of erudition, Parke equates the boxing boys of Akrotiri with the legend of a semi-divine set of twins who come to blows over a swan, the hypostasis of this sea-mother.[46] The parallels to stories of the Dioscuri in this account—and their connection to pugilism—merit close attention in the mythopœia of western boxing.

Much is ambiguous about the boys' punching technique. Has Beta delivered a wherret to the left ear of his opponent, or has he missed? Or does the artist avoid occluding Alpha's face with Beta's striking fist, even though that is precisely the action that he intended to portray? Much is lost by the damage at the end of Alpha's arm: does he strike his opponent with a fist or an open hand? Is he grasping one of Beta's forelocks or does his hand disappear behind Beta's head, the way Beta's disappears behind Alpha's? As we have seen before with this Minoan masterpiece, the crucial piece of the puzzle is missing.

If we acquiesce that both boys wear a single glove, then it seems most likely that each wears this gauntlet on his right hand (Marinatos 1984, p. 109). (The enantiomorophic variety of gloving is attested in other ancient depictions.) There can be no question that Beta wears a glove on his right hand. As we have already noted, close inspection of Alpha's necklace, which is discontinuous at his right shoulder, provides evidence the painter meant to indicate that Alpha is gloved on the right hand, as well. Without this detail, which demonstrates the artist's "understanding of the separation of planes," the gloved hand would have been ambiguous (Immerwahr 1990, p. 52).

What are the implications of both fighters wearing a glove only on one hand, and on their right hand, in particular? Perhaps the only modern parallel is dambe, the traditional pugilism of the Hausa people in Nigeria (Figure 19). A dambe boxer wraps cords[47] around his dominant fist while leaving his non-dominant hand open. The dominant hand is used for offense (it is called *mashi* 'spear') and the weak hand is used for defense (*garkuwa* 'shield'). The combatants stand with the dominant hand furthest away from the opponent, as in modern sport boxing. If, as seems likely, the Akrotiri boys are both right-handed (and if the same functional primitives of dambe apply) then their stronger arm is gloved and their weaker arm is unequipped. In dambe, the gloved fist is used for striking while the open hand can (defen-

---

[44] Interestingly, this practice is not true of professional boxing, where, on occasion, boxers may be dressed almost identically, from the color of their gloves to the color and style of their trunks.

[45] At modern amateur boxing matches it is not at all uncommon to hear spectators calling out encouragement and chastisement to "Blue" and "Red."

[46] In possible parallel to the boys' belt, a muay Thai fighter's protective *pra jiad*, mentioned above, is traditionally made of strips of cloth from a sarong once worn by the boxer's mother.

[47] It appears that a single, modern boxing glove may serve in some cases, as well.

sively) catch, block, and hold or (offensively) push, grasp, and gouge. The glove appears to be the only physical constraint on what a man or a boy can do with his hands in the dambe ring, where a great variety of regulation (including almost none) seems to prevail. There is evidence for a proscription against striking with the closed fist of the weak hand, although this hand is by no means idle. The fingers of the open hand are routinely forced into the face of the opponent, with no taboo on gouging or fish-hooking the eyes, nostrils, and mouth. For all its utility, the *garkuwa* never appears to form a striking fist.

It seems likely that the boys of Akrotiri fought in a similar style. A Theran pugilist could use the open hand to seize his opponent by the belt or hair and yank him 'inside' to receive an even sounder drubbing with the gloved hand.[48] While the inpainter of the 'Boxing Boys' fresco imagined a club-like boxing glove much like the Hausa *mashi*, it is possible that the boys wore an even more dangerous, sharp glove like the ones depicted on the Boxer Rhyton. The threat of grave injury in the Minoan 'ring' may have changed the boys' technique substantively. Given the fearsome nature of the *mashi*,[49] dambe boxers often assume an extraordinarily wide stance at the onset of a bout, leaning backward to keep their heads as far away from the dreaded 'spear' as possible. By contrast, the boys of Akrotiri approximate one another, gently cambré,[50] and their stance is relatively narrow, suggesting their eagerness to mix it up.[51] We learn from dambe that single-gloved boxing provides for a unique level of brutality, which may have been *de rigueur*—practiced even by young boys—on Bronze Age Thera.

While elusive in its interpretation and oblique in some of its most basic graphic characteristics, the 'Boxing Boys' is hardly a *locus desperatus* in our history of boxing. According to Marinatos (1971), the boys are "depicted boxing in most perfect earnestness" and "rendered... with an amazing dexterity and discretion" (p. 49). We cannot help but agree with the archæologist's summation and find in this work of art a powerful expression of boxing's mysterious duality—what Robert Graves, in his memoir of boyhood pugilism, called "the pain not felt as pain" (1985, p. 47). Though in a heavily reconstituted form and across millennia of forgetting, the fresco still speaks volumes to contemporary boxers. Moreover, the unique forms represented in the fresco further evince the malleability of boxing as cultural praxis. While Marinatos (1971, p. 49) argued that the boys were "young princely brothers", he did not rule out the possibility that they represented "divine beings", further acknowledging that "divine children and divine twins abound in Mycenæan mythology" (p. 49). Thus, he likewise suggested the numinous power of boxing itself, which the Minoans may have understood better than any other culture, ancient or modern.

---

[48]Repeated attempts to withdraw from such a clinch, especially when pulled towards an opponent at the hips, may have resulted in "acute arching of the lumbar area," a dysthetic posture which Ferrence and Bendersky (2005) observe in Beta (p. 109).

[49]There are reports that the 'spear' hand was once coated in resin and then rolled in broken glass but only, we are assured, in a bygone era.

[50]Davis (1977) notes that the boys bend "backward from the waist," like (some of) the fighters on the Boxer Rhyton (p. 31). This is particularly true of Beta, whose posture was of interest to Ferrence and Bendersky (2005).

[51]Obviously, dambe boxers must close the distance eventually, and this could be precisely the moment of the fight that we observe in the fresco.

Figure 19: Dambe boxers (Jeremy Weate, 2010, CC BY 2.0). The two boxers on the left are armed on the right hand (*mashi* 'spear') while the left hand (*garkuwa* 'shield') is open. The three boxers on the right are gloved in opposing fashion, i.e., with the left hand armed. Dambe boxing may be the closest modern parallel to the fight depicted in the 'Boxing Boys' fresco of Akrotiri.

2.6.2   Other frescoes

Another fresco found at Tylissos, on Crete, has been reconstructed as including a boxer with an extended, striking arm, with a hand that is evidently ungloved (Figure 20). The figure was first identified as a boxer by Evans (1921–1935, vol. 3, p. 35). The fighter's posture contrasts with that of the victorious boxers of the Boxer Rhyton: his stance is inverted horizontally so that his right arm is outstretched and his left is (most likely) bent and lowered. Detail is insufficient to asses whether the boxer is gloved or bare-fisted, but there are no marks that might accompany the various forms of the Minoan boxing glove. From what we can infer from the fragmentary evidence, the boxer's legs have a narrower stance with respect to the Hagia Triada boxers.

The boxer in the Tylissos fresco wears an apron-like loincloth. Its shape strongly resembles that of a similar garment worn by a boxing figurine found at Palaikastro (Figure 5). Indeed, it may be the distinctive form of this loincloth and its relation to the Tylissos boxer that presents the strongest evidence for the identification of the Palaikastro figurine as a pugilist.

Another possible example of a boxing scene in Minoan art comes from the "Grand Staircase" fresco in the palace complex at Knossos (Blakolmer 2016, pp. 49–53). The reconstructed fresco (Blakolmer 2016, Fig. 11, p. 51) is imaginatively based on a single fragment that shows a human face looking closely at what Blakolmer regards as the backside of a boxer's loincloth. According to the reconstruction, the face belongs to a fallen pugilist who gazes at the nether regions of his victorious rival.

Figure 20: Reconstructed boxer from Tylissos fresco (Shaw 1972, p. 184, Fig. 13).

3   Written evidence? The Phaistos Disc

There is a sign for a boxing glove or *cæstus* on the Phaistos Disc, a fired clay object found in a Minoan palace on Crete and possibly dating to the second millennium (Kober 1948). The disc is inscribed with a variety of symbols that have been named and numbered but not yet deciphered. Sign No. 8 (Figure 21) has been given the name GAUNTLET and resembles a hand (palm facing the viewer) wrapped round the wrist and the thumb with the fingers free (Godart 1995).[52] It has much in common with the high-relief stucco arm housed at the Heraklion Archæological Museum (Figure 9).

Figure 21: Phaistos Disc sign GAUNTLET (Sign No. 8). Like the rest of the corpus of Cretan hieroglyphs, this sign is undeciphered; it has the form of a wrapped fist and may be equated with a Minoan *cæstus* or Greek *himantes*.

GAUNTLET may well be associated with Minoan boxing, perhaps as a logogram representing the activity.[53] Because helmeted pugilists appear on the Boxer Rhyton, it may be worth noting that GAUNTLET appears after HELMET (Sign No. 7) in three of the five instances it occurs on the Phaistos Disc (though HELMET is admittedly a frequent sign, appearing a total of 18 times).[54] Whether GAUNTLET represents the idea of boxing or, more likely, a syllable of the (unknown) spoken language associated with the characters, the inclusion of this sign in the writing system bespeaks the profound cultural importance of boxing to the composers of the disc.

4   Conclusion

It is astonishing that so much evidence of pugilism survives from the Bronze Age Ægean and we naturally wonder, how much more has been lost? Boxing was undeniably a prestige activity on Crete and Thera in the second and third millennia before Christ. The practice merited faithful rendering by craftsmen skilled in numerous artistic traditions (Rethemiotakis 2001, pp. 128–129). The prestige of Minoan boxing is further supported by the deposition of intricately crafted *ex-voto* figurines in religious contexts at Kophinas and Palaikastro, the strong association of boxing with the opulent palace culture of Knossos, and the jewelry worn by at least one of the Boxing Boys at Akrotiri. Ægean pugilism was also heavily bound up in cultic activity, as suggested by the attire of fighters, by the production of votive boxer figurines, and by the ritual libations most likely poured from the Boxer Rhyton (Koehl 2006, p. 165).

---

[52] The sign is rendered in Unicode as U+101D7.

[53] Such a logogram existed in Sumerian and was passed on to Akkadian and Hititte (Dioscurus and Dioscurus 2022).

[54] GAUNTLET also occurs next to CLUB (No. 13), SMALL AXE (No. 44), and CAT (No. 29).

We must not forget that boxing in the Ægean spanned more than ten centuries and that the numerous innovations in Greek and Roman boxing observed during a comparable period, e.g., between 800 BC and 400 AD, may be expected just as well in the little kingdom on Crete. Because the dating of the relevant Ægean artifacts is not at all precise, we have opted to emphasize the variation in Minoan boxing culture rather than its diachrony. In the case of the boxing glove alone, we have secure evidence of bare-handed boxing, boxing with a cup-shaped glove, and boxing with a type of fingerguard. There is less secure but still discernible evidence of bracelets and 'gloves' that extended all the way to the bicep, as in much later Mediterranean pugilism.

Did boxing arrive in the Ægean or did it emerge autochthonously? Contact between the civilizations of the Near East, Egypt, and the Ægean during the Bronze Age is all but assured. Elites in all three centers likely maintained communications "through the active mediation of material culture and/or the exchange of correspondece in Akkadian, the *lingua franca* of the time" (Knapp 1998, p. 205). It is not difficult to imagine that courtly exhibitions of boxing were held for visiting dignitaries, whether at Knossos or Ugarit. As Ægean traders and Minoan ambassadors traveled to Egypt and the Near East their knowledge and experience became "invisible commodities that motivated trade, modified cultural attitudes towards the maritime seascape, and continuously transformed socio-ideological practice in the wider world of the Bronze Age Mediterranean" (ibid.).

Was boxing one of these "invisible commodities"? There is so little evidence of boxing as a deeply-ingrained cultural practice in Egypt we are skeptical the Minoans could have derived their boxing traditions from the land of the pharaohs. Comparison with the relatively copious iconography of pugilism in the ancient Levant also makes us doubtful that contact, in regards to boxing, was particularly influential. For example—and with the possible exception of the Naxos Plaque—we find no representation of a referee or official in any Minoan boxing art. This is a remarkable lacuna, given the near ubiquity of a 'third man in the ring' in similar art of the ancient Near East (Dioscurus and Dioscurus 2022). The absence of any 'prize' situated between Minoan boxers is another significant difference. We have described the considerable variety found in Minoan boxing, particularly in terms of attire, gloves, and posture. All that said, there can be no doubt that cultural contact with Egypt and the Near East was generally pervasive in the ancient Ægean. For this reason, we believe that autochthonous fist fighting, perhaps like the primitive form pocked into the marble of the Naxos Plaque, was known in the truly ancient Cyclades. As it developed, mundivagant Minoans became aware of boxing in the mystical city states of the Levant and Egypt, if not in the heart of Mesopotamia. Perhaps some of the pageantry of Near Eastern boxing was incorporated into the Ægean variety but we believe Minoan boxing was fundamentally auturgical. It fulfilled unique cultic, even magical, needs for the residents of the Ægean islands.

Minoan boxing appears to have been lost at the end of the Bronze Age, evidently exerting little direct influence on the iconography of pugilism in mainland Greece. Though similar in function to the Minoan gauntlets, for example, the Roman *cæstus* is almost certainly an example of convergent evolution rather than direct inheritance. While oral traditions of the most brutal forms of Bronze Age boxing may have persisted in the Iron Age Mediterranean (like the stories of Minos and his Minotaur), there is little iconographic evidence that the Greeks directly adopted the fistic practices of their Ægean predecessors. As we will see, it is the Greeks who were more directly influenced by Near Eastern models of boxing. If we are correct, the singularity of Minoan boxing provides evidence of boxing's polygenesis in the ancient Mediterranean.

We cannot restrain ourselves from giving the last word to the great archæologist, who deftly stitches the rich and strange fabric of Bronze Age boxing together with that of its more celebrated classical inheritors, our forthcoming foci:

> [T]he lords of Mycenæan Knossos glutted their eyes with violent displays, just like their cultural descendants, the Greeks and the Romans... The sports of the amphitheatre, which have never lost their hold on the Mediterranean world, may thus in Crete at least be traced back to prehistoric times. It may well be that, long before the days when enslaved barbarians were 'butchered to make a Roman holiday,' captives, perhaps of gentle blood, shared the same fate within the sight of the 'House of Minos' and the legends of Athenian prisoners devoured by the Minotaur preserve a real tradition of these cruel sports (Evans 1900–1901, pp. 95–96).

References

James Baikie. *The Sea-Kings of Crete*. Adam and Charles Black, London, 2nd edition, 1913.

J. Benson. A new Boxer-Rhyton fragment. *Boston Museum Bulletin*, 64(335):36–40, 1966.

Fritz Blakolmer. Ein Prozessionsfresko im 'Grand Staircase' von Knossos oder im Banne von Persepolis? Zum minoischen Freskofragment einer Boxerszene. In F. Blakolmer, M. Seyer, and H. D. Szemethy, editors, *Angekommen aus Ithaka. Festgabe für Jürgen Borchhardt zum 80. Geburtstag*, pages 37–53. Vienna, 2016.

J. Coulomb. Les boxeurs minoens. *Bulletin de Correspondance Hellénique*, 105:27–40, 1981.

E. Davis. Youth and age in the Thera frescoes. *American Journal of Archaeology*, 90(4): 399–406, 1986.

E. N. Davis. *The Vapheio Cups and Aegean Gold and Silver Ware*. Garland, New York, 1977.

Castor Dioscurus and Pollux Dioscurus. The development of boxing: The ancient world (Western Asia and Egypt). *Scholia Pugillātōria*, 1:23–71, 2022.

Christos Doumas. *The Wall Paintings of Thera*. Thera Foundation, Athens, 1992.

Christos Doumas. La répartition topographique des fresques dans les bâtiments d'Akrotiri à Théra. In I. Bradfer-Burdet, B. Detournay, and R. Laffineur, editors, *Κρής Τεχνίτης. L'artisan crétois. Recueil d'articles en l'honneur de Jean-Claude Poursat, publié à l'occasion des 40 ans de la découverte du Quartier Mu*, volume 26 of *Ægæum*, pages 73–82. Liège, 2005.

Arthur Evans. The palace of Knossos: Provisional report of the excavations for the year 1901. *The British School at Athens*, 7:1–120, 1900–1901.

Arthur Evans. *The Palace of Minos at Knossos*. Macmillan and Co., London, 1921–1935. 4 vols.

S. C. Ferrence and G. Bendersky. Deformity in the 'boxing boys'. *Perspectives in Biology and Medicine*, 48(1):105–123, 2005.

Fragoula Georma. The wall paintings from Building Beta, Akrotiri Thera: A new approach to the iconographic programme. *Δωδώνη*, 47:31–49, 2019.

Louis Godart. *The Phaistos Disc: The Enigma of an Ægean script*. Itanos, Heraklion, 1995.

J. Walter Graham. Egyptian features at Phaistos. *American Journal of Archaeology*, 74(3): 231–239.

Robert Graves. *Good-bye to All That*. Doubleday, New York, 1985. 2nd. ed. rev.

Hans Gustav Güterbock and Timothy Kendall. A Hittite silver vessel in the form of a fist. In J. B. Carter and S. P Morris, editors, *The Ages of Homer: A Tribute to Emily Townsend Vermeule*, pages 45–60. University of Texas Press, Austin, TX, 1995.

Sinclair Hood. *The Arts in Prehistoric Greece*. The Pelican History of Art. Penguin Books, New York, 1978.

S. A. Immerwahr. *Ægean Painting in the Bronze Age*. Pennsylvania State University Press, University Park, PA, 1990.

A. Bernard Knapp. Mediterranean Bronze Age trade. In Eric H. Cline and Diane Harris-Cline, editors, *The Ægean and the Orient in the Second Millennium: Proceedings of the 50th Anniversary Symposium*, number 18 in Ægæum: Annales d'archéologie égéene de l'Université de Liège et UT-PASP, pages 193–205. Université de Liège, Liège, 1998.

Alice E. Kober. The Minoan scripts: Fact and theory. *American Journal of Archæology*, 52(1):82–103, 1948. ISSN 00029114, 1939828X. URL http://www.jstor.org/stable/500554.

R. Koehl. The Chieftain Cup and a Minoan rite of passage. *The Journal of Hellenic Studies*, 106:99–110, 1986.

Robert B. Koehl. *Ægean Bronze Age Rhyta*, volume 19 of *Prehistory Monographs*. Institute for Ægean Prehistory Academic Press, Philadelphia, PA, 2006.

Tomaž Lazar. The Fighting techniques of the Hallstatt period boxers: An attempt at reinterpretation of the situla art. *Arheološki vestnik*, 62:261–288, 2011.

Nanno Marinatos. *Art and Religion in Thera: Reconstructing a Bronze Age Society*. D. & I. Mathioulakis, Athens, 1984.

Spyridon Marinatos. *Excavations at Thera I: First preliminary report (1967 season)*. Number 64 in Vivliothēkē tēs en Athēnais Archaiologikēs Hetaireias. Archaiologikē Hetaireia, Athens, 1968. Reprinted 1976.

Spyridon Marinatos. *Excavations at Thera IV (1970 season)*. Number 4 in Archaioi Topoi kai Mouseia tēs Hellados. Archaiologikē Hetaireia, Athens, 1971. Reprinted 1977.

Spyridon Marinatos. *Excavations at Thera I–III: 1967–1969 seasons*. Number 178 in Vivliothēkē tēs en Athēnais Archaiologikēs Hetaireias. Archaiologikē Hetaireia, Athens, 2nd edition, 1999. 3 vols.

Jeremy McInerney. Bulls and bull-leaping in the Minoan world. *Expedition Magazine*, 53 (3):6–13, 2011.

Lyvia Morgan. Of animals and men: The symbolic parallel. *Bulletin of the Institute of Classical Studies*, 40:171–184, 1995.

Lyvia Morgan. Form and meaning in figurative painting. In Susan Sherrat, editor, *The Wall Paintings of Thera: Proceedings of the First International Symposium*, pages 925–946. Hidryma Theras, Athens, 2000.

Christine Morris. Configuring the individual: Bodies of figurines in Minoan Crete. In Anna Lucia D'Agata and Aleydis Van de Moortel, editors, *Archæologies of Cult: Essays on ritual and cult in Crete in honor of Geraldine C. Gesell*, pages 179–187. American School of Classical Studies at Athens, Prineceton, NJ, 2009.

H. W. Parke. A Note on the fresco of the 'Boxing Boys' at Akrotiri. *Journal of Prehistoric Religion*, 1:35–38, 1987.

Alan Peatfield. The topographay of Minoan peak sanctuaries revisited. In Anna Lucia D'Agata and Aleydis Van de Moortel, editors, *Archæologies of Cult: Essays on ritual and cult in Crete in honor of Geraldine C. Gesell*, pages 251–259. American School of Classical Studies at Athens, Prineceton, NJ, 2009.

Michael Baron Poliakoff. *Combat Sports in the Ancient World*. Yale University Press, New Haven, CT, 1987.

George Rethemiotakis. *Minoan Clay Figures and Figurines: From the Neopalatial to the Subminoan Period*. Number 219 in Archæological Society at Athens Library. The Archæological Society at Athens, Athens, 2001. Trans. by A. Doumas.

Giorgos Rethemiotakis. Images and semiotics in space: the case of the anthropomorphic figurines from Kophinas. *Κρητικά Χρονικά*, 34:147–162, 2014.

Nick Saunders. Jaguars, rain and blood: Religious symbolism in Acatlán, Guerrero, Mexico. *Cambridge Journal of Anthropology*, 9(1):77–81, 1984.

M. Shaw. The miniature frescoes of Tylissos reconsidered. *Archäeologischer Anzeiger*, 2: 171–88, 1972.

Steven Soetens. Juktas and Kophinas: Two ritual landscapes out of the ordinary. In Anna Lucia D'Agata and Aleydis Van de Moortel, editors, *Archæologies of Cult: Essays on ritual and cult in Crete in honor of Geraldine C. Gesell*, pages 261–268. American School of Classical Studies at Athens, Prineceton, NJ, 2009.

Oğuz Soysal. Did a Hittite acrobat perform a bull-leaping? *Nouvelles Assyriologiques Brèves et Utilitaires*, pages 105–107, 2003.

Karl Taube. The Ballgame, boxing and ritual blood sport in Ancient Mesoamerica. In Colin Renfrew, Iain Morley, and Michael Boyd, editors, *Ritual Play and Belief in Evolution and Early Human Societies*, pages 264–301. Cambridge University Press, Cambridge, 2018.

Karl A. Taube and Marc Zender. American gladiators: Ritual boxing in ancient Mesoamerica. In Heather Orr and Rex Koontz, editors, *Blood and Beauty: Organized Violence in the Art and Archæology of Mesoamerica and Central America*, pages 161–220. Cotsen Institute of Archæology Press, Los Angeles, CA, 2009.

Shirley S. Wang. Boxing group bans headgear in bid to reduce concussions. *Wall Street Journal, Eastern Edition*, 261(61):A3, 2013. March 15.

Peter Warren. *Minoan Stone Vases*. Oxford University Press, Oxford, 1969.

John G. Younger and Paul Rehak. Minoan culture: Religion, burial customs, and administration. In Cynthia W. Shelmerdine, editor, *The Cambridge Companion to the Ægean Bronze Age*, pages 165–185. 2008.

Zach Zorich. Fighting with jaguars, bleeding for rain. *Archaeology*, 61(6):46–52, 2008.

Changelog

- ~2022.7.1 First public release.
- ~2022.8.14 (Younger and Rehak 2008) reference, footnote added; fixed pagination.
- ~2023.6.10 Boxer rhyton foot wraps noted.
- ~2023.9.29 Spelling of *dambe* regularized; minor proofreading edits.

The Development of Boxing: The Ancient World (Classical Greece)

Castor Dioscurus; Pollux Dioscurus

Contents

Scholia Pugillātōria 1 (2022): 113–190.

Address author correspondence to scholia@protonmail.com.

Abstract

The development of boxing on the Greek mainland marked a turning point in the history of ancient pugilism. From the Late Bronze Age to the beginning of the Hellenistic era, ancient boxing emerged in a form increasingly recognizable to the modern observer. The evidentiary record, including both literary and visual depictions, permits us an increasingly pellucid vision of the practice in the Mycenæan, Archaic, and Classical eras. In this article, we address the rich resources available for studying Greek boxing into the fourth century BC and limit ourselves to artifacts discovered in Greece and Cyprus (excluding even those items produced in Greece but destined for a foreign clientele). During this period and within these geographic bounds, boxing possessed a richness and variety of form that laid the groundwork for boxing as a coherent athletic practice.

1 Introduction

As we have labored to demonstrate previously (Dioscurus and Dioscurus 2022a;b;c), boxing was not invented by the Hellenes. By the time pugilism was introduced into the Olympic games in the early seventh century before Christ, boxing was "neither new nor specifically Greek" (Puhvel 1988, p. 30). Instead, boxing was already more than a thousand years old, during which time it had been "fully present in the Hellado-Anatolian orbit" of the mid-to-late Bronze Age (ibid.). This is not to say that the ancient Greeks were only casually invested in the sport. Visual depictions of and/or literary references to boxing are consistently found in mainland Greece from the eighth century BC well into the first millennium of the Christian era. Even though the Greeks by no means invented boxing, their deep cultural affinity for the practice lasted, conservatively, a thousand years.

Fast-forward almost 1500 more years to the "Fight of the Century" between Jack Dempsey and Georges Carpentier when a critic in Paris wrote a defense of boxing by referring to its deep Western roots:

> What *laudator temporis acti* shall dare to pretend that boxing contests are modern inventions, degrading and unworthy of a civilization that lays claim to the beauty of antiquity?[1]

Nordmann argues that, as a vestige of *la beauté antique*, boxing should be revered by educated moderns as it was by the ancient Greeks. In those days, boxing was regarded as an avenue to perfect the body and the mind. Despite this, the ancient Greeks also acknowledged, often obliquely, its potential for degradation.[2] Their values were tightly wound up in their boxing praxis. We see in Greek depictions of pugilism courage and strength, of course, but also the glory of the naked male body and the calculating logic of the warrior at work. Indeed, the embrace of boxing by the Greeks "owes a great deal to the new presence of Indo-European-speaking aristocratic warrior cultures" that evidently prized the deeply resonant virtues of hand-to-hand combat for educating men and boys (Puhvel 1988). Of all the ancient cultures that boxed, the Greeks leave us an account that is at once imminently erudite

---

[1] "Quel *laudator temporis* acti osera prétendre encore que les combats de boxe sont des inventions modernes et dégénéérescentes, indignes d'une civilisation qui se réclame de la beauté antique?" (Nordmann 1921, p. 456, translation ours).

[2] While we do not deny that some Hellenistic authors satirized the sport as disfiguring, their critiques were evidently unpersuasive, since boxing was practiced widely and for a long time.

and visually astonishing.[3] Greek art is undoubtedly the *locus classicus* for naturalistic depictions of athletic boxing in the ancient world. Not only did the Greeks elaborate and refine the equipment and convention of boxing, they mused on its value to the individual and to society. It is in Greek depictions that we first observe boxers engaged in activities other than fighting: they wrap their fists; they hear instructions before the beginning of the bout; they sit, contemplative. The ancient Greeks are rivaled only by the early-modern English, Welsh, Scots, and Irish in their celebration of the paradoxical brutality and humanity of boxing.

Turning once more to Nordmann's classically-influenced panoply, we find a potential explanation for the Greeks' enduring commitment to pugilism:

> The fine and delicate flowers of poetry and science bloom more readily in brains
> that crown healthy bodies, robust and winsome.[4]

Greek *Leibeskultur* anastomatized naturally with boxing, which when practiced at its highest level, requires near perfection in limb, joint, and muscle. The glory achieved in athletics was widely celebrated. As explained to the man of twists and turns by his Phæacian host in Book 8 of the *Odyssey*, "[T]here is no greater glory for a man so long as he lives than that which he achieves by his own hands and his feet" (Murray 1919).[5] Boxing became the *sine qua non* of athleticism, a perch that it retains among the boughs of western culture to this day—though its popularity may wax and wane.[6] Given the comparatively rich resources available for studying boxing in the Hellenic world before the death of Alexander, we will attempt in the present article to study pugilism from the ancient Greek perspective.

2 Representations of boxing in Greek myth and legend

Elsewhere we have argued that boxing developed as a ritual practice (Dioscurus and Dioscurus 2022a) and remarked at length on its association with worship in the ancient Near East (Dioscurus and Dioscurus 2022b). According to Graf (2009), "Running and boxing were not just athletic disciplines in Greece, they were the *ritual* core disciplines of archaic education" (p. 121; emphasis ours). Given its great antiquity and persistence in human society, boxing may be regarded as one of the oldest rituals still extant in Western (now global) civilization. We should not be surprised, therefore, to learn that boxing was closely linked to Greek religion, including its divinities.

Among the Olympians, the oracular god Apollo[7] was the deity most closely associated

---

[3] As two examples only, consider the richly-detailed (Hellenistic) *Gymnasticus* of Philostratus of Athens and the magnificent bronze *Boxer at Rest* to be reviewed in Dioscurus and Dioscurus (2023b).

[4] "[L]es fleurs délicates et fines de la poésie et de la science naissent plus aisément dans les cerveaux qui couronnent des corps sains, robustes et beaux" (Nordmann 1921, p. 462, translation ours).

[5] οὐ μὲν γὰρ μεῖζον κλέος ἀνέρος ὄφρα κ' ἔῃσιν, | ἢ ὅ τι ποσσίν τε ῥέξῃ καὶ χερσὶν ἐῇσιν (*Odyssey* 8.146–147).

[6] We note, for example, that boxing is routinely ranked as the "most difficult sport" by the Entertainment and Sports Programming Network (ESPN), among other oracles. This by no means corresponds to contemporary boxing viewership, which is still low relative to the mid-twentieth century.

[7] While Apollo's solar association arose in the fifth century BC and has been considerably strengthened in the post-classical tradition, the earliest provinces of Apollo seem to have been far more polytropic: he is associated with oracles, music, archery, plague, healing, and youth, in addition to light (Graf 2009, pp. 151–153). One functional hypothesis for linking the sun and boxing has become apparent to us while holding our own bouts out of doors, particularly when the sun is low on the horizon. One does well in these situations to put oneself between one's adversary and the sun, effectively blinding him. For any opponent of Phœbus Apollo himself, this doleful situation would have been unavoidable.

with pugilism.[8] Venerated particularly among the Ionians (the Greeks that inhabited the middle region of the Ægean islands and the west coast of Anatolia), Apollo is the subject of a Delian Hymn (149–152) that refers to boxing in the context of his worship:

> There [at Delos] in remembrance of you they give you delight with their box-ing | matches and dancing and singing, whenever they set competitions. | One would suppose them immortal and ageless forever and ever, | he who had come upon those Ionians meeting together[.][9]

Boxing was the only combat sport cultivated by the Ionians on Delos (Graf 2009, p. 29). As with the Hittites, who evidently delighted their own divinities through pugilism (Cammarosano 2014, Dioscurus and Dioscurus 2022b), boxing at Delos was viewed as an entertainment for the gods.[10] Moreover, it was related to dancing and singing—activities that also fell squarely among Apollo's prerogatives. Boxing and music had gone hand in hand since at least the third millennium in Mesopotamia (Dioscurus and Dioscurus 2022b) and continued to do so in Etruria and Lucania well into the first millennium before Christ (Dioscurus and Dioscurus 2023a). It has been noted that dancing and singing in honor of a god are uniquely ephemeral acts of devotion (Graf 2009, p. 17). Unlike clearly defined and consistently executed rituals, a boxing match can never be repeated step by step or blow for blow.[11] Much like ecstatic dance or incantation, boxing must always be *ex tempore*. In this regard, boxing bouts pattern with acts of dancing and singing to constitute unique votive offerings intended for Apollo.

In the Delian hymn, boxing is associated with ἀθανάτους καὶ ἀγήρως the 'ageless quality' of its participants, presumably invigorated by pugilistic activity. There are, of course, strong associations between adolescent boys and the eternally youthful Apollo. It has been noted by at least one critic, however, that Athena acted as a more consistent protector of the ephebes than her divine sibling (ibid., p. 13). After all, Apollo was frequently responsible for the sudden death of young men, e.g., the six sons of Niobe. It is perhaps the cold lethality of Apollo that draws him closest to the boxing ring. In a match between two young men, only one can be Apollo's protegé: the youthful god is just as implicated in the victory of one as in the defeat of the other.[12] In Greek accounts, defeat in the boxing 'ring' is typically gruesome, even grotesque, reminding us in some respects of the devastating plague unleashed by cruel Apollo in the opening act of the *Iliad*. Apollo's aspect as an archer is perhaps not too far removed from his aspect as a boxer. The archer stealthily fires arrows into the void between

---

[8] The Anatolian origins of Apollo are controversial (Graf 2009, pp. 136–137), but nonetheless find support among a variety of recent scholars, including those who associate the Greek god with the Hittite divinity *Apaliuna* (Rutherford 2020, p. 110, fn. 71). If Apollo is indeed an Anatolian god, this presents intriguing possibilities for a connection between Hittite and Greek boxing (Dioscurus and Dioscurus 2022b). Hittite boxing was associated with mountain deities who were in turn associated with hunting; while tenuous, this may provide a link via the panurgic Apollo's patronage of archery.

[9] οἱ δέ σε πυγμαχίῃ τε καὶ ὀρχηθμῷ καὶ ἀοιδῇ / μνησάμενοι τέρπουσιν, ὅτ᾽ ἂν στήσωνται ἀγῶνα. / φαίη κ᾽ ἀθανάτους καὶ ἀγήρως ἔμμεναι αἰεί, / ὃς τόθ᾽ ὑπαντιάσει᾽, ὅτ᾽ Ἰάονες ἀθρόοι εἶεν. "A Homeric Hymn to Apollo." Trans. Rodney Merrill. In Pepper, Timothy, ed. 2011. *A Californian Hymn to Homer*. Hellenic Studies Series 41. Washington, DC: Center for Hellenic Studies.

[10] The inhabitants of Delos were also known for their appreciation of cockfighting (Blaine 1840, p. 1206).

[11] "[T]out combat de boxe est un pièce qui est toujours une première" (Nordmann 1921, p. 460).

[12] Though respected by Homer's Achæans when not entirely trusted, Apollo was decidedly in the Trojan camp. It seems to us that Pæan Apollo picks sides in boxing matches, as in war.

two armies while a boxer hurls his fists into the void between two bodies. In both cases, a well-aimed strike can maim or slaughter. These are both provinces of Apollo, who "killed softly with his silver arrows" (*Iliad* 24.578).

While in all likelihood composed much later, the Hymn to Delian Apollo serves as a festal counterpoint to the brutality of boxing that is portrayed in the *Iliad* and *Odyssey*.[13] According to Plutarch (*Quæs. Conv.* 724c / 8.4.4), writing in the first century of the Christian era but presumably referring to matters of greater antiquity, an epithet of Apollo was πύκτης 'boxer' and offerings were made to him at Delphi under that name (Poliakoff 1987, p. 82).[14] Plutarch describes Apollo as φιλόνεικος 'eager for strife' and mentions his evocation in the Iliadic boxing match (Section 3.1.1).

A boxer was reportedly entombed in the sanctuary of Apollo Lykeios (Wolf-Apollo)[15] at Argos (Graf 2009, p. 121). This was highly unusual, since graves were not normally permitted inside the city, let alone inside a god's sanctuary. The burial of a boxer in the temple of Apollo Lykeios is an outstanding indication of the Apolline association with pugilism. A depiction of the famous Greek boxer Kreugas was also found in the temple (*Paus.* 8.40.5).

In many mythic vignettes, boxing is practiced by barbarians[16] on the periphery of the (early) Greek world (e.g., Bebrycia and Phlegyas) while divine and semi-divine beings worshiped by the Greeks (Apollo and Polydeuces) are revealed as the true masters of the craft. This suggests a kind of ambivalence towards boxing: rejecting, on the one hand, its raw brutality (epitomized by barbarians like Phorbas and Amycus); while celebrating, on the other, the skill, agility, and power manifest by all successful pugilists.

Another association between boxing and the divine comes from a fragment written by the Greek poetess Corinna: "For your [Tanagra's] sake Hermes boxed against Ares".[17] This suggests a nearly-forgotten tale in which Hermes boxed Ares to settle a dispute over a Naiad-nymph, the daughter of Æolus.[18] If the match went the same way as the contest between Apollo and Ares, we assume Hermes went home happy.[19] A euhemeristic approach to boxing in this myth might suggest that boxing arose from competition for females. It may even evoke a system whereby the fittest males were coupled with the worthiest females based on victory in formal boxing matches, at least in some localities (Dioscurus and Dioscurus 2022a).[20]

---

[13] According to Burkert (1979), the Hymn to Delian Apollo may have been composed as late as 522 BC.

[14] Plutarch, himself a priest of Apollo at Delphi, would have been intimately aware of Apollo's association with boxing, though he does not appear to have discussed the matter at length in any of his surviving works. The relevant passage is: κούφων δὲ καὶ βαρέων ἀγωνισμάτων ὄντων, πύκτῃ μὲν Ἀπόλλωνι Δελφούς, δρομαίῳ δὲ Κρῆτας ἱστοροῦσι θύειν καὶ Λακεδαιμονίους. It claims that Apollo was worshiped as a boxer at Delphi and as a runner by the Cretans and the Spartans.

[15] Wolves were reportedly sacrificed at the sanctuary. Wild animals were uncommon sacrificial victims in Greek religion (Marcinkowski 2008, p. 47).

[16] The triumph of Polydeuces in the *Argonautica* has been interpreted as "a victory for skill over sheer power, youth over maturity, good over evil, Greek over barbarian" (Nelis 2001, p. 18).

[17] "περὶ τεοῦς Ἑρμᾶς πὸτ Ἄρεα πουκτεύει" (fragment 666)

[18] Tanagra is also the name of a town in Bœotia where the inhabitants were known for their devotion to cock-fighting (Blaine 1840, p. 1206).

[19] John William Waterhouse's pre-Raphaelite masterpiece *Hylas and the Nymphs* (1896) gives some idea of the prize that awaited Hermes for his fistic superiority.

[20] In an evaluation of post-Mycenæan Greek art, one critic has written of "young marriageable females" depicted in scenes of contest, like boxing: "[They] are precisely that sector of the population whose control is critical for the well being of the community, especially to the elite households of the nascent state" (Langdon 2008, pp. 226–227). Moreover, the depiction of these women on domestic pottery is a didactically astute way of reflecting "the power of the elites to exert their mastery over the household and the community" (ibid).

Another story about a mortal boxer straddles the threshold between myth and legend and attracted the attention of Plato, Pausanias, Pliny, and Augustine (Burkert 1983, pp. 84–93). A fighter named Damarchus (or Demænetus) of Parrhasia (or Arcadia) was said to have won the Olympic boxing competition around 400 BC (*Paus.* 6.8.2). Damarchos was changed into a wolf at the sacrifice of Zeus Lykaios (Wolf-Zeus), a secret ritual held high on a mountain slope in Arcadia. The ritual may have involved human sacrifice and cannibalism at some point in the legendary past; it was certainly geared towards the initiation of adolescent males. It is fitting, perhaps, that once transformed into an animal, Damarchus should return to humanity in the form of a boxer. The legend suggests that the brutality and potential lethality of boxing made it, by some lights, a liminal activity for humans. In addition, the close association of pugilism with male initiation rituals (boy becomes wolf, wolf becomes boxer), as hypothesized based on the material culture of the Minoans (Dioscurus and Dioscurus 2022c), is here confirmed textually among the ancient Greeks.

The Greeks practiced boxing for so many centuries that they naturally grew curious—and likely inventive—regarding its origins. They became the first scholars of boxing, leaving us written accounts of where they thought the activity came from. Philostratus (*Gym.* 9) claimed that boxing was invented by the Spartans only to be adopted later by the Bebrycians. As we detail in Section 3.2, according to *Argonautica* 2, a legendary ruler of the Bebrycians, Amycus, was said to have engaged in a boxing match with Polydeuces, the semi-divine twin of Castor.[21] This is a relatively late source; the *Argonautica* was written in the third century BC. Polydeuces is referred to as πὺξ ἀγαθὸν 'good with his fists', in the much older *Iliad* 3.237 and *Odyssey* 11.300. The Greeks strongly associated him with boxing, as did the Romans. We will discuss the cult of Polydeuces (whom the Romans called Pollux) in a future article on boxing in Italy (Dioscurus and Dioscurus 2023b).

Theseus is attributed as the legendary inventor of wrestling, boxing, and/or *pankration* (cf. the *Scholia in Pindarum, Nemean Odes v*:89a–b, which passage is variously translated by different authors).

In his *Description of Greece* Pausanias (5.7.10) claims that Apollo beat Ares in boxing at the first Olympic games (which were held either to celebrate the victory of Zeus over his father Cronos, or to set the stage for them to wrestle for supremacy).[22] The match is not described in any detail, but it is an indication of Apollo's dominion over boxing and boxers. That Ares is defeated in boxing by the youthful and adroit Apollo suggests that the Greeks did not necessarily conceive of boxing as a form of war, but as something connected to Apolline attributes and associations: archery, music, dance, truth, prophecy, healing and disease, the sun, light, and poetry. What does this list have to do with boxing? Music and dance may be the Apollonian features most closely associated with pugilism. A boxer's movements are analogous to those of a dancer and music had a strong association with boxing acrosss ancient Mediterranean and Near Eastern cultures.

The Spartans incorporated boxing among adolescent boys into the *Gymnopaidia* festival

---

[21] See the Ficoroni Cista in Dioscurus and Dioscurus (2023a). The Dioscuri were regarded as kings of the Spartans (Sens 1997).

[22] The stephanitic games, so-called for their award of a crown rather than a prize of monetary value, included the Olympic, Nemean, Pythian, and Isthmian games. Delightfully, each awarded a characteristic crown: for the Olympic, a garland of olive branches cut from behind the temple of Zeus with a golden sickle; for the Nemean, a crown of wild celery in mourning for Opheltes; for the Pythian, a crown of laurel branches; for the Isthmian, a garland of pine leaves (Broneer 1962).

honoring Apollo Pythæus (Apollo the Python-slayer)[23] and Apollo Karneios (Ram-Apollo) (Graf 2009, pp. 116–117).[24] The *Gymnopaidia* also included the γυμνοπαιδικὴ ὄρχησις, a "boy's dance that is performed naked" (ibid.). Thus, singing, nude dancing, and boxing were all aspects of the Spartan adoration of Apollo.

3 The Language of *pygmachia*

3.1 Homeric

The boxing matches recounted in the *Iliad* and the *Odyssey* explain the proceedings of formal agonistic encounters and allow us to infer why boxing mattered to ancient people. In the *Iliad*, the game is motivated as a show of funereal reverence for a fallen comrade where prizes are offered and fighters volunteer to compete for them. In the *Odyssey*, the combatants are goaded into fighting each other for the pleasure of spectators, though both fighters have their own objectives in mind.

What, if anything, can these ancient narratives tell us about the deep-time origins of paired human combat? In the *Iliad*, the prizes are not necessary for survival (and in any case each competitor gets something). There are no females present, which rules out (direct) sexual selection. In both fights, at least one of the combatants seeks status, although the wily Odysseus arguably subverts this paradigm.[25] For Odysseus, defeating his rival is merely a means to gain the trust of the suitors, whom he will later defeat, as well. Engaging in paired combat to achieve status among males may be the civilized, uniquely human (or hominin?) version of gathering in a lek to court female conspecifics. The absence of females in Homer's boxing vignettes is puzzling, however, given that competition for access to the enslaved women Briseis and Chryseis arguably drives the entire Iliadic narrative (Schadewaldt 1951). Perhaps formal combat between males, watched and adjudicated by other males, developed so that higher-status males could select the most fit lower-status males for privileged access to females under their authority (Dioscurus and Dioscurus 2022a).

As we point out below, the loser in the Iliadic boxing match still receives a prize and the loser in the *Odyssey* is at least offered one. In Near Eastern literature and Minoan iconography, by contrast, the vanquished is either ignored or shown in all his humiliation. While Homer does not spare us the details of Euryalos' downfall in the *Iliad* (he spits thick clots of blood, his head hanging to one side) we are also edified to see him treated with respect and awarded his prize. Even metheless Iros, who deserves little of our sympathy, is shown some respect by Odysseus after their encounter in the *Odyssey*.

We can learn a great deal about the ancient audience's regard for boxing by closely studying Homeric texts. In what follows, we will discuss lexical choices that illuminate boxing as it was practiced in Greece (and western Anatolia) during the Iron Age and perhaps as early as the late Bronze Age—to the extent that the poem preserves traces of earlier Mycenæan culture.[26] However, scholars are by no means in agreement about what culture or time period

---

[23] Apollo's sister Artemis and mother Leto were also honored at the *Gymnopaidia*.

[24] Here we find a link to Hittite boxing, which was accompanied by ram-fighting called *tarpa* (Dioscurus and Dioscurus 2022b).

[25] There is a body of literature suggesting such subversion is the main purpose of Odysseus (Zieliński 2020).

[26] The chronology depends heavily on when the works of Homer were composed and set down in the form we have them today; estimates for the *Iliad* and the *Odyssey* range from 800 to as late as 630 BC. The central conflict of

is represented in the poetry of Homer. One critic insists that "the epic was not some kind of bad history. It was a poetic creation, what *some* eighth-century Greeks thought the heroic world *ought* to have been like" (Morris 1997, p. 558). Another scholar opines, "[I]t seems risky to assume that Homeric poems give a reliable, let alone comprehensive, depiction of any single historical society" (Dickinson 2006, p. 240). While currently it may be fashionable to conclude that the boxing scenes in Homer were mere fantasies of a late Iron Age mind,[27] we also cannot be entirely certain that they were uninformed by legend or knowledge of a more ancient, heroic past (Van Wees 1992). It has been argued that Homeric references are perhaps most appropriately connected to individual, "prosaic" features of Mycenæan society—those that were not likely "intended to attract attention" in the Homeric narrative (Dickinson 2006, p. 240).[28] We believe that some aspects of the Homeric boxing matches, e.g., wearing a loincloth, may be unobtrusive enough to suggest their great antiquity along these lines. Homer's account likely offers a glimpse of boxing as it was practiced well before it became an Olympic sport in 688 BC.

3.1.1 *Iliad* **23**

A boxing match between two Greek soldiers is described in 45 lines of dactylic hexameter in Book 23 of the *Iliad*. The context is a series of funeral games for the fallen warrior Patroclus. Boxing is immediately preceded by a chariot race and followed by wrestling. While funeral games were practiced widely among the Etruscans late into the first millennium (Dioscurus and Dioscurus 2023a), there is no evidence that the Greeks, outside of those depicted in the *Iliad*, incorporated boxing into their funerary cultus (Corrigan 1979, p. 210). We suspect that the context of combat sports among the Mycenæans changed over time, gradually becoming disassociated from funerals in Greece while retaining this feature in Etruria, perhaps due to more archaic Mycenæan influence. It is also possible that funeral games were widely practiced by Indo-European invaders of southeastern Europe and it is their influence and/or inheritance that we observe in both Etruscan and Mycenæan practice.

The scene opens with Achilles' offer of prizes (ἄεθλα) to entice potential combatants: a mule (ἡμίονος) for the winner and a special cup for the loser. The cup, which is called δέπας ἀμφικύπελλος, is often translated as "double-cup", or a "cup with two handles". It is not clear if the cup is valued because of its composition (we do not learn, e.g., if it is made of some precious metal), its utility to a warrior, its ceremonial value, or something else.[29] It is remarkable that prizes are made available to both the winner and the loser before the bout even begins. This offers a point of comparison with earlier, Near Eastern boxing. In a Mesopotamian poem called the "Marriage of Martu," the victor of the boxing match is offered treasure (ultimately opting for a bride instead), while the losers are noted only for

---

the *Iliad*, the Trojan War, was likely waged by the Mycenæan Greeks as early as 1200 years before Christ. Thus, it is hardly extreme to claim that Homer is "no guide at all" to Mycenæan civilization (Finley 1982, p. 232).

[27] According to (Dickinson 2020), Greek tradition "is more likely to represent how later Greeks wanted to imagine the past than to incorporate any accurate and detailed memories" (p. 158).

[28] A thought experiment: how might naïve twenty-first century authors reconstruct a bout from the seventeenth century? The narrative would likely be filled with anachronisms—references to contemporary rather than contemporaneous pugilism. Accordingly, our expectations for Homeric 'history' should not be too high, since the collapse of Mycenæan culture occurred some fifteen generations before "the process of shaping the Homeric epics into their present form" even began (Palaima 2008, p. 348).

[29] The value of a mule in a Bronze or Iron Age agrarian culture requires less explication.

the devastating wounds they suffer under the hero's fists (Vanstiphout 1998, Dioscurus and Dioscurus 2022b). As we will see, the defeated boxer in the *Iliad*, though *hors de combat* and soundly thrashed, is neither humiliated nor deprived his due. He thus leaves the scene with a kind of dignity that we do not see in "Martu" or the many depictions of recumbent, defeated boxers created by Minoan artists (Dioscurus and Dioscurus 2022c).[30]

In introducing the fight and calling out the fighters, Achilles refers to the one who will ultimately lose the bout by using a passive form of the verb νικάω 'conquer'. The eventual winner is described in a more circumlocutory, though revealing, manner. He is the one who will demonstrate καμμονίη 'steadfastness' or 'endurance', which is said to be a gift from Apollo himself (line 661).[31] Thus we learn that victory in boxing was understood to proceed from outlasting one's opponent even more so than beating him into unconsciousness. Though a knockout indeed ends this particular match, it seems that the ideal boxer in this culture was the one who could withstand the most punishment. We also have early evidence that Apollo was regarded as the patron of boxers. No other god is mentioned in relation to the Iliadic boxing contest.

The first to take up Achilles' challenge was Epeius,[32] a man of pantagruelian proportions said to 'know boxing' (εἰδὼς πυγμαχίης) but relatively unskilled in warfare.[33] Here, for the first time, we encounter the word πυγμαχία or *pygmachia*, literally, a 'fist fight', the term of art for Greek boxing well into late antiquity.[34] The participial form of οἶδα 'know how to', which describes Epeius, suggests that *pygmachia* was a learned skill—hardly the province of mere pothouse brawlers. Epeius calls on a potential adversary with the phrase 'let him draw nearer' (ἆσσον ἴτω). But where was this opponent to join him, exactly? Homer provides no special word for the space sanctified by the blood of the combatants—what we call the 'ring'. Instead, the phrase ἐς μέσσον ἀγῶνα 'into the midst of the assembly' is used (line 685) to describe the path of motion. The operative noun is ἀγῶν; its English transliteration *agon* has come to mean the contest itself. Here, however, it refers to the crowd of warriors eager to watch a bout between two of their comrades. The welter of bodies formed the boundaries circumscribing the boxers. Like a great lung, contracting and expanding, the crowd surged and withdrew, turning the 'ring' into an organic participant in the fight itself. When the men pushed forward, the boxers were compelled to strike at closer quarters and with greater vigor; when they stepped back, the fighters could separate and consider their actions more carefully.

On entering this 'ring', Epeius calls for a challenger, sanctifying the space with a solemn

---

[30] Blandishments for the loser are still featured in professional boxing, thousands of years later, when fighters sign contracts with legally enforcible provisions as to the distribution of monies generated by the fight.

[31] Etymologically, the term appears to be a compound of κατα+μονή, suggesting someone that remains, or stays put.

[32] Epeius was the son of Panopeus, who, according to Hesiod, fought his twin brother Crissus while still in the womb. It is said that Epeius built the Trojan horse under the inspiration of Athena.

[33] In lines 670–671, Epeius boasts that he is the 'best' (ἄριστος), a term "normally reserved for elite warrior heroes," then ironically proceeds to acknowledge his shortcomings as a soldier (μάχης ἐπιδεύομαι) (Scanlon 2018, p. 9). He addresses this by reasoning that man "may not...prove him a man of skill in every work" (ἐν πάντεσσ' ἔργοισι δαήμονα φῶτα γενέσθαι). While this may make Epeius a "comic scapegoat" akin to Thersites in Book 2, his eventual victory in the boxing 'ring' allows the audience to identify with his down-to-earth claim that men cannot be skilled in all deeds (ibid.).

[34] The forms πύξ *pyx* (an indeclinable adverbial form meaning 'with the fist') and πυγμή *pygmē* 'fist' are commonly associated with phrases including "boxing" or "boxer" in translation, including *Iliad* 3.237 and *Odyssey* 11.300 (Murray 1919; 1924).

vow or prayer (εὔχομαι) to rend (ῥήγνυμι) the flesh and break (ἀράσσω) the bones of his opponent. He colorfully remarks that his adversary's closest comrades will be responsible for removing what remains of the unlucky man at the conclusion of the fight. The term he uses for these comrades (κηδεμόνες) is, throughout Homer, reserved for those who attend to the dead, so 'pallbearers' might be an apt translation in English—and more in keeping with Epeius' outrecuidance. Epeius uses a passive participial form of the verb δαμάζω 'overpower' or perhaps 'kill' to describe the final state of anyone audacious enough to meet him (line 675). The lexical evidence suggests that Epeius was threatening his opponent (hyperbolically, we think) with death, not just defeat. This has implications for understanding the deep-time relationship of boxing to human sacrifice, a connection which seems likely among the Minoans and was all but certain among the Etruscans and the Classic Mayans (Corrigan 1979, Taube and Zender 2009). As we will see at the conclusion of this episode, however, death was not the preferred outcome sought in the Achæan boxing 'ring'.

Despite these threats—or perhaps incited by them—one Euryalus[35] rises (ἀνίστημι) to the occasion. We learn that he prevailed (νικάω) in boxing matches at Thebes where he beat all of the locals following the death of Œdipus (a sort of *mise en abyme* suggesting the history of funerary pugilism long before the burning roof and tower of Ilium).

We then encounter another remarkable innovation—or at least first attestation. A man referred to as the "son of Tydeus" appears to serve as Euryalus' second or cornerman.[36] This man, who is equated with the warrior Diomedes earlier in the epic, performs a number of important functions, psychological and physical. Pyschologically, he encourages (θαρσύνω) Euryalus and wishes him victory (βούλομαι νίκην). These may be cover terms for brief cultic rites like prayer and anointing, as observed in the corner of a modern Muay Thai bout, and occasionally a western boxing match, as well. Diomedes attends (ἀμφιπονέομαι) to Euryalus in more practical matters, too. He clothes (παρακαταβάλλω) Epeius in a boxing garment, the *zōma* (ζῶμα),[37] and binds (δίδωμι) his hands in the 'boxing gloves' that will receive more attention below. The active voice of the verbs παρακαταβάλλω and δίδωμι makes it relatively clear that Diomedes dressed Euryalos and put his gloves on for him.[38] If the boxer performed these actions himself, we might expect the verb to appear in the middle voice instead. The loincloth or *zōma* that Diomedes puts on Euryalos is a truly archaic feature of the match. Greek boxing art (including early examples like the Copenhagen Kantharos, see Figure 12) almost always depicts the combatants naked but for their gauntlets and, occasionally, a κυνοδέσμη *kynodesmē* securing their foreskin (e.g., Figure 22). A related word is mentioned in the Iliadic wrestling match, between Ajax and Odysseus (23.710) where the verb ζώννυμι is usually translated as 'gird'. Some form of covering about the waist is typical of both Near Eastern and Minoan boxing, however, suggesting that Mycenæan (or early Greek) boxing was influenced by either or both of these cultures (Dioscurus and Dioscurus 2022b;c).

The 'boxing gloves' bound to the hands of Euryalus are the famous leathern straps or thongs known as *himantes* (ἱμάντες). The same word can also mean 'dog leash', 'whip', and

---

[35] Euryalus was one of the Argonauts, which links him to another famous boxing match, viz., one between Polydeuces and Amycus. According to Hesychius, Euryalus is also a surname of Apollo, the divine patron of boxers (Schmidt 1867, p. 655).

[36] No such figure is reported in Epeius' 'corner'.

[37] We will henceforth transliterate ζῶμα as *zōma* without providing the Greek spelling.

[38] The inflected forms are παρακάββαλεν (line 683) and δῶκεν (line 684), respectively.

'rope', inter alia.[39] We are told on line 684 that the straps are 'well-cut' (ἐύτμητος). The text does not resolve for us whether the *himantes* are bound to one or both hands since the hands are not mentioned at all in this respect. However, the narrative does make explicit the material from which the *himantes* are fashioned. We are told the strips come from a 'field-dwelling bull' (βοῦς ἄγραυλος).[40] The significance of the adjective ἄγραυλος is unclear. While it is possible that the adjective was included merely for metrical purposes, it is more likely that the bovid's origins were significant to ancient boxing. Even though the *himantes* are widely known, their original purpose is not altogether transparent. No explicit mention is made of how Epeius is graithed for the combat.[41]

As with modern boxing gloves, there seems to be no consensus view as to why hand-coverings should be used during a fistfight. This is because there seems to be no agreement on whether it is more or less injurious (and to whom) to wear such coverings on the hands. Frost (1906, p. 214) writes:

> Professional pugilists seem to agree that fights [at the turn of the twentieth century] in which very light gloves are used are more severe than if bare fists were allowed: the gloves have not enough padding to make any appreciable difference, while they prevent the knuckles from swelling and deadening the blows. This must have been the case to an even greater extent when strips of leather were employed.

Accordingly, we propose three reasons for using the *himantes* in the boxing ring: (1) to protect the (hands of the) striker; (2) to protect the stricken; or (3) to injure the stricken more gravely. As with modern boxing gloves, there seems to be no consensus[42] as to the 'true' purpose of the *himantes*.[43] We present another option for consideration: the practical utility of the *himantes* in the fight was secondary, while their primary purpose was telesmatic. They were perhaps used to bind the boxer to the animal spirit of the field-dwelling bull, βοῦς ἄγραυλος. From the bull of heaven in the Epic of Gilgameš to the *tarpa* blood sport among the Hittites, to bull-leaping among the Minoans, bulls and boxing were closely connected in the ancient world.[44] In trying to imagine why ancient men first wrapped their fists in leather

[39] The term is specific enough that we will transliterate and use *himantes* to denote this ubiquitous piece of boxing equipment.

[40] Though Homer is not explicit on this point, commentators appear to agree that the *himantes* are a product of the hide rather than, e.g., the intestines of the bull.

[41] An Attic neck amphora from Tell Dafana (Daphnæ) in Egypt shows a boxing scene in which, arguably, only one fighter is gloved—and only on his right hand (British Museum, No. 1888,0208.102; Figure 20).

[42] Connor (1995, p. 102) proposes that the *himantes* were "intended to strengthen hand and wrist rather than to hurt an opponent" but the evidence for this claim is doubtful.

[43] Even option (3), increased injury, is possible with modern gloves. Reports of using the exposed laces of the glove to abrade an opponent's face, or to twist the leather of the glove on impact in order to make the skin tear and bleed, are not uncommon in the modern sport (Thomas 1997, pp. 9–15). The case is argued repeatedly, particularly by enthusiasts of mixed martial arts, that boxing gloves facilitate more strikes and thereby more cumulative damage to an opponent in the ring. Even cosmetic damage, like a black eye or bloody nose, is not prevented by gloves. Besides distributing the force of the blow to a relatively wide surface area (at least in very modern, foam-padded gloves), there is no real consensus as to what good they do (Chadli et al. 2018). We cannot deny that boxing gloves bear some mystical power in the modern ring, as well.

[44] The use of pigskin in constructing the *himantes* was explicitly forbidden (Phil. *Gym.* 10): ὅθεν τοὺς ἱμάντας τοὺς ἀπὸ τῶν συῶν ἐκκρίνουσι τῶν σταδίων ὀδυνηρὰς ἡγούμενοι τὰς ἀπ' αὐτῶν πληγὰς καὶ δυσιάτους. A relatively late source suggests this is because it was too hazardous to fighters but we find this claim implausible. Despite being somewhat bumpier, pigskin is regarded by leather workers as more supple than bull hide, particularly after it has gotten wet and

thongs to fight each other with their fists, we must be open to all of these possibilities and continue to scour the sources for the best evidence we can obtain. Unfortunately, it seems that ancient critics themselves were only guessing at their ancestors' intentions.

Both boxers are girt in the *zōma*, as we learn from the dual form of the verb ζώννυμι (line 685). Their procession into the *agon* is marked by the verb βαίνω 'walk' or 'step'.[45] The initial description of the fight seems like it has been drawn directly from a seal impression at Ugarit or a terracotta plaque in Mesopotamia. Homer tells us that fighters 'lift their hands on high'—the same attitude struck by boxers at least a thousand years before the *Iliad* was composed—with at least one hand raised high above the head. The verb is a middle voice form of ἀνέχω 'hold up, lift up' and applies to the boxers' hands. Two more evocative verbs are used, viz., πίπτω 'fall violently upon, attack' (active voice) and μίγνυμι 'mix up, mingle'. The latter verb, in the passive voice, specifically describes the action of the boxers' 'heavy hands' (βαρεῖαι χεῖρες) and is used elsewhere to denote the mixing of different liquids. The colloquial English expression 'mix it up' could have no more august a predecessor, albeit a presumably non-etymological one.

The description of the fight is particularly evocative in the original Greek. It is laced with dramatic language that is still compatible with the experience of modern boxers and their audience. A 'fearful crashing sound' (δεινός χρόμαδος) emanates 'from the jaws' (γενύων) of the boxers (line 688). Murray (1924) translates this as a 'grinding of teeth', apparently assuming a mereological relationship between teeth and jaws. It is perhaps more likely that Homer referred simply to the pounding of fists on jaws. The thud of a punch landed flush is an unforgettable auditory sensation and one that the poet could conjure easily among listeners accustomed to watching these bouts. It is also possible that, without mouth guards (gum shields), ancient boxers were more likely to experience injuries to their jaws and that these were accompanied by dreadful, loud noises.[46]

Homer also incorporates the visual and, to some extent, tactile quality of a boxing match in his description of ἱδρώς 'sweat'. The poet says it 'flows' (ῥέω) 'from every quarter' (πάντοθεν). The source of this perspiration is regarded as the boxers' 'limbs' (ἐκ μελέων), presumably because they were understood to be the hardest-working parts of the body during the match. However, the term μέλος may also be rendered more generally as 'body part' and thus includes the face, back, and torso, which are all diaphoretic loci in their own right. Given the boxers' deliquescent state, we may infer that their punches occasionally slipped off the mark and that any form of orthograde wrestling or clinching (if allowed) was difficult to execute in so lubricious a company.

The poet describes the detailed sequence of only one blow[47] and it is, fittingly, that of the knockout punch. We are told that Epeius 'lets loose', 'awakens', or is otherwise 'aroused' (ὄρνυμι) during the course of the action. He 'glares' (παπταίνω) at his opponent. Some translators prefer to render this verb as 'casts a searching glance', suggesting the boxer's mental

---

dried out again. The taboo on using certain materials in their construction suggests that the *himantes* themselves had a cultic importance. Moreover, it seems that pigs, unlike bulls, were not to be associated with boxing.

[45] This calls to mind the verb used in Hittite texts, when boxers 'step' (*tiya-*) into the act of GEŠPÚ 'boxing' (Cammarosano 2018, Dioscurus and Dioscurus 2022b).

[46] A review of evidence from early modern boxing, before the introduction of the mouth guard, could be helpful in clarifying the meaning of δεινός δὲ χρόμαδος γενύων γένετ᾽ (line 688).

[47] At least one commentator has inaccurately concluded that Epeius won after throwing a single punch, a misreading of the hard-fought battle that precedes the blow or perhaps a confusion with the bout described in the *Odyssey* (https://sententiaeantiquae.com/2017/05/26/less-strength-more-skill-homeric-boxing/).

craft at work. However, anyone who has boxed another man in earnest knows that 'glare' is perfectly adequate. Murray offers a somewhat ornate gloss arising, we can only imagine, from contemporaneous pugilistic vernacular: "as he peered for an opening" (ibid.). Epeius then strikes (κόπτω)[48] Euryalus on the cheek or jaw (παρήιον). Given the aftermath of the punch, we believe that the best translation here is indeed 'jaw'. Laterally-directed punches to the jaw or the chin are often the cause of a failure in equilibrium and can result in devastating knockouts.

And so, for Euryalus, champion of Thebes, the lights went out. The poet seems to relish the episode's dénouement most of all. In an instantaneous transformation, as if the sudden object of a sorcerer's spell, the mighty Euryalus loses not just some of his strength but all of it. He can no longer stand (ἵστημι). His beautiful, glistening limbs (φαίδιμα γυῖα), once the cynosure of athletic prowess, now fail him utterly (ὑπερείπω). Down he falls, and in a complicated simile that seems to evade even the most artful and erudite of interpreters, the fallen boxer writhes on the ground like a fish suffocating in air.[49] In other words, he has a seizure.[50]

The somewhat adscititious piscine simile is more than a little puzzling. Translators like Murray suggest that Euryalus leaps up after being struck. However, this is an uncommon if not unencountered physical reaction to even a powerful blow in the boxing ring. It is even stranger since Euryalus' legs had just gone limp, robbing him of any power to thrust himself upward. Perhaps the poet wished to depict Epeius delivering an uppercut so *puissant* that it lifts Euryalus off his feet.[51] Despite the unlikelihood of such an event occurring in the boxing ring, it is possible that Homer believed such an event could occur, as we saw in the fanciful depiction of an uppercut at Knossos (Dioscurus and Dioscurus 2022b). The crucial verb seems to be ἀναπάλλω which can be analyzed morphologically as 'up' (ἀνα) and 'sway a missile before it is thrown' (πάλλω). Other definitions include 'oscillate', 'vibrate', and 'swing to and fro', suggesting a horizontal path of motion. Line 694 is more consistent with a seizure on the ground, i.e., he 'swung to and fro' (ἀνέπαλτ').[52] Fagles (1990) was tempted to use the

---

[48] This verb can also mean 'cut' in Ancient Greek. In other Indo-European languages, like Old Church Slavonic *skopiti* 'castrate' and English *hatchet*, slicing or hewing seems to be the dominant sense.

[49] Lines 692–694 read, in part: ὡς δ' ὅθ' ὑπὸ φρικὸς Βορέω ἀναπάλλεται ἰχθὺς | θίν' ἐν φυκιόεντι, μέλαν δέ ἑ κῦμα κάλυψεν, | ὡς πληγεὶς ἀνέπαλτ'. In his translation, Fagles (1990) puts it thus: "[A]s under the ruffling North Wind a fish goes arching up | and flops back down on a beach-break strewn with seaweed | and a dark wave blacks him out..." (p. 581).

[50] A reminder of this possibility occurred in a September 2021 fight between Callum Smith and Lenin Castillo at the aptly-named Tottenham Hostpur Arena in London. The light heavyweight matchup ended when Smith dropped Castillo with a right hand to the temple. Castillo began to seize on the blue stretched canvas. Ingemar Johansson experienced a similar seizure in his 1960 rematch with Floyd Patterson after the former dealt him a left hook to the chin. Patterson reportedly cradled the supine Swede, unconscious and bleeding from the mouth, while promising him a rematch. Their next encounter occurred about a year later when Johansson was again defeated.

[51] This is by no means a common outcome in modern boxing. However, an anecdote has circulated claiming that George Foreman lifted his opponent, Joe Frazier, off the ground with an uppercut in their first title matchup in 1973. We find the evidence for this fairly unconvincing, having carefully reviewed the film ourselves. For example, with 18 seconds remaining in the first round, Frazier moves his right (back) foot retrograde when an uppercut is delivered to his left side, but his left (front) foot does not leave the ground under the force of the blow. In the second round, approximately one minute and ten seconds after the opening bell, Foreman lands another right uppercut and a few moments later Frazier lurches to his right; Foreman's hands are already fairly relaxed at his own waist. The punch that causes this awkward movement is probably the one that has given rise to the dubious claim that Foreman lifted Frazier off the ground. It also effectively ended the fight.

[52] The verb is a simple indicative where a medio-passive might be expected, further complicating the translation.

penultimate phrase θίν᾽ ἐν φυκιόεντι, μέλαν δέ ἑ κῦμα κάλυψεν to allude to unconsciousness: "a dark wave blacks him out". Its significance may be even simpler, however. The clause is most literally translated as "a dark swelling covers him." Perhaps this refers to the bruises appearing on Euryalus' stricken body, an indication that the fight had dragged on for some time before the knockout punch was delivered. A final possibility is that the phrase forms a metalepsis or kenning for the recitator by appropriately matching rhythm, perhaps an instance of an unattested Homeric-style epithet used rhapsodically.

The concluding scene contains the hitherto-unprecedented moral center of the boxing match and captures, *multum in parvo,* one of the most fascinating psychological aspects of western boxing, viz., the empathy of a victor for his fallen opponent. In a gesture repeated countless times since the revival of boxing in the early modern era, Epeius shows genuine concern for Euryalus. He takes him up in his arms (χερσὶ λαμβάνω) and 'straightens him out' (ὀρθόω), perhaps attending to his crippled posture resulting from the seizure, perhaps setting him back on his feet, as Murray has it (op cit.). At this moment, Homer recommends Epeius to us as μεγάθυμος, which can be rendered as 'great-hearted', 'high-minded', or perhaps 'high-spirited'. None of these glosses, however, does justice to the concept of *thymos*—a combination of passion, loyalty, rage, and lust for glory. Whatever *thymos* is, we are told that Epeius has it in abundance. Epeius may be read as struggling with his desire to brutally defeat his opponent while at the same time feeling deep compassion and loyalty to him in his fallen state. Volumes could be written on the *thymos* of boxing in the western tradition, from Epeius vs. Euryalus in the late Bronze Age to Ray Mancini vs. Duk Koo Kim in 1982.[53] Each boxer knows that he can only win at the bodily expense of his opponent; there is no other way. It is this terrible knowledge that binds the adversaries to one another so closely.[54]

Finally, we watch as Epeius' prophecy is fulfilled and Euryalus' beloved comrades (φίλοι ἑταῖροι) surround him (ἀμφίστημι) then 'lead', 'carry' or 'fetch' (ἄγω) him from the midst of the assembly, his feet trailing behind him (ἐφελκομένοισι πόδεσσιν) while he "spit[s] clots of blood" (αἷμα παχὺ πτύοντα) (Fagles, op. cit.). According to Murray (op. cit.) Euryalus "wander[s] in his wits" or perhaps simply 'gives no heed' (ἀλλοφρονέω) to what is going on around him. His taut muscles at last relaxed and his mind rummy from the blows, Euryalus' head lolls to the side (κάρη βάλλονθ᾽ ἑτέρωσε). His fellows return to fetch the cup, now almost an afterthought.

Inventive English translations have sought to close the gap between contemporary readers and ancient epic by introducing modern boxing terminology. In so doing, they suggest conventions and techniques that are unattested in the original and may mislead. We have already mentioned that there is no 'ring'. There is also no term for a 'corner' in which the fighters rest and receive assistance and advice. No specific word for 'second' is used, despite our conclusion that Diomedes functions as such for Euryalus. There is certainly no bell to initiate or close a round; in fact, there are no rounds and no pauses in the action. From the description of the boxer's perspiration, we might assume that they fought for more than just a minute or two but Homer gives us scant evidence as to the duration of the battle. There

---

[53] Mancini's defeat of Kim resulted in the latter's death. The brutality of the televised match, along with public knowledge of the outcome a few days later, pushed boxing out of the mainstream in the United States for more than a generation. Though deeply troubled by his opponent's death, Mancini continued to box at the highest levels of the sport for ten more years.

[54] One notable perversion in the modern era of boxing is the (usually fabricated) escalation of 'bad blood' between boxers for an audience increasingly unaware of the deep fraternal bonds that exist inside the ring.

are absolutely no terms of art for specific offensive or defensive manœuvers like jabs, upper-cuts, slips, or any type of guard. Finally, the designation of the *himantes* as boxing 'gloves' should be treated with caution. As we have pointed out, the structure of the *himantes* is not particularly glove-like nor is their purpose as straightforward as one might assume.

3.1.2 *Odyssey* 18

Homer's *Odyssey* (Book 18) presents us with a different kind of boxing match.[55] In some ways this event stands as the tragicomic counterpart to the heroic bout we witnessed in the *Iliad*. Odysseus, in the guise of a beggar, is picked on by an authentic vagrant named Arnaios,[56] called Iros because he often serves as a messenger for Ithaca's upper crust. Protective of his turf, the bombastic Iros menaces and threatens Odysseus. The men angling for a crack at Odysseus' wife are delighted by the diverting prospect of a fist-fight between two men of such low rank; accordingly, they urge them on.[57] Of course, no one knows that the "man of twists and turns" sits before them dressed in a beggar's weeds, about to prove himself as skilled and wily a boxer as he is a wrestler, a runner, and a warrior.

We start by examining Iros' challenge to Odysseus. In a rodomontade that must have been just as amusing to the ancient Greeks as it is to the modern reader, Iros threatens to knock (ἐξελαύνω) the teeth out of Odysseus' jaw like the tusks of a corn-ravaging boar.[58] In an overlap with the language of the boxing match outside the walls of Ilium, Iros commands his rival to accinge himself for their fight by putting on the *zōma* (ζώννυμι). Here, the nominal form has been incorporated into a verb.[59] This makes it clear that pugilists clad in loincloths at the funeral games of Patroclus were no fluke and that early Greeks did not box naked like their classical counterparts.[60] Donning the *zōma* seems to be a symbolic act, as well, suggesting readiness for the fight.[61]

Iros boasts that he will smite his rival left and right (κόπτων ἀμφοτέρῃσι; line 28), using the same verb the narrator employs to describe the knockout punch in the *Iliad*. However, the word *pygmachia* is not used in this episode. Instead, Iros employs the verbs μάχομαι and μάρναμαι to describe the forthcoming action (line 31).[62] Any semantic differences between these two terms are lost on the modern reader. They are both glossed merely as 'fight' or

---

[55] Boxing is referenced but not described in Book 8, lines 100–103, when the Phæacian ruler Alcinous makes claims as to his people's great skill in boxing. The games held during Odysseus' visit to Phæacia/Scheria (modern Corfu) included 'boxing' (πύξ, line 103) but Odysseus did not participate. After startling his hosts with a powerful throw of the discus, they declined his request to enter the other competitions, including boxing. By some lights, this episode was intended to prefigure the boxing episode of Book 18, setting up expectations for violence Odysseus later unleashes on Iros (Scanlon 2018, p. 18).

[56] Derived from either ἄρνυμαι 'get' or ἄρνα 'lamb' (cf. the Haggis-prize mentioned later in the narrative), the name Arnaios is suggestive of a greedy character (Scanlon 2018, p. 15).

[57] A similar phenomenon has arisen in twenty-first century America, notably expressed in the video series *Bumfights* (2002–2006) which features homeless men fighting each other (Bunds et al. 2016). Claims that the men were instigated to fight one another have been disputed (Stahl 2018).

[58] The pejorative allusion to pigs may be related to the apparent (and much later attested) prohibition of pigskin in the fabrication of Greek boxing gloves (Phil. *Gym.* 10).

[59] The Iliadic *zōma* is the object of the verb παρακαταβάλλω 'clothe', *ut supra*.

[60] Compare, for example, the verb for athletic preparation (including boxing) used by Philostratus the Elder, writing during the early Roman Empire. He explains simply that Phorbas ἀποδύω 'strips' (in the medio-passive) before commencing the agon (*Imagines* 2.19).

[61] The linguistic and cultural relevance of the *zōma* is still found in the English expression 'gird (up) one's loins', though the garment is not itself mentioned.

[62] Later, in line 52, Odysseus also uses μάχομαι.

'battle', though the latter may have its etymological roots in a Proto-Indo-European word meaning 'seize'. (The stem of μάχομαι is of doubtful origin.)[63] Iros calls for spectators to watch (ἐπιγιγνώσκω) the main event. We find another usage of *thymos* in the description of the beggars' escalating fury: the adverb πανθυμαδόν 'in full *thymos*', "in high dudgeon" describes the manner in which they become enraged at each other (ὀκριάομαι; line 33).[64]

The suitors find the beggars' truculence a 'delight' or 'rare sport' (τερπωλή). A prominent member of the group, Antinous, calls their encounter 'wrangling' ἐρίζω. He refers to the fight that is brewing as χερσὶ μάχομαι. In the dative case, the plural χερσὶ (which we encounter frequently in *Iliad* 23, as well) suggests the most faithful translation of this phrase might be 'hand-to-hand combat'. Agig, Antinous bids his friends drive the two beggars together (συνελαύνω) as one might crowd two fighting dogs or gamecocks into an enclosed space to watch the fur or feathers fly. This is to be done quickly (ἀλλὰ ξυνελάσσομεν ὦκα; line 39), presumably so their pugnacity does not dissipate or discharge prematurely, before a true spectacle can be made of it.

As we have come to expect in Near Eastern and Greek boxing, prizes are offered to the fighters. In the case of the *Odyssey*, these are two goat stomachs (γαστέρες αἰγῶν) filled with blood and fat (line 44). The man who conquers (νικάω) the other and shows himself mightiest (κρείσσων), Antinous declares, will get to choose the best one for himself (the loser, presumably, gets the gastronomic residuum). Compared to the mule and the goblet offered to the contestants in the *Iliad*, the haggis-prize of the *Odyssey* is a much humbler token of victory. Despite the humor in this, the ensuing boxing match is still deadly serious.

Before the fight begins, the crafty Odysseus interdicts any behavior on the part of the suitors that might cause him to lose the fight (lines 51–57).[65] This is the first textual evidence we have of what might be considered illicit in ancient boxing, though the focus is on the audience's actions, not the fighters'. Intervention of the audience was perhaps a more common situation than is now possible in today's sport boxing, given the distant and elevated position of the modern ring.[66] The operative term describing the unwanted "foul blow" is ἀτασθάλλω 'to be insolent' or 'arrogant' (Murray 1919). According to Odysseus, such a foul would allow him to be 'overcome' (δαμάζω) 'by force' (ἶφι). Terms not found in the Patroclan boxing match, ἶφι and ἀτασθάλλω may carry with them the suggestion of unacceptable behavior in *pygmachia*. By contrasting the fair and honorable unwinding of a boxing match with 'insolence' and 'force', the poet may suggest to us that these concepts are not legible within the ethos of ancient Greek boxing. Given the violent character of boxing, it is possible that ἶφι had a more nuanced meaning through its association with an unwelcome practice in the ring.

The oath sworn, most-blameless Telemachus steps forward, extolling the καρδία καὶ θυμὸς 'heart and *thymos*' of his disguised father (line 61).[67] Once more, we see how *thymos* is an

---

[63] The verb may be related to Old Armenian *mak'arim* 'come to blows'.

[64] We note here the continuing puzzle of *thymos*, a derivative of which was used to describe the benevolent actions of Epeius after defeating his rival in the ring, here attached to the quarrel of two pathetic mendicants.

[65] Some read in lines 52–53 a "reasoned attempt to dissuade [Iros] from fighting" (Nelis 2001, p. 10). To us, this seems another example of Odysseus' craft, suggesting he is too old to fight when he knows he is about to clean the other man's clock.

[66] USA Boxing rules, for example, prohibit spectators—including extra cornermen—from approaching the ring during a sanctioned fight. Similarly, audience participation is sedulously avoided during Peruvian *takanakuy*, lest it give rise to a general brawl (Ttito and Ttito Tica 1999).

[67] Fagles (1996) renders the phrase "spine and fighting spirit" (p. 377).

operative component of the boxing match, though here it is allied with the fighter's 'heart' (καρδία). These are agents, Telemachus opines, that together stir (ὀτρύνω) the stranger to manly defense (ἀγήνωρ ἀλέξασθαι) against the overweening Iros (here reduced to the deictic τοῦτον). Telemachus uses the verb θείνω 'strike' in reference to the action of anyone who might intervene irregularly in the match. We did not encounter this verb in the Iliadic boxing match, perhaps because it also designates an action illicit in the boxing ring. Telemachus promises that anyone who strikes (θείνω) Odysseus in this fashion will have a fight (μάχομαι) on his hands. Telemachus' role in protecting the combatants from audience interference may be related to the function of the stick-wielding 'third man' ubiquitous to depictions of boxing throughout much of the ancient world, including Greece. The stick may have served a double-purpose, i.e., to discipline the fighters as well as the crowd.[68]

Next, Odysseus girds himself (ζώννυμι) about his genitals (περὶ μήδεα) in ragged garments (ῥάκος). Certain parts of his body are brought into focus and described as strong and sturdy: his thighs (μηροί), his shoulders (ὦμος), his chest (στήθεα),[69] and his arms (βραχίονες). In these lines (67–69), Homer appears to be highlighting for us the body parts perceived to be of greatest importance to an ancient boxer. If so, his preferences align fairly well with those of the modern boxing trainer.

The goddess Athena, functioning in her role as personal guardian of the vagrant Odysseus rather than as a patroness of boxing *per se*, strengthens (ἀλδαίνω) his limbs. Awed by the beauty of Odysseus' body, the suitors remark especially on the well-developed muscle just above his knee (ἐπιγουνίς)[70] and how it sings awk for his opponent. The ancient Greeks well understood the value of strong legs in building a fine boxer "from the ground up," as one might hear in a modern gym. At the sight of his glorious opponent, stripped and ready to fight, the *thymos* of Iros 'stirred badly' (κακῶς ὠρίνετο). Laborers (δρηστῆρες)—presumably servants of the suitors—then girt him (ζώννυμι) for the fight using force (ἀνάγκη). Antinous prescribes hideous punishment for the trembling Iros if he is conquered (νικάω) in the 'ring' by the mightier (κρείσσων) man. It is not a good way to start the contest.

Following the pattern from the *Iliad*, the boxing match begins in the nondescript 'midst' (μέσος) as the fighters raise (ἀνέχω) their hands. In lines 91 and 92, the poet lets us in on Odysseus' thought process: should he deal a blow (ἐλαύνω) so powerful that it kills his enemy or strike him (once more, ἐλαύνω) just hard enough to stretch him out (τανύω) on the ground? The verb ἐλαύνω, with its consequent of a fallen, prostrate adversary, is the closest we will come to a special word for 'knockout' in Homeric boxing. ἐλαύνω is not found in the Iliadic boxing match and is elsewhere associated with pounding metal in a forge, an apt metaphor for a sweltering boxing ring. It appears to be a rather generic term for punching in the *Odyssey*. Odysseus resolved to hit his opponent only slightly (ἦκ) in order to accomplish his larger purposes.[71]

With the fighter's hands still raised (ἀνέχω, this time in the middle voice), Iros threw the first punch, driving at Odysseus' right shoulder (ἤλασε δεξιὸν ὦμον). In all but the most playful of bouts, the shoulder is a curious target for a boxer. We speculate that Odysseus' shoulder was doing exactly what it would do in a modern boxing match: it was thrust forward towards

---

[68] C.f. Herodotus 8.59, ὦ Θεμιστόκλεες, ἐν τοῖσι ἀγῶσι οἱ προεξανιστάμενοι ῥαπίζονται, "Themistocles, at the games those who start before the signal are beaten with rods" (Godley 1920).

[69] This form appears in the plural, suggesting the poet's awareness of the paired nature of this body part.

[70] Likely the quadriceps femoris muscle.

[71] It is presumably on the basis of the adverb alone that Fagles (1996) translates this option as a "light jab" (p. 378).

his opponent and his chin was tucked behind it. If we are correct and it was Odysseus' right shoulder that Iros aimed for, then we can reasonably claim that Odysseus was a southpaw. In any event, a punch to the shoulder could do no damage (as the poet and audience well knew) and Odysseus took the advantage immediately while his opponent's hand was extended well beyond guard position.[72] Odysseus threw what was most likely a hook,[73] probably his right; it landed on Iros' neck (αὐχήν) just beneath his ear (ὑπ' οὔατος), crushing (θλάω) his bones.[74] The striking verb is once more ἐλαύνω. Bleeding from the mouth, down went Iros, shrieking (μηκάομαι) like a wounded boar. He gnashed his teeth (ἐλαύνω, again) and kicked (λακτίζω) the dirt, presumably lying on the ground. Both motions are highly suggestive of a seizure, much like the one Euryalos experienced at the end of the boxing match in the *Iliad*.

In an apparent parallel to the Iliadic bout, Odysseus attends to his fallen opponent while the suitors yield to paroxysms of laughter at Iros' expense. But Odysseus is no Epeius and his magnanimity has limits. In any event, Iros is by no means Odysseus' peer. He unceremoniously drags (ἕλκω) Iros by the foot through a doorway into a courtyard where he seats (ἵζω) him and leans (ἀνακλίνω) him up against a wall. Odysseus puts a staff (σκῆπτρον) in the braggart's hand and a leather pouch (πήρα) around his neck. He commands him to scare off wild swine and dogs and to cease lording it over other vagrants while "playing the beggar king," in Fagles' (1996) translation (μηδὲ σύ γε ξείνων καὶ πτωχῶν κοίρανος εἶναι). Iros did not, in fact, receive his haggis.

Victorious Odysseus, on the other hand, was treated to the great goat stomach (μέγας γαστήρ), juicy with blood and fat (ἐμπλείην κνίσης τε καὶ αἵματος). He was saluted (δεικανάω) by the suitors who toasted how he had put an end to Iros' nuisance. They reiterated their threat to ship the "insatiate fellow" away to the land of King Echetus, the "maimer of men" (βροτῶν δηλήμονα πάντων), who would feed to the dogs his nose, ears, and testicles (Murray 1919). It is the last we hear of Iros.

There are many useful points of comparison between the boxing matches in the *Iliad* and the *Odyssey*. Now that we have commented on the language used in both—and leaving aside the possibility that lexical items were chosen for metrical purposes only—we can make a few assertions about Homer's fighting words. The vocabulary used to describe the action is limited and, while a handful of words are used for 'strike' or 'punch', there is nothing in their respective etymologies or their usage in Homer that suggests they mean anything like 'jab', 'hook', or 'knockout blow.' Rather, they seem to be used interchangeably, though the poet shows a strong preference for ἐλαύνω in the *Odyssey* (it does not appear in the Iliadic boxing episode). Both narratives use the verb νικάω 'conquer' to reference what a successful boxer does. There are no *himantes* in the *Odyssey*, suggesting that these were indeed specialized pieces of equipment, suitable only for solemn occasions (like funeral games) and among trained boxers. Despite the lack of specialized gauntlets in the *Odyssey*, the boxers in both stories use their hands in similar ways, lifting them (ἀνέχω) at the beginning of the match in

---

[72] From what follows we can have little doubt that Iros knew nothing of keeping his guard up after punching.

[73] We are here in agreement with Fagles (1996, p. 378). The original verb is once again the relatively bland ἐλαύνω; Homer seems to have no specialized vocabulary for different types of punches, *ut supra*.

[74] The poet made an astute choice in picking the mastoid process as Odysseus' target. A pneumatized structure, the mastoid process is full of air pockets and could indeed shatter in the way Homer describes. Blunt force trauma to the this bone would also damage the middle and inner ear, resulting in a loss of equilibrium and a precipitous collapse. It is less clear whether trauma to the mastoid process would result in blood pouring from the mouth, but we are willing to accept the poet's judgment on the matter. He had clearly seen (if not participated in) a boxing match or two.

a gesture well-known to later Greek vase painters.

The *zōma* is another highly salient, shared feature of the Homeric boxing episodes. That the low-rent boxers of the *Odyssey* wear the *zōma* (or some raggedy version thereof) suggests that the ancient Greeks strongly associated this manner of dress with boxing competition, even more so than they associated the *himantes* with boxing. Supporters appear in both narratives: Diomedes girds Euryalos and puts on his *himantes*; the laborers put on Iros' *zōma*; Odysseus and Epeius (the winners of their respective bouts) appear to take care of themselves.[75] Telemachus offers the psychological boost to Odysseus that Diomedes provides Euryalos in the *Iliad*. There is no specialized Homeric vocabulary for a 'second' or a 'cornerman'. There is no Homeric word for a boxing 'ring'; the *locus in quo* is rendered generically as the 'midst' or the 'place of assembly'. The word *pygmachia* does not appear in Odysseus' boxing episode while other, perhaps more generic terms for fighting are included. This may suggest that *pygmachia* was at this time a cultic rite, only associated with the *himantes*, or carried out exclusively by trained boxers.

Scholars such as Snell (1960) have argued that the Homeric conception of the body is less unitary than that of classical antiquity and modernity. Feyerabend (2010, pp. 186–188) summarizes the case thus:

> The *additive treatment* of events [due to rhapsodic parataxis] becomes very clear in the case of (human) motion. ...Many of the similes assume that the parts of a complex entity have a life of their own and can be separated with ease. Geometrical man is a visible list of parts and positions; Homeric man is put together from limbs, surfaces, connections which are isolated by comparing them with inanimate objects of precisely defined shape. ...Thus the poet repeats the formal features used by the geometric and the early archaic artists. Neither seems to be aware of an 'underlying' substance that keeps the objects together and shapes their parts so that they reflect the 'higher unity' to which they belong. ¶Nor is such a 'higher unity' found in the concepts of the language. For example, there is no expression that could be used to describe the human body as a single entity. ...All we get is a puppet put together from more or less articulated parts.

Snell's views have been criticized, but in this case we find the hypothesis supported by the description of the fight scenes from the Homeric œuvre as cited above and the subsequent early Greek corpus: hands raise up high to 'mix' or 'mingle' (μίγνυμι); jaws make sounds; sweat flows; limbs are strengthened (ἀλδαίνω). The body of Odysseus is described as plural in form, consisting of a catalogue of well-formed parts. A Homeric boxer, presumably, as body-puppet inserted into a fight, thus manifests the will of the gods as much as he himself personally triumphs. We find later accounts such as the *Argonautica* to portray the outcome as more a function of skill and will than divine favor.

---

[75]Could this be a subtle indictment of the seconds? Perhaps Homer saw them as parasitic attachments to the true champion, who inevitably won his glory alone and without aid.

3.2 Classical

3.2.1 Pindar

In his fifth-century epænetic to Diagoras of Rhodes (*Olympian 7*), Pindar uses the term εὐθυμάχης 'straight-fighting' to praise the boxer's pugilistic style (line 29). The term is a curious one. It could mirror the verb εὐθυπορέω (line 69) 'walk straight forward' which is used to denote Diagoras' other virtues, like his lack of arrogance and willingness to hearken to the wisdom of his ancestors; thus, to fight without guile. It may also suggest the manner in which Diagoras fought, e.g., continually moving forward against his opponent or throwing straight punches (rather than hooks or hammer blows) but there is insufficient evidence to make a strong claim in this regard.

An allusion to an assistant or perhaps a trainer is made in Pindar's ode to Hagesidamus (*Olympian* 10). Pindar recommends that the victorious Hagesidamus also thank 'Ilas' (Ἴλᾳ, dative), just as Patroclus thanked Achilles.[76] Gildersleeve (1885) suggests that 'Ilas' is another name of Hylas (Ὕλας), the servant and companion of Heracles in his many adventures (p. 213). Hagesidamus, victorious in the boy's boxing, owes some of his glory to this figure, whom Gildersleeve equates with a 'trainer' ἀλείπτης (lit. 'anoint'; ibid., p. 215–216). As a youth boxer, Hagesidamus would not have had a young male companion like Patroclus (or Hylas), so it would seem that Pindar exhorts the young man to thank his older mentor. On the other hand, even a princely youth in the games would have been attended by servants, making the allusion to Ὕλας more reasonable. Pindar seems to suggest that victorious boxers rely on others to achieve glory in the 'ring', but he does not specify whether these are trainers, sparring partners, or even corner men: "With the help of a god, one man can sharpen another who is born for excellence, and encourage him to tremendous achievement" (Svarlien 1991).

3.2.2 Plato and Xenophon

Living in the late fifth and fourth centuries BC, the philosopher Plato, who was reportedly a talented wrestler (perhaps eponymously so), made occasional references to boxing, wrestling, and pankration in his works. E.g., on the rules of boxing: τὸν δέ γε οἶμαι κατὰ τὴν πυκτικὴν πυκτικόν "And the rules of boxing, I suppose, make a good boxer?" (Plato, *Alcibiades* 2:145d, tr. Lamb). Elsewhere he warns boxing does in no way supersede honor: ὅτι ἔμαθεν πυκτεύειν τε καὶ παγκρατιάζειν καὶ ἐν ὅπλοις μάχεσθαι, ...οὐ τούτου ἕνεκα τοὺς φίλους δεῖ τύπτειν οὐδὲ κεντεῖν τε καὶ ἀποκτεινύναι "just because one has learnt boxing ...gives one no right to strike one's friends" (Plato, *Gorgias* 456d, tr. Lamb). Plato occasionally has his authorial stand-in, Socrates, exclaim along the lines of a boxer: ἐγὼ μὲν οὖν, ὥσπερ πληγεὶς ὑπὸ τοῦ λόγου, ἐκείμην ἄφωνος "Here I must say I was knocked out, as it were, by the argument, and lay speechless!" (*Euthydemus* 303a).

Boxing is also mentioned by Xenophon, another student of Socrates, in the *Anabasis* (4:6) as a celebratory sport engaged in by the mercenary army as they camped by the Euxine Sea (Black Sea).[77]

---

[76] πύκτας δ' ἐν Ὀλυμπιάδι νικῶν Ἴλᾳ φερέτω χάριν Ἀγησίδαμος ὡς Ἀχιλεῖ Πάτροκλος (lines 21–23).

[77] The current article, with the exception of the commentary on the *Argonautica*, closes at the end of the Classical period in 323 BC, and Hellenistic sources will be treated in a subsequent publication.

3.2.3 *Argonautica*

The *Argonautica* was written by Apollonius of Rhodes in the early third century BC.[78] It includes a boxing match that echoes, in some ways, the pugilistic poetry of Homer. However, the boxing vocabulary of the *Argonautica* is more diverse than Homer's and its narrative arc differs somewhat from the episodes in the *Odyssey* and *Iliad*, which parallel one another.[79] Apollonius was almost certainly familiar with boxing terminology that had come into fashion among the classical Greeks who, by the time the *Argonautica* was written, had long ago professionalized the sport at Olympia.

At the inception of Book 2 we are introduced to the 'manly' (ἀγήνορος) and 'huge' (ὑπεροπλος) Bebrycian King Amycus, who demanded through the institution of a 'shameful ordinance' (ἀεικής θεσμός) that any visitor to his realm engage him in a boxing match (lines 2–5).[80] More specifically, guests to his kingdom on the Anatolian coast of the Black Sea were required to 'try him in *pygmachia*' (πειράω ἑοῖο πυγμαχίης; lines 6–7). In the middle voice, as it appears here, the verb πειράω can also mean 'test one's skills'.

Upon receiving intelligence of the Argonauts' disembarkation on Bebrycian soil (the sailors were merely seeking fresh water), Amycus goes to meet them. He commands them to make their 'best (man)' (ἄριστος) to 'stand' (ἵστημι) in *pygmachia*. Amycus demands that this warrior, selected from the throng of Greeks, 'raise up' (ἀνὰ ἀείρω) his hands against his own 'on the spot' (καταυτόθι) in order to 'wrangle' (δηριάομαι) together (line 16).[81] The verb ἀείρω is unfamiliar to us so far; the oft-repeated Homeric term for lifting the hands in boxing was ἀνέχω.

The emotions that grip the boxers may be different from those we encountered in Homer. Instead of being washed in *thymos*, Amycus (or perhaps Polydeuces) is μέγα φρονέων, a participial form derived from the verb φρονέω 'be spirited or bold' (line 19).[82] It seems this fills the role of Homeric *thymos*. Polydeuces (the object of the clause) is 'made to stand' (ἵστημι) by the others and submits (ὑπείκω) to the 'rule' (θεσμός) that Amycus proposes. While this may be a general reference to Amycus' demand that they box, it may also be specific term for the rule-set of *pygmachia*, which Amycus has obliquely described. Thus Polydeuces assents to meet (ἀντιάω) his adversary.

The poet next offers us a complex simile describing Amycus' glare: it is like that of a wounded lion singling out the hunter who struck (τύπτω) him.[83] The combatants then disrobe, but do not don the *zōma*, which had clearly fallen out of fashion in boxing contests

---

[78] We include discussion of the *Argonautica* in this article because it was most likely written before the death of Alexander in 323 BC. It is regarded as the only surviving Hellenistic epic poem.

[79] Nelis (2001, p. 9), writes that Apollonius' "skillful reworking of Homer is marked by precise verbal allusion as well as related techniques of imitation such as distribution of features of the model texts, and both variation and deliberate inversion of Homeric detail."

[80] Much later in Book 2 (lines 783–785) we learn that Heracles boxed a Mysian name Titias, contending with him for a prize (ἀθλεύω) and 'vanquished' (ἀποκαίνυμαι) him, 'dashing' (ἐλαύνω) his teeth to the ground: ἀθλεύων Τιτίην ἀπεκαίνυτο πυγμαχέοντα | καρτερόν, ὃς πάντεσσι μετέπρεπεν ἠιθέοισιν | εἶδός τ' ἠδὲ βίην: χαμάδις δέ οἱ ἦλασ' ὀδόντας. "He entered the lists with Titias in boxing and slew him, mighty Titias, who surpassed all the youths in beauty and strength; and he dashed his teeth to the ground" trans. Seaton (1912). In this text we find the verb πυγμαχέω 'practice boxing, be a boxer'.

[81] Among the many allusive elements in the subsequent narrative, "The fight between Polydeuces and Amycus is related to the confrontation between Jason and the bulls of Aeëtes and the Earthborn men" (Nelis 2001, p. 20).

[82] "Thus [Amycus] spoke haughtily" (Cuypers 1997, p. 51). The reading is highly contextual.

[83] One commentator notes that the simile reflects how Amycus' routine "fight with a ξεῖνος [guest, stranger] has now become a challenge" (Cuypers 1997, p. 55)

long ago. The fighters select a 'pleasing piece of ground' (χῶρος ἐαδότος) that presumably satisfies the requirements for a boxing ring. This is a major difference from Homeric epic. While the ring still has no specific name in the *Argonautica*, it is nonetheless selected based on its compatibility with the requirements of *pygmachia*. Indeed, the space was discovered because the men 'looked about with a sharp, searching glance' (παπταίνω).[84]

Next they made their comrades sit 'in two' on the beach-sand: ἷζον ἑοὺς δίχα πάντας ἐνὶ ψαμάθοισιν ἑταίρους. According to Seaton (1912), they were arrayed "in two lines"; we find no clear indication of this arrangement, but it is plausible, since seating the spectators in pairs, for example, seems less appropriate for the context (p. 105).[85] More significant is the orderly positioning of the spectators, an innovation first attested here. The problem this level of organization resolved is foreshadowed in the *Odyssey*, where the pell-mell arrangement of spectators at the fight gave Odysseus cause to worry that one of them might interfere. Organized seating betokens the professionalization of Greek boxing in the first millennium BC and its evolution into a true spectator sport. It also severely limited the audience's natural urge to join the fray, whether to change the outcome of the fight or to discharge their own thymotic energy.[86]

The author contrasts Polydeuces and Amycus in terms of their physical features, accentuating the brute character of Amycus and the refined beauty of Polydeuces.[87] The fight between Polydeuces, as a representative of the Olympians, and Amycus, a representative of the Titans, may be a recapitulation of the ancient battle of order over chaos (Hardie 1993).[88] It is clear which pugilist met the Classical ideal of manly virtue and comeliness: the poet describes Polydeuces as a 'heavenly star' (οὐράνιος ἀστήρ; lines 40–41).[89] Nevertheless, his 'strength' (ἀλκή) and 'passion' (μένος) 'rose up' (ἀέξω) as if in a 'beast of prey' (θήρ). Once again, the author declines to mention *thymos* where Homer would have almost certainly included it.

Next Polydeuces 'swings' (πάλλω)[90] his hands in a motion that likely indicates shadowboxing.[91] More evidence for shadowboxing comes from lines 46–47 where we learn that through this exercise Polydeuces intends to 'prove' (πειράζω) his hands are still 'quick-moving' (εὐτρόχαλος).[92] The Son of Zeus was concerned lest his fists had been made heavy from 'toil'

---

[84] Intriguingly, this is the same verb used to describe how Epeius set up his knockout punch in the *Iliad*.

[85] Green (2007) translates this difficult adverbial as "well apart from each other" (p. 80).

[86] Male spectators at a modern boxing match are frequently observed throwing punches, presumably to mirror the action they perceive or desire to see in the ring. We believe this mimesis stems from the hormonal shifts males experience when watching other males fight. The prospect of fighting is powerful—naturally enhanced by partiality towards one of the fighters—and necessitates the presence of security guards and watchful officials even at amateur boxing matches.

[87] In the poem, Amycus is explicitly related to the earth and Polydeuces, implicitly, to the sky (i.e., Zeus, his father). In this sense it is an encounter of weather god versus earth god, parallel in some ways to Hercules' encounter with Antæus: "The one [Amycus] seemed to be a monstrous son of baleful Typhœus or of Earth herself, such as she brought forth aforetime, in her wrath against Zeus" (Seaton 1912, p. 105).

[88] Here the author refers to the Vergilian battle between Hercules and Cacus, but the logic applies to the duel in the *Argonautica*, as well.

[89] "The comparison of Amycus to Typhœus and of Polydeuces to a shining star is relevant here also as it evokes the idea of a struggle between the forces of heaven and hell and fits into an important thematic pattern in the poem as a whole" (Nelis 2001, p. 19, fn. 78).

[90] A derivative of this verb was used to describe the motion of Euryalus during his piscine seizure in the *Iliad*.

[91] It is routine for modern boxers to throw punches at the air in preparation for the bout just minutes away.

[92] We find Seaton's (1912) translation rather vague here: "He poised his hands to see if they were pliant as before..." (p. 105). Green's (2007) translation is closer to the mark: "[H]e shadowboxed | testing whether his hands were as

(κάματος) and 'rowing' (εἰρεσία).

The first reference to *thymos* in this episode relates to Amycus. The king of the Bebrycians smolders from afar while glorious Polydeuces clothes himself for the agon. The *thymos* swells up (ὀρεχθέω) darkly within Amycus who yearns to 'spatter' (κεδάννυμι) Polydeuces' (or his own?) chest with blood: οἱ ὀρέχθει | θυμὸς ἐελδομένῳ στηθέων ἐξ αἷμα κεδάσσαι (lines 49–50). It may be that Apollonius' reluctance to refer to *thymos* in this vignette is suggestive of its negative, perhaps bloodthirsty, connotations at this stage in Greek literary history.

A number of seconds are named and their specific functions are described in the *Argonautica*. Amycus' assistants are referred to as his 'henchmen' or 'squires' (θεράποντες) and, given his royal status, there is probably no special association between this term and boxing; they were merely his servants. However, we conjecture that men of high status, when they boxed, employed their manservants to assist at ringside. Their main function seems to be to lay out (τίθημι) the *himantes*, to bind them to the fighters' hands, and to offer words of encouragement before the fight. All of these functions, but for the ceremonial presentation of the gauntlets, we also observe in Homer. Polydeuces is attended to by his comrades-in-arms. Amycus' servant places at the feet of the two combatants a pair of 'raw' or 'undressed' (ὠμός) *himantes*. The adjective, taken figuratively, might also mean 'savage' or 'cruel'. We also learn that the *himantes* are 'dry' or perhaps 'cured' (ἀζαλέος) and ἐσκληῶτες, likely another word describing the means by which they were dried—perhaps using smoke (line 53).

Amycus appears to refer to a practice by which boxers selected their *himantes*. He presents Polydeuces with two pairs of gauntlets and magnanimously explains that it will not be necessary to cast lots (πάλον ἐγγυαλίζω) to determine who will wear which pair. This leads us to speculate that casting lots was indeed conventional in this context. Some quality of the rawhide probably accounted for the ability of the *himantes* to lacerate an opponent and Amycus' display of good sportsmanship suggests that such properties could be manipulated in their production. While Amycus is no philoxenist, this detail suggests he could be fair-minded, as well—or perhaps it merely demonstrates his hubris. Under typical conditions, casting lots for the *himantes* assured participants of fair play. Under these conventions it would be to no one's advantage to intentionally arrange a pair with injurious qualities, since they might wind up on the other man's fists. Modern amateur boxing matches also require boxers to receive gloves inspected and cleaned by an official at the 'glove table'. In the early twentieth century, the boxing gloves were unwrapped in the ring and put on the boxers' hands just before the bout.[93]

Amycus boasts[94] that he is able to spatter blood on the cheeks of his boxing rivals.[95] The barbarian king also styles himself an expert leather-worker, indicating how well he has cut

---

quick as they'd been before" (p. 80).

[93] Ceremonial presentation of the gloves was a feature of boxing as late as the 1920s. For example, in the celebrated "Long Count Fight" between Jack Dempsey and Gene Tunney (1926), the gloves were brought out in a package wrapped in a bow.

[94] Each boxing narrative we have reviewed includes a braggart: Epeius in the *Iliad*, Iros in the *Odyssey*, and finally Amycus. Only in the *Iliad* is the braggart presented in a positive light, perhaps because it is exclusively in that narrative that the trash-talk accompanies victory.

[95] The syntax is a tangle, with 'blood' in the dative case and 'cheeks' in the accusative. The verb translated as 'spatter' by both Seaton (1912) and Green (2007) is more typically glossed as 'mix' or 'mingle' (φύρω). παρηίδας is a late, accusative plural form of παρήιον 'cheek'.

(τέμνω) the ox hides (ῥινός βοῶν) for the *himantes*.[96] This presents the interesting possibility that early Greek boxers tanned animal hides by trade.[97] We can imagine two young apprentices wrapping their fists in the cuttings on the floor of a tanning house, then squaring off to settle a score, impress a nubile young lady, or just let the best man win.

Polydeuces' brother Castor, along with another Argonaut named Talaus, undertakes precisely those duties Diomodes performed for Euryalos in the *Iliad*: they 'bind' (δέω) their boy's hands with the *himantes* and (in Green's 2007 translation) "exhort him to display his prowess" (μάλα πολλὰ παρηγορέοντες ἐς ἀλκήν). Amycus' 'seconds' are Aretus and Ornytus, who are said to perform the 'binding' (δέω) for their doomed champion.

Duly 'fitted with' (ἀρτύνω) the *himantes* and standing apart from one another (διασταδόν), the proper fight begins (line 67). From Homer we expect to see the boxers 'raise' (ἀνέχω) their 'heavy hands' (χεῖρες βᾰρεῖαι), and in this regard we are not disappointed. We are, however, given non-Homeric information regarding the boxers' guard: their hands are positioned 'in front of' (προπάροιθε) their 'faces' (ῥέθεᾰ). However, ῥέθεᾰ may also refer to 'limbs'. If this is the proper translation of line 68, then the Hellenistic guard position may have been more open, with the arms extended and the hands in front of them, as is well represented in illustrations of early modern boxing, particularly of the bare-knuckle variety (e.g. Figure 1). The boxers 'met' (ἀντιάω), 'bearing' (φέρω) 'might' (μένος) 'to one another' (ἀλλήλοισ), or rendered more harmoniously by Green, they "set about one another with eager fury" (2007, p. 81).

We next encounter the second Apollonine simile of the boxing episode. Amycus is compared to a fierce 'wave' (κῦμα, κλύδων) crashing[98] over a ship and Polydeuces is compared to the crafty pilot who each time narrowly 'avoids' (ἀλύσκω) being struck.[99] There may be some connection here to the piscine simile in the Iliadic boxing vignette. We conjecture that the dark wave (κῦμα) in Homer represents unconsciousness driven by head trauma. Here, too, the wave crashing over Polydeuces' bark would result in his debilitation and defeat. Thus Amycus pursued (ἕπομαι) and menaced (φοβέω) his opponent (line 74). 'He did not suffer him to tarry' (οὐδέ μιν εἴα δηθύνειν), i.e., Amycus gave him no respite.

Yet 'unwounded' (ἀνούτατος), Polydeuces continues to demonstrate 'wisdom', 'skill', or 'craft' (μῆτις).[100] He 'darts' (ἀΐσσω) and 'avoids' (ἀλεείνω), most likely referring to the art of 'getting in and getting out' without getting hit. A thinking boxer, Polydeuces quickly 'figures out' (νοέω) the king's 'rough boxing (style)' (ἀπηνής πυγμαχία), assessing his strength and weaknesses, lit., his 'inviolable power' (κάρτος ἄατος) and his 'inferior (power)' (χερείων). Polydeuces 'stood' (ἵστημι) and with his rival 'mixed' (μίγνυμι) hands—the Homeric formulation for trading punches.

Now we reach the third periergia of the *Argonautica*'s boxing episode. Once more with

---

[96] Amycus had a reputation as an inventor of the *himantes*, which may be precisely why Apollonius goes to the trouble of mentioning his leather-working skill (Leigh 2010, p. 122).

[97] As a perhaps tangential comparison, African dambe boxing is said to have originated among traveling butchers.

[98] The verb κορύσσω, the action of the wave, may be translated as 'crest'. It can also mean 'furnish with a helmet', perhaps an Apollonine *jeu d'espirt* in the context of a boxing match where a helmet could come in handy.

[99] Were it not for the author's positive assessment of Polydeuces, we might conclude from the verb ἀλύσκω that he was running from a fight. However, we suspect that this is instead an oblique reference to slipping, dodging, and rolling.

[100] The word derives from the Indo-European root for 'measure'. Modern boxers are routinely counseled to 'measure out' their punches to determine the distance needed to strike their opponent while remaining outside the other man's 'reach'.

Figure 1: "The fundamental position", a modern open boxing stance favored by 20th-century boxing instructor Edwin Haislett (1940, p. 4). Compare this stance with those depicted in visual media later in this article.

echoes of Homer, who apprised his listeners of the crashing sounds of jaws and teeth,[101] Apollonius offers us a bespoke simile comparing the fighters to shipwrights (or perhaps carpenters) who 'strike' (ἐλαύνω, θείνω) their blows with hammers (line 80).[102] The hammers and the boxers both make 'dull and heavy sounds' (δοῦπος). The fighters' cheeks (παρήια) and jaws (γένυες) 'ring', 'resound', or 'crash' (κτυπέω) on being struck 'from both sides' (ἀμφοτέρωθεν). In the *Odyssey*, Iros' teeth merely 'struck' (ἐλαύνω) each other, but in the *Argonautica* the boxers 'gnash' (βρυχή τέλλω, line 83). Amycus and Polydeuces 'wound' (οὐτάζω) each other 'successively' (ἐπισταδόν) before 'deadly, short-drawn breath' (οὐλοός ἄσθμα) 'overpowers' (δαμάζω) them.[103]

---

[101] "The phrase χρόμαδος γενύων gave rise to discussion among ancient commentators over whether Homer is referring to the noise made by the grinding teeth of a hard-fighting boxer (the generally accepted solution) or the noise made by teeth when the jaw receives a heavy blow. Apollonius seems to describe both kinds of noises with παρήια…γένυες κτύπεον and βρυχη…ὀδόντων. The fact that the word γένυες is applied to the noise understood by the second explanation of the Homeric phrase suggests that this was how Apollonius understood the words χρόμαδος γενύων" (Nelis 2001, p. 12).

[102] θείνω seems to be the verb most closely related with 'hammers' σφῦραι. One etymologist has noted the curious resemblance and possible etymological connection between 'hammer' and 'sphere' and thus an association with *sphairai*, the ball-like boxing gloves we describe elswhere in this article (Frisk 1954–1972). The muscular body of the boxer Amycus in Theocritus' *Idyll* 22.47 is described as being 'σφυρήλατος', 'forged by a hammer', perhaps a play on words.

[103] δαμάζω is found in both the *Iliad* and the *Odyssey*, where it is used to denote the activity of victorious boxers. In this passage, Apollonius has provided an effective example of how boxers must battle their own physical limitations and control their bodies, in this instance, by breathing properly.

The next few lines (86–87) refer to an interval between 'rounds' but it is important to point out that the boxers rest *mero motu*, with no external signal directing them to do so and with no indication that a pause is formalized in the rule set. They briefly 'stand a little apart' (ἵστημι βαιὸν ἄπωθεν), 'wipe off' (ἀπομόργνυμι) the 'copious sweat' (ἱδρώς ἅλις) from 'between their eyes' (μέτωπον) all the while 'panting toilsome breath' (καματηρὸν ἀυτμένα φυσιάω). Once again in each other's sights (συνόρουσαν ἐναντίος) and 'bearing a grudge' (κοτέω), they 'wrangle' (δηριάομαι) like two bulls fighting for access to the same heifer. This allusion reminds us of the consistent association between boxing and bulls that we have observed in the ancient Near East, Anatolia, and Crete. It is followed by the last—and once more bovid-adjacent—Apollonine boxing simile. Amycus 'rises on tiptoe' (ἐπ' ἀκροτάτοισιν ἀείρω), dropping his heavy hand in an attempt to 'make tremble' (πελεμίζω) his rival (line 92). Green (2007) puts it thus: "rising on tiptoe... and bringing | his heavy hand slamming down on him" (p. 81). In this passage, Amycus is likened to an 'ox butcher' (βουτύπος),[104] a term used for the priest at the Buphonia festival.[105] As part of this celebration, traditionally held in late summer at Athens in honor of Zeus Polieus, bulls were driven toward an altar covered with various edible enticements. The first bull to take a nibble was ceremonially slaughtered with an axe. In Dioscurus and Dioscurus (2022a) we speculate at some length regarding the ritual nature of boxing, and will do so again in a future summary of our thoughts on the meaning of boxing. Boxing and ritual slaughter have been closely connected since well before the time of the Greeks. We must credit Apollonius with being the first to draw the comparison explicitly in writing.

Ever fleet of foot, Polydeuces (surely the Sugar Ray Leonard of his age) dodges (ἀίσσω) the murderous blow and thereby 'lies in ambush' for his foe.[106] By moving his head to the side (παρακλίνω), Polydeuces 'caught' or 'took up' (ἀναδέχομαι) the blow from Amycus' forearm (πῆχυς, accusative) on his shoulder (ὦμος, dative). By 'whipping in' (Green 2007) or 'coming near' (Seaton 1912) (ἀμσίβων, line 94)[107] and positioning his knee with respect to Amycus',[108] Polydeuces 'follows closely' (μεταίσσω) then throws a punch (κόπτω), landing it 'above the ear' (ὑπὲρ οὔατος) and 'shattering' (ῥήγνυμι) the bones within (just as in the *Odyssey*). "And the king in agony fell upon his knees.... And his life was poured forth all at once" (Seaton 1912).[109] The term 'pain of body' (ὀδύνη) is used to describe Amycus' condition *in articulo mortis*. He expires amid the ecstatic cries (ἰαχέω) of Polydeuces' compatriots. The original Greek indicates that it is Amycus' *thymos* that flows out of him at the end: τοῦ δ' ἀθρόος ἔκχυτο θυμός (line 97).[110]

---

[104] Apollonius uses the word once more, applying it to Jason when he slays Apsyrtus by the Temple of Artemis (*Argo.* 4.468), as noted by Leigh (2010, p. 128).

[105] The butcher simile has an unintended echo in the founding of modern Nigerian *dambe* by a butcher's guild.

[106] The full clause reads ὁ δ' ἀίξαντος ὑπέστη (line 92).

[107] This is probably a corrupted form of ἀμείβω 'exchange' or 'shift', used to describe footwork, for example, in the much later account of a boxing match in *Dionysiaca* (37.526) and apparently copied (with correction) by Quintus of Smyrna in *Posthomerica* 4.347.

[108] The translations for the knee position vary. According to three different translators, the knee might be 'pressed' against the other knee *kolenem koleno tiskna* (Jaroš 1924) or slipped 'past' the other knee (Seaton 1912, Green 2007). We note the preposition παρέξ might also mean Polydeuces positioned his knee 'outside' the other.

[109] "In the *Iliad* it is the challenger Epeius who wins, but in both the *Odyssey* and the *Argonautica* the tables are turned and it is the person challenged, Homer's Odysseus and Apollonius' Polydeuces, who defeats his arrogant opponent" (Nelis 2001, p. 12).

[110] Iliadic *thymos* is often associated with the breath of life itself, particularly as it is expired from a dying warrior (4.522–524, 13.653–654), horse (16.468–469), or sacrificial animal (3.293–294).

4   Boxing in the visual arts

4.1   Mycenæan vase painting

4.1.1   Mainland Greece

There is some visual evidence that boxing was practiced on mainland Greece during the late Bronze Age, at a time when the activity is attested elswhere in the Ægean. However, attestations of boxing on the Greek mainland at this early date are exceptionally meager, consisting of only a handful of pottery sherds, none of which represent a complete scene.[III] We will start with the firmest evidence of orthograde, unarmed combat among mainland Mycenæans before presenting some less convincing evidence.

Boxers are acknowledged as a "new" subject in the (Late) Helladic IIIB period, covering the first part of the thirteenth century BC (Vermeule and Karageorghis 1982, pp. 43). On the mainland, pottery from this era is associated with the Linear B script, which was used to write Mycenæan Greek. One fragment from this period (Figure 2) shows a strangely-clad figure with his left fist raised, the muscles of his bicep and forearm bulging (Archæological Museum of Mycenæ, No. 60-327). His opponent, whose nose and raised arm are visible, does not close his hand in a fist. His arm, which looks rather like that of a post-traumatic Gregor Samsa, has five branching fingers suggesting the hand is open. It is juxtaposed with the fist of the principal figure, whose hand is curled neatly into a fist. The primary combatant wears a helmet and some attire around his neck. Helmets were used by Minoan boxers, as depicted on the sixteenth-century Boxer Rhyton. We have no evidence for a gorget or 'neck guard' elsewhere in the world of ancient boxing, but there seems to be no other explanation for this strange piece of equipment. The fighter wears a three-banded belt at or just below the level of the chest, which is adorned with a circular shape that may indicate the nipple (curiously, another circle appears below the belt, perhaps representing his navel, though admittedly in an almost cubist distortion of perspective).

While the context of the fragment's excavation is assuredly Helladic IIIB, the style is so "bizarre" that one critic believes it may have been produced as late as the twelfth century, during the "transitional" phase of Mycenæan art (Vermeule and Karageorghis 1982, p. 93). The painting's details are unprecedented and full of puzzles awaiting resolution by comparison with other, fuller depictions—if such items ever come to light. Still, the confrontation of the figures, the angle of their arms, as well as the retrograde position of the principal combatant's torso and his clearly identifiable fist all lead us to the conclusion that this is a depiction of boxing, albeit with some highly idiosyncratic elements.

Another fragment from this period (Figure 3) is housed at the National Archæological Museum of Athens (No. 1272). It depicts boxers during a bout, with their arms stretched out to fight. The boxer on the left is preserved from the crown of his head to his waist whereas all that appears of the boxer on the right are his fists. This seems to be a bare-knuckle match, with no indication of gauntlets signaled, e.g., via enlargement of the hands. The hands are rendered using conventions found in other Mycenæan vase paintings (cf. Figure 11) where

---

[III] While Homer's epics, dating most likely to the eighth century, may describe boxing matches as they took place centuries earlier among the Mycenæan Greeks, it is also possible that they were retrofitted in some respects to include much later innovations (see Section 3.1). There is sufficient archæological evidence, *nos judice*, of boxing in Greece and Mycenæan Cyprus during the late Bronze Age that it requires no special pleading to conclude that Greeks of the early Iron Age correctly viewed pugilism as part of the heroic past.

Figure 2: Fragment of a krater (?) from the Citadel House on the acropolis at Mycenæ, ca. 1300–1230 BC. The fighter is attired in unprecedented fashion: he wears a helmet, a high collar or neck guard, and a belt around his chest. His own hand is curled into a fist whereas his opponent's fingers are outstretched (Archæological Museum of Mycenæ, No. 60-327).

the fingers (as one) and the thumb are differentiated as two curved lines, one (presumably the thumb) terminating in a finial. The boxer's face is rendered in an elegant contour that indicates the nose, mouth and chin. A rosette surrounded by dots, perhaps representing the sun, fills the space above the boxers' arms. Vermeule and Karageorghis (1982) have called this piece "welcome evidence for the continuance on the Greek mainland of the old Minoan athletic vogue" (p. 93). While we agree that the fragment depicts boxers, there is little in the posture or attire of the pugilists to indicate a close relation to antecedaneous representations of boxing on Crete and the Cyclades.[112]

Two more pottery fragments from Mycenæ dated 1230–1200 BC may be associated with boxing but the connection is far more tenuous. In these depictions (Figure 4a–b), the solitary figure, who may be facing another boxer, raises his hand in a "commanding gesture" with the fingers pointing upward and the thumb curled towards the palm 4(a) or pointing forward 4(b) (Vermeule and Karageorghis 1982, p. 216). The gesture in 4(a) is remarkably similar to (much later) depictions of the open hand in Greek and Etruscan boxing (e.g., the left-hand boxer in a sixth-century black figure oinocohoe, Figure 27). We have seen an open hand—however coarsely rendered—in Mycenæan boxing, as well (Figure 2). The figure in 4(a) wears a helmet, which has precedent in both Minoan and Mycenæan representations of boxing. We are not alone in arguing that the figures represent boxers (Vermeule and Karageorghis 1982, p. 110). However, given the absence of an opposing figure in these fragments, there is nothing besides the hand gesture to recommend their interpretation as depictions of Mycenæan pugilism. Other interpretations, e.g., that the figures represent charioteers (ibid.), are certainly viable.

---

[112] There is circumstantial evidence that Minoan spectacle made a deep impression on the Mycenæans. During the thirteenth century BC, they also produced representations of bull-leaping, which, with boxing, was popular in the Minoan sphere of influence (cf. a Mycenæan pottery fragment held at National Archæological Museum of Athens, No. 2675).

Figure 3: Mycenæan depiction of boxing from mainland Greece with solar filling ornament (National Archæological Museum of Athens, No. 1272). The arms are both extended in a manner reminiscent of a better-known krater from Cyprus now held at the British Museum (Figure 5).

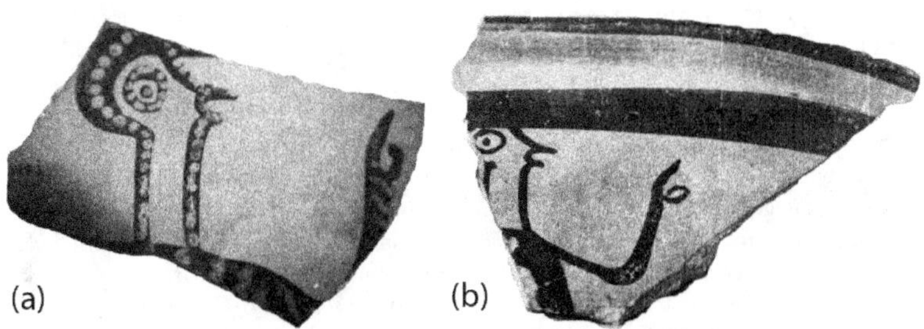

Figure 4: Two krater fragments from Mycenæ: (a) National Archæological Museum of Athens No. 2681; (b) Archæological Museum of Nafplio No. 15-37. The figure's gestures are suggestive of an open-hand gesture attested in much later illustrations of Greek and Etruscan boxing (1230–1200 BC).

4.1.2 Cyprus

Based on as few as two illustrations (Section 4.1.1), it is a tall order to argue that boxing was widely practiced by people on the Greek mainland during the late Bronze Age. There is, however, abundant and unmistakable evidence of Mycenæan boxing on Cyprus, where the activity was a popular subject of vase painting during the thirteenth century BC.[113]

Cyprus was settled by Mycenæans during the same century in which pugilistic scenes began appearing on Cypriot vases. According to legend, Achæans returning from the Trojan War were the tip of the Hellenic spear on Cyprus, where Mycenæan culture subsequently flourished. In a prime position with access to Anatolia, the Levant, and the baths of all the western stars, Cyprus was of course already populated when the Greeks arrived. The local culture mingled with theirs, no doubt drawing in considerable influence from the Near East and Anatolia. According to one historian, "[F]irm ties bound Cyprus to the Peloponnese, so that religious ideas, deities and cult were passing both ways across the Ægean before the Bronze Age had been rung out" (Dietrich 1978, p. 8). It seems likely that these diaægean transmissions included boxing. They also included the cult of Apollo, whose origins, as we have already pointed out, are likely Anatolian. The god was worshiped on Cyprus as Apollo Alasiotas, where he was represented aniconically as a pillar (ibid., pp. 9–10).[114]

The best-known Cypriot boxing depictions come from two Late Helladic IIIB amphoroid kraters found at Enkomi and now held by the British Museum (Nos. 1897,0401.1287 and 1897,0401.928). The vessels are dated to the early thirteenth century BC (see Figures 5 and 6) and belong to "the period of the greatest Mycenæan expansion" emanating from the Argolid peninsula of the greater Peloponnese (Sherratt 1980, p. 175, citing Furumark). Kraters like these found on Cyprus were "a specialist product of the Argolid" on the mainland of Greece; as such, they are regarded as Mycenæan (Crouwel and Morris 2015, p. 171). This has been determined through archæometric analysis (Jones 1986) of the unique Argive clay used in their construction as well as a close stylistic study of the painting suggesting "only a small number of producers painting this material" (Crouwel and Morris 2015, p. 171). It has been speculated that Mycenæan vessels of this type were intended for male users in the context of drinking and feasting (ibid., p. 172).

Influences of Minoan art are evident in the exaggeratedly narrow waists of the pugilists on both kraters. They lack some of the dynamism and much of the detail found in the older Boxer Rhyton (Dioscurus and Dioscurus 2022c). A similar vegetal motif stands directly between the antagonists on both vessels, in the spot where prizes or representations of divinities are to be found in glyptic depictions of pugilism likely executed a few hundred years earlier across the sea in nearby Syria (Teissier 1984, Thompson 2013, Dioscurus and Dioscurus 2022b). The fighters are bare-headed and, from the absence of detail, presumably naked. The torso, arms, legs, and feet of the figures are brown while the face, neck, and hands are

---

[113]The Hittites laid claim to Cyprus, if only as a vassal state, from the 15th century BC. Around the time the Cypriot boxing kraters were produced, the Hittites engaged in a naval battle with the residents of the island, which they called *Alḫašiya*. The possibility of cultural transmission between Cyprus and the realms of the Hittite king should not be ignored. The contemporaneous attestation of boxing in both locations may prove significant as more archæologial discoveries are brought to light.

[114]Several cylinder seals from Ugarit show boxers sparring with a column between them (Schaeffer-Forrer 1983, Dioscurus and Dioscurus 2022b). This space was frequently reserved for the representation of a divinity in astral or animal form. The column in the Ugarit cylinders may have been a representation of Apollo's Ugaritic predecessor/analog (probably Ršp, imported to Cyprus as Resheph), whose cult was also observed on Cyprus.

Figure 5: Body fragment of an amphoroid krater found at Enkomi Cyprus; 1300–1250 BC / Late Helladic IIIB1 (British Museum, No. 1897,0401.1287). Painted in the Pictorial style, the vessel originated on the Argolid, in Greece. The boxers appear to wear some form of boxing glove.

uncolored. The artist may have left the faces untinted to provide details of the eyes and ears. The hands, however, are not filled in, nor do they bear any detail. This contrasts with the hands of the archers (not pictured in Figure 6; British Museum, No. 1897,0401.928) that stand to the left of the boxers. The archers have three extended brown fingers. To leave the hands of the boxers blank while filling in the arms was likely intended to suggest the fighters wear some form of boxing glove. Indeed, their fists are rendered as simple ellipses, suggestive of the club-like gauntlets postulated for the 'Boxing Boys' of Akrotiri (Dioscurus and Dioscurus 2022c).

In the body fragment shown in Figure 5, each boxer raises his arms up and stretches them out towards his adversary in a gesture perhaps signaling the start of the battle. In the krater pictured in Figure 6, however, the boxers both face the same direction and "make menacing gestures with their left arms, like boxers warming up for the punch" (Vermeule and Karageorghis 1982, p. 44). The figures lean dramatically retrograde with their arms bent so their right hand touches the small of their back. The knee of the leftmost boxer is bent curiously backwards. While the archers pictured on the same vase have smooth hair, the boxers' hair is rendered in jagged outline to indicate curls. Each boxer's left elbow is bent with his fist raised to his face in a gesture typical of a boxing guard, though with one hand only. Since they are clearly not fighting, this illustration may represent a dance that took place before the contest. The evidence for boxing gloves, such as it is, can be found only on the boxers' raised, left hands; the detail of their right hands disappears into the modeling of their backs.

The other side of the vase depicts creatures which, despite heavy erosion, appear to be sphinges. For this reason, Vermeule and Karageorghis (1982) conjectured that the vase was associated with funerary rites. The "devourer of the dead" was pictured on one side and participants in funeral games (archers and boxers) were limned on the other.

Given that these depictions of late Bronze Age boxing were arguably produced on the Peloponnese then later exported to Cyprus, we are left to wonder whether they illustrate boxing praxis in Greece, on Cyprus, or even on Crete. At Hala Sultan Tekke, an archæological site situated, like Enkomi, on the east side of Cyprus, around 2% of the pottery from the Late Helladic has been classified as of Mycenæan origin; less than 1% is considered Minoan (Mee 2008, p. 375). Settlement of Cyprus by Mycenæans has been ruled out based on other evidence. Markings characteristic of pottery manufactured on Cyprus also appear on pottery manufactured on the Argolid, suggesting that Cypriots were the ones producing their own pottery in Greece, whence it was shipped back home (ibid., pp. 375–376). If this rather elaborate hypothesis is correct, then what we see on the kraters is not Mycenæan boxing at all, but Cypriot boxing likely influenced by both Levantine and Minoan models.

Another amphoroid krater from Cyprus includes boxers facing one another, with the pairs separated by large anserine birds (Figure 7). The vase is said to be painted by an artist from Aradippou, in eastern Cyprus. Long locks of hair on the boxers may have been "stimulated by some intermediate reflection of an older style...dependent on the Boxer Rhyton" (Vermeule and Karageorghis 1982, p. 44). The boxers are naked: the penis of the leftmost pugilist in the central pair is indicated. The stance is exaggerated in a manner similar to that of the Boxing Boys.

The other side of the vase shows boxers in a different attitude (Figure 8). They are no longer fighting nor do they appear particularly martial in their gestures. Their hands consist of a two-pronged fork representative of the fingers (as one unit) and the thumb. They sway from the hips and their hair falls back in a single, curling lock reminiscent of the Minoan

Figure 6: Detail of a Late Helladic IIIB amphoroid krater found at Enkomi, Cyprus and dated 1300–1200 BC (British Museum, No. 1897,0401.928). The figures have been identified as boxers.

Figure 7: Detail from an amphoroid Krater from eastern Cyprus with long-haired boxers (G. G. Pierides Collection, No. 35). The vase is dated between 1300 and 1230 BC.

hairstyle depicted on the Boxer Rhyton or perhaps the Boxing Boys of Akrotiri (Dioscurus and Dioscurus 2022c).

A single figure from a pair of sparring partners is preserved on a pottery fragment found at Kition, in southeastern Cyprus (Figure 9). Dated to the first two-thirds of the thirteenth century BC, the painting contains a figure whose 'Mycenæan' boxing stance is by now familiar to us: hips thrust forward, torso leaning back, arms forward in a defensive posture (Figures 6 and 7). According to Vermeule and Karageorghis (1982, p. 202), the fragment is housed on Cyprus, possibly at the Larnaca District Archæological Museum (Kition Area II, No. 14/2418). The figure reminds us of mainland depictions found at Mycenæ (Figure 4) though the flat-topped head and long nose are doubtless associated with another style, attested at Ugarit (Vermeule and Karageorghis 1982, pp. 44).[115] In this case, however, the raised hand is more clearly rendered as a fist (an ellipse) with the thumb projecting from the side. The torso leans backwards as if to avoid an (unseen) opponent's onslaught and the hips are rendered in a style reminiscent of both Figures 7 and 11.

In a fragment of an amphoroid krater found at Maroni (British Museum, No. 1898,1201.137), a series of "very mannered" boxers, sparring in pairs, are separated by vegetal motifs, perhaps "dejected palms" (Vermeule and Karageorghis 1982, p. 44). The fighters' "legs are emphasized for length and thrust, the chests are relatively thick, the heads are held straight up, and the fists are curled" (ibid.) They hold one arm up and one arm down with thumbs projecting from the fist.[116] Estimates of the vase's date vary: the British Museum assigns it to the fourteenth century while Vermeule and Karageorghis (1982) assign it to the thirteenth. The more natural rendering of the hips, stance, and fists, with an added detail of slighly lumpy knees

---

[115] A modern observer may be forgiven for seeing in this Bronze Age pugilist shadows of Matt Grœning's cartoon character Bart Simpson.

[116] A much later (sixth-century BC) depiction of boxing on a Eubœan amphora shows the thumbs extended during striking (Vatican Museum, No. MV.34976.0.0). Poliakoff (1987) reasons that the extended thumbs were intended to gouge the eyes (p. 87).

Figure 8: Detail of amphoroid krater from the G. G. Pierides Collection (see Figure 7 for the object's other side). The striding boxers sport locks of hair reminiscent of Minoan pugilists. Dated to the first two-thirds of the thirteenth century BC.

Figure 9: A fragment from a deep bowl found at Kition, in southeastern Cyprus, and dated between 1300 and 1230 BC (Kition Area II No. 14/2418). The posture assumed by the fighter is similar to that observed in other depictions from Cyprus.

differentiates it from all other styles of Mycenæan boxing art we have observed, so placing it in an earlier century does not seem too drastic a conclusion.

Figure 10: Painting from fragmentary amphoroid krater found at Maroni, on Cyprus (British Museum, No. 1898,1201.137). Pairs of boxers are visible form the shoulders to the feet; each has drawn one arm up and left the other hanging. The lowered hands are curled into fists with an extended thumb. Dated 1375–1300 BC.

Figure 11 provides detail from an amphoroid krater (Boston Museum of Fine Arts, No. 01.8044). The painting has been described as exhibiting "new grotesquerie" and "awkward details" like a creature part avian, part cetacean, as well as chariots with oval wheels (Vermeule and Karageorghis 1982, p. 39). By one account, the vessel came from Rhodes but it has been grouped with Cypriot pottery of the late Bronze Age, nonetheless. The figures of interest to us have been described as belt wrestlers (ibid.) but we find this interpretation vexed. Belt wrestling is amply attested in the ancient and modern world: the practice involves grasping the belt of one's opponent in order to throw him. However, in every version of this sport we have encountered, including in antiquity, each wrestler wears his own belt, not a single belt that binds them together (Gordon 1950–1951). Moreover, in the painting in question, the hands do not reach for this communal belt at all. Instead, they are raised in precisely the gesture we have come to expect among Mycenæan boxers (this is acknowledged by Vermeule and Karageorghis in their description: "the arm gestures are those of sparring boxers," p. 39). The hands are also indisputably curled into fists (we note the similar shape of the charioteers' hands, on the same vessel, as they grasp the reins, along with the formal similarity to the hands of the boxers in Figure 3).

Thus, we are presented with a novel form of boxing, one which directly addresses the absence of a ring in the ancient world.[117] In this form of boxing, the fighters are constrained by the belt to stay near one another and slug it out, thus obviating the need for a constrained space to contain them. A similar technique is still used by modern boxing trainers who tie the two boxer's lead ankles together, giving them only a short distance (less than an arm's

---

[117] A ladder or a pole may have been used to restrain boxers, as depicted in two sixth-century vase paintings found in Italy, one of Attic origin. The practice is also mentioned by Pausanias and Eustathius, writing in a later era. The evidence will be reviewed in Dioscurus and Dioscurus (2023b).

length) to range apart from one another. The painting could represent a boxing match or a training session in which this technique is applied.[118]

4.2 Geometric vase painting

Whether boxing was introduced to the Greek mainland by Cypriots, Minoans, or both during the Bronze Age, there is scant evidence that it ever really caught on.[119] If it did, it was not depicted robustly in visual art for several hundred years (we noted only two fragmentary vase paintings that clearly depict boxers in Section 4.1.1). After the collapse of the Mycenæan palace culture at the end of the Bronze Age, there is a gap in information about Mediterranean boxing (including the Greek mainland) that lasts approximately five centuries. After the relatively large number of vase paintings from thirteenth-century Cyprus, we find no pictorial depictions of boxing again until the eighth century BC. This lacuna is roughly coterminous with the period known traditionally as the Greek Dark Ages. During this poorly understood period, it seems that extensive famine, depopulation, dissolution of overseas trade networks, and decentralization of palace economies left few resources for artistic output.

Boxing may have continued on a smaller scale during the Dark Ages, albeit stripped of the pageantry, spectacle, and religious implications associated with it at Knossos and (probably) on Cyprus.[120] If we take fist-fighting as a kind of human primitive, then the apparent resumption of boxing in eighth century Greece is more likely indicative of increased access to artistic resources, not pugilistic ones. As in the much longer disappearance of boxing from the historical record beginning in Late Antiquity (approximately 500–1600 AD), to argue that boxing vanished entirely is to argue *ex silentio*. Any new archæological discovery could easily subvert the claim that boxing ceased to be practiced during this period. In other words, we know nothing about the Greek Dark Ages that would limit the practice of fist fighting *a priori*. Given the thin evidence of boxing among mainland Mycenæans, it is possible that Bronze Age people never adopted it in what we know today as Greece and that the eighth-century Geometric vases indicate the first substantial foothold boxing gained in mainland Europe.[121]

One line of thinking has it that in the aftermath of the Mycenæan collapse the Greeks adopted many elements of Near Eastern religion. If this is so, then it may have been during this period of great transition that boxing—as a cultic practice if not as a form of athletics— was imported from the east (Kirk 1990). However, this hypothesis has been criticized on

---

[118] We are reminded of portrayals of knife duels where the opposing hands of the fighters are tied to one another, leaving the knife hand only free to strike and limiting the space between the antagonists.

[119] Apollo, as we noted above, is regarded as the divine patron of boxing in Homer. Apollo is not mentioned by name among the attested divinities of Mycenæan religion (Palaima 2008, pp. 348–350). Aspects subsequently associated with Apollo, such as healing, may have been the province of the Mycenæan god *Pa-ja-wo*; a later epithet of Apollo, Pæan, may be etymologically related to this Mycenæan name.

[120] According to one commentator, "[I]t is very dangerous to assume that ancient-seeming practices [attested in ancient Greece] must have been inherited unchanged from the B[ronze] A[ge]" (Dickinson 2006, p. 221). We agree that Mycenæan boxing, if it had ever been adopted in the first place, must have changed while Dark Age Hellenic communities were "continually coming into being, then failing" again (Dickinson 2020, p. 158). However, given the indeterminate character of boxing on the Greek mainland before the eighth century BC, this must remain speculative for now.

[121] The small number of mainland Mycenæan depictions could represent a Mycenæan take on Minoan boxing as seen through the eyes of travelers, for example, and were perhaps never intended as illustrations of 'native' pugilism. This could account for the paucity of such representations on the mainland.

Figure 11: Detail of painting on an amphoroid krater with boxers bound at the waist and bleeding from the nose and mouth, 1350–1250 BC (Boston Museum of Fine Arts No. 01.8044).

multiple grounds, including the absence of "any ancient parallel for such a wholesale adoption of foreign religious ideas" (Dickinson 2006, p. 221). Regardless of what may or may not have happened during the Greek Dark Ages, we observe a steady increase in depictions of Hellenic boxing at their conclusion.

The Dresden kantharos (Figure 13), Louvre œnochoe (Figure 17), and the pedestaled krater (Figure 18), along with the Copenhagen kantharos (Figure 12), are among the earliest depictions of 'Greek' boxing after the thirteenth-century kraters found on Cyprus. Additional examples of Geometric boxing include an Argive pottery fragment held in the National Museum at Athens (Waldstein 1902, pl. 57, 11) and a fragment of unknown provenance (though most likely from mainland Greece) held at Sarajevo (Hampe 1936, Fig. 25).

It is beyond the scope of this article to present and evaluate hypotheses about the usage of each piece of pottery that includes on its face a depiction of pugilism. However, we note that the use of pottery, and decorated pottery in particular, was manifold in ancient Greek society. Boxers painted on vessels might have been associated with funerals or male initiation rituals, as there are numerous examples of vase paintings that seem interested in precisely these activities (Langdon 2008, Gadolou 2015). Pugilists might also have been included as a means of self-representation (Mikrakis 2015): boxing was likely an elite activity, as it probably had been among the Minoans. The users of these vessels had an interest in seeing the valiant activities of themselves and their sons depicted. Pottery was also used in association with heroic, ancestral, and even chthonic cults (Kourou 2015, pp. 98–100). Associations between boxing and cultic practices are of interest to us. However, we will necessarily take them up in a forthcoming article wherein we attempt to interpret the significance of boxing in western culture, ancient and modern.

Figure 12: Detail from a Geometric kantharos housed at the National Museum of Denmark (No. 727) and dated to around 750 BC. The boxing figures are surrounded by sword fighters, dancers, and a person being torn apart by two lions. Scholars speculate that the scene represents a sports competition or a funeral ritual.

An Attic Geometric kantharos held at the National Museum of Denmark (No. 727) is dated to the eighth century, around the time some scholars believe the Homeric epics were first set down. However, the kind of boxing represented does not seem to meet the Iliadic ideal. Among dancers, sword fighters, an abducted female,[122] and a person being torn asunder by two lions, two boxers confront each other (D'Acunto 2016, p. 214). As with Geometric figurative art more generally, details are sparse but the artist shows a keen interest in various anatomical aspects of the fighters, including their calf muscles (Figure 12). The arms of the left boxer are somewhat confused and both are unnaturally lengthened to reach the head of his opponent, where the glaze is unfortunately missing. Under one interpretation, the excessively long arms are intended to indicate the impact of the blow, which would not otherwise be identifiable, given the position of the torsos (Ahlberg-Cornell 1987, pp. 62–63). The artist most likely wished to indicate that this was indeed a fight, since less brutal (unarmed) exercises, like dancing and acrobatics, are also represented on the same kantharos.

The figure on the right has an engorged left hand with some indication of the thumb on top.[123] Given the smaller, more naturalistic hands of other figures on the same vessel, it is probable that the painter of the Copenhagen Kantharos intended to represent "some special pugilistic equipment," most likely a glove, based on its shape (Ahlberg-Cornell 1987, p. 63). No such glove is evident on the same boxer's right hand, leading us to believe that the kantharos depicts a single-glove contest.[124] The boxers' phalli are represented (as on the Dresden Kantharos, see Figure 13), revealing that nudity was already a feature of Greek boxing in the Iron Age. Since this remained a characteristic of Greek boxing for another thousand years, the use of a loincloth (*zōma*) in Homeric boxing suggests that girding one's loins to box was indeed the more ancient practice, as we have argued above.[125]

The Dresden Staatliche Kunstsammlungen holds an early—and distinctive—depiction of boxers on an Attic kantharos (No. 865499). The scene is electric and lively, with wavy vertical lines[126] drawing the viewer's attention to the waist-level of the figures and above. Eight-pointed astral ornaments fill the empty space above the four figures' heads. Two gigantic figures armed with swords across their hips raise one hand in the air and appear to cheer with delight, their wide-open eyes drinking in the spectacle before them.

The main event in the Dresden kantharos consists of two figures with a slight bend in their knees, triangular chests facing the viewer, heads in profile to confront one another resolutely. Their back arms are raised and crossed in a gesture familiar to us from scenes of

---

[122] This interpretation is offered by Langdon (2008, pp. 197–233), who claims that, "The agonistic displays in their range of sport...recall similar exercises held at public betrothals and paralleled in tyrant histories." This makes her interpretation of boxing on the Copenhagen kantharos close in spirit to the ancient Near Eastern "Marriage of Mardu" (Dioscurus and Dioscurus 2022b).

[123] This projection may also be related to the Minoan boxing glove, which consisted in some cases of a curved plate that fit over the back of the hand and projected beyond the knuckles and fingers curled into the palm (Dioscurus and Dioscurus 2022c).

[124] Unfortunately, damage to the vessel makes it impossible to determine if the boxer on the left wears one or two similar gloves—or any at all.

[125] The *zōma* reappears in later Greek depictions of boxing, though we argue (Dioscurus and Dioscurus 2023b) that such images were rendered to suit Italic tastes. For example, a stamnos held at the Bibliothèque Nationale de France (No. De Ridder.252) shows boxers wearing loincloths. This late sixth-century vase was produced in Attica but was evidently intended for export to Etruria since it was discovered at Vulci, north of Rome.

[126] One such segment is, uniquely, compartmentalized into a rectangle that floats between the boxers, in the spot where prizes and gods are also known to appear in other depictions of boxing. We cannot discount the possibility that this wavy line is set apart for its anguine association with Apollo Pythæus.

boxing in the ancient Near East (Dioscurus and Dioscurus 2022b). The other arm is bent at the elbow and the fist, a delicately enlarged glob, points to the waist. The raised hands take two different forms; both possessed of five projections. In one case the fingers radiate from the palm like a star, in the other they all project from one side of the arm's terminus, like a fearsome rake pointed directly at the opponent's eyes.

Figure 13: A boxing scene depicted on an eighth-century Attic kantharos (Dresden Staatliche Kunstsammlungen, No. 865499). Boxers are enantiomorphically gloved on one hand only. Dancers and a musician are depicted on the other side of the vessel.

A fragment of Argive pottery (National Archæological Museum of Athens, no item number) shows two boxers bedeviling one another over or in front of a tripod supporting a cauldron (Figure 14). Their arms and hands are highly stylized; one looks remarkably like the tip of an asparagus stem. The confused projections from the hands may indicate fingers, the depiction of which seems to have presented a puzzle to Geometric vase painters in general, given the wide variety of attested solutions to the problem—some more appealing to the modern eye than others. Ahlberg-Cornell (1987), however, has argued that these flourishes indicate "a special piece of equipment," by which the author presumably meant some form of gauntlet (p. 63). Indeed, a pronged boxing glove with an asparagoid sensibility is attested among Minoan figurines (Dioscurus and Dioscurus 2022c, Fig. 4c). The crooked, unnaturally long arms of the boxer are familiar to us from another ancient Ægean source: a third-millennium marble plaque (Hood 1978, p. 94), also depicting boxers, found on Naxos (Dioscurus and Dioscurus 2022c, Fig. 1).

What made tripods, like the one depicted on a fragmented vase painting found at the Argive Heraion (Figure 14) and the one pictured on the seal in Figure 15, such fantastic prizes, worthy of risking life and limb in the ancient boxing 'ring'? As the means of holding a cauldron above a fire, tripods enabled people to cook food more easily. The tripod cauldron awarded as a prize may also have been filled with meat as part of the reward.[127] As we discuss elsewhere (Dioscurus and Dioscurus 2022b), one of the earliest depictions of boxers

---

[127] This hearkens back to the haggis-prize for the victorious boxer in *Odyssey* 18.

Figure 14: An Argive pottery fragment depicting boxers with a tripod cauldron as a prize and dated most likely to the seventh century BC. The piece was found at the Heraion of Argos (Waldstein 1902, pl. 57, No. 11) and is now housed in the National Archæological Museum of Athens (no item number).

Figure 15: A seal impression depicting boxers with a tripod cauldron as a prize. Seventh century BC. Ashmolean Museum, Oxford University, No. 1895.130.

was integrated into the design of a meat-hook used for fetching boiling flesh from a cauldron (Trifonov et al. 2021). According to Langdon (2008, p. 271):

> With roots in Bronze Age cooking utensils and movable hearths, the bronze tripod in the Early Iron Age was transformed from practical to magnificent, becoming an object of display and ritual importance. By the end of the eighth century, it was a symbolic nexus proclaiming status, power, and political authority...[T]ripods represented both personal excellence and divine favor.

Tripods also had religious significance, as an altar for offering sacrifices. The Delphic oracle sat on a tripod, covered with a slab, while she received prophetic emanations from Apollo, the divine patron of boxing.[128] Herakles and Apollo got into a scuffle when the former tried to abscond with the same tripod in Apollo's temple at Delphi. The three-way association between Apollo, boxing, and tripods may have had cultic significance to ancient observers.

Figure 16: Fragment of a stamnos held at the National Museum of Bosnia and Herzegovina at Sarajevo (no item number). Provenance and date unknown, most likely from mainland Greece, probably early seventh century BC.

In a fragment of a stamnos (a two-handled jar used for mixing liquids and for storage) now held at Sarajevo (Figure 16), two boxers approach one another with an elaborate, massive

---

[128] Langdon (2008, p. 272) argues for "a special connection" between Apollo and tripod cauldrons "not only in their mantic role but also in their continuing association with competition."

tripod betwixt them. They are both gloved on the hand nearest the viewer and the fingers of the other hand are extended.[129] The boxer on the left wears a boxing glove shaped much like the Minoan gloves with "perimetric rim" observed in Minoan figurines (Rethemiotakis 2001, p. 128) and on the Boxer Rhyton (Dioscurus and Dioscurus 2022c). The shape of the other boxer's gauntlet is less clear and directly abuts a diamond-shaped filler ornament, which obscures the gloves leading edge. The date and provenance are unknown, but similarities in the modeling of the fingers remind us of a pedestaled krater (Figure 18) from the early seventh century BC. The boxer on the right has an exposed phallus and, while there is some damage at the relevant site, this appears to be true of the leftmost boxer, as well. An eight-pointed star floats in the midst of the cauldron, which itself takes the form of a crescent moon. The configuration is similar to an ornament that appears between boanthropic pugilists on a hematite cylinder seal, most likely from Cyprus (Dioscurus and Dioscurus 2022b, Fig. 21).

The long legs of the boxers in the Sarajevo stamnos are echoed in those of muscular boxers that appear on an eighth-century œnochoe held at the Louvre. Originally from Thebes, the vessel has a long neck that frames the boxers, who are surrounded by the vertical wavy lines also observed on the Dresden kantharos (Figure 13). Another similarity to that piece presents itself in the apparent single-gloving of the boxers. On the Louvre œnochoe, the lowered fist, brought in front of the waist, is depicted as a significantly enlarged glob. The other hand (of the leftmost boxer only; the rightmost boxer's raised hand is obscured by damage) is narrow and pointed. Fingers are not depicted on either hand. The boxers' massive thighs seem to attract the painter's attention. The heads are quite small, though there is some indication of a beard (or extremely sharp chin) on both fighters. The arms farthest from the viewer cross in the classic, symmetric gesture.

Large pedestaled kraters like the seventh-century exemplar shown from both sides in Figures 18 and 19 served as grave markers for men or boys.[130] The juxtaposition of horses and boxing in this piece reminds us of the twin dominions of Castor and Pollux, whose cult we will discuss in greater depth in Dioscurus and Dioscurus (2023b). The pedestaled krater, which is held at the National Archæological Museum of Athens (No. 12896) is originally from Thebes. As in other Geometric scenes of boxing, the representation of the fingers in this piece continues to surprise. Here, they emerge from one side of a triangle (the hand) or branch twig-like from the arm. Spectators armed similarly to those on the Dresden kantharos are here shorter than the boxers, though dwarfed by their charmingly-rendered equine companions, who also appear to watch the fight.[131]

The boxers on the Theban pedestaled krater do not raise their hands in the symmetrical gesture familiar to us in other Geometric portrayals. Instead, they mix it up with their hands between the shoulders and waist. The armed figure to the right of one pair of boxers (Figure 19) lifts his left arm as if to encourage or cheer for the fighters. The figure to the right of the boxers in Figure 18 does something similar with his left hand. These figures may represent assistants like the "son of Tydeus" in the Iliadic boxing vignette.

---

[129] The symmetry of the rightmost boxer's raised hand suggests it may bear the same gauntlet noted on the Heraion fragment (Figure 14, *ut supra*).

[130] A hole in the bottom of the krater indicates that it was used for this purpose: libations offered in the krater would drain through the bottom and thence, presumably, to the underworld. We have not examined this piece in person and so do not know if such a hole exists.

[131] Two figures to the right of the sparring pair in Figure 19 look away from the boxers, disrupting the symmetry and focal point of the scene.

Figure 17: Boxers appear on the neck of an eighth-century œnochoe from Thebes housed at the Louvre (No. A568), dated 735–720 BC. As on the Dresden kantharos (Figure 13), the boxers appear to wear only one glove, which is lowered, while they strike with the open hand.

Figure 18: Boxers, flanked by armed horsemen, on a pedestaled krater from Thebes (National Archæological Museum of Athens, No. 12896). The depiction, dated 690–670 BC, illustrates single-gloved boxing.

Figure 19: Boxers, flanked by armed horsemen, on a pedestaled krater from Thebes (National Archæological Museum of Athens, No. 12896). This is the other side of the vessel shown in Figure 18.

In the pedestaled krater we see perhaps the clearest evidence of a boxing glove in Geometric vase painting. The lowered hands are massive and globular but not ellipsoid. Instead, a lump on the underside appears, perhaps representing the bound thumb. The glove of the rightmost boxer in Figure 18, for example, bears a notable resemblance to a modern sixteen-ounce boxing glove. It even seems that the artist has here rendered a subtle difference between the glove's cuff and the forearm.

On one side of the krater, the boxers are separated by a large prolate spheroidal object, most likely intended to represent a shield, that floats between their knees. Eight-pointed broken-legged asterisms,[132] dotted lines, wavy lines, and stacks of chevrons fill up the empty spaces in less focal positions. The shield, horses, and swords all indicate that the boxing match on the pedestaled krater takes place in a martial context. In the seventh century, the most famous example of such an event was undoubtedly the boxing match between Epeius and Euryalus, whom we suspect are depicted here.[133]

We summarize by posing the following questions: Where is boxing attested in eighth- and seventh-century Greece and is there any evidence that boxing was preserved in an unbroken tradition from the Bronze Age at these sites? The Dresden and Copenhagen kantharoi come from Attica, the latter likely produced by either the Burly or Rattle Workshop (Ahlberg-Cornell 1987, p. 55). The Louvre œnochoe and the pedestaled krater (No. 12896) are both from Thebes. Thus, the earliest depictions of boxing occur in a fairly small area of mainland Greece: the Attic Peninsula and the region that borders it directly to the north. It has been argued that "'collapse' is too dramatic a term for what happened at the end of the Bronze Age in Athens and Attica, but 'transformation' is too anodyne" (Osborne 2020, p. 142). The author concludes that the Attic Peninsula faced significant "pressures brought about not directly by other humans but by factors beyond human control" (ibid.).

While evidence of wholesale collapse is scant in Attica, the Mycenæan palace at Thebes was clearly destroyed by fire (Magiddis 2020, p. 116).[134] Thus the Bronze Age 'collapse' affected two contiguous regions (where boxing later emerged) differently: while life on the Attic Peninsula "sustained continuity and achieved substantial revival with their [erstwhile] limited production and trade capacity" in the late twelfth century BC, the more complex palace economies of places like Thebes disintegrated (ibid.). The palace at Thebes was "partially repaired and reoccupied" but it, too, was "gradually abandoned" as the Dark Ages wore on (ibid.). On the Argolid, where pottery with depictions of boxing had been produced and exported (to Cyprus) during the late Bronze Age, what has been called "collapse" elsewhere in the Mediterranean is described more moderately as "radical culture change" (Mühlenbruch 2020, p. 130).

If boxing existed in Mycenæan Greece and if it was exclusively tied to the Bronze Age palace cultures, then it almost certainly disappeared with the dissolution of the palace economies and their advanced foreign trade networks. As Magiddis (2020) writes:

[I]t was the Mycenæan elite and its diagnostic elements (palatial administration

---

[132] The asterisms may represent the revolving sun, in which case they may be linked to Phœbus Apollo.

[133] The presence of armed men on the Dresden kantharos (Figure 13), along with its numerous formal similarities to the Theban pedestaled krater, lead us to wonder whether or not this earlier vessel, too, depicts the Iliadic boxing match.

[134] The destruction of Thebes is even recorded in the *Iliad*, shortly preceding the Trojan War. Homer tells us that Euryalus, the defeated champion in the Iliadic boxing match, fought magnificently at Thebes before the war began, suggesting that Thebes was legendary for its pugilism.

and writing, ideology and ritual, foreign contacts and luxury goods, monumental art and megalithic architecture, representational arts and crafts) that suffered the most from the system metltdown; paradoxically, the same societal and cultural forces of transformation that caused their demise, fossilized the Mycenæan kings and warriors in the realm of a heroic past, elevated them in the sphere of myth and preserved them in collective memory (pp. 116–117).

If, on the other hand, boxing had permeated Mycenæan Greece as a folk custom more or less independently of the palatial "diagnostic elements" of Thebes, for example, then it likely survived, changing gradually over five centuries of practice as part of the "basic material culture and cultural practices" of the "remaining core of Mycenæan society" (ibid., p. 117). It should be stressed, however, that there is hardly any evidence that boxing was a core element of (Bronze Age) Mycenæan society.

Modern scholars do not encourage the view that Greek society of the post-Mycenæan era consisted of "one social order, or one set of 'human thing entanglements', but [of] many... [T]here was neither one homogeneous society nor one homogeneous culture (Whitley 2015, pp. 122–123). Based on this thinking, we would not expect depictions of boxing to be uniform during this time period and, indeed, they were not.

So what did boxing look like when it fully reëmerged on mainland Greece? In nearly all Geometric depictions,[135] boxers of the new era fought with a single glove, one combatant wearing it on the left hand and the other on the right so that the boxers mirrored each other. There is insufficient detail in any of these renderings to determine whether the gauntlet worn on one hand had the structure of the Homeric *himantes*. In one case (the Sarajevo stamnos) the evidence points to a much more ancient boxing glove, the one used at Knossos in the sixteenth century BC. In Geometric depictions, the ungloved hand appears unencumbered by any gauntlet and the fingers are often extended either to make this evident or perhaps even to suggest their function in defensive manœuvres like deflecting blows, or perhaps offensive ones like grasping, raking, and clawing.

Remarkably absent from both Mycenæan and Geometric boxing scenes is the 'third man in the ring,' the official or trainer, armed with a stick, ubiquitous in Near Eastern depictions as well as later Greek depictions, as we shall see. The reappearance of this figure in boxing scenes of later centuries can almost certainly be attributed to the orientalization of Greek vase painting.

There is significant evidence from the Geometric vase paintings that boxers of this period fought in the nude like their much later descendants. This is perplexing, because the *zōma* 'loincloth' is referred to explicitly in the boxing scenes of both the *Iliad* and the *Odyssey*. Yet nowhere in Geometric art do we find clear evidence of an artist's interest in depicting this noteworthy bit of pugilistic attire. Geometric painting did not normally involve any kind of painting over the silhouette—this is an innovation of the so-called "black-figure" era (see below). However, other conventions were possible for representing clothing,[136] and none of these are used on Geometric boxing figures (who often manifest an exposed penis, in any event). Mycenæan boxers on Cyprus apparently fought naked (see Figure 7). Beyond Cyprus

---

[135] When single-gloving is not obvious, it is due to a lack of detail or damage to the painting. In other words, there is no clear representation of dual-gloved boxing in the Geometric period.

[136] For example, on the Theban pedestaled krater (Figure 18), the sword-bearing figures are painted with two thin strokes flaring out on each side of their body, from abdomen to hips, arguably indicating a short tunic.

we have no depiction of a Mycenæan boxer that includes the waist, so we cannot be sure if mainland pugilists of that era wore the loincloth or not. Homer insists on the *zōma* in boxing contests of the heroic age, yet we know of no illustration of such a garment in Mycenæan art. Therefore, we conjecture that the *zōma* is an element of Homer's poetry that has a truly ancient origin in Minoan civilization, the only place (besides the ancient Near East) where a loincloth is attested in boxing scenes up to that time.[137]

4.3   Black- and red-figure vase painting (ca. 700–300 BC)

Beginning in the seventh century BC, Greek artisans began employing a new technique for decorating pottery. Known as "black-figure," this style incorporates figures and ornaments that were painted with slip on the vessels before they were fired. These were sometimes highlighted by colors like white and red, painted on after firing, but figures mostly appeared in black silhouette. Details were scratched away from the slip, which sometimes resulted in jagged, angular lines. The renderings of the human figure gradually became more and more sophisticated and naturalistic until the "red-figure" technique emerged in the late sixth century. This technique, in which the negative spaces were painted with slip and details were applied with a fine brush, resulted in a heightened degree of naturalism. Perhaps freed up by their new found ability to produce finer contours, painters began experimenting with a less orthodox approach to the human form, presenting it less frequently in strict profile and even using foreshortening to capture depth in a two-dimensional form.[138] Especially in the black-figure depiction of boxers, certain manneristic tendencies (like extra-long fingers in an open-hand gesture) remained from the Geometric, but on the whole, the new techniques in vase painting give us much more leeway to take the stance, swing, and punch of the fighters at face value and thus better apprehend the kinetics of *pygmachia*.

The Classical Art Research Centre at Oxford University maintains a database of Greek pottery.[139] It contains 532 items under the subject term "boxing." These are dated between 600 and 300 BC. While many appear to be duplicate entries and the database itself is not comprehensive, this approximates the number of post-Geometric Greek vases that are adorned with pugilistic scenes. We comment on only a few of these in order to establish *termini ante quem* for certain innovations or to examine other peculiarities.

An Attic neck amphora found at Daphnæ (Tell Dafana) on the long-lost Pelusiac branch of the Nile (British Museum, No. 1888,0208.102) shows two boxers fighting over a tripod (Figure 20). The trunks of their bodies are painted purple, but the genitals of the rightmost boxer are exposed—incised in the slip or painted in white—as are features of the chest and abdomen, including some muscles and the nipples. While the British Museum concludes that the boxers wear purple chitons, we disagree based on the incisions made in the silhouettes; these are intended to show features that would be obscured by a tunic.[140] Instead, we argue that the purple coloring on the body represents blood (as it does in the scene of a boar

---

[137] Another possibility is that the loincloth was entirely fanciful. Perhaps the poet included this element as part of the heroic *imaginaire*, with no evidence or tradition that the *zōma* was ever used in boxing at all.

[138] Techniques like foreshortening were eventually applied to late exemplars of black-figure, with sinuous white lines painted on (see the boxers' feet in Figure 32).

[139] https://www.beazley.ox.ac.uk/carc/Home, accessed August 27, 2022.

[140] If the boxers are indeed painted with clothed torsos, the Daphnæ amphora would be the only such depiction we have encountered in the ancient record.

hunt in the upper register of the same vase).[141] The fighters wear necklaces. The amphora also bears a clear representation of a stick-wielding official (though he presides over an adjacent pair of wrestlers, not the boxers). Finally, the boxer on the left appears to wear the *himantes* on his right hand: it is indicated by a strip around the wrist and another across the knuckles or palm and excluding the thumb.[142] The piece is dated 580–560 BC.

By the late sixth century, the *himantes* are depicted as a white cross-hatch pattern incised across the fists, sometimes with a cuff or bracelet at the wrist. This can be seen in a black-figure skyphos discovered at Corinth, held at the Louvre (No. MNC-332), and executed between 550 and 525 BC. The skyphos shows two naked boxers, one charging his opponent from the left, the other fleeing to the right while holding up his right hand with fingers extended in what may be a gesture of defense (Figure 21). Two streams of blood are ejected from the nose of the boxer in flight; the word πυκτα appears between them, surely a morphological variant of πυκτεύω 'box' or 'spar'. With black-figure painting like the Louvre skyphos we see the earliest depictions of boxers whose genitals are illustrated within the silhouette of their bodies, viz., against their inner thigh. In Geometric art, unless the penis projected beyond the outline of the thigh (as it does, e.g., in the Theban pedestaled krater, Figure 18), it was necessarily subsumed in the silhouette. Thus, by the sixth century BC, we have unambiguous indications that Greek boxers did *not* wear the *zōma* referred to in Homer.[143] A red-figure tondo shows two nude boxers, including one wearing a κυνοδέσμη, with *himantes* indicated as cuffs along the wrists (Figure 22). Another depiction shows a boxer wrapping his hands ahead of his match, presumably examining the bindings (Figure 23). A wonderful red-figure kylix shows boxers preparing for their *agon* as others fight (Figure 24).

Depictions of Greek boxing often include clothed figures, probably trainers, judges, or other officials, standing near the boxers. Another figure is sometimes illustrated, as well. This figure holds extra *himantes* and sometimes what appear to be the garments of the boxers, though he is also nude (cf. a Panathenaic amphora at the Metropolitan Museum, No. 06.1021.51; and an Attic hydria at the Penn Museum, No. 51-32-1). In some cases, this may be the *ephedros*, i.e., the boxer who has received a bye and is waiting to fight the winner of the ongoing bout. One rendering of the *ephedros* attributed to the Eucharides painter has him clenching one fist and raising it to his abdomen as if to mimic the action of the boxers or perhaps to demonstrate a punch he would like to have thrown (Figure 25). In one case, Athena herself stands brandishing the admonitory reed (Figure 26).

As late as the sixth century, Greek boxers still appear to have experimented with removing the *himantes* from one hand.[144] This experimental attitude towards boxing gloves is a

---

[141] Another example of painting over the bare chests of boxers occurs on an Athenian skyphos found at Corinth and dated 575–525 BC (Archæological Museum of Ancient Corinth, No. CP881).

[142] It is not clear whether the painter intended the viewer to see the knuckles of the hand or the palm. A natural overhand right, which may be depicted, would have the thumb on top. If the image is interpreted strictly based on the position of the thumb then we must observe the palm of the hand, perhaps being used in a defensive gesture to laterally deflect the striking right hand of the adversary.

[143] We understand that the conventions of Geometric vase painting did not normally provide for detail to be expressed within the silhouette of the human body (though this is clearly not true of animal forms, like the birds in Figure 7); this may account for the absence of the *zōma* in Geometric art. However, besides the fact that projecting penises are sometimes depicted in these boxers, it should also be noted that in Geometric low relief, where the upper thighs and hips are clearly modeled (Figures 14 and 35), there is no indication of a loincloth.

[144] Given evidence from Geometric painting, it may also be an archaic feature of Greek boxing with an ancestry stretching as far back as the Minoans (Dioscurus and Dioscurus 2022c).

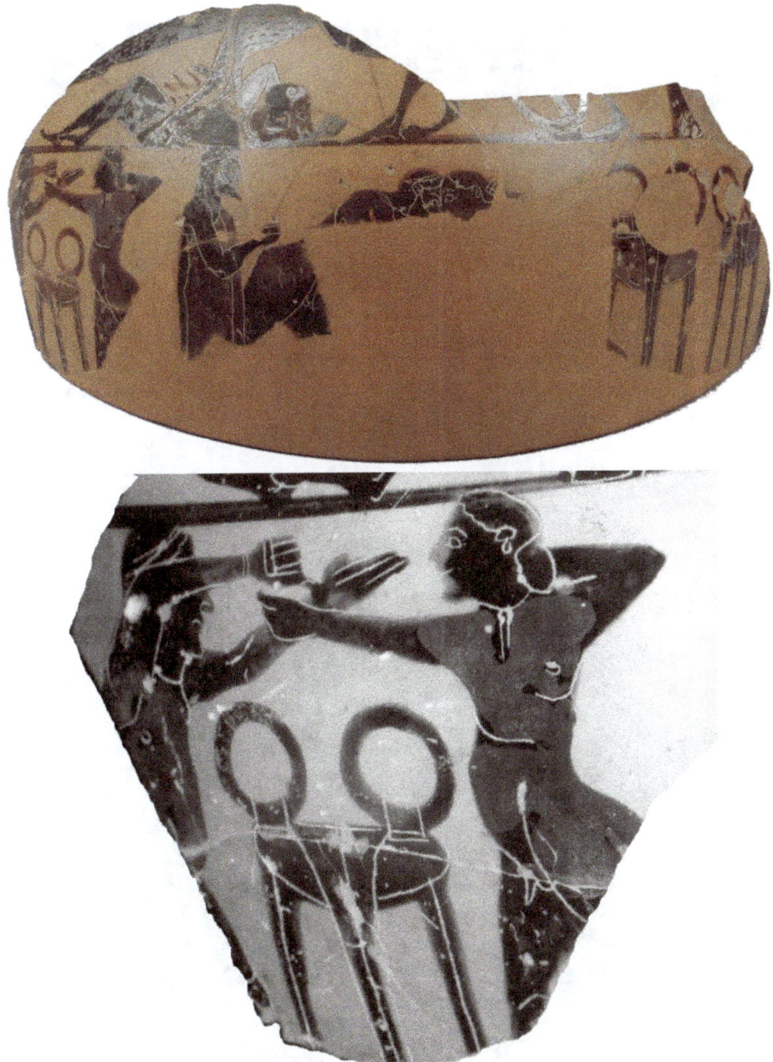

Figure 20: Found at Tell Dafana in Egypt, this fragmented Attic neck amphora contains either an unprecedented depiction of boxers awash in (purple) blood or (less likely, in our opinion) of boxers wearing clothing on their torsos (British Museum, No. 1888,0208.102; 580–560 BC). Note that the rightmost boxer's genitals are exposed, despite the chiton that some posit he is wearing. The boxer on the right wears the *himantes* on his right hand only.

Figure 21: A sixth-century skyphos depicting two boxers, one fleeing his adversary and bleeding profusely from the nose, hand raised in a gesture of defense. The word πυκτα, inscribed between them, is likely a morphological variant of πυκτεύω 'box' or 'spar' (Louvre, No. MNC-332 / L-179; 550–525 BC).

Figure 22: Red-figure tondo in the manner of Euergides; 510–500 BC (Museo Civico Archeologico of Bologna, No. 28655).

Figure 23: Red-figure tondo in the manner of Epidromos; 520–500 BC (Hood Museum of Art, Dartmouth College, No. C.970.35).

Figure 24: Red-figure kylix by the Triptolemos Painter; c. 490 BC (Toledo Museum of Art, Toledo, Ohio, No. 1961.26).

Figure 25: Detail of an Attic black figure amphora (National Archæological Museum, Athens, No. 447). The *ephedros*, naked and holding *himantes* in his right hand, stands to the right of two other athletes engaged in a boxing match (note also the extended fingers of the leftmost boxer, partially visible). From Exarchos, Locris. By the Eucharides Painter, ca. 500 BC. Photo courtesy Nemeæus.

Figure 26: Black-figure panathenaic amphora from the Nikomachos series; c. 336–335 BC (British Museum, London, No. 1873,0820.371).

theme that runs through late Antiquity, until the disappearance of boxing in the West.[145] It is possible that the artist simply chose not to render the stylized *himantes* on the silhouette of the open hand but artists who wished to include this detail were by no means prevented from doing so by available techniques. A black-figure neck amphora dated to the second half of the sixth century and attributed to Nikosthenes demonstrates this clearly (Fitzwilliam Museum, No. GR3.1962). In this depiction, the fighter on the right holds up his left hand, fingers extended, with abundant indications of the *himantes* wrapped around his wrist, thumb, knuckles, and fingers. His right hand, similarly equipped, is balled tightly into a fist. Per one commentator, "The fingers were left free so that the boxer could clench his fist to deliver a blow, and open his hand to catch a punch. Both these attitudes of the hands—offensive and defensive—are frequently seen in the portrayal of boxing matches, and both are often displayed by a single boxer" (Miller 2004, pp. 51–52).

Figure 27: Detail of a black figure œnochoe (Cleveland Museum of Art, No. 1916.1062), dated 550–540 BC. The lack of *himantes* on the left hand of the boxer on the left suggests fights could be organized under a variety of conventions.

The appearance of *himantes* on the hands of fighters is not dispositive of pugilism, however. A sixth-century rendering attributed to the Theseus Painter (Metropolitan Museum of Art, No. 06.1021.49) shows pankratiasts (they are manifestly engaged in pronograde combat) wearing the leather thongs (Figure 28). A panathenaic amphora decorated by the Marsyas

---

[145] We note that experimentation with boxing gloves continues today with the reëmergence of bare-knuckle boxing in the United States and the United Kingdom, as well as the development of "hybrid boxing" rule sets that use lightweight gloves. Despite this ferment, we are not aware of any promotion that licenses fighters to wear only one glove or a glove specially engineered to inflict greater injury.

Painter also depicts pankratiasts with their hands wrapped (National Archaeological Museum of Athens, No. 20045; 360–359 BC). On the amphora, excavated at Eretria near a gymnasium, one fighter leans over his prone opponent in a posture typical of pankration representations.

Figure 28: Pankratiasts wear the *himantes* (ἱμάντες) on an Attic black-figure skyphos (Metropolitan Museum of Art, No. 06.1021.49). The work is attributed to the Theseus Painter, ca. 500 BC.

The often observed, stick-wielding official may have been called παιδονόμος 'warden' or 'educator' or perhaps κύριος 'lord, master', whose right it was to 'separate' διαλύω the boxers (Xen. *Const. Lac.* 4.6). Another possible term for this individual is βραβεύς or βραβευτής 'umpire', related to the βραβεῖον 'prize'. He begins to appear clearly only in the black figure period, perhaps only in the sixth century. One early depiction of this official comes from an Athenian skyphos found at Corinth (575–525 BC), where the figure holds a long thin staff and looks on at the boxers to the viewer's right. In another depiction, an eagle appears to be flying between two boxers in a badly fragmented black figure hydria (Ashmolean Museum, Vase No. 350345; 600–550 BC). An official, a bearded ephedros, and another official stand to the right of the dueling pair. The position of the bird is reminiscent of Levantine cylinder seals discussed in Dioscurus and Dioscurus (2022b) and may represent a deity.

A standard depiction of boxing from this era is painted on a skyphos held at the Carlsberg Glyptothek in Copenhagen (No. 2677) and attributed to the Camel Painter (575–525 BC). The illustration contains two naked boxers surrounded by two bearded, robed men (Figure 29). Behind one of them stands another boxer, naked and outfitted with *himantes* (represented as stylized cross-hatching on the fists, with cuffs).

Around the early fifth century we begin to see evidence of a change in the iconography

Figure 29: Boxing scene from an Athenian skyphos held at the Carlsberg Glyptothek in Copenhagen (No. 2677).

and perhaps the rule-set of boxing. Vanquished boxers raise their finger indicating they have lost and, presumably, that the pummeling should cease. This is the case in a red-figure cup attributed to Epiktetos, held at the Agora Museum (No. P24110) and illustrated in Figure 30.

Some black- and red-figure paintings have been identified as depicting boxers, even though the fighters clearly do not wear *himantes*. In the case of the painting by Epiktetos (Figure 30) mentioned above, the posture of the bodies may suggest *pankration* but the fists are closed and neither fighter appears to seek a hold on his opponent. Similarly, on one leg of a Bœotian (Tanagra) claw-footed pyxis stand (Antikensammlung Berlin, No. F1727), naked black-figure athletes raise both their hands, clenched in fists, high above their heads (570–560 BC). One figure bears naturalistic detail of the thumb overlapping the fingers at a right angle. There can be no doubt from their posture that they are boxers but neither wears the *himantes*. The boys tussling with one another on a miniature red-figure wine jug or chous[146] (Boston Museum of Fine Arts, No. 95.53) are identified as boxers though they are not fitted with the gauntlets (Figure 31). Their hands are open and we cannot rule out the possibility that they represent wrestlers or pankratiasts frozen at a preliminary, non-grappling stage of the match.[147] The scene is framed by two short columns (not included in Figure 31) which may represent the boundaries of the boxing 'ring' or may merely have served as a conventional boundary of the scene for the vase painter.

---

[146] A small wine jug like this would have been presented to a young boy at the Anthesteria festival in Athens. As the boys grew older, the size of the wine jug did, as well. The function of the detail on the vessel was likely aspirational. Just as modern parents in the West may dress their children in printed T-shirts suggestive of sports they might one day take part in, or top a birthday cake with a toy boxing ring, parents of children in this period likely wished to encourage their young boys to emulate the older boys and men already slugging it out in the *palaistra*.

[147] Two pugilists with wrapped hands appear in an Athenian red-figured cup dated to the second half of the fifth century (Musées Royaux d'Art et d'Histoire, Brussels, No. R335). Unconventionally, however, none of their hands are balled into fists though their hands are in striking position.

Figure 30: The fallen boxer signals his defeat and the end of the match by holding up his right index finger just as his opponent lands a hammer fist to his head (Agora Museum, No. P24110). Detail from a red-figure cup, 525–475 BC, attributed to Epiktetos.

Figure 31: Detail of a a chous (miniature wine jug) depicting two boys who are identified as boxers, despite the fact that they wear no *himantes* and have open hands (Boston Museum of Fine Arts, No. 95.53). The item is dated to about 425 BC and is said to be from Athens.

As a subject of vase painting, boxing seems to have captured the interest of Greek artisans (or, more likely, the elites who consumed their productions) from the end of the sixth century to the beginning of the fourth century BC. While rendering of boxing scenes continued well into the third century, the number of such pieces decreased significantly.[148] This may also be attributed to a general decrease in artistic depictions of athletes—or even painted vases—in general. Depictions of wrestling and *pankration*, never as popular as portrayals of boxing, also peaked in the sixth and fifth centuries, then dwindled substantially by the Hellenistic era. Connor (1995) confirms that boxing was a "popular [motif] in middle to late black figure, [but] of less interest in red figure" (p. 101).

4.4   Relief sculpture

Boxing was not a popular theme of Greek sculpture before the Hellenistic era. We know of no Greek representations of boxers in the round before 325 BC and we are aware of only a few examples of early reliefs, which we review in this section.[149]

An eighth-century bronze tripod leg from Olympia arguably presents us with the earliest sculptural depiction of boxing in Greek art (Archæological Museum of Olympia, No. B-1730). In a clever *mis en abyme*, the principals battle over a tripod cauldron (Figure 34).[150] Lower on the same leg, lions fight each other. The boxers wear helmets and plumes—a remarkable parallel to the helmeted figures on the much earlier Boxer Rhyton found at Knossos.

A terracotta plaque depicting a boxing scene was found at the Heraion of Argos (Figure 35) and has been dated to the beginning of the seventh century (Waldstein 1902, pp. 52–53). Little can be discerned about the boxers. They are naked and appear to wear their hair long. Insufficient detail and/or erosion make it impossible for us to say much about their hands, e.g., whether they wear a gauntlet. The Heraion was dedicated to the goddess who oversaw marriage. We note that votive plaques depicting boxing were also found in temples in Mesopotamia, where it has been argued that they were associated with betrothals (Dioscurus and Dioscurus 2022b).

Grave reliefs appear to have been the most common sculptural form devoted to boxing in the Classical era. Along with soldiers, athletes were the only group identified by their profession on funeral steles (Osborne 2018, p. 58). Boxers can be picked out on some of these by their *himantes* and by traces of disfigurement occasioned by a career in the 'ring'. One such example[151] is an Attic funerary stele (560–530 BC) housed in the Kerameikos Archæological Museum (No. P1054). The stele, which is fragmented, now reveals only the boxer's face and part of his raised arm (Figure 36). Here there is abundant evidence of a carefully executed

---

[148] A back-of-the-envelope calculation using the database of Oxford's Classical Art Research Centre suggests that the number of vases depicting pugilism decreased as much as 90% from 550 to 300 BC.

[149] We discuss Greek contributions to the sculptural corpus in (Dioscurus and Dioscurus 2023b). This will include a discussion of the well-known Boxer at Rest.

[150] The scene is identified by some as representing a battle between Herakles and Apollo over the tripod of the Delphic oracle. There is not much to recommend this interpretation besides the tripod, however. Boxers in other depictions fight over tripods without being identified as Apollo or Herakles (e.g., Figure 16). Moreover, tripods were common prizes in Greek athletics, *ut supra*. Finally, there is nothing about the iconography of the figures on this tripod leg to suggest they represent either son of Zeus. According to Burkert (1983, p. 121), clearly identifiable representations of this myth are not attested before the sixth century BC.

[151] Several others are attested in Richter (1965).

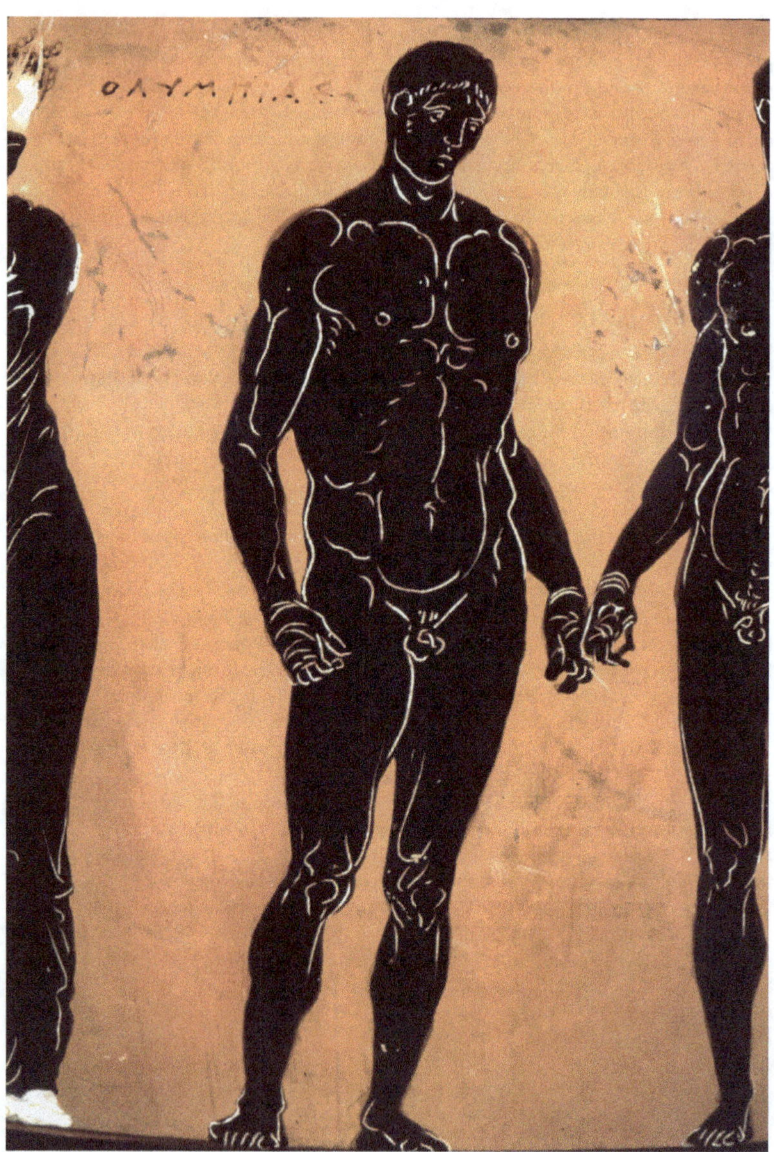

Figure 32: Detail from an Attic black figure Panathenaic prize amphora (340–339 BC). The fighter stands next to another boxer, on the right, and an official who appears to deliver instructions. A personification of the Olympic games stands to the left (Harvard University Art Museums, No. 1925.30.124).

Figure 33: Detail of a Panathenaic prize amphora (J. Paul Getty Museum, No. 93.AE.55). Boxer crowned by winged Nike, with the *himantes* removed and dangling from the crook of his left arm (363–362 BC).

Figure 34: A low-relief boxing scene on a bronze tripod leg (Archæological Museum of Olympia, No. B-1730), eighth century BC. The boxers appear to wear plumed helmets as on the Minoan Boxer Rhyton, produced some eight centuries earlier.

Figure 35: A terracotta plaque found at the Heraion of Argos. The figures appear to be boxing in a manner familiar to us from ancient Near Eastern depictions: one hand raised aloft, the other at chest level (Dioscurus and Dioscurus 2022b).

Figure 36: Funerary stele depicting a boxer with raised fist (Kerameikos Archæological Museum, No. P1054). Found in Attica and dated 560–530 BC, the figure appears to suffer from a broken nose and cauliflower ear.

himas. The straps cross in an 'X' just below the wrist and a cuff fits snugly around the forearm. The gauntlet covers about one-third of the space between wrist and elbow. Critics have noted that the boxer's nose has been broken and repeated trauma to the side of his head has resulted in auricular hematoma or cauliflower ear. Greek artisans were evidently interested in representing boxing injuries, including hemorrhage, from the sixth century onward (Figure 20, 21) and the tradition would continue well into Late Antiquity.

5 Conventions

Having reviewed literary and visual attestations of Greek boxing from the Archaic to the Classical era, we can now summarize some of the major features of the activity that can be inferred from the evidence: the gloves and the form of boxing.

5.1 Gloves

The Greeks were not the first to cover their hands in order to engage in unarmed, orthograde combat. There is some evidence that this practice was known in the ancient Near East and it was irrefutably the case among the Minoans (Dioscurus and Dioscurus 2022b;c). It can be challenging to determine whether a bare or covered fist is intended in Mycenæan and Archaic depictions, given the formal simplicity that was adopted in rendering the human form. For example, in a Late Bronze Age krater from Enkomi (Figure 5), the 'glove' is rendered as an ellipse, larger than the hands of other comparable figures (Figure 5). Close inspection does make it clear, however, that in the Archaic period, boxers typically wore only one glove—something that Homer's poetry neither describes explicitly nor rules out. The gloved hand is substantially enlarged but still lacks the detail necessary to assess its character fully, for example, in the Dresden kantharos (Figure 13). In at least one instance, the Greek gauntlet looks similar to the Minoan glove depicted on the Boxer Rhyton (Figure 14). It is also possible that Greek boxers fought bare-knuckled as on the Tanagra pyxis stand (Antikensammlung Berlin, No. F1727).

By the sixth century, Greek vase painters rendered the *himantes* in a stylized cross-hatch pattern covering the fist and/or wrist. This was evidently a visual shorthand meant to indicate the layered wrapping of the fists in the leather thongs. By the Late Archaic and Classical eras, the *himantes* were illustrated with greater naturalism. It appears they were wrapped across the knuckles, crossing at the wrist, and were tied at a position slightly above the mid-forearm (Figure 36).

By the fourth century, the *himantes* were rendered at various stages of their use, including after removal. From one such depiction (Figure 33), we learn that the leather thong was pierced at each end and threaded with a long string, doubled over. The resulting four ends were most likely tied in some fashion to secure the *himantes*. It is possible that more than one leather strip was used on one hand, but the fastening strength conferred by one long, single strip would have made this arrangement preferable, in our opinion.[152]

In some Archaic representations like the Louvre skyphos (Figure 21), the hand appears to be bound tightly as a club. This style of boxing glove has been posited for the Boxing Boys of Akrotiri and is known in contemporary African *dambe* boxing (Dioscurus and Dioscurus 2022c). Depictions like one on a fifth-century amphora (Figure 25) demonstrate that the fingers on a hand bound with the leather thong could still be extended, presumably to catch a blow.

The changing representation of the *himantes* does not necessarily mean that their appearance changed over time. Their depiction is also closely linked to innovations in artistic tastes and techniques. Greek artists may have grown more interested in the *himantes* as subject matter, perhaps as popular interest in boxing increased among their elite patrons. Our clearest view of the structure of the *himantes* emerges only in Hellenistic sculpture. Unfortunately, during this period we learn from textual sources that the gauntlets had already undergone modification and differentiation. For these reasons, we must be cautious in assessing the appearance of Archaic and even Classical *himantes* and in rectifying our judgments with much later literary sources that claim to typologize and explain the differences in boxing gloves. These sources, like Philostratus' third-century AD *Gymnasticus*, were infused with their own ideology (Reid 2016), as we will explore in Dioscurus and Dioscurus (2023b).

In the late fifth century, Plato (*Laws*, 8.830B) described boxing gloves known as *(epi)sphairai*, which were used "to imitate as nearly as possible the fighting in the ring... so that we could

---

[152] In modern sport boxing, the gauze bandages known as hand wraps are routinely secured with a layer of adhesive tape, but ancient boxers, who could not avail themselves of such a convenience, likely invented a variety of solutions to the problem of keeping the *himantes* secure under the stress of impact and struggle.

practice striking and the avoidance of blows as much as possible" (Sweet 1987). We are un-aware of any depiction of these gloves before the Hellenistic era.[153]

Practiced for centuries among the ancient Greeks, boxing probably experienced diachronic change. One of the few ways we can verify this hypothesis is to closely examine visual depictions of boxing over time. Fortunately, Greek vase painters were enthusiastic about depicting pugilism and there are many scores of examples available for study today.

It should be noted immediately that boxers are not always bilaterally 'gloved' in Greek depictions. For example, a sixth-century black-figure œnochoe (Figure 27) shows a boxing match where one fighter wears the *himantes* on both hands while his adversary wears them on his right hand only. Not only is the boxer's left (lead) hand ungloved, but his fingers are elongated and extended upward (a gesture seen in Etruscan tomb paintings, as well). An official is present, seated, to the left; and another observer stands to the right, suggesting the encounter is a legitimate boxing match and not merely a practice session. Such an image allows us to infer that different conventions were applied to boxing praxis synchronically. This is remarkably like our own day, when a variety of conventions govern the use of boxing equipment such as gloves and headgear. The asymmetry in this depiction is particularly remarkable, however. Whether the arrangement confers an advantage or disadvantage on the left-hand figure is debatable. Parrying blows was probably easier with his ungloved hand. If permitted to do so, the unilaterally-gloved boxer could grasp his opponent, assail him with fingers jabbed into his eyes, nose, or mouth, or even pull his hair. The bones of the hand, however, were subject to increased risk of injury and so it is likely that his left-hand strikes, if unbuttressed by the *himantes*, were less forceful.

In several early depictions, Greek boxers are gloved on only one hand. Three vase paintings from the seventh and eighth centuries show much simpler figures but it is still clear that the boxers are unilaterally gloved. The Geometric depiction of the hands, though certainly not naturalistic, has the advantage in several instances of showing each of the five fingers; these are represented as twig-like projections from the stem of the arm or as star-like emanations from the hand. The other hand is depicted as a ball. Though working in the simplified Geometric style, the artist seemingly intended to depict closed and gloved fists. In an eighth-century Kantharos, Geometric boxers stand chest-forward, with the ungloved hand raised and the gloved hand lowered (Figure 13). When it comes to their gloved hands, the boxers are laterally inverted images of each other, i.e., one boxer wears a glove on his left and the other wears a glove on his right.

In another eighth-century vase, this time an œnochoe, the boxers appear on the neck of the vessel (see Figure 17). Their struggle is somewhat more dynamic than the one depicted on the Dresden kantharos. The boxers' lowered hands are depicted as balls, most likely representing a boxing glove. The figure on the left throws a left at his opponent's head. His hand ends in a point, not a globe (his fingers are not expressed, however). The figure on the right also throws a punch, but damage to the object prevents us from examining the shape of the hand directly. The Louvre œnochoe thus presents a somewhat deprecated case for single-glove boxing in that only one pugilist definitively engages in it.

More convincing evidence of unilaterally gloved boxers comes from the illustration on an early seventh-century pedesttalled krater (Figure 18). Here, the artist emphasizes the fin-

---

[153] A Greco-Roman terracotta caricature of a boxer shows him wearing large round gloves (Skulpturensammlung Dresden, No. ZV803).

gers on the hands of each figure and clearly shapes one hand of each boxer into a ball. For the combatant on the right, the glove even appears to have a cuff, suggestive of the artist's intention to render the shape of the gauntlet accurately.

5.2 Form

Aside from the unique hand-coverings, can we judge from visual depictions and literary sources how early Greek boxers fought? Homer indicates that boxers raised their hands (ἀνέχω) and we have certainly observed visual examples of this behavior (Figs. 27 and 29). However, the visual record is hardly indicative of a single, orthodox style. We see lead hands up and back hands down (Fig. 13), both arms extended (Fig. 5), a leading open hand and a back-hand fist at waist level (Fig 16). Early depictions, in particular, were likely to communicate the idea of boxing through stylized conventions like the raised and crossed arms of the Dresden kantharos (Figure 13; compare Homeric language about 'mixing' hands). With the advent of more naturalistic portrayals in black- and red-figure, artists seem more sensitive to depicting an actual match. Still, a confused jumble of hands is not easy to capture and not every punch is thrown with precision. Some of the more awkward renderings of fighting (e.g., Figure 20) may have been closer to reality than we might at first suppose.

Was there a single convention for making a fist? Again, in the visual record we see much diversity: fists with thumbs extended (Fig. 10); thumbs held close but parallel to the fingers (Fig. 30); and thumbs closed over the fingers (Antikensammlung Berlin, No. F1727). Perhaps some of this variation may be attributed to an absence of naturalism in depicting the closed human fist—a challenging subject to render in any medium.

Assessing the stance of Greek boxers in Geometric and black-figure vase painting is fraught with difficulty because of a general tendency to depict the human form in the 'Egyptian style', with the lower half of the body in profile and the chest and shoulders rotated towards the viewer. In the Geometric phase, it is complicated by an interest in the symmetry of the opposing forms. Still, in some cases we can detect the artist's awareness of how the body moved during a fight. For example, in the black-figure Cleveland œnochoe (Figure 27), the leftmost combatant raises his back heel and pushes off the ball of his foot, suggesting that he is turning his body to deliver the right-hand punch. Even in the relatively early Geometric Louvre œnochoe (Figure 17), the boxer on the right naturalistically lifts his back heel slightly to deliver a punch (this time, his right). The boxers in the Louvre skyphos (Figure 21) make much more exaggerated movements with their legs due to the (possibly comic) flight of the retreating pugilist.

Greek vase painters seemed to avoid a naturalistic depiction of the defensive guard position in which boxers hold both forearms in front of their face and close to the head, offering protection from oncoming blows. In the early Archaic, this avoidance may have been due to the technical difficulty of representing depth in this fashion. However, an accurate rendering of this form was achieved by at least the end of the sixth century BC, confirming the presence of modern defensive technique in the Greek boxing repertoire of the Late Archaic. A black figure amphora at the Musées Royaux d'Art et d'Histoire in Brussels (No. R336, dated 510–490 BC) includes a depiction of a bleeding boxer with his hands in guard position while his opponent thrusts a jab between them (Figure 37). The sophistication of the illustration is such that we can tell the blow has landed from the length and angle of the arm, despite the fact that the point of contact is occluded from the viewer by the raised arm of the stricken fighter.

Figure 37: Detail of a black-figure amphora depicting bleeding fighters, Musées Royaux d'Art et d'Histoire, Brussels (No. R336, dated 510–490 BC). The lead jab of the boxer on the left and the guard of the boxer on the right are remarkably modern.

6 Boxing history

For the first time in our study of pugilism in the ancient world, we can mention the *history* of boxing. "Greek history begins, traditionally, with athletics" (Osborne 2018, p. 53) and for some scholars, the division between history and pre-history is 776 BC, the date calculated for the first Olympic games. Accordingly, we might say that 688 BC, the year boxing was included in the Olympic games, represents the end of boxing's long pre-history.

The history of boxing, however, was not written contemporaneously. The facts, such as they could still be remembered, were not put down until much later (at least in the form we have them today). Same as it ever was, facts are influenced by the ideologies of the times in which they are recorded. For this reason, we leave our discussion of boxing's written history to a subsequent article on boxing in the Roman era (Dioscurus and Dioscurus 2023b), when the historians lived. For now, we can say that they attributed the rules of boxing to one Ono-mastus of Smyrna, himself an Olympic champion. According to Poliakoff (1987, p. 80), "No description of his system has come down to us." Speculation about Onomastus' rules can be found in the preceding pages of the present article. Miller (2004, pp. 21–23) goes so far as to argue that any lineal descent of athletic tradition is more hagiography than archæology; he leaves a slight caveat for boxing, which evidence cited in Dioscurus and Dioscurus (2022c) addresses. These rules were considered apt: τὸν δέ γε οἶμαι κατὰ τὴν πυκτικὴν πυκτικόν "And the rules of boxing, I suppose, make a good boxer?"[154] (Plato, *Alcibiades* 2:145d, tr. Lamb).

Olympic boxing was decidedly a combat between individuals. "One man won and everyone else lost. We hear of no one taking solace in being a runner-up" (Miller 2004, p. 19). Greek Olympic boxing saw its share of champions including the remarkable Theagenes, who won more than 1,300 fights in 22 years (equivalent to one competitive fight every two weeks during that period). The legendary Diagoras of Rhodes, victorious boxer in the Olympic, Isthmian, Nemean, and Pythian games, was celebrated not only for his own victories, but for those of his sons and grandsons. Other names of victors are preserved as well for posterity. Hearkening back to the funeral games of Patroclus, "The funeral games of Patroclus [and hence boxing] celebrate life in the face of death, but more than anything else they express a basic joy of living. As the individual athlete exerts himself physically, mentally, and emotionally in the competition, a statement is made: 'I am alive!'" (Miller 2004, p. 30).[155]

Olympic boxing matches took place inside the stadium in a *skamma*, or wrestling pit with softened earth to allow safer falls. Matchups were determined by casting lots, with no rounds and no time limits, although after a long bout opponents could agree to exchange blows.[156] Pictorial evidence (e.g. Figures 24 and 26) suggests that waiting boxers were allowed to prepare and watch ongoing bouts. Strikes on fallen opponents were forbidden.[157]

616 BC (the 41st Olympiad) serves as the *terminus ante quem* for stratification of competitive boxers into classes, albeit in terms of age rather than weight. At this time a boys' boxing event was included in the Olympic games. We can be all but certain that civilizations, including the Minoans, Egyptians, and Mesopotamians, segregated youth from adult boxing for practical reasons wherever youth boxing was permitted. Though conclusive evidence of children boxing occurs only on Thera (Dioscurus and Dioscurus 2022b), it is hard to imagine that boxing fathers did not teach their sons how to fight from an early age—or that those sons did not enthusiastically imitate their fathers.[158]

With the commencement of the historical record, we have for the first time contemporaneous narratives of specific bouts of note (rather than literary or procedural records). One of the most celebrated accounts is the fight between Coragus and Dioxippus before Alexander (Diodorus Siculus, *Bibliotheca Historica* 17:100–101). The contest takes place between Coragus as Macedonian soldier clad in armor and Dioxippus as Greek boxer carrying only a

---

[154] A bit tautological!

[155] Contrast the opprobrium of Demosthenes: τοὺς δὲ τὴν πυγμὴν καὶ τὰ τοιαῦτ' ἀσκήσαντας πρὸς τῷ σώματι καὶ τὴν γνώμην διαφθείρεσθαι, "those who practice boxing and the like ruin their minds as well as their bodies" (Demosthenes 61:24, tr. DeWitt and DeWitt).

[156] For example, the bout of Kreugas and Damoxenus, *q.v.*.

[157] We can imagine that techniques such as maneuvering an opponent into the blinding sunlight and exploiting terrain obstacles would have formed the valid "dirty tricks" of that age.

[158] Indeed, among the ranks of Olympic boxing champions we find the name of Diagoras of Rhodes and his three sons, all of whom were boxing and *pankration* champions. Pindar memorialized Diagoras' 464 BC victory in Olympia 7, ἄνδρα τε πὺξ ἀρετὰν εὑρόντα, "to the man who has found excellence as a boxer" (lit. πὺξ 'with the fist'). Consider also Chilon the Lacedaemonian, of whom Diogenes Laertius records that he died stricken of joy upon hearing that his son had gained the prize in boxing.

club. Dioxippus deftly overcomes Coragus by κινήσας ἐκ τῆς βάσεως τὸν ἀντίπαλον ὑπέσυρε τὰ σκέλη "upset[ting] the man's balance and [making] him lose his footing", surely aided by his boxing skills.[159]

Another instructive contest is the agon of Kreugas and Damoxenus. Pausanias (8:40, *ll.* 2–5, tr.) relates the story thus:

> The Argives too gave to Kreugas after his death the crown in the Nemean games, because his opponent Damoxenus of Syracuse broke their mutual agreement. For evening drew near as they [Kreugas of Epidamnus and Damoxenus of Syracuse] were boxing, and they agreed within the hearing of witnesses, that each should in turn allow the other to deal him a blow. At that time boxers did not yet wear a sharp thong on the wrist of each hand, but still boxed with the soft gloves, binding them in the hollow of the hand, so that their fingers might be left bare. These soft gloves were thin thongs of raw ox-hide plaited together after an ancient manner.
>
> On the occasion to which I refer Kreugas aimed his blow at the head of Damoxenus, and the latter bade Kreugas lift up his arm. On his doing so, Damoxenus with straight fingers struck his opponent under the ribs; and what with the sharpness of his nails and the force of the blow he drove his hand into the other's inside, caught his bowels, and tore them as he pulled them out.
>
> Kreugas expired on the spot, and the Argives expelled Damoxenus for breaking his agreement by dealing his opponent many [five, i.e., one per finger] blows instead of one.

The agreement merits a special convention. As Gardiner (1910, p. 432) has it, "when a fight had continued long without any result, the combatants sometimes agreed to exchange free hits without guarding." The tragicomic outcome of an open-handed strike being considered five blows is unlikely to bear heavily on what was actually considered conventional in boxing praxis, given the partisan nature of the bout's judges.

Internal evidence (the soft gloves) suggests that this contest took place during the Classical Greek period or possibly the early Hellenistic age. The transition between rule sets and the exchange of blows are suggestive of broader conventions between boxers whose bouts lasted overlong: "evening drew near".

Finally, as much of the history of the Olympic games took place and was recorded during the Hellenistic and Roman eras, we reserve much of our commentary on Olympic boxing for our discussion of that era (Dioscurus and Dioscurus 2023b). While a roster of known Olympic champions can be drawn up (and would stretch to late antiquity), we elide such a tabulation in favor of topical analysis on what certain incidents reveal to us of ancient boxing.

7 Conclusion

Ancient Greek boxing was never characterized by ropes, rounds, point systems, or even weight categories. The first formalized rule set appears to have been adopted in 688 BC, but we can-

---

[159] As described, the contest sounds more like armed *pankration* than boxing, and we include it more for Dioxippus' personal history as a boxer than for any insight it provides into pugilistic practice.

not be certain what it included. Despite the absence of many of the formalities we consider essential to boxing today, the epic poetry of Homer and a wealth of Greek art, particularly vase paintings, suggest a variety of normative behaviors, if not rules, integrated into the praxis. At some point, boxers may have fought in a loincloth, according to Homer, but visual depictions of this are rare; we will review counterexamples, largely Etruscan, in Dioscurus and Dioscurus (2023a). Boxers typically covered at least one hand with a kind of gauntlet but early vase paintings do not render these gauntlets in enough detail to discover whether they consist of the leather-strap *himantes* of the late Archaic and Classical eras. Adjutants are attested in Homer and can be descried among the figures who accompany boxers in art. Spectators, it seems, were always drawn to the fights. Prizes were awarded.

Later Greeks considered boxing, along with wrestling, a "hard" or "distressful" (ἀλεγεινός) competition, an adjective derived from ἄλγος 'pain'. Along with their Minoan predecessors, the Greeks, particularly those of the fifth and sixth centuries BC, were gripped by a passion that Juvenal might later have termed *insanabile cacoēthes pugillandī*. Enthusiastic embrace of the fight game characterized the Minoan and Greek civilizations for well over a thousand years. During that time, many fundamental characteristics of boxing appear to have changed but the core characteristics of orthograde personal combat remained.

References

G. Ahlberg-Cornell. Games, play and performance in Greek geometric art: the Kantharos Copenhagen NM 727 reconsidered. *Acta Archæologica*, 58:55–86, 1987.

Delabere P. Blaine. *Encyclopædia of Rural Sports.* Longman, Orme, Brown, Green and Longmans, London, 1840.

Oscar Broneer. The Isthmian Victory Crown. *American Journal of Archaeology*, 66:259–263, 1962.

Kyle S. Bunds, Joshua I. Newman, and Michael Giardina. Bum Fights: Dehumanizing the homeless for profit. *Communication Currents*, 11(1):1–2, 2016.

Walter Burkert. Kynaithos, Polycrates and the Homeric Hymn to Apollo. In G. W. Bowersock, W. Burkert, and M. C. J. Putnam, editors, *Arktouros: Hellenic studies presented to B. M. W. Knox*, pages 53–62. De Gruyter, Berlin, 1979.

Walter Burkert. *Homo Necans: The Anthropology of Ancient Greek Sacrificial Ritual and Myth.* University of California Press, Berkeley, CA, 1983. Trans. by Peter Bing.

Michele Cammarosano. Rejoicing in the gods: the Verb *dušk-* and Hittite cheese fighting. In Piotr Taracha, editor, *Proceedings of the Eighth International Congress of Hittitology*, pages 138–170. Wydawnictwo Agade, Warsaw, 2014.

Michele Cammarosano. *Hittite Local Cults.* Society of Biblical Literature, Atlanta, GA, 2018.

Samir Chadli, Noureddine Ababou, Amina Ababou, and Nazim Ouadahi. Quantification of boxing gloves damping: Method and apparatus. *Measurement*, 129:504–517, 2018. doi: https://doi.org/10.1016/j.measurement.2018.07.036.

Peter J. Connor. 'Boxing on' a Lucanian red-figured skyphos in the University of Melbourne. *Mediterranean Archæology*, 8:101–105, 1995.

Eileen H. Corrigan. *Lucanian Tomb Paintings Excavated at Pæstum 1969–1972: An Iconogrpahic Study*. PhD thesis, Columbia University, 1979.

J. H. Crouwel and C. E. Morris. The Minoan amphoroid krater: From production to consumption. *The Annual of the British School at Athens*, 110:147–201, 2015.

M. P. Cuypers. *Apollonius Rhodius Argonautica 2.1-310: a commentary*. PhD thesis, Leiden, 1997.

Matteo D'Acunto. Dance in Attic and Argive Geometric pottery: Figurative imagery and ritual contexts. In Giulio Colesanti and Laura Lulli, editors, *Submerged Literature in Ancient Greek Culture*, volume 2, pages 205–242. De Gruyter, Berlin, 2016.

Oliver Dickinson. *The Ægean from Bronze Age to Iron Age: Continuity and change between the twelfth and eighth centuries* BC. Routledge, New York, 2006.

Oliver Dickinson. The irrelevance of Greek 'tradition'. In Guy D. Middleton, editor, *Collapse and Transformation: The Late Bronze Age to Early Iron Age in the Ægean*, pages 153–159. Oxbow Books, Oxford, 2020.

B. C. Dietrich. Some evidence from Cyprus of Apolline cult in the Bronze Age. *Rheinisches Museum für Philologie*, 121(1):1–18, 1978. Neue Folge.

Castor Dioscurus and Pollux Dioscurus. The development of boxing: Origins in biomechanics and social mechanics; The ancient world (Prehistory). *Scholia Pugillātōria*, 1: 1–22, 2022a.

Castor Dioscurus and Pollux Dioscurus. The development of boxing: The ancient world (Western Asia and Egypt). *Scholia Pugillātōria*, 1:23–71, 2022b.

Castor Dioscurus and Pollux Dioscurus. The development of boxing: The ancient world (The Ægean). *Scholia Pugillātōria*, 1:73–111, 2022c.

Castor Dioscurus and Pollux Dioscurus. The development of boxing: The ancient world (The Eastern Alps, Pre-Roman Italia, and Sardinia). *Scholia Pugillātōria*, 1:191–247, 2023a.

Castor Dioscurus and Pollux Dioscurus. The development of boxing: The ancient world (The Hellenistic world and Rome). *Scholia Pugillātōria*, 1:249–375, 2023b.

Robert Fagles. *The Iliad, Homer*. Penguin, New York, 1990.

Robert Fagles. *The Odyssey, Homer*. Penguin, New York, 1996.

Paul Feyerabend. *Against Method*. Verso, London, 4th edition, 2010.

Moses I. Finley. *Economy and Society in Ancient Greece*. Viking Press, New York, 1982. B. D. Shaw and R. P. Saller, editors.

Hjalmar Frisk. *Griechisches Etymologisches Wörterbuch*. Carl Winter Universitätsverlag, Heidelberg, 1954–1972. 3 vols.

K. T. Frost. Greek boxing. *The Journal of Hellenic Studies*, 26:213–225, 1906.

Anastasia Gadolou. Narrative art and ritual in the Sanctuary of Poseidon Heliconius in ancient Helike, Achæa. In Vicky Vlachou, editor, *Pots, Workshops and Early Iron Age Society: Function and Role of Ceramics in Early Greece*, volume 8 of *Études d'Archéologie*, pages 267–276. Centre de Recherches en Archéologie et Patrimoine, Brussels, 2015. Proceedings of the International Symposium held at the Université libre de Bruxelles 14–16 November 2013.

E. Norman Gardiner. *Greek Athletic Sports and Festivals*. Macmillan and Co., London, 1910.

Basil L. Gildersleeve. *Pindar: The Olympian and Pythian Odes*. Harper's Classical Series for Schools and Colleges. American Book Company, New York, 1885.

A. D. Godley. *Herodotus*, volume 5 of *Loeb Classical Library*. Harvard University Press, Cambridge, MA, 1920.

Cyrus H. Gordon. Belt-wrestling in the Bible world. *Hebrew Union College Annual*, 23(1): 131–136, 1950–1951.

Fritz Graf. *Apollo*. Gods and Heroes of the Ancient World. Routledge, London, 2009.

Peter Green. *Apollonios Rhodios, Argonautika*. University of California Press, Berkeley, CA, 2007. Expanded edition.

Edwin L. Haislett. *Boxing*. The Ronald Press Company, New York, 1940.

Roland Hampe. *Frühe griechische Sagenbilder in Böotien*. Deutsches archäologisches Institut, Athens, 1936.

P. Hardie. *The Epic Successors of Virgil: Studies in the dynamics of a tradition*. Cambridge University Press, Cambridge, 1993.

Sinclair Hood. *The Arts in Prehistoric Greece*. The Pelican History of Art. Penguin Books, New York, 1978.

Jozef Jaroš. *Apollonius Rhodius, Argonautica*. B. Ryba, Prague, 1924.

Richard E. Jones. *Greek and Cypriot pottery: A review of scientific studies*, volume 1 of *Fitch Laboratory Occasional Paper*. British School at Athens, Athens, 1986.

G. S. Kirk. *The Iliad: A Commentary*, volume 2. Cambridge University Press, Cambridge, 1990.

Nota Kourou. Early Iron Age mortuary contexts in the Cyclades: Pots, functions and symbolism. In Vicky Vlachou, editor, *Pots, Workshops and Early Iron Age Society: Function and Role of Ceramics in Early Greece*, volume 8 of *Études d'Archéologie*, pages 83–105. Centre de Recherches en Archéologie et Patrimoine, Brussels, 2015. Proceedings of the International Symposium held at the Université libre de Bruxelles 14–16 November 2013.

Susan Helen Langdon. *Art and Identity in Dark Age Greece, 1100–700 B. C. E.* Cambridge University Press, Cambridge, 2008.

Matthew Leigh. Boxing and sacrifice: Apollonius, Vergil, and Valerius. *Harvard Studies in Classical Philology*, 105:117–155, 2010.

Christofilis Magiddis. Glas and Bœotia. In Guy D. Middleton, editor, *Collapse and Transformation: The Late Bronze Age to Early Iron Age in the Ægean*, pages 107–120. Oxbow Books, Oxford, 2020.

Alexandre Marcinkowski. Sanctuaire et culte d'Apollon Lykeios à Argos: un état de la question. In Alain Bouet, editor, *D'Orient et d'Occident: Melanges offerts à Pierre Aupert.* Ausonius, Bourdeaux, 2008.

Christopher Mee. Mycenæan Greece, the Ægean and beyond. In Cynthia W. Shelmerdine, editor, *The Cambridge Companion to the Ægean Bronze Age*, pages 362–386. 2008.

Manolis Mikrakis. Pots, early Iron Age Athenian society and the Near East: The evidence of the Rattle Group. In *Pots, Workshops and Early Iron Age Society: Function and Role of Ceramics in Early Greece*, volume 8 of *Études d'Archéologie*, pages 277–289. Centre de Recherches en Archéologie et Patrimoine, Brussels, 2015. Proceedings of the International Symposium held at the Université libre de Bruxelles 14–16 November 2013.

Stephen G. Miller. *Ancient Greek Athletics.* Yale University Press, New Haven, CT, 2004.

Ian Morris. Homer and the Iron Age. In Ian Morris and Barry Powell, editors, *A New Companion to Homer*, pages 535–559. Brill, Leiden, 1997.

Tobias Mühlenbruch. The Argolid. In Guy D. Middleton, editor, *Collapse and Transformation: The Late Bronze Age to Early Iron Age in the Ægean*, pages 121–135. Oxbow Books, Oxford, 2020.

A. T. Murray. *The Odyssey of Homer.* Harvard University Press, Cambridge, MA, 1919. 2 vols.

A. T. Murray. *The Iliad of Homer.* Harvard University Press, Cambridge, MA, 1924. 2 vols.

Damien Nelis. *Vergil's Æneid and the Argonautica of Apollonius Rhodius*, volume 39 of *ARCA Classical and Medieval Texts, Papers, and Monographs.* Francis Cairns, Cambridge, 2001.

Charles Nordmann. Revue scientifique: A propos de boxe. *Revue des Deux Mondes*, 64(2): 452–462, 1921.

Robin Osborne. *The Transformation of Athens: Painted Pottery and the Creation of Classical Greece.* Princeton University Press, Princeton, NJ, 2018.

Robin Osborne. Collapse and transformation in Athens and Attica. In Guy D. Middleton, editor, *Collapse and Transformation: The Late Bronze Age to Early Iron Age in the Ægean*, pages 137–144. Oxbow Books, Oxford, 2020.

Thomas G. Palaima. Mycenæan religion. In Cynthia W. Shelmerdine, editor, *The Cambridge Companion to the Ægean Bronze Age*, pages 342–361. 2008.

Michael Baron Poliakoff. *Combat Sports in the Ancient World*. Yale University Press, New Haven, CT, 1987.

Jaan Puhvel. Hittite athletics as prefigurations of Ancient Greek games. In Wendy J. Raschke, editor, *The Archaeology of the Olympics: The Olympics and other festivals in Antiquity*, pages 26–31. University of Wisconsin Press, Madison, WI, 1988.

Heather L. Reid. Philostratus's 'Gymnasticus': The ethics of an athletic æsthetic. *Memoirs of the American Academy in Rome*, 61:77–90, 2016.

George Rethemiotakis. *Minoan Clay Figures and Figurines: From the Neopalatial to the Subminoan Period*. Number 219 in Archaeological Society at Athens Library. The Archaeological Society at Athens, Athens, 2001. Trans. by A. Doumas.

Gisela Marie Augusta Richter. *The Portraits of the Greeks*. Phaidon Press, London, 1965.

Ian Rutherford. *Hittite Texts and Greek Religion: Contact, interaction, and comparison*. Oxford University Press, Oxford, 2020.

Thomas Francis Scanlon. Class tensions in the games of Homer: Epeius, Euryalus, Odysseus, and Iros. *Bulletin of the Institute of Classical Studies*, 61:5–20, 2018.

Wolfgang Schadewaldt. *Von Homers Welt und Werk*. K. F. Koehler, Stuttgart, 1951. 2nd Ed.

Claude F.-A. Schaeffer-Forrer. *Corpus des Cylindres-Sceaux de Ras Shamra-Ugarit et d'Enkomi-Alasia*. Éditions Recherche sur les civilisations, Paris, 1983.

Moritz Schmidt. *Hesychii Alexandrini Lexicon*. Libraria Maukiana. Sumptibus Hermanni Dufftii, Jena, 1867.

Robert Cooper Seaton. *Rhodius Apollonius, Argonautica*. Heinemann, London, 1912.

Alexander Sens. *Theocritus, Dioscuri (Idyll 22): Introduction, Text, and Commentary*, volume 114 of *Hypomnemata*. Vandenhoeck & Ruprecht, Göttingen, 1997.

E. S. Sherratt. Regional variation in the pottery of Late Helladic IIIB. 75:175–202, 1980.

B. Snell. *The Discovery of the Mind*. Harper Torchbooks, New York, 1960.

Michael Stahl. Subversion gone wrong: Inside 'Bumfights'. *Rolling Stone*, 2018. October 2. https://www.rollingstone.com/culture/culture-features/bumfights-homeless-men-fight-activists-730393/.

Diane Arnson Svarlien. *The Odes of Pindar*. Yale University Press, 1991. In Perseus Project 1.0 `perseus.tufts.edu`.

W. E. Sweet. *Sport and Recreation in Ancient Greece: A Sourcebook with Translations*. Oxford University Press, New York and Oxford, 1987.

Karl A. Taube and Marc Zender. American gladiators: Ritual boxing in ancient Mesoamerica. In Heather Orr and Rex Koontz, editors, *Blood and Beauty: Organized Violence in the Art and Archaeology of Mesoamerica and Central America*, pages 161–220. Cotsen Institute of Archaeology Press, Los Angeles, CA, 2009.

Beatrice Teissier. *Ancient Near Eastern Cylinder Seals from the Marcopoli Collection*. University of California Press, Berkeley, 1984.

J. C. Thomas. *Boxing's Dirty Tricks and Outlaw Killer Punches*. Loompanics Unlimited, Port Townsend, WA, 1997.

Gail D. Thompson. *A comparative study of Near Eastern and Ægean glyptic art, 2000–1400 BC: Combat, hunt, chariot, boar, goat, bird, and bull scenes*. PhD thesis, State University of New York at Buffalo, 2013.

V. A. Trifonov, N. I. Shishlina, A. Y. Loboda, and V. A. Khvostikov. The flesh-hook featuring a scene of fist fighting from a Maikop culture dolmen near the village of Tsarskaya in the northwest caucasus. *Kratkiye Soobshcheniya Instituta Arkheologii*, (251):25–42, 2021.

Máximo Cama Ttito and Alejandra Ttito Tica. Peleas rituales: la waylía takanakuy en Santo Tomás. *Anthropologica*, 17:151–185, 1999.

H. Van Wees. *Status Warriors: War, Violence and Society in Homer and History*. Gieben, Amsterdam, 1992.

Herman L. J. Vanstiphout. The Marriage of Martu, 1998. Unpublished manuscript.

Emily Vermeule and Vassos Karageorghis. *Mycenaean Pictorial Vase Painting*. Harvard University Press, Cambridge, MA, 1982.

Charles Waldstein. *The Argive Heræum*, volume 2. Houghton Mifflin, Boston, 1902.

James Whitley. Agency, personhood and the belly-handled amphora: Exchange and society in the ninth century Ægean. In Vicky Vlachou, editor, *Pots, Workshops and Early Iron Age Society: Function and Role of Ceramics in Early Greece*, volume 8 of *Études d'Archéologie*, pages 107–126. Centre de Recherches en Archéologie et Patrimoine, Brussels, 2015. Proceedings of the International Symposium held at the Université libre de Bruxelles 14–16 November 2013.

Karol Zieliński. Odysseus—trickster and the issue of the compatibility of the image of the hero with its function in the traditions of the oral epic. *Studia Religiologica*, 53(3):187–208, 2020.

Changelog

- ~2022.9.16 Preprint release.
- ~2022.10.13 Preprint release, more on Olympic boxing.
- ~2022.10.25 First public release.

- ~2022.11.15 Note on Theocritus' *Idyll* 22.47.
- ~2022.11.20 Notes on the Phæacian games, Epeius, and Iros.
- ~2022.11.27 Note on ἀμσίβων / ἀμείβων.
- ~2023.6.17 Expansion on Pausanias; footnote on stephanitic games; explanation of Olympic games in Dioscurus and Dioscurus (2023b).
- ~2023.6.24 Minor proofreading edits.
- ~2023.7.8 Repagination in anticipation of printing.
- ~2023.9.29 Minor proofreading edits.

The Development of Boxing: The Ancient World (The Eastern Alps, Pre-Roman Italia, and Sardinia)

Castor Dioscurus; Pollux Dioscurus

Contents

Abstract

Long before Roman rule, boxing in Italy, the Eastern Alps, and Sardinia had a particularly sanguinary character. The visual culture of Etruscan, Celtic, and Hallstatt artifacts depicts unique local developments in the sweet science. For instance, the Etruscan funeral cult embraced boxing to the death to the accompaniment of music, a strong association unseen since the days of the Hittites. Ultimately, this field of boxing points to the Hellenistic and Roman unification of pre-Roman Italic *pygmachia* into uniquely violent manifestations as Greek influence in Italy grew.

1   Introduction

Italy proved fertile ground for the dissemination and hybridization of boxing as practiced by the Greeks. Diverse forms of orthograde combat sport almost certainly predated Hellenic colonization of the Appenine Peninsula, with possible influences from the Phœnicians and Minoans. Unfortunately, boxing in the Roman world has generally been dismissed as a degradation of Greek athleticism. We approach the problem differently, recalling the brutal aspects of boxing that existed long before the ascent of Rome, including in Italy. In the absence of extensive written records about boxing in this region of the world, the visual culture shows forth an abundance of boxing genius.[1]

---

[1] We recollect to your mind the genesis of *genius* as the Greek spirit of place.

Scholia Pugillātōria 1 (2023): 193–249.

Address author correspondence to `scholia@protonmail.com`.

2   Eastern Alps

Toreutic[2] representations of stylistically similar boxers are found on more than a dozen objects, primarily bronze situlæ,[3] distributed in a region from Vienna to Bologna and from the Austrian Tyrol to Lower Carniola in southeastern Slovenia (Figure 1). There is no suitable modern geographic descriptor for this area: Bologna is not Alpine and Vienna is not Adriatic. Nor do ethnic terms provide a clear delimiter: The relevant situlæ were discovered at Iron age sites associated with the Etruscans (Bologna), Veneti (Este, Kobarid), Celts (Fließ, Sanzeno, Mechel), partakers of the Hallstatt culture[4] (Kuffarn, Kleinklein), and Illyrians (Vače, Magdalenska Gora, Dolenjske Toplice). Even ancient regional names provide no more clarity: The Romans called the sites of situla deposition Noricum, Rhætia, Pannonia, Illyricum, Venetia, and Cisalpine Gaul. A circle drawn around these sites has its center approximately at the three-way border of modern Italy, Slovenia, and Austria in the Julian Alps. Recognizing that that toreutic boxers were widely disseminated, if not rendered, in a large and ethnically diverse region, we call this section 'Eastern Alps' and will occasionally characterize the situla boxers as 'Alpine'.[5]

Though it is sometimes claimed that situla art was an Etruscan export to this region,[6] the quantity and distribution of evidence may suggest the opposite: the Etruscans were introduced to East Alpine art and the autochthonous cultural conventions that it depicted. Based on the deposition of toreutic artifacts, the situlæ most likely originated in the Eastern Alps. When some of the decorated situlæ became burial goods of the Etruscan elite (e.g., the Certosa and Benvenuti Situlæ), these had presumably been preserved in Etruria as exotic treasures from the northeast.

Boxers are among the most common figural motifs found in situla art (Frelih 1989, p. 104). One particulalry well-known example comes from the Vače Situla (National Museum of Slovenia, No. P-581, Figure 11). According to Frelih, the poses of the situla boxers, along with the presence of a prize tripod in at least one exemplar (the Matrei Situla, Tyrolean State Museum, No. 2274, Figure 5), "offer concrete proof that the early toreutic workshops ... were inspired by Greek templates" (1989, p. 105, translation ours). However, there is reason to be skeptical of a direct connection between the form of boxing represented in situla art and Greek *pygmachia*. The most notable difference is that the boxers on the situlæ hold objects

---

[2] Toreutic art uses embossing and chasing in metal to form fine details in relief.

[3] A situla is essentially an elaborate bucket or pail, usually equipped with a handle on top and sometimes a lid.

[4] Participants in the Hallstatte culture were probably Celtic-speaking; they spread across western and central Europe during the Iron Age.

[5] If we remove the outlying Kuffarn situla, the geographic center of the situlæ's distribution is perhaps at Trieste (where no situlæ have been found). We are unsatisfied with the assertion (Poliakoff 1987a, pp. 75–76) that the toreutic boxers are "Illyrian," since perhaps only four relevant artifacts (three situlæ and one belt buckle) were deposited in the region of ancient Illyria, though they do, admittedly, form a tight cluster there. Elsewhere, the objects are described as "Veneto–Illyrian" (Merhart 1932), but this excludes Celtic and Etruscan influence. We believe that reluctance by some scholars to characterize the toreutic situla art as "Alpine" stems from their hesitance to associate these objects with Iron Age Celtic culture(s)—well outside the influence of Etruria, not to mention Greece. Some confidently assert that the artifacts are Hallstattian, referring to the (probably) Eastern Celtic culture of the Iron Age, linked to the town of Halstatt in Upper Austria (Egg 1980, Lazar 2011). Frelih (1989, p. 104) argues that the depictions of boxers were produced by the Este (sometimes called Paleo-Venetic) culture, under influence from Greek colonizers of the Appenine peninsula.

[6] "[I]t should be possible to find in Etruria alone, motifs which could explain the origin of situla art in its particular form" (Mansuelli 1965, p. xxix).

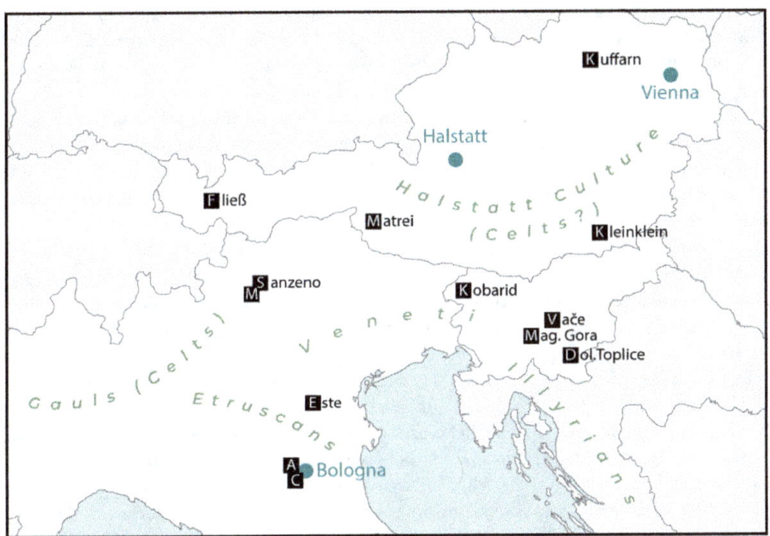

Figure 1: Map showing Iron Age sites where visual representations of boxers (primarily tore-utic decoration on situlæ) have been found in Italy, Austria, and Slovenia. Occupation by various Iron Age cultures is indicated along with modern political boundaries. M = Mechel; A = Necropoli Arnoaldi; C = Necropoli della Certosa. Fließ and Landeck appear only as "Fließ". The map does not include Rome, though two (most likely imported and/or copied) artifacts depicting Alpine boxers were found there.

shaped like dumbbells, which they appear to wield against one another as fist-load weapons[7] capable of inflicting serious injury in a single blow.

The distal ends of these dumbbell-shaped objects are rounded, if not spherical. It seems likely that a bar extends between the ends and that the fingers are wrapped around it with the thumb projecting (Figure 11, *inter alia*).[8] In other depictions, it appears that a strap runs across the knuckles (e.g., in the Kuffarn Situla, Natural History Museum Vienna, No. 17036, Figure 8). Because none of these dumbbell-shaped objects have been recovered "in archæological contexts," it has been assumed by many that they "must have been made of organic material such as wood or leather" and thus, by now they have decomposed completely (Rebay-Salisbury 2012, p. 190). English-speaking scholars seem to have settled on the term 'dumbbell' to denominate the object. The (plural) *hanteln* is used in German; in Slovenian, *ročke*; in Italian, *manubri*.[9] One author calls them *venetisch Cæstus* 'Venetian cæstus' (Merhart 1932, p. 61, fn. 1). The aim of the fight may have been to knock the dumbbell out of an opponent's hand, as suggested by the Arnoaldi Situla (Figure 10), in which the fighter on the right may have dropped one of his *hanteln* (Rebay-Salisbury 2012, p. 191). Egg (1980, p. 55) refers to the dumbbell as *Faustschutz* 'fist guard', under the hypothesis that the objects were not offensive weapons but merely protection for the hands. It seems unlikely that these objects were suitable for protection, however, since they cover almost none of the hand.

We concur with others who regard the dumbbells as relatively heavy weapons that the boxers used to strike each other in earnest (Thuillier 1985, Lazar 2011). In our opinion, the *hanteln* were sacrificial implements that added heft to the fists; they would have been particularly effective at smashing the skull of one's opponent and spattering his brains. In the words of one scholar, the weapons were "terrifying and murderous" *terrifiantes et meurtrières* (Thuillier 1985, p. 265). Others will doubtless disagree with our interpretation, but we find little evidence to support the counterclaim that the dumbbells were illæsive.[10] Lucke and Frey (1962, p. 27), for example, refuse to see in the dumbbells a deadly weapon. For an unacknowledged reason, they dismiss this possibility as a "thoroughly barbaric affair" (*eine durchaus barbarische Angelegenheit*). They argue that the dumbbells are "nothing more than protection for the hands and at the same time protection from excessive injuries, just like our modern boxing gloves."[11] No rationale is given for this conclusion, however, other than the alternative seems too "barbaric" a competition.[12] They suggest that the objects must be made of leather or cloth rather than bronze because of the strap that can be seen across the back of the hand in some depictions (e.g., the Matrei Situla, Figure 5). This, we are assured, could not be made of bronze (ibid.).[13] They offer the interesting hypothesis that the dumbbells were

---

[7] An example of another such weapon, highly similar in form to the dumbbell of the Iron Age Alps, is the Japanese *yawara*.

[8] We have considered and do not decisively reject a hypothesis that the dumbbell is a doubly-knotted rope, which would stabilize the fist and be slightly more dangerous than a gloved fist. We prefer another interpretation of the visual evidence, however, due to corroborative cultural predilections discussed below.

[9] The term *manopla*, which has the sense of 'knuckle-duster', is used sometimes used in reference to Mayan boxing (Taube and Zender 2009, Taube 2018).

[10] Gardiner (1930, p. 121) writes, "[I]t is hard to conceive any people inventing a weapon so clumsy and so inappropriate for boxing." This claim is weakened if one consideres that the East Alpine boxers fought for their lives.

[11] *Die hantelförmigen Gegenstände sind nichts anderes als ein Schutz für die Hände und zugleich Schutz vor zu harten Verletzungen genau wie unsere heutigen Boxhandschuhe* (Lucke and Frey 1962, p. 27)

[12] We note that it is relatively easy to convince scholars that similar objects wielded in boxing matches were indeed meant to maim and kill—as long as the evidence comes from the New World (Taube and Zender 2009).

[13] *... man sich diese kaum in Bronze vorstellen kann.*

used to force the fighters to make a fist: the open hand seen in Greek depictions would be impossible if the phalanges were curled around the dumbbell throughout the fight.[14] According to the authors, this would have resulted in "a more subtle, agile arm technique" (ibid.).[15] While we are not convinced that the dumbbells would add much in terms of subtlety or agility, we agree that holding the dumbbells likely prevented the fighters from relaxing their clenched fists. Along with the belt, which by their interpretation served as a boundary for low punches,[16] and the wrist straps, which provided some support and protection to the boxer's wrists, Lucke and Frey (1962) claim the 'hand protectors' must have ensured that Alpine boxing never devolved into "barbaric brawls" (*barbarische Schlagerei*), though admittedly less skillful than a modern boxing match. We argue the contrary: the *hanteln* matches were arranged to leave one man dead and the other, perhaps, gravely injured.

While the dumbbells themselves are not described in any literary account, the dashing of skulls is a common leitmotif in Latin epic boxing matches, including the ones recounted in the *Æneid*, the Valerian *Argonautica*, and Book 6 of the *Thebaid* (Dioscurus and Dioscurus 2023). We believe that dumbbell boxing spread south from the Eastern Alps by way of the Etruscans, who were evidently interested in boxing as a form of ritual killing (Section 3). While the dumbbells were probably known to the Romans only as an archaic device (e.g., in the Corsini Chair, found at Rome), their capacity for mayhem in the boxing 'ring' of the Alps was remembered and eventually transduced into the cruel *cæstus* described hundreds of years later by the poets Vergil, Valerius, and Statius. It is easy to see shadows of the *hanteln* in the hammer-like *cæstus* featured in all these narratives.

We have found reference to eighteen situlæ or sheet bronze fragments, five relief figurines, and one clay relief fragment depicting boxers of the East Alpine variety.[17] We will discuss each of these items briefly before comparing features relevant to the scenes of pugilism. The eighteen toreutic pieces, their provenance, and their approximate dates of production (when available) are listed here:

- Kleinklein Schmiedkogel Vessel (Austria): 700–600 BC
- Kleinklein Kröllkogel Vessel (Austria):
- Certosa Situla (Bologna): 600–550 BC
- Matrei Situla (Austria) 600–500 BC
- Magdalenska Gora Belt plate (Slovenia): 600–400 BC
- Benvenuti/Este Situla (Este): ca. 600 BC
- Kuffarn Situla (Austria): 550 BC
- Providence Situla (Bologna): 530–525 BC

---

[14] Modern boxing gloves, made of molded open cellular polyurethane foam covered by a bit of leather, achieve a similar effect, by forcing the fingers to remain curled slightly at all times, though not necessarily balled into a tight fist.

[15] *... eine bewegtere, fintenreichere Armtechnik.*

[16] Thuillier (1985, pp. 380–381) muses on the possibility that a cord—tied to the belt on one end and the foreskin on the other—was used to infibulate the fighters.

[17] Poliakoff (1987a, p. 75) states that "Horseshoe shaped gloves show up at least eighteen times in Illyrian and Italic art" between 700 and 300 BC. He evidently refers here to the dumbbells, since he exemplifies his claim with detail from a fourth-century Roman/Etruscan sarcophagus lid (Figure 36) and the fifth-century Matrei Situla (Figure 5), both of which clearly show fighters using the *hanteln*. In his estimate, Poliakoff almost certainly includes the sarcophagus lid as well as the well-known Corsini Throne (Figure 35), which we exclude from our count and present as Etruscan artifacts in Section 3.

- Arnoaldi Situla (Bologna): 500–400 BC
- Vače Situla (Slovenia): 500–400 BC
- Kobarid Situla (Slovenia): 500–400 BC
- Magdalenska Gora Situla (Slovenia): ca. 500 BC
- Magdalenska Gora lid (Slovenia): 500–400 BC
- Dolenjske Toplice (Slovenia)
- Sheet bronze fragments (Santuario Orientale, Este)
- Sheet bronze fragments (Fließ, Austria)
- Mechel Situla (Italy)
- Sanzeno Situla (Italy)

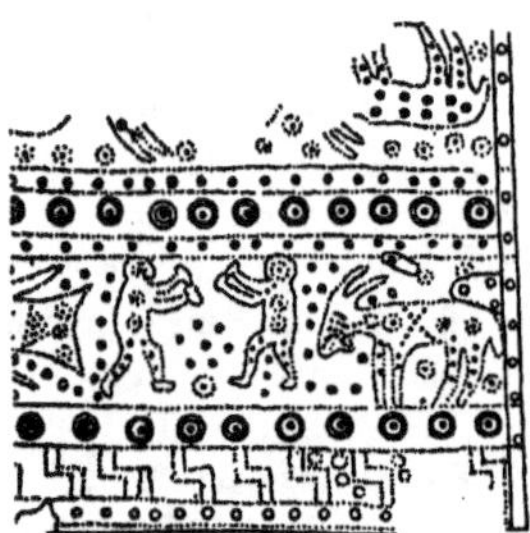

Figure 2: Detail from a seventh-century vessel found in the Schmiedkogel at Kleinklein and described by Schmid (1933) (museum unspecified, No. 1998). The decoration includes images of boxers wielding the *hanteln*.

Hanteln are implied even in the "primitive" boxers visible on two early, point-bossed cistæ (Ger. *zister*) found at Kleinklein in lower Austria (Frey 1969, p. 68). In the example found at Schmiedkogel (Ziste VIII), the fists are widened unnaturally at the knuckles, suggestive of the dumbbells (Figure 2). Both objects are wielded at the opponent simultaneously, as in the Benvenuti Situla (Figure 7). This is the earliest known image of dumbbell boxing, dated to the seventh century BC. The object is described in greater detail by Frey (1999). On another exemplar of a point-bossed vessel discovered in the nearby Kröllkogel, the boxers do not appear to use the *hanteln* (Figure 3).

The toreutic art on the Certosa Situla (Museo Civico, Bologna, no inventory number; Figure 4) arguably represents a funeral ceremony with individual scenes from everyday life. In the panel of interest, two musicians are seated on an elaborate couch with armrests in the shape of vorant beasts: one consumes a hare and the other, a person. Atop each armrest a boxer swings one fist forward at his adversary on the opposing side. The elaborate couch has at least one literary/archæological model, suggesting that the diminutive boxers are intended to represent statuary that adorn the furniture (Bonfante 2011). Frelih (1989, p. 110), who seems most puzzled by the fact that boxers are separated from one another,[18] proposes

---

[18] Frelih (1989, p. 110) notes the boxers' vigorous posture (*razgibani telesni drž*).

Figure 3: Detail from a seventh-century (?) vessel found in the Kröllkogel at Kleinklein and described in Schmid (1933) (museum unspecified, No. 10711). The boxers do not appear to hold anything in their hands.

that the they are included on the situla as mere ornament and not as integral parts of the scene. The composition, Frelih reasons, did not provide enough space to include the standard toreutic boxing scene and so the artist simply crammed them in where he could—a rather elaborate, and in our estimation improbable, example of *horror vacui*.

The boxers on the Certosa Situla have been misjudged as boys tossing items into the bucket that floats above the center of the panel (Lucke and Frey 1962, p. 28). While the tableau is certainly an odd one, most scholars have no trouble believing that the figures represent boxers, given the prevalence of similar figures in East Alpine situla art. The Certosa fighters wear the Alpine boxing belt observed in other toreutic representations. Moreover, the position of their legs and arms is consistent with the posture necessary to throw a punch, though they pitch forward at the waist in a manner distinct from that of the boxers on other situlæ. It is difficult to discern whether the Certosa boxers use the *hanteln*, however.

The boxers on the Matrei Situla (Tyrolean State Museum, No. 2274; Figure 5) adhere more closely to the common template for a scene of Alpine pugilism. They are nude but for a belt and one armband. They clutch the dumbbells, one of which appears to have a strap crossing the knuckles. The fighter on the left has a prominently extended thumb. In the 'prize position' known from much older Near Eastern models (Dioscurus and Dioscurus 2022b) stand a horned helmet with a plume and a spear.[19] A circular ornament occupies the space between the waist of the fighter on the right and the helmet prize. The boxers' genitals are in full view—a feature that has received some comment (see below).

A unique belt plate depicting toreutic boxers (Natural History Museum Vienna, No. 22962; Figure 6) was discovered at Magdalenska Gora, Slovenia, in 1893 (Frelih 1989, p. 99). In the upper left-hand corner of the plate an aquatic bird (Cro. *barske ptice*, lit., 'pond bird') holds a writhing serpent in its mouth. According to Stipčević (1981, pp. 23–29), the bird was a well-known symbol of the sun god throughout Illyria. He supposes that the confrontation between the bird and the serpent is a recapitulation of the contest between celestial and infernal forces, as in the fight between Apollo and Python in Greek myth. Frelih (1989, p. 99) claims that the motif is 'exceptional' (*izjemen*) and argues that the fight between the 'eagle' and snake symbolizes the eternal struggle between light and darkness, good and evil (p. 100).

---

[19] Thuillier (1985, p. 206) has argued that the spear may serve as a demarcation of the boxing ring, citing similar lances found on the Corsini Throne (see Section 3).

Figure 4: Detail of the Certosa Situla with boxers standing on the theriomorphic armrests of an elaborate couch. Museo Civico, Bologna (no inventory number), 600–550 BC.

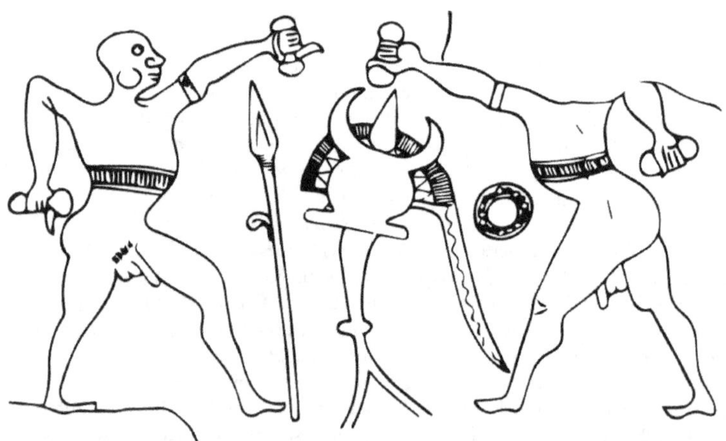

Figure 5: Detail from the sixth-century Matrei Situla, Tyrolean State Museum (No. 2274).

The agonism of bird and snake is complemented by that of the two naked boxers to the right. They clearly hold *ročke* and swing dynamically at one another, their back legs bent in a stance associated with body blows. Nevertheless, they seem to direct the dumbbells at each other's heads.

Figure 6: The Magdalenska Gora *Gürtelblech* 'belt plate', depicting dumbbell-wielding boxers (Natural History Museum Vienna, No. 22962). The object is dated 700–600 BC.

Figure 7: Detail from the Benvenuti Situla, Museo Nazionale Atestino, No. 6182, ca. 600 BC.

The scenes limned on the Benvenuti Situla (Museo Nazionale Atestino, No. 6182; Figure 7) are heavily orientalizing, with fantastical creatures like griffins and sphinges—one striding directly towards the boxers from the right (Frelih 1989, p. 109). Because the boxing match appears to lack a trophy, Frelih argues that is derived from "some proposal [*predlog*] not directly influenced by the Greek variant" (ibid., translation ours). According to him, boxing in the Eastern Alps must have had several origins, going so far as to suggest that it first reached the Appenine Peninsula by way of Phœnician traders.

The Kuffarn Situla, found in Austria, contains a depiction of two naked boxers who also wield *hanteln* (Natural History Museum Vienna, No. 17036, Figure 8). Figures, perhaps referees, stand on the right and left, bearing forked rods. A plumed helmet appears between the adversaries, on a stand. The form of the boxers is particularly supple, emphasizing their swollen calf muscles. The boxers are bald.

Figure 8: Detail from the Kuffarn Situla, Natural History Museum Vienna (No. 17036).

While some critics characterize the Providence Situla (Rhode Island School of Design #32.245; Figure 9) as an Etruscan artifact, its boxing scene is highly similar to those found on other East Alpine situlæ. The object is dated between 530 and 525 BC. It was found in Bologna and, according to its curators, it is "said to be from Certosa Necropolis," an Etruscan site. The situla bears an inscription about its rim in the Rhætic language, recently argued to be a close relative of Etruscan (Schürr 2003).[20] Another proposal is that the inscription is in fact Etruscan. Translated from that language, the inscription *irχie śiati kaianin mvlvainice* reads, "This was given to Irchi by Kaian" (Olzscha 1962, pp. 85–86). The boxers on the Providence Situla wield the familiar *hanteln* and wear a belt and armband but are otherwise naked. They stand above neatly-folded robes, topped by their hats. Onlookers in cloaks and hats appear to bear no special mark of their office. In the 'prize position' we find a ceremonial vessel on an elaborate stand with avian heads. A curious bird perches on the bowl to refresh itself and take in the action.

According to Huth (2003), the Arnoaldi Situla (Archæological Museum of Bologna, no inventory number; Figure 10) may be dated as late as 400 BC. The boxers are rendered rather simply and with less attention to proportion and physiognomy than we observe in other examplars. The pugilsts lack armbands but both wear a belt. As mentioned previously, the boxer on the right holds a dumbbell in his right hand only. The other one has perhaps dropped. Given the somewhat crude modeling of the anatomy, it possible that the dumbbell/fist was also rendered poorly (we note the small size of the *hantel* in the corresponding, back hand of the boxer on the left). The artist has taken some pains to limn a hairline, cap or perhaps even a helmet on both fighters. They are not, in any event, capitally unencumbered as are the glabrous boxers in other toreutic representations. The familiar plumed helmet stands between them.

The Vače Situla, found in modern-day Slovenia and today a celebrated artifact of the region, shows two boxers in the classic two-dimensional pose known from Sumerian times (National Museum of Slovenia, No. P-581; Figure 11). Both are naked but for a belt or rope

---

[20]Others have argued that Rhaetic is Indo-European and that its speakers were heavily influenced by Celtic and Illyrian tongues (Scullard 1967, p. 43).

Figure 9: Detail from a situla associated with an Etruscan site in Bologna, now housed at the Rhode Island School of Design (No. 32.245) and known as the Providence Situla.

Figure 10: Detail from the Arnoaldi Situla, Archæological Museum of Bologna, no inventory number.

stretching across mid-abdomen and an armband of similar material on one (uplifted) arm. Their genitals are unencumbered and visible, even on the right-hand boxer, where the thigh of his projecting left leg partially obscures them. The fighters grasp the *ročke* tightly with their thumbs extended. The fighter on the left appears to show the tops of his knuckles, over which a strap extends.

Like most of their toreutic brethren, the Vače boxers are depicted in an offensive posture, with one arm extended to strike and another lowered to the side and/or back. The anatomical rendering of the fighters is somewhat naïve, with improbable placement of the feet vis-à-vis the twisted shoulders and torso. Also, the thumbs of the striking hands are incorrectly rendered on the bottom, rather than the top of the fist (unless the knuckles face the viewer, in which case the arms are rotated in a manner that would make a strike so awkward as to be ineffectual).

Figure 11: Boxing scene from the Vače Situla, National Museum of Slovenia, No. P-581.

A fragment of a bronze situla from Kobarid (Caporetto/Karfreit), dated to the fifth century BC, is held at the Civico Museo di Storia ed Arte, Trieste (no inventory number) (Lucke and Frey 1962, p. 70). The item presents little information that is new but confirms the high frequency of such features as nudity, the plumed helmet, armband, and *ročka* in representations of boxers in situla art (Figure 12).

The boxers on the Magdalenska Gora Situla (National Museum of Slovenia, No. P-4280; Figure 13) are more lithesome than their counterparts on other East Alpine objects. Instead of a prize, there floats between the pugilists a large rosette surrounded by eighteen petals. The internal structure of the boxers' belts is more evident, consisting of a top and bottom band with vertical striations in the middle. The *ročke* have relatively small, spherical ends. The fighters appear to stride forward. Their noses are pointed up and their chins are sticking out in a vulnerable gesture. Cloaked men wearing hats stand on either side holding long staffs that look almost like hockey sticks.

Fragments from the lid of a floor vessel found at Magdalesnka Gora (National Museum of Slovenia, No. P-4282; Figure 14) confirm the basic elements of the toreutic boxing scenes we have observed so far. The belt is clearly present but the raised arms are generally missing, so we cannot be sure if an armband was rendered or not. The plumed helmet appears to rest on a stand. The boxers are bare-headed and bald. An observer, wearing a cap, stands behind the boxer on the left. The lid is apparently not associated with the situla found at

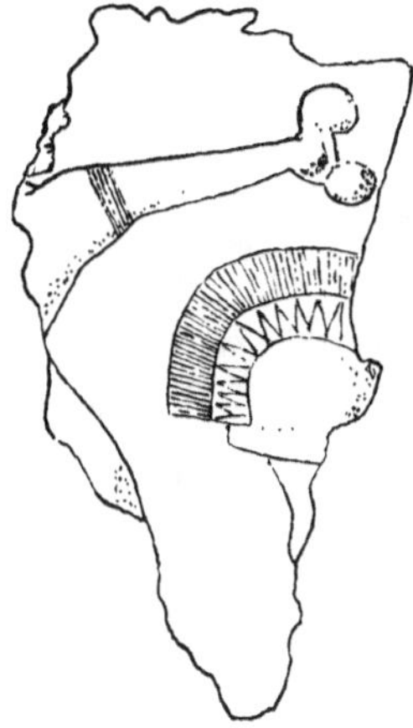

Figure 12: A fragment from a fifth-century bronze situla, found at Kobarid, Slovenia, in 1886. The piece is held in the Civico Museo di Storia ed Arte, Trieste (no inventory number).

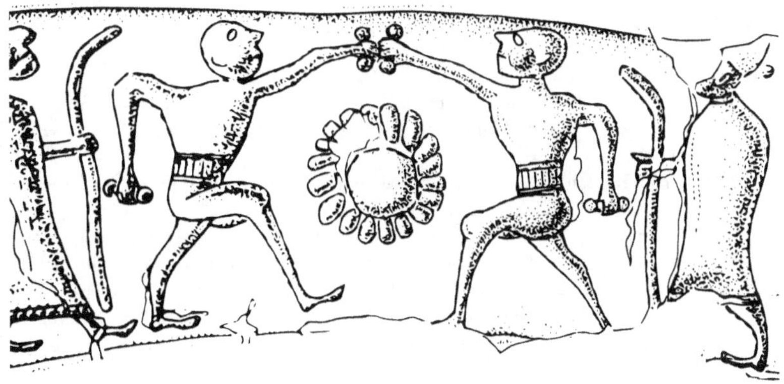

Figure 13: Detail from the Magdalenska Gora situla, National Museum of Slovenia (No. P-4280).

Magdalenska Gora (Figure 13).

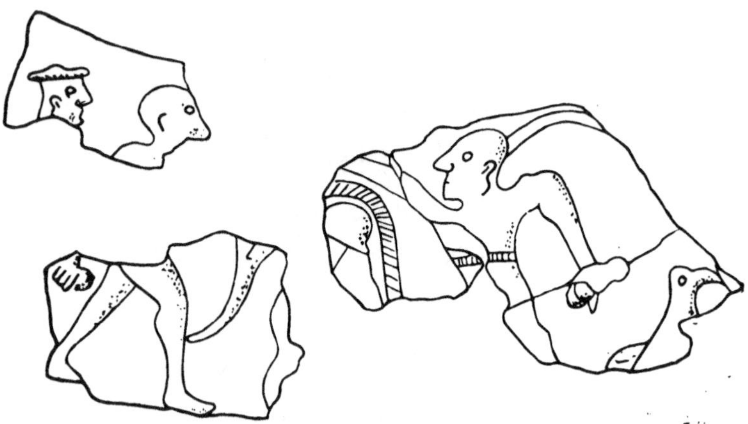

Figure 14: Detail from the lid of an *Etagangefäß* 'floor vessel' from Magdalenska Gora, National Museum of Slovenia (No. P-4282). Note: the lid belongs to another vessel which is *not* the same as the one for which detail is provided in Figure 13.

A bronze fragment from Dolenjske Toplice (Natural History Museum Vienna, No. 56801; not pictured here) shows the leg of the boxer on the right along with one of his *ročke*. A 'second' (*sekundanten*) in a long robe stands behind him (Lucke and Frey 1962, p. 28). Another bronze fragment from Mechel, in northeastern Italy, is held at a museum in Trento identified by Lucke and Frey (1962, p. 67) as the Museo Nazionale (No. 1772).[21] The Mechel fragment, which measures only 2.7 × 1.5 cm, contains the right side of a prize helmet, a bit of the stand it rests on, as well as an arm and a leg of the fighter on the right (Lucke and Frey 1962, p. 67). The dumbbells are not visible. We have not been able to observe the fragmentary boxing scene discovered on pieces of Bronze at Fließ, Austria and have no further information about the object(s).

The boxers in the Sanzeno fragments (Tyrolean State Museum, Innsbruck, No. 16700; Figure 15) are found near an erotic scene, which Frelih (1989, p. 112) equates with the story of Hephæstus capturing Ares and Aphrodite *in flagrante delicto*. Because the Phæacians, in Book 8 of the *Odyssey*, sing of this episode before holding games, including boxing, Frelih makes the argument that the Sanzeno situla celebrated the Phæacian games themselves. The upright and fairly stiff-legged stance of the boxer on the left can be inferred; his dumbbells are visible, as well as a plumed helm on a stand. The raised *hantel* of the boxer on the right is barely visible.

A clay relief fragment similar in style to the toreutic boxers, was found at Saccheto in Contrada Sostegno, Italy (Museo Nazionale Atestino, No. 3760; Figure 16). The object comes from a large, thick-walled, yellow vessel, suggesting that the boxers were a popular mo-

---

[21] This is most likely now known as the Museo Nazionale Storico degli Alpini.

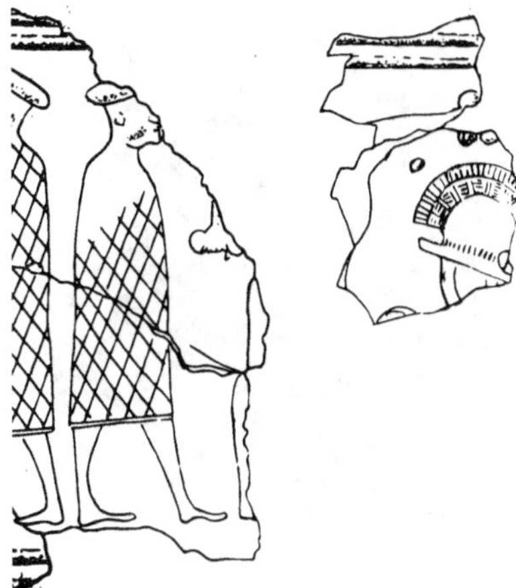

Figure 15: Fragments from a bronze situla, found at Sanzeno, Italy. The pieces are held in the Tyrolean State Museum, Innsbruck (No. 16700). The dumbbells are visible partially above the helmet and in the lowered right hand of the boxer to the left of the helmet. The left arm and right leg of the boxer on the left are also partially visible.

tif on clay vessels, as well. In the relief, a bald, naked pugilist (the left-hand figure of a pair) stands with exposed genitalia in the familiar East Alpine boxing pose, wielding the dumbbells. Hoernes (1893, p. 108) calls the implement a *schlagwaffe* 'blunt weapon'. A dumbbell, forearm, and the forward leg of the right-hand boxer are also visible. The fragment has been dated to between 500 and 400 BC (Thuillier 1985, p. 173).

As we have seen, the toreutic artists worked within a fairly strict set of conventions in their depictions of boxing.[22] The Mesopotamian and Greek antecedents of these symmetrical fighting figures with a trophy placed between them have been noted by Frelih (1989, p. 100ff.). While there is some variability, these scenes all have much in common. In most cases, the boxers raise one hand, aimed at their opponent, while the other hand is lowered behind them. Details of the chest are absent, so it is not always clear whether we are seeing the torso or the back of the fighter on the right. The detail of the thighs, groin, and buttocks on the Providence Situla, for example, suggests that the fighters have turned their chests towards the viewer, their left feet forward.[23] One foot (when discernible, it is typically the left) projects,[24] the other remains behind—a standard boxing posture that ensures stability in throwing and

---

[22]Lucke and Frey (1962, p. 27) argue that the pose of the boxers "is not so much an arbitrary possibility of representation, but rather a specific moment of the fight, perhaps a starting position." They further claim that "the clear juxtaposition of the fighters without overlapping is partly due to the technical situation of the bronzeworker" (translation ours).

[23]Only on the Magdalenska Gora belt plate (Figure 6) does it appear that the boxer on the right is showing his back to the viewer.

[24]The boxer on the right-hand side of the Certosa Situla (Figure 4) appears to put his right foot forward, his genitals faintly visible.

Figure 16: A clay relief fragment from Sacchetto in Contrada Sostegno, Este (Museo Nazionale Atestino, No. 3760).

receiving blows. Indeed, the wide stance assumed by the boxers is one of the reasons we believe they were not merely scuffling to knock a dumbbell out of their opponent's hands. Surely this would not require the wide stance we see in all the toreutic boxers.

Still, there are noteworthy differences between the postures of the East Alpine pugilists. For example, according to Lucke and Frey (1962), the boxers on the Matrei and Vače situlæ have a "slack posture" (*schlaffe Haltung*) while those on the Providence situla have an "intermediate" one (*eine Mittelstellung einnehmen*). The wide lunge and energetically bent arms of the Kuffarn boxers suggest that it was possible for the artist to capture the temperament of the fight (Lucke and Frey 1962, pp. 27–28). The Vače Situla, on the other hand, shows the boxers in much more static pose: figural symmetry here seems to have been of greater concern to the artist than naturalistic movement.

The character of the Matrei boxers' genitalia has been noted (Merhart 1932, p. 61). Despite the forward swing of the body of the man on the right, his penis and scrotum hang plumb. This contrasts with the boxer on the left, whose genitals seem to move together with his left leg as he strides forward. In most other Alpine boxing depictions, the genitals are either absent (e.g., the Arnoaldi Situla), obscured by the leg (e.g., the Magdalenska Gora situla) or "their immobility stands in contrast to the swing of the body" (e.g., the Magdalenska Gora belt plate).[25] The Matrei Situla is also notable in that the prize includes a lance in addition to the ubiquitous helmet.

Are the ithyphallic boxing figures in some situla art, as on the Magdalenska Gora belt plate, intended apotropaically? Stipčević (1981, pp. 68) regards such figures in Illyrian art as "closely related to the cult of the dead."[26] The horse on the belt buckle is also considered a chthonic animal in Illyrian art (ibid., pp. 59–65).

---

[25] *steht ihre Unbeweglichkeit in einigem Gegensatz sum Schwung des Körpers* (Merhart 1932, p. 61).
[26] "... usko je pozevan sa kultom mrtvih."

Frelih (1989, p. 107) regards the Sanzeno, Kobarid, and Vače situlæ as belonging to the same group because they all appear to fight for a similar helmet, which the author describes a plume attached to a piece of wool with triangular ornaments. In these examples, Frelih observes, the boxers all wear narrow belts and their left arms are tied below the shoulder with a decorative ribbon. The author believes (p. 1114) the appearance of the plumed helmet in the prize position may be a cultural innovation, post-dating those representations without it.

The toreutic boxers occur in the context of feasts, ceremony, and music also limned on the situlæ. One critic has written that such "scenes from life are are selected whose character, being episodic, places them beyond time and a given milieu" (Mansuelli 1965, p. xxviii). While we agree that the teurotic erotica, for example, are indeed timeless, this is less true of the boxing, which subscribes to conventions (e.g., the *hanteln*, the belts, the armbands) unique to the Alpine Iron Age. We also tend to disagree with the author when he writes that toreutic art "consciously held to a concrete, everyday reality" (Mansuelli 1965, p. xxx). This claim seems to disregard the the fantastic beasts that appear, e.g., on the Benvenuti Situla. As for oft-cited Greek influence on the "formal toreutic culture" of the Alps, while it is plausible, "we have no assurance beyond the fact that the AdriaticSea [sic.] was the medium by which such influence was transferred" (Mansuelli 1965, p. xxx).

Frelih (1989, p. 114) opines that the boxing scene originally possessed some older mythic background (*starejše mitsko ozadje*) but that repetition of the scene in toreutic art led to loss of important details. This "disintegration" came about due to an "increasingly weak awareness of the primary substantive basis of the motif" (translation ours).

Though some have claimed that the Alpine boxers carry *halteres*, i.e., Greek jumping weights, these had both a different shape and a different purpose (Thuillier 1985, p. 263). Lucke and Frey (1962, pp. 26–27) refer to them as 'hand protectors' (*Handschützern*) and argue that the dumbbells never had the same shape as Greek *halteres* (*nie genau diese Form gehabt haben*). Merhart (1932, p. 61, fn. 1) wonders whether Alpine people confused different forms of Greek athletics in their representations, and so mixed the *halteres* in with boxing. We find this solution inadequate, particularly because there are other indications that the practice was ubiquitous throughout the region and included non-Greek conventions, including the belt, the armbands, and the pectoral crosses of the figurines, as well as the baldness of situla boxers. According to one author, Mediterranean boxing was "probably adjusted to local preferences and rules" in Iron Age Central Europe, and this included the use of the hammer-like *hanteln* (Rebay-Salisbury 2012, p. 194).

Per Lucke and Frey (1962, p. 29), when Greek representations of boxing finally penetrated the southeastern Alps, pugilism already existed there. While efforts to depict boxing on vessels may have been influenced by Greek culture, perhaps mediated by the Etruscans, Alpine boxing was itself autochthonous.[27] Hoernes (1893, p. 110) ponders whether Alpine representations of boxing were not directly influenced by the stylistically similar cylinder seals of Cyprus and the ancient Near East (Dioscurus and Dioscurus 2022b;d).

Lucke and Frey (1962, p. 29) make strong claims about the social status of the Alpine pugilists, paying special regard to the clothes carefully folded beneath them on the Providence Situla and the war helmets that appear frequently in many of the other depictions. These, they argue, are sure signs that the boxers could not have been slaves.[28] We are not

---

[27] *Als bei diesen südliche Darstellungen emdrangen, war ihnen der Faustkampf längst bekannt, allerdings ohne daß sie bis dahin gestrebt hatten, ihn bildlich wiederzugeben.*

[28] The authors exhibit this concern about social status, we suppose, because of the later Italic development of

convinced by this. We have no evidence that slaves wore no clothes, or even hats, in this culture. In fact, the only naked figures on the situlæ are either in the act of making love or boxing. Hats are worn even by figures regarded as attendants. Lucke and Frey (1962, p. 29) wonder, "What did a helmet mean to the victor if he wasn't a free man who was allowed to take up arms himself?" We question this reasoning, which seems overly influenced by Greek notions of citizenship. Perhaps in this culture enslaved men, victorious in a ritual boxing match, were set free and then sent to war. Or perhaps slaves were routinely used as warriors. While we do not stake much on the status of the fighters (the boxers on the Providence Situla may have been prestigious duelists settling a score), we are skeptical that this can be determined based on the scant evidence about Eastern Alpine culture during the Iron Age.

We agree with Lucke and Frey (1962, p. 29) when they claim that the helmets distinguish situla art from Greek models.[29] Only the Matrei Situla seems to reflect a kind of tripod or cauldron, the typical Greek prize from the era. The prize object in the Providence Situla may be a kind of drinking vessel, but the stand it rests on, adorned with avian heads, is reminiscent of Celtic and La Tène art. Moreover, the position of the Alpine boxers' arms does not correspond to any Greek models. Long crooks and double-rods appear in the hands of some participants in the boxing scenes, which is more suggestive of Greek influence than perhaps anything else. We note, however, that in New World boxing traditions, whipping or lashing the fighters is not uncommon, and is almost certainly uninfluenced by Ancient Greek custom (Zorich 2008).

The dumbbells represent an important albeit neglected innovation in the history of western boxing. Though many classicists appear to have discounted them as fantastic weapons not actually used in fights, their attestation is frequent enough in situla art to suggest that they were an important element in boxing of northern Italy and the eastern Alps. Indeed, we argue that these instruments are functionally related to the later development of the various weaponized *cæstus* used throughout the Mediterranean into Late Antiquity. The slaughter of the bull at the conclusion of the Æneidean boxing match (Dioscurus and Dioscurus 2023) may suggest a repudiation of ancient Italic custom, by which the brains of a man would be scattered using the dumbbells. Better to do this to a an animal, Vergil opines, and his victorious boxer does just this to the bull.

The so-called 'Celtic hypothesis' has suffered recently based on the genetic diversity of mainland European populations (including the Hallstatt people) known to scholars for hundreds of years merely as 'Celts'. Despite this, we adopt the traditional view that the culture which produced the boxing situlæ had some cultural affinity with the Celts of Gaul described in Classical Antiquity. Customs of the Gaulish Celts were committed to history by the Greek polymath Posidonius in the first century BC, though his observations survive only in fragments copied by others. One such fragment describes single combat that took place at Celtic festivities (*deipnon* 'meal') (Athenaeus, *The Deipnosophists* 4.40). The author uses terms associated with pugilism elsewhere in Greek literature, viz., *skiamachy* 'shadow-boxing' and *monomachy* 'single-combat'. Interestingly, the account does not explicitly mention weapons in the duel.[30] Instead, the rivals were said to 'struggle at arm's length' *akrocheirizomai*, the same term used by Philostratus in connection with the Greek combat sports (*Gym. 36*). This

---

gladiatorial contests between slaves and criminals.

[29] *Die Art des Kampfpreises erweist somit erneut die Selbstandigkeit der Darstellungen auf den Situlen.*

[30] A *xiphos* 'sword' is referenced later in the anecdote, but this weapon is used in connection with a sacrificial victim remunerated (in advance) for having his throat slit—not one of the mutual combatants.

struggle roused the Celtic fighting blood (*erethizo*) to the point where the two men verged on killing each other if not prevented by the gathered spectators. Evidently, the spectators did not always intervene. The festive nature of Gaulish monomachy is likely mirrored in the Benvenuti (umbewhile Este) and Providence Situlæ, where spectators drink as they watch the fights.[31]

It is possible that the Celtic monomachy Posidonius witnessed was in fact a boxing match, though it bore little resemblance to Greek *pygmachia* in terms of its conventions. It is unfortunate that Posidonius (or his copyist) has not provided us with more details regarding this uniquely Celtic agon.[32] While the evidence is not particularly strong, the account of Posidonius gives us some reason to suppose that the Gaulish Celts boxed, perhaps aided by the deadly *hanteln* engraved on numerous situlæ of the eastern Alps and northern Italy, argued by many to be the Celtic homeland.

We next mention several bronze relief figurines[33] discovered in Austria's Tyrolean Oberland and today housed at the Tyrolean State Museum, Innsbruck (Nos. 3752–3755; Figure 17) and at the Römisch-Germanisches Zentralmuseum, Mainz (no inventory number; Figure 18). These are by all indications sculptural examples of the same boxers depicted on the situlæ (Egg 1980). The figures hold the *hanteln* with their arms outstretched. The objects have enlarged, rounded ends in one case (Figure 17-c) but are merely cylindrical in others. One of the boxers wears a helmet (Figure 17-c), while the others are bare-headed, if not bald (Figure 18, for example, is probably depicted with a head of hair, given the striations on what might otherwise be regarded as a cap). The figurines, characterized as *Caestuskämpfer*, were discovered at Landeck in the Austrian Tyrol (Merhart 1932, pp. 57–58).[34] They were likely used as votive offerings (Egg 1980, p. 57). One author argues that their erect penises are intended to indicate that they are naked rather than aroused (ibid., p. 61).[35] Unfortunately, Merhart does not suggest a date for these objects, known as the *Landecker Caestuskämpfer*; however, he does refer to them as descendants of the situla boxers (p. 63) and this view is also espoused by Egg (1980, p. 58).[36] Egg concludes his presentation of the relief figurines by stating that they are "a part of the tradition of the Hallstatt period" and their production indicates "the survival and further development of Hallstatt-age elements in the younger Iron Age Alpine region" (ibid., translation ours).

Several of the figurines (Figure 17 a–c) wear a pectoral cross (*brustkreuz*) but no armband or belt as on the situlæ. The boxer in Figure 17-b does not hold the dumbbells; his fingers are represented, though somewhat hastily (his left hand appears to have six digits). His scrotum is distinguished, as it is in most cases of situla boxers, at least when the genitalia are rendered. The other *Cæstuskämpfer* lack a scrotum. For the same figure, there are traces of iron on the

---

[31] One appears to have fallen asleep (Rebay-Salisbury 2012, p. 191).

[32] Posidonius goes on to recount that in times past, two brave Celts might wind up fighting to the death (*mechrî thanaton*) in this manner for no greater reason than to claim a thigh-bone at table.

[33] The reverse side of the figurines is flat and bears no detail.

[34] The site is very close to Fließ, where a bronze sheet depicting boxers was also found. In Figure 1, only Fließ is shown.

[35] Merhart's (1932) argument is that the figurine artists did not have the skill to limn the genitals within the outline of the body, as in several of the toreutic representations, and so they rendered the penis in silhouette. We note that a somewhat unsatisfactory attempt (*ziemlich mißglückt*, p. 61) has been made to render the genitals within the outline of the body for Figure 17-b, the only figure for which a scrotum has been depicted, as well. A belt may also be represented across this figure's waistline (ibid., p. 62).

[36] *...ihre abstammung von diesen bleibt doch klar* (Merhart 1932, p. 63).

left side of the pectoral cross, suggesting how the detail was laid in at the time the bronze was still molten (Merhart 1932, p. 59). The details of the faces, though subtle, were probably cut in to the figurines after being cast (ibid., pp. 58–59).

The bronze figurines carry their arms differently than the situla boxers, who characteristically raise one arm to the opponent and maintain the other fist pointed at the ground, elbow bent. The bronze figures, by contrast, have outstretched arms with level shoulders. While the gesture of the figurines could be an authentic representation—perhaps indicating wide, looping hooks—it seems to us more likely that the artist simply wished to represent the formal notion of striking with the outstretched fists. It is also possible that rendering a more naturalistic pose was beyond his ability.

The helmeted boxer depicted in Figure 17-c also has no parallel among the situla pugilists. The boxer in (b) may wear a cap, whereas the amorphous head of (d) is most likely overfilled and somewhat botched (like the penis). The glabrous head of (a) suggests he is bald, like his boxing brethren on the situlæ. The pectoral cross is unique to the figurines; cross-shaped designs are also featured on several bronze pendants representing adorants, with their hands raised (Merhart 1932, p. 62). Given this evidence, it is hard to characterize the boxers as mere athletes. We believe they are engaged in fist-fighting as a form of devotion—the sacrifice of their own body or that of their opponent—to satisfy the numina that brooded over the bent world of their 'ring'.

We conclude that a coherent boxing practice was attested as late as the fifth century BC in the Eastern Alps. By this time, Greek colonists had reached up the Balkan coastline, perhaps as far as modern-day Croatia. Their influence on East Alpine boxing cannot be ruled out. However, the culture that produced the bronze situlæ and other toreutic and figural representations of boxers in that region evidently held to a set of conventions that differed greatly from that of Greek *pygmachia*. Most importantly, the boxers used fist-load weapons which cannot be discounted as fantastical or as a misinterpretation of the Greek *halteres*. If the ubiquitous dumbbells of the Eastern Alps were heavy, as we suspect, then we can reach no other conclusion than that boxing among Iron Age Alpine people entailed the deliberate fracturing of skulls, like boxing among the ancient Maya (Taube and Zender 2009, Taube 2018). Boxing in the Iron Age Alps had an overtly sacrificial character and its influence was widespread. We believe that this deadly form of boxing was transmitted to the Etruscans, who appear to have valued situla art enough to include it among their own grave goods. As we will see in the next section, the Etruscans developed a form of boxing associated with ritual killing and funerary ritual consistent with our hypothesis regarding the boxers represented in the bronze artwork of the Eastern Alps.

3   Etruria

The Etruscans were a non-Indo-European-speaking people whose core homeland was located in central Italy. Their origins have remained mysterious despite millennia of speculation (including by Herodotus, who reported their ancestors were Lydian refugees of famine). As the Iron Age wore on, the Etruscans spread far enough northeast to interact with the culture that produced the toreutic art of the Eastern Alps (Section 2). The Etruscans included East Alpine situlæ among their own precious grave goods in locations like the Arnoaldi and Cerstosa Necropoli (Figures 10 and 4). This has led some to speculate that the Etruscans were

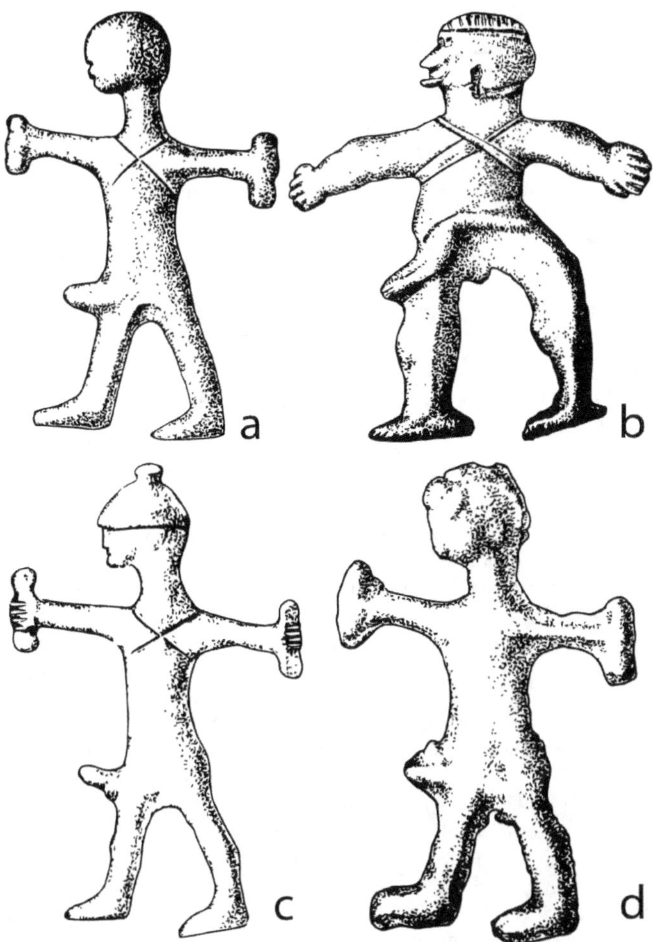

Figure 17: Bronze relief figurines of boxers held at the Tyrolean State Museum, Innsbruck (a = No. 3754; b = 3752; c = 3755; d = 3753). The reverse side of the figurines is essentially flat, with no detail.

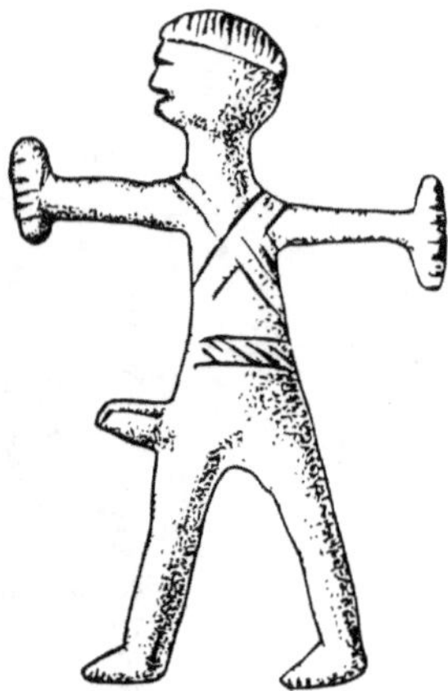

Figure 18: Another *Cæstuskämpfer* relief figurine, housed at the Römisch-Germanisches Zentralmuseum, Mainz (no inventory number). The item was reportedly found in western Hungary but this is disputed (Egg 1980).

themselves the producers of the situla art. While we have taken the position that the situlæ were fabricated by an autochthonous Alpine culture that engaged in dumbbell boxing, the evidence is still insufficient to reach a definitive conclusion on the matter. Others will doubtless continue to characterize the situla art, and therefore dumbbell boxing, as Etruscan.

Even for those who consider the use of the curious *hanteln* peripheral to Etruria, boxing was "by far the most popular sport" among the Etruscans (Thuillier 1985, p. 267). In the present section, we will explore the material culture of boxing in pre-Roman central Italy. While not everyone agrees that East Alpine boxing was a bloody affair intended as a form of human sacrifice, there is less ambivalence about Etruscan boxing. There is more support for the view that it included elements of ritual killing. These elements were magnified by the Romans, who ultimately assimilated their Etruscan rivals in the late first millennium BC.

The story of Etruscan boxing—indeed, of Etruscan culture in general—cannot be told without some reference to the centuries-long encounter between the Etruscans and their Greek neighbors. Hellenic settlers began arriving in Italy in the eighth century BC and surely commenced interactions with the Etruscans (whom they called Tyrrhenians) soon after. Nearly thirty thousand pieces of Greek pottery, many produced in Attica and shipped to Italy, have been reclaimed from Etruscan tombs. Indeed, it is widely believed that the Greeks produced pottery explicitly for their Tyrrhenian clientele, painting them with themes of local interest— including boxing (Osborne 2001). We argue that some features of Etruscan boxing were highlighted in Greek pottery destined for the Italian market, including the shedding of blood and, occasionally, the clothing of the boxers. We therefore include in this section some pottery manufactured on the Greek mainland because it was discovered in central Italy and may have reflected Etruscan tastes in the depiction of boxing. To separate Greek and Etruscan representations of boxing on any item produced in Greece, however, is surely a tenuous proposition. We admit that, with good reason, some may prefer a general discussion of Hellenic boxing that includes all Greek pottery, regardless of its findspot.

Despite the *non liquet* of binding Greek pottery to Etruscan culture, we can be reasonably certain that frescoes painted on tomb walls in pre-Roman central Italy represent an *echt* Etruscan notion of boxing. Here, too, the lines blur as these representations extend farther south into Lucania, given the stronger Hellenic influences of *Magna Græcia* (Section 4). We provide no alcahest for debates concerning the depth of Greek influence on Etruscan material culture, noting merely the patterns we observe among artifacts associated with boxing in pre-Roman central Italy.[37]

The Plicaśna[38] Situla (Figure 19), found at Chiusi, is a gilt-silver vessel that may depict boxers. The boxers, wearing a garment across their buttocks that may represent a loincloth, approach each other on the sides of a larger-than-life chalice (the position where prizes are frequently found in Greek and Etruscan depictions of pugilism). Both arms are uplifted; the boxer on the right seems to direct his fists towards his opponent. Perhaps because the figures are separated from one another, it is not obvious to all critics that they are, in fact, boxing (Thuillier 1985, pp. 65–68).[39] Nevertheless, the aggressive posture of the boxers, as well as the presence of aolists (nearly ubiquitous in later Etruscan and Lucanian depictions)[40] and the chalice-prize make a fairly strong case that what we observe on the Plicaśna Situla is indeed a representation of pugilism. The visual momentum of the scene, with the boxers and prize as centrally-located elements, also lead to this conclusion. Figures surrounding the boxers include musicians, as previously mentioned, as well as warriors wearing plumed helmets and armed with sword and spear, as well as men carrying sheep on their shoulders, as to a sacrifice. The figures immediately adjacent to the boxers have no particular identifying features. They are dressed as the boxers are, with their hands in a lowered albeit aggressive gesture. They may represent a second set of boxers eager to fight.

Figure 19: Detail of the Plicaśna Situla, found at Chiusi. Dated to around 650 BC, not all agree that the central figures are in fact boxing. If they are, however, then this is certainly one of the earliest representations of pugilism in Etruria.

Another candidate for the oldest representation of boxing among the Etruscans is found on a bucchero amphora now in Wiesbaden (Figure 20). The boxers, presumably naked, cross

---

[37] We take the position that fist fighting need not be borrowed by any group since orthograde, ritual combat is likely a primitive of our erect, symbolically-oriented species (Dioscurus and Dioscurus 2022a). So, while we may be accused of "splitting" rather than "lumping" when it comes to the typology of ancient boxing, one advantage of our approach is to clearly separate the evidence according to the geographic region, if not culture, that produced it. Those who come after us may reasonably decide to merge some of the distinctions we found boethetic.

[38] The Etruscan name *Plicaśna* appears twice on the object.

[39] Frelih (1989, p. 110) argues that the vessel is not Etruscan, but a Phœnician–Cypriot product dating to the initial contact between the Etruscans and traders from the Middle East in around 650 BC.

[40] The flute player was known in Etruscan as *suplu*, arguably derived from Latin *subulo* (Thuillier 2017, p. 226).

uplifted arms while maintaining the other arm lowered, elbow bent, at waist level. The prize position is occupied by a tripod holding a cauldron. A *suplu* plays his pipes to the left of the fighters.[41] To their right appears a representation of Theseus slaying the Minotaur. To the left of the musician we find an extensive scene depicting Orestes' slaughter of Clytemnestra and Ægisthus (Thuillier 1985, p. 112). The mythological contest is intriguing, suggesting that the boxing itself represents a mythological scene, perhaps the bout between Apollo and Hercules over the Delphic tripod (Dioscurus and Dioscurus 2022d).

The presence of aolists in these early Etruscan depictions of boxing may represent the origins of a long tradition seemingly unique to Italy, if not to Etruria. While various forms of music are found in representations of boxing going back to the ancient Near East (Dioscurus and Dioscurus 2022b), the Etruscans were particular to include the *suplu* wherever boxers were duking it out.[42] Flute players appear repeatedly in Etruscan and Lucanian tomb painting, for example (see below). According to Thuillier (2017, p. 226), several ancient authors, including Eratosthenes and Alcimus, noted the Etruscan penchant for combining music and fighting, a trait they called τρυφή, suggesting Etruscan softness and effeminacy. Thuillier draws an apt connection to (modern) Thai kickboxing, in which musicians "provide a rhythm for the blows of the two combatants and even...stir up their zeal for the fight" (ibid.).

Pausanias, in his *Description of Greece*, briefly renders a scene depicting the funeral games of Pelias. He refers to a flute player in the context of a boxing match (5.17.10): "Those who have boldly ventured [ἀποτολμάω] to box [πυκτεύω] are Admetus and Mopsus, the son of Ampyx. Between them stands a man playing the flute [ἐπαυλέω], as in our day they are accustomed to play the flute when the competitors in the pentathlon are jumping" (Jones et al. 1918). This may suggest that Pausanias regarded musical accompaniment (at boxing matches) as archaic; he is believed to have written during the second century AD. To be sure, the aolist is not exclusive to Etruscan sport (Thuillier 1985, p. 231) but the connection between boxing and flute-playing in Etruria was *plus étroite* 'tighter' than anywhere else in the ancient world (ibid., p. 246). While flute-playing seemed to generally accompany athletics in Greece, among the Etruscans it was strictly associated with boxing (ibid., p. 247–248).

Two other early (seventh-century) visual representations of pugilism are found on Etruscan pottery. A bucchero olpe found at Cerveteri (Figure 21) includes on its surface a depiction of the Medea myth. Figures carry what may be the golden fleece. Nearby, two boxers throw punches, landing them on each others' chest or shoulders.[43] The figures wear their hair long and may be girt in loincloths (Bonfante and Bonfante 2002, p. 134).[44] The front legs are bent sharply at the knee, effectively communicating the posture of a boxer as he strikes. The back feet are poised on the ball or tiptoe. The boxer on the right even raises his foot slightly off the ground as he throws a right hand—a technique abjured by modern boxing coaches since it weakens the blow. The olpe is evidence, for Thuillier (2017, p. 222), of "Etruscan

---

[41] The sack hanging from the instrument is interpreted as their 'carrying case' (*étui*) by Thuillier (1985, p. 112).

[42] The Tomba delle Bighe, notable for heavy Greek influence on its iconography, is one of the few exceptions, where boxers are depicted without a musical accompanist (Thuillier 2017, p. 626). Demonstrating the perennial confusion over terms for ancient boxing handgear, Skutsch (1985) claims that the boxers in the Tomba delle Bighe wear the Roman *cæstus*, then parenthetically clarifies: "or perhaps only leather strips."

[43] The relation between the golden fleece and boxing recalls the *Argonautica*'s boxing match between Polydeuces and Amycus may be represented here. However, there is nothing in the iconography of the boxers themselves to further substantiate this hypothesis. There is no clear difference in age or size between the fighters, for example.

[44] The stylization of the male breasts on the left figure suggest that the circles drawn on the hips are meant merely to communicate roundness and depth, not clothing.

Figure 20: Detail of a bucchero cylindrical amphora dated to 600–575 BC. Now in a collection in Wiesbaden, the piece originated in Chiusi. While the scenes to the left and the right of the boxers are probably mythological, it is not clear which mythological boxing match may be represented by the pugilists.

interest in pugilism already in the 630s."

Figure 21: Two boxers fight on a seventh-century bucchero olpe found at Cerveteri. Depicted are scenes of the Medea myth and attendants carrying what may be the golden fleece and there are inscriptions in Etruscan.

A bucchero vase found at Veii (Figure 22) is dated to the last third of the seventh century BC. Boxers on the vase wear armbands, suggesting some relation to the Alpine boxers described in Section 2. Unlike those fighters, however, these have hair. They are naked, though no genitalia are limned. The boxer on the right has some indication of a garment wrapping around his loins, but it does not fully circumscribe his waist.[45] The prize position contains an elaborate, winged stand with nothing placed atop it. Is it a tripod (there are only two feet) or a chair? Thuillier (1985, p. 61) suggests that it may be a curule seat (*sella curulis*), a foldable and transportable chair used by certain office holders in Ancient Rome. A vegetal motif, perhaps a leafy cypress branch, stands to the left.[46] Each boxer bears one hand aggressively aloft, with the other bent at the chest, fist raised. The legs are bent and the fighters stand on the balls of their feet or on tiptoe.

---

[45] Thuillier (1985, p. 60) regards the boxers as clothed in a *maillot-tunique* 'jersey-tunic' but we are not convinced. Thuillier goes on to claim that this garb is "doubtless of Minoan origin" (ibid., translation ours). Unfortunately, the Veii vase has been lost, so closer inspection of the artifact is currently impossible. In a later publication (in English), Thuillier (2017, p. 223) states that the Veii boxes wear "singlets."

[46] "It is well known that the cypress has long been associated with death" (Thuillier 1985, p. 61, translation ours). This element, coupled with the fantastic predators surrounding the boxers, may suggest a funereal and/or sacrificial character to the match.

Surrounding the boxers on the vase are a number of fantastic beasts, including griffins and sphinges, many in the act of devouring other animals or people. A gracefully-rendered human leg dangles from the mouth of a lion, for example. Here too, we find a connection to toreutic art of the Alps, viz., the Cerstosa Situla, on which boxers stand atop beasts of ravin—though in that case the animals appear to be sculptural features of the furniture.[47]

Figure 22: Drawing of boxers on a bucchero vase found at Veii and dated to between 633 and 600 BC. The original has been lost, but a detailed drawing was produced by S. Campanari in 1839.

Two sixth-century bronze belt-buckles found near Siena (Figure 23) are decorated in repoussé with boxers. The scenes are influenced by both Greek and Near Eastern models. We note, in particular, the loincloths,[48] characteristic of the earliest Near Eastern anctecedents (Dioscurus and Dioscurus 2022b); as well as the tripod and carefully-rendered *himantes*, both Greek features. Thuillier (1985, p. 574–575), who notes the conspicuous length of the boxers' tresses (down to their shoulders), argues that long hair is disruptive to the unfolding of a boxing match, as we have observed in more general terms elsewhere (Dioscurus and Dioscurus 2022a).

A bronze vessel (British Museum No. 1855,0816.1; Figure 24) known as the Barone Lebes contains images of beasts wild and fantastical, chariot races, wrestlers, and at least one pair of boxers. These are flanked on the left by an official wielding a rod and a looped object and on the right by a *suplu* playing his instrument. The looped object is perhaps a victor's wreath, but it may also represent the *himantes*. Curiously, the official is nude, an unprecedented characteristic for such a figure. He may be another boxer, waiting his turn to fight and acting *emethen* as a referee on an improvised basis (Thuillier 1985, p. 153, fn. 45).

The leftmost pair of boxers, flanked by the officiator and the musician, are evidently *in articulo pugnæ*, with both hands raised and their feet spread apart. The boxer on the left, who is throwing a punch, has also raised his back foot onto its ball. The fighter on the right raises both hands in an apparent gesture of defense. The other set of boxers have reached the climax of their contest; the crouching figure on the right appears to raise one finger in sign of his defeat. All of the boxers are naked.

---

[47] Thuillier (1985, p. 59) regards this iconography as characteristic of Etruscan culture.

[48] Thuillier (1985, pp. 117, 671) claims the garments are *crétois* (by which he means 'Minoan') in part because they leave the buttocks largely uncovered. See Dioscurus and Dioscurus (2022c) for discussion of the athletic dress of Minoan boxers.

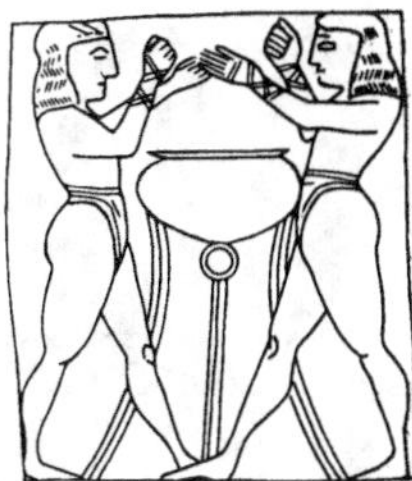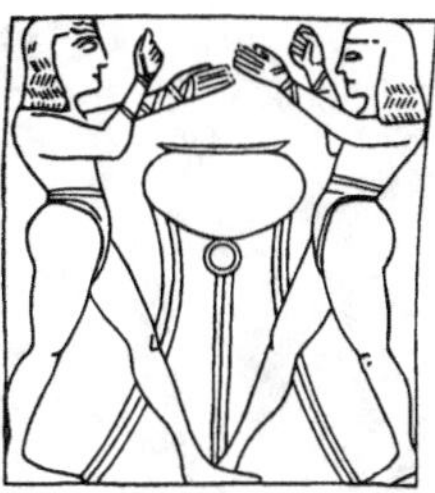

Figure 23: Etruscan belt buckles found near Siena (Casole d'Elsa), dated 575–550 BC. The iconography of the boxing scenes appears to draw from a variety of ancient traditions.

The conventions of the fights on the Barone Lebes—including the raised finger that signals submission—leave no doubt as to the pollent Greek influence on the vessel's decoration. However, the surrounding chariot races, the *suplu*, and the preoccupation with fantastic beasts all mark the vessel definitively as an Etruscan artifact. The Barone Lebes was found at Capua and is dated to the beginning of the fifth century BC.

Figure 24: Detail of the Barone Lebes featuring boxers (British Musem No. 1855,0816.1). Evidently Etruscan, the Lebes was found at Capua and is dated 500–480 BC.

The boxer's *hanteln*, described in Section 2, reappear in the hands of a gorgon in Etruscan art.[49] The scene on a sixth-century Etruscan amphora (Figure 25) depicts a fugacious sister of Medusa wielding the dumbbells. From Medusa's decapitated trunk, at right, spring the aliferous horses Pegasus and Chrysaor. Why Medusa's sister holds these implements remains a puzzle. Is she chasing after Perseus, her sister's murderer, preparing to deal him a deadly blow? The gorgons were known to have brass hands (Oktapoda 2011, p. 538), which may link them to the (presumably metal) *hanteln* used in the Alpine boxing tradition (Pseudo-Apollodorus, *Bibliotheca* 2.38–46).

A late sixth-century Attic stamnos found at Vulci is remarkable in its depiction of boxers accoutred in the *zōma* (Figure 26). This feature stands out because the evidence of clothing in Greek boxing scenes is otherwise quite rare (Dioscurus and Dioscurus 2022d). The painting does not likely represent the Iliadic games: the other side depicts satyrs and mænads and the upper register, a symposium. Another late sixth-century boxing scene (this time on a kantharos with one handle; Bibliothèque National de France, No. DE RIDDER.354) shows the

---

[49] The dumbbells are reportedly visible in art discovered in Asia Minor, as well (Bonfante 2011).

Figure 25: Detail of an Etruscan amphora formerly held at the J. Paul Getty Museum and now repatriated to Rome. The Gorgon at left holds the *hanteln*. The depiction is attributed to the Painter of Tityos, likely produced at Vulci, and dated to 530–510 BC.

boxers naked but the *ephedros* wears a *zōma*. The runners and jumpers in the scene also wear a loincloth. The preference for clothed athletes may reflect local tastes, as the one-handled kantharos was also discovered at Vulci, though apparently manufactured in Attica. It is worth noting, however, that in this depiction, even with plenty of loincloth-wearing athletes, the boxers are still naked. The Etruscans used nudity to suggest divinity or for apotropaic purposes (Bonfante 2011). Boxers are clothed in relatively few representations but the frequency of clothed boxers in Etruria seems greater than in Greek art destined for the Greek market (Dioscurus and Dioscurus 2022d).

A Panathenaic amphora dated to around 510 BC (Museo nazionale etrusco di Villa Giulia, No. 50680) shows a referee or trainer striking a boxer who has gotten his opponent in an indefensible position (which the English boxers would later term *chancery*), presumably to motivate the other boxer's release (Poliakoff 1983, p. 85). The vessel was found at the Cerveteri Necropolis though it was produced in Athens by the Munich Painter (Beazley 1956, 394.10).

An Etruscan bronze statuette (Bibliothèque Nationale de France, No. BRONZE.101), probably of Apollo, may depict him in the form of a boxer (Figure 27).[50] He wears on his right arm (the left is missing) a garment that has been described as a mutilated chlamys. We interpret this object as five strips dangling from the figure's forearm, as in a Greek vase painting illustrated in Dioscurus and Dioscurus (2022d). We believe these are *himantes*. The figure wears a necklace, a bracelet on the left arm, laced boots, and a garland on his head. The left leg bears an inscription in Etruscan: "I am the statue, or votive offering, (which)

---

[50] Because it was once in the collection of the Dukes of Ferrara, the piece is known in French as "Apollon de Ferrare".

Figure 26: A late sixth-century Attic stamnos depicting boxers wearing the *zōma* (lower left). The vessel was found in Vulci and is now held by the Bibliothèque Nationale de France (No. DE RIDDER.252).

Fast Rufriś gave according to ritual to Artemis Spulare on behalf of her son".[51] The figure is dated 350–300 BC.

Figure 27: The Apollon de Ferrare (Bibliothèque Nationale de France, No. BRONZE.101). This late fourth-century Etruscan bronze may be the only surviving representation of Apollo the Boxer. The figure arguably holds *himantes* on his right arm and wears laced boots, as well as a necklace and a bracelet on his left bicep.

Boxers depicted on at least four Etruscan funerary stelæ found at Bologna are arguably participating in games intended to celebrate the deceased (Sacchetti 2011).[52] The more than 230 stelæ from Bologna—sometimes described as 'tombstones'—may be dated from as early as the eighth century to as late as the fourth century BC (Whitehouse 2013). They are made of sandstone and carved in low relief. On Ducati Stele 10 (Figure 28), the boxer on the right appears to hold an oblong object in his left hand (Thuillier 1985, p. 145). The pillar that stands between the fighters recalls the iconography of Near Eastern cylinder seals (Dioscurus and Dioscurus 2022b).

Boxing in Etruria is well documented in frescoes painted on the walls of thirteen tombs (540–480 BC).[53] These boxing matches have attracted considerable attention because of their ubiquity. There is no critical consensus on whether the boxers painted in these tombs were regarded metaphorically, e.g., as guardians of the deceased, or as depictions of actual events, like funeral games (Jannot 1985, Jazwa 2020). It could be both. Like Thuillier (1985), we prefer the simple explanation that the frescoes depict actual boxing matches associated with Etruscan funerals. While many have argued that boxing—and the concomitant shedding of human blood—is a central aspect of the Etruscan mortuary cultus, others are more reticent.

---

[51] *mi flereś spulare artimi fasti rufriś t(u)rce clen cecha* (Bonfante and Bonfante 2002, p. 165).

[52] The stelæ include Nos. 2, 10, 15, and 169, described originally by Ducati (1911; 1943) and later by Thuillier (1985, pp. 144-147).

[53] The tombs are Àuguri, Iscrizioni, Cardarelli, Olimpiadi, Mæstro delle Olimpiadi, Fustigazione, Bighe, Teschio, Citaredo, Scimmia, Montollo, Colle Casuccini, and Poggio al Moro (Jazwa 2020, p. 32).

Figure 28: Detail of an Etruscan funerary stele (Ducati No. 10, Face B), including boxers (Museo Civico Bologna), 390–360 BC.

Krauskopf (2006, p. 66), for example, has argued that "we will never be able to fit … every picture painted on a tomb wall into the framework of a logically consistent and uniform [Etruscan] conception of the Underworld and of the transition into that realm." There can be no doubt, however, that boxing kythed bright in the Etruscan *imaginaire* of death and afterlife.

Spectators of a boxing match in a fresco in the Tomba delle Bighe in Tarquinia are shown in a variety of activities, including lovemaking. Grandstands appear to be set up to observe the spectacle. Various (clothed) figures on top are seated and cheering while some figures beneath the grandstand are naked and include one couple in the throes of an amorous act.[54] Boxers from a fresco in the Tomba delle Bighe, which is badly damaged, are reconstructed in Figure 29. Two young men watch another boxing match in the same fresco (Figure 30). Evidently ready to participate in a match themselves, one appears to give advice to the boy who will be his adversary in a few short moments.

On the right wall of the Tomba del letto Funebre, in Tarquinia, a man appears to interact with a defeated boxer who holds a sponge to his head (Thuillier 1985, p. 128) in order to absorb a profusion of blood, which drips to the ground (Figure 31). The victor stands to the right, facing the other direction, and throws yet more punches in triumph at the air; a *suplu* stands between the loser and the winner. In the Tomba della Scimmia (Figure 32), the fighters are flanked on the right by an athlete preparing to throw a javelin and a diminutive male[55] holding a palm branch and an aryballos full of oil, perhaps to smear on the fighters.

The boxers painted in the Tomba dell'Iscrizioni (Figure 33) are separated by a curious object shaped like an I-beam (Thuillier 1985, p. 207). One possible antecedent for this object is the pillar that frequently appears between boxers in Cypriot and Ugaritic cylinder seals (Dioscurus and Dioscurus 2022b;c). This may be the aniconic representation of a divinity. In Greek and Alpine depictions, this position is typically reserved for a prize, but in the cylinder seals, it is often a more abstract element—arguably representing a numinous being presiding over the match. The prize that stands between the fighters in the Tomba della Scimmia is also unexpected. A low stand (below the fighters' knees) holds a richly-decorated

---

[54] The grandstands occupy a corner of the tomb, and are depicted on two adjacent walls. Boxers flank the grandstands on one side, pankratiasts on the other.

[55] Thuillier (1985, p. 132) identifies the small figure as a slave.

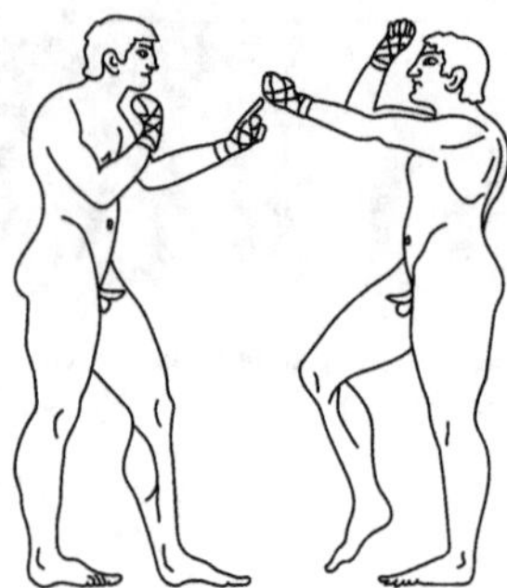

Figure 29: Reconstructed detail of two boxers having it out from Tomba delle Bighe di Tarquinia, ca. 490 BC.

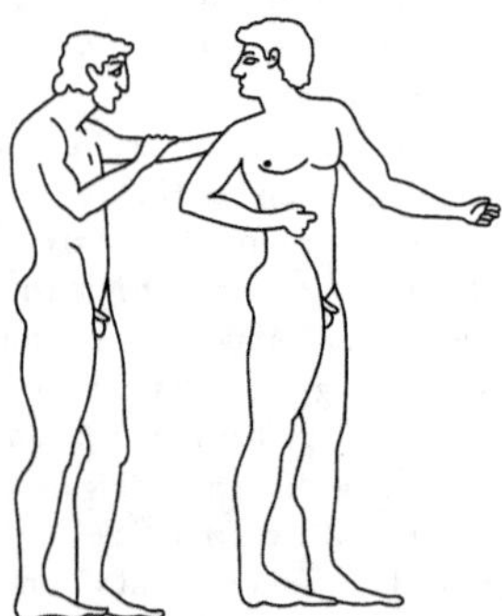

Figure 30: Reconstructed detail from Tomba delle Bighe di Tarquinia, ca. 490 BC. Two young men prepare for a match as they watch two older men slugging it out just to their right.

Figure 31: Detail from Tomba del Letto Funebre, right wall, ca. 460 BC. The figure on the right is a nude boxer who holds a sponge up to his face, which drips blood. The figure to the left, perhaps a servant, looks at the boxer over his shoulder.

Figure 32: Detail from Tomba della Scimmia, 480–470 BC. Note the extraordinarily elongated fingers of the boxers' lead hands.

piece of fabric that may conceal another object (Thuillier 1985, p. 132).

The names[56] that appear near the Iscrizioni boxers are of particular interest in distinguishing Etruscan from Hellenic boxing. Thuillier (2017) argues that because the boxers (here as well as in the Tomba degli Àuguri) receive a single name instead of two (a prænomen plus a gentilic), the fighters necessarily "stand outside the class of gentlefolk" (p. 224). He goes farther, claiming that "[T]hese were real sports stars, and the deceased (or his family) wanted these individuals ... to accompany him in image to the beyond" (p. 225). In cases where two names appear next to fighters, as in the Tomba Cardarelli, the author reasons that these must have been the names of fighters' *domini*, i.e., their owners. He acknowledges that they may have fought "during the funeral games" (ibid.). Thus, Thuillier alludes to the possibility that boxers, owned by their masters, were forced to fight in Etruria, and that they did so in conjunction with funeral games. This has little to do with the traditions of Greek *pygmachia*.

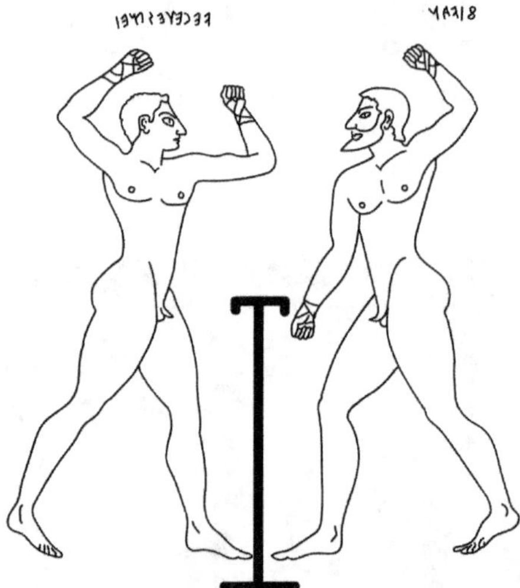

Figure 33: Drawing of the now-damaged boxers in the Tomba dell'Iscrizioni, 520 BC. The words above the fighters, most likely their proper names (read right to left), may be transliterated as *Vecenes Mei* (L) and *Fivan* (R).

Boxers painted in Etruscan tombs are generally naked, with the possible exception of the fighters depicted in the badly damaged Tomba dell'Iscrizioni. Thuillier (1985, p. 122–123) describes these boxers as wearing a loincloth that, while covering their genitals, leaves their buttocks exposed. In the Tomba degli Àuguri, the boxer on the right is infibulated (Thuillier

---

[56] Transliterating the characters left to right, the fighter on the left-hand side of the fresco appears to be named Vecenes Mei (likely the names of the boxer by his father and by his mother) and his adversary is named Fivan (Gray 1840, p. 185).

1985, p. 123–124). The boxer on the left in the Tomba della Scimmia (Figure 32) is similarly protected. Here, a cord around the waist provides an anchor for the suspending cord tied to the boxer's foreskin (Thuillier 1985, pp. 378–379).

A naked man (Figure 34) identified as a boxer stands to the left of the entrance door in the Tomba della Fustigazione (Thuillier 1985, p. 129). A similar, though comically ventripotent, boxer is found painted in the same position in the Tomba Cardarelli (Thuillier 1985, pp. 128, 557–558). The boxers that surround doors in Etruscan tombs were perhaps intended to "threaten any unwanted visitors" (Thuillier 2017, p. 226).

Figure 34: Detail from Tomba della Fustigazione, entrance wall, left of the door, ca. 490 BC.

While boxers are often paired in Etruscan depictions, this is not always the case: a single boxer appears in the Tomba del Colle Casuccini (Thuillier 1985, p. 133). In this fresco, the figure assumes the characteristic posture often associated with boxers in Etruscan art (Jazwa 2020, p. 30). His front foot is raised with toe pointed down while he balances on the ball of his back foot. His front arm is also raised with an open hand and his back hand is raised, elbow bent, with his fist cocked back to his ear. The Colle Casuccini boxer is accompanied by a *suplu*, to his left. A stick-wielding official oversees a wrestling match to the right. It is possible, as argued by Jannot (1985, p. 74), that isolated boxers in Etruscan tomb paintings had a "symbolic or magical role" (translation ours).

The Corsini chair (Galleria Corsini, No. 666) is most likely a first-century Roman copy of a fifth-century Etruscan throne, one with decoration that incorporates elements of East Alpine situla art (Bonfante 1977). Two boxers, wearing short chitons, appear on the throne (Figure 35). The prize, which floats between the boxers, is a Roman helmet, perhaps modified

Figure 35: Detail from the marble Corsini Throne (Galleria Corsini, No. 666), evidently a first-century Roman replica of a fifth-century Etruscan original. The boxers wear short chitons and hold the dumbbells known to situla art (Section 2).

from the Etruscan original. Most remarkably, the boxers carry some version of the *hanteln*.[57] Lucke and Frey (1962, p. 47) argue that the habits and customs (*Sitten und Gebräuche*) of the Eastern Alps did not necessarily end with their own material culture and may have been adopted by the Etruscans, as evidenced in the chair's decoration. Bonfante (1977, pp. 115–116) finds in the Corsini chair "proof" of "direct descent" from "northern models." Lucke and Frey (1962, p. 28) dismiss claims that the *hanteln* depicted on the throne are an Etruscan innovation. The original chair, they argue, was decorated in the late fourth century, too late to have influenced toreutic art of the Alps. Frelih (1989, p. 114, fn. 46) points out that the theme of martial revue (*borilni revkvizit*) also connects the Corsini chair to toreutic art.

Described as a boy's boxing match (*Knaberingkampf*) by Matz and von Duhn (1881, vol. 2, p. 2), the scene on the lid of a "Greek" marble sarcophagus held at the Villa Carpegna in Rome depicts fighters holding dumbbells in gloves that resemble oven mitts (Figure 36). The rest of the scene (not pictured) includes pairs of cherubic figures (probably Erotes) wrestling and boxing, accompanied by a double-flute player, connecting the scene to Etruscan iconography (ibid.). On the sarcophagus lid, a similarly youthful official bears a palm branch that he seems to swing at the standing boxer, presumably for committing the *supercherie* of stepping on his fallen opponent's leg. On the other side of the sarcophagus, a woman is depicted with a "broad braid" hairstyle characteristic of the late third and fourth centuries. Etruscan ash caskets (*aschenkisten*, small sarcophagus-like repositories for cremated human remains) are included in the image, as well. The object is most likely Etruscan.

Boxing Erotes appear on funeral objects going back as far as the fifth century BC in Greece (Scanlon 2002, p. 317).[58] "The metaphor comparing Eros, the human phenomenon of desire,

---

[57] The curved form of the dumbbells has been cited to argue that these are, in fact, Greek jumping weights. That this curvature was intended by the artist has been challenged, however (Thuillier 1985, p. 264).

[58] The tradition continued into the second and third century AD (Newby 2005, p. 41). Boxing was not an uncommon theme in the decoration of children's sarcophagi, well into the second century AD (e.g., Museo Gregorio

Figure 36: Detail of a sarcophagus lid housed at the Villa Carpegna, Rome (no inventory number). The boxers hold dumbbells in their gloves. Probably Etruscan, based on surrounding iconography, and dated to ca. 400 BC.

with the tension, the struggle, and the agonistic spirit of the contest is thus married explicitly on the Roman sarcophagi with the theme of death, risk, and hazard present in the life of any person who acts on his or her desires" (Scanlon 2002, p. 317).

The sarcophagus lid from the Villa Carpegna (Figure 36) has been cited to argue that kicking was allowed in some forms of boxing (Jüthner and Mehl 1962). It appears to show the victorious fighter stepping with his right foot on the right leg of his fallen opponent. We agree with Crowther (1990, p. 177), who points out that "this does not necessarily represent the kick which led to the fall."

Numerous objects depicting boxing were made in Greece and exported to Etruria. Others were produced in Italy, perhaps by Greek artisans. Both types of artifact arguably reflect Etruscan tastes and interests. One intriguing example is a kylix made at Chiusi, featuring a minotaur (Figure 37). The beast appears to have large boxing gloves on his hands. These are presumably the *himantes*, since the one on his right hand is unraveling. This object makes for an interesting comparison with a Levantine cylinder seal depicting boanthropic boxers (Dioscurus and Dioscurus 2022b) and reminds us of the long history of boxing's association with bulls, including among the Minoans (Dioscurus and Dioscurus 2022c). The image could be related to Theseus, slayer of the minotaur and legendary originator of boxing by some Greek accounts (Dioscurus and Dioscurus 2022d).

Another vessel, a red-figure cup attributed to the Villa Giulia Painter (Figure 38), suggests that the Etruscans had an interest in the disfigurement of boxers, like the Greeks. The boxer on the left is noteworthy for the appearance of a facial injury—a large hematoma under the

Profano, No. 1019).

Figure 37: Detail of a black-figure kylix from Chiusi (Boston Museum of Fine Arts, No. 76.235). The figure appears to be a minotaur wearing Greek-style boxing gloves, one of which is unraveling. The vase is dated 525 to 475 BC.

eye called a 'mouse'.

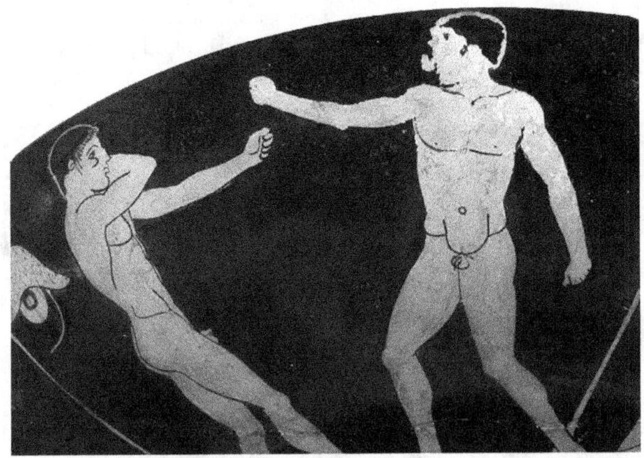

Figure 38: Red-figure cup, attributed to the Villa Giulia Painter. The vessel was discovered at Tarquinia and is dated 460–450 BC. Staatliche Museen zu Berlin, No. F-2522.

Two vases from Italy, one evidently of Attic origin, suggests that the boxers might be kept within bounds through apparatus (Poliakoff 1987a, Figs. 81 and 82). Both objects are now held in museums in Italy.[59] It seems premature to conclude from this evidence that the notion of a boxing ring was first developed in Italy, only to be modeled by Greek artisans on vases that they designed to suit Etruscan tastes. Nevertheless, depictions of boundaries are so uncommon in the iconography of ancient boxing that this should be entertained as a possibility.[60]

There is some evidence that the Etruscans liked boxing dirty (Thomas 1997), and included digging into the eye with the thumb among their tricks. Presumably with this purpose in mind, the fighters' thumbs are extended on a Eubœan amphora now housed in the Museo Gregoriano Etrusco (No. MV.34976.0.0).[61]

The Ficoroni cista (Figures 39, 40) is another Greek-influenced object found in Etruria. The cista is handsomely engraven with a synoptic portrayal of Polydeuces' boxing match with

---

[59] Poliakoff (1987b) argues that the story of Melancomas (Dioscurus and Dioscurus 2023) is fictional on the grounds that Greeks enforced proximity with a barrier to promote striking. He cites Hesychius (fl. c. 500 AD) that the Greeks used a "ladder" κλῖμαξ and boxers fought "from the ladder" ἐκ κλίμακος, some sort of wooden device in which the boxers would presumably stand (Poliakoff 1987b). Furthermore, he cites Eustathius (c. 1115–c. 1195/6 AD) for a late corroboration. We acknowledge the existence of apparatus to restrain boxers to mutual proximity (Dioscurus and Dioscurus 2022d), but do not consider this expedient to be universal or perhaps even widespread in classical and Hellenistic boxing. While certainly not dispositive evidence against Melancomas, it does highlight a practice of enforced proximity in training if perhaps not in competition.

[60] References to a delimited space for a boxing match are challenging to descry in epic poetry. The best (though admittedly controversial) example is rather late: the *cavea* mentioned in the Valerian *Argonautica* (Dioscurus and Dioscurus 2023); see also the 'confined space' χῶρος στενός of Theocritus' *Idylls* (Dioscurus and Dioscurus 2023).

[61] The item is shown in Poliakoff (1987a, Fig. 90).

Amycus. The engraving of the himantes demonstrates *ad unguem* the artist's close attention to their layering and structure. Partially occluded by the ropes that bind him to a tree, they are also visible on Amycus. It is easy to imagine that members of the Etruscan elite, who appear to have had considerable reverence for the Dioscuri, found the story of the Amycian boxing match as compelling as these superb images (Thuillier 1985, p. 488–489).

Figure 39: Detail of the Ficoroni cista (ca. AD 340) showing the preparations of Polydeuces (at left, striking the κώρυκος barefisted) for his boxing match with Amycus. Silenus sits at the fountain (Museum of Villa Giulia, No. 24787).

Despite evidence of Greek-influenced boxing artifacts in Etruria, Thuillier (2021) argues that Etruscan sport was by no means merely derivative of Greek athletics.[62] In Etruria, for

---

[62] The view is not universally shared. Lucke and Frey (1962, p. 29), for example, argue that the Tuscan 'ring' was strongly influenced by the Greek model. Jazwa (2020, p. 35) finds sufficient heuretic evidence to conclude, "The presence of boxing in Etruria need not be explained by Greek or other external influences...[A]n independent invention in Etruria is most likely."

Figure 40: Detail of the Ficoroni cista (ca. AD 340) showing the aftermath of Polydeuces' boxing match with Amycus, whom Polydeuces ties to a tree (Museum of Villa Giulia, No. 24787).

instance, blood was spilled during boxing matches to benefit the recently deceased. Thuillier (2017, p. 230) notes as early as the seventh century BC, several tombs at Tarquinia[63] were designed with a wide entrance, "resembling a small public square, often ringed on several sides with benches to accommodate spectators." Gathered to send their deceased relative to the next world, an elite Etruscan clan would there be able to "watch dance performances as well as boxing or wrestling matches, within the context of funerary games" (ibid.). The author notes that, "Other religious ceremonies, such as sacrifices, could of course be performed there as well" (ibid.).[64] Human sacrifice was a part of Etruscan culture and it also typified their northern neighbors, including the Celts and the paleo-Venetians (Bonfante 1984; 2011).

Brandt (2015) cites the late Roman author Arnobius,[65] who mentions the Etruscan funerary cult described in the lost *Acherontic Books*.[66] From Arnobius' statement, Brandt surmises that among the Etruscans it was understood that "a blood sacrifice was able to give immortality to dead souls" (p. 125) and Krauskopf (2006, p. 66) goes even farther, arguing that "the Etruscans believed that certain...sacrifices...could transform human souls into gods."[67] Jannot (1998, p. 67) suggested that the blood shed in boxing matches might have been intended to furnish the deceased with longer life in the great beyond. Brandt notes that while animal blood sacrifice is not depicted in Etruscan tomb paintings, "scenes with the flowing of human blood are not infrequent," including scenes of boxers (p. 127). The author muses, "Could such blood-thirsty scenes have served the same purpose as the animal sacrifices, to give immortality to the deceased's soul? At death the blood stops running; flowing blood in a ritual context would thus be a symbol of life" (ibid.). Brandt perceives in the "cognitive world" of the Etruscans (and later the Romans) "a tension between death and the life-giving blood, procured through fighting" (ibid.).

4   Lucania (Pæstum)

Around 600 BC, Greek settlers established a southern Italian colony they called Poseidonia; later, the Romans called it Pæstum. Perhaps one hundred years after its founding, an Italic, Oscan-speaking group known as the Lucanians conquered the city. Rather than drive out the Greeks, the Lucanians seem to have mixed relatively easily with them and forged a thriving culture. The Italiote art that resulted from this concrescence is known to us from vase paintings and from a relatively large number of decorated tumuli, where stone slabs formed the four walls and pitched ceiling. The interior sides of the slabs were richly decorated with frescoes. The tombs were the resting places of the Lucanian elite, and the art adorning the slabs is arguably a pastiche of Italic and Greek elements. Given the strong possibility that the Lucanians were influenced culturally by the Etruscans, living farther to the north on the Appenine peninsula, many scholars seem to regard the Lucanian tombs as 'Etruscan'. Indeed,

---

[63] These tombs include the tumuli of Doganaccia, Poggio del Forno, Poggio Gallinaro, and Infernaccio.

[64] As Jazwa (2020, p. 31) has noted, comments by Livy (1.35, 5.1) suggest that Etruscan boxers participated in Roman athletic events, so their association with the Etruscan funerary cultus was by no means exclusive.

[65] Arnobius was a Christian apologist who wrote in the fourth century AD. He comments (dismissively) on blood sacrifice among the Etruscans in *Adversus nationes* 2.62.

[66] Krauskopf (2006, p. 66) notes that we have only the barest evidence for what was contained in these books, known in Latin as *Libri Acheruntici*.

[67] The resulting gods were known (in Latin) as *dii animales* and were related to the Roman household / ancestral gods called the *Penates*.

both groups decorated their tombs with images of boxers. At the risk of being too precise, we differentiate Lucanian representations of boxing from Etruscan ones (Section 3), though it is entirely possible that both belong to the same supercategory.

About 55% of the Lucanian tomb frescoes include representations of boxing (Pontrandolfo Greco and Rouveret 1992, p. 68). Armed gladiatorial duels are even more common (over 90% of tombs include such depictions). Pugilistic scenes are frequently juxtaposed on the same slab with gladiatorial contests. The corpus of Lucanian tomb paintings is rather large and relatively understudied. We list all of the images of boxing we have been able to identify (see Table 1).

The Lucanian depictions of boxing differ considerably from the Etruscan variety. However, the emphasis on blood flow and the association with funerary ritual is common to both. Another similarity is the presence of an aolist in the Lucanian boxing matches.[68] We interpret this to mean that associations between boxing, blood, music, and human sacrifice were strongly linked in Archaic and post-Archaic Italy, with roots reaching back to the Iron Age in the north (see Chapter 2), if not even further to the ancient Near East (Dioscurus and Dioscurus 2022b). The Lucanian approach to boxing stands in contrast to the more eastern (i.e., Hellenic) focus on athleticism and individual glory to be won in boxing. It seems to hearken back to the even more ancient cultic boxing practiced in Bronze Age Anatolia and Mesopotamia.

Painted tombs at Pæstum feature boxers who are more often than not bloodied in combat. There are at least twenty-two pugilistic scenes form this corpus. The major features of each scene are cataloged in Table 1.

The fighters in all but one case are entirely naked (the exception is a fresco now found in the collection at Tufts University; the boxer in question wears a decorated loincloth). Blood is evident in most of the frescoes (17/22) and flows prodigiously in many. An aolist is present in most examples (15/22). Typically, the fists are tightly wound, claviform, in strips of cloth or leather (14/22).

Blood was not unknown in Greek depictions of boxing (Figure 41), but blood seems to have played a special role in Italic pugilism. Thuillier (2017, p. 222) notes that the boxing scenes at Pæstum bear "a pronounced Etruscan stamp."

In general, the action in the Lucanian boxing frescoes appears to be of a serious nature. However, the burlesque is evident in up to one-third of the compositions. This is clearly signaled by the presence of a fodgel, satyr-like aolist (4/22). It may also be expressed by deformed boxers (3/22; including one with no genitalia) and the single example of an ithyphallic fighter. Here, we may see a connection to Etruscan depictions of boxers, where big-bellied fighters depicted in some tombs (e.g., the Tomba Cardarelli and the Tomba della Fustigazione) were perhaps deliberately juxtaposed with the skilled athletes painted in others (Thuillier 1985, pp. 129, 557–558).

The Lucanian boxers were occasionally distinguished from one another by skin tone (6/22). In Andriuolo 24, for example, a black pugilist has received a damaging blow to the face; one critic has argued that the portly figure in this fresco is a pygmy (Zuchtriegel 2020, p. 395). The dark-skinned boxers do not in all cases bear other features suggestive of African origin (cf. Vannullo, Tomb 4 in Figure 44). For this reason, it has been argued that the skin tone is not intended to be realistic, but merely to distinguish the fighters from one another. How-

---

[68] Thuillier (1985) notes that this is *favorable à l'influence étrusque* (p. 225).

Loc.	An	An	An	An	An	An	An	An	An	La	La	Ar	Ar	PA	Li	G	G	V	V	V	SF	T
Num.	12	18	32	90	104	104	48	1	24	64	3	1	271	1	8	7	1	2	4	3	1	?
Slab	S	S	N	N	S	E	E	S	W	S	N?	N?	S	N	N	N	S	N	N	S	?	?
Aolist	?	+	+	+	+	-	-	+	+	+	-	+	+	+	+	+	+	-	+	-	-	+
Dwarf	-	?	+	-	-	-	-	+	-	-	-	+	-	-	-	-	-	-	-	-	-	+
Blood	+	+	+	+	+	-	+	+	+	-	+	+	+	+	?	+	+	-	+	-	+	+
Wraps	?	?	+	+	?	-	-	+	+	+	+	+	+	?	?	+	?	+	+	+	+	+
Caestus	?	?	?	-	?	?	+	?	-	?	+	-	+	?	?	-	?	?	-	-	-	+
Black	?	?	?	-	-	?	+	?	+	-	-	-	-	-	?	+	-	+	+	+	-	-
Wreath	?	?	?	-	?	-	-	+	-	-	-	+	+	-	-	-	?	-	-	-	+	+
Striking	-	+	-	+	-	-	-	-	+	?	-	-	-	?	-	+	?	-	-	-	-	-
X-arms	+	-	-	+	-	-	-	-	+	?	+	-	-	?	-	+	?	-	+	+	-	-
Beard	?	?	?	+	-	+	+	-	-	+	+	+	+	-	?	-	?	+	+	+	+	+
Judge	?	?	?	-	-	-	-	-	-	-	-	-	+	-	+	-	-	-	-	-	-	-
Naked	+	+	+	+	+	+	+	+	+	+	+	+	+	?	?	+	?	+	+	+	+	-

Table 1: Lucanian tomb paintings (location, tomb number, slab) that include scenes of pugilism (N = north, etc.). The matrix indicates whether or not particular features are present or absent (X-arms = crossed arms). The question mark is used when the best available image does not permit determination (usually due to fresco deterioration). Locations: An = Andriuolo; La = Laghetto; Ar = Arcioni; PA = Porta Aurea; Li = Licinella; G = Gaudo; V = Vannullo; SF = Sequestro Finanza; T = Tufts.

Figure 41: Boxers on a Nikosthenic amphora (British Museum #1867,0508.968) found at Agrigento, Sicily and dated 550–540 BC. The bleeding pugilist is represented widely in Italic art, including the funerary frescoes discovered at Pæstum, in southern Italy.

ever, we note that there are no black gladiators in any of the Lucanian tomb frescoes. It is possible that Lucanian boxing was reserved for low-status individuals, perhaps slaves.

Vegetal motifs are common in the Lucanian tomb frescoes. While by no means exclusive to the scenes of boxing, balaustas are frequently found floating around the pugilists (Ferrari et al. 2018, p. 826). Pomegranates are likely symbolic of death and rebirth, appropriate for the funerary setting. Indeed, this may give us some clues as to why boxing of this particularly sanguinary type is included so frequently in the tomb frescoes.

The depiction of boxers in Tomb 3 of Laghetto (Figure 43) may include the earliest known representation of the kind of weaponized *cæstus* that became commonplace in Late Antiquity (Dioscurus and Dioscurus 2023). While the precise form of the weaponized *cæstus*, which appears on the left (lead) hand of each boxer, is not altogether clear in the fresco as it remains, we can say for sure that the left and right hands of the boxers are outfitted differently. On the right hand we see the tightly wrapped, club-like gauntlet (apparent on both hands in most boxers of the Pæstum tomb paintings). The left hand, which holds particular interest for us, is equipped with a different material, rendered by the artist with tighter cross-hatching than we see on the boxers' right hands. This material covers the knuckles and the back of the hand up to the wrist. The cross-hatching suggests a thinner strip, designed perhaps to carry pieces of metal referred to in later forms of Roman boxing glove. Extensions from these gloves are most likely the finger and thumb. Why are the fingers free?

To approach this question, let us consider a modern analogy. A relatively recent innovation in western combat sports is the mixed martial arts or MMA glove. In some cases MMA gloves bear a thick pad across the knuckles; in others, the padding is inconsiderable. Striking

Figure 42: Boxers on the south slab of Vannullo Tomb 3. Fists are tightly wrapped, including the forearm. Unlike other Lucanian depictions of boxing, blood is not featured prominently here.

is permitted while wearing either type.[69] In all gloves of this type, the fingers and thumb are free. In MMA, this allows a fighter to grasp his standing opponent in order to wrestle him to the ground and more easily subdue him using a variety of holds. This form of fighting would be greatly deprecated if opponents wore modern boxing gloves—or the right-handed gloves of the Laghetto Tomb 3 boxers—due to the restraints imposed on the fingers and thumb.

Are the Laghetto boxers practicing something more akin to MMA? The culture that produced this image was doubtless already familiar with Greek *pankration*, the ancient combat sport most similar to MMA. It was practiced among the Greeks as early as the seventh century BC. *Pankration* fighters did not wear gauntlets of any kind and depictions of the sport typically show the fighters struggling on the ground or, if standing, then kicking. Indeed, it seems to be the presence of gauntlets in ancient depictions of the combat sports that allows us to conclude that boxing and not *pankration* is taking place (Dioscurus and Dioscurus 2022d).

Given the emphasis on bloody combat in the Lucanian tomb paintings, it is likely that the liberated fingers on the left (lead) hands of the Laghetto boxers allowed them to gouge the eyes, mutilate the ears, and "fish-hook" the mouth and nostrils of their adversaries—all banned in modern MMA and rendered more or less impossible with the modern boxing glove (at least since the immobilization of the thumb in the mid-twentieth-century). What we see at Laghetto Tomb 3 is an experiment that may not have lasted, or was perhaps simply replaced by the far more lethal spiked gauntlets often depicted in Roman-style pugilism of Late Antiquity.

Lucanian boxers depicted in Tomb 3 of Vannullo present evidence of claviform, wrapped fists on both hands (Figure 42) much like those often presumed to be worn by the Boxing Boys of Akrotiri (Dioscurus and Dioscurus 2022c). In Vannullo 3, the light-skinned boxer (on the right) naïvely thrusts both hands forward. Both are tightly wound up in bandages or strips, perhaps of leather, like Greek *himantes*. The left (lead) hand of the dark-skinned boxer is equipped in the same fashion. Unfortunately, it is not possible to make out the details of this boxer's right hand, raised in front of his chest. Similarly indeterminate is the equipage on the right (back) hands of the boxers depicted in Tomb 4 of Vannullo (Figure 44). Though no fingers can be seen, it is possible that the artist wished to depict a closed fist unencumbered by any glove, or perhaps wearing a glove like the one seen on the lead hands of the Laghetto Tomb 3 boxers but curled into a fist (Figure 43). At the very least, we can argue that the Lucanians innovated boxing through differential outfitting of the lead and back hands. At Laghetto we have indication of mobile fingers on the lead hand, while at Vannullo Tomb 4, the lead hand is the blunter instrument and the back hand bears a different type of *cæstus*, if not a fingerless glove.

The Iliadic funeral games notwithstanding, one critic notes: "Bloody combat at funeral games has no direct precedent in Greek sepulchral art" (Corrigan 1979, p. 210). The particularly sanguigenous pugilism depicted in tombs of pre-Roman Italy, including the frescoes at Pæstum, suggests the presence of an autochthonous Italic death cult, perhaps connected to or even derived from the bruising battles featured on East Alpine situlæ, where the dumbbells would have provoked significant bloodshed and traumatic injury (Section 2). There is thus strong evidence for a link between funerals, human sacrifice, propitiation of the dead, and boxing in pre-Roman Italy. Given the absence of evidence for a similar pugilistic death

---

[69] Gloves without the knuckle pad are sometimes called 'grappling gloves' while the gloves with the knuckle pad are sometimes called 'striking gloves'.

Figure 43: Boxers on the north(?) slab of Laghetto Tomb 3. The boxers appear to wear weaponized *caestus* on their left (lead) hands. Their right (back) hands are wrapped in the club-like fashion observed in other Lucanian tomb frescoes. Blood streams from the face, abdomen, and legs of the boxers.

Figure 44: Boxers on the south slab of Vannullo Tomb 4. The boxers have tightly wrapped fists. While not flowing freely as in other Lucanian tomb frescoes, blood is indicated on the face and breast of the dark-skinned fighter; also on the abdomen, left arm, and left thigh of the light-skinned fighter.

cult in post-Homeric Greece, it is possible that Italic associations between boxing and human sacrifice are in fact quite ancient, and stretch back to early Celtic settlement of Italy and Greece, if not to the earlier Indo-European dispersion.[70]

Boxing in Lucania was also represented by more traditional Greek depictions, like the one on a Skyphos described by Connor (1995). A fine example of the red-figure style (Figure 45), the boxer represents the bold graphic style of Greek artisans able to capture the dynamics of fighting and the tension of the male bodies engaged in it. On the other side of the skyphos, a boxer raises both arms at an angle, with the fingers extended. Stylistically, the depiction has little in common with the Lucanian tomb frescoes, further evidence of the unique cultural exchange that took place here before the ascendancy of Rome.

Figure 45: Lucanian red-figure skyphos (University of Melbourne, No. MUV75: 1989.0070). The object is dated 410–400 BC.

5 Sardinia

Dated to as late as 750 BC, the statues of Mont'e Prama in western Sardinia are the oldest life-size human sculptures of the western Mediterranean (Tronchetti and Pauli 2016, p. 63). Some of these statues allegedly represent boxers (see, for instance, Figure 46).[71] They are

---

[70] We suspect that Hittite boxing may have been influenced as much by this hypothetical Indo-European substratum as by Babylonian and Sumerian precedents.

[71] Two torsos perhaps belonging to representations of pugilists—not the torsos pictured here—were discovered as late as May 2022 (Unattributed 2022).

accoutred after a fashion that resembles the strange garb we observed in Mycenæan depictions of boxing (Dioscurus and Dioscurus 2022d). Some of the statues identified as boxers wear belts around their upper-chest and one bronze archer wears a gorget reminiscent of the one worn in Mycenæan pottery fragment (Minoja and Usai 2011, p. 37). The fighters carry shields and wear a kind of arm-length *cæstus*. They are often bare-chested.

The upper body of one of the boxers is naked and he wears a pointed loincloth (Tronchetti and Pauli 2016, p. 65). The clothing recalls the loincloth worn by a Minoan boxer figurine found on Crete (Dioscurus and Dioscurus 2022c). Above his head, one Nuragic boxer holds a shield that was probably originally made of leather (Tronchetti and Pauli 2016, p. 65).

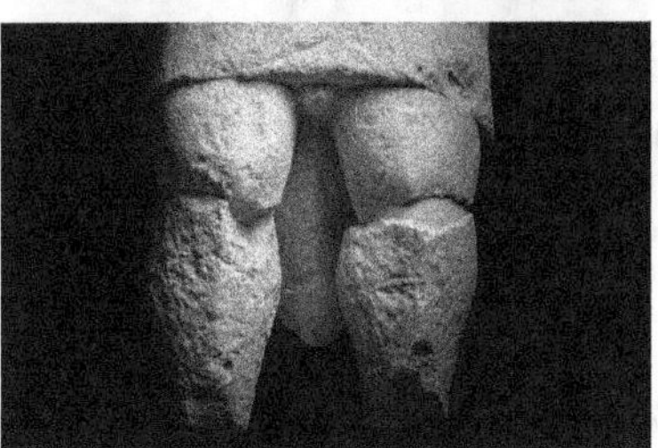

Figure 46: Sandstone Nuragic boxer figures from Mont'e Prama (Museo archeologico nazionale—Cagliari, no inventory numbers). Dated between 1100–750 BC.

These little-studied monuments were associated with burials along a path—a kind of *via sacra* (Tronchetti and Pauli 2016, p. 64). There are a total of seventeen statues that have been categorized as 'boxers' among the ruins of Mont'e Prama (intriguingly, eight other statues represent archers).

It is believed that the Sardinian boxers were created by the Nuragic culture between 1100 and 750 BC. But are these really boxers or is "boxer" just a label that has stuck? The fact that the fighters are routinely depicted with shields makes us wonder if they fit our self-imposed definition of unarmed orthograde combat (Dioscurus and Dioscurus 2022a). The term 'boxer' has perhaps been applied to these statues by convention as it is generally supposed that the fighters were in fact armed. Two authorities on the subject summarize:

> The 'boxers' make up the most uniform group, showing only minor variations in size. All represent bare-chested males wearing loin-cloths with the rear trimmed to a triangle. In some cases, shallow grooves depict the strings used to tie the loin-cloths. The boxer's heads are covered by a smooth cap that suggest the use of cloth or leather. A curved oval shield presumably made of leather on a wooden frame covers one of the boxers' arms from elbow to fist. It is invariably held on the left arm and raised above the men's head, while a leather sleeve running from the elbow down protected their right arm (Tronchetti and van Dommelen 2005, p. 190).

While separated by a yawning gap of time, it is worth considering what influence the fighting culture of Archaic Sardinia may have had on developments on the Appenine Peninsula, including among the Etruscans (Section 3), Lucanians (Section 4), and the Romans themselves (Dioscurus and Dioscurus 2023). The fighting style represented by the Nuragic statues corresponds most readily to gladiatorial combat, though it seems that too little is as yet known about the culture that created these statues to even suggest how their version of 'pugilism' might have influenced recreational bloodletting elsewhere in the ancient Mediterranean.

6 Conclusion

Many of the depictions we have reviewed in this article force us to wonder, once more, what makes boxing boxing? The Lucanian tomb painting at Laghetto (Figure 43) presents us with the problem *in nuce*: The upright posture of the fighters and their gloved hands are almost certainly suggestive of ancient boxing (rather than *pankration*). However, the inclusion on the hands of sharp elements problematizes boxing as an 'unarmed' combat. As we will see in Dioscurus and Dioscurus (2023), boxing gloves were ostentatiously weaponized by the Romans in Late Antiquity, yet boxing remained distinct from gladiatorial combat. As we have demonstrated here, the ontological boundary between the reinforced and weaponized fist began long before the Roman ascendancy. Furthermore, the ritual focus on funeral games is both of long vintage and yet a departure from nearby Greek athleticism. The unique features of these European boxing cultures show the sempiternal genesis of boxers (and their patrons) playing with the rules and generating new forms: either ancient forms independently rediscovered or obscurely transmitted, or novel forms that tested the limits of what orthograde personal combat could become.

Although traditionally treated as a minor sidelight in the history of boxing, the blood-thirsty nature of East Alpine, Italic, and Sardinian boxing together produced a fertile terroire for Roman gladiatorial boxing soon upon the import of Hellenistic boxing practices. Without these unique, pre-Roman forms of boxing, combat sport in the Roman world may never have achieved its gory apotheosis.

References

John D. Beazley. *Attic Black-Figure Vase-Painters*. Oxford University Press, Oxford, 1956.

Giuliano Bonfante and Larissa Bonfante. *The Etruscan Language: An Introduction*. Manchester University Press, Manchester, 2nd edition, 2002.

Larissa Bonfante. The Corsini Throne. *The Journal of the Walters Art Gallery*, 36:110–122, 1977.

Larissa Bonfante. Human sacrifice on an Etruscan funerary urn. *American Journal of Archæology*, 88(4):531–539, 1984.

Larissa Bonfante. The Etruscans: Mediators between northern barbarians and classical civilization. In Larissa Bonfante, editor, *The Barbarians of Ancient Europe: Realities and Interactions*, pages 233–281. Cambridge University Press, Cambridge, 2011.

J. Rasmus Brandt. Passage to the underworld: Continuity or change in Etruscan funerary ideology and practices (6th–2nd centuries bc)? In J. Rasmus Brandt, Marina Prusac, and Håkon Roland, editors, *Death and Changing Rituals. Function and meaning in ancient funerary practises*, pages 105–184. Oxbow Books, Oxford, 2015.

Peter J. Connor. 'Boxing on' a Lucanian red-figured skyphos in the University of Melbourne. *Mediterranean Archæology*, 8:101–105, 1995.

Eileen H. Corrigan. *Lucanian Tomb Paintings Excavated at Pæstum 1969–1972: An Iconogrpahic Study*. PhD thesis, Columbia University, 1979.

Nigel B. Crowther. The evidence for kicking in Greek boxing. *The American Journal of Philology*, 111:176–181, 1990.

Castor Dioscurus and Pollux Dioscurus. The development of boxing: Origins in biomechanics and social mechanics; The ancient world (Prehistory). *Scholia Pugillātōria*, 1:1–22, 2022a.

Castor Dioscurus and Pollux Dioscurus. The development of boxing: The ancient world (Western Asia and Egypt). *Scholia Pugillātōria*, 1:23–71, 2022b.

Castor Dioscurus and Pollux Dioscurus. The development of boxing: The ancient world (The Ægean). *Scholia Pugillātōria*, 1:73–111, 2022c.

Castor Dioscurus and Pollux Dioscurus. The development of boxing: The ancient world (Classical Greece). *Scholia Pugillātōria*, 1:113–190, 2022d.

Castor Dioscurus and Pollux Dioscurus. The development of boxing: The ancient world (The Hellenistic world and Rome). *Scholia Pugillātōria*, 1:249–375, 2023.

P. Ducati. Le pietre funerarie felsinee. *Monumenti antichi dei Lincei*, 20:360–724, 1911.

P. Ducati. Nuove stele funerarie felsinee. *Monumenti antichi dei Lincei*, 39:374–446, 1943.

M. Egg. Ein Cæstuskämpfer im Römisch–Germanischen Zentralmuseum. *Archäologisches Korrespondenzblatt*, 10:55–59, 1980.

Giorgia Ferrari, Giovanna Bosi, Ivano Ansaloni, Luigi Sala, Aurora Pederzoli, Pietro Baraldi, Laura Mussi, Matteo Nannini, Paolo Zannini, and Marta Bandini Mazzanti. Images and colors from the tombs of Paestum: A multidisciplinary study of the pigments in the flora and fauna iconography. *Journal of Archaeological Science: Reports*, 20:818–833, 2018.

Marko Frelih. O motivu dveh boksarjev v situlski umetnosti. *Zbornik za Umetnostno Zgodovino*, 25(25):99–114, 1989.

Otto-Herman Frey. *Die Enstehung der Situlenkunst: Studien zur figürlich Verzierten toreutik von Este*. Walter de Gruyter, Berlin, 1969.

Otto-Herman Frey. Il Veneto e il mondo di Hallstatt-la tène. In O. Paoletti, editor, *Protostoria e storia del 'venetorum angulus'*, pages 17–27. Poligrafici Internazionali, Pisa, 1999. Atti del XX Convegno di Studi Etruschi ed Italici, Portogruaro-Quarto D'Altino-Este-Adria.

Norman E. Gardiner. *Athletics of the Ancient World*. Clarendon, Oxford, 1930.

Elizabhet Caroline Johnstone Gray. *Tour to the Sepulchres of Etruria, in 1839*. Hatchard, London, 1840.

Moriz Hoernes. *Prähistorischen Formenlehre: Bericht über den Besuch einiger Museen im östlichen Oberitalien*. F. Tempsky, Vienna, 1893.

Christoph Huth. *Menschenbilder und Menschenbild: Anthropomorphe Bildwerkeder frühen Eisenzeit*. Reimer, Berlin, 2003.

Jean-René Jannot. De l'agôn au geste rituel: L'example de la boxe étrusque. *L'Antiquité Classique*, 54:66–75, 1985.

Jean-René Jannot. *Devins, dieux et démons: Regards sur la religion de l'Etrurie antique*. Picard, Paris, 1998.

Kyle A. Jazwa. A Late Archaic boxing-dance in Etruria: Identification, comparison, and function. *Etruscan Studies*, 23(1–2):29–61, 2020.

W. H. S. Jones, D. Litt, and H. A. Ormerod. *Pausanias. Description of Greece*. Harvard University Press, Cambridge, MA, 1918.

Julius Jüthner and Erwin Mehl. Pygme (pugilatus). In Konrat Ziegler, editor, *Paulys Realencyclopädie der classischen Altertumswissenschaft*, volume S9, pages 1306–1352. Alfred Druckenmüller Verlag, Stuttgart, 1962.

Ingrid Krauskopf. The grave and beyond in Etruscan religion. In Erika Simon and Nancy Thomson de Grummond, editors, *The Religion of the Etruscans*, pages 66–89. University of Texas Press, Austin, TX, 2006.

Tomaž Lazar. The Fighting techniques of the Hallstatt period boxers: An attempt at reinterpretation of the situla art. *Arheološki vestnik*, 62:261–288, 2011.

W. Lucke and Otto-Herman Frey. *Die Situla in Providence (Rhode Island). Ein Beitrag zur Situlenkunst des Osthallstattkreises*, volume 26 of *Römisch–Germanische Kommission, Forschungen*. Walter de Gruyter, Berlin, 1962.

Guido Mansuelli. The East, the Adriatic, Etruria, and situla art. In Jože Kastelic, editor, *Situla Art: Ceremonial Bronzes of Ancient Europe*, pages xxvii–xxxii. McGraw–Hill Book Company, New York, 1965.

Friedrich Matz and Friedrich Karl von Duhn. *Antike Bildwerke in Rom: mit Ausschluss der grösseren Sammlungen*. K. W. Hiersemann, Leipzig, 1881. 3 vols.

G. von Merhart. Venetoillyrische Relieffigürchen aus Tirol. *Mannus*, 24, 1932.

Marco Minoja and Alessandro Usai. *La Pietra e gli Eroi: Le sculture restaurate di Mont'e Prama*. Accademia di Belle Arti "Mario Sironi", Sassari, 2011.

Zahra Newby. *Greek Athletics in the Roman World: Victory and Virtue*. Oxford University Press, Oxford, 2005.

Efstratia Oktapoda. Sirenes, gorgones, meduse et les monstres marins: Les Évolutions d'un mythe dans la littérature et l'art. *Economics, Management and Financial Markets*, 6:532–551, 2011.

Karl Olzscha. Die Inschrift auf der Situla Providence. In W. Lucke and Otto-Herman Frey, editors, *Die Situla in Providence (Rhode Island). Ein Beitrag zur Situlenkunst des Osthallstattkreises*, volume 26 of *Römisch–Germanische Kommission, Forschungen*, pages 85–86. Walter de Gruyter, Berlin, 1962.

Robin Osborne. Why did Athenian pots appeal to the Etruscans? *World Archæology*, 33(2):277–295, 2001.

Michael Baron Poliakoff. *Studies in the Terminology of the Greek Combat Sports*. PhD thesis, University of Michigan, 1983.

Michael Baron Poliakoff. *Combat Sports in the Ancient World*. Yale University Press, New Haven, CT, 1987a.

Michael Baron Poliakoff. Melankomas, ἐκ κλίμακος, and Greek boxing. *The American Journal of Philology*, 108(3):511–518, 1987b.

Angela Pontrandolfo Greco and Agnès Rouveret. *Le Tombe Dipinte di Pæstum*. Franco Cosimo Panini, Modena, 1992.

Katharina Rebay-Salisbury. It's all fun and games until somebody gets hurt: Images of sport in early Iron Age art of Central Europe. *World Archæology*, 44(2):189–201, 2012.

F. Sacchetti. Charu(n) et 'les autres' : le cas des stèles étrusques de bologne. *Revue archéologique*, 52:263–308, 2011.

Thomas Francis Scanlon. *Eros and Greek Athletics*. Oxford University Press, New York, 2002.

W. Schmid. Die Fürstengräber von Klein Glein in der Steiermark. *Præhistorische Zeitschrift*, 24:219–282, 1933.

Diether Schürr. Die rätische inschrift der situla in providence. *Studi Etruschi*, 503:243–255, 2003.

H. H. Scullard. *The Etruscan Cities and Rome*. Cornell University Press, Ithaca, NY, 1967.

Otto Skutsch. *The Annals of Quintus Ennius*. Oxford University Press, Oxford, 1985.

Aleksandar Stipčevič. *Kultni Simboli kod Ilira: Građa i Prilozi Sistematizaciji*. Akademija Nauka i Umjetnosti Bosne i Hercegovine, Sarajevo, 1981.

Karl Taube. The Ballgame, boxing and ritual blood sport in Ancient Mesoamerica. In Colin Renfrew, Iain Morley, and Michael Boyd, editors, *Ritual Play and Belief in Evolution and Early Human Societies*, pages 264–301. Cambridge University Press, Cambridge, 2018.

Karl A. Taube and Marc Zender. American gladiators: Ritual boxing in ancient Mesoamerica. In Heather Orr and Rex Koontz, editors, *Blood and Beauty: Organized Violence in the Art and Archæology of Mesoamerica and Central America*, pages 161–220. Cotsen Institute of Archæology Press, Los Angeles, CA, 2009.

J. C. Thomas. *Boxing's Dirty Tricks and Outlaw Killer Punches*. Loompanics Unlimited, Port Townsend, WA, 1997.

Jean-Paul Thuillier. *Les Jeux Athlétiques dans la Civilisation Étrusque*. École Française de Rome, Rome, 1985.

Jean-Paul Thuillier. Sports. In Alessandro Naso, editor, *Etruscology*, pages 221–232. De Gruyter, Berlin, 2017.

Jean-Paul Thuillier. Etruscan events. In Thomas Francis Scanlon and Alison Futrell, editors, *The Oxford Handbook of Sport and Spectacle in the Ancient World*, pages 74–84. Oxford University Press, Oxford, 2021.

Carlo Tronchetti and Rainer Pauli. Gräber und Monumentalstatuen vom Monte Prama auf Sardinien. *Antike Welt*, 3:63–68, 2016.

Carlo Tronchetti and Peter van Dommelen. Entangled objects and hybrid practices: Colonial contacts and elite connections at Monte Prama, Sardinia. *Journal of Mediterranean Archaeology*, 18(2):183–208, 2005.

Unattributed. Two Iron Age fighter statues exhumed in Sardinia. *Noticias Financieras*, 2022. May 7.

Ruth D. Whitehouse. 'Tombstones' in the North Italian Iron Age: Careless writers or athletic readers? In K. E. Piquette and R. D. Whitehouse, editors, *Writing as Material Practice: Substance, surface and medium*, pages 271–288. Ubiquity Press, London, 2013.

Zach Zorich. Fighting with jaguars, bleeding for rain. *Archaeology*, 61(6):46–52, 2008.

Gabriel Zuchtriegel. Isocrates and the paideia of the Lucanians. *Mélanges de l'École française de Rome - Antiquité*, 132(2):383–401, 2020.

Changelog

- ~2023.6.19 First public release.
- ~2023.7.8 Repagination in anticipation of printing.
- ~2023.10.1 Minor proofreading edits.

The Development of Boxing: The Ancient World (The Hellenistic World and Rome)

Castor Dioscurus; Pollux Dioscurus

Contents

Abstract

While Hellenistic boxing maintained an athletic aesthetic and tradition of performance well into the common era, Roman boxing synthesized many of the more brutal Italic aspects of the activity. Ultimately, Roman boxing blurred the boundaries between armed and unarmed orthograde combat. We propose a logical classification of boxing into ritual, athletic, and gladiatorial strands. Roman boxing is frequently criticized as a degraded or decadent form of Greek pugilism. We find this frame unhelpful for understanding the true nature and evolution of boxing in Late Antiquity. Instead, we argue that the final stage of ancient boxing was a synthesis of Homeric *pygmachia* and Italic

Scholia Pugillātōria 1 (2023): 251–377.

Address author correspondence to `scholia@protonmail.com`.

funeral cult, sharing features with, but still distinguished from, armed gladiatorial combat.

1   Introduction

Historically, boxing waxes and wanes in its degree of violence, as evoked poetically in the fifth book of Vergil's *Æneid*. Boxing was ultimately eclipsed by gladiatorial combat and other forms of spectacle while elite participation in the sport dwindled. There is little evidence that boxing disappeared because it was banned by any ruling elite. Synthesizing the story of boxing to date, we propose a notional taxonomy: in Late Antiquitiy, boxing activities can be sorted into ritual, athletic, and gladiatorial forms. Ritual boxing encompasses pugilism undertaken to perform or commemorate before onlookers and the gods, such as the funeral games of Patroclus. Athletic boxing reaches its characteristic apex in the Hellenic Olympics, although the Hellenistic Olympics continue to produce notable boxers and boxing stories well into the common era. Gladiatorial boxing has ancient roots but comes into its own as a violent performance in the Roman Colosseum and other contemporaneous arenas.

2   Hellenistic and Roman Greece

While boxers of the ancient Near East, Egypt, and the Ægean (Crete and the Cyclades) almost certainly adhered to rule sets and norms, the sheer wealth of information about Greek boxing allows us to infer much more about the regulation of pugilism in the late first millennium (Dioscurus and Dioscurus 2022d). In many cases, no inference is needed, since ancient writers described the activity *eo nomine*. Not only did the Greeks discourse upon the methods and manners of the sport they called *pygmachia*, they created works of art from those bloody, bruising battles that still exercise a transfiguring effect on the modern viewer. The Greeks set orthograde and pronograde bounds to the previously murky field of unarmed personal combat, and then obscured those bounds again with the invention of the *pankration*. We discuss literary, laudatory, and documentary sources for Hellenistic Greek boxing.

The Greeks and the Romans were interested in perpetuating two types of boxing stories,[1] derived to a great extent from Homeric models, though with considerable variation. Type I includes the funeral games stories,[2] in which two peers engage in a prize fight to honor a fallen comrade. One combatant is often older than the other but enmity (beyond a little trash talk) is not usually part of the equation.[3] Type II, on the other hand, seethes with ill will. It is the story of a bully who challenges all comers to fight him, then loses to a virtuous figure who is skilled in and represents the finer points of boxing.[4] In most cases, the bully is also a barbarian, i.e., one who does not represent the values of the Greco-Roman world. The bully is usually called Amycus and his antagonist is typically Polydeuces (Roman Pollux), one of the semi-divine twins known in Latin as the Dioscuri. While Type I funereal boxing is clearly

---

[1] Vian (2008, p. 400) considers boxing so ubiquitous an element as to call it an "epic motif."

[2] After Homer the funeral games are considered *un épisode obligé dan l'épopée grecque et romaine* (Thuillier 1996, p. 151).

[3] Statius' account of boxing in Book 6 of the *Thebaid* (Section 3.4.2) is the exception that proves the rule.

[4] Hagopian (1955, p. 57) sees in this type of story an underdog David vs. Goliath or Jack the Giant Killer motif. Indeed, the physical size of the bully is often accentuated in the epics, though his antagonist is never characterized as diminutive.

ritual, Type II agonistic boxing partakes of a generally athletic attitude, including praise of the superior skill of the victor and protagonist (Dioscurus and Dioscurus 2022d, pp. 126ff., 132ff.).

Hellenistic Greeks recognized that other cultures had their own boxing traditions, and they generally belittled them. The fourth-century BC orator and statesman Demosthenes, in *Philippic I*, 4.40, offered a scathing critique of the Athenian military by comparing it to a barbarian pugilist:

> But you, Athenians, possessing unsurpassed resources—fleet, infantry, cavalry, revenues—have never to this very day employed them aright, and yet you carry on war with Philip exactly as a barbarian boxes [πυκτεύω]. The barbarian, when struck [πλήσσω], always clutches [ἔχω] the place; hit him on the other side and there go his hands. He neither knows nor cares how to parry [προβάλλω][5] a blow or how to watch [βλέπω] his adversary [ἐναντίος] (Vince 1930).[6]

Demosthenes' simile serves not only as an indictment of how non-Greeks boxed, it also indicates what Greeks valued in a good boxing match. They appreciated solid defensive technique, including careful scrutiny of one's opponent.[7] These characteristics redound through all the Greek (and Roman) epic boxing vignettes (including Homer and the *Argonautica*, reviewed in Dioscurus and Dioscurus, 2022d) as emblematic of successful boxers.

However, the esteem was not universal. Sparta (betimes the legendary inventors of boxing) rejected the sport for its individualist nature: "In time, however, they [the Spartans] abandoned boxing and likewise the pankration, believing that it was disgraceful to compete in these events, in which it is possible, through just one person admiting defeat, for the whole of Sparta to be reproached for lack of courage" (Philostratus, *Gym.* 9).

Why are there so many expressions of athletic boxing in Greek epic poetry? The Greeks recognized a close connection between athletes and soldiers. The Greeks found a dim echo of war in athletics but they acknowledged the differences. According to one critic of Greek sport:

> The ritual ordeal of the athlete reënacts the ordeals of the warrior, and, like heroic deeds, athletic activity compensates for the athlete's mortality as the athlete figuratively dies a ritual death in recurrent festivals. The origin of athletics is related both to initiation and to funeral games, and real or symbolic death and rebirth is common to both activities. Epinikian songs refer to those done 'in compensation for' (*epi*) the ordeal involved in winning the victory (Nagy 2021).

For the Greeks, then, there was glory in war and there was glory in sport.[8]

---

[5] The verb, here in the mediopassive voice, probably means 'to cover or protect oneself'.

[6] ὑμεῖς δ', ὦ ἄνδρες Ἀθηναῖοι, πλείστη δύναμιν ἁπάντων ἔχοντες, τριήρεις, ὁπλίτας, ἱππέας, χρημάτων πρόσοδον, τούτων μὲν μέχρι τῆς τήμερον ἡμέρας οὐδενὶ πώποτ' εἰς δέον τι κέχρησθε, οὐδὲν δ' ἀπολείπετε, ὥσπερ οἱ βάρβαροι πυκτεύουσιν, οὕτω πολεμεῖν Φιλίππῳ. καὶ γὰρ ἐκείνων ὁ πληγεὶς ἀεὶ τῆς πληγῆς ἔχεται, κἂν ἑτέρωσε πατάξῃ τις, ἐκεῖσ' εἰσὶν αἱ χεῖρες· προβάλλεσθαι δ' ἢ βλέπειν ἐναντίον οὔτ' οἶδεν οὔτ' ἐθέλει (Butcher 1903).

[7] It is still common in early modern and modern boxing to spend a round "feeling out" an opponent cautiously, in particular when fighting a new adversary.

[8] The bloodier-minded Romans seemed to never quite wrap their heads around this universalizing attitude (cf. Section 3.5).

2.1   *Idyll 22*

Writing the *Idylls* in the third century BC, Theocritus gives us his account of the boxing match between Polydeuces and Amycus in Book 22. The narrative, written in hexameter, is "probably an imitation" of the Apollonine version of the same episode found in the *Argonautica* (Nelis 2001, p. 9fn. 41).[9] The resemblance between the two works is "reinforced by verbal similarities and coincidences of detail" (Gow 1942, p. 11). The same commentator reasons that the Theocritean "poem is the later of the two" and that the author "deliberately set[...] out to improve on A[pollonius]," though this is much debated (ibid.).

The second part of *Idyll 22*, roughly between lines 27 and 134, describes the boxing match between Polydeuces and Amycus.[10] Book 22 is itself a hymn to the Dioscuri—those "boxer bards" (ἀεθλητῆρες ἀοιδοί, line 24) and "helpers twain of men" (ἄμφω θνητοῖσι βοηθόοι, line 23) according to Edmonds (1912)—with the first part devoted to Polydeuces.[11] The second half of the diptych pertains to Castor. In it the brothers abduct the rightful fiancées of two other men (their cousins, the Apharidæ) and Castor kills one of them gruesomely in an armed duel.[12]

"[R]uddy as the wine" (οἰνωπός, line 34),[13] Polydeuces wanders through a pleasant woodland (the *locus amœnus* of the poem) in search of fresh water for himself and his crew. He comes upon Amycus, the warden of a crystal spring, a man "both huge and terrible." Amycus is described in terms that "assimilate him to the landscape": "down from the top of his shoulders the muscles on his solid arms stood like round boulders which a winter-flowing river spun and polished with great eddies" (Chaldekas 2020, p. 20).[14] His ears (οὖς) were tough (σκληρός) and rendered shapeless (τεθλασμένος) by the fist (πυγμή), an early reference to perichondrial hematoma, an occasional subject of Greek boxing art (e.g., Figure 2). The round contour of his mighty chest is emphasized in line 46: στήθεα δ' ἐσφαίρωτο πελώρια .... The flesh of his broad back appears to be constituted of iron (σιδήρεος), giving the impression that Amycus is a gigantic statue, a veritable colossus (κολοσσός).[15]

Theocritus calls the giant ὑπέροπλος 'insolent' (line 44)[16] and the ensuing conversation (presented to the reader as a formal stichomythia, lines 54–74) brims with insulting lan-

---

[9] See Dioscurus and Dioscurus (2022d, pp. 132ff.) for a full discussion of the boxing episode by Apollonius of Rhodes.

[10] Line numbers in this section come from Cholmeley (1901) unless otherwise indicated.

[11] ὑμνέων Πολυδεύκεα πρῶτον ἀείσω (line 26).

[12] The problematic nature of Castor's section of the poem, which lacks the literary finesse of Polydueces' and shows us the Dioscuri participating in a morally questionable adventure, has been pondered at some length (Gow 1942, Chaldekas 2020).

[13] The adjective likely refers to Polydeuces' age, at the cusp of manhood, not quite ready to grow a beard (Sens 1997, p. 104).

[14] ἐν δὲ μύες στερεοῖσι βραχίοσιν ἄκρον ὑπ' ὦμον | ἔστασαν ἠύτε πέτροι ὀλοίτροχοι, οὔστε κυλίνδων | χειμάρρους ποταμὸς μεγάλαις περιέξεσε δίναις (lines 48–50)

[15] The term κολοσσός most likely suggests a "statue of archaic or archaizing type" (Sens 1997, p. 115). Both Williams (1945b) and Sens (1997) claim that Theocritus refers to a particular statue. According to Williams (1945b), it is the famed Terme Boxer (Figure 26). Sens (1997, p. 115) argues that "Amycus is compared not merely to any statue, but to a specific archaic antecedent," perhaps a statue of Zeus dedicated at Olympia by a member of the (Corinthian) Cypselid dynasty. The matter is by no means settled.

[16] Sens (1997, p. 113) contends that ὑπέροπλος has no "unambiguously moral implications" here, but "principally refers to Amycus' size." Hunter (1996, p. 62) notes that ὑπέροπλος may refer to "both moral and physical excess." The portrayal of Amycus "is based on the monstrous Homeric shepherd Polyphemus," also a son of Poseidon (ibid., p. 95).

guage.[17]   The exchange arguably has descendants in the highly publicized 'trash talk' that precedes modern boxing matches. In essence, Amycus "refuses to treat the Dioscuri hospitably" (Sens 1997, p. 95). But as one critic has observed, "To fight with the Tyndaridæ is no light matter" (Moulton 1973, p. 41). Polydeuces tries to bargain for access to potable water but instead of an exchange of silver, the louring Amycus challenges him to 'lift up' (ἀείρω) his hands to 'oppose' (καθίστημι) each other 'man to man' (ἐναντίος ἀνδρὶ) in a boxing match.[18]

The model "Hellenistic gentleman" (Sens 1997, p. 95), Polydeuces politely inquires if the combatants will also (ἠ καὶ) kick each other's legs (lit. 'strike legs with feet'), or if the contest will consist of *pygmachia* alone.[19] Amycus tersely clarifies that the fight will be 'with the fist' (πὺξ) and that the utmost exertion (διατείνω) and cunning (τέχνη) will be required, consistent with the Greek understanding of pugilism in the late first millennium.[20] Before Amycus' reply, at the end of line 66, we find a few words, ὄμματά γ' ὀρθός, from which one critic argues "no sense can be extracted" (Gow 1952, p. 392). Presumably spoken by Polydeuces (though attributed betimes to Amycus, e.g., by Edmonds, 1912), the line may suggest that one of the combatants proposes eye-gouging (Gow 1952, p. 392) but the corrupted line remains something of a *mauvais pas* (Thomas 1993, pp. 254–256). Those who find it unsettling that Polydeuces might propose ungentlemanly conduct in the 'ring' should remember that eye-gouging was an acceptable move in *pankration*, as Sens (1997, pp. 126–127) observes.

A step behind the reader, it would seem, Polydeuces then asks Amycus who his opponent is to be: for whom does he bind on (συνερείδω) the leather thongs?[21] In a bit of poorly understood levity or perhaps an obscure kenning, Amycus claims that the boxer (πύκτης) "may be called a woman."[22] The statement may be intended to goad Polydeuces, suggesting he is too weak to fight a real man, though the selfsame statement appears to humiliate his rival, as well. Perhaps this is for comic effect.[23] We prefer Sens' simpler interpretation of Amycus' gibe: "Not being a sissy [like Polydeuces], he [the opponent, i.e., Amycus] will be called 'The Boxer'" (Sens 1997, p. 128).[24] Polydeuces wonders aloud if the two will wrangle (δηριάομαι) for a prize (ἄθλον). Amycus proclaims that "the vanquished will be the victor's slave."[25] Polydeuces asks if this is not too much like a cockfight (κυδοιμός) but Amycus dis-

---

[17] The "remarkable" stichomythia in *Idylls* 22 is "a complete surprise" (Hunter 1996, p. 58).

[18] "Up hands fight me man against man" εἰς ἑνὶ χεῖρας ἄειρον ἐναντίος ἀνδρὶ καταστάς (line 65), trans. Edmonds (1912). The series of misunderstandings, enshrined in the stichomythia between Polydeuces and Amycus has been read as a clash between Greek cultural norms—specifically those related to the treatment of strangers and those of the barbarians (Chaldekas 2020). Greek hospitality conventions, *xenia* ξενία, are illustrated elsewhere in the *Argonautica*, e.g. by King Kyzicus of the Doliones. These eventually became the Greco-Roman standards of *hospitium* and were culturally enforced by tales of Zeus Xenios, the chief god who, in his role as protector of strangers, effectively put his hosts to trial.

[19] πυγμάχος, ἠ καὶ ποσσὶ θενὼν σκέλος; (line 66). See Thomas (1993, p. 254–255) for the interpretation that Polydeuces alludes to *pankration*.

[20] πὺξ διατεινάμενος σφετέρης μὴ φείδεο τέχνης (line 68).

[21] Sens (1997, p. 128) argues that the expression with συνερείδω probably means "with whom I shall join my hands in combat," though readings of the συνερείδω as 'clench' (of a fist) and 'bind' are also possible.

[22] ἐγγὺς ὁρᾷς: οὐ γύννις ἐὼν κεκλήσεθ' ὁ πύκτης (line 69). The term γύννις may mean 'effeminate man' and is used in that sense by Chaldekas (2020, p. 17): "He's no girly man and he will be called 'The Boxer'." The translation with a definite article is intentional here and suggests Amycus' jactance (Sens 1997, p. 129).

[23] The Bebrycian goon was perhaps widely seen as a comic figure, attested for example in a lost comedy by Epicharmus and a fragmentary satyr play by Sophocles, both entitled *Amycus* (Sens 1997, p. 96).

[24] This obfuscation is in keeping with Amycus' haughty refusal to reveal his identity.

[25] Gow (1942, p. 11). Line 71 reads σὸς μὲν ἐγώ, σὺ δ' ἐμὸς κεκλήσεαι, αἴκε κρατήσω. Sens (1997, p. 129) points out that Polydeuces, referred to as the 'champ' (ἀθλοφόρος) on line 53, is "somwehat coy" in asking about the prize.

misses his protest (or perhaps his *jeu d'esprit*), averring that this is the "only stake" (ἄθλον) on which they will fight.[26]

The blow of a conch summons Amycus' supporters (lines 75–80).[27] Most eminent Castor (ὑπείροχος ... Κάστωρ), Polydeuces' divine twin, gathers the Argonauts from the hull of their ship. The crowd assembles ὑπὸ σκιερὰς πλατανίστους 'under the shade of the plane trees', where the fight presumably takes place, as well.[28] The contenders harden or strengthen (κρατύνω) their hands with leathern coils (σπεῖρα ... βοείαις).[29] These σπεῖραι are arguably different from the *himantes* which are mentioned in the subsequent line and may be related to the similarly-spelled *sphairai* described by Plato (Gow 1942, p. 13fn.). Given the clear differentiation between the two handwraps, we agree with Sens (1997, p. 135) that Theocritean σπεῖραι most likely refer to the "coils of heavy leather that after the fourth century boxers wore over their knuckles ... distinct from the more pliant thongs they used to reinforce their forearms." These coils are portrayed, for example, on the hands of the Terme Boxer (Figure 27). The combatants then wind (ἑλίσσω) the long *himantes* (μακρός ... ἱμάς) around their hands and 'limbs' (γυῖον), most likely their arms.[30] Though the boxers' comrades carry out this function in the Apollonine vignette, here the fighters clearly tie on their own thongs, a practice which "seems to have been normal in antiquity" (Sens 1997, p. 135). Gathering together ἐς μέσσον 'in the midst', the combatants breathe out murder against one another.[31]

The fighters first tussle for position to determine "which should have the sunshine [φάος ἠελίοιο, line 84] at his back." Forthwith Polydeuces gets the advantage (παρέρχομαι, with connotations of outwitting his opponent by craft or deceit), such that the beams (ἀκτίς) "fall full" in Amycus' face, a presagement of the facial beating he is about to receive (Edmonds 1912).[32] His *thymos* aroused (ἐν θυμῷ κεχολωμένος), Amycus dashes forward (ἵημι πρόσω), aiming straight (τιτύσκομαι)[33] with his hands at the mark before him. Hagopian (1955, p. 38)

---

[26] οὐκ ἄλλῳ γε μαχεσσαίμεσθ' ἐπ' ἀέθλῳ (line 74). Amycus may propose the two will fight to the death (a more natural outcome for a cockfight), though he uses oblique language, viz., that the victor will 'call' (καλέω) the vanquished 'mine' (ἐμός), hence Gow's allusion to enslavement. Sens (1997, p. 130) muses "that the losing bird ... follows the victor as though his servant ... and was likely called a δοῦλος ['slave']." The author notes that "roosters were proverbially pugnacious as well as boastful" in antiquity (ibid.). We find in this passage more evidence for a latent connection between animal fighting and boxing as truly ancient human activities (Dioscurus and Dioscurus 2022a;b;c).

[27] Greek writers sometimes included the conch, re-purposed as a kind of trumpet, to suggest the primitive state of those who blew it, in this case, the uncouth Bebrycians ruled by an "uncivilized son of Poseidon" (Sens 1997, p. 133).

[28] Sens (1997, p. 132) notes the connection to the grove of plane trees where young Spartans would hold their own fights (*Paus.* 3.14.8), which perhaps included boxing. Sparta was the legendary homeland of the Dioscuri. A plane-tree cult associated with Helen, sister of the Dioscuri, is mentioned by Theocritus in *Idyll* 18 (Hunter 1996, p. 158).

[29] The verb κρατύνω unfortunately does not do much to clarify exactly what function the Greeks understood the σπεῖρα to serve. Did the coils 'strengthen' the hands in their ability to withstand or deliver punishment? Unfortunately, much debate as to the function and terminology of boxing hand gear in Greece has not settled the matter (Sens 1997, p. 135).

[30] χεῖρας καὶ περὶ γυῖα μακροὺς εἵλιξαν ἱμάντας (line 81). The verb ἑλίσσω 'wind round' "would be slightly more natural" if it appeared here in the middle voice since the action affects the subjects, i.e., the boxers. In Homer, the active voice form of ἑλίσσω is used only "of turning horses round a turning post" (Sens 1997, p. 136). Another commentator sees a clear difference between the *cæstus*/σπεῖρα, which fortify the hands, and the *himantes*, which are wrapped around the arms (Hagopian 1955, p. 37).

[31] ἐς μέσσον σύναγον φόνον ἀλλήλοισι πνέοντες (line 82). The phrase ἐς μέσσον is used elsewhere (Soph. *Trach.* 513–514) "of combatants approaching one another" (Sens 1997, p. 136).

[32] One commentator has argued that the sun is already setting, thus low in the West, when the bout begins, since the Argonauts had earlier prepared their beds and fires for the evening (line 33) (Sens 1997, p. 137).

[33] The Indo-European root for this term, *$d^h ewg^h$*, is realized in Old Armenian as *y-an-dugn* 'bold, rash'. The expression χερσὶ τιτυσκόμενος may be based on a "Homeric use of the verb with the dat[ive] of a weapon" such as a

surmises that Amycus was enraged because he had the sun in his face.

Unfazed by this intempestivity, Polydeuces strikes (τύπτω) his adversary on the point of the chin (ἄκρος ... γένειον). This further incites (ὀρίνω) Amycus so that his fighting blood (μαχάω)[34] is stirred up (ταράσσω) even more.[35] Overwrought, Amycus stumbles,[36] perhaps tackling his opponent to the ground: ... πολὺς δ' ἐπέκειτο νενευκὼς | ἐς γαῖαν ... (lines 90–91). The verb νεύω 'incline in any direction' suggests "that Amycus keeps his head down as he launches his attack, an imprudent practice for any boxer, ancient or modern" (Sens 1997, p. 141).[37] The Bebrycians 'shout in applause' (ἐπαυτέω) suggesting that whatever Amycus did, it was effective, or at least entertaining. Feeding off the energy of the crowd, Polydeuces is emboldened (θαρσύνεσκον) by the crowd's cheers, though apparently in favor of his opponent. Some of the multitude fear that Polydeuces will fall (ἐπιβρίθω),[38] being overpowered (δαμάζω) by Amycus, whose resemblance to Tityus is noted by Theocritus at this turn.[39]

The boxing match takes place in a χῶρος ... στενός (line 94). The term χῶρος is glossed as 'a definite space' while στενός is glossed as 'confined'. This, then, is the first clear literary reference to the confinement exerted on boxers when they fight. Thus, we submit that χῶρος στενός 'confined space' in Theocritus is the earliest literary reference to a boxing ring.[40]

Polydeuces (here called Διὸς υἱὸς 'the son of Zeus') steps in on his rival here and there (ἔνθα καὶ ἔνθα παρίστημι), 'lacerating' (ἀμύσσω, line 96)[41] him on either side (ἀμοιβαδίς) and 'holding fast' (ἔχω), perhaps suggesting a clinch. Amycus, the child of Poseidon (παῖδα Ποσειδάωνος) once splendid in his coxcombery (ὑπερφίαλόν),[42] found himself "drunken with his drubbing" (πληγαῖς μεθύων)[43] and expectorating (πτύω) crimson blood (αἷμα φοίνιος).[44] The crowd exulted (κελαδέω) loudly over the wounds (ἕλκος) appearing around his mouth and jaw (περὶ στόμα τε γναθμούς τε, line 100). The swelling (οἰδέω) of his face (πρόσωπον) was so great that it stretched his skin and narrowed (ἀποστενόω) his eyes.

Using the adjective ἐτώσιος 'to no purpose, fruitless' to describe Polydeuces' hands, Theocritus makes reference to punches that are "intentionally unsuccessful and misleading, i.e.,

---

lance (ἐγχείη) or a spear (δόρυ) instead of the hands (Sens 1997, p. 139).

[34] Literally, 'wish to fight' (verb).

[35] Sens (1997, p. 140) points out that "a wild and artless boxing style was considered characteristic of non-Greek pugilists." The verb ταράσσω suggests such a style in this passage.

[36] In the charming diction of Edmonds (1912), "[It] did ... make him to betumble his fighting."

[37] In our experience, boxers must be carefully trained to avoid looking at the ground, both when they 'roll' underneath punches (generally hooks) and when they rush their opponent. In the latter case, it is common for a beginner to expose the top of his head like a ram and barrel into his adversary's chest. This detail in Theocritus' vignette suggests to us that Amycus, an experienced boxer, was indeed transported in his wrath.

[38] The verb ἐπιβρίθω may also mean 'press close around' or 'attack' (Sens 1997, p. 142).

[39] A giant of the earth, Tityus attempted to rape Leto, the mother of Apollo (himself the divine patron of boxing, Dioscurus and Dioscurus 2022d), and was thereafter subjected to the same torture as Prometheus (Sens 1997, p. 144).

[40] The reader should cast his or her mind back to antecedents such as the crowd gathered round a fight, as at the funeral games of Patroclus.

[41] The use of the verb ἀμύσσω 'lacerate' strongly suggests that the fighters use the *himantes oxeis*, as these "tear at Amycus' face" (Sens 1997, p. 145).

[42] The boxing match between a son of Zeus and a son of Poseidon is suggestive of the larger conflict between sailors, special protégés of the Dioscuri, and the sea, the province of Amycus' father.

[43] The term μεθύων is used elsewhere to suggest grogginess, as well as mental states associated with love and success (Sens 1997, pp. 145–146).

[44] The adjective φοίνιος is a Homeric *hapax*, used only to describe the blood of Iros in the Odyssean boxing match (Sens 1997, p. 146).

feints," on line 102 (Sens 1997, p. 147). These 'fruitless fists' perform the action προδείκνυμι 'show by example', which by Theocritus' time may have been a technical pugilistic term for feinting (ibid.). On line 103 the narrator refers to Polydeuces as 'lord' or 'master' (ἄναξ). While regularly applied to Homeric heroes, the term is of special significance in this context since the Dioscuri were known by the cult title Ἄνακ(τ)ε(ς) in various localities (Sens 1997, p. 147). Correctly perceiving his opponent to be confused (ἀμηχανάω), Polydeuces "let drive at him to the bone" (Edmonds 1912). In the original Greek, he drops a fist from above, striking Amycus "in the middle of the forehead just above the bridge of the nose" (Sens 1997, p. 148).[45] The outcome of this blow seems to recall a Warner Brothers cartoon: Amycus falls flat, stretched out (ὕπτιος ... ἐκτανύω) in a bed of springing flowers (ἐν φύλλοισι τεθηλόσιν), perhaps with a halo of little birds twittering around his cracked skull.

But the disgruntled son of Poseidon is by no means knocked out—not yet, at least.[46] The boxers continue to wreak havoc (ὀλέκω) on each others' bodies, pounding (θείνω) with their hardened (στερεόω) gauntlets. In lines 109–111, the reader is treated to a blow-by-blow commentary: while the king of the Bebrycians lands shots (χεῖρας νωμάω, line 109) to Polydeuces' chest and neck,[47] the son of Zeus succeeds at head-hunting.[48] The description gives no indication that landing blows to the body was illegal (Poliakoff 1987a, pp. 84–85).

The blows (πληγή) to Amycus' face are considered 'unseemly' or 'disgraceful' (ἀεικής, line 110). Hellenistic writers were in some cases amused by the facial swelling and disfigurement that occurred concomitant with boxing (see below). Artists of the period also found it a noteworthy and likely comical subject (cf. Figure 38 in Dioscurus and Dioscurus (2023)). It is possible that Theocritus hints at this perspective in his use of ἀεικής to describe the blows delivered to Amycus' nose. He may also be suggesting that boxers should be ashamed of what they do to one another in the ring; however Gow (1952) argues that in using ἀεικής the poet "probably means 'disfiguring' rather than 'disgraceful' and attaches to the blow the epithet which belongs more strictly to the wound," not the activity that causes it. Sens (1997, p. 151) notes that the adjective is used in the *Iliad* to describe how Achilles disfigures Hector's body "without ... any moral condemnation of Achilles." Both interpretations were known in arethede via debates over the "physical corruption of Hector's corpse" (ibid.). Another interpretation presents itself: Amycus was shamefully beaten not due to some moral failure of Polydeuces but as a result of Amycus' own disgraceful lack of skill in the boxing 'ring'. This suggests a moral stance towards boxing in which the observer regards the loser as getting what he deserves. To us, this seems altogether consistent with the ancient (and modern) attitude towards the sport.[49]

The poet next makes a curious observation: the physical size of one of the boxers (presumably Amycus) begins to diminish due to sweating.[50] Contrarily, as Polydeuces' exertions

---

[45] μέσσης ῥινὸς ὕπερθε κατ᾽ ὀφρύος ἤλασε πυγμῇ (line 104).

[46] Hagopian (1955, pp. 37–38, 51–52) separates the action of the boxing match into two 'rounds' [Ger. *Ganger*] punctuated by the knockdown of Amycus.

[47] At least one commentator seems to suggest that these blows are below the belt (Ahrens 1887), but Sens (1997, p. 150) is skeptical given their ineffective nature.

[48] The expression used here is συμφύρω πρόσωπον 'knead together the face' as if it were a lump of bread dough.

[49] On line 131, Amycus is called 'reckless' ἀτάσθαλος, an adjective that Sens (1997, p. 164) elaborates as denoting "behavior for which men not only suffer but deserve to suffer."

[50] In the Greek, his 'flesh sank to sweat' (σάρκες ... ἱδρῶτι συνίζανον). The verb is common in Hellenistic medical writing and proceeds from the Greek belief that perspiration caused a loss of strength since "liquid ... gave the flesh its substance" (Sens 1997, p. 152).

increased, "so waxed his limbs ever more full and round and his color ever better" (Edmonds 1912).[51] In the ring, a boxer naturally looks for any sign of weakness in his opponent. Theocritus' peculiar commentary here corresponds to our own experience as veterans of the ring. The physical appearance of an adversary seems to change—at least in the eye of his sparring partner—as he experiences success or failure during the course of a bout. What Polydeuces regarded as the wilting of Amycus, regardless of its etiology, likely cheered the son of Zeus more than even the clamor of the crowd, as it assured him of victory. The physical transformation of godlike Polydeuces, which no doubt disheartened Amycus, should be the aspiration of all students of the sweet science. We become different people in the ring; Theocritus (or those poets he emulated) was aware of the subjective response a fighter experiences as he witnesses the physical changes to his opponent during a bout.

The poet interrupts the narrative (lines 115–117) with an appeal to the Muse—a standard Hellenistic conceit—imploring her to describe how Polydeuces finally 'took down' (καθαιρέω) the 'glutton' (ἀδηφάγος) Amycus.[52] As the fight reaches its conclusion, Amycus leans forward (κλίνω), keeping his guard up (προβολή, line 120), and seizes (λαμβάνω) Polydeuces' left hand with his own left.[53] This manœuvre, most likely an illegal tactic (Hagopian 1955, p. 38), would result in the fighters' left arms crossing in front of their bodies or perhaps their faces. Availing himself of the pell-mell, Amycus throws a right hand "from his right flank" (δεξιτερῆς ... λαγόνος). This seems like a description of a shovel hook or uppercut[54] thrown from the hip except for the rather confusing use of πλατύς γυῖον which literally means 'flat fist' or 'flat forearm' (line 121).[55] If this is an open-handed offensive gesture, then it may force us to reconsider the ubiquitous generalization that the open hand in Greek depictions of boxing is a defensive tactic.[56] One commentator regards the term πλατύς γυῖον as referring to "the whole forearm girt with the cæstus" and claims that "[t]he Greeks used this swinging blow much more than the modern prize-fighter" (Cholmeley 1901). At the same time, Polydeuces slips (ὑπεξαναδύομαι)[57] his head to the side and throws his own sturdy (στιβαρός) hand (presumably his right). He attacks Amycus with a blow delivered squarely from his shoulder

---

[51] The comparative adjective used to describe Polydeuce's improved limbs, πασσονα 'stouter', also appears throughout the *Odyssey* on occasions when Athena miraculously enhances the hero's appearance (Sens 1997, p.152). The term that Edmonds translates as 'color' is properly 'skin' χροιά. A variant of this word, χρόα, surfaces in Epeius' taunt issued to his potential rivals before the Iliadic boxing match when he threatens to "rend their flesh" (Dioscurus and Dioscurus 2022d, pp. 120–121).

[52] Sens (1997, p. 154) notes that "boxers and other athletes had proverbially large appetites" in Greek literature. It may be attractive to consider Amycus a "glutton for punishment," eating the many punches that Polydeuces served up.

[53] The adjective προβολή, relating to anything held up as a screen or bulwark, is an important bit of fight game terminology, suggesting just how advanced the Greeks had become at using language to describe boxing techniques by Theocritus' era. Sens (1997, p. 158) notes that the term is used in the "sense of weapons in military context" but also of boxers holding up their fists.

[54] Commentators have elaborated on the Theocritean reversal of Apollonius here. In the *Argonautica*, Amycus drops a punch from above, missing his opponent. In the *Idyll*, the corresponding punch from Amycus is an errant uppercut (Sens 1997, p. 158).

[55] The verb is ἐγγυάω, which might be translated as "Polydeuces answered" his opponent with a punch or, even more colorfully, "pledged" the blow "for security".

[56] An alternative is presented by Poliakoff (1983, pp. 112–113), who argues that πλάτος refers to 'broadness' and is "a very common epithet for the bodily parts of participants in combative events," including the neck and feet. The name 'Plato' itself may be implicated. Greek and Etruscan depictions of boxers occasionally limn the open hand with inordinately long fingers, e.g., in the Tomba della Scimmia (Dioscurus and Dioscurus 2023, Fig. 32).

[57] Elsewhere (*Iliad* 13.351–352), the verb means 'rise up out of', but that does not fit the context here.

(ἐπεμπίπτω ὦμος),[58] striking him under the left temple (σκαιός κρόταφος). This opens up a 'gaping' (χάσκω, line 125) wound from which the blood quickly pours (χέω). The injury is consistent with the use of the sharp thongs—the Theocritean σπεῖρα—and is reminiscent of the verb ἀμύσσω 'lacerate' employed to describe the action earlier in the narrative (line 96).

His left hand now freed, Polydeuces follows up with a jab, i.e., a punch from the left (λαιῇ ... κόπτω)[59], to his adversary's mouth, rattling (ἀραβέω) his teeth.[60] Then he lets loose with his fists in a torrent of punches. The noun πίτυλος characterizes the barrage; in another context it refers to the sweep of oars (Euripides, *Iphigenia in Tauris* 1050) and may have resonance here with the Dioscuri's role as protectors of sailors. The adjective ὀξύς 'sharp' is used here in the dative, presumably to clarify that Amycus' faces is not only being struck, it is being slashed to ribbons. Indeed, the onslaught 'spoils' (δηλέομαι) his countenance, or in Edmonds' parlance, the king was mauled "till his visage was all one mash" (Edmonds 1912). At last the brute falls (κεῖμαι), dazed (ἀλλοφρονέω, lit. 'giving no heed'.)[61] Amycus then raises (ἀνεσχέθομεν) his hands to call off the fight (νεῖκος ἀπαυδάω, line 129). The verb 'raise' is a variant form of ἀνέχω familiar from Homer as the term used for boxers when they begin their battles. Here, Theocritus cleverly provides a coda to the fight with this otherwise proemial signal.[62] All this did Amycus because the fearsome Polydeuces had brought him near the gates of death: ... ἐπεὶ θανάτου σχεδὸν ἦεν (line 130).

The resolution of the boxing match is perhaps the most salient reason one commentator has called the Theocritean episode "light" (Sens 1994, p. 126). Unlike the Apollonine version of the Bout in Bebrycia, in this one Amycus does not die. Instead, Polydeuces merely compels his adversary to swear an oath to be more hospitable to strangers, giving the vignette the apological feel of a Saturday morning cartoon.[63] The ending may not be entirely original. A comparison has been drawn with the "sarcastic remark" Odysseus makes to Iros after knocking him silly in the *Odyssey* (Sens 1994, p. 124). *Odyssey* 18.106 includes Odysseus' admonition that the gasconading Iros cease to lord it over strangers. Amycus, spared from death by Polydeuces, swears to cease doing annoyance to strangers (line 134). It has been noted that Theocritus' Amycus is "something of a comic buffoon" akin to the Odyssean Iros (Sens 1994, p. 126). Indeed, the villainous king takes on a much more menacing aspect in other versions of the story, particularly the one written by the Flavian poet Valerius Flaccus (see below).

Theocritus' depiction of boxing is notable for the poet's concentration on the left and

---

[58] Here 'shoulder' appears in the dative. It may be rendered as "fell upon him with his shoulder" (Sens 1997, p. 160). The related verb ἐμπίπτω can have the special meaning "fall upon an opponent" in the context of combat sports (Poliakoff 1983, pp. 107–108).

[59] To call the punch a jab here assumes that Polydeuces is an orthodox boxer. There is still no unique verb for 'jab' in Theocritus' time.

[60] There is some disagreement as to whether the sound of the teeth is caused by the fact that they are loosened by previous punches or if this particular punch causes Amycus' teeth to gnash (Sens 1997, p. 161).

[61] ἀλλοφρονέω also characterizes Euryalus when he is carried away at the end of the Iliadic boxing match.

[62] Amycus' gesture of submission should not be confused with the single raised finger evident among boxers, wrestlers, and pankratists of Greek vase-painting. In this instance, Theocritus goes to some trouble to clarify that both hands (ἀμφοτέρας χεῖρας) are raised at once (ἅμα, line 130). Sens (1997, p. 163) suggest that the poet is recalling the gesture made by the moribund Diores in *Iliad* 4.523, among others, "offering supplication or appealing for aid."

[63] Though unmentioned by Theocritus, in other sources it appears that Amycus was bound to a tree or rock as a preliminary to his oath-swearing (Gow 1942, pp. 12–13fn. 2). This is depicted on the Ficoroni Cista (Dioscurus and Dioscurus 2023, Fig. 40) and on a red-figure Lucanian hydria (425–400 BC) held in the Cabinet des Médailles in the Bibliothèque nationale de France (No. DE RIDDER-442) (Figure 1).

Figure 1: Amycus punished after his defeat at the hands of Polydeuces. Detail of red-figure vase by the Amycus Painter, c. 420–400 BC. Located in the Bibliothèque nationale de France (No. DE RIDDER.442).

right sides of the body. In the *Idyll*, punches and their landing sites are frequently described in these terms, providing further evidence that by Theocritus' time boxing had evolved a highly technical praxis. The advantages and disadvantages of throwing lefts and rights, hooks and straights under a variety of circumstances were understood even by a general audience; it is almost certain that boxers were taught these skills explicitly. Nor were the more archaic, obumbrative hammer blows yet forgotten. Theocritus does not benefit from a fully developed boxing orismology: specialized vocabulary still did not exist for the punches themselves, though the poet describes subtleties like feinting, slipping, and holding up one's guard in a sophisticated style. Theocritus entertains his audience with an account remarkable for its athletic realism despite some of its more cartoonish embellishments.

2.2   The Pauline Epistles

Combat sport is mentioned in some of the earliest writings included in the New Testament, viz., the Apostle Paul's first epistle to the Corinthians, his second epistle to Timothy, and his epistle to the saints at Ephesus. There is considerable doubt that the epistle to the Ephesians was written by Paul himself, and may have been composed up to 25 years after his death (as late as 90 AD). First Corinthians was almost certainly written by Paul around 54 AD. The case for the authorship of II Timothy is somewhat dubious; it may have been written by an unknown follower of Jesus as late as 140 AD. For our purposes, the authorship is not so important as the date of the New Testament's references to boxing. These were put down sometime between the middle of the first and the middle of the second century AD. In the epistles, Hellenistic boxing is regarded from the perspective of early (Pauline) Christianity.

In I Corinthians 9:26, Paul contrasts boxing (πυκτεύω) with shadowboxing or 'flaying the air' (ἀέρα δέρω). One who follows Jesus will engage in the former, not the latter in his fight with evil.[64] Paul's explicit allusion to boxing was doubtless intended to impress his audience with the realism of his fight with the natural man. It was not for show and the blows were real. In the next verse (27), Paul uses the highly specific verb ὑπωπιάζω 'strike under the eye' to indicate how a follower of Jesus will beat back his own carnal nature.[65] While Paul could have used a general term for fighting, he explicitly chose boxing in this passage, presumably because the saints at Corinth understood the conventions of Hellenistic pugilism. Paul probably counted on their familiarity with the common epic formula of wasting one's punches on the air (e.g., *Æneid* 5:446).[66]

In II Timothy 4:7, the author writes of fighting "the good fight". The term for the 'fight' is ἀγῶνα and the verb of 'fighting' is the related term ἠγώνισμαι. The KJV phrase "we wrestle not against flesh and blood" (Ephesians 6:12) invokes the term πάλη 'wrestling'.

2.3   *Orations* **28, 29**

Dio Chrysostom memorializes in his twenty-eighth and twenty-ninth orations the history of Melancomas (Μελανκόμας) motivated by an incidental encounter with Iatrocles his onetime opponent. Melancomas was notable as a defensive boxer, able to maintain his hands up as a guard for long periods of time, up to two days. Ultimately he leveraged this skill to garner victory in the 207th Olympiad (A.D. 49). The first descriptive passage of note concerning boxing spans sections 7 and 8:

> At any rate, although boxing was his specialty, he remained as free from marks as any of the runners; and he had trained so rigorously and went so far beyond others in toilsome exercising that he was able to remain for two whole days in succession with his hands up, and nobody could catch him letting them down or taking a rest, as athletes usually do. Then he used to force his opponents to give up, not only before he himself had received a blow but even before he had landed one on them. For he did not consider it courage to strike his opponent or to receive an injury himself, but thought this indicated lack of stamina and a desire to have done with the contest. ¶But to last out the full time without either being done up by the weight of his arms, or becoming out of breath, or being distressed by the heat — that, he thought, was a splendid achievement.[67]

---

[64] γὼ τοίνυν οὕτως τρέχω ὡς οὐκ ἀδήλως, οὕτως πυκτεύω ὡς οὐκ ἀέρα δέρων "I therefore so run, not as uncertainly; so fight I, not as one that beateth the air" (KJV).

[65] The same verb is used in Luke 18:5, a parable in which a judge relents to the remonstrations of a widow lest she 'harass' ὑπωπιάζω him.

[66] *Entellus vires in ventum effudit ...*

[67] πυγμὴν γοῦν ἀγωνιζόμενος οὕτως ὑγιὴς ἦν ὥσπερ τῶν δρομέων τις, οὕτω δὲ σφόδρα γεγύμναστο καὶ τοσοῦτο περιῆν τοῖς πόνοις, ὥστε δυνατὸς ἦν καὶ δύο ἡμέρας ἐξῆς μένειν ἀνατετακὼς τὰς χεῖρας, καὶ οὐκ ἂν εἶδεν οὐδεὶς ὑφέντα αὐτὸν ἢ ἀναπαυσάμενον, ὥσπερ εἰώθασιν. πρότερον δὲ ἠνάγκαζε τοὺς ἀνταγωνιστὰς ἀπειπεῖν, οὐ μόνον πρὶν αὐτὸς πληγῆναι, ἀλλὰ καὶ πρὶν πλῆξαι ἐκείνους: οὐ γὰρ τὸ παίειν καὶ τιτρώσκεσθαι ἀνδρείαν ἐνόμιζεν, ἀλλὰ τοῦτο μὲν εἶναι μὴ δυναμένων πονεῖν καὶ ἀπηλλάχθαι βουλομένων: τὸ δὲ ἀνέχεσθαι τοῦ χρόνου καὶ μήτε τοῦ βάρους τῶν χειρῶν ἡττᾶσθαι μήτε τοῦ πνεύματος ἐνδεᾶ γίγνεσθαι μήτε τῷ καύματι ἄχθεσθαι, τὸ δὲ εἶναι γενναῖον.

Firmly within the Greek athletic tradition, Dio focuses on the glory of Melancomas' technical accomplishment. Being at leisure to strike an exhausted opponent rather than play for his yielding, Melancomas (in Dio's conception) refused in favor of the principle of maintaining his defensive stance. "He held that it was the truest victory when he forced his opponent, although uninjured, to give up; for then the man was overcome, not by his injury, but by himself." Dio sees in this the mark of *aretē*, personal excellence.

Melancomas' boxing appears to be highly technical, relying on an ability to block with his arms rather than counterstrike his opponent. He appears to have regarded this form of winning as a sort of private game. The phrase "with his hands up" μένειν ἀνατετακὼς τὰς χεῖρας denotes an abiding discipline of the hands in order, resisting their weight. The duration of two days in boxing would appear to refer to multiple bouts against opponents, likely throughout an entire athletic competition. The opponents were forced "to give up" ἀπειπεῖν, to exhaust themselves against his prodigious display.

The other technical passage in Dio Chrysostom, from 29:11–12, elaborates on his expertise:

> Furthermore, a person might have been amazed at this — that he won all his victories without being hit himself or hitting his opponent, so far superior was he in strength and in his power of endurance. [12]For often he would fight throughout the whole day, in the hottest season of the year, and although he could have more quickly won the contest by striking a blow, he refused to do it, thinking that it was possible at times for the least competent boxer to overcome by a blow the very best man, if the chance for making it were offered; but he held that it was the truest victory when he forced his opponent, although uninjured, to give up; for then the man was overcome, not by his injury, but by himself; and that for an adversary to give up because of the condition of his whole body and not simply of the part of his body that was struck, meant brilliant work on the part of the victor; whereas the man who rushed in to win as quickly as possible by striking and clinching was himself overcome by the heat and by the prolonged effort.[68]

"To hit" here is παίω and derivatives, "to strike, smite" or "to dash together". Indeed, Dio Chrysostom lavishes praise on Melancomas' boxing but expresses little of *how* Melancomas operationally realized his absolute mastery. Dio rather prefers to use Melancomas as the occasion for a discussion of athletic beauty and the favor of the gods in taking the young before they are marred by time.[69] The celebration of athleticism following is among the best philosophical expositions of athletic boxing that has yet been written.

Dio Chrysostom strongly distinguishes athletic sport boxing from a soldier's combat. Dio argues for two ways in which boxing ranks as superior:

---

[68] ἔτι δὲ καὶ τόδε ἄν τις αὐτοῦ κατεπλάγη, τὸ μήτε παιόμενον αὐτὸν μήτε παίοντα νικᾶν: τοσοῦτο τῇ ῥώμῃ περιῆν καὶ τῷ δύνασθαι πονεῖν. πολλάκις γὰρ δι' ὅλης τῆς ἡμέρας ἠγωνίσατο ἐν τῇ σφοδροτάτῃ wρα τοῦ ἔτους, καὶ δυνάμενος θᾶττον ἂν περιγενέσθαι παίων οὐκ ἐβούλετο, νομίζων τὸ μὲν πληγῇ νικῆσαι καὶ τοῦ φαυλοτάτου ι ἔσθ' ὅτε εἶναι τὸν βέλτιστον, εἰ τύχοι: τὴν δὲ ἀληθεστάτην νίκην, ὅταν ἄτρωτον ἀναγκάσῃ τὸν ἀντίπαλον ἀπειπεῖν: οὐ γὰρ τοῦ τραύματος, ἀλλ' ἑαυτοῦ ἡττῆσθαι: καὶ τὸ ὅλῳ τινὰ τῷ σώματι. ἀπειπεῖν, ἀλλὰ μὴ τῷ πληγέντι μέρει, λαμπρόν. τὸν δὲ € ἐπειγύμενον ὡς οἴών τε τάχιστα μικῆσαι καὶ παίοντα καὶ συμπλεκόμιενον αὐτὸν ἡττῆσθαι τοῦ καύματος καὶ τοῦ χρόνου.

[69] This is congruent with the mood of classicist A. E. Housman's ode "To an Athlete Dying Young".

1. The soldier conquers an enemy once for all, while the athlete must maintain his superiority. "In war the man who once conquers slays his antagonist, so as not to have the same opponent the second time; whereas in athletics the victory is just for that one day, and afterwards the victor has for his opponents, not only the men he has beaten, but anyone else who cares to challenge."

2. The soldier's use of technology obscures personal excellence, while the athlete epitomizes it. "In athletics the better man proves superior to the inferior man, since he must conquer with nothing else but his courage and physical strength; while in war the might of steel, which is much superior to mere human flesh, does not allow the excellency of men's bodies to be tested and often takes the side of the inferior man."

Self-control ἐγκρατείας is set apart for particular praise, and Melancomas' training and performance merit his adoption as the proximate symbol of ἐγκρατείας. Boxing is portrayed as an exercise of aesthetics as well as mastery, and chance (favor of the gods) enters in, as well.[70]

2.4 *Imagines 2*

According to Philostratus the Elder[71] (*Imagines* 2.19), writing in the second or third century AD, Apollo once took vengeance on a wicked ruler in a boxing match. The conceit, as with the other sections of the ekphrastic *Imagines*, is that Philostratus describes a painting to a young companion. He indicates that the scene is near the Bœotian stream Cephisus, οὐ τῶν ἀμούσων "not unknown to the Muses."[72] Phorbas, the tallest and most savage of the Phlegyans,[73] was also their king. He took control of the road[74] to Delphi, preventing veneration of the oracular god at one of his holiest shrines. Phorbas routinely abducted travelers on the road and competed with the strongest of them in wrestling and *pankration*. He unheaded the vanquished and hung his grisly trophies from a great oak, where they swung from the boughs in various states of decomposition.[75]

Apollo appears on the scene in the form of a youthful boxer with his hair "fastened-up [ἀναλαμβάνω] so that he may box with girt-up [εὔζωνος] head," perhaps using the hairstyle we observe among later Roman boxers, viz., the *cirrus*. "Rays of light rise from about his brow and cheek." No fancy footwork could get the sun out of Phorbas' eyes and into those of his opponent. He emits a "smile mingled with wrath" that a modern boxer could recognize in the ominous glare of his adversary.[76] Apollo throws (βολή) his eye keenly (εὔσκοπος) on his opponent and raises both his hands together (συνεξαίρω). The prefix συν- is critical here, indicating a gesture with not one hand raised, but both. The *himantes* bound (ἐνάπτω) on his

---

[70]See Poliakoff (1987b) and discussion in Dioscurus and Dioscurus (2023) on whether the story of Melancomas is fictional or fictionalized.

[71]Philostratus of Lemnos, nephew of Philostratus *simpliciter*, the author of the *Gymnasticus*.

[72]Translations in this section come from Fairbanks (1931) unless otherwise indicated.

[73]The Phlegyans were considered autochthons of Bœotia, in central Greece. Noted for their hostility to surrounding tribes, they once plundered Apollo's temple at Delphi (Franchi 2013, p. 453). Philostratus the Elder calls them βάρβαροι πόλεις οὔπω ὄντες "barbarian people who do not yet live in cities."

[74]This sounds like a job for Apollo Agyieus!

[75]Writing on the general mistreatment of corpses in ancient literature and modern media, McClellan (2019, p. 4) notes, "Spectacularized violence of this sort is intended to invoke audience gaze."

[76]The passage reads: μειδίαμα θυμῷ ξυγκεκραμένον ἡ παρειὰ πέμπει. An alternative translation might be, "He smiles with a cheek trembling with restrained *thymos*".

hands are "beautiful" (ἡδύς)—a far cry from those that are dripping with blood in the much later *Dionysiaca* or caked with the brains of former opponents in the *Æneid*. In the words of the poet, his gauntlets made so pleasant a picture, his hands may as well have been wreathed in garlands (στέφανος). Boxing (a reduplicative form of πυκτεύω), the god throws in (ἐμβάλλω) his right hand (δεξιά) and lays Phorbas low (καταλύω). The Phlegyan king is stretched out (κεῖμαι) on the ground with a wound (τραῦμα) on the temple (κρόταφος), "blood gushes forth [ἐκδίδωμι] ... as a fountain." With that, the boxing match is over. Philostratus gives his audience little of the drama that characterizes epic treatments of the subject.

The story of Phorbas and Apollo has some similarities to the tale of Amycus and Polydeuces, a popular Hellenistic theme.[77] In both, a ruler blocks access to some resource: for Amycus, it is freshwater, while for Phorbas it is the road to Apollo's oracle. The bully challenges all comers to fight him in order to obtain their goal. The facinorous[78] king gets his comeuppance when someone *au fait* in boxing finally takes a swing at him. The two myths may be imitations of one another or are perhaps based on on a deeply internalized story connected to a real event. A ruler who challenges his subjects in single combat is a trope as old as Gilgamesh. As in Gilgamesh, the wicked king meets his match in a supernatural (if not divine) being sent to topple him. In the Greek versions the king is often killed, whereas Gilgamesh lives to tell the tale and make peace with his own mortality. It is worth noting that in the various examples of the Amycus story (including Philostratus' version *mutato nomine*) the unworthy king challenges others with his fists, not some kind of blade—a weapon presumably available to even the least consequential of Bronze Age gangsters. Chiromachy seems to have had a deep and abiding significance for ancient cultures of the Mediterranean. These are tales about men settling differences among men, in the most time-honored manner possible: with bare (or barely covered) fists.

2.5 *Posthomerica* 4

Quintus Smyrnæus' *Posthomerica* accounts for events after the *Iliad* and before the *Odyssey*, including the fall of Troy.[79] The poem is regarded skeptically by many modern critics based on its style, but its preservation between the two Homeric poems throughout the Middle Ages suggests "it was considered worthy" of this honor by audiences across many generations (Maciver 2012, p. 9). We are interested, of course, in what Quintus, who may have written as late as the 4th century AD and was probably a Christian,[80] had to say about boxing. His boxing episode is closest in form to the one presented in the *Iliad*, a relationship which is generally true of all the *Posthomerica*:

> [F]rom the very start of [Quintus'] epic, the reader is made very aware of the inextricable conjunction of the *Posthomerica* with the *Iliad*. This fact, together with the overwhelmingly Homeric nature of the poem's language and style, adds to the perceptive reader's impression that the aim of the poem is to be

---

[77] Scandinavian folktales involving trolls guarding bridges may have the same Indo-European origin (Hartmann 1936).

[78] Philostratus describes Phorbas as "savage" (ὠμός) and "swinelike" (συώδης), highlighting the dichotomy between civilized Greek and brutish barbarian that typifies the Amycus narratives, as well.

[79] Line numbers and translations of passages in this section come from Way (1913) unless otherwise indicated.

[80] Quintus was the father of a Christian priest named Dorotheus who was executed by Diocletian (James and Lee 2000).

Figure 2: Terracotta figure of a boxer wearing the Roman *cæstus* (second or first century BC, provenance unknown). The fighter's right ear is cauliflowered. National Archæological Museum of Athens, No. 5764.

'still the *Iliad*'. This illusion—the reader knows this poem is not the *Iliad*, and that this poet is not Homer, but a much later writer of a different cultural and literary background—influences reading of the whole of the *Posthomerica*. A studied attempt on the part of the poet to make the poem as 'Homeric' as possible makes any differences in the epic technique in relation to the Homeric epics all the more noticeable and worthy of discussion (Maciver 2012, p. 33).

With this cue in mind, we pay special attention to what is *not* Homeric about the boxing match presented in Quintus' Book 4, wherein are described the funeral games of Achilles.[81] Indeed, there are many innovations not attested in the Iliadic or Odyssean boxing matches. These include:

- In the proem to the fight, an older boxer receives a (lavish) prize uncontested.
- Blood is mentioned during the fight, not just at the end; it streaks the boxers' faces and pours forth from their eyes.
- The fight is stopped prematurely by the boxers' comrades (as in the *Æneid*).
- Both fighters receive the same type of prize (a silver krater).
- Sponges are used to bathe the fighter's brows.
- The fighters are compelled to kiss each other and mend their friendship after the combat is terminated.
- Attention is paid to how the boxers' wounds are treated, including methods of squeezing, sewing, and applying medicine.

In Book 4, Quintus offers his readers a description of the funeral games not of Patroclus, but of his friend Achilles. After a wrestling match has taken place, an older commander named Idomeneus[82] rises to engage in *pygmachia* (line 284). Idomeneus' *thymos*, the poet says, has already been perfected in many prizefights (ἐπεί οἱ θυμὸς ἴδρις πέλε παντὸς ἀέθλου, line 285). True to the Homeric model, a dramatic silence takes hold and "none come forth to meet him" (κατέναντα κίω, line 286). Given the lack of a challenger, Idomeneus receives from Thetis, Achilles' divine mother, the grand prize:[83] a chariot and horses (Patroclus' own), which he sends to the ships by means of his servants while he remains in the glorious boxing 'ring' (κλυτῷ ἐν ἀγῶνι, line 292).[84]

When Phœnix, Achilles' erstwhile tutor, steps up to recruit some fighters (thus fulfilling Achilles' Iliadic role), he indicates that the fighting will "gladden great Pelaides' soul," lit. 'warm' (ἰαίνω) the *thymos* of the departed hero. He invokes hands leveled at the opponent like weapons, skilled in 'straight' (ἰθύνω)[85] boxing: χεῖρας ἐπ' ἀλλήλοισι δαήμονας ἰθύνοντες | πυγμαχίης ... (lines 298–299). While Idomeneus was given the boxing prize (ἄθλον, line 294) uncontested—a bloodless (ἀναιμωτί) victory (τίοντες)—[86] the younger men will have to

---

[81] The *Posthomerica* is notable for including an epic account of *pankration*, though the prize goes uncontested to Ajax Major.

[82] A Cretan king, Idomeneus was known for promising to Poseidon the first living thing he laid eyes on when returning to his home country. This oath forced Idomeneus to sacrifice his own son.

[83] The funeral games "serve to divide Achilles' riches among those worthy of them" (Scheijnen 2018).

[84] ἀγών is used for the site of the boxing match, as in the Iliadic episode (23.685).

[85] Homer (*Odyssey* 22.8) uses the verb to characterize arrows shot 'straight' at their target, reminiscent of our earlier claim that archery and boxing (two domains of Apollo) were not unrelated in the minds of the ancient poets, especially if the fists are regarded as missiles launched at the adversary (Dioscurus and Dioscurus 2022d).

[86] The participle here used to suggest victory in Way's (1913) translation comes from the form τίω 'to pay honor'.

fight each other for glory. Phœnix urges them on though they are "loth to essay the contest [ἄθλος]," bidding them take part in the 'exalted' (ἐπήρατος) bruising (ἀλέω), the skill (δαήμων) that 'delights' (τερπωλή)[87] young men (νέος, line 304). Boxing, the poet tells us, forges a link between 'glory' (κῦδος) and 'toil' (κάματος, line 305).

Phœnix laments his own advancing age (cf. Nestor in the *Iliad*) and reminisces about fighting Polydeuces himself in a long-ago boxing match held at the funeral games of Pelias.[88] Lines 309–310 read: ἀμφήριστος ἐγώ Πολυδεύκεϊ δίῳ | πυγμαχίη γενόμην ... 'When I came to contend evenly-matched with Polydeuces in boxing'. The adjective ἀμφήριστος 'evenly-matched' is particularly eyebrow-raising: Not only was Polydeuces a son of Zeus, his skill in boxing had been acclaimed in the ancient world for generations. To ensure that the audience gets the point, the indomitable Phœnix then recounts how he got the better of Ancæus[89] in παλαισμοσύνη 'the wrestler's art', when the latter "shrank from me, and dared not strive with me that day." Here, hand-to-hand fighting is invoked using the term ἀγχεμάχοισιν (line 314). Reaching even farther back into the heroic past, Phœnix explains how he "dashed" Ancæus "to the dust" (ἐκονίσατο 'make dusty', line 315) on a previous occasion at the site of a grave (σῆμα, line 316) belonging to Amarynceus.[90] Thousands, we are assured, marveled at Phœnix' bodily strength (βία) and courage (κάρτος).[91] Ancæus certainly did, since he subsequently refused to raise (αἴρω) his hands against him and thus walked away Phœnix with an uncontested (ἀκόνιτος, line 319) prize. The adjective ἀκόνιτος means 'without dust' which is here taken to mean 'without getting dirty', i.e., without struggle or combat.

Phœnix' account highlights his prowess as both a boxer (in his match with none other than Polydeuces) and as a wrestler (in his realized match with Ancæus). It is not clear if his aborted re-match with Ancæus was to consist of boxing, wrestling, or even *pankration*: it is called ἀγχεμάχοισιν 'hand-to-hand fighting' (line 314) and we are told that on this occasion Ancæus refused to 'raise' (αἴρω) his hands, a verb commonly associated with pugilistic encounters elsewhere. While the aged Phœnix may be forgiven for letting his mind wander across all his combative experiences, it may be telling that Quintus, writing in Late Antiquity, blurs the lines between boxing, wrestling, and perhaps even *pankration* in Phœnix' rambling history. There is evidence that the Romans had done precisely this and that the various combat sports were more eclectic by Quintus' era (Remijsen 2015).[92]

Noting once more his advanced age (and thus excusing himself from fighting), Phœnix bids the young guns in the audience to 'lift the prize with their hands' ἀέθλια χερσὶν ἀρέσθαι

---

[87] τερπωλή (line 305) is the same term used for the 'rare sport' that oblectates the suitors when they compel Odysseus and Iros to fight (*Odyssey* 18.37). A related term is used to describe the 'delight' experienced by Apollo in watching the boxing matches mentioned in the Homeric Hymn to Apollo: ἐπιτέρπεαι (146), τέρπουσιν (150).

[88] Pelias, legendary king of Iolcus, was a son of Poseidon like Amycus, the adversary of Polydeuces in the *Argonauticas* of Apollonius of Rhodes and Valerius Flaccus, as well as *Idyll* 22. The funeral games of Pelias, including a boxing match between Mopsus and Admetus, are mentioned briefly by Pausanias in his *Description of Greece* (5.17.9–10).

[89] This Ancæus is most likely the son of Lycurgus and father of Agapenor, who led the Arcadians to Troy.

[90] Nestor also took part in these Amaryncean games, once more affirming the long tradition of funeral games that included combat sport (*Iliad* 23.269). Quintus almost certainly put this lengthy rodomontade in the mouth of Phœnix to make of him a humorous parallel to the æolian king of Pylos.

[91] The latter term reminds us of καρδία καὶ θυμός 'heart and *thymos*', used to praise Odysseus the disguised boxer in *Odyssey* 18.61. Modern commentators routinely extol boxers for their "heart," understood as their willingness to fight, particularly in the face of uneven odds.

[92] Similarly, future historians may regard all-in wrestling and mixed martial arts in the twentieth- and twenty-first-century West as a parallel to the farrago of Late Antique fighting sports.

(line 321), a clever *jeu d'esprit* employing the same verb 'raise' (αἴρω) used just three lines earlier to describe the combat itself. He assures glory (κῦδος) to the victor. The poet writes, κῦδος γὰρ νέῳ ἀνδρὶ φέρειν ἀπ᾽ ἀγῶνος ἄεθλον "Glory on the temple of he who bears away the agon-prize" (line 322, translation ours).

At long last, the audience may have a fight to watch, and a familiar figure to cheer on. The son of 'haughty' (ὑπέρθυμος)[93] Panopeus, Epeius, strides forth. The victor in the Iliadic boxing match, Epeius is once more the first to take up the challenge (Dioscurus and Dioscurus 2022d). In Homer's account, Epeius notes that he is not skilled in warfare.[94] Likewise, Quintus points out that "in deadly craft of war, when Ares rusheth through the field, he was not cunning." Nonetheless, his pugilistic conquests are such that "none dared meet him now in play of fists."[95] The interplay between the art of war and the sweet science of bruising is a feature to note from Homer to Quintus. From the beginnings of the Greco-Roman world to its twilight, boxing was kept distinct from war-like behavior, though the Romans arguably did much more than the Greeks to smudge the boundary (Section 3.5). Ares is occasionally brought into myths about boxing, but never as it its patron. One indicates that the bloody god of war was a tomato can in the ring while the other is too fragmented to inform us of the victor (Dioscurus and Dioscurus 2022d). Epeius, the poor soldier but terrific fighter, personifies the disjuncture between 'baneful, wretched' (λευγαλέος, line 328) war and 'delightful' (τερπωλή, line 305) boxing.

We are on the cusp of witnessing yet another uncontested (ἀνιδρωτί, lit., 'without sweat') match when Acamas, the son of Theseus (by some accounts the inventor of boxing, see below), strides forth to meet Epeius (σχεδόν ἔρχομαι). What's more, he is wrapped and ready to go, Agelaus having already wound the cured leather thongs (ἀζαλέος ἱμάς)[96] around the prince's hands. The verb used for putting on the gauntlets is ἀμφιβάλλω, a general term for items of clothing. The hands are here indexed with the specialized term παλάμη denoting 'hands used in deeds of violence' instead of the echt χερσι. A 'second' in the tradition of Diomedes (*Iliad* 23.683–684), Agelaus also 'excites' or 'stirs up' (ἐποτρύνω) his fighter. The comrades (ἑταῖρος) of Epeius, likewise 'encourage' (θαρσύνω)[97] their boy, who stood forth like a lion 'in the midst' (ἐν μέσσοισι)—another remarkably persistent Homeric expression for the still anonymous boxing 'ring'. While the comparison between a boxer and a lion in epic poetry is novel, Quintus has not forgotten the cultic importance of the bull in pugilism: εἱστήκει περὶ χερσὶν ἔχων βοὸς ἶφι δαμέντος | ῥινοὺς ἀζαλέας ... "Epeius stood there while around his hands were thrown by force the overpowering dried flesh of bulls" (lines 338–339, translation ours).

The cheers of the crowd ring out to 'stir up' (ἐποτρύνω) the fighters as they 'mix' (μίγνυμι) hands.[98] The intention, the poet tells us, is for the fighters to stain those untiring paws in blood: ἐν αἵματι χεῖρας ἀτειρέας (line 341). We imagine the cagey fighters hopping up and down, shadowboxing. Epeius and Acamas are eager for the anguish of the 'ring': μαιμώωντες

---

[93] Compare this term to μεγάθυμος, used to describe Epeius' magnanimous behavior towards his fallen opponent at the end of the Iliadic boxing match.

[94] Quintus credits Epeius with building the Trojan Horse.

[95] ἀλλ᾽ οὖ οἵ τις ἐτόλμα ἐγγὺς ἱκέσθαι | εἵνεκα πυγμαχίης ... (line 326–327).

[96] Vian (2008, p. 392) finds in this expression a parallel to *Argonautica* 2.52.

[97] This is the same term Diomedes uses to fortify Euryalus in *Iliad* 23.682.

[98] The verb μίγνυμι 'mix' is used of liquids and is unmistakably Homeric in its application to the hands of boxers. As has been argued for Greek wrestling in ancient poetry, boxing also routinely "dissolves the borders of the body—causing even human matter to liquefy" (Zilcosky 2019, p. 93).

ἐνὶ ξυνοχῇσιν ἀγῶνος (line 342). They throw out initiatory punches (πειράω), like Polydeuces in the Apollonine *Argonautica*, to ensure "their arms were limber and lithe, unclogged by toil of war."[99]

Suddenly, they raise their erstwhile hanging hands at each other (... ἀλλήλοισι καταντία χεῖρας ἄειραν). With hands in close (ταρφύς), the adversaries cast sharp glances (παπταίνω), presumably searching for an opening.[100] Poised on the 'extremities' (ἐπ' ἀκροτάτοις ... πόδεσσι) of their feet—most likely the balls—Quintus' boxers adopt a stance familiar to modern fighters, who still balance on their metatarsal joints for increased agility.[101] As they walk around (βαίνω), the fighters shift from knee to knee (γόνυ γουνὸς ἀμείβω),[102] trying not to expend too much effort (ἀλέομαι μέγα κάρτος),[103] while calling each other on (βοάω, line 347) to fight. This is notable as the only instance in epic poetry where the boxers vocalize to one another during the match.

Like a mass of clouds (νεφέλη) driven (βάλλω) swiftly (αἰψηρός, line 349) by the wind (ἀνεμόω), the boxers leap (θρῴσκω, line 350) forward, hurling (ῥίπτω) themselves at one another. The fighters send forth (προίημι) lightning (ἀστεροπή), an allusion to their punches. Heaven (αἰθήρ) is stirred (ὀροθύνω), the clouds agitated (θηγομένως), perhaps a reference to the dust rising at the fighters' feet. Heavy, whirling winds (ἄελλα) crash (κτυπέω) like the dry hide (ἀζαλέα ... ῥινόν)[104] resoundingly (περικτυπέω) slapping the combatants' chins (γένειον, line 353). The Quintean tempest simile (lines 349–354) seems to be his own invention, comparable to the elaborate similes in other epic boxing episodes (Dioscurus and Dioscurus 2022d).

Blood flows down (καταρρέω) from their foreheads (ἐκ ... μετώπων, line 354), their full cheeks (θαλερὰς ... παρειάς) flushed (ἐρύθαινε) with bloody sweat (ἰδρὼς αἱματόεις).[105] The boxers 'stay busy' (πονέομαι) the whole time, bent (μέμαα, line 356) on their savage purpose. Epeius does not stay put (λήγω), always pushing forward (ἐπισεύω) in his vigorous wrath (ἑῷ μέγα κάρτεϊ θύων, line 357). Acamas' judgment in the heat of the fight remains clear: ... ἐΰφρονέων ἐν ἀέθλῳ (line 358). He frequently 'parries' (ἐς κενεὸν ... τίθημι, lit. 'place in emptiness') Epeius' powerful straight hands (κρατερὰς χέρας ἰθύνεσθαι).[106] Here Quintus provides a remarkable description of "opening up" an opponent by forcing his hands away laterally: ... ἰδρείῃσι διατμήξας ἑκάτερθε | χεῖρας ldots (lines 360–361). Acamas adroitly (ἰδρείῃσι) 'cuts in half' his opponent's hands, surely a synechdoche for his guard. This allows Acamas to spring (ἐφάλλομαι) on his adversary, landing a well-timed blow (τύπτω) directly to Epeius' brow (ὀφρύη), lacerating him deeply: ... ἄχρις ἱκέσθαι | ὀστέον ... (lines 361–362).[107] Conse-

---

[99] ἄμφω χεῖρας ἑὰς πειρώμενοι, εἴπερ ἔασιν | ὡς πρὶν ι ἐΰτρόχαλοι, μηδ' ἐκ πολέμου βαρύθοιεν (lines 343–344).

[100] The action of παπταίνω is attributed to Epeius in the *Iliad* right before he knocks out his adversary and to the combatants in the Apollonine *Argonautica* as they try to locate suitable ground to box on.

[101] In *Argonautica* 2.90 a similar expression is used at the critical moment when Amycus tries to slaughter Polydeuces with a hammer-blow, though it is usually translated as "on tiptoe" (Vian 2008, p. 392).

[102] The expression appears to be lifted directly from the Apollonine *Argonautica* 2.94 (Dioscurus and Dioscurus 2022d).

[103] Way (1913) translates this phrase as, "[E]ach still eluding other's crushing might." He makes no mention of what the knees are up to or of the vocalizing verb βαίνω.

[104] The *himantes* are not mentioned here, only the 'hide' ῥινόν.

[105] The suggestion here may be that their cheeks are swollen from being battered, as in Dionysiaca 37.

[106] Here the mediopassive form of the verb ἰθύνω 'guide in a straight line' suggests the path of motion Epeius' hands travel.

[107] Polydeuces similarly cuts his opponent "to the bone" with his σπεῖραι in the Theocritean boxing match (Section 2.1).

quently, blood ran out of his eyes: ... ἐκ δέ οἱ αἷμα κατέρρεεν ὀφθαλμοῖο (line 362).[108] Despite the gore, Epeius' 'heavy hand' (βᾰρεῖᾰ χείρ) 'reaches' (τυγχάνω) Acamas, 'smiting' (τύπτω) him on the temple, whereupon the Cretan prince takes a dive into the dirt: χαμαὶ δέ οἱ ἤλασε γυῖα (line 364).[109] The adverbial 'down on the temple' κατὰ κροτάφοιο suggests the punch is a hammer-blow, coming from above. This may also explain why Epeius' hands are described as heavy (one alternative is that βᾰρεῖᾰ χείρ simply means 'fist'). By falling down half-way through the fight, Acamas takes on the role of Amycus in his duel with Polydeuces and the audience's expectation that he will lose the contest is heightened.

Still undaunted, the son of Theseus springs up (ἀνορούω), leaping (ἐνθρῴσκω) on the 'mighty man' (φώς κραταιός) and striking (πλήσσω) his head. He (probably Epeius) darts (ἀίσσω) backward, swerves a little to the left (βαιὸν ὑποκλίνας σκαιῇ, line 367) and plants (τύπτω) his fist between his opponent's eyes (μέτωπον). Immediately he springs forward (ἐφάλλομαι), striking (ἐλαύνω) his nose (ῥίς). He (probably Acamas) skillfully 'reached out' (ὀρέγω) his hands in various ways: ... ὃς δὲ καὶ αὐτὸς | μήτι παντοίη χέρας ὤρεγε ... (lines 368–369). This could refer to offense or defense.

At this less-than-dramatic moment in the narrative, the Achæans prevail upon (ἔλδομαι, lit. 'desire') the fighters to 'desist' (ἀπερύκω) from their 'toil' (πονέομαι) for 'beloved victory' (νίκη ἐρατη, line 371). The fighters' pursuivants (θεράπων)[110] hurry to the scene to remove (ἀπό ... λύω) the bloody 'skins' (ῥινός, i.e., the *himantes*) from their mighty (σθεναρός) hands.[111] The fighters exhale (ἀποπνέω) from their toil (κάματος, genitive) and wipe (μόργνυμι) their brows (μέτωπον, previous landing site of punches) with "sponges myriad-pored" (σπόγγος πολύτρητος, line 374).

The boxers' comrades (ἑταῖρος) and friends (φίλος), fulfilling a role markedly different from that of the lowly attendants (θεράπων), appear to broker a peace between the erstwhile combatants. They draw (ἄγω) them face to face (ἄντικρυς ἀλλήλων, line 376)[112] and exhort (παρηγορέω) them to hastily forget (λανθάνω) their grievous wrath (χόλος ἀλγινόεις) and make up (ἀρέσκω φιλότητι).

The boxers, we are told, hearken to the councils of their friends and kiss (κυνέω) one another, forgetting (ἐπιλανθάνομαι) their baneful strife (ἔρις ... λευγαλέη). Curiously, in this construction it is the fighters' *thymos* that appears to be the agent of their forgetting: ... ἔριδος δ' ἐπελήθετο θυμὸς | λευγαλέης ... (lines 380–381). The token of friendship symbolized by the kiss has no antecedent in epic boxing. While it has been argued that the *Posthomerica* shows no signs of Christian belief (James and Lee 2000), the kiss-and-make-up at the end of Quintus' boxing match stands out to us as a potential counterexample despite the poet's strong Homericizing tendencies. To be sure, displays of magnanimity to a fallen opponent are found throughout epic boxing, including in the *Iliad*, *Odyssey*, and the *Idylls* (much harsher resolutions are described in other epics, including Apollonius' *Argonautica* and the *Æneid*). But the Quintean kiss seems different. The explicit forgiveness of a grudge in the Posthomeric boxing match feels like an overtly religious expression entirely consistent with

---

[108] This gruesome detail is omitted entirely by Way (1913).

[109] γυῖα, though in the plural here, seems to have its singular meaning (γυῖον), i.e., the 'whole body'. According to Way (1913), "[Epeius] hurled him to the ground."

[110] This is the same term used by Apollonius of Rhodes to characterize the henchmen of Amycus.

[111] It is still true that exhausted boxers, having finished their work in the ring, are first unencumbered of their gloves before any (other) post-fight ceremonies.

[112] The related form ἀντικρύ 'against, opposite' is used by Epeius in his threat against Euryalus in *Iliad* 23.673: ἀντικρὺ χρόα τε ῥήξω σύν τ' ὀστέ' ἀράξω "I will rend his flesh and crush his bones."

contemporaneous teachings regarding the duties and character of Christians.[113] The comity achieved by Quintus' quondam combatants has implications for the development of conventionalized 'repair strategies' that take place at the end of modern Western boxing bouts.[114]

The fighters both receive a dark-blue silver (κυανοκρήδεμνος ἀργυρέους) krater from the godesss Thetis, who appears to serve as the matron of her son's funeral games, bestowing prizes on the winners.[115] After an extended discussion of the kraters' provenance (lines 381–393),[116] Quintus returns to the exhausted combatants.

More than other epic poets, Quintus concerns himself with the aftermath of the boxing match. He concludes the account by discussing how the fighters' wounds are treated. Podalirius, a son of the medicine god Asclepius and a legendary healer in his own right, sedulously (ἐνδυκέως) tends to (ἀκέομαι) the boxers' gashes (ἀμφιδεδρυμμένα τύμμα).[117] It is possible that the Quintean inclusion of a 'ringside' doctor was drawn from his own experience watching Late Antique matches, where a physician may indeed have been present. There is no other account of an ancient boxing match that includes medical treatment, besides perhaps "The Marriage of Martu" (Dioscurus and Dioscurus 2022b). Podalirius first squeezes (ἐκμύζησεν) the lacerations, presumably to remove infection, then he sews them up (ῥάπτω). He next applies a drug (φάρμακον), perhaps a salve or an herb, "given him by his sire of old" and famed for its immediate virtue over all kinds of 'incurable wounds of men' (ἀναλθέα τύμματα φωτῶν). The epulotic philtre did the trick, healing (ἀπαλθαίνομαι) the wounds on their faces (πρόσωπον) and beneath "their clustering hair" (εὐκομόωντα κάρηνα, lit. 'well-curled heads'). Quintus does not remark on wounds to any other part of the boxers' bodies, though he concludes by noting that Podalirius' ministrations generally assuaged (κατηπιάω) them of their distress (ἀνία, line 404).

2.6 *Dionysiaca* 37

Nonnus of Panopolis was a Greek poet living in Egypt, probably in the fifth century AD. Most likely a Christian, he was deeply familiar with the New Testament (Vian 1997). His contribution to the epic tradition, an astoundingly lengthy hexametric affair known as the *Dionysiaca*, concerns—among other topics—the military expedition of the wine god Diony-

---

[113] St. Paul wrote in his epistle to the Colossians (3.13): "Forbearing one another, and forgiving one another, if any man have a quarrel against any: even as Christ forgave you, so also do ye" (KJV). This epistle, as only one example of the Christian doctrine of forgiveness, was written, at the latest, near the end of the first century AD and would have been in wide circulation by Quintus' era. See also literature on the contemperaneous "kiss of peace" (εἰρήνη).

[114] We have observed the following conventional gestures directed towards an opponent: embracing; smiling warmly; shaking hands or bumping fists; clapping hands; lifting him in the air; cupping a hand behind his head and bringing foreheads together; holding his hand aloft; speaking congenially and at close proximity; holding the ropes to ease his exit from the ring; and greeting members of the opposing corner.

[115] Thetis appears to take on the role of the goddess Nike who is depicted garlanding victorious fighters on numerous vases (Dioscurus and Dioscurus 2022d).

[116] The kraters were fashioned by Hephæstus as a wedding gift for Dionysus, who filled them with nectar and turned them over to his son, Thoas, the king of Lemnos. Hypsipyle inherited them from her father and gave them to Euneus, her son by Jason. Euneus in his turn gave the kraters to Achilles as a ransom for Lycaon, the half-brother of Hector. Homer tells the story a bit differently in *Iliad* 23.747: Patroclus receives one krater in exchange for releasing Lycaon, who was by then his slave. Achilles killed Lycaon after the death of Patroclus. Quintus was presumably interested in making sure the boxing prize had significant connections to the story of Achilles and Patroclus, the honorees of the Posthomeric and Iliadic funeral games, respectively.

[117] The noun τύμμα can also refer to a snakebite or an insect sting. The adjective ἀμφιδεδρυμμένα is a rare one, perhaps meaning 'torn all around'.

sus to India. This war, "fought by the generation of the Iliadic heroes' grandfathers" is understood by Nonnus to be morally and æsthetically superior to the Trojan War (Verhelst 2016, p. 157). It has been suggested that Nonnus saw Homer as his poetic rival.

Book 37 (lines 485–545)[118] of the *Dionysiaca* features a boxing match between two semi-divine beings named Melisseus and Eurymedon at the funeral games of a fallen soldier named Opheltes: "There are contests about the tomb," we are told.[119] While closely linked to the boxing vignette in *Illiad* 23, the Nonnian boxing match is "influenced by contemporary realities" of Late Antiquity which arguably affect the way it is presented (Frangoulis 1995, p. 145).[120] It has even been argued that "Nonnus wrote ... for a mixed audience, comprised mainly, but not exclusively of Christians" (Agosti 2016, p. 657). This leads us to wonder, what, if anything, is uniquely Christian about the boxing match in the *Dionysiaca*?

While, like other post-Homeric epics, Nonnus' ergasy languished for many generations, it has experienced renewed interest since the middle of the twentieth century. One commentator writes, "The whole story is imaginative, even visionary, and full of fanciful details, sprinkled with fantastic imagination" (Bannert and Kröll 2016, p. 503). As to its supposedly derivative nature, the same authors note, "Nonnus rarely includes whole verses from [the] *Iliad* and *Odyssey* but prefers to insert references and allusions to be recognized and decoded by the reader. He uses single words bearing literary effect, pointing at certain scenes or situations in the Homeric epic ..." (ibid., p. 503). Indeed, while there is much evidence that Nonnus studied other epic boxing matches carefully, it is undeniable that he infused the funeral games of Opheltes with his own imagination, perhaps leavened by his Christian worldview and elements of boxing relevant to a Late Antique readership.[121] Thus, the Nonnian boxing match, written at a time shortly before boxing would "go dark" for over a thousand years, is a critical link in our understanding of boxing's evolution. Below are a few of the elements that make Nonnus' contest stand out from those of his predecessors:

- Hermes appears to be the divine patron of the match, having bestowed on one boxer his hand gear.
- One boxer wears armor over his loins.
- There is reference to a defensive hand, compared to a shield, and an offensive hand, compared to a spearhead.
- One fighter lands a 'lucky punch'.
- The boxer's sharp teeth are mentioned.
- A clinch takes place.
- Body blows are thrown: A boxer is struck on the chest; another below the nipple.
- Footwork is described in some detail.
- Swelling occurs around the eyes and on the cheeks during the fight.
- A fighter's brother acts as his 'second'.
- An ox-hide shield serves as one of the prizes.

---

[118]Line numbers in this section come from Rouse (1940–1942) unless otherwise indicated.

[119]ἧχι τριηκοστὸν πέλεν ἕβδομον, εἵνεκα νίκης | ἀνδράσιν ἀθλοφόροις ἐπιτύμβιοί εἰσιω ἀγῶνες (no line numbers: proem to Book 37).

[120]*...influencées par des réalités contemporaines...*

[121]"Ces innovations lui ont peut-être été inspirées par des spectacles de pugilat contemporains" (Frangoulis 1999, p. 42).

The episode begins with Dionysus setting up (ἵστημι) a contest (ἀγών)—the cruel (χαλεπός) boxing (line 485). Like Achilles in *Iliad 23*, Dionysus inaugurates the action by presenting the prizes (δῶρον): a bull from an Indian stall (ταῦρος ἀπ' Ἰνδῴοιο βοαύλου) and an exotic, barbarian ox-hide shield (βοείη)[122] fashioned by black-skinned (μελάρρινος) Indians. The ancient cultic relationship between bulls and boxers (Dioscurus and Dioscurus 2022b) is evident in these tauric funeral gifts (κτέρεα). The god calls for prizefighters (ἀεθλητῆρας), urging (ἐπείγω) two skillful (εὐπάλαμος) men to contend (ἐριδμαίνω)[123] for victory (περὶ νίκης, line 490).

This is the contest of the unyielding (ἀτειρής) fist (πυγμή), the god proclaims. The one who conquers (νικάω, active) will receive the shaggy (δασύθριξ) bull, the one who is conquered (νικάω, passive) will bear off the shield (ἀσπίς) with many folded layers (πολύπτυχος) of hide.[124] At the end of Dionysus' speech, warlike (σακέσπαλος) Melisseus arises (ὄρνυμι). Melisseus is identified among the Kuretes, a group of mystical dancer–warriors who, on Crete, protected the infant Zeus from his cormorant father. Melisseus was also a rustic demigod associated with honey[125] and bee-keeping (his name means 'honey bringer'). According to *Dionysiaca* 28.318, Melisseus imitated the bee, wielding its sting (κέντρα μελίσσης) in battle.[126] He was both accustomed to (ἠθάς) and cultivated in (ἐπιμελέομαι) *pygmachia*. Seizing (ἅπτω) the 'beautifully-horned' (εὐκέραος) bull, the god of apiaries exclaimed, "This way anyone who wants a painted shield! For I will not let another have the fat bull as long as I can hold up [ἀείρω] my hands!" (line 497).[127] Melisseus further mimics Epeius, who in *Iliad* 23 likewise commands all rivals to suit themselves with second place.

Silence, as usual, greets the upstart. Finally, Eurymedon, a son of Hephæstus by a Thracian woman, rises (ἀνίστημι). Hermes himself furnished (πόρω) the lad with the tools (ὄργανον) of boxing, intended for the 'strong of limb' (γυιαλκέος). The term 'tools' is novel in this context. We must assume that it refers to the *himantes*, which he mentions later, but it may also apply to the Theocritean *spherai*, which are differentiated from the *himantes* in *Idyll* 22, or even the two-pronged Late Antique *cæstus* (see below).

Casting Hermes as the divine benefactor of boxing gear is another innovative choice. When it comes to Olympians involved in epic boxing, Apollo is invoked in the Iliadic match, while Poseidon and Zeus are mentioned as the fathers of Amycus and Polydeuces, respectively. Eryx, the semi-divine son of Aphrodite, granted his brain-spattered *cæstus* to Entellus in the *Æneid*, and was said to have sparred with Heracles. Hermes as boxer is not entirely without precedent.[128] He appears in a matchup against Ares in a fragmentary poem by Corinna (Dioscurus and Dioscurus 2022d), but Nonnus' choice is still unusual. It has been argued that Hermes and Christ are elsewhere related in the work of Nonnus (Dijk-

---

[122] A shield appears in the prize position (i.e., between the combatants) in at least one Geometric depiction of boxing, a Theban pedestaled krater held at the National Archæological Museum of Athens, No. 12896 (Dioscurus and Dioscurus 2022d).

[123] Another meaning for ἐριδμαίνω is 'provoke to strife.'

[124] The adjectives used to describe the bull and the ox-hide shield seem to make them more comprarable.

[125] Large jars of honey are placed around Opheltes' funeral pyre (line 50).

[126] As we will see by the end of the episode, if ever there were a classical antecedent to the dictum "float like a butterfly, sting like a bee," it must—almost by definition—be embodied in the boxer Melisseus.

[127] In *Idyll* 22.65, Amycus challenges Polydeuces to put up his dukes using the same verb, ἀείρω (see Section 2.1).

[128] DeLaine (1997, p. 80) notes that in the Roman world, Hermes, along with Hercules, was the "presiding deity of the *palæstra*" and according to Philostratus, "The *palaistra* of Hermes was the first" (*Gym.* 16): παλαίστρα γένοιτο Ἑρμοῦ πρώτη (Kayser 1871).

stra 2016, pp. 84–85, 88). Nonnus clearly broke with the epic tradition by invoking Hermes, leading us to speculate that he did so to highlight Christ's role as the patron of the dionysian boxing match. Indeed, it has been observed that Nonnus' "fruitful dialogue" between Christianity and Hellenism "ensured the instant popularity and lasting legacy of [his] œuvre throughout Late Antiquity, and beyond" (ibid., p. 88).

A bit of background on Eurymedon: He "used to remain busy beside his father's furnace hammering [σφυρήλατος] away at the beaten [τύπτω] anvil." Does Nonnus here cleverly suggest the boxer's art in pounding his opponent? As we mentioned in Dioscurus and Dioscurus (2022d), ancient poets may have amused their audiences with the alliterative similarity between the words 'hammer' and *sphairai* or *spherai*, which may refer to one or more types of Greek boxing glove. In any event, Apollonius Rhodius conjures hammers in one of his elaborate boxing similes (*Argonautica* 2.80) and Nonnus likely recalls it here.

Acting in the Iliadic role of Diomedes, Alcon attends (ἀμφιέπω) his brother Eurymedon "full of excitement" (ἐριπτοίητος).[129] Alcon lays out (παρατίθημι)[130] his brother's *zōma* and fastens (ἁρμόζω) a μίτρα (see below) snugly around his loins (line 505). We have not observed the anatomical term 'loins' (ἰξύς) in any other boxing match.[131] Nonnus' utilization of the *zōma* and his concern with covering the boxers' nether regions may arise from the pudeur of his Christian audience, though we certainly cannot make the same argument for the *zōma*'s appearance in both the *Iliad* and the *Odyssey*. The term μίτρα is curious. In Homer it refers to a 'piece of armor, apparently a metal guard worn around the waist'.[132] In context, it appears to be a synonym for the *zōma* (Frangoulis 1999, p. 154).[133] We are left to wonder whether Nonnus wished to reassure his audience of the boxers' ample protection in the genital area. If the meaning of the words were synonymous in his time, it is not clear what Nonnus intended: a bit of armor or a cloth garment.[134] If μίτρα refers to armor, then we must conclude that strikes to the groin were common in Late Antique boxing, though we need not presume that they were legal (Brophy and Brophy 1985).[135]

Alcon joins together (συνάπτω)[136] and binds (σφίγγω) his brother's 'long hands' (δολιχή

---

[129] The adjective ἐριπτοίητος might also mean 'scared' or 'aroused'. Frangoulis (1999, p. 93) renders Alcon *plein d'inquiétude* 'full of worry' and reasons elsewhere that Melisseus' reputation as a boxer has left Alcon bestraught over his brother's fate (ibid., p. 154).

[130] The servants of Apollonine Amycus similarly execute the *mise en place* (τίθημι) of their master's *himantes* before his boxing match with Polydeuces in the *Argonautica*.

[131] The term appears in *Odyssey* 5.231, when Calypso dons a golden girdle.

[132] In a strange reversal, μίτρα is the ancestor, via Latin *mitrā*, of English *mitre*.

[133] Another possibility is that the boxers wear both a loincloth and a piece of armor, as we have conjectured in a sculptural pair of boxers from the second or third century (Figure 25).

[134] In *Dionysiaca* 37.55, Nonnus again refers to a μίτρα, though now metaphorically, in describing how the fat of slaughtered horses encircled (κυκλόω) Opheltes' corpse on the pyre. In the same book (line 670) μίτρα almost certainly refers to a piece of armor and not a mere loincloth, since it is offered as a second-prize (after two spears and a helmet) in the stone-throwing competition.

[135] Modern boxing competition requires a foul protector to be worn over the genitals even though repeated and/or flagrant blows "below the belt" may result in the offending boxer's disqualification. USA Boxing regulations, however, indicate that the offended fighter will lose the match if he is unable to recover from a first—or second—accidental punch to his privates.

[136] Surely this cannot mean the hands themselves were bound together. The verb presumably suggests the action of joining the hand more securely to the wrist, or the fingers to the hand, etc.—one function of boxing handwraps to the present day.

παλάμη)[137] with the dried (ἀζαλέος)[138] and coiled (περίπλοκος) *himantes* (line 507). He also calls the thongs ὁλκός meaning 'drawn to oneself'. This may suggest the manner in which they were tied: as the attendant cinches the straps, this naturally draws the boxers' hands closer to the attendant. The adjective ὁλκός probably indicates that the boxer held his hands aloft or at least away from his body as the attendant performed the binding. In any event, this is a level of detail we have not observed previously in the epic boxing matches.

Then the 'foremost man' or 'champ' (πρόμος)[139] sets out (ἔρχομαι) into the midst (εἰς μέσον),[140] carrying (φέρω) his left hand thrown forward (προβλής) before his face (πρόσωπον, genitive).[141] Nonnus calls the arrangement a "natural shield" (σάκος ἔμφυτον, line 509), leaving no doubt as to the defensive nature of this gesture. The lead hand is juxtaposed with the other (the right), which is adorned with the flesh-cutting (ταμεσίχροας) *himantes* and made into a kind of spearhead (λόγχη). The mayhem inherent in this boxing gear is highlighted by the adjective ταμεσίχροας, derived from τέμνω, meaning 'cut', 'hew down', 'maim', 'butcher', or 'sacrifice'. While the adjective (and verb) is unprecedented in epic boxing matches, its polysemy recalls the sacrificial scene at the end of the Vergillian boxing match, as well as the facial lacerations in *Idyll* 22. The spearhead (λόγχη) reference would likely be identified by a Late Antique audience as the pronged *cæstus* worn by boxers of that era (Figures 16, 18, 17). This may be as close as we come to a literary reference to these gruesome boxing implements.

One of the boxers constantly wards off (φυλάσσω) the challenging (δύσμαχος, lit. 'hard to fight with') onslaught (ὁρμή) of his adversary. Here, 'adversary' is rendered as the one he is 'wrestling against' (ἀντίπαλος).[142] Derived from the noun πάλη 'wrestling', the application of this adjective may suggest the blurring of the boundaries between boxing, wrestling, and *pankration* in Nonnus' world. It may also suggest that the adjective had undergone semantic bleaching and meant only 'rival' or 'antagonist' more generally.

Names and identifying epithets are in short supply during the boxing battle. Moreover, it is hardly clear who is called the 'champ' (πρόμος) at the beginning of the bout (*ut supra*). By this point in the narrative, the audience would have almost certainly lost the thread as to who was throwing what punch when. That was, perhaps, Nonnus' intention: the identity of the fighters has become mingled (cf. μίγνυμι, line 527), just like the boxers' hands in Homero–Nonnian epic or perhaps even individual members of the body of Christ. It may be that the Nonnian approach here is another example of the Late Antique tendency in art and literature called "dematerialization, intended to supersede naturalistic representation, in favor of a spiritual weightlessness conferring symbolic meanings," and "typical of Nonnian

---

[137] Nonnus' adjective δολιχή is novel of hands in boxing matches. Is it possible he was familiar with much older, manneristic depictions of boxers on Greek vase paintings (Dioscurus and Dioscurus 2022d) and in Etruscan tombs, in which the defensive hand, raised aloft, is frequently dolichomorphic?

[138] The term is also used to describe the leathern thongs in the *Posthomerica* and in Apollonius' *Argonautica*.

[139] It is not altogether clear who Nonnus refers to as πρόμος. Is it Melisseus, cultivated in the sweet science and audacious to claim the bull? Or is it Eurymedon, who received his boxing gear from a deity? Nonnus is perhaps toying with his audience's perception of the fighters as individuals (see below).

[140] By the fifth century AD there was still no definitive word for the boxing ring. Clearly the Greeks and Romans did not conceive of it as a defined space in the manner of their early modern and modern counterparts.

[141] The syntax is somewhat touchy, with no preposition to make the relation between the hand and face explicit: … ἑοῦ προβλῆτα προσώπου | λαιὴν χεῖρα φέρων … (lines 508–509). Nonnus may be influenced here by the allusion to a guard position in *Posthomerica* 4.360–361 and in *Idyll* 22.120. Nonnus' description conforms to Gardiner (1910, p. 204–205), where he explains how Greek boxers used the right (back) hand for striking and the left (lead) hand for defense, though Poliakoff (1987a, pp. 83–84) notes exceptional depictions in Greek vase painting.

[142] αἰεὶ δ' ἀντιπάλοιο φυλάσσετο δύσμαχον ὁρμήν (line 511).

descriptions" Agosti (2016, pp. 661–662).

We are next treated to a rich mosaic of boxing injuries, whether potential or realized, Nonnus does not specify.[143] First, the punch (πλήσσω) down (κατά, probably suggesting a hammer-blow) to the brow (ὀφρύος) or the forehead (μέτωπον). Next, the bloodying (αἵμαξις) punch landed (τύπτω) to the ἄρθρον (line 513), an anatomical term which generally means 'joint' but can have the specialized denotations of 'eyes', 'mouth', or even 'genitals'; Rouse (1940–1942) translates ἄρθρον as "face", Frangoulis (1999) as *oreille* 'ear'. How about a blow to the temple (κρόταφος) that cuts it in half (διατμήγω)? Here, the verb is τυγχάνω 'happen', suggesting, as Rouse (1940–1942) has it, a "lucky blow." We conjecture that it may point to a haymaker—a wide-looping hook—which, if landed, indeed spells good fortune for the puncher. Next, a shot that "tear[s] away to the very center of his busy brain."[144] Here, Epeius' Iliadic taunt to 'crush' his opponent's bones resurfaces in the verb ἀράσσω and Late Antique boxing is revealed in all of its terrible glory: What kind of a boxing punch can crush the skull and reveal the 'innermost' brain within? Nonnus describes boxing at its most brutal— the doom of the Æneidean bull now meted out on a man. The kind of violence Nonnus describes could be carried out only with specialized boxing gear—the most vicious forms of the Roman *cæstus*—intended for just such mayhem. Nonnus' boxing poetry is steeped in the gore of the arena and alludes to the kinds of particularly nasty injuries that were common in the pugilism of his era.

But wait, there's more! How about a 'savage hand' (παλάμη τρηχεῖα, line 516) stretched out (τιταίνω) so hard to the side of the head[145] that it strips (γυμνόω, lit. 'strips naked') the eyes from the adversary's blinded (λιπόγληνος) countenance?[146] Finally, there's a smashing (ἀράσσω) punch to his bloodied (δαφοινήεις) jaw meant to 'strike' or 'expel' (ἐλαύνω)[147] his many sharp (ὀξυτέρως)[148] teeth in a row (ὄγμος).[149]

Nonnus supplied his audience with a catalog of epic boxing's greatest hits, each with an antecedent somewhere in the Greco-Roman literary tradition that, by Nonnus' time, was already over a thousand years old. The laundry list seems to us a playful way for Nonnus to outdo all of his predecessors,[150] by including not just one punch, but all of them. However, despite the relatively late date of its composition, the *Dionysiaca* still contains no specialized lexical items like 'jab' or 'hook' to characterize blows. Instead, the poet relies on striking verbs like ἐλαύνω, literally as old as Homer. Throughout the epic tradition, punches are de-

---

[143]It is probably a list of injuries that a boxer could avoid with good defensive technique. The list lends itself to the "encyclopedic aspect" or "jeweled style" of Nonnus (Geisz 2016, pp. 173, 192).

[144]εἰς μέσον ἐγκεφάλοιο νοήμονος ἄκρον ἀράξας 'Smash in to the innermost middle of an intelligent head' (line 515).

[145]One text has βλεφάροισι 'eyelids' instead of κροτάφοισι 'temple' (Frangoulis 1999).

[146]Nonnus may here be echoing Valerius Flaccus' description of the fight between Otreus and Amycus in which the ogre "dashed out" the eyes of his opponent (*Argonautica* 2.167–168; see Section 3.3).

[147]In *Odyssey* 18.91–96, this is the verb used to describe Odysseus' knockout blow of Iros. It is fitting that Nonnus uses it as the last in his list of punches.

[148]Why sharp teeth? Nonnus may be alluding to the possibility that boxers bit one another in the Late Antique ring. If so, on June 28, 1997, Mike Tyson may have recreated history by gnashing on Evander Holyfield's right ear and expectorating the gruesome remnants on the ring apron during a heavyweight championship fight in Las Vegas. Tyson claimed the offense was retaliation for headbutting.

[149]One sense of this word, perhaps intended here by the poet, is a swathe that has been previously reaped. This is somewhat complicated by the use of the adjective πολύστιχος meaning 'of many lines'. The most likely translation is 'many teeth in a row'. Nonnus may be playing with another reading of πολύστιχος 'prolix', an attribute rendered comically implausible for someone whose teeth have just been knocked out.

[150]Throughout the *Dionysiaca*, "[T]he propriety of the past is infused with the mischief and irreverence of [Nonnus'] own time" (Bannert and Kröll 2016, p. 504).

nominated based primarily on their landing sites and only occasionally based on their path of motion and origin: a punch to the temple or side of the head, often invoked, must be a hook; a punch to the forehead or nose, a straight. Strikes accompanied by the preposition *kata* are most likely hammer blows whose vertical trajectory is made most explicit in the *Æneid* and the Apollonine *Argonautica*. In at least one instance, Theocritus tells us the origin of the punch and its landing site, allowing us to infer the trajectory of an uppercut (see Section 2.1).

On with the fight. Melisseus rushes (ἐπισεύω) Eurymedon, striking (ἐλαύνω) him on the top (ἄκρος) of the chest (στῆθος, line 521). He (probably Eurymedon) reaches (τιταίνω) toward his opponent's face in vain (μάτην), failing in his purpose (ἁμαρτάνω) and striking (τύπτω) nothing but air. Trepidant (τρομέω, in some senses 'from fear') and running round and round (περιτρέχω), one of the boxers (again, probably Eurymedon) repays (ἀμείβω) his fellow with a right hand (δεξιτερός) reaching out (τιταίνω) to the hollow of his bosom (κόλπος, accusative). The punch lands below (κάτω) the nipple (lit., 'naked chest' γυμνός μαστός, genitive).

In the most explicit reference we have seen to a clinch in any epic boxing match, Nonnus describes the technique this way: 'the incomers came' (ἵκανον ἐπήλυδες) 'one against the other' (ἄλλος ἐπ' ἄλλῳ, line 525). With sparing footsteps (ἴχνεσι φειδομένοισι) the fighters slip (ἀμείβω) their feet past each other (ποδὸς πόδα τυτθὸν, line 526).[151] Unable to resist the Homeric boxing trope *par eminence*, the poet writes χερσὶ ... χεῖρας ἔμιξαν 'hand mixes with hand'.

By successive (ἐπασσύτερος) swinging motions (ῥιπή) the *himantes* plaited (ὁμοπλεκέων) round the surface of their hands (ἀκροτάτην περὶ χεῖρα)[152] made an awful (φρικτός), booming (ἐπιβομβέω), thud (δοῦπος, lines 527–528). Now a list of outcomes: cheeks torn asunder (χαρασσομένης); *himantes* stained red (φοινίσσω) and dripping with blood (αἱμαλέαις λιβάδεσσιν); heavy sounds emanating from the jaws (γενύων πέλε δοῦπος); and facial swelling[153] into which the eyes sink deep.[154]

Eurymedon toils (κάμνω) against Melisseus' skillful cunning (ἴδμονη τέχνη), facing (ἀντωπέω) the irresistible (ἄσχετον) might of the sun's rays (αἴγλη) which shine into (καταυγάζω) his eyes. This recalls the jockeying for position between Polydeuces and Amycus (*Idyll* 22.535–536), and does not bode well for Eurymedon. Melisseus 'plays like a child' (παίζω),[155] perhaps taunting his opponent. With a sharp (ὀξυτέρη) pivot (στροφάλιγξ), he treads lightly (ἀείρω) with a raised foot (μετάρσιος ἴχνος).[156] While difficult to reconstruct, this passage may suggest the quick stomping motion, sometimes accompanied by a feint, that a modern boxer

---

[151] It has been remarked that Nonnus, in his *Paraphrase*, "pays particular attention to Christ's feet, which might be related to the popular cult of Jesus' footprints" (Agosti 2016, p. 652). The careful description of footwork in this passage, unprecedented in boxing epic (the closest is Apollonius' expression describing knee position in *Argonautica* 2.94 and emulated by Quintus in *Posthomerica* 4.347), may reveal a coded element intended to draw the attention of Nonnus' Christian audience. It may also be related to "the special meaning feet had in the Egyptian religion, a meaning resumed by Christians" (ibid.).

[152] Rouse (1940–1942) translates this expression as 'fingers', i.e., the extremities of the hands.

[153] This particularly difficult passage reads: ... ἐπὶ θρωσμῷ δὲ προσώπου | εὐρυτέρου γεγαῶτος ἐκυμαίνοντο παρειαί "On the rising ground (θρωσμός) of the broad face the cheeks arose like waves (κυμαίνω)" (lines 531–532, translation ours). The oblique reference to waves may hail from Homer's fish simile (*Iliad* 23.692–694) or Apollonius' ship simile (*Argonautica* 2.70–71), both used to describe some aspect of boxing (Dioscurus and Dioscurus 2022d).

[154] We translate ὀφθαλμοὶ δ' ἑκάτερθεν ἐκοιλαίνοντο προσώπου as "The eyes hollow out (κοιλαίνω) the face on either side" (line 533).

[155] The verb may also be 'rush at' (ἐπαΐσσω), as in Frangoulis (1999). "Nonnus is very sensitive to movement and he creates a rich system of ideologically oriented oppositions, as movement vs. immobility, swiftness vs. slowness, etc., to convey also the idea of prompt belief in Jesus' words ..." (Agosti 2016, p. 652).

[156] Line 537 reads: ὀξυτέρη στροφάλιγγι μετάρσιον ἴχνος ἀείρων. This may be another example of Nonnus' peculiar

may use to startle his opponent. Suddenly he strikes (τύπτω) the other's jaw (γναθμός) under the ear (ὑπ' οὔατος, line 538) right where the knockout blow is landed in the *Odyssey*.[157]

Suffering (κάμνω) and lying down on his back (ὕπτιος) Eurymedon rolled (αὐτοκύλιστος) around, planted firmly (ἐρείδω) in the dust (κονία, dative). Bereft of his *thymos* (θυμολιπής),[158] he was like in all points (πανείκελος) to one 'drunken with wine' (μεθύω, line 540). Carrying his head to one side (εἶχε δὲ κόρσην κεκλιμένην ἑτέρωσε) he spat out (ἔπτυω) a "thickish" (λεπτός παχύνω) bloody foam (ἄχνη).[159] Seizing (λαμβάνω) Eurymedon, his kinsman (σύγγονος) Alcon conveyed (μετάγω) him out of the gloomy gathering (ἐκτὸς ἀγῶνος στυγνὸς).[160] The astonied boxer was deprived of his reason (ἀμερσίνοος) and weighed down (βαρέω) by the blow (πληγή, dative). Alcon, presumably, eagerly (ἐσσύμενος) "lifted the great Indian shield" (line 545).

2.7 Features of boxing in Hellenistic and Roman Greece

In this section we present features of boxing as attested in Greek texts and visual art of the Hellenistic and Roman eras. It is a challenge to describe Greek boxing during this period in consistent terms and to do so separately from developments that took place in Italy at roughly the same time. While it may be useful to separate objects based on their findspot, as we have done elsewhere, there can be no doubt that boxing cultures in Greece and Italy exerted significant mutual influence. The distinction between Roman and Greek boxing in the imperial period and during Late Antiquity seems particularly artificial, since what we style 'gladiatorial' (Roman) boxing was practiced in Greece at the same time Greek 'athletic' boxing was practiced at Rome. While we hesitate to make the distinctions too stark, we will attempt to present here features of boxing that seem particularly 'Greek', either because they are attested in objects of Greek provenance or because they are written about by Greek authors.

Any cultural practice will necessarily change over time and space. This is doubtless true of boxing in Hellenistic and Roman Greece. Depictions of boxing, visual and literary, provide ample evidence of different techniques and equipment but in a less-than-methodical fashion. Visual depictions do not come with captions. Words—if they were ever defined in the first place—take on new meanings and shed their old ones. This is the primary reason for the extraordinary parviscience that still surrounds Greek terms for boxing hand gear, despite considerable effort to decode the sources (Jüthner and Mehl 1962, Poliakoff 1983; 1987a, Thuillier 2019). While we do not counsel despair when it comes to the potential clarification of boxing terms in Greek, it is still imprudent to declare what a particular type of boxing glove was called or what it looked like across centuries of cultural flux. At best, we may be able to reason what type of glove is used in a particular image based on its structure or its effect on an opponent. Using a text, we may be able to do the same, if the author provided detail *quantum sufficit*. To know for sure what a Greek boxer called that glove at the time a painter

---

fascination with feet (*ut supra*).

[157] Polydeuces strikes Amycus above the ear in the *Argonautica*.

[158] Frangoulis (1999) translates the adjective as *inconscient* 'unconscious'.

[159] This passage is remarkably similar to Oppian *Cynegetica* 4.204, as noted by Frangoulis (1999, p. 43). In his description of an expugnate boxer (a simile for a captured lion), Oppian refers to the head lolling to one side, the thick foam of blood, and the appearance of drunkenness: *peut-être le modèle de Nonnos ici* (ibid.)

[160] The gloominess may also be attributed to Alcon, as in the translation of Frangoulis (1999), who explains that the adjective *désigne simplement la tristesse que ressent le frère du vaincu*.

rendered it, or what the glove looked like when the author conjured it up with words, may indeed lie beyond our discernment. And yet the urge to classify, categorize, and typologize the material culture of boxing remains, if for no other reason than the sheer abundance of evidence, messy and incomplete as it may be. There remains in us the hope that by considering all of this evidence, we may reach some new conclusions. In this section, we will attempt to summarize what we have learned and what we still do not know about boxing from literature and art produced in Greece (or the Greek language) from around the third century BC to around the fifth century AD. We reserve comment about boxing's characteristics in Italy and elsewhere in the Roman world for a later section of this paper.

Why did the Greeks box? We have a better answer to this question than we do for the same question as it relates to any Bronze Age people: the Greeks wrote volumes about their own values. According to Scanlon (2002, p. 17):

> The primary athletic virtue, like that of the heroic warrior, was *aretē* (ἀρετή), an untranslatable term, including notions of "manly excellence," "merit," "achievement," and "accomplishment." The fact that *aretē* was so pervasive a concept in all aspects and in all eras of Greek culture does not dilute its importance in the sphere of athletics; it suggests that athletic *aretē* shared the essential qualities of the generalized notion of *aretē* and could therefore have widespread symbolic importance.

> In the traditional view of Pindar, *aretē* was something obtained by nature, improved by practice, and seen through to success with the assistance of the gods, as expressed in this ode to a victor in boys' boxing: "Sharpening one who is naturally excellent [φύοντ' ἀρετᾷ], a man [as trainer], with the guiding hand of god, can rouse him to enormous fame. (Ol. 10. 20–21)

> The chief purpose of *aretē* within the social contest system was "to win fame" (κῦδος [κλέος, εὖχος] ἀρέσθαι), to obtain a measure of immortality, and to do so in accordance with the prosperity of one's family and community.

Greek athletics emerged from religious festivity and "one's performance in [athletic events] was taken as a measure of status and honor" (Scanlon 2002, p. 12). For this reason, boxing and other competitions were "pursued with deadly seriousness and with one eye on our human relation to the divine cosmos" and the other eye on one's opponent (Scanlon 2002, p. 12).

In his *Description of Greece* Pausanias (5.7.10) claims that Apollo beat Ares in boxing at the first Olympics (which were held either to celebrate the victory of Zeus over his father Cronos, or to set the stage for them to wrestle for supremacy). The match is not described in any detail, but it is an indication of Apollo's dominion over boxing and boxers. That Ares is defeated in boxing by the youthful and adroit Apollo suggests that the Greeks did not necessarily conceive of boxing as a form of war, but as something connected to Apolline attributes and associations: archery, music, dance, truth, prophecy, healing and disease, the sun, light, and poetry. What does this list have to do with boxing? Music and dance may be the Apollonian features most closely associated with pugilism. A boxer's movements are analogous to those of a dancer and music had a strong association with boxing across ancient Mediterranean and Near Eastern cultures.

While we should be skeptical, Philostratus (*Gym.* 9) asserted that the Spartans developed boxing because they chose not to wear helmets in battle (preferring shields). Thus boxing gave them an opportunity to practice how to protect themselves from being struck in the face, and how to endure it when such blows inevitably occurred. The Spartans, who claimed to have invented boxing, quickly abandoned it and did not take part in boxing competitions. The true origins of boxing, as we have demonstrated, are fare less tractable (Dioscurus and Dioscurus 2022a;b).

Boxing was first listed as an Olympic event in 688 BC and a boys' version was differentiated sixty years later. The rules of boxing were ascribed to the first Olympic champion, Onomastus of Smyrna.[161] Hellenic boxing arguably emphasized strikes to the head; some have argued that they were not permitted to strike the body during this period of development.

Hellenic boxers were not censured if they killed their opponents in the bout, but they were usually denied victory. Slaughtering an opponent in the 'ring' was treated like accidentally killing a comrade during war, according to Athenian law (Scanlon 2002, p. 307). The killer still had to be relieved of blood guilt, an expression of catharsis perhaps helpful to the subsequent social acceptance—if not the emotional welfare—of the survivor. The boxer Kleomedes of Astypalæa killed his opponent, went mad[162] and then went on to kill again (Paus. 6.9.6–8).[163] Notably, he was censured not for the death of his antagonist, Ikos of Epidauros, but for using a foul blow. (Unfortunately the details of the blow are not specified.)

While athletic boxing may not have assured one contestant of death, it was nevertheless gravely dangerous and the Greeks were well aware of boxing's vicissitudes. They acknowledged boxing as the 'heaviest' of the athletic contests, even more so than their *pankration*. Agathos "the Camel"[164] Daimon of Alexandria died at Olympia, 35 years old (Riele 1964, pp. 185–187). The Nemean champ's inscription (Scanlon 2002, p. 305) reads:

ἐνθάδε πυκτεύων ἐν τῷ σταδίῳ ἐτελεύτα,
εὐξάμενος Ζενὶ ἢ στέφος ἢ θάνατον

Boxing here in the stadium I died,
praying to Zeus for either the wreath or death.

What was the nature of this man's sacrifice? Did he really lose the match by dying at the hands of his opponent? Or are the wreath and death, in fact, equivalent prizes?[165] Agathos' inscription raises these profound questions with a great economy of words, cleverly concealed in what appears to be a narrative statement about one man's attitude. No boxer has the right to step between the ropes without the conviction of Agathos or his pellucid appraisal of the mystery that boxing represents. "'The wreath or death' was more than a hyperbolic boast" in the cultus of Greek boxing (Scanlon 2002, p. 11). Indeed, it is the omnipresence of

---

[161]Boxing was more developed as a rule-governed practice in Asia Minor at the time of its introduction to the Olympics; this may be inferred reasonably from the fact that its thesmothete was Onomastus of Smyrna (Thuillier 1985, p. 268). Onomastus is discussed in more detail below in comments on Philostratus.

[162]Savica et al. (2017) speculate that Kleomedes suffered from *dementia pugilistica* rather than some other form of psychological or neurological trauma.

[163]The introduction of the cruel *cæstus* in Roman 'gladiatorial' boxing (Section 3.5) must have increased the body count considerably, but we are aware of no contemporaneous mention of the mortality rate or its social impacts in Italy.

[164]The nickname may have suggested strength, endurance, or heaviness.

[165]To kill a man in the ring may be to experience an agonizing draw, as suggested, for example, by the remarkable life of Ray "Boom-Boom" Mancini after he beat his opponent to death in a boxing ring at Caesars Palace in 1982 (Kriegel 2013).

death that made (and makes) boxing a powerful cultic activity, one that has outlasted (and will outlast) the greatest civilizations.

Prizes are of considerable importance throughout the history of boxing; they are nearly ubiquitous in its iconography and appear frequently in literary attestations, as well. In all boxing competitions of the funereal type, such prizes are offered: precious vessels, livestock, and a shield are among the guerdons of epic pugilism.[166] With regard to other traditional athletic events, the prizes for the 'heavy' events of boxing, wrestling, and *pankration* became increasingly valuable during the Roman era. This was arguably a function of the growing prestige of combat sport (Scanlon 2002, p. 56).

After AD 37, contestants were no longer allowed to enter both boxing and the *pankration*.[167] The winner of both events was previously known as the 'Successor of Heracles'. Perhaps this was to avoid immoderation (can there be too much of fighting?) or perhaps "officials simply wished to avoid too many 'sweeps' by specialized heavy athletes in these events" (Scanlon 2002, p. 52).

Surprisingly, perhaps—at least for a modern sensibility—there are few attestations of boxing matches where the victor gets the girl.[168] According to a tale told by Pausanias (6.6.9–10), Euthymus of Lokroi, who boxed victorious at the Olympics, fell in love with an Italian maiden from Temessa. To win her, however, he first had to fight the local ghost. In life, the spirit had been a comrade of Odysseus; in death he haunted the locals and demanded that a local virgin be sacrificed to him as his wife each year. Euthymus succeeded in getting the girl after the ghost simply fled, unwilling to meet him in combat. "The hero or athlete who has successfully demonstrated his excellence is a most suitable candidate for husband" (Scanlon 2002, p. 226).[169]

In *Heroicus* (p. 678), Philostratus the Athenian explains that a boxer named Plutarch consulted the cult hero Protesilaus about how to win an upcoming match. Puzzlingly, he was instructed to pray to Achelous, the chief river god. During the fight, when Plutarch was exhausted from thirst, a storm erupted over the stadium, engorging the fleece (κώδια, diminutive of κώδιον) on his forearms (πῆχυς)[170] with water, which he drank, winning the match and revealing the meaning of the oracle's advice. The κώδια mentioned here is probably equivalent to the sheepskin (*vellus*) that absorbs Capaneus' blood in the *Thebaid* (Section 3.4.2). It was likely used "as a sweatband or as a protective cover for the forearm, and would have served as a convenient sponge for the boxer Plutarch" (Scanlon 1986, p. 111). By the age of Philostratus the Athenian, boxers routinely wore a kind of boxing gauntlet that covered a good deal of the arm, and was notable for its lanuginous cuff.

Philostratus (*Gym.* 34) expounds at length on physical desiderata for boxers:

> The boxer should have large hands and well-built forearms, and upper arms
> which are not lacking in vigor and strong shoulders and a high neck. Thick
> wrists give a heavier punch; those that are less thick are flexible and punch with
> ease. Let him also be supported by well-built hips, for the forward projection
> of the hands drags the body downwards, unless it is supported on firm hips.

---

[166] In the Valerian *Argonautica* (4.216–217), Amycus wickedly offers death as the *donum* in his boxing matches, suggesting that 'gladiatorial' boxing had already captivated the author's imagination.

[167] According to Philostratus, *pankration* was imperfect wrestling combined with imperfect boxing (*Gym.* 11).

[168] For a Near Eastern example, see the Marriage of Martu in Dioscurus and Dioscurus (2022b).

[169] See also Plato, *Rep.*, 468c, in which it is recommended that a victorious warrior receive the beloved of his choice.

[170] ... περὶ τοῖς πήχεσι κώδια ...

I think that those who have bulky calves that are not well suited to any of the disciplines, but least of all to boxing. For these athletes will be slow to kick against the shins of their adversaries, and easily kicked in turn. The boxer should have calves that are straight and well-proportioned, while the thighs should be well distanced and separated from each other. For the shape of the boxer is more suited to attack if his thighs do not come together.[171] The best kind of stomach for a boxer is slim; for these athletes are light and have good breathing. Nevertheless there is some advantage in the stomach for a boxer, for a stomach of this kind can ward off blows against the face by sticking out in a way that impedes the forward motion of the punching opponent.

Later (*Gym.* 36), he expands on size, assigning a relative disadvantage to small stature for a boxer: "They are hit from above by their opponents and have to raise themselves up in the air in a comical fashion whenever they themselves throw punches." From these passages we can extract the somatotype of the classical Greek and Roman boxer:

- big hands
- well-built forearms
- an upper arm that did not lack vigor
- strong shoulders
- high neck
- strong wrists giving a harder blow
- well built hips
- strong but not voluminous calves (kicks slow and easily kicked back)
- thighs well apart and apart separated
- thin belly (ἀθληταί: lighter, better respiration)
- of average height or taller

This is the most extensive physical description of the boxing physique that has survived from the ancient world; compare it to the *Boxer at Rest, q.v.* and the many illustrations included here and in Dioscurus and Dioscurus (2022d). It would not be unwarranted to extrapolate from Philostratus' prose description that the chief boxers of the Greek world, such as Onomastus, would have resembled this ideal.

Blood, gore, sweat, and bruises (the telluric heart of boxing) were ever-prized in pugilism, even among the Greeks. One anonymous poet whose work is now found in the *Greek Anthology* (12.123) wrote:

When Menecharmus, Anticles' son, won the boxing match [πυγμῇ νικήσαντα]
I crowned [στεφανόω] him with ten soft fillets,
And thrice I kissed [φιλέω] him all red [φύρω] with much blood,
But the blood was sweeter [μελιχρός] to me than myrrh [σμύρνα][172]

To argue that the Greeks were too sensitive or civilized to revel in the blood-and-guts of the ring is to deny their own textual history. The Greeks were fascinated by the physical deconstruction of individual boxers. If they laughed at a boxer's cauliflower ear or his twisted

---

[171] As boxing was conducted in the nude, this seems anatomically appropriate.
[172] Translated by Scanlon (2002, p. 218).

nose, perhaps they thought it was better for him to die gloriously in the ring than to tramp about town with a disfigured face. One author mocked a boxer named Stratophon (*Greek Anthology*, 11.77): "[A]fter boxing for four hours, [you] have become not only unrecognizable to dogs but to the city" (Paton 1918, p. 111). Hellenistic artists, at least, seem to have been amused by the disfigurement that accompanied a boxing career. The terracotta statue of a boxer shown in Figure 2 is one example of a Greek boxer manifesting cauliflower ear (ὠτοκλαδίας). The deformity is represented in a variety of other statues of boxers, including little-known works like a grotesque terracotta head housed at the Bergama Museum in Izmir, Turkey (Inv. A 3472); and the celebrated *Boxer at Rest* found at Rome in the late nineteenth century (Section 3.5). According to one critic, "mangled ears" became a hallmark of boxers as depicted in statuary of the Roman imperial period (König 2005, p. 115).

In discussing boxing handgear among the Greeks, we draw on an extensive literature. Before the invention of the well-known Roman *cæstus* (Section 3.5), the Greeks engaged in a good deal of experimentation with boxing gauntlets or *himantes*, the earliest forms of which are mentioned in Dioscurus and Dioscurus (2022d).

Philostratus cites the development of the hand covering from a band wrapping the four fingers with a strap, to a cowhide "sharp, projecting boxing glove" (πυκτικὸν ὀξὺν καὶ προεμβάλλοντα) (*Gym* 10). Lee (1997) attributes a three-stage evolution of (Greek) boxing gloves to Jüthner and Mehl (1962). This includes:

1. Soft thongs, simple leather straps, *himantes meilĭchai* (literally, the sweet, mild, or gentle straps);

2. padded inner-glove or sleeve with leather wrapping, which had arisen by at latest 324 BC (Jüthner called these the *sphairai*);

3. The *himantes oxeis* ὀξεῖς or 'sharp thongs' worn by the bronze boxer at Terme (Section 3.5): thick rings of leather encircled the fingers, but not the thumb, including a knuckle pad under the rings of leather.

The meaning of the Greek word μύρμηκες (*myrmēkes*) is not entirely clear.[173] While Poliakoff (1987a, p. 73) reasons that the term, which literally refers to (biting) ants, is the name for the 'sharp thongs', Jüthner and Mehl (1962) suggests that *myrmēkes* instead refers to the dumbbells featured in Alpine situla art (Dioscurus and Dioscurus 2023). The most convincing iconographic representation of of *myrmēkes* as 'biting ants' may be in the cruel *cæstus* of the Trier Mosaic (Figure 17) or the boxing mosaic from Ostia (Figure 23) where the prongs of the weaponized glove look like the antennæ or perhaps the jaws of an ant. While these gloves are relatively late Roman artifacts, so is the attestation of *myrmēkes* in Pollux' late second-century *Onomasticon*. Though a Greek term, the 'biting ants' are perhaps more related to what we call 'gladiatorial' boxing than 'athletic boxing' (Section 3.5).

The *himantes* were not likely understood to protect the hands of the boxer.[174] As evidence for this claim, they do not appear on the hands of Polydeuces[175] as he hits the punching bag in the Ficoroni Cista (Dioscurus and Dioscurus 2023, Fig. 39). On the same object,

---

[173] The term is attested in Pollux, *Onomasticon* 3.150), writing in the second century AD.

[174] In at least one depiction (late sixth century BC, Archæological Civic Museum of Bologna, No. 433), only the wrist was bound (Poliakoff 1987a, Fig. 71).

[175] For the identification of this figure as Polydeuces, see Williams (1945a, p. 351).

Polydeuces wears the *himantes* while tying Amycus to a tree (ibid., Fig. 40), suggesting that the artist did not intend to indicate a bare knuckle bout and was also purposeful in omitting the *himantes* for the training scene.[176]

Himantes made of pigskin were prohibited, as it was thought that they caused too much injury (Phil. *Gym.* 10). This is perhaps because pigskin is thinner than cow leather and may suggest a tacit recognition of what we might call 'weight' for boxing gloves. But did using pigskin risk damage to the wearer, his opponent, or both? Greek commentators naturally seem to focus on the damage that boxing did to the visage of the pugilists, not the injuries to their hands.[177] Based on this, as well as the evidence from the Ficoroni Cista, it seems likely that *himantes* were intended to limit the disfigurement of the person being punched, not to protect the hands of the fighter doing the striking. Perhaps this is why later Roman innovations to the *himantes* were so appealing, since they would have performed the opposite function, to wit, disfiguring an opponent more quickly and effectively.

Based on inspection of vase paintings, Thuillier (1985, p. 259) dates the invention of the sharp thongs to 339–336 BC. As Jüthner and Mehl (1962) explained, these included a thick leather strap that encircled the knuckles. Their purpose was almost certainly offensive in nature. The epithet *oxeis* suggests that it was intended to lacerate an opponent and thus were perhaps cognate with the Roman *cæstus* (derived from the verb *cædo* 'cut').

In an extended simile in which Plutarch (*Præcepta* 32) compares public debate to a boxing match, he mentions ἐπισφαίροι (*episphairai*)[178] 'round muffles' intended, he explains, to avoid "any fatal accident", rendering the blows "soft and such as can do no great harm"(1874, p. 155). The gloves (σφαῖρα) were mentioned much earlier by Plato (*Laws* 8.830B) for mimicking the real distribution and reception of blows. The *episphairai* represent yet another Greek variation on the boxing glove.

According to Philostratus, writing in the third century of the Christian era, kicking (the shins) was allowed in boxing, though it is infrequently attested in visual art (Rusten and König 2014, p. 419, fn. 59). Moreover, Philostratus regarded those with bulky calves as being incapable of delivering and avoiding kicks in boxing. In Philostratus (*Gym.* 34), much hinges on the interpretation of the verb προσβαινω, translated by some, including Jüthner (1909, p. 210–211) and Robinson (1955, p. 216), as 'kick'. Others prefer to translate προσβαινω as 'advance' or 'lunge' (Gardiner 1910, p. 426fn. 2) or simply 'approach' (Crowther 1990, p. 179). By this reasoning, "Philostratus is stating not that the boxer kicks against the shins of his opponent, but that he takes up his stance close to the shins of the opponent" (ibid.).

Eusebius, who lived in the late third and early fourth centuries AD, appears to offer the clearest evidence for kicking in boxing (*Præp. Evang.* 5.34). He employs the term λακτίζω in his comments critical of the honors given to athletes, including Cleomedes, whom Eusebius may have confused with Damoxenos (Crowther 1990, p. 179–180).[179] Eusebius also writes

---

[176] The Roman *cæstus*, on the other hand, was worn during shadow-boxing, as clearly indicated in the Latin *Argonautica* by Valerius Flaccus (*Argo.* i, 420): "The hero of Sparta wears thongs of bull's hide studded with wounding lead, that to the empty airs at least he may deal his random blows, and that the Pagasean ship may ... watch his harmless sport" (trans. J. H. Mozley, 1934, p. 35).

[177] The injured boxer as a motif arises in black-figure vase painting but arguably reached its zenith in the Hellenistic sculpture known as the Boxer at Rest, discussed below.

[178] Note the vowel [o] in the original. In the boxing literature, at least, the term is generally transliterated with [α], as we have done.

[179] ἐκεῖνο δὲ εἰδέναι, ὅτι ἡ πυκτικὴ τῆς λακτικῆς οὐδὲν διαφέρει (*Præp. Evang.* 5.34.2).

that asses, especially wild ones, make good boxers, the implication being that kicks were essential in the boxing 'ring' (*Præparatio Evangelica* 5.34.7). Eusebius, though regarded as one of the most learned Christians of Late Antiquity, was perhaps "not the most reliable witness on Greek boxing" (Crowther 1990, p. 180). By including kicks, he may have been "confusing a form of Roman boxing from his own time with Greek boxing" (ibid.). The literary and visual evidence for kicking in Greek boxing has been thoroughly reviewed (Crowther 1990). Some images may show boxers "stepping on" their opponents "perhaps to prevent [them from] getting up" (ibid., p. 177).

According to one translation of Lucian, in his second-century *Demonax*, biting, though foul, was known to occur in boxing (Harmon 1913, p. 167). From Harmon's translation of *Demonax* (49) we read:

> When he saw many of the athletes fighting foul and breaking the rules of the games by biting instead of boxing, he said: "No wonder the athletes of the present day are called 'lions' by their hangers-on!"[180]

Lucian uses the verb κακομαχέω 'fight unfairly'. He refers to παγκρατιάζω 'practice *pannkration*' rather than *pygmachia* or a similar term, so this passage seems to have nothing to do with boxing at all. The word for 'bite' is δάκνω. "Rules of the games" is (νόμος ... ἐναγώνιος).

Writing in the second century AD, Artemidorus of Ephesus included in the *Oneirokritikia*, his book on the interpretation of dreams, a brief section on dreams involving the heavy sports, including boxing (*On.* 1.61). Artemidorus concluded that a dream of boxing means universal harm (Harris-McCoy 2012):

> To box is harmful for all. For it signifies damage to one's honour and harm. For in fact the face becomes misshapen and blood comes forth, which is considered to be like money. But it is good only for those who make their living from blood, and by that I mean doctors, sacrificers, and cooks.[181]

A more sophisticated praxis of boxing has begun to emerge in the terminology used by historians and essayists as well. Unlike the relatively sparse and obscure descriptions and metaphors used in Homer, Philostratus is able to identify a specific coaching call and connect it to a strike we would recognize as heirs of the tradition:

> When Glaucus of Carystus was giving way to his opponent in the boxing at Olympia, his trainer Tisias led him to victory by encouraging him to strike "the blow from the plow". This meant a right-handed punch against his opponent; for Glaucus was so strong with that hand that he once straightened a bent plowshare in Euboea by hitting it with his right hand like a hammer (*Gym.* 20).

A kind of training activity called σφαιρομαχια is attested as early as 394 BC in Aristomenes' *Dionysus Asketes* (Borthwick 1964a, fn. 8). In this context, the activity is related to the athletic training of Dionysus and the reference may have been deployed to humorous effect.

---

[180] ἐπεὶ μέντοι πολλοὺς τῶν ἀθλητῶν ἑώρα κακομαχοῦντας καὶ παρὰ τὸν νόμον τὸν ἐναγώνιον ἀντὶ τοῦ παγκρατιάζειν δάκνοντας, Οὐκ ἀπεικότως, ἔφη, τοὺς νῦν ἀθλητὰς οἱ παρομαρτοῦντες λέοντας καλοῦσιν.

[181] Πυκτεύειν παντὶ βλαβερόν· πρὸς γὰρ ταῖς αἰσχύναις καὶ βλάβας σημαίνει· καὶ γὰρ ἄσχημον γίνεται τὸ πρόσωπον καὶ αἷμα ἀποκρίνεται, ὅπερ ἀργύριον εἶναι νενόμισται. ἀγαθὸν δὲ μόνοις τοῖς ἐξ αἵματος ποριζομένοις, λέγω δὲ ἰατροῖς θύταις μαγείροις.

The activity is most likely related to punching a ball, perhaps like modern speed-bag or even double-end-bag training.[182]

Philostratus cites weightlifting, sprinting, bending metal, wrestling with animals, and swimming as being used in training boxers and other combat athletes (*Gym.* 43). In *Gym.* 48–52 he counsels athletes (*a fortiori* boxers) to abstain from sexual intercourse, overeating, and alcohol before exercise and competition.

Ear-guards (ἀμφωτίδες, related to the term for a two-handled pail) are also a relatively poorly attested piece of boxing equipment.[183]

A light punching bag is cited in *Gym.* 57:

> A punching bag should be hung up also for boxers, but all the more so for those who compete in the *pankration*. The punching bag for the boxers should be light, since the hands of boxers are to be trained only for opportune punching, but the punching bag for pankratiasts should by [*sic*, be] heavier and bigger ....[184]

No details of the construction of a punching bag κώρυκος are provided by Philostratus. An item called κώρυκος is sometimes regarded as a leathern sack hung up for punching (it also means 'scrotum').[185]

Philostratus mentions Onomastus[186] of Smyrna (*Gym.* 12) as the originator of the rules of Greek boxing[187] and four-time boxing champion at the seventh-century BC Olympics.[188] Their adoption is doubly notable to Philostratus because of Onomastus' origin in Smyrna (modern Izmir in Turkey): his mastery was such that the stain of his Anatolian background was overwhelmed by his reputation for the mainland Greeks, establishing his ruleset as the Olympic standard. Unfortunately, no direct trace of these rules serves as such.

Finally, we note the etymologies of Greek combat sports as these etymologies were understood in antiquity. In an extended discussion with Sosicles of Coronea over the antiquity of wrestling versus other sports, Plutarch (*Quæs Conv.* 2.4) reports that Philinus etymologized wrestling as having to do with the *palaistē* 'palm' while boxing had to do with the *pygmē* 'fist'. While Plutarch disagreed, these folk etymologies are revealing as to how people understood the sports at some point in the long history of Greek boxing: the action of the open hands in wrestling versus the closed fists in boxing.[189] Plutarch goes on to conclude that wrestling is derived from a verb meaning 'draw near together', which makes sense to him, because, he claimed, ancient Greek boxers were not permitted to hold each other.

---

[182] The possibilities are still more numerous for the Romanized version of the activity, *sphaeromachia* (3.5).

[183] References to the ἀμφωτίδες include: Plu. 2.38b, 706c, cf. Paus.*Gr.Fr.* 52., *Pollux* 2.82.

[184] Κώρυκος δὲ ἀνήφθω μὲν καὶ πύκταις, πολὺ δὲ μᾶλλον τοῖς ἐπὶ τὸ παγκράτιον φοιτῶσιν. ἔστω δὲ καὶ κοῦφος μὲν ὁ πυκτικός; ἐπειδὴ κωρύκου γυμνάζονται μόναι αἱ τῶν πυκτῶν χεῖρες, ὁ δὲ τῶν παγκρατιαστῶν ἐμβριθέστερος καὶ μείζων ....

[185] References to the κώρυκος include: *Sor.* 1.49, *Antyll. ap. Orib.* 6.33.1, *Gym.* 57, and Luc. *Lex.* 5.

[186] The name bears no relation save coincidence to Pollux' *Onomasticon*; it merely means "a name of note" in circular fashion.

[187] καὶ νόμους ἔγραψεν ὁ ἀθλητὴς οὗτος πυκτικούς, οἷς ἐχρῶντο οἱ Ἠλεῖοι διὰ σοφίαν τοῦ πύκτου, καὶ οὐκ ἤχθοντο οἱ Ἀρκάδες, εἰ νόμους ἔγραψεν αὐτοῖς ἐναγωνίους ἐξ Ἰωνίας ἥκων τῆς ἁβρᾶς.

[188] Onomastus of Smyrna was victorious in the games of 688, 684, 680, and 676 BC.

[189] The open-hand gesture, emphasized through the exaggerated length of the extended fingers, is found in Greek vase paintings (Dioscurus and Dioscurus 2022d, Fig. 27) as well as Etruscan tomb paintings, notably the Tomba della Scimmia.

3 Rome

The Romans "recognized the paradoxical combination of the productive and destructive in gladiatorial combat" (Feldherr 2002, p. 71). The fights were "grim but necessary" according to the Emperor Julian, who reigned in the fourth century of the Christian Era.[190] If we can extend the same logic to boxing, as seems appropriate given the blurred line between boxing and gladiatorial fights in Late Antiquity, then we must ask, "Necessary for what?" Watching the fights was certainly an aspect of Roman socialization (Figure 3). However, Feldherr (2002) argues for more: personal combat as a form of sacrifice must be equated with Livy's "unendurable remedies".[191] Livy argues that the young, in particular, will be moved to identify with the executed but the execution will nonetheless have salubrious effects on those same disgusted youth as they reach maturity.[192] Boxing is still seen as an "unendurable remedy" to a variety of problems in the modern West: these include gun violence, the father's absence from family life, the dissolution of social bonds, and the displacement of traditional manly virtues. To know exactly which problems were solved by the version of boxing held in the grisly embrace of Rome we will undertake a thorough review of the literary and visual evidence in this section.

We agree with Deremetz (2011, p. 54), that Latin epics, in particular, are not completely reliable documents for those interested in the history of boxing. Instead, they "freely mix realities belonging to different historical strata, both Greek and Latin, and are mixed with data from the mythological imagination" (translation ours). Still, by carefully reviewing these epic stylizations of ancient boxing, we hope to infer something about boxing and boxing values in the Roman world, or at least to generate new questions worthy of inquiry elsewhere.

3.1 *Æneid* 5

In Book 5 of the *Æneid*, the eponymous hero gathers his comrades together to celebrate the *jahrzeit* of his father, Anchises, with contests that feature a "battle with gloves of raw hide" (line 69).[193] After eight days of sacrificing wine, blood, flesh, and flowers, athletic competitions begin on the ninth. During the prodromal sacrifices, participants are crowned with wreaths. The description of the boxing competition, which occurs after a foot race and before an archery event, is lengthy (122 lines of dactylic hexameter) and thus offers us a great deal of lexical and grammatical material to review in order to better understand how boxing was regarded by Vergil and his audience in the first century BC. At least one critic has argued that the boxing match is central to the games and thus to the *Æneid* itself, functioning as a bridge between its two halves (Feldherr 2002).

To construct his own boxing episode, the poet appears to have drawn on at least two boxing narratives in Greek literature that we reviewed in a previous article (Dioscurus and

---

[190] σκυθρωπῶν μέν, ἀναγκαίων δὲ ὅμως (*Or.* 4.156b–c).

[191] ... quibus nec uitia nostra nec remedia pati possumus peruentum est (Liv. 1 *præf* 9).

[192] *triste exemplum sed in posterum salubre iuventuti erimus* (Liv. 8.7.17).

[193] The line reads: *seu crudo fidit pugnam committere caestu.* The adjective *crudus*, here modifying the ablative plural *cæstu*, is frequently translated as 'raw' or 'rawhide' (Ruden 2008) but might be just as appropriately translated as 'bloody', 'bleeding', or 'trickling with blood' (Fairclough and Brown 1919). Indeed, we later learn that the *cæstus*, to which blood and gore still cling, have been used previously (line 413). Line numbers in this section come from Greenough (1900) unless otherwise indicated.

Figure 3: Fistfighting (probably *pankration*) with young spectators. Detail of sarcophagus, Roman, AD 450–425, Museo Torlonia, No. 478.

Dioscurus 2022d).[194] These are found in *Iliad* 23 and the second book of the *Argonautica* by Apollonius of Rhodes.[195] As in the proem to the Iliadic boxing match, Æneas (as a substitute for Achilles) calls on fighters to volunteer or 'be at hand' (*adsum*) (lines 363–364). These must "have valour in their breast and a stout heart" (*virtus animusque in pectore præsens*). Here, *animus* appears to function for the equally polysemous Greek *thymos*: it may also be defined as 'the rational soul'. Fairclough and Brown (1919, p. 421) decode *animus … præsens* as "the spirit of resolution that supports one in the hour of danger … more than mere presence of mind, being active, not simply passive." The would-be fighters' arms must be 'lifted up' (*attollo*), their 'flat hands' or 'palms' (*palma*) 'bound' (*evincio*). The binding material is not yet mentioned in the narrative, despite the efforts of some proleptic translators.

Like his predecessor Achilles, Æneas sets out a 'double-prize' (*geminus honor*), careful to provide a 'consolation' (*solacium*) for the defeated fighter.[196] The winner will receive a 'bullock' (*iuvencus*) while the loser gets a 'distinguished', probably 'engraved', helmet (*insignis galea*)[197] and sword (*ensis*). The victor's prize bovid is decked with gold[198] and garlands (*velatus auro vittisque*), suggesting its cultic importance to be revealed in the narrative's stunning denouement.

A soldier named Dares[199] immediately and vigorously (*cum viribus*) presents himself (*effero*). We are told that he was once the sparring partner[200] (*solitus contendo contra*) of the Trojan prince Paris.[201] Dares' record also includes a beat-down (*percello*) of Butes, a kinsman of the boxing Bebrycian king Amycus.[202] Vergil informs us that this bout took place in a funereal context, as well—at a match held in honor of Hector, another prince of Troy.[203]

In his preparations, Dares throws punches at the air (*verbero ictibus auras*) in the same

---

[194] With some exaggeration, Servius Auctus (Verg. *Æn.* 5.426) wrote of the Vergilian boxing episode, *est autem hic totus locus de Apollonio translatus* "The whole thing is copied from Apollonius" (Dunkle 2005, pp. 170–173). Hedging his bets, he also wrote of Book 5, *pars maior ex Homero sumpta est* "most of it is taken from Homer."

[195] In composing *Æneid* 5, Vergil arguably referred to *Odyssey* 8, in which the man of twists and turns participates in an athletic competition on Phæacia (Dunkle 2005, pp. 154–155). The games include πύξ 'boxing' but the activity is not described in any detail (*Odyssey* 8.103, 130, 205). Odysseus' pugilistic encounter with Iros in *Odyssey* 18, which we review carefully in Dioscurus and Dioscurus (2022d), is not universally regarded as an influence on Vergil's boxing vignette but see Nelis (2001, p. 9) for a different perspective. Another source may have been the second-century *Annals* of Ennius. However, the putative reference to boxing in this work, at funeral games established by Romulus, is fragmentary and depends crucially on a controversial reading of *cæstibus* versus *cælestibus* (Skutsch 1985).

[196] According to Nelis (2001, p. 13), "Vergil's opening scene" of the boxing match "is closely modeled" on its Iliadic predecessor.

[197] Helmets are one of the most common motifs to appear situated between boxers in situla art of northern Italy and the eastern Alps (Dioscurus and Dioscurus 2023).

[198] Ruden's translation (2008) suggests that the horns are gilded and that the bullock is beribboned (p. 101).

[199] The name is etymologically related to δέρω 'beat' and particularly the aorist passive participle δαρείς 'the beaten (one)' (McGowan 2002, p. 87). Vergil's use of two different accusative forms, *Daren* and *Dareta*, arguably signals the boxer's shifting role from bully to battered over the course of the vignette (ibid.).

[200] *solus qui Paridem solitus contendere contra* "[W]ho alone was wont to spar with Paris" (McGowan 2002, p. 81).

[201] Paris was regarded as an excellent athlete, perhaps even a boxer, in Roman verse, whereas Homer regarded him as "showy and effeminate" (Fairclough and Brown 1919, p. 421).

[202] This is the same Amycus slain by Polydeuces in a boxing match narrated in *Argonautica* 2 (Dioscurus and Dioscurus 2022d). By referring to a Bebrycian boxer, "the Vergilian bout immediately evokes its [Apollonine] counterpart" (Nelis 2001, p. 13). In what follows, imitations of Homer and Apollonius are "almost inextricably intertwined" but ultimately "[t]here is no complete identification between Vergil's characters and any single model, whether Homeric or [Apollonine]" (ibid., pp. 14, 16).

[203] *ad tumulum, quo maximus occubat Hector* (line 371). The funeral games of Hector are mentioned at the conclusion of the *Iliad*, but there is no reference to a boxing match. After the barrow is constructed over Hector's remains a banquet is given (δαίνυμι) but Homer alludes to no games of any kind (24.802).

proemial show of skill boxers exhibit to the present day. Poliakoff (1985) suggests that this show of shadowboxing is not vainglory; it is, rather, a virtuous form of preparation and a "precaution" in Apollonius and Vergil, associated with Polydeuces in the former and Dares in the latter (pp. 229–230). Another commentator notes how, in a simile comparing Turnus to a bull preparing to fight (Verg. *Æn.* 12.105–106), the animal lashes out at the air; the language used (... *ventosque lacessit* | *ictibus* ...) recalls the language of Dares shadowboxing in Book 5 (Leigh 2010, p. 130). Vergil emphasizes the fighter's broad shoulders (*umerus latus*) but is reserved in describing any other anatomical features.

No one takes up the challenge immediately and the *cæstus*[204] are mentioned for the first time inasmuch as no one else wishes to put them on (*manibus induco*). The crickets chirp for so long that Dares finally places his left hand on the bullock and claims it for his own, absent a viable challenger. In line 383, Dares remarks that none dare lend himself to the battle (*credo se pugnæ*). Translators like Fairclough (1916) and Ruden (2008) agree that the spectators cheer his bravado, but the lines that follow (384–385) are ambiguous as to the crowd's disposition: *Cuncti simul ore fremebant* | *Dardanidæ, reddique viro promissa iubebant.* The Dardans (i.e., the Trojans) howl (*fremo*) all at once, demanding (*iubeo*) that the prize (*promissa*) be given up (*reddo*, in the passive). The key to understanding this outcry lies in the translation of *vir* 'man'. Do the Dardans demand that the prize be given up *to* the man who deserves it or *by* the man who usurps it? Inflection is of little help here, since *viro* is a syncretic form for both ablative and dative. It falls to the translator to decide which thematic role is most appropriate given the context. We believe it is more likely that the crowd is incensed that they will not get to see a fight and so they jeer Dares for his presumption. In our experience, once gathered to see two men brutalize each other in the ring, the canaglia do not regard no-shows graciously. Much less do they cheer magnanimously for someone who takes home a prize without fighting for it first.[205] Would an audience of battle-hardened soldiers, wound up by their leader to witness an epic battle, gladly acclaim an uncontested "victory"? Hardly. Dares is playing the heel by goading both a potential rival and the crowd—and the crowd is not having it.

Vergil then turns to a conversation between Acestes, the local Sicilian ruler, who sits next to his comrade Entellus on the grass.[206] Acestes chides his Sicilian companion, who we learn was once a prize-winning[207] boxer, trained by divine Eryx,[208] the son of Aphrodite.[209] Acestes does not disparage Dares but does wonder out loud how Entellus can let the prize walk

---

[204]Budrovich (2011, p. 33) points out the anahcronism of including the *cæstus* in a story set in the Late Bronze Age. Injurious boxing handgear was in fact attested during this period, albeit on Crete (Dioscurus and Dioscurus 2022c).

[205]In his *Posthomerica*, Quintus plays repeatedly with the tension of a potential no-contest (Section 2.5). In one case, the "bloodless victory" is awarded to Idomeneus, who is arguably too old to fight, anyway.

[206]Entellus later refers to Acestes as his *auctor* (line 418). According to Ruden (2008) this means 'supporter'; to Fairclough (1916), 'patron'.

[207]The unspecified prizes, perhaps dried viands, could be hung within Entellus' shelter: *spolia illa tuis pendentia tectis* (line 393).

[208]This made Eryx a half-brother of Æneas. Vergil tells us that Eryx was killed by Heracles in a boxing match—a mythic encounter for which we evidently have no earlier source. Servius Auctus (Verg. *Æn.* 1.570) writes that Eryx, like the Apollonine Amycus, challenged strangers to box and then murdered them.

[209]The celebrated temple of Venus at Eryx, in western Sicily, was described by Ælian in the late second or early third century AD (*De Natura Animalium* 10.50). Ælian wrote: τά γε μὴν ἱερεῖα ἑκάστης ἀγέλης αὐτόματα φοιτᾶ καὶ τῷ βωμῷ παρέστηκεν "And the sacrificial victims from every herd come up and stand beside the altar of their own accord" (Scholfield 1958–1959). Via Eryx, the boxing son of Aphrodite who founded the western Sicilian town in which Vergil's boxing match takes place, the parallel to the sacrifice of the bull in *Æneid* 5 is worthy of note. The legend of bovine self-sacrifice in the Temple of Erycinian Venus may be linked to the understanding that boxers,

away without a fight. It is a classic call to return to battle as old, at least, as the provocations of Achilles. Entellus protests that he is no coward; he is simply too old to climb back into the 'ring'.[210] "If only I had the juice I used to ..." Entellus muses.[211] But even if that were the case, he still wouldn't fight for prizes, he assures Acestes. Vergil thus leads the reader to wonder, what would he fight for?

The Sicilian, who it seems did protest too much, suddenly and with no explanation for his change of heart, produces the giant *cæstus* of his semi-divine master and casts (*proicio*) them into the field of play.[212] Significantly, the gauntlets are 'twins' (*geminus*) so there can be no doubt that boxing gloves were worn on both hands in the Roman 'ring'. Though often assumed, this was made explicit by neither Homer nor Apollonius. Vergil intends that the reader gape, awestruck (*obstipesco*, line 404; *stupeo*, line 406) at the *cæstus*, which are 'of monstrous weight' (*immani pondere*). Unless we are to consider Entellus (or Eryx) a giant, we must assume that this impressive characteristic of the *cæstus* derives not from the size of the *cæstus* (a function of a boxer's hand size, presumably) but from the cumulative weight of lead and iron studs sewn into the leather, so much of it that the leather is stiff (*plumbo insuto ferroque rigebant*, line 405).[213]

The act of casting the *cæstus* into the 'ring' deserves comment, as it has no antecedent to Vergil in literature or art—so far as we are aware. By throwing a representative object which belongs to him into the space consecrated for fighting, Entellus commits himself to the battle. Like signing a fight contract in the modern world, this abstraction has an even closer equivalent in the nineteenth-century, when boxing rivals pitched their hats into the ring as the ultimate token of their gameness, even when the fight had long been planned.[214]

Returning to the construction of the *cæstus*, the poet explains that they were constituted of 'seven hides of oxen' (*septem terga boum*). Given the odd number, we reckon that each gauntlet must have been composed of all seven strips. Why so long? The length of the Erycian *cæstus* suggests that it swathed the fist and forearm entirely and in multiple layers. It is not easy to determine the length of a typical Greek boxing *himas*. A low estimate for a single ox-hide thong is about two feet, based on a Panathenaic amphora where an ablated *himas* dangles from the arm of a victorious boxer (Dioscurus and Dioscurus 2022d, Fig. 28). Another representation, from an undated vase painting, shows one strip stretched out longer than the armspan of an adult male, perhaps six feet (Walters et al. 1893–1925, Vol. 3, E 78). This means the *cæstus* described by Vergil—a series of seven ox-hide strips stitched together end to end—was between fourteen and forty-two feet long. The lower estimate comports roughly (though on the high end) with another scholar's visual inspection of vase paintings, in which

---

too, "stand beside the altar [i.e., the 'ring'] of their own accord" (ibid.).

[210] *Non laudis amor, nec gloria cessit | pulsa metu; sed enim gelidus tardante senecta | sanguis hebet, frigentque effetae in corpore vires* (lines 394–396).

[211] *Si mihi, quae quondam fuerat ...* (line 397). Entellus' reluctance to fight mirrors that of Odysseus, who reflected on his erstwhile "sporting expertise" when demurring to take part in the Phæacian games described in *Odyssey* 8.166–85 (Nelis 2001, p. 14).

[212] Like Homer, who apparently had no specific lexical options for referring to a boxing 'ring', Vergil here uses the cohibitive term *medium* 'midst, center, middle' for the space in which the contest will take place. Note, however, that later in the narrative (line 456), the poet uses *æquor* to refer to the space circumscribed for boxing (see below).

[213] An alternative possibility is that the enormous hides were wrapped around and around the fighter's fists enough to make them gigantic, but the result would be comically unwieldy. We prefer the argument that it is the weight of the *cæstus* that makes them so remarkable.

[214] "The stakes were drove, the ropes were hitched | Into the ring my hat I pitched" (Masefield 1911).

Greek *himantes* "appear to have been ten to twelve feet long" (Gardiner 1910, p. 197).[215] The girth of a 1.5-ton ox can be be reckoned at about nine feet and its length about 6.5 feet, putting the maximum length of the Erycian *cæstsus*—taken from the circumference of the bullock's torso at the point of the heart—at a whopping 63 feet.[216]

It was perhaps a Roman innovation to develop a much longer bandage than those worn by the Greeks and it is also conceivable that it was intended to cover the arm all the way to the armpit,[217] as suggested in many depictions (e.g., Figure 2). Greek boxing frequently appears to depict hands so thoroughly wound in the *himantes* that no flesh is visible (e.g., the cross-hatch of fifth- and sixth-century black-figure vase painting, though highly stylized). Other depictions demonstrate that the *himantes* merely crossed the back of the hand and then wound round the wrist a few times (e.g., the sixth-century boxer on a funeral stele found at Kerameikos), leaving much of the skin exposed. A longer wrap would have afforded more surface coverage and more points of contact for potential strikes, suggesting that the forearms, elbows, and even triceps may have been used not merely to defend from but also to inflict damage on an adversary. We assume that the bits of metal were sewn into the terminal segment(s) of a composite strip. Once the strip was wound around the hand and arm, only spikes and studs at the distal end would surface atop the other layers, the prime location for inflicting laceration and other trauma.

We are told that 'savage' (*acer*) Eryx used these *cæstus* in his boxing matches (*proelium*). It is suggested that they were bound to both his hands and arms: in bouts he was wont to lift (*fero manum*) his hands in the monstrous *cæstus*, stretching out his arms (*intendere brachia*) in the 'hard leather' (*durus tergum*) (lines 401–403). This degree of coverage is consistent with a bandage as short as fourteen feet. It is also possible that Vergil's reference to seven ox hides was not meant literally, but to convey the hefty character of the gloves. Alternatively, the poet may have chosen the number seven for its telesmatic associations, perhaps in reference to Apollo, the Greek patron of boxing (Dioscurus and Dioscurus 2022d). According to Clark (1913, pp. 28–31), the number seven was connected to the cult of Apollo at Delphi and has links to Orpheus and titanomachy. There is some evidence that Vergil was familiar with these associations. Then again, Vergil may have chosen the number seven more generally because it is "uneven and sacred" (ibid., p. 31).

With good reason it seems, these *cæstus* are the cause of alarm (*obstipesco*) in the Dardan gathering. Vergil evidently hoped for the same reaction in his audience.[218] Upon seeing the *cæstus*, valiant Dares is struck dumb (*stupeo*) and either objects to their usage or otherwise becomes reluctant to fight; he may even back out (*recuso*).[219] Great-souled[220] Æneas inspects

---

[215] Modern cotton hand wraps for boxers can be purchased in lengths of nearly 17 feet (200 inches).

[216] http://bairnsley.com/, accessed September 18, 2022.

[217] Junkelmann (2000, p. 76) argues that a parallel development occurred with the gladiatorial *manica*: "there was a tendency for the *cæstus* worn by boxers to be elongated in the course of the imperial period into something like a sleeve ..."

[218] There may be, in the vision of these extraordinary *cæstus*, "cosmic and gigantomachic imagery" (Morgan 1998, p. 188).

[219] *longe recusat*: "from a distance declines"; *longe* implies "shrinking back" (Fairclough and Brown 1919, p. 423). According to one commentator, "Either Dares actually recoils many paces from the weapons and will not come near them, or metaphorically shrinks from them utterly and declines the contest" (Conington 1876). One critic notes that Dares' sudden fear of fighting connects him to the braggart Iros in the Odyssean boxing vignette (Nelis 2001, p. 15).

[220] The adjective *magnanimus* is a Latin calque for Greek *megathymos*, used by Homer to describe victorious Epeius in the Iliadic boxing match.

the gauntlets, perhaps because he, too, is gobsmacked by them, or maybe it is his job as arbiter to ensure that they are fair for the contest. While Æneas conducts his examination, Entellus speaks up, explaining that his mentor Eryx fought Hercules on the very beach where they now stand.[221] The *cæstus* he wore, which lie ponderously before the gathered crowd, are stained with ancient blood and brains (of the latter, perhaps, the defeated Eryx' own, as surmised by Servius Auctus): *sanguine cernis adhuc sparsoque infecta cerebro* (line 413).[222]

This reference to spattered brains, while unimaginable to most modern readers, is noteworthy for precisely this reason. It is evidence for the true character of ancient boxing hidden, as it were, in plain sight. No regular blow of hide-bound fist could split open another man's skull. It is essential to recognize that boxing gloves like the *cæstus* were instruments of execution: one man—or perhaps both—would necessarily die from their injuries, and likely on the spot. Critics loath to admit[223] the reality of these unsettling scenarios fail to descry in boxing its relationship to human sacrifice or ritual killing.[224] The mute witnesses of boxing in the ancient Minoan, Etruscan, and eastern Alpine cultures make it somewhat more challenging—though not impossible—to reach the same disturbing conclusion. But when an Augustan poet refers to dried cerebral matter caked on a pair of boxing gloves, we could only delude our readers by willfully ignoring the explicitly homicidal nature of the contest.

Vergil uses the terms *cæstus* and *arma* 'weapons, tools, implements' when describing the material culture of boxing. We will try to understand what distinction, if any, the poet intends between these two critical words. For example, Vergil indicates that the boxing match between Hercules and Eryx involved both *cæstus* and *arma*: "What if any had seen the gloves *and* arms of Hercules himself ...?" (Fairclough 1916, emphasis ours).[225] The use of *arma*, translated here as 'arms' by Dryden (1697) and Fairclough (1916) but elided by Ruden (2008), suggests weapons were used as complements to the *cæstus*. This recalls the Nuragic *pugillatori* of ancient Sardinia (Dioscurus and Dioscurus 2023) and foreshadows the fearsome pugilists of Late Antiquity, hands fitted with prongs as if their limbs were socketed spears (Figure 16). The generic term *arma* could be used for the implement(s) combined with the *cæstus* (e.g., in Figure 11). Unfortunately, it is not so straightforward, for in other cases the poet appears to use *arma* as a synonym for *cæstus*, for example, in referring directly to Eryx' gauntlets in line 412: *Haec germanus Eryx quondam tuus arma gerebat* "These arms your brother Eryx once wore" (Fairclough 1916).[226] The term *arma* is used again, most likely to refer to Dares' Trojan *cæstsus* (line 418), which Entellus bids him put down (*recuso*). At next mention, Entellus again refers to the gauntlets, this time as *Troiani cæstus* (line 420). The only strong evidence for a true juxtaposition of *cæstus* and *arma* is in reference to the mythic battle be-

---

[221] The fight between Eryx and Hercules seems to have its source in *Argonautica* 2.783–785, in which Lycus tells of how Heracles defeated Titias, a Mysian, in a boxing match years earlier.

[222] In *Hercules Furens*, Seneca writes that Heracles dashed Eryx to pieces (*fracto*) with his gauntlets and that Antæus shared the same fate: *ipsius opus est cæstibus fractus suis | Eryx et Eryci iunctus Antæus Libys* (lines 481–482).

[223] When it comes to the cruelty of Roman spectacle, there is often a "scholarly reluctance to accept the unpalatable truth that our sources provide" (Coleman 1990, p. 63). Some scholars simply "cannot accept the brutality implicit" in Roman literature and visual art that make that same brutality abundantly clear (ibid., p. 66).

[224] Kyle (1998) distinguishes these two "forms of homicide": "In human sacrifice[,] societies feel that a god or its cult requires the regular offering of human life. In ritual killing ..., in reaction to circumstances ..., societies carry out the killing of humans in ritualized and sacralized ways, in hopes that the consecration of the victim to the god(s) will sanction or legitimize the violence, prevent pollution, and bring a restoration of order" (p. 36).

[225] *Quid, si quis cæstus ipsius et Herculis arma | vidisset ...* (lines 410–411).

[226] Neither does the verb *gero* offer us much help. It can mean either 'bear' or 'wear' and would work equally well with a weapon or a piece of clothing as an object.

tween Eryx and Hercules (line 410). In other cases, *arma* is most likely a hypernym for the boxing gauntlets.

Zarker (1972, p. 44) equates the Vergilian *herculis arma* with the well-known club of Hercules. The connection between the Herculean cudgel and the *cæstus* is rendered graphically on the opposing faces of several third-century BC Umbrian coins from Tuder (modern Todi) which bear an image of a boxing gauntlet on one side and two clubs on the other (Häberlin 1967, pl. 80, nos. 9–13). Local legend has it that Hercules defeated the fire-breathing giant Cacus at Tuder. We cannot discount the possibility that in the boxing match of Eryx and Hercules, the latter used his club while Eryx used the *cæstus*, a donnybrook perhaps memorialized in the iconography of these Umbrian coins (Figure 4).

Figure 4: Front and back of a third-century BC Umbrian coin from Tuder inscribed with the image of a right hand in a *cæstus* much like the one worn by the Boxer at Rest, with a raised strap over the knuckles. On the back of the coin two clubs appear, likely an iconographic reference to Hercules. The toponym '[T]utere' (modern Todi) is inscribed in the Neo-Etruscan alphabet, right-to-left (in the image, top-to-bottom).

Doubtless noting his rival's reluctance, perhaps even refusal, to fight if he insists on wearing the terrible Erycinian *cæstus*, Entellus offers a bargain: he will 'send back' (*remitto*) the gauntlets of Eryx if Dares in turn 'removes' (*exuo*) his Trojan gloves (lines 419–420).[227] Vergil provides us with no description of the Trojan gloves, but they were evidently inferior to those of Entellus in terms of their destructive potential.[228] Entellus "gives up his personal advantage" by proposing to have two equal pairs of gloves provided by a third party if this is agreeable to Æneas, the captain of the wandering Dardans, and to Acestes, the local magistrate (Poliakoff 1985, p. 229). Entellus wishes to make the fight even (line 419).[229] Then,

---

[227] The reference to a uniquely Trojan *cæstus* leaves open the possibility that Vergil recognized a variety of boxing practices in the heroic past. This may have been rooted in an understanding of historical reality. As we argue elsewhere (Dioscurus and Dioscurus 2022b), boxing was practiced in Anatolia by the Hittites, who almost certainly had some connection to the Bronze Age inhabitants of Ilium.

[228] The Trojan gauntlets may have had their own cruel devices. This may explain why Entellus bargains for Dares to relinquish them.

[229] *æquemus pugnas* 'equalize the fight'. We conjecture that in boxing, as in gladiatorial fights, it was a "disgrace to be matched with an inferior" opponent. Seneca writes (*Prov.* 3.4): *ignominiam iudicat gladiator cum inferiore componi*. It is not clear why *pugna* 'fight' here appears in the plural. It may be only to preserve the dactyl | nās.ĕ.rў |

in a passage reminiscent of Odysseus in the build-up to his fight with Iros (*Odyssey* 18.68–69), Entellus sheds his cloak with a dramatic flourish, revealing his "great bones and thews" (Fairclough 1916).[230] Next, with a father's care, Æneas brings out gloves of equal weight and wraps both pairs of hands (lines 424–425).[231]

As in *Argonautica* 2, the boxers in *Æneid* 5 appear to have some choice as to which gauntlets they will wear. It is perhaps worth pausing here to reflect on a boxing culture in which the size, shape, and potential lethality of gauntlets is determined not by a neutral arbiter, judge, fight organizer, or even divinatory rite, but by the fighter himself.[232] In the earlier era presented to the reader in the *Argonautica*, lots were cast to determine who wore which pair of gloves. Any two pairs must therefore have differed in some regard, otherwise the casting of lots would be vacuous. In Vergil's *Vorstellung* the gauntlets are obviously different but the fighters seem to have the option to proceed if they wish. It is Entellus, the owner of the more intimidating pair, who proposes the deal to be fitted with equal gloves. From this we infer that Entellus had the right to use whatever boxing gauntlets he brought with him to the fight, even if this put his adversary at a disadvantage. This suggests that not only were the *cæstus* personal property of a fighter, but they could be used in battle just like a personal sword or buckler, regardless of their idiosyncratic attributes and without the adjudication or approval of an official. Perhaps this *laissez-faire* attitude is precisely what resulted in the arms race of Roman boxing, with gauntlets of increasing lethality apparently developed and deployed through Late Antiquity.[233]

According to Poliakoff (1985), Vergil deliberately links Entellus to the noble bruiser Euryalus of the *Iliad* and to Odysseus himself in his boxing match with Iros (*Odyssey* 18). But Vergil creates a paradox by also linking Entellus to "the [Apollonine] ogre Amycus" in order to stress the theme, repeated throughout the *Æneid*, "that the corrupting forces of anger and violence take hold easily and in unexpected places, and that responsible people must constantly labor to subdue them" (Poliakoff 1985, p. 227).

At long last (if not for Dares and Entellus, then at least for our patient readers), the bout begins. The description of the combatants' stance is brief but evocative: "Straightway each took his stand, poised on his toes, and, undaunted, lifted his arms high in air. Raising their heads high and drawing them far back from blows" (Fairclough 1916).[234] Both stand upright (*arrectus*) on their toes (*in digitos*), their forearms (*bracchium*) extended (*effero*) above

---

which, without the 's' would result in three short syllables (line 419). If not, it may be intended to suggest that Vergil's boxers saw their fight as a series of encounters, similar to modern rounds, though untimed. Only Apollonius comes close to indicating an interval between rounds, and this obliquely (Dioscurus and Dioscurus 2022c).

[230] *magna ossa lacertosque* (line 422). Vergil pays special attention to the *lacertus* 'upper arm' of the boxer, recalling the polysemous Sumerian term ɢᴇŠᴘᴜ́ (Dioscurus and Dioscurus 2022b).

[231] *Tum satus Anchisa caestus pater extulit æquos, | et paribus palmas amborum innexuit armis.* The term *pater* indicates Æneas' "careful superintendence of the games" (Fairclough and Brown 1919, p. 424).

[232] We wonder what changes to sport boxing might be occasioned by a similar inversion of responsibility. Inspected and sanitized with a bleach solution, gloves are loaned to fighters according to (modern, amateur) USA Boxing rules.

[233] As we note elsewhere, weaponized *cæstus* were common in the ancient Mediterranean from the Bronze Age (cf. the Minoans and the Nuragians) but the tradition seems to have been lost by the Archaic Greeks, who may have sublimated this form of violence in the softer but still injurious *himantes*. As is evident to any student of history, however, what's old is always, eventually, new again and it was almost certain that brutal hand implements would once more find their way back into the ancient boxing 'ring'. Nor should future observers be surprised at their return decades or centuries after this writing.

[234] *Constitit in digitos extemplo arrectus uterque, | brachiaque ad superas interritus extulit auras. | Abduxere retro longe capita ardua ab ictu* (lines 426–428).

(*ad superas*), in proper Homeric fashion (Dioscurus and Dioscurus 2022d). Both men are magnificently unafraid (*interritus*) of the terrific punishment that awaits them, though their heads, as a practical matter, are drawn back and away (*abduco retro longe*) from the blows (*ictus*). Even in this defensive posture, their heads are still held gallantly aloft (*capita ardua*). In a definitive allusion to Homer, the fighters mix their hands (*immisceo*), though the nominative–dative construction *manus manibus* 'hand-to-hand' is a splendid innovation of Vergil's alone (line 429).[235] In this manner, Dares and Entellus goad each other to fight more fiercely (*pugnam lacesso*).

Entellus shows his age almost immediately, marked by difficulty breathing (*anhelitus*) and shaking knees (*genua labuant*). The boxers throw a great many futile punches into the void between their bodies *multa viri nequiquam inter se vulnera iactant* (line 433) as in the preliminaries of any modern boxing match. At length they redouble (*ingemino*) their efforts by attacking each other's 'hollow flanks' (*cavus latus*). These are undoubtedly hooks thrown at the body.[236] Loud sounds (*sonitus*), presumably of punches landed, thunder from their broad chests (*pectus vastus*, ablative). The hands flew thickly (*erratque ... crebra manus*) at the ears (*auris*) and around the temples (*tempora circum*). The verb *erro*, suggesting a scrithel path of motion, may indicate that these blows missed the target: "A storm of strokes, well-meant, with fury flies | And errs about their temples, ears, and eyes" (Dryden 1697). With blows raining down on both the head and body, fighters would need to learn to defend both targets, as in the modern sport. Reference is made to a rattling (*crepito*) of wounded jaws (*vulnus malæ*), reminding us of gnashing teeth and shattered mandibles in Homer and Apollonius (Dioscurus and Dioscurus 2022d). Entellus does not move his body quickly: he is heavy (*gravis*) and 'rooted in place' (*immotus eodem*) despite his exertion (*nisus*) (line 437). He dodges (*exeo*) Dares' punches (*telum*, lit., missile) using his body and his keen eyes (*corpus ... atque oculi vigilantes*, ablative).[237]

Vergil next applies a simile: Dares' onslaught is compared to that of one who besieges (*oppugno*) a 'lofty city' (*celsa ... urbs*), with its 'massive walls' (*moles*, ablative).[238] Entellus is further compared to a 'mountain stronghold' (*montanus ... castellum*). The metaphorical battle takes place 'at arms' (*sub armis*), recalling the terminology used to describe the *cæstus* earlier in the poem.

The poet is aware of how much time boxers spend merely looking for the opportunity to strike, often fruitlessly. The boxer 'draws near' (*adeo*) to his adversary, 'wandering' (*pererro*) hither and thither: *nunc hos, nunc illos aditus, omnemque pererrat* (line 441). He leaps forward (*adsultibus ... urgeo*)[239] from time to time but the attack is always 'of no significance' (*inritus*).[240]

---

[235] In *immisceo*, Fairclough and Brown (1919, p. 424) envision "the preliminary sparring which provokes the real encounter" later.

[236] *multa cavo lateri ingeminant* (line 434).

[237] *corpore tela modo atque oculis vigilantibus exit* (line 438). Fairclough and Brown (1919, p. 424) interpret the adverbial as "merely with his body and eyes, i.e., without changing his place." One commentator has referred to Entellus' style at this early stage of the fight as "turtling" a technique by which the fighter "shield[s] himself with his arms instead of dodging, and observ[es] his opponent in order to find an opening for a knockout blow" (Secci 2009, p. 38).

[238] The ablative of *moles* in this context is ambiguous. If it is a complement of the verb *oppugno* then it describes the manner of the attack, i.e., using great siege ramps or the like. The reading we use is also preferred by Williams (2015), *inter alia*.

[239] In the sense 'press in' or 'confine', *urgeo* might also suggest a kind of clinch technique.

[240] "Now and then he springs forward to close the gap, but in vain" (translation ours): *arte locum, et variis*

On lines 443–444 we are treated to a description of a punch disallowed in modern sport boxing: a hammer or guillotine blow (Thomas 1997, pp. 111–134). Lifting himself up (*insurgo*), Entellus stretches out (*ostendit*) his right hand, but his opponent dodges (*effero*) the blow, which came from above (*ictus veniente a vertice*). As in Theocritus' *Idyll* 22, we find in the Æneidean boxing match mention of specific hands—an innovation that post-dates both Homer and Apollonius. The cultic importance of the right hand in Roman religion may play a greater role here than the dynamics of punching, but if we assume that Vergil is faithfully describing a boxing move, then striking a hammer blow with the right hand carries with it a number of interesting implications. If Entellus is right-handed,[241] then the tactic suggests that the boxers did not point their lead (i.e., left) shoulders towards one another. To land a hammer blow in the way described, Entellus was most likely 'squared up' in front of his opponent, a strategy discouraged in the modern ring because it maximizes the target area for an opponent to land his punches. Recalling the earlier description of blows striking the fighters' chests (line 434), we may safely assume that in matches of this type, boxers confronted each other with their chests forward. From another passage, we might also conclude that the hammer blow was much sought after, since from the first moment of the fight, the boxers raised themselves on their toes *in digitos extemplo arrectus* (line 426).

Vergil describes boxing with the *cæstus* in an impressively comprehensive fashion. We learn from the *Æneid* that the boxers strike at both the head and the body; they throw hooks as well as straight punches; they spend much time merely searching for an opening; they evade punches by moving their head and body; they jump in and out of the action; they hold their hands aloft; they stand on their toes; they throw hammer blows; and the adversaries face one another frontally instead of at an angle.[242] But for the last three features, the match looks similar to a modern one in terms of its dynamics. The material in the boxing vignette, while drawing on Greek sources, nonetheless suggests the poet had a keen eye for pugilism and was aware of its distinctive rhythms.

Dares' defensive movements also merit examination. The poet writes: *ille ictum venientem a vertice velox | prævidit, celerique elapsus corpore cessit* (lines 444–445). Thus, Dares foresees (*prævideo*) the blow as it hurtles from above (*a vertice velox*), 'gliding away' (*elabor*) while 'withdrawing' (*cessit*). The word 'body' (*corpus*) is here used in the ablative, suggesting the defensive move is made with Dares' whole frame, not just his head. The two lines are alliterative, first in *v* and then in *c*, perhaps to reinforce the rapidity of the boxers' movements. Dares slip was effective enough that Entellus 'poured out' (*effundo*) his 'strength' (*vis*) 'on the air' (*in ventum*). Off-kilter and as heavy as he was, Entellus fell even heavier.[243] Vergil arguably alludes here to the fall of Troy with a simile likening Entellus' caducity to that of a great conifer on Mount Ida[244] (in the Troad region of western Anatolia), uprooted thanks to the persistent effort of farmers.[245] The cries of the crowd suggest that the fight is won ("a

---

adsultibus inritus urguet (line 443).

[241] If Entellus were left-handed then he would be striking the hammer-blow with his weaker hand, which seems less plausible to us.

[242] The latter may have subtle resonance in Vergil's formulation *sto contra* (line 414).

[243] *... et ultro | ipse gravis graviterque ad terram pondere vasto | concidit ...* (lines 446–448).

[244] Earlier in the epic, Anchises prays for a sign that he should abandon Troy; subsequently, he witnesses a meteor fall on Mount Ida and interprets this portent as his answer.

[245] *ut quondam cava concidit aut Erymantho, | aut Ida in magna, radicibus eruta pinus.* (lines 448–449). Fairclough and Brown (1919, p. 425) translate *cava* as "hollow from age."

shout mounts to heaven"), but the poet has a reversal in mind (Fairclough 1916).[246]

Showing pity (*miserans*), Acestes hastens (*accurro*) to lift his friend 'of equal age' (*æquævus*) from the dirt (*ab humo*).[247] Entellus, however, is in no sorry state (*non tardatus … neque territus*) and he sets to beswinging Dares with an extraordinary fury (*acrior ad pugnam redit ac vim suscitat ira*) (lines 453–454).[248] Vergil explains what motivates Entellus in his comeback: *pudor … et conscia virtus*. The former could be his desire for approval or his shame at being knocked down, the latter a "conscious valor" in the formulation of Fairclough (1916), i.e., the recognition that his *virtus* 'manliness' is being judged by his opponent and all those who look on. Accordingly, he drives (*ago*) 'headfirst Dares' (*præceps Dares*, accusative) from the 'whole level surface' (*æquor totus*, ablative).[249]

This line appears to contain the earliest specific reference to the 'ring' in literature: *æquor*, 'an even, level surface'. Homeric and Apollonine references to the site of a boxing match referred to it only as the 'midst' of a gathering (Dioscurus and Dioscurus 2022c). While we may take for granted the idea that the 'field of play' in boxing should be flat, even, and unencumbered, Vergil offers us the first literary characterization in this regard. By using the ablative expression *æquore toto*, Vergil also suggests that the area had limits that Entellus transgressed when pummeling Dares beyond them. This indicates that by the first century BC the notion of fighters confronting one another in a delimited space had been operationalized, though there is still only minimal evidence of physical barriers serving as bounds.[250]

Vergil refers to Entellus' right (*dextera*) and left (*sinistra*) hands as the origins of the blows (*ictus*) with which he hatters Dares.[251] The use of both left and right hands here is presumably intended to highlight Entellus' two-fisted fury rather than any technical prowess. The verb associated with the activity is *ingemino* 'repeat' or 'redouble'. No longer is there pause (*mora*) or rest (*requies*)—Entellus is closing in on victory. Entellus' punches have become so many hailstones raining down on the roof of Dares' crumpling body.[252]

Æneas once more fulfills his father-like role, this time by stepping in to preserve Dares from the onslaught of Entellus. He will not suffer the latter's rage to "flame beyond bound" (Williams 1908).[253] Æneas puts a stop (*finem impono*) to the battle (*pugna*, dative) by snatching away (*eripio*) the weary (*fessus*)[254] Dares, whom he softly rebukes (*mulcens dico*) in lines 465–467:

---

[246] *Consurgunt studiis Teucri et Trinacria pubes; | it clamor caelo …* (lines 450–451).

[247] Entellus experiences "fall and resurrection" during the fight. This is regarded by some commentators as "the collective history of the Trojans/Romans themselves, and the plot of the *Æneid* as promised in the proem" (Feldherr 2002, p. 73).

[248] According to Nelis (2001, p. 18), this "is a surprising turnaround for the reader who knows the [Apollonine] model" in which a hammer blow is lowered on Amycus, who does not survive (Dioscurus and Dioscurus 2022d). *vim suscitat ira* has been translated as "awakes violence with anger" (Fairclough and Brown 1919, p. 425). Entellus, who no longer seems to be a sympathetic character, may here be drawing from the example of his master, Eryx, who according to one commentator was seized by murderous impulses (Leigh 2010, pp. 148–149).

[249] *praecipitemque Daren ardens agit aequore toto* (line 456).

[250] The softening of a piece of ground or *skamma* with axes, accomplished prior to Greek boxing, wrestling, and *pankration* bouts, also suggests a circumscribed zone for fighting, as do a handful of Greek vase paintings in which some marking on the ground or a low horizontal barrier is indicated.

[251] *nunc dextra ingeminans ictus, nunc ille sinistra* (line 457).

[252] *… quam multa grandine nimbi | culminibus crepitant, sic densis ictibus heros | creber utraque manu pulsat versatque Dareta* (lines 458–460).

[253] *Tum pater Aeneas procedere longius iras | et saevire animis Entellum haud passus acerbis* (lines 461–462).

[254] Conington (1876) argues that it means "sick of fighting" in this context.

> Infelix, quæ tanta animum dementia cepit?
> Non vires alias conversaque numina sentis?
> Cede deo ...

No other ancient text so movingly casts pugilism in the divine glow.[255] Specifically, Æneas highlights the numinous role of the gods who may switch allegiances from time to time but who (ultimately crown the victor. Dares, who has no chance of winning, is entreated to "submit to (the) god," perhaps Entellus's semi-divine patron, Eryx (Conington 1876) or maybe Apollo, to the extent the poet invokes the Iliadic boxing match (Dioscurus and Dioscurus 2022d). In line 465, Æneas mentions the madness (*dementia*) of the ring, which can overcome even the rational soul (*animus*) and make one miserable (*infelix*), as with Dares. Line 466 is poignant and familiar to anyone who has met defeat in the ring: "Do you not sense the divine presence that has altered the contest?"[256]

Thus speaking, Æneas disrupts the fight (*proelia ... dirimo*) using his voice (*vox*, ablative); this might be translated more literally as 'separates the combatants'.[257] Dares' friends (*fidi æquales*) drag (*traho*) him back to the ship on shaking knees (*genua ægra*) all the while he vomits (*ejecto*) a gore (*cruor*) of blood mingled with his own teeth. His head tosses (*jacto*) from side to side (*utroque*). Dares' attendants accept (*accipio*) the promised prize[258] of helmet and sword on his behalf. Naturally, they leave behind (*relinquo*) the bullock and a palm branch—not previously mentioned—for Entellus, the victor (line 472).

The concluding scene (lines 473–484) finds Entellus triumphant.[259] He strides forward, musing on his strength and what would have befallen Dares had he been permitted to keep fighting him. "Behold," he exclaims, "What strength was mine in youth, and from what death | ye have delivered Dares" (Williams 1908).[260] As if pantomiming his adversary's forestalled doom, Entellus drops his heavy fist, still bearing the *cæstus*, between the horns of the

---

[255] By compelling Dares to yield, Æneas recalls Poseidon in *Iliad* 20.332–339, when the former strove with Achilles. As the victor, Entellus occupies "the role of the god Hercules" (Feldherr 2002, p. 74) and Æneas takes on the role of Iliadic Poseidon. He is "simultaneously playing a god and revealing the workings of the divine within the spectacle" (ibid.). In the *Æneid*, "The gods are sometimes seen as natural forces or human psychological impulses. This particular function, sometimes called 'double motivation', shows clearly [when] Æneas comforts the beaten and bleeding Dares, and saves his dignity" in lines 465–467 (West 1998, p. 314–315).

[256] We reflect on a tableau of the modern ring in which the referee, having delivered a standing eight-count, asks the dazed boxer: "Can you still fight?" The stricken man nods sincerely, eyes wide, and holds his hands aloft in an earnest gesture of gameness. Then, Like Pater Æneas, the referee looks intently at the boxer for a moment and waves off the contest—to the disappointment of the bloodied adversaries who want nothing more than to settle it their own way.

[257] Though it generally means 'battle', there are other instances where *proelium*, in the plural, means 'fighters', e.g., Stat. *Th.* 1, 8.

[258] The term *donum* 'gift' is used to refer to the bullock in line 478; presumably it could have been applied equally to the *galea* and *ensis*.

[259] For Fairclough and Brown (1919, p. 426), *superans animis* yields "triumphant in spirit".

[260] ... *cognoscite, Teucri, | et mihi quæ fuerint iuvenali in corpore vires, | et qua servetis revocatum a morte Dareta* (lines 474–476).

bull,[261] smashing its skull[262] and ostensibly sacrificing it to his patron Eryx.[263] He then proclaims, "Victorious I now repose my art and my *cæstus*" (line 484), suggesting he will never box again.[264]

Immediately after he slays the bullock and just before he hangs up his gloves for good, Entellus clarifies the relationship between boxing and sacrifice. His speech, which we do well to consider closely, is as follows (lines 483–484):

> Hanc tibi, Eryx, meliorem animam pro morte Daretis
> persolvo ...

Addressing the goddess-born Eryx, Entellus states that in the sacrifice of the bull he renders (*persolvo*) a better spirit (*melior anima*) than that of Dares, or perhaps, in the formulation of Fairclough and Brown (1919, p. 426), "[I]t is better to offer a bull than the life of a man." Williams (1908) translates it thus: "This victim due | I give thee, Eryx, more acceptable | than Dares' death to thy benignant shade."

The *Æneid* is not merely a story about the past, it is a story about the past in which its characters break with their own pasts. This includes Entellus, who appears to change the trajectory of boxing from its brutal origins by choosing not to kill his opponent.[265] The irony, of course, is that when Vergil wrote his poem, gladiators and armed boxers were routinely killing one another in amphitheaters across the Roman world.[266] Does Vergil argue that boxing should be any different? Or is he suggesting that combat sports were cruel in the mythic past (Hercules vs. Eryx), then became more humane in the heroic past (Entellus vs. Dares), only to become cruel again in the poet's own time? Perhaps Vergil recognized the cyclical nature of combat sport, oscillating between lethal violence and kayfabe over the centuries. According to one critic, the sacrifice of the bull "returns us to the beginning of the cycle," suggesting that animal sacrifice predated human sacrifice in the 'ring' (Feldherr 2002, p. 69). He continues, "[T]he substitution of the bull for Dares ..., far from marking an

---

[261] The sacrifice of the bull in the *Æneid* reminds one commentator of an episode in the *Argonautica* (1.425–431) "where Heracles kills a sacrificial bull by hitting it on the forehead ... with his club" (Nelis 2001, p. 19).

[262] *effractoque inlisit in ossa cerebro* (line 480). By performing this action, Entellus is comparable to Amycus in the *Argonautica*, who plays the ox-slayer to Polydeuces, but fails. "If Apollonius connected the slaying of Amycus with the transition from lawless barbarism to Jovian order, the sacrificial differences in Vergil's text in turn civilize his predecessor by substituting ritual for slaughter" (Feldherr 2002, p.68). In other words, Vergil "transformed Apollonius' simile of sacrifice into real sacrifice" (ibid., p. 79).

[263] As far as Olympians go, Eryx is most closely linked to Venus, as is Anchises, her erstwhile lover and the father of Æneas (Feldherr 2002, p. 73).

[264] *hic victor cæstus artemque repono*

[265] Gardiner (1910, pp. 431–432) argued that Vergil's anachronistic placement of the Roman *cæstus* in the heroic past was intended to highlight that "heroes of the past must have excelled [the men of today] in the bloodiness of their fights and the murderous brutality of their weapons." Poliakoff (1985, p. 229) offers a critique of this claim, arguing instead that the anachronism allows Vergil's characters, "led by Entellus, to demonstrate their enlightenment in abandoning the savage customs they have inherited." Another author concludes, "[Entellus] rejects the brutal and gratuitous violence of celebrated boxing matches of the heroic past" (Dunkle 2005, p. 172).

[266] Poliakoff (1987a) entertains the possibility that Entellus' words are "the brutal scoff of the conqueror" (Henry 1881, p. 121) and that "the Romans were not so delicate and refined as to say, or to think, it was better to spare the human being and kill the beast" (Conington 1876, p. 377). Poliakoff notes that another critic is unwilling to choose between an interpretation in favor of either Entellus' humanity or his brutal sarcasm (Williams 1960, pp. 135–136). Ultimately Poliakoff (1987a, p. 231) concludes that Entellus' statement is consistent with an attitude that eschews the "promiscuous destruction of human life" and that "Vergil was sufficiently delicate and refined" to account the life of a man worthier than that of an animal.

advance over the shedding of human blood, in fact serves to reveal the ox in every boxer. ... Boxers, after all, prepare for battle by donning the hides, *terga*, of bulls" (ibid.).[267] The bull is killed "not as a sacrificial victim, but as a boxing opponent", blurring the lines between whatever boxing represented to Vergil's audience—including its associations with the heroic past—and religious sacrifice (Feldherr 2002, p. 69).[268]

By juxtaposing the (averted) death of Dares with the real death of the bullock,[269] Vergil is contrasting some earlier or imagined version of boxing where the loser dies with a more humane one practiced under the watchful eye of pious Æneas.[270] But is this intended to be a comment on first-century boxing at Rome? Was Vergil celebrating the victory of science over brutality, or was he subtly condemning the brutality he himself saw in contemporaneous fights? Suetonius reports that Vergil's patron, Augustus, was fond of boxing—including the Odyssean type, which took place in the alleyways of the capital.[271] Does the Æneidean boxing match serve as a recommendation for how boxing matches should be conducted in a perfect world, or as a celebration of how they were (righteously) conducted in Augustan Italy? Perhaps the *cæstus*, which was clearly already known, fell out of favor briefly at the time that Vergil wrote the *Æneid*. He seems to refer *quand même* to some virtuous, perhaps even latent, characteristic of a Roman (i.e., Trojan) man who does not need to kill his boxing opponents, even if the brutal gauntlet was in ure widespread—and primed to become even more savage in the decades ahead (Section 3.5). The boxer in the *Æneid* is both victim and sacrificant, as we observe in the changing roles of Dares, Entellus, and finally, the bullock.[272]

Vergil's "extensive allusions" to Apollonius allow him to draw out characterizations and ethical issues that are more complex than they are in any preceding boxing episode, Homeric or Apollonine (Poliakoff 1985, p. 229). The poet does this by assiduously linking the heel in one version with the face in the other—enough to blur the lines between who is virtuous (the Polydeuces role) and who is vicious (the Amycus role). Perhaps most remarkable in this regard is the animalistic rage of Entellus, formerly of noble stature and heroic comparison, at the conclusion of the Vergilian bout: *saevire animis ... acerbis* (line 462). Once self-effacing, he exits the 'ring' in a show of arrogance: *victor superans ... superbus* (line 473). The moral, according to Poliakoff (1987a), is clear: the Vergilian boxing match is "an emphatic rejection

---

[267] Kraggerud (1960) points out that the name of Dares' victim/opponent, Butes (Βούτης), is suggestive of βου 'ox'. Moreover, according to Lycophron's cryptic fourth-century poem *Alexandra* (regarded by Liberman (2009) as "what may be the most illegible piece of classical literature" ever written), the semi-divine Eryx was known as the 'bull' in the 'inhospitable wrestling arena' (cf. Tzetzes, *ad Lyc.* 866). Lines 866–867 from *Alexandra* read: ἥξει δὲ ταύρου γυμνάδας κακοξένους | πάλης κονίστρας, ὅν τε Κωλῶτις τεκνοῖ.

[268] According to Feldherr (2002), "[T]he lines that describe the trembling cow hurled lifeless to the ground suggest the image of Entellus himself collapsing after his mistimed blow and the verb used of the fighter on that occasion was *concidit* (line 448), which, as Hardie (1993, p. 52) points out, is particularly associated with the death of the sacrificial victim" (p. 69).

[269] It has been noted that the ox is a particularly salient substitute for man in sacrifice because the plough-ox works as man's partner in agricultural endeavor (Leigh 2010, p. 128).

[270] Musing on "the interpretative choice of the reader of the poem ... as a representation of the past," Feldherr (2002) remarks that "the sacrificial overtones of [the boxing match] invite discordant responses" as the reader struggles to resolve "sacrificial ambiguity", i.e., "the choice between participation and detachment" in the boxing vignette (p. 75).

[271] *spectauit autem studiosissime pugiles et maxime Latinos, non legitimos atque ordinarios modo, quos etiam committere cum Graecis solebat, sed et cateruarios oppidanos inter angustias uicorum pugnantis temere ac sine arte* (*Aug.* 45.2).

[272] Because each boxing match may potentially result in a fatality, it is "possible for the loser to be figured as a sacrificial victim" (Leigh 2010, p. 118).

of uncontrolled violence" which "highlights the corrupting effects that violence works upon Entellus" (p. 231).

What of the narrative arc of the Æneidean bout and its influence on how we understand modern boxing in the West? Vergil's account combines elements of the Iliadic and Apollonine versions but it is more dramatic than both. Vergil is more expert at playing with his reader's expectations than his predecessors. In fact, he does so in a way that has become *de rigeur* in underdog boxing cinema. Entellus is unlikely to win because of his advanced age and genuine reluctance to enter the ring. Vergil "stacks the deck" against him (Dunkle 2005, p. 171). While boastful, like Dares, Apollonius' Amycus is older than his opponent, like Entellus. But the Bebrycian's malignant nature leads the reader to correctly predict his downfall. In the case of Dares versus Entellus, it feels rather like a toss-up: Dares should win according to the Iliadic formula (might makes right), Entellus by the Apollonine (virtue wins the day). Ultimately, Vergil adopts the more 'modern' of the two scenarios, awarding the victor's laurel to modest but powerful Entellus while casting a shadow on Entellus' own character. The narrative still has reverberations two thousand years later in American cinema. In features like "Somebody Up There Likes Me" (1956), "Rocky" (1976), "The Champ" (1979), and "The Fighter" (2010) the down-on-his-luck fighter wins it all. This seems to be the boxing story that most resonates with modern audiences. On the other hand, narratives like "Raging Bull" (1980) and "Hands of Stone" (2016) follow Vergil more closely in exploring the ways in which violence degrades the victor.

The dark thread of degradation merits closer inspection. As Leigh (2010) summarizes, "[I]f the choice of an animal over a human victim is to be applauded, the decision of Entellus to make the bull an offering to his former trainer Eryx raises questions about what Eryx himself represents. One half of the mythological tradition offers some distinctly uncomfortable answers" (p. 149). The "half" the author refers to undoubtedly includes Eryx' chthonic role as "dealer of death" to his rivals in the 'ring' (ibid. p. 125). We find in the *Æneid* yet more evidence for what we have referred to elsewhere as the "hyper-violence" of boxing, both ancient and modern (Dioscurus and Dioscurus 2022a, p. 15).[273] Modern boxing matches turn instantly from a show of amiability between opponents to a feud of pure, though carefully circumscribed, hostility.[274] Leigh (2010) points out the same "tension ... between the spirit of amity and hospitality prevalent in Vergil's games as a whole and the murderous spirits unleashed in the course of the boxing match in particular" (p. 151). To box in the modern ring is to unleash those same animal spirits. There can be no amity between boxers when boxing. To consciously lighten the blows or deliver fewer of them is to suggest that one's adversary is too weak to fight and, as Seneca wrote of gladiatorial combat, it is a "disgrace to be matched with an inferior [opponent]."[275] Moreover, it is imprudent for a boxer to "go easy" even on a flagging adversary, who can turn from lamb to lion at a moment's notice. A stumbling fighter may even have won previous rounds and so must be beaten decisively in the here and now. When a fighter falls to the ground, that is the signal to stop the onslaught, and the only such signal apart from a referee's intercession. In the modern ring, the referee is

---

[273]This includes modern boxing gloves which are, as we argue elsewhere, offensive weapons popularly misunderstood as protective devices.

[274]According to Poliakoff (1985, p. 231), later in Book 11 of Æneid, the controlled boxing match is juxtaposed with human sacrifices (arranged by Æneas) at the funeral of Pallas (line 81). Messapus offers a Roman life on the altar in 12.296 even using the familiar taunt heard in the arena, "Hoc habet" upon observing the victim's fatal wound.

[275]*ignominiam iudicat gladiator cum inferiore componi* (*Prov.* 3.4).

present to protect the boxers' welfare while each boxer is there to inflict maximal damage on his adversary. The referee acts as the externalized conscience of whichever boxer is currently dominating his rival; the dominant fighter needs no conscience of his own. For a fighter to exercise mercy in the ring contradicts the basic premises of boxing and is, in any case, redundant. Æneas as *pater pugilis*, i.e. as Entellus' externalized conscience or the good referee, may be one of Vergil's most enduring contributions to the ethos of Western boxing.[276] All in all, Vergil memorializes the longstanding essence of ritual boxing by tying in the discipline of athletic boxing, prefatory to the Roman onslaught of gladiatorial boxing.

3.2 *Metamorphoses*

Boxing is mentioned briefly in Ovid's *Metamorphoses*, written in AD 8.[277] The poet takes up the subject of two boxers in Book 5. They are victims of Phineus, a rival of Perseus later turned to stone by gazing at the severed head of the gorgon Medusa. The brothers, Broteas and Ammon, would have been able to withstand their murderer, we are told, "if boxing gloves were able to overcome swords." The poet seems to make a comment on the fragility of the human body, even when trained to athletic perfection, if an opponent carries a deadly weapon. To wit, don't bring boxing gloves to a sword fight:[278]

> Hinc gemini fratres Broteasque et cæstibus Ammon
> invicti, vinci si possent cæstibus enses (lines 107–108).

3.3 *Argonautica* **of Valerius Flaccus, 4**

Dead by the dawn of the second century AD, the Flavian poet Valerius Flaccus was mourned by the rhetorician Quintilian—this, even though Valerius' work was long regarded as "imitative and inferior to Virgil and showing signs of a secondary belatedness" (Heerink and Manuwald 2014, p. 1). The *Argonautica*, Valerius' only attested work, tells the story of Jason and the other voyagers aboard the Argos. Critics have only recently begun to consider the significance of the text.

Book 4 of the Valerian *Argonautica* contains a lengthy reworking of the contest between Polydeuces (Pollux) and Amycus, known to us from the Apollonine *Argonautica* (Dioscurus and Dioscurus 2022d) as well as the *Idylls* of Theocritus (Section 2.1). The bout belongs to Type II of the epic boxing match (the beatdown of a bully), though it mixes in funereal elements, too, most notably the theme of human sacrifice. Amycus, erstwhile sacrificer, becomes the sacrificant.

The poem is easily the most aureate of the epic boxing episodes. For example, Valerius paints a lurid image of Amycus' lair and makes of him a bloodthirsty monster. However, the boxing match itself is rather brief and provides fewer opportunities to explore the vocabulary of Roman-era pugilism than either Statius' *Thebaid* (Section 3.4.2) or Nonnus' *Dionysiaca*

---

[276] Deremetz (2011, p. 64) argues that Æneas' intervention in the bout may be interpreted as the *aition* of a custom well known in gladiatorial combat: the so-called 'droit de grâce' (instituted by Augustus, according to Suetonius) that allowed the president of the games to spare a valiant fighter when vanquished and on the point of death.

[277] We are grateful to Nemæus for reminding us not to overlook Ovid.

[278] The anecdote is also likely a Roman indictment of Greek athletics in favor or (Roman) martial prowess, a theme that is also found in the Statian boxing match (Section 3.4.2).

(Section 2.6). Still, there are a number of truly remarkable features in the Valerian boxing match that merit special mention:

- Human sacrifice is an explicit element of boxing, with victims offered to Neptune and gauntlets placed on his altar.
- Cleromantic selection of the *cæstus* is mentioned, but dispreferred.
- A multitude of ghosts are released from the underworld in order to attend the match.
- The space designated for boxing is referred to as *cavea*, suggesting an enclosure.
- The fight is won due to a rabbit punch delivered to the bowed head of one of the boxers; there is no suggestion that this blow is ignoble or illegal.

A major theme of the Valerian *Argonautica* is the civilizing mission of the sailors, including three sons of Jupiter, viz., Hercules, Castor, and Pollux. As representatives of their father, they spread civilization and turn humanity from the ignave Saturnine world to the energetic world of Jove—the Iron Age (Bernstein 2014, p. 241ff.).[279] Cowan (2014, p. 241) writes, "Though the conquest of chaos by order can be seen as underlying most epic narratives, and is a particular feature of quest epics in which voyaging heroes civilize barbaric peoples and barbaric lands as they pass, Valerius' *Argonautica* remains exceptional in the extent to which it exploits this motif as its central organizing principle."

In Valerius' work, "The mythic narrative of the Argonautic saga takes on aspects of a cultural commentary by importing key societal constructs and tensions from contemporary— that is to say, late Flavian—Rome" (Zissos 2003, p. 660). These include the "arena motif as a framing device for a number of important episodes," including the fight between Pollux and Amycus (ibid.).

Sailing through the Bosporus, the Argonauts come upon the shores of Bebrycia, "a land of fertile soil and a good friend to sturdy bulls [*taurus*, line 100]."[280] Ancient Bebrycia has been identified with the Bay of Beicos, hence the Beykoz district of modern Istanbul (Dewing 1924, p. 470). The bull is introduced early on in the narrative, reminding the reader of the mythpoeic relation between bulls and boxing spanning millennia (Dioscurus and Dioscurus 2022b). Zissos (2003, pp. 667–668, fn. 29) conjectures that Valerius is also having a bit of fun with his audience, remarking that the bulls are indeed friends of the Bebryces, since their master offers human sacrifice in place of the taurine variety.

As Valerius' readers would have known from, *inter alia*, the Apollonine *Argonautica* and Theocritus' *Idylls*, the Bebrycian king is named Amycus and dealing with him is no walk in the park. According to Cowan (2014, p. 231), Valerian villains are either tyrants or monsters. Amycus is both. Valerius tells us that the local population believes so much in Amycus' "destiny and power divine" that they chose not to build walls or "observe ... conditions of treaties or laws." This attachment to their doubly-primitive ruler means their own downfall is imminent.

Valerius establishes the visiting Argonauts as "culture-hero ushers of the Jovian Iron Age" pitted against "Titanic, Earth-born, Sun-spawned and Neptune-sired monsters of Saturnian

---

[279]Valerius "sketch[es] a ... submerged conflict between divine brothers. Jason's mission advances Jupiter's side in his conflict with his brother Neptune and his father Saturn. ... Jupiter's ambitions bring him into conflict with his brother Neptune, who is made to open his sea" to the commercial activities of humans (Bernstein 2014, p. 163). Leigh (2010, p. 127fn. 44) regards the boxing match between Pollux and Amycus as a battle between the sky and the sea: "a neat encapsulation of cultural advance."

[280]Line numbers in this section come from Kramer (1913).

primitivism" (ibid.). In the ensuing conflict between Pollux and the son of the earth-shaker, Valerius presents an "emblematic encounter ... in which the new overcomes the old" and chaos is supplanted by order. His audience was expected to find satisfaction in this resolution, and in the defeat of the monster. Indeed, Amycus is compared to the Odyssean cyclops Polyphemus (another spawn of the *enosichthon*),[281] hungering for shipwrecked strangers— "grim fodder and wretched victims for [his] feasting." Not explicitly anthropophagous, Amycus typically hurls his victims from a cliff into the sea (*æquor*, line 110).[282] Like Bram Stoker's energumen Renfield, the solicitous Bebryces "drag captive bodies to their king."

The miserable men so disposed of are described as offerings (*sacrificus*, line 110) to Neptune, Amycus' father. Amycus prefers to sacrifice those of "finer build" (*forma ... præstantior*, from *præsto* 'be excellent', line 111) in a more sportive fashion. These athletic types he commands to "take arms" (*arma sumo*, line 112) and 'run up against' him (*ocurro contra*) wearing the boxing gauntlets (*cæstus*).[283] "That, for the hapless men, is the fairest doom of death": *haec miseri sors est æquissima leti* (line 113). Though anachronistic, a hint to late Flavian gladiatorial combat is strongly suggested in this line. Instead of being executed outright, prisoners of Amycus must fight him for their lives, doomed to die in a manner that, in the Roman world view, was far more equitable or perhaps even impartial (*æquus*).[284]

In a somber digression, Valerius presents the perspective of Neptune himself, with foreknowledge of his son's defeat in the boxing ring.[285] He considers the "fields [*campus*] that once rejoiced in their master's [sc., Amycus] contests [*certamen*]." Here we note that the location of boxing matches is called *campus* and the competition is designated as *certamen*, derived from *certo* 'struggle'. Given Neptune's rosy, even nostalgic, outlook on his son's butchery, Cowan (2014, pp. 243–244) reads this passage as "a glimpse at an epic written by the monstrous losers," i.e., one in which the pre-Jovian order exults in its glory days and suggests to the reader "that epic morality is relative." Neptune even laments that Amycus' mother, Melie, had not been seduced by his resurgent brother, Jupiter, instead of himself: "'Tis pity thou wast long ago carried off by me beneath the waves, and didst not rather yield to the Thunderer." Cowan (2014, p. 244) argues that Neptune's regard for Amycus' "brutal pugilism" as *virtus* "valor" (line 124) is another example of moral relativism in Valerius' epic. The sea god counsels his son that confidence (*fiducia*, line 124) in his father is misplaced and should no longer afford him any courage (*ops*, line 125) in the fight. "Now other might [*vis*, line 126] has the mastery, and the destinies of Jove, more eager to protect his own, are too strong for blood of mine." Given that he can "in aught delay thy death," Neptune admonishes Amycus to abjure a contest with any of the Argonauts: "Make lesser kings thy prey." Here Valerius uses the verb *premo*, 'to press', the same verb used to describe the action dur-

---

[281] According to Cowan (2014, p. 241), "Valerius self-consciously draws parallels between his monsters, ... depicting them less as individuals than as instantiations of the almost abstract 'type' of the monster. The clearest, and arguably least subtle, example of this is the simile comparing Amycus to Polyphemus, ... an equation of epic characters as much as of mythical figures."

[282] The noun *æquor* is used by Vergil to designate the location of the boxing match—with sacrificial overtones— between Dares and Entellus. The word generally means a flat place, including a body of water.

[283] At least one critic understands the sacrifices to Neptune to include the boxers (Leigh 2010, p. 127fn. 44).

[284] Ironically, perhaps, Amycus, who is supposed to represent a primordial world of disorder and injustice, runs a fight game similar to that of the Flavian elite. Perhaps Valerius' audience could distinguish Amycus' bloodsport from their own or perhaps Valerius intended to hold up Amycus' boxing match as a mirror to the gladiatorial fights of his day. It is fairly certain that the poet saw some relation between the two, as argued by Zissos (2003).

[285] "Hostility to strangers, murderous intent expressed through the practice of combat sport, perverse rituals of human sacrifice: this, it seems, is how to know a son of Neptune" (Leigh 2010, p. 142).

ing the boxing match between Alcidamas and Capaneus (*Thebaid* 6.770). In a baleful, final flourish, Neptune looks away, "leaving his son and the ill-starred combat [*tristia ... proelia*, lines 131–132][286]" and laves the Bebrycian coast "with a tide of blood" (*sanguineus ... æstus*, line 132).

Once ashore, the Argonauts are hailed as "doomed" (*perdo*, line 140) by the lone survivor of a previous expedition to Bebrycia. He warns them to flee, characterizing Bebrycia as "no friendly land" (*hospita ... terra*, lines 145–146) and assuring the Greeks that the locals are impious: ... *non hic ullos reverentia ritus | pectora ...* (lines 146–147). "This shore," he continues, "is the home of death and cruel combats" (*mors habitat saevæque hoc litore pugnæ*, line 147). The stranger, named Dymas, tells them of Amycus, the local potentate who will bid them raise (*tollo*) the "dread gauntlets" (*dirus ... cæstus*, line 148). He highlights Amycus' gigantic stature, noting that he "strikes the clouds with overtopping head" (*vasto qui vertice nubila pulset*, line 149).[287]

Dymas warns the Argonauts that Amycus rages (*furo*, line 151)[288] against all travelers in his territory. Those whose manliness does not match Amycus' own (*æquæ virtutis*, line 151) he "stations [*constituo*] like sluggish bulls [*segnis ... taurus*, line 152] at the cruel altars of the gods [*superum ... iniqua altaria*, line 152], only that he may wet his weapons in the wretches' brains [*lavo arma cerebro*, line 153]." This passage is strongly reminiscent of the bull sacrifice at the end of the Æneidean boxing match, including the reference to cerebral matter. Given the Valerian (and Vergilian) tendency to call the boxing gauntlets *arma*, it is likely that Amycus' sacrifice of the weaker men also involves the *caestus*, though it would seem only Amycus wears the gauntlet during this ritual.

Beat a hasty retreat, Dymas tells the sailors. No one would dare engage (*concurro*, line 155) Amycus and, in any case, there is no pleasure (*voluptas*, line 156) in the fight.[289] Naturally questioning the *bona fides* of this messenger, the Argonauts interrogate him. Is he a Bebrycian or a stranger? If a stranger, "Why, then, has Amycus not shattered thy face with his gauntlet? (*et tua cur Amycus cæstu nondum obruit ora?*, line 160). The verb *obruo* means 'to bury, overwhelm, oppress, or consign to oblivion'. The same verb is used, with *cæstus* in the ablative, in Statius' *Achilleid* (1.190–191): ... *crudum quo Bebryca caestu | obruent Pollux* ... "Pollux with his glove smote down the cruel Bebryx" (Mozley 1928b).

Dymas, a resident of Mariandynia, recounts how he followed an Anatolian leader named Otreus who, "in search of the enjoyment of a Phrygian bride," was forced to stand against Amycus (*Amycum contra iussus sto*, line 165). The passage recalls the Apollonine *Argonautica* 2.778. There we learn that Otreus sought to marry the Trojan princess Hesione and, passing through Bebrycia, was summarily beaten to death by Amycus in a boxing match. Dymas "enlaced the hands" (*palmas implico*, line 165–166) of his master for that fight. He tells the Argonauts, "Scarce had Otreus drawn nigh and lifted (*levo*) his head when Amycus with lightning blow [*fulminea dextera*, line 167][290] dashed out the eyes from his shattered brow [*disjecta fundo lumina*, lines 167–168]." This gory tidbit indicates the use of a cruel *cæstus*, indeed. The match between Otreus and Amycus suggests that boxing could sometimes

---

[286] The form is in the plural.

[287] The verb *pulso* is elsewhere used to indicate beating (repeatedly) with a hammer, as in a boxing match.

[288] This verb adumbrates the boxer and anti-hero Capaneus in Statius' later *Thebaid*.

[289] The reference to *voluptas* suggests that in some circumstances, at least, boxing was regarded as pleasurable—just not in a ring with Amycus (cf. *Achilleid* 2.155–156).

[290] The punch is specifically named as as 'right' *dextera*.

serve as an obstacle to *gaudia nuptæ* (line 164), though this theme is hardly a prominent one in ancient boxing poetry.[291] For some reason, Dymas himself was "never deemed worthy [*dignatus*]" of death in the Amycian ring or at the altar of Neptune; both are suggested by the phrase *leto … armis* (line 168).

The Argonauts listen to this ghastly tale unperturbed (*non … formidine moti accipio*, lines 174–175) and "with unimpaired resolve" (*dura sic pergere mente*, line 175) they follow Dymas to a cave (*spelunca*, line 177), "a grim abode that trembled with the roaring of the deep" (*infelix domus et sonitu tremibunda profundi*, line 180). A veritable treehouse of horrors[292] (*metus*, line 180) lay at its mouth: mutilated (*truncus*) arms snatched (*rapio*, line 182) from the sockets of men whom Amycus had "sent flying" (*roto*, also 'whirl about' line 181). The limbs, still bound tight (*stringo*, line 182) with the boxing gauntlet (*cæstus*, ablative, line 182) were strewn about "this hideous abditory" (McClellan 2019, p. 193) with bones "foul and mouldering, and heads in a dismal row": *ossaque tætra situ et capitum mæstissimus ordo* (line 184).[293]

Some of the decomposing noggins bore signs of a frontal wound (*adversus … vulnus*, line 184) that "left nor name [*nomen*, i.e., a means of knowing] nor visage [*facies*]." Boxing with Amycus could literally result in having one's face ripped off. Only a savage *cæstus* could cause such mayhem. Indeed, Amycus' holy boxing gauntlets (*arma sacra*, lines 185–186) are mentioned next, sanctified "through fear" (*metus*, ablative, line 186) and lying in honor "on the altar of his mighty sire" (*magnique aris imposta parentis*, line 186).

Some in the company are stricken by fear (*pavor*, line 188) but not plucky Pollux. "With starry countenance undismayed" (*sidereo Pollux interritus ore*, line 190) he threatens the absent monster. "I will cause this wood of thine to bear thee anon, whoever thou art, if thou have but blood and limbs withal": … *modo sint tibi sanguis et artus* (line 192).[294] Aroused by their comrade's *cri de cœur*, the other sailors likewise call for (*exopto*) the man (*vir*) "to try the issue in valiant fight" (*decerno pugna*, ablative, line 193). They want to "challenge him face to face" (*contra … ocurrere posco*).[295] Valerius treats his audience to a simile comparing Pollux and his companions to a bull (*taurus*, line 196) that first tests "untried waters," hence leading the herd (*pecus*, line 197) into the swirling eddies, their terror (*formido*, line 197) at once forgot.

At the same time, "the ruthless giant" (*sævus gigans*, line 200) strides towards his cave in a fury (*furens*, line 204) and straightaway informs his unwelcome visitors,[296] "Here it is my law to raise gauntlet and arms in opposing combat": *hic mihi lex cæstus adversaque tollere con-*

---

[291] One exception is the poetess Corinna's mention of a boxing match between Ares and Hermes for the love of a certain water nymph (Dioscurus and Dioscurus 2022d).

[292] The cave of Amycus, described in lines 177–185, is "a horror show of corporal abuses. The venue is appropriately a *locus horridus* modeled on Cacus' cave in Vergil (*Æneid* 8.193–197) where too the monster has decorated the entryway with severed heads" (McClellan 2019, p. 193).

[293] Valerius is aware "that a much darker sense of a pre-Jovian civilization might exist in the universe. … [T]he most shocking example of such barbarity is the primitive Amycus" (Buckley 2014, p. 323).

[294] "His [sc., Amycus] spectacle of abuse elicits a threat of retaliatory corpse abuse from Pollux, who will take up the gauntlets against Amycus in a boxing match to the death" (McClellan 2019, p. 197). The author provides his own translation of this passage: "[W]hoever you are, I will nevertheless see to it that your trees bear *you* on account of this horrific display, provided you have blood in your limbs" (ibid.).

[295] This is the third time we have found some variant of the verb phrase *ocurrere contra* in the Valerian boxing episode.

[296] "Amycus' perversion of *xenia* ['hospitality'] constitutes a violation of duties analogous to treachery" (Cowan 2014, p. 233fn. 12).

tra | bracchia ... (lines 210–211).[297] According to one commentator, Amycus thus substitutes "agonism for hospitality" (Bernstein 2014, p. 167). Lamenting his unyore lack of sparring partners, Amycus notes that his "gauntlets lie idle, and the ground is cold and dry, and but few teeth bestrew it": *iam pridem cæstus resides et frigida raris | dentibus aret humus* ... (lines 214–215). He mockingly asks, "Who will strike [*jungo*] a bargain [*fœdus*, plural, line 215] with me?" Valerius toys with his audience's expectations of an epic boxing match when Amycus goads his guests further, "To whom may I hand the prize [*donum*, line 216]? The same guerdon [*honor*, line 217] will come to all in time." The prize, by twisted Amycian convention, is death.[298] They are trapped, he tells them, and he has no patience for "grovelling prayers" or "appeals to heaven." In a final bit of blasphemy that surely sings awk, the son of Neptune bellows, "'Tis elsewhere Jupiter counts for king": *aliis rex Iuppiter oris* (line 219).

At this foul provocation, several sailors leap forward to fight but none as quickly as Pollux, who has already stripped off his clothes—at least partially (*nudus ... pectus*, ablative, line 225)—and taken his stand (*sto*). Pollux' brother, Castor, is gripped by fear (*pavor*) and "icy chill of blood" (*gelidus ... sanguis*, line 226) recognizing this hand-to-hand fight (*pugna*, line 227) would not be like the ones back home in Greece. Valerius imagines games attended by nobility with applause (*favor*, line 228) resounding off the slopes of Taygetus and into the Spartan ring: *nec sonat Œbalius caveæ favor aut iuga nota | Taygeti* ... (lines 228–229). *Cavea* is the first word we have found in epic poetry denoting a space for boxing that suggests more than a flat piece of ground (e.g., *æquor*, *campus*) or a clearing in a crowd (e.g., *in medium*). The term *cavea*, which is used elsewhere to characterize an enclosure for animals,[299] instead calls to mind a constructed space in which the fighters torment one another. Valerius associates the *cavea* with Sparta.[300] The noun *cavea* may also refer to the part of the theater in which the spectators sat; if Valerius describes the cheers coming from the *cavea*, it is possible this is what he meant. However, the form used in the poem is either genitive or dative, so applause reaching the *cavea* is grammatically just as likely as applause emanating from it. Thus, we cannot rule out the possibility that Valerius imagined some form of Spartan pit fighting, as is strongly implied by *cavea*, ultimately derived from *cavus* 'hollow'.[301]

Valerius writes that on Bebrycia's "accursed" sand (*sacra harena*, line 230),[302] the prize (*pretium*) is not "a bull or a steed with sounding hooves, but the guerdon [*præmium*, line 231] is man's life [*Manes*, line 231][303] and the gate of death unbarred [*reclusa ... ianua leti*, line 231]." While the Amycian bouts take place on the shore, it is hard to miss Valerius' double-entendre: *harena* 'sand', e.g., in the amphitheater, was by Valerius' time a synecdoche for the place of combat itself.

With an ominous smile (*ora renidens*, line 234) not unfamiliar to boxers, Amycus sizes up

---

[297] Given our particular interest in the contrast (or lack thereof) between *cæstus* and *arma*, we note that Mozley (1928b) need not have included "and arms" in his translation of this passage because *arma* does not appear in it.

[298] We see in Amycus' cruel *donum* the shadow of what we call 'gladiatorial' boxing, in which one of the boxers is likely to die, given the nature of the cruel *cæstus* used throughout the imperial period and Late Antiquity (Section 3.5).

[299] It has been translated in other contexts as 'cage', 'stall', 'coop', or even 'beehive'.

[300] Œbalia, another name for Sparta, is so designated based on the name of an early king.

[301] Modern cage-fighting will perhaps one day reckon its debt to Valerius Flaccus.

[302] The adjective *sacer* 'sacred' can also mean 'execrable' in poetry and post-Augustan prose. While the context here suggests the pejorative (and was also chosen by Mozley), the notion that the sand was consecrated by spilled blood is also not out of the question.

[303] *Manes* refers to the ghost of a person, also the underworld generally.

(*lustro*) his opponent, who is "neither fierce of brow [*nec frons trux*, line 232] nor terrible in bulk [*moles tremenda*], scarce as yet showing signs of earliest manhood [*primæ spargentem signa iuventæ*, line 233]." Amycus rages (*fremo*) at the youth's audacity (*ausum*), and "in blazing fury rolls his bloodshot eyes": *sanguineosque rotat furiis ardentibus orbes* (line 235).[304] Valerius compares the ogre to Typhœus, a monstrous serpentine giant defeated by Jupiter in order to secure supremacy over the cosmos. Amycus attempts to psych out (*terreo*, line 239) his opponent using some old-fashioned trash talk (*rabidus murmur*). He blusters, "Make haste, whosoever thou art, unhappy boy [*infelix ... puer*, line 240]; no longer shall the beauty of that fair brow [*pulchra ... frons*, lines 240–241] remain to thee, nor shalt thou take back to thy mother the face she knew [*haut ... decus orave matri | nota feres*, lines 240–242]." His final threat makes it clear that their fight will be to the outrance: "Wilt thou, the choice of cruel comrades, wilt thou die by the and of Amycus?"[305] Amycus "exemplifies from the very beginning ... an arrogant and furious behavior that distances him significantly from all previous boxers" in the epic tradition, "mak[ing] the reader wish to see him not only defeated, but also dead" (Antoniadis 2017, p. 164).

No more messing around now, the son of the earth-shaker "displays his huge shoulders [*ingens umerus*, line 244] and the spacious breast-bones [*spatiosa ... pectoris ossa*] and the unsightly sinews [*toris informis*, line 245][306] of his terrible [*horreo*] limbs [*artus*, line 245]." As when Irus watched Odysseus drop his cloak, the Argonauts sputter at the sight. Their brief revery is interrupted by their pugnacious host who presents Pollux with "hardened wrappings" (*durus volumen*, line 250). This novel term for the *cæstus* suggests they may have been rolled up for storage. As usual, they are made of the 'raw' or 'bloody' hide of a bull (*taurus*, ablative, line 250).[307] Amycus discounts the option of choosing gauntlets by cleromancy: "Seek not [*nec peto*, line 251][308] the aid of chance [*sortis ops*, line 251], but put on [*induo*, line 251] what gloves [*cæstus*] thou canst." As in the Apollonine *Argonautica*, the possibility of sortition for the *cæstus* is mentioned but it is summarily rejected. This puzzling detail leads us to wonder if the practice was recalled from distant memory or if it was a mere fiction.

As oblivious to his expiatory fate (*piaculum*) as any Titan about to be hurled headlong into Tartarus, Amycus gives his flat hands (*palma*, line 253) to his servant (*famulus*), line 254).[309] The servant's task is to to 'bind' or 'weave' (*innecto*, line 253) the *arma* (in the ablative or dative), a clear indication that here, at least, *cæstus* and *arma* are synonymous.[310] Pollux does the same; the phrase is *dat et inde*, so it is not clear if Pollux wraps up his own hands or extends them to a comrade to do the job.

Valerius provides a timeless insight into the psychology of boxing when he writes that ferocious hatred (*odium asper*, plural) gathers to a greatness (*surgo*, line 254) in the breasts

---

[304] "Amycus' ... madness remains unexplained and unjustified" (Antoniadis 2017, p. 168).

[305] *... tune a sociis electus iniquis? | tune Amyci moriere manu? ...* (lines 242–243).

[306] The phrase may be translated 'shapeless muscular protuberance'. Evidently, Amycus was to be respected for his bulk, not his pulchritude.

[307] Valerius uses no word for 'hide' in this passage.

[308] The form is first person singular, which means Amycus is talking about himself, *pace* Mozley (1928b), who renders it a command. Another manuscript appears to have *petae*. Arguably, this may be a corruption of the second person singular imperative *pete*.

[309] The noun, appearing in the dative form *famulis*, could be singular or plural in the masculine, plural only in the feminine.

[310] Perhaps intent on the possibility that Amycus and Pollux are about to wrestle, Mozley (1928b) translates *arma* as "harness".

of those who were strangers only moments before (*ignotus prius*). Their minds eschaufed (*incensa mens*, line 255), the combatants hurl themselves (*fero*, line 256) "into the midst" (*in medium*, line 256). Here the poet touches on one of the abiding mysteries of personal combat. What transpires in the mind of a boxer when he realizes that only he or the stranger standing before him can leave the ring in victory? How can *odium asper* be born so quickly in the heart of man? Is it hatred, after all, or something else?

The next passage has unique implications for a theory of the psychagogic origins of boxing. In a tense silence "strung taut by suspense and hope [*votum*, 'vow']", a multitude of ghosts (*umbra*)[311] entreat (*oro*, line 258) the lord of the underworld to grant them seats at this special fistfight: ... *ad meritæ spectacula pugnæ | emittit* ... (lines 259–260).[312] So many shades emerge from Tartarus and find their seats that "the mountain-tops grow black with them." While Mozley (1928b) suggested that these phantoms were victims of Amycus' cruelty during their mortal lives, there is little support for this interpretation in the original text. The presence of ghosts is clearly related to the Roman view of boxing as a cultic endeavor. We note the close connection between boxing and funerals in southern Italy and among the Etruscans (Dioscurus and Dioscurus 2023), including the notion that blood must be spilt near the entrance of a tomb to the benefit of the deceased. Zissos (2003, p. 663ff) argues that the ghosts take their seats on the tops of mountains surrounding the boxing ring, suggesting the natural equivalent of a Roman amphitheater, with spectators seated in the nosebleeds, high above the action.[313]

"Like a hurricane [*turbo*, line 262] sweeping down from Malea's roaring summit,"[314] Amycus "scarce suffers the hero to raise his head, scarce to lift [*tollo*, line 262] his arms" before his attack.[315] Amycus drives Pollux 'headlong' (*præceps*), encompassing (*involvo*, lit. 'roll upon') him in a rainstorm (*nimbus*, line 263) and torrent (*torrens*) of attack (*ago*).[316] The bigger man pursues (*insequor*) the smaller one "over all the ground" (*harena*, lit. 'sand', line 264).[317] Pollux is alert (*vigil*) with fear (*metus*). He turns (*redeo*, line 268) his breast and boxing gloves (*arma*, line 265) repeatedly, always "with head drawn back" (*cervix reducta*, ablative, line 266) and "ever a-tiptoe" (*in digitis*). The manner in which boxers stood on their toes is the focus of other epic poets, notably Apollonius of Rhodes (Dioscurus and Dioscurus 2022d) and Nonnus of Panopolis (Section 2.6). Standing on tiptoe suggests that the boxer is attempting to increase his height. However, minimizing the surface area of contact

---

[311] Mozley (1928b) renders the noun phrases "shades of the slain" but we find no indication in the text that these are spirits of victims, e.g., of Amycus. Though that seems to be the sense of Mozley's translation, there is not a great deal of evidence for it in Valerius' original words.

[312] Again, Mozley (1928b) intends to explain the presence of the ghosts by suggesting that their human forms were slaughtered by Amycus: "to view at last the well-earned retribution." It is difficult to read 'retribution' into the original.

[313] Citing Zissos (2003), Antoniadis (2017, p. 177fn. 36) observes that Valerius "gives prominence to the gladiatorial aspects of the fight, i.e., its amphitheatrical setting and its aristocratic self-fashioning, as well as to the psychodramatic involvement of spectators." This is no longer a ritual performance, even if nominally a sacrifice.

[314] Valerius refers to a peninsula and cape in the southeast of the Peloponnese, known for its lousy weather.

[315] It was also said of Otreus, Amycus' prior victim, that he hardly had a chance to raise his head before Amycus swung at him. This might mean that the boxers initiated combat with bowed heads, or may refer to them rising from a seated position where, perhaps, they accoutred themselves with the *cæstus*.

[316] "Valerius is faithful to the message of Apollonius, who turns the battle into a *mise en abyme* of a new epic whose defining topos is the storm, a topos that shows a capacity to integrate material from 'earlier' epics into a new and more accomplished semionarrative model" (Deremetz 2014, p. 65).

[317] This is undoubtedly another reference to the Roman arena.

between the foot and the ground in this way would be an unreliable technique in the modern boxing ring, as it leads to poor balance. We surmise that references to boxing *in digitis* or the like may indicate that the fighter attempts to land a hammer-blow from above by increasing his vertical dominance over his opponent. If, on the other hand, *in digitis* really means "on the balls of the feet" then this description fits nicely with the praxis of modern sport boxing, where boxers are encouraged to stand in this position in order to remain nimble in avoiding punches and springing back and forth at one's adversary. Indeed, the same passage refers to the boxers lunging forward (*proicio*).

Valerius compares Pollux to a raft (*ratis*, line 269) in a restless (*trepidus*) sea (*æquor*).[318] This is remarkably consistent with modern boxing terminology, in which this motion is referred to as 'bobbing'. All the while, the son of Jupiter "warily watches the blows": ... *Pollux sic providus ictus | servat* ... (lines 271–272).[319] With a skill that Valerius considers uniquely Spartan (*Œbalius*), Pollux "withdraws his head from the peril": *dubium caput eripio* (line 272).[320] By doing so, he causes Amycus to pour out (*effundo*) his "urgent wrath" (*urgente* ... *ira*, line 273, plural) and fury (*ardor*) on the clouds (*nubes*, dative/ablative). Pollux is already winning.

Pollux rises (*insurgo*) gradually (*palautim*) to strike, as yet untouched (*integer*) by his already exhausted (*fessus*, line 274) opponent. He brings down (*deduco*, line 275) the *cæstus* with "uplifted arms" (*summa manus*, plural ablative, line 275). This is another clear example of how important the hammer-blow was to ancient boxing. While Pollux waxed, Amycus waned. His limbs drooped (*æger artus*), he was covered in sweat (*sudor*), and breathed with halting (*cuncto*) and parched (*areo*) gasps: *arenti cunctantem vidit hiatu* (line 277).[321] Amycus is, in a word, "weary " (*defatiscor*, line 278), so much so that his own people do not recognize him.

In what appears to be a kind of break between rounds (reminiscent of Greek athletic pauses by mutual agreement), both combatants take a breath (*respiro* ... *paulum*, line 279) and let their arms fall (*repono*). Valerius imagines another *æquor*[322] where Gradivus (a surname of the god Mars) revives (*refoveo*, line 281) the Lapiths[323] or the Pæonians while "leaning silent upon his fixed spear."[324]

The interval was short (*vix*) but we are told the combatants stood (*sto*) throughout it. Once more unto the breach, they fall (*ruo*) on one another with violence, their gloves reverberating (*terga sonant*) at the reciprocal infliction (*infligo*, line 282) of blows. Quickened (*nova vis*) with "fresh bodies" (*novum corpus*) they stand erect (*surgo*, line 283). The poet gives his audience a rich psychological insight into the boxers: shame (*pudor*) motivates (*instimulo*) one (presumably Amycus), while the other (presumably Pollux) feels hope (*spes*).

---

[318] Valerius referred to the boxing 'ring' as *campus* 'flat plain', just a few lines earlier (267). Reference to the 'ring' as *æquor* in epic poetry is not unknown, as we have mentioned earlier. Its most general sense the noun means 'a flat surface'.

[319] Antoniadis (2017, p. 175) argues that Valerius, "beside re-working epic boxing scenes, is also alluding to some basic tenets of stoic philosophy" by describing Pollux as *providus* and possessed of reasoning that "justifies even his own fear ... as a means of restraining his anger."

[320] A slip.

[321] This line is difficult to translate. In particular, we are puzzled as to the meaning of *vidit hiatu*. Mozley (1928b) seems to interpret it as 'gasp', though 'look for an opening' is also possible—lexically, at least.

[322] 'War' is not mentioned explicitly, *pace* Mozley (1928b).

[323] The Lapiths were known for their role as the human side of the centauromachy, a legendary brawl at a wedding feast that pitted the Lapiths against the disorderly, drunken sagittaries.

[324] This attitude recalls the Hellenistic Prince, often paired with the Quirinal Boxer as a sculptural duo.

Amycus' performance in the ring so far has disappointed him; he knows that he must recover and therefore presses forward out of shame for his failure to defeat his opponent any sooner. Pollux, on the other hand, is more confident (*audeo*, line 284) as he learns (*notus*) more about his enemy (*hostis*, line 284). He has hope that he will win and this provides its own positive motivation. As boxers, we recognize the singular importance of this psychological peripateia in a match, viz., the moment when it dawns on a fighter that he understands his opponent and that he is, in fact, beating him.

The muscle that parts the chest and abdomen, the *præcordia* (line 285), is steaming (*fumo*) from punch after punch (*creber pulsus*, line 285). This image, unique to epic boxing, suggests that Valerius was a studious spectator himself and had observed such steam arise from the bodies of pugilists, presumably on chilly days in the arena or the *palaestra*.

The fighters vocalize (*gemitus*)—something that is relatively uncommon to epic boxing episodes. Typically, the only sounds the boxers make emanate from their jaws as they gnash together or receive heavy blows. In a second reference to Polyphemus, Valerius creates an auditory representation of the cyclopean forge. The monster "prepares the metal for the thunderbolt [*fulmen*]."[325] The emphasis here is on the "clang" (*strepito*, line 288) of "stricken [*pello*, line 288] anvils" and their resemblance, presumably, to the punches the two fighters unload on each other. Pollux next "leaps forward" (*emico*, line 289) and makes ready (*paro*) his right hand in a menacing (*mino*) gesture. Distracted by this threat ("that way go the eyes"), Amycus "lunges" (*pondus*, 'weight', ablative) based on his (miscalculated) reckoning (*reor*) of Pollux' next move. "With swift left" (*celeri ... sinistra*, line 291), Pollux tears (*rapio*) his opponents face or perhaps his mouth (*ora*, line 291). At this signal of dominance, Pollux' comrades (*socius*) shout (*conclamo*) for joy (*gaudia*).

Disordered (*turbo*, line 293) and enraged (*furo*) by his opponent's "unexpected guile" (*insperata fraus*), Amycus retreats (*refugo*, line 294) until he can thunder forth (*detono*) his wrath (*ira*).[326] He is also described as alarmed (*terreo*) and "conscious of his great daring" (*ingentis conscius ausi*, line 295).[327] The behemoth of Bebrycia is described as 'helpless' (*inops*, line 296) in his ferocity (*sævio*), never a good look for a boxer. Amycus heedlessly (*nullo discrimine*) "hurls himself forward" (*præcipito*).[328] He is "greedy for his foe" (*avidus ... viri*) when he see the Argonauts rejoicing (*ovo*) in the distance. He raises both his gauntlets (*cæstu elatus*) and casts them down (*inruo*) on both sides (*utroque*, line 298) of his adversary. Pollux "slips" (*subeo*, lit. 'come under') between them (*hos inter Pollux subit*, line 299) and flies (*advolo*, line 300) at his grim (*trux* opponent's face (*ora*).[329]

Valerius allows one blemish to appear on Pollux' boxing record. Though his hope (*spes*, line 300) was presumably to drive his gauntlets into Amycus' face, both fists (*manus*) fall

---

[325] Elsewhere in epic poetry, we have seen boxers' hands compared to lightning.

[326] The Flavian Amycus, perhaps conceived by the poet in relation to Stoic theory, manifests a "self-destructive ... vulnerability to anger" (Antoniadis 2017, p. 177).

[327] Alcidamas, a boxer in Statius' depiction of epic pugilism, "grew pale at [his own] success" at a certain moment during the match (*Thebaid* 6.805). Amycus' alarm, dismay, or fear in the Valerian *Argonautica* may have a similar etiology.

[328] "Seneca [in *De Ira*] devotes considerable space to demonstrate that anger is by no means necessary in order to carry out virtuous deeds and exemplify one's courage or bravery. His reference to the irrevocable effects of rage seems to be fully confirmed in Valerius' account of the boxing match at Bebrycia. Against Amycus who is hurling himself in helpless rage ..., Pollux' self-control and imperturbability now seem to bear Stoic connotations" (Antoniadis 2017, p. 174).

[329] The term *ultro*, 'on the other side' is used in this passage (line 299) but it is not evident in Mozley's translation.

(*cado*) on the other man's chest (*in pectus*). Even the son of Jupiter does not have perfect aim. Enraged (*sævio*) at this affront, Amycus punches (*ago*) "at random" (*inconsultus*, lit. 'unasked, not consulted', line 302), striking nothing but air (*vacua aura*, plural). Discerning (*sentio*, line 303) that Amycus is at this point 'wanting reason' (*rationis egens*),[330] Pollux makes his move: he sets his knee (*genu*) close (*jungo*)[331] and "presents his side" (*do ... latus*). This is strong evidence that Roman-era pugilists angled their bodies to reduce the area that an opponent could strike, a fundamental posture in modern sport boxing, as well.

Pollux pours out (*effundo*) punishment and follows (*sequor*) his opponent, preventing him from recovering his position (*revoco gradum*). He makes an uproar (*turbo*, line 305) and presses (*premo*, line 305) his opponent repeatedly (*creber*) "in his perplexity" (*anceps*, lit., 'one who has two heads', line 306). Pollux heaps together (*congero*) blows from above (*desuper*) and from behind (*aversus*). In the general mayhem, it appears Amycus has turned his back on his opponent and will suffer a lethal penalty for this improvident move. The blows (*ictus*) are delivered at will (*liber*), suggesting that Amycus can no longer defend himself or offer any resistance. The giant's head is bowed (*vertex ... inclinis*, lines 307–308) and like a drum it reverberates (*sono*) "with all manner of wounds" (*vulnus*). The haughty son of Neptune "sinks beneath [*cedo*] the punishment [*mala*, line 308]." His temples stream (*mano*) with blood and his ears are hidden (*lateo*, line 309) in gore (*sanguineus*). At last, a heavy blow with the right hand (*dextera gravis*) loosens or releases (*solvo*, line 311) the "vital bond" (*vitalis vinculum*) the cervical joint (*cervix*). This is, evidently, a rabbit punch delivered to the back of Amycus' head. While outlawed in modern sport boxing,[332] this punch appears to have been perfectly acceptable in Valerius' time: The punch is thrown by the hero, after all.[333]

As Amycus slides (*labor*, line 311), Pollux knocks (*propello*) him to the ground (another rather ungentlemanly maneuver). Exultant, the son of heaven stands over his opponent (*super insisto*, line 312) and thunders:

> ...'Pollux ego missus Amyclis
> et Iove natus' ait; 'nomen mirantibus umbris
> hoc referes: sic et memori noscere sepulchro' (lines 312–314)

"Pollux am I, who hail from Amyclæ and am born of Jove; this name shalt thou bear down to the wondering shades; thus shall it be told of thee on thy recording tomb." No epic boxing match is as explicitly concerned with the world of the dead as the Valerian *Argonautica*. The spirits came to watch the fisticuffs and Pollux sends Amycus back with them, insulting him further by proclaiming that even Amycus' tombstone will bear the adversary's name.

A few lexical considerations from the story's denouement are worth our attention. Pollux' hand is said to have warded off (*arceo*, line 317) Amycus from his ambition. This verb

---

[330] The phrase may refer to Amycus being punch-drunk, too enraged to think rationally, or perhaps both.

[331] We suspect this means that he brings his knee close to the knee of his adversary.

[332] Referees are alert to warn boxers who turn their backs on their opponents and to stop the action when the fighters do so. This makes strikes to the back of a boxer's head relatively uncommon. Though a hook may still land (with considerably less force) at this site, a straight punch to the back of the head is vanishingly rare in the modern ring.

[333] Though the death blow is demonstrably vicious, the Valerian boxing match is nevertheless regarded as "symboliz[ing] the triumph of civilized art over brutal archaic force" (Deremetz 2014, p. 64). Has Pollux not become something of a monster in the way he defeats Amycus? Valerius' original audience presumably had no such qualms about the Tyndarean character.

may have been associated with defensive tactics in Roman-era boxing. Poignantly, Amycus desired "youth's enduring vigour" (*vis juventæ continua*, lines 318–319) like many boxers past their prime. Outstretched (*tendo*) on the field, the son of Neptune, "'that vast terror of men" (*ingens hominum pavor*, line 320) is compared to "a portion of ... Eryx" (*pars Erycis*, line 322), a reference to the semi-divine patron of the Æneidean boxing match and a formidable boxer during his life. Pollux cannot get enough (*expleo*, line 323) of the physical emblem of his victory, "the huge prostrate mass " (*moles jacentis*, line 322) lying before him. The son of Jove marvels at his opponent's body from close at hand (*comminus*, line 324).[334] Once more, this detail may have been taken from the Roman arena, where the victor's visible response to the corpse of his fallen opponent likely made for a compelling tableau.

Pollux' comrades "throng him" (*urgeo*, 325) and give him "emulous embraces" (*densus ... amplexus*, ablative, line 325). They carry (*ferro*) his gauntlets (*arma*) and "raise his weary arms" (*attollo palmas*, lit. hands, line 326). A version of this gesture of victory is repeated in the modern ring when the referee holds aloft the hand of the prevailing boxer.[335] The myrmidons cry, "Hail, true offspring, ay, true offspring indeed of Jove [*vera Iovis ... proles*, line 327]!" They continue, "Hurrah for Taygetus [i.e., Sparta], renowned for great-hearted wrestling-schools [*magnanima ... palæstra*, line 328], and for the fruitful lessons (*felix labor*, line 329) of thy earliest teachers [*magister*, line 329]!" Given the context, we see no reason why *palæstra* should not be translated as 'boxing gym' in modern English and *magister* as 'coach'.

In the aftermath, a thin (*tenuis*, line 330) stream (*cruor*, plural) of blood flows (*eo*) down Pollux' forehead (*frons*). Unfazed, the hero dries (*sicco*, line 332) the wound (*vulnus*) with the back of his glove (*aversus cæstus*, ablative).[336] Using the same verb for plaiting (*implico*, line 334) employed earlier to describe wrapping the hands with the *cæstus*, Valerius writes that Castor entwines his brother's head and his weapons (*arma*, line 333) with leaves of the laurel tree. While placing a garland on the head of the victor is hardly novel, we are unaware of another reference to this festive treatment of the *cæstus* itself. After a brief prayer to the goddess requesting a safe return home,[337] the sailors slaughter (*cædo*, 337) "with strong axe" (*valida ... bipennis*, line 337, ablative) steers (*armentum*, plural of the herd). The verb characterizing the sacrifice, *cædo*, has the same root as the boxing gauntlets, *cæstus*. Valerius surely recognized in the gauntlets instruments of laceration and cutting, as well as striking. His readers may also have connected them to sacrifice, remembering the events that close the Æneidean boxing match.

Having made their offering of blood, the Argonauts bathe, (*perfundo*) "in the sacred water" (*sacer ... gurges*, line 338) of a river (*amnis*, ablative, line 338) that they have appeased (*placo*, line 338), suggesting that their religious observances were directed towards a river deity. Next they lie down (*sterno*, line 339) upon the grassy ground (*gramineus humus*), perhaps

---

[334] This term is used elsewhere to refer to hand-to-hand combat, line 324.

[335] Boxers will occasionally hold both hands aloft unaided when introduced in their corner or shortly before a decision while standing in the center of the ring, to indicate a presentiment of victory—or a sympathetic magic in hope of it.

[336] The absorptive qualities of the fleece lining of the Roman *cæstus* will be more explicitly drawn out by Statius (Section 3.4.2).

[337] Castor prays that the "foliage" (*frons*) and the garland (*corona*, line 336) "speed over the sea." The term *frons* 'leafy branch' is homonymous, at least in the nominative, with 'forehead', a term referenced in the immediately preceding lines. The religious significance of this prayer, and the vegetal decoration of the *cæstus* is worthy of closer inspection.

to rest, perhaps in emulation of the fallen Amycus. During a sacrificial feast (*daps* line 339), they place *libum* 'cakes' (line 339) "upon leaves" and give the best cuts of meat (*tergum ... pecudum*) to Pollux. We note that the noun *terga* is used elsewhere to refer to the *cæstus*.

During this solemn banquet, Pollux exults (*ovo*, line 342) with joy (*lætus*) at the praise (*laus*) directed towards him and at the honoring song (*carmen*) of the bard or soothsayer (*vates*, line 342). Two times he pours out (*gemino*)[338] a krater, presumably filled with wine, to his victorious (*victor*) father (*parens*, line 343). The celebrants turn their attention to the true winner of the boxing match, viz., Jove himself. While the purpose of these devotions, rich in detail, are not entirely clear, we speculate based on Valerius' abundant wordplay that they are closely related to the boxing match and draw rich, anagogical parallels between the shedding of human and taurine blood; between the *cæstus* and the flesh of the living bull; and between human and animal sacrifice.

Valerius' "access to Seneca's *De Ira* gives him a framework that is distinctly Roman, imperial and post-Vergilian" (Antoniadis 2017, p. 178). The boxing match of this *Argonautica* partakes of ritual (through Amycus' foul intent), athletic (through Pollux's display of ἀρετή), and gladiatorial elements, a fitting laurel for the tale of boxing in late classical antiquity.

3.4   *Thebaid* 1, 6

The *Thebaid*, a brooding and at times unhinged reflection on the moral and military perils of civil war,[339] was composed in hexameter by the Roman poet Statius and published in the last decade of the first century AD. Though deeply influenced by both Homer and Vergil, Statius should be regarded as far "more than a second-rate or maladroit plagiarist" (Vessey 2010, p. 2).[340] His work lay in the penumbra of the *Æneid* throughout antiquity but the *Thebaid* was much admired and studied during the Middle Ages when it was translated into a variety of languages and richly illustrated.

Statius' epic contains two episodes of unarmed orthograde combat. The first, a rixation between two princes down on their luck, is arguably not boxing at all but is perhaps close enough to merit our attention. It has much in common with the fistfight in *Odyssey* 18. The second, a reconstitution of Homeric funereal boxing familiar to Statius from both the *Iliad* and the *Æneid*, is unquestionably relevant to our theme. While considered derivative by some, the boxing match in *Thebaid* 6 is rendered with a realism and attention to detail likely distilled through Statius' intimate familiarity with the arena of his day (Grimal 1994, pp. 448–454).

3.4.1   Polynices vs. Tydeus, Thebaid 1

In Book 1 of Statius' *Thebaid*, the exiled princes Tydeus[341] and Polynices[342] engage in a grim unarmed fight that contains some elements of boxing, though it arguably veers into the realm

---

[338] This verb designates a repeated but non-specific action.

[339] One critic has called the *Thebaid*, "[A]n apocalyptic relocation of Roman epic tradition within the framework of ancient Greek civil strife" (König 2005, p. 239).

[340] Legras (1905), for example, dismissively (and incorrectly, *nos iudice*) describes most of the Thebaidic boxing match as an imitation of Vergil.

[341] Tydeus is the father of Diomedes, the 'second' to Euryalus in the Iliadic boxing match. Tydeus was also reportedly the first inexpugnate boxer of the Nemean Games (Apollodorus 3.6).

[342] Because the central conflict of the *Thebaid* is between the two sons of Œdipus, Polynices and Eteocles, the contest between Polynices and Tydeus is arguably "a venting of fratricidal rage on the substitute [Tydeus] who, like

of Greek *pankration* as well. In other words, it is an unarmed brawl but the opponents appear to remain mostly upright. If we force a comparison between the epic boxing matches and whatever takes place in *Thebaid* 1, then the latter most closely evokes the encounter between Odysseus and the beggar Iros in *Odyssey* 18. Indeed, both wandering princes in the *Thebaid* are homeless, so the bout in that poem is suggestive of what might have happened had Odysseus met his match in Iros. The fight between the two vagrant princes is sloppy and violent; its baseness is almost comical, were the contest not so grisly. The fight includes knees to the groin and eye-gouging, in addition to the usual mixing it up expected in an epic boxing match.[343] According to one commentator, "There is no obvious reason for this event; the passion is irrational and sudden" (Vessey 2010, p. 95).[344]

Contending over "a dry place to sleep on the doorsill of the palace of Argos" (Bonds 1985, p. 225), Tydeus and Polynices are driven into a bloody rage against each other: *ambobus rabiem … cruentam | adtulit …* (lines 408–409).[345] As in the central conflict of the *Thebaid*, it is not the prize that matters so much as "the sheer urge for domination" (ibid., p. 233). Polynices and Tydeus "tarry with exchange of threatening words" until their "taunts swelled [*intumesco*] their anger to the pitch [*satis*]" they stood up, bared their shoulders (*exserto umeros*), and challenged (*lacessere*) each other "to naked combat" (*nuda … pugna*).[346] The reference to bared shoulders (line 413) is most likely a reminiscence of the scene in *Odyssey* 18 in which Odysseus casts off his cloak to reveal his massive deltoid muscles. Given that it is the only part of the body that is explicitly bared during the boxing, we might infer that the Thebaidic combatants were stripped only to the waist, though the phrase *nuda pugna* (line 414) may be tautegorical. It is likely consistent with the late Roman *imaginaire* of how two ancient Greek nobles might have duked it out *al fresco*. The "Theban" (Polynices) is "taller … with long stride [*gradus procerus*] and similarly (long) limbs [*membra simulque*]." Though possessed of a bold spirit (*virtus*), Tydeus has the smaller frame (line 417).

The two princes throw punches (*ictus*) 'in close', 'repeatedly' or 'thick' (*creber*) at each other's 'hollow temples' (*cavus temporus*), suggesting hooks or haymakers. However, the blows are described as "showers of darts [*telus*]" or "Rhipæan hail [*grando*]," perhaps indicating staight paths of motion, vertical and horizontal. Line 420 *…flexoque genu vacua ilia fundunt* suggests they "pound" (*fundo*, lit., 'pour out') on each other in the "unprotected loins" (*vacua ilia*) with their bent knees (Shackleton Bailey 2004).

Statius then draws a provocative analogy between the fighters and ceremonial competi-

his brother [Eteocles], threatens to usurp his [Polynices'] place" (Bonds 1985, p. 227). Polynices, "the expression of a monstrous family," is "[f]aced with the unnatural craving for related blood which is his inheritance" (Bonds 1985, p. 235). Fratricidal rage and its society-level embodiment, civil war, lie at the dark heart of the *Thebaid*.

[343]Unlike an epic boxing match, the duel between Polynices and Tydeus is "devoid of any fighter's art" (Bonds 1985, p. 231). The fight has been described as "natural, mundane, without psychological overtones" (ibid.). We do not agree with the last descriptor. The savage baseness of the fight says much about the psychology of the two fighters, erstwhile noblemen of their respective kingdoms reduced to fighting like mendicants in the street. Statius' gritty scene, with its shiftless bare-knuckle boxers, reminds us of Charles Bronson's film "Hard Times" (1975), in which the main character's brutal occupation belies his dignified, if mysterious, origins.

[344]Another critic has observed that it is "easy to see the fight as arising from the madness of Polynices" (Lovatt 2001, p. 109fn. 16). The encounter may have been designed to demonstrate the irrationality of the fighting spirit—an urge that arises from neither a social affront nor the enticement of a prize, but from a much deeper atavistic impulse. Polynices, like his modern brethren of the ring, need not be 'mad' to find themselves so transported.

[345]Line numbers and translations in this section come from Mozley (1928a) unless otherwise indicated.

[346]Some prefer *unda* 'wave, billow' to *nuda*—an orthographic tangle, no doubt—but this is almost certainly a corruption, given the context.

tors, gathered at the end of a "lustral term" to honor Jupiter, the Thunderer, with their agon (lines 421–426). Their mothers are excluded from the place of combat, waiting for their sons to carry home the prizes:

> Even as when his lustral terms return to the Pisæan Thunderer and the dust warms [*ardeo*] with the crude sweat [*crudus sudor*] of men—but yonder the discord of the crowd [*caveae dissensus*] spurs on [*concito*] the tender youths [*ephebus*] and their excluded mothers wait for the prizes [*praemium*] (Shackleton Bailey 2004).

Just as lively (*alacer*) as such striplings, though inspired by hate (*odium*) instead of any desire for athletic glory (*cupido laudis*), the princes attack (*incurro*) each other. There is no audience, there are no "excluded mothers," there is no significant prize—just a bloody fight between two vagrants.[347]

Then things gets ugly. "The sharp nails probe [*scrutor*, line 426] far into their faces and force their way into the yielding eyes." Surprisingly, the poet explains, the two bruisers had "swords girt [*accingo*, line 428] to their sides" the whole time. Perhaps the poet conceived of this battle as a simulacrum to a combat sport, hence the allusion to ceremonial games. How common was it for men of Statius' time to engage each other in such a bloody combat without drawing even those swords they had at their disposal? Perhaps it was a tradition stretching back at least to Suetonius' account of boxing *sine arte* in the backstreets of Rome during the first century (*Aug.* 45.2).

The Argive king, Adrastus, awoken by the boys' "clamor and the fierce panting groans deep-heaved [... *pectore ab alto* | *stridentes gemitus* ..., lines 431–432]," stumbles from his bed to the site of their agon. There he beholds "a sight terrible to tell, faces torn [*lacero*] and cheeks disfigured [*putreo*] with streaming blood [*sanguineus ... imber*, line 438]."[348] Adrastus interrogates this "fury [*furor*]"[349] and the "implacable desire [*implacabalis ardor*] to let your hate [*odium*] disturb [*exturbo*] the tranquil silence of the night." The king seems more disconcerted by the fact that the fight is taking place at night than that it is taking place at all: "Has then the day so little room ...?" Next he asks, "[W]hat may be your quarrel [*iurgium*, line 444]? Mean of soul ye cannot be—such anger [*ira*] proves it—even through bloodshed [*effundo ... cruor*, line 446] the noble signs of proud race show clear."[350]

There are no explicit tokens of pronograde combat in the fight between Polynices and Tydeus: no reference to grappling on the ground; no grasping, seizing, choking or throwing.[351] The formal differences between this fight and the one between Iros and Odysseus are the lack of a loincloth (the Thebaidic combatants are most likely naked), the bent-knee strikes to the "unprotected loins," and the eye-gouging. We believe that Statius had in mind a kind of Roman boxing that is not adequately described in texts, but is amply attested in

---

[347] Bonds (1985) explains that the climactic battle between the brothers Polynices and Eteocles takes place in front of a large gathering and with a more substantial prize at stake, viz., the kingdom of Thebes. The proemial bout between Polynices and Tydeus foreshadows and contrasts with it, he argues.

[348] *lacera ora putresque* | *sanguineo videt imbre genas* (lines 437–438).

[349] Vessey (2010, p. 96) equates *furor* with "the insatiable madness of beasts."

[350] *... quae iurgia? nam vos* | *haud humiles tanta ira docet, generisque superbi* | *magna per effusum clarescunt signa cruorem* (lines 444–446).

[351] Polynices is represented as a lion, Tydeus as a boar, in an oracle in which Apollo predicts Adrastus' future sons-in-law (lines 395–397). These animal representations do not, *nos iudice*, make either a boxing or wrestling scenario any more likely.

figurative art and which his audience would have recognized: the boxing match with sharp projections on the *cæstus* (cf. Figures 18, 19, 11, among others). Statius seems to allude to at least one function of these projections—removing the eyes—but makes it clear that is it is the nails of the hand (*unca manus*, line 427) that do the dirty work in *Thebaid* 1.[352] Statius highlights the vulnerability of the eyes in unarmed combat, something that generations of fighters (including gloved boxers) seem to intuit naturally (Thomas 1997) and upon which the Romans appear to have capitalized.[353]

Their *mauvais quart d'heure* concluded, the two princes are eventually reconciled and married to the daughters of the Argive king. But their status as mere brothers-in-law cannot account for Polynices' emotional unraveling when he attempts suicide out of grief for Tydeus' death much later in the narrative.[354] The fraternal bond forged between Tydeus and Polynices is a direct outcome of their nasty fight in *Thebaid* 1. As Adrastus observes, "[The fight] that has passed is not in vain, nor were the gods elsewhere" (Shackleton Bailey 2004).[355] The old king goes on to prophesy that their wrath [*ira*] will turn to strong friendship [*amor*]. The fact that devoted brothers may be born in an unarmed match like this one is mirrored and rendered ironic when Polynices and his biological brother Eteocles succeed in killing one another in an (armed) fight at the conclusion of the poem.

3.4.2 Capaneus vs. Alcidamas, Thebaid 6

In Book 6 of Statius' *Thebaid*, we encounter nearly one hundred lines in dactylic hexameter dedicated to a boxing match (6.729–825)[356] Thuillier (1996) has argued for the influence of contemporary "sporting reality" on Statius' presentation of athletic competition, including boxing; he notes that Statius' epic is "imprinted" by first-century athletic practice (p. 167).[357] Having reviewed many examples of epic boxing, we have a good idea of what to expect. Yet some details still surprise:

- The nudity of at least one of the boxers is strongly suggested.
- Pollux is the divine patron/trainer of one of the boxers.
- Something akin to a face-off occurs before the action starts.
- Slipping is described as quickly and nimbly 'nodding' the head.
- The boxers wear sheepskin or fleece on their arms.
- The interval between rounds seems to start and end with a signal.
- The boxing 'ring' is designated as *arvum* 'ploughed land'.
- The fight ends preëmptively, leaving one fighter denying his own victory and threatening his rival with morthdeed.

---

[352] Eye-gouging was a common technique in North American "rough and tumble" dueling through at least the nineteenth century (Gorn 1985).

[353] Vessey (2010, p. 95) has remarked that the reference to eye-gouging also "points back at once to Œdipus" and is "generically linked to [his] turbulent passions."

[354] Polynices' attempted suicide is prevented by his father-in-law (9.76–81).

[355] *non haec incassum divisque absentibus acta* (line 471).

[356] Line numbers and translations from the *Thebaid* in this section come from Mozley (1928a) unless otherwise indicated.

[357] "On peut donc penser que Stace était très proche de cet univers sportif, qu'il a pu être amené à suivre de près des compétitions et que ces circonstances ont finalement laissé leur empreinte sur une épopée que était à priori très éloignée de l'Urbs du 1er siècle."

While the Argive army is delayed at Nemea, a local child named Opheltes dies, struck by the tail of a gigantic and apparently clumsy serpent that protects the sanctuary of Nemean Jupiter: *occidis extremæ destrictus verbere caudae | ignaro serpente puer* ... (lines 5.538–539).[358] The child, who was the son of the priest Lycurgus, is buried "in an elaborate ceremony that serves as the founding moment of the Nemean games" (McNelis 2007, p. 91).[359] These games, described in *Thebaid* 6, include a boxing match in the tradition of the *Iliad*.

Capaneus and Alcidamas are among the last in a long series of contestants to enter the boxing 'ring' of epic poetry. Capaneus looms large in the *Thebaid* and other ancient sources as a character notorious for his procacity.[360] Capaneus seems a variation on the theme of Amycus; his description suggests a giant and his final, doomed-from-the-beginning show-down with Jupiter in Book 10 suggests a titan (Franchet d'Espèrey 1999, p. 198–203). A contemptuous blasphemer of the gods, including supernal Jupiter, Capaneus meets his end in a Jovian fulmination (10.295).[361] Before that event, however, Statius' audience gets to see him box.

Pugilism at funeral games requires a master of ceremonies. In the *Thebaid*, this role is filled by King Adrastus, the separator of princely boxers in Book 1. Just like his earliest literary forerunner, Achilles, the son of Talaus announces the boxing, which he describes sparingly as the 'work of wrath' (*opus ... animis*).[362] He calls for men to raise (*tollo*) the dangerous *cæstus* (*infestus cæstus*, plural) in close or 'hand-to-hand' combat (*comminus*). He further remarks that the manliness (*virtus*) boxing requires is close to the kind required for warfare (*bellum et ferrum*, line 730). The juxtaposition of war and boxing—the martial and athletic—is arguably a theme of great importance to Statius and his Late Antique audience.

A megalith of a man (*immanis cerni immanisque*, line 731), Capaneus first agrees (*consto*) to put on (*induo*) the *cæstus*, which are described as 'coverings of raw hide' (*tegmina cruda boum*) made black with lead (*nigrantia plumbo*, lines 732–733). This is presumably Statius' way of telegraphing that pieces of lead were stitched into the straps, as made more explicit in *Æneid* 5.405. However, the reference is generic enough that it may mean that lead, perhaps in strips, provided an extra layer. Such devices are pictured, for example, in a number of Gallo-Roman mosaics depicting Dares, Entellus, and the Bull (Figures 24, 9), described by Budrovich (2011).

According to one commentator, "Capaneus enters with the express intention of killing" (Vessey 2010, p. 222). This is exhibited by the giant's demand that he fight an Aonian (i.e., Theban)[363] adversary, someone he could lawfully murder (*fas demitto leto*). As an Argive

---

[358] There may be here a connection to the Pythian Games, celebrated in honor of Apollo's "cosmogonic victory" over Python (McNelis 2007, p. 94).

[359] If the Iliadic funeral games were, as one critic supposes, intended to exemplify the "enduring friendship" of Achilles and Patroclus and Achilles' "resolved anger," the Thebaidic celebration fails in this regard: The brothers Eteocles and Polynices still kill one another, despite the presence of the games in Statius' narrative (McNelis 2007, p. 157).

[360] According to Æschylus, Capaneus carried a shield embossed with the figure of an unarmored man withstanding fire, bearing a torch, with the inscribed vow, "I will burn the city."

[361] "Capaneus is best likened to legendary rebels against Jupiter, symbols of a chaotic force now tamed by celestial power" (Vessey 2010, p. 223). There is a hint of Capaneus' electrified future in Statius' reference on lines 751–752 to the boxers' *fulmineas ... manus* (ibid., p. 222).

[362] The noun *animus* is here in the plural, suggesting the provocative variant 'work of souls'. Both Mozley (1928a) and Lesuer (1991) translate *animus* here as 'courage'.

[363] Given Statius' general interest in the theme of civil war, it is perhaps not surprising that Capaneus demands a Theban opponent so that conflict between countrymen may be averted (lines 735–737). His eventual opponent, a

(line 732), Capaneus could avoid blood guilt by boxing (to the death) a member of a different tribe; his *virtus* would remain in tact so long as it "were not stained with kindred blood": *nec mea crudelis civili sanguine virtus* (line 737).[364] According to one commentator, Capaneus "wants to drag the games into the arena of war," which is arguably Statius' intention, as well (Lovatt 2001, p. 111).

The crowd is "aghast" (*obtipesco*), in fact stricken with fear (*fecitque silentia terror*, line 738) by the hulk baying for an opponent to meet him at the scratch.[365] At last a heleth named Alcidamas leaps forward (*prosilio*) from among the naked Spartans (*nuda de plebe Laconum*), a phrase suggesting Alcidamas, too, finds himself in the buff. We learn that Alcidamas was tutored in boxing by none other than Pollux, that semi-divine galactico of pugilism known to the Greeks as Polydeuces. Moreover, he was raised in 'holy gymnasia' (*sacras ... palæstras*, line 742), i.e., those associated with the divine twins. Pollux placed (*pono*) the hands of Alcidamas, teaching him to assume the correct gestures and throw punches the right way. He "molded" (*fingo*, lit. 'form by instruction' also, 'adorn', e.g., with the *cæstus*) his arms. Much later in the epic, when Alcidamas dies, we learn that he was in fact "the first on whom Pollux fastened [*ligo*] the *cæstus*."[366] Pollux urged (*suadeo*) his charge in love (*amor*) of the "sport" (*materia*, lit. 'material'). A more modern reading, exemplified by the translation of Shackleton Bailey (2004, fn. 82) surmises that *materia* refers to Alcidamas' own body and thus makes him the object of the god's lust.[367] Pollux appears to have sparred with Alcidamas, i.e., 'putting (him) in close combat' (*loco comminus*) with him. In these sparring sessions, Pollux admires how his student is "caught up in like mood [viz., wrath]" (*simili stantem miratus in ira*, line 745), suggesting Alcidamas is learning to box with all the cunning and aggression of his teacher. After their exercises, they embrace in the state of undress common to ancient boxers.[368]

Lovatt (2005, p. 157) claims that the "passage emphasizes the erotics of pedagogy, reading boxing as lovemaking." However, modern boxers frequently embrace after sparring, particularly after a hard-fought match; a boxer does so with warm-heartedness (cf. *exsulto*, line 746) rather than amorous intent towards his opponent. Naturally, this embrace takes place with the fighters clothed (or unclothed) as they were during the bout.[369] As we have demon-

---

Spartan, was allied with the Argives agains Thebes but still represented a heritage distinct from that of Capaneus.

[364] The adjective *crudelis* (line 737) is obelized by Garrod (1904) perhaps because 'cruel', 'fierce' and 'severe' do not match what translators of the era, including Mozley (1928a), believed Statius meant. Vessey (2010, p. 210) argues that the line should read: *ne mea crudescat civili sanguine virtus* 'lest my *virtus* grow violent with an ally's blood'. Another possibility is that Statius meant *crudus* 'raw', 'bloody', 'bleeding' but used *crudelis* for metrical purposes.

[365] Legras (1905, p. 88) notes that the initiation of the fight is similar across Homer, Vergil, and Statius. As in the *Iliad*, one contestant issues an orgulous challenge that inspires a terrified silence in the crowd. According to Legras, Capaneus is *plus insolent encore* than Iliadic Epeius (ibid.). Lovatt (2005, p. 141) aptly summarizes the proem to nearly all the epic boxing matches: "[A] champion issues a challenge in supreme confidence, and expectations are aroused."

[366] *... primis quem cæstibus ipse ligarat | Tyndarides ...* (10.500–501).

[367] While plausible in the context of classical *paideia*, such a (Roman) attitude stands in contrast to the Greek ethic as propounded by Philostratus in *Gymnasticus*, wherein he abjures any overlap of sexual interest with athletic excellence (*Gym.* 45, 48) (Reid 2016, pp. 79–80).

[368] Line 746 reads: *sustulit exsultans nudumque in pectora pressit* "Exultant Pollux lifted him naked against his chest" (translation ours).

[369] Modern boxers, usually professionals participating in fights with a large audience, will occasionally return to their corners before the announcement of a victor to don a t-shirt or baseball cap emblazoned with the logos of their sponsors. Their reasons for clothing themselves immediately at the conclusion of the fighting have little to do with modesty and much more to do with the economics of modern (professional) sport boxing.

strated elsewhere (Dioscurus and Dioscurus 2022d), in almost every ancient example, boxers wear only a loincloth or nothing at all. Statius' reference to a bare-chested embrace may simply highlight the author's knowledge of boxers' 'exultant' behavior in greeting one another after a match when they still happen to be stripped of clothing. To sexualize the post-fight greeting in Statius seems to us unnecessary and may tell us more about modern critics than ancient boxers.[370] Nor are we alone in our opinion—regarding line 744, Lesuer (1991, p. 151, n. 60) prefers glossing *materia* as *matière de son art* (sc., boxing) instead of his sparring partner's body, stating, "It seems preferable to us because boxing is the exercise in which Pollux excels" (translation ours).[371]

As noted by Vessey (2010, pp. 222–223), Capaneus sneers (*rideo*) at his rival, the story's *jeune premier*.[372] The same verb is used to describe how Alcidamas' comrades regard Capaneus at the end of the boxing match (line 825). Finally, *rideo* characterizes how Jupiter looks on the marauding Capaneus as he scales the heights of heaven in a blasphemous rage (10.907). "It is as if Capaneus wants competitors more worthy of his attention... His desire to win is so great that he seeks an impossible competition" (Lovatt 2001, p. 113). "Capaneus' madness in the games" is "inspired by his desire for more than victory, his desire to go beyond the normal context and achieve glory greater than manhood, forever to push out the boundaries of his world, to re-make his reality" (ibid., p. 115). Capaneus even demands another adversary (*posco alium*, line 748) before, at last, he and Alcidamas are forced to oppose one another (*tandemque coactus resto*). Statius offers a curious detail: Capaneus' "languid neck swells" due to the 'incitement' (*stimulus*, dative/ablative) of being set before his rival.[373] We imagine this scene depicting something like a modern face-off in boxing, when two fighters stare intently at each other at the center of the ring while they are given final instructions before the bell. They naturally puff out their chests, stand taller, etc., in an attempt to look more menacing. Whether the tumescence of Capaneus' neck was effected *mero motu* remains a mystery.

The fighters are "poised at their full height" (*alte suspensi corpora*, line 750) on the soles of their feet (*planta*, dative/ablative)[374] and lift up (*erigo*) their lightning-fast (*fulmineus*) hands. They remain at a distance from one another behind their weapons, viz., the *cæstus*: (... *procul ora recessu | armorum* ..., line 751-752).[375] They watch each other closely (*tueor ... in speculis*) and each forms a barrier against the blows of his opponent: Literally, they 'frustrate', 'delude', or 'deceive' (*eludo*) the other's 'entrance' (*aditus*) to injury (*vulnus*, line 752). The fight will be characterized, in the words of one commentator, "by a structure of sudden narrative reversals" (Lovatt 2005, p. 141).

Statius compares the fighters in lines 753–759. The "alarmingly brutish" Capaneus is the "embodiment of brute rage" and "bestial discord" (May 2016, p. 44). In the formulation of Mozley (1928a), he is "great in broad expanse of every limb and terrible in size of bone."

---

[370] We are unaware of a similarly inflected commentary on the post-fight kiss in the *Posthomerica*.

[371] *nous paraît préférable du fait que la boxe est l'exercice où Pollux excelle.*

[372] The relevant passage is *... ridetque vocantem | ut miserans ...* (lines 747–748).

[373] *stimulis iam languida colla tumescunt* (line 749).

[374] Lesuer (1991) places the fighters *sur la pointe de leurs pieds.*

[375] Hall (1992, p. 296) argues against *armorum* as a reference to the *cæstus*: "[T]he expression is strained, ... even for Statius, and I am much drawn to the idea of replacing *armorum* with *ulnarum*, a word very well suited to represent the cradling effect of the fighters' uplifted and extended arms." However, we noted earlier that Vergil may have used *arma* as a term for the boxing gauntlet, e.g., at *Æneid* 5.412, and the supremely injurious—indeed, weapon-like— nature of the Late Antique *cæstus* is also amply depicted in contemporary artwork.

Statius compares Capaneus to the giant Tityus (line 753), harking back to Theocritus, who compares Amycus to the same Stygian ogre (*Idyll* 2.94). Alcidamas, by contrast, is just a lad (*hic paulo ante puer*). Despite this, he has some quality (probably strength) of an ancient oak (*robur*) and "his youthful vigor gives promise of a mighty manhood" (*ingentes spondet tener impetus annos*, line 757). The audience, it seems, did not "wish to see [Alcidamas] defeated [*vinco*, passive] nor stained with cruel gore [*sanguini...tinguo*]." To avert such a conclusion was the object, we are told, of their supplications (*erigo ... voto*) to divine agency. By assimilating Capaneus to Amycus and Alcidamas to Polydeuces, Statius seems to suggest the battle is another example of gigantomachy—the eternal struggle between chaos and order, the duel between the chthonic and the heavenly (Deremetz 2011, p. 58).

The boxers measure (*permetior*) each other with their eyes, hoping for (*spero*) the first opening (*locus*, lit., 'place'). They fall to neither wrath (*ira*) nor blows (*ictus*) immediately: (*non protinus ira nec ictus*, line 761). Suspended in a state of mutual dread (*timor*), their fury (*furor*) is mingled (*misceo*) with deliberation (*consilium*).[376] Their contrary lower arms (*contrarius ... bracchium*) bend (*inclino*) by throwing (*iactus*, ablative) them, presumably against each other.[377] This activity, rarely seen in modern boxing, must have taken advantage of the densely wrapped material covering their forearms. We can imagine, for example, strikes and feints with the front forearm intended to distract from a blow delivered by the back fist. They search one another out (*exploro*) with their *cæstus*, obtunding the implements (*hebeto*) in the way they bear (*fero*) them. Mozley (1928a) discerns that the boxers "dull ... them with mere rubs" while Lesuer (1991) conjectures that they land *coups qui les émoussent* 'strikes that blunt them'. Much specificity is derived from the generic verb *fero*. The sense seems to be that the fighters threw relatively light blows at one another, perhaps glancing off their targets and thus figuratively 'dulling' the sharp edges of the *cæstus*. Unlike the sparring with forearms described directly before, this movement probably involves straight punches thrown from a greater distance.

Alcidamas' training (*doceo*) is such that he sets aside (*differo*) his fury (*animus*) and "takes thought for" (*metuo*) what will come next. He prudently delays (*cuncto*)[378] dispersing (*dispenso*) his energy (*vis*). Capaneus, on the other hand, is "prodigal of harm" (*nocendi prodigus*) and "reckless" (*incautus*, line 768). Heedless, he tumbles forward with all his force (*ruo omnis*), both his hands 'devouring' (*consumo*) without order (*sine lege*) and without consequence (*irritus*) to his adversary. Epic boxing is incomplete without some form of gnathic emanation (*frendo*); Capaneus satisfies this Homeric exigency on line 769. He lifts himself up (*insurgens*), pursues (*sequor*) his rival, and presses in (*premo*, line 770), all to little avail, it would appear. "The contest may be epitomized as one between *furor* and *prudentia*, between skill and brutish frenzy" (Vessey 2010, p. 222).

Plucky and provident (*providus*), Alcidamas is alert (*vigil*), exhibiting the adroitness (*astu*) of his fatherland. Here Statius reminds his audience that the Spartans were known

---

[376] *ternus paulum timor et permixta furori | consilia ...* (lines 762–763).

[377] From the barest of lexical evidence in lines 763–764, *... inclinant tantum contraria iactu | bracchia...*, Lesuer (1991) divines the verb *boxer* and Mozley (1928a) 'spar'.

[378] Much can be made of the verbal form *cunctatus*, which Hall (1992) notably applies to Capaneus, not Alcidamas (line 766). "Capaneus, being more experienced, husbands his strength at the outset of the fight. Most manuscripts give *cunctatus*, but the Puteaneus offers *cunctatur*, from which Bæhrens elicited *cunctator* ['one who delays'], thus generalizing about Capaneus' style of fighting. If, however, a particular tactic was here in Statius' mind, he might well have chosen to write *cunctanter* ['slowly']" (Hall 1992, p. 296). Like Polydeuces in his fight with Amycus, Alcidamas "conserves his energy with greater care" during the bout (Vessey 2010, p. 222).

for their vigilance and agility in the 'ring'. These are also attributes of Pollux/Polydeuces, himself late of Laconia, in his epic encounters with Amycus.[379] Sometimes Alcidamas hurls back (*reicio*) punches (*ictus*) and sometimes he is on guard (*caveo*, line 771). Occasionally he slips (*nutus*, ablative, lit. 'nod'), quickly and flexibly (*obsequium*, ablative) moving his head, unscathed (*integer*, line 772).

Now their hands meet (*obvio*) like missiles (*telum*) shattering (*discutio*, line 773) on impact. Mozley (1928a) sees in this action the 'parry' familiar to a modern boxer, whereby he strikes the adversary's hand just as it is about to connect. Statius' metaphor of exploding missiles is particularly innovative and appropriate for the context. One of the boxers (presumably Alcidamas, based on his agility and an upcoming reference made more explicitly to Capaneus) takes a step (*insto gressu*) and pulls his face backward (*recedo*).

Capaneus (the 'foe' *hostis*) musters up (*confero*) unequal force (*injusta vis*, line 774). The proof (*experientia*) of his brute strength (*vigor ingenio*) is in his right hand (*dextera*, line 775). While critics seem eager to chastise Capaneus for his arrogance, perhaps they would not want to tell him so to his face. He is courageous (*audax animis*) as he enters (*intro*) Alcidamas' guard (a noun for which there is no equivalent in the original passage). Capaneus overshadows (*obumbro*) and attacks (*adsilio*, line 777) from above, suggesting the powerful hammer blow we have surmised elsewhere in epic boxing.

Even though the latest punch is thrown by Capaneus, Statius weaves a simile that appears to compare Alcidamas to a wave (*unda*) leaping (*salio*) headlong (*præceps*) on a menacing (*minor*) rock, arguably a reference to Capaneus.[380] The simile is suggestive of how Alcidamas avoids the falling blow of his rival while landing a shot of his own. However, there are no references that make it explicit who is the rock and who the wave:

> Just as a mass of water hurls itself headlong [*præceps*] on a threatening rock, and falls back [*redeo*] broken [*frango*], so does he wheel round [*circumeo*] his angry foe, breaking his defence; look! he lifts[381] his hand and threatens a long time his face or side,[382] and thus by fear of his hard weapons [*rigida arma*] diverts [*avoco*, lit., 'call away'] his guard [*caveo*, accusative participle] and cunningly [*callidus*] plants [*intersero*] a sudden [*necopinus*, lit., 'unexpected'] blow, and marks [*designo*] the middle of his forehead with a wound [*vulnus*]; blood flows, and the warm stream [*rivus*, line 784] stains [*signo*] his temples (Mozley 1928a).

In this passage, we note the reference to the *cæstus* as 'hard weapons' (*rigida arma*). This may help clarify Vergil's used of the same noun to describe the *cæstus* in the *Æneid*. Forms of the verb *caveo* 'be on one's guard' are used to suggest a basic defensive position that by Late Antiquity apparently needed no further description. The verb *intersero* literally means 'sow in between'—perfectly suited to the context of landing a blow between another fighter's eyes.

---

[379] "Alcidamas is successful in his fight with Capaneus for the same reason that his *magister* Pollux was" (Vessey 2010, p. 222).

[380] Theocritus (*Idyll* 22.49) referred to Amycus' shoulders as boulders washed in a spring (Section 2.1).

[381] Hall (1992) replaces *leuat* with *læua* (sc. *manu*) 'left hand' on line 779 and *manibus* with *dextra* 'right hand' on line 781. He writes, "No one who has ever watched a boxing match can fail to recognize this picture: the fighter first jabs with his left so as to distract his opponent's attention, and then comes in suddenly with his right in the hope of a knockout" (Hall 1992, p. 297).

[382] Another translator approaches lines 779–782 differently, noting, "Alcidamas protects his face first" *Alcidamas protège son visage en priorité* (Lesuer 1991, p. 151, n. 61; translation ours).

This blow causes Capaneus to hemorrhage, though at first he is not aware of it. He "wonders at the sudden murmur of the crowd [*agmen*]" and learns of his wound only by "draw[ing] his weary hand across his face." The blood from his temple incarnadines the fleece (*vellus*, line 786) he is wearing on his arms. This reference to sheepskin (not "cowhide," *pace* Mozley 1928) is congruent with visual depictions of the arm-length Roman *cæstus* which are constructed in part out of a lumpy material that reaches up almost to the shoulder (cf. Figure 2).[383] The use of *vellus* in this context is evidence of how Statius projected features of the late Hellenistic and Roman boxing familiar to him onto the boxing of a bygone (Greek) era represented in the *Thebaid*.

Capaneus' reaction to discovering his own blood is anything but demure. Like a lion or tiger wounded (*indignor*) by a javelin (*iaculum*),[384] he drives (*ago*) Alcidamas "before him in headlong retreat [*retro*] over the whole field [*arvum*, line 788]." The location of the boxing match is described as an *arvum* or 'ploughed field'. This is reminiscent of Vergil's *æquor* but it is still hardly specific to a boxing 'ring'. Breaking with Homer's circumclusive 'midst of an assembly', Statius instead brings into focus the surface on which they contend. So vicious is the beating that Capaneus delivers, his opponent finds himself *in terga supinat* 'reclining on his back' (line 789).[385] For Statius—and presumably for boxing in his time—the lines between orthograde and pronograde combat had become blurred.

The boxer's teeth make 'harsh noises' (*dentibus horrendum strido*, line 790). Is this the sound of Capaneus grinding his teeth as he exerts his fury on his adversary (Mozley 1928a)? Perhaps it is the rattle of Alcidamas' teeth as they are knocked loose in his head. Statius restrains himself from clarifying, but the evocation of dental cacophony in boxing is as old as the *Iliad*. The aggressor swings (*roto*) his hands in repeated blows (*gemino...multiplico*). These incoming exertions simply 'hurry on' or 'snatch' (*rapio*) though the main verb seems to have no goal or object (*rapio conanima venti*). Some of the punches land (*cado*, line 792) on the *cæstus* of the adversary, a situation rendered more plausible if the poet understood the *cæstus* to extend from the hands to the shoulder, as we presume he did.

Alcidamas ("the Spartan"), with sharp movement (*motus ... acutus*) and the help of his feet (*auxilium ... pedum*, ablative), eludes (*caveo*) the thousand deaths (*mille ... mortes*) that glide (*labor*) around his hollow temples (*circum cava tempora*). Litotically, the poet persuades the reader that Alcidamas was "not unmindful of his art" (*non tamen immemor artis*, line 794). Though he fled, he kept fighting, meeting the adversary's blows with his own: *adversus fugit et fugiens tamen ictibus obstat* (line 795). Statius' recognition of boxing as *ars* is of particular note.

The next passage suggests something like an interval between rounds. This is not entirely without precedent: Amycus and Pollux pause, for example, in the *Argonautica* of Apollonius

---

[383]Lesuer (1991) omits any reference to the lanuginous portion of the gauntlet: *il vit des taches sur la surface du ceste*. This type of gauntlet may also be mentioned by Trebellius Pollio in the *Historia Augusta, Life of Gallienus* (8.3) where it is called *flacculis*—perhaps a misspelled version of several other proposed forms (Scanlon 1986). A clearer reference to fleece as part of a boxing glove comes from Philostratus the Athenian's *Heroicus* (p. 668), where a boxer named Plutarch uses the κώδια 'fleece (diminutive)' as a sponge to soak up rainwater during a particularly exhausting match.

[384]The javelin in this context recalls how Nonnus referred to the offensive hand in boxing as a 'spear' (λόγχη) and may be evidence that Statius here alludes to a particularly lethal form of the *cæstus* equipped with spikes (cf. Figure 17).

[385]In a modern boxing match, such a posture would never be permitted. It is more congruent with a mixed martial arts bout, where a man may be beaten even while he lies on the ground.

(Dioscurus and Dioscurus 2022d). They seem to do so out of exhaustion, as do the boxers in Statius.[386] Their strengths wane: one pursues (*premo*) slowly, and the other fails to escape (*absisto*) swiftly. Their knees give out (*deficio*) and at last they rest (*quiesco*). The adherescent simile (lines 799–801) gives a suggestion—however oblique—that Late Antique boxing may have incorporated, if not an interval between rounds, then at least a goad to renew the violence:

> Thus when long wandering o'er the sea [*æquor*] has wearied [*lasso*] the mariners, the signal [*signum*] is given from the stern and they rest their arms awhile [*pono parumper bracchia*]; but scarce have they taken repose [*requies*], when another cry [*vox*] summons [*cito*] them to the oars again (Mozley 1928a).

Statius' thalassic *imaginaire* is more suited to the ancient boxing context than it may first appear to the casual reader. We noted earlier (Section 2.1) that Theocritus used the term πίτυλος to refer to a barrage of punches in *Idyll* 22. The same term was used by Euripides to characterize the motion of oars on a ship. It is also significant that Statius uses the term *æquor* as a reference to the sea, the sailors' field of play, since Vergil employs the same term for the boxing 'ring' in Sicily. The voice accersing the combatants to the agon is like that of the coxswain calling to his rowers. In this *vox citans* we may hear the first sound reminiscent of a boxing bell and the first literary suggestion that the interstices between rounds is never sufficient to find rest.

One of the boxers, evidently Capaneus, makes a "furious dash" (*immodice venio*, line 802) for the second time. Alcidamas engages in a bit of treachery by lowering (*ruo*) his shoulder in such a way that he buries (*mergo*) it into the oncoming Capaneus, who forthwith takes a tumble on his head (*effundo ... in caput*).[387] As if the "ignominy" of Capaneus' fall is not enough (Hall 1992, p. 297),[388] while struggling back to his feet (*assurgo*), Alcidamas—that 'shameless boy' (*puer improbus*)—strikes his rival again (*ictu percello*), evidence that Late Antique boxers, like modern professional wrestlers, had no interest in the neutral-corner rule. In one of Mozley's more evocative turns of phrase, Alcidamas "himself grew pale at [his] success" (*impallesco secundo*, line 805).

The Inachians (to wit, a general ethnonym for the Greeks that could include the Argive supporters of Capaneus as well as those of the Spartan Alcidamas) raise shouts (*clamorem ... tollo*) *inconnues des rivages et des bois* (Lesuer 1991). The ethnic ambiguity of the term 'Inachian' leaves it unclear whether they jeer Capaneus for his fall or reprove Alcidamas for his

---

[386] "And now both are wearied with the toil and their exhausted panting" *Et iam utrumque labor suspiriaque aegra fatigant* (line 796).

[387] The labyrinthine syntax of the passage permits at least one other interpretation, though we find it much less satisfactory: *Alcidamas déjoue l'attaque et lui échappe en se précipitant à terre, la tête enfoncée dans les épaules* "Alcidamas thwarts the attack and escapes it by rushing to the ground, his head buried in his shoulders" (Lesuer 1991, translation ours). Another commentator similarly argues that Alcidamas does not rush, but drops "with his head tucked into his shoulders; Capaneus goes right over the top of him, falling head first, and as he gets up, is felled *alio...ictu*. Not at all surprisingly, Mozley was troubled by *alio ictu*, which he tried vainly to defend" with the argument that Capaneus' fall was in fact the first blow (Hall 1992, p. 297). Mozley "would have done much better to resort to one of the easiest of all emendations, *alto* for *alio*," suggesting the blow came from above (ibid.). The author also suggests *expalluit* for *impalluit*. We find this unnecessary since both verbs signify the subject growing pale, though Hall's suggestion does appear to enjoy greater lexical frequency.

[388] We note that a tumble during a boxing match usually results in a psychological disadvantage to the boxer who has fallen. He knows that the crowd knows he has suffered a setback, and this may force him to change his approach, perhaps improvidently, out of wounded pride.

dirty trick. Indeed, it could be both. Capaneus "struggl[es] from the ground" (*ab humo conor*, line 907), raising up his hands (*tollo manus*) and "intent on hideous deeds" in Mozley's (1928) translation. Lesuer (1991) makes Capaneus' intent more explicit: he is *prêt à une vengeance intolérable*. Statius is rather conservative on this point, characterizing Capaneus merely as *non toleranda parantem* 'prepared for the intolerable'. Nor deeds, nor intents, nor vengeance are mentioned explicitly by the poet. We pause to take note of Capaneus' gesture. Were his hands raised to deliver a deadly hammer-strike? What in his gesture may have suggested the 'intolerable' to the Late Antique reader? In any event, according to Lovatt (2001, p. 112), "It is the wound to Capaneus' pride, caused by Alcidamas' successful knockdown blow, that sends him over the edge."

Royal Adrastus, seeing Capaneus thus eschaufed, declares him mad (*furo/furio*) and calls for the boxers' right hands (*dextera*) to be lowered (*oppono*, line 809).[389] This unassuming detail, overlooked in the translations of both Mozley and Lesuer, suggests that the right hand was considered more injurious. As if to soothe the savage breast, the king calls for "the palm and the prizes" (*palma ... et præmium*) to be distributed immediately. He believes that the dread giant will not otherwise desist (*absisto*) until he breaks (*effringo*) the skull and mixes (*misceo*) the brains of the "doomed [*moriturum*] Laconian[.]" With his talk of brittle skulls and mucilaginous cerebral matter, Statius ecphores the sacrificial rother in the Æneidean boxing match, which meets the fate Adrastus foresees for Alcidamas. As with Vergil's anecdote, we recall that no ordinary blow of the fist could so punish the human body: the *cæstus* all but guaranteed the lethality of Roman boxing, particularly in Statius' era when the gauntlet had become a veritable weapon.

Executing their liege's command, Tydeus (a quondam brawler himself) and Hippomedon bind (*restringo*) both of Capaneus' hands (not just his right) and urge him to depart, having already conquered (*vinco*). They aver that it is indeed glorious (*pulchrum*) to spare (*vitam donare*, lit. 'give life') the 'smaller ones' (*minor*, dative). Hippomedon and Tydeus extend their appeal by citing their relationship with Alcidamas as brothers at arms (*noster et hic bellique comes*, line 817).

Having lost "his grip on sanity in the boxing" (Lovatt 2001, p. 109), the harageous Argive is having none of it (*nil frangitur heros*). Rejecting the prizes of victory—a branch (*ramus*) and a cuirass (*thoraca*)—he spews a Steliteutic at Alcidamas (lines 819–822):

> Let me free! Shall I not smash in gore and clotted dust those cheeks whereby
> that eunuch-boy gained favor, and send his unsightly corpse to the tomb and
> give cause for mourning to his Œbalian masters?[390]

Capaneus' parting lines suggest a deep resentment towards his adversary that seems to go beyond the realm of normal athletic competition. This is unprecedented in depictions of

---

[389] Adrastus cries, *ite, oro, socii, furit, ite apponite dextras | festinate furit ...* (lines 809–810). The "staccato words" and the palilogy of both *ite* and *furit* "evoke Adrastus' alarm" (Vessey 2010, p. 222). "Adrastus highlights the madness of Capaneus, the victor, by repeating the verb" *furo* (Maugier-Sinha 2010, p. 97; translation ours).

[390] *liceat! non has ego pulvere crasso | atque cruore genas, meruit quibus iste favorem | semivir, infodiam mittamque informe sepulcro | corpus et Œbalio donem lugere magistro?* Hall (1992, p. 298) writes, "Capaneus' vociferation, as regularly now printed, changes tack with an abruptness difficult to register on the inner ear, shifting with one word from entreaty to blustering threat. I find myself wondering whether Statius did not settle for an easier run of words and couch the whole of Capaneus' outburst in the form of an entreaty," replacing *non* (line 819) with *nunc* and ending line 822 with an exclamation instead of a question mark.

boxing at funeral games, though perhaps Statius read it under the surface of earlier pugilistic vignettes.[391] Threats of extraordinary physical harm are *de rigeur* among epic boxers, including in the *Iliad*, but elsewhere these take place before the match.[392] Capaneus imagines murdering his opponent after the fight has ended. Lugubrious imagery in this passage doubles the linkage between boxing and funerals: a boxer, who has fought to the death at the grave of a fallen hero, is to be carried off to his own tomb.

The episode ends on a raucous note, with the comrades of Capaneus leading him away, swollen (*tumidum*)[393] with rage and "protesting that he has not conquered" (*vicisse nego*, line 823). In the *Thebaid* the natural order of the boxing match has been profoundly disrupted. There can be no winner because there is no loser.[394] This is why Capaneus denies his own victory and continues to menace his rival.[395] Meanwhile, the Spartans praise (*laudo*) their own Alcidamas, "the nursling [*alumnus*] of famed Taygetus," and (nervously, perhaps) laugh off Capaneus' threats (*minæ*).

On the matter of Capaneus' madness, we wonder if Statius does not offer a subtle critique of Roman boxing rather than an instance of *dementia pugilistica*. As noted above, Capaneus smeared in blood the lines between war and boxing,[396] but had Roman society not done the same thing, for example, by turning the Greek *himantes* into *arma*, equipping them even with spearheads by Statius' era? According to Lovatt (2001, p. 103), the *Thebaid* "is the maddest of Roman epics" in which "the boundaries between appropriate heroic fervor and unacceptable *furor* are impossible to place securely and are often blurred." Does a mad athlete make a good warrior, or vice versa? The Romans did not appreciate Greek athletics so much as they appreciated war (Section 3.5). So, it would seem, they transformed the former into the latter, just as Capaneus did.[397]

Capaneus' approach to boxing was evidently not the only one possible in the Late Antique imagination, however. Statius himself, writing in his unfinished *Achilleid*, provides an alternative (2.155–156). In recounting the glories of his youth, Achilles mentions that, along with hurling weights and wrestling, "to scatter blows with the boxing-gloves [was] sport and rest to me" (Mozley 1928a).[398] The phrase from *Achilleid* 2.156, *ludus erat requiesque mihi…*, suggests a Greek ideal of recreational pugilism presumably lost in Late Antiqiuty and subsumed by the gore of battle. Mars had eclipsed Apollo as the genius of Roman boxing.[399]

---

[391] Capaneus approximates Amycus in his "animal fury and blasphemous pride" (Vessey 2010, p. 222).

[392] According to one commentator, in boxing Capaneus betakes himself to that "same *furor* that leads [him] into his insane battle with Jupiter in [B]ook 10, the same *furor* that destroys him … On that occasion there is no Adrastus to save Capaneus from the consequences" of his intempestivity (Vessey 2010, p. 222).

[393] Perhaps Statius here recalls Capaneus' tumescent neck during his initial face-off with Alcidamas.

[394] Legras (1905, p. 89) notes that it is not clear that Capaneus has won, since Alcidamas leaves the ring "safe and sound, mocking his rival's blustering threats" *sain et sauf, se moquant des menaces fanfaronnes* (translation ours).

[395] According to one critic, "Victory for [Capaneus] is symbolized not just by the palm and the prize, but by the violent death and disfigurement of his opponent. He has imported the values of war into the context of the games; his desire to win has become a desire to kill; it is this that shows his madness" (Lovatt 2001, p. 112).

[396] König (2005, p. 246) notes that the games of Statius, including the boxing match, "return obsessively to the image of warfare threatening to burst open the funeral celebrations…"

[397] Later in the epic, Alcidamas' death is emblematic of Roman skepticism of athletic prowess. Despite being the student of Pollux and proving successful (*specto … felix*) in all *palæstræ* and in the dust of the Nemean Games (10.498–499), Alcidamas does not exactly impress in his encounter with Capaneus. When Alcidamas dies entering the gates of Thebes, it "cast[s] doubt on [his] heroism" (Cannizzaro 2020, p. 295).

[398] The verb that Mozley translates as 'scatter' is *spargo* which may also mean 'strew', 'cast', or 'hurl'. Mozley's "boxing-glove" is, naturally, the *cæstus*.

[399] Pollux, too, is reduced to a sinking star in the vault of heaven, the cynosure to which Alcidamas poignantly

3.5 Pugilatus

While there is a wealth of textual and visual information on boxing in Italy during the period of Roman ascendancy,[400] it is still vexing to perceive the conventions of and attitudes towards boxing as it was practiced at Rome over the centuries. How was it related to other native Italic (East Alpine, Etruscan, and Lucanian) varieties of orthograde personal combat (Dioscurus and Dioscurus 2023)? How was Roman boxing related to gladiatorial spectacle? Was it associated with military training? Did it have particular meaning to Romans as their own practice, or was it always marked for its alterity, i.e, perceived as 'Greek'? Was boxing a form of ritual killing? How did boxing handgear change in the Roman context, and why? The answers to many of these questions are still speculative. In this section we will describe Roman boxing (*pugilatus*), recognizing that it is not entirely defensible to separate the practice from either Greek athletics (Section 2) or gladiatorial spectacle (Section 3.6). As we have done elsewhere with regard to regional forms of boxing in particular time periods, we find it helpful to assess the evidence for distinctively Roman boxing separately, at least as a hypothetical proposition.

In our extensive review of Roman epic boxing (*ut supra*), we do not encounter a single instance of the word *pugilatus*, a derivative of *pugnus* 'fist'. In epic poetry, circumlocutions—often revolving around the *cæstus*—are used to denominate boxing. Where does the term *pugilatus*, then, occur? Plautus includes *pugilatus* in a list of other sports (*Bacchides*, 3.3.24), written in the early second century BC. Pliny's *Natural history* (8.83) glosses Greek 'boxing' as *pugilatus* in AD 77. Writing in the early third century AD, Tertullian (*Spect.*) refers to *pugilatus* along with *luctatus* 'wrestling' in his criticism of Roman entertainments, juxtaposing them with more Christian pursuits. The term is again used by Sidonius Apollinaris in his *Letters* (2.2, to Domitius) in the late fifth century. The term *pugil* 'boxer' is much more frequent in Latin texts, though it seems more limited diachronically. The term is attested from as early as Statius Cæcilius' (lost) play, *Pugil* (ca. 150 BC) to Quintus Curtius in the first century AD. The term *spectaculum pugilum* refers to 'combat spectacle' (lit., 'spectacle of boxers') in later inscriptions found in Tunisia (Khanoussi 2006, p. 79). Elsewhere, *pugilum certamina* was used (Khanoussi 1991, p. 316).[401]

Of all the material features of boxing in the ancient world, the Roman *cæstus* is undeniably the most celebrated (for one example, see Figure 5). It features prominently in both Roman visual and literary culture. Despite this, the functional and formal properties of the *cæstus* are poorly understood and often overgeneralized. The visual record clearly establishes that boxing handgear throughout the Roman Empire took multiple gnarly forms, some of which seem only distantly related to the Greek *himantes* (Section 2). These are all referred to as *cæstus* in modern commentary. Roman authors seem to have had no special vocabulary for differentiating their boxing handgear and none have been invented by modern critics.

The allotropic manifestations of the Roman *cæstus* in the visual record present us with

---

casts his dying gaze: "dying thou lookest toward the vault where thy master shines; straightway the god sinks with averted star" ... *nitidi moriens convexa magistri | respicis: averso pariter deus occidit astro* (10.501–502).

[400] According to one scholar, "Boxing (*pugilatus*) was easily the most popular form of heavy athletic contest among the Romans," surpassing both wrestling and the *pankration* (Junkelmann 2000, p. 75).

[401] Boxing was "widespread in Tunisia during the Roman era" (Khanoussi 2006, p. 79), beginning, more specifically, during the Severan dynasty in the late second century AD and declining by the beginnings of the fourth (Khanoussi 1991, p. 322).

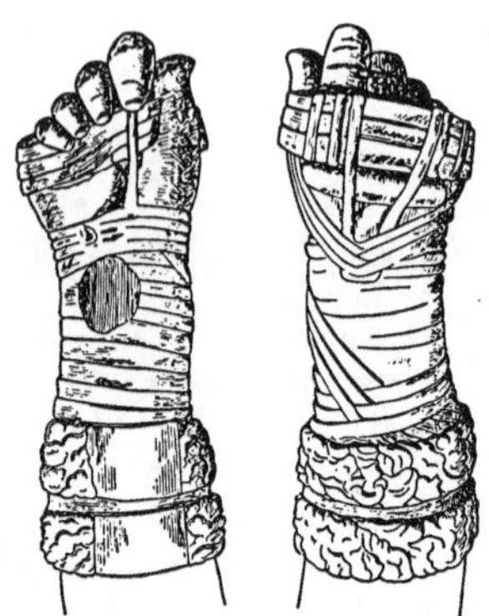

Figure 5: A modern drawing of the Roman *cæstus*, presumably based on a sculptural model.

a puzzle. There is no explicit[402] literary description of a *cæstus* equipped with prongs, for example, even though this bit of boxing tackle is widely attested in Late Antique art found throughout the empire (e.g., Figures 16, 19, 18). The Latin word for boxing handgear is derived from *cædo* 'cut'.[403] If etymology is any guide, this may suggest awareness that the primary purpose of the *cæstus* was to lacerate an opponent, as reflected in epic accounts. More prosaically, the verbal derivation may simply point back to the fact that the *cæstus* was structured from strips cut from the hide of a bull.

In 2018, two second-century Roman "boxing gloves" were discovered by archæologists at Vindolanda, a Roman fortress just south of Hadrian's Wall in Northumberland, England (Figure 6). They have been dated to around AD 117–119 (Lobell 2018). The gloves were discovered in "a cavalryman's barrack alongside a pile of horse gear, shoes, wooden bath clogs, gaming counters, and a nearly complete sword" (ibid., p. 68). The two gloves have different structures. One is more soft and pliable; the knuckles of the fighter's hand have left an imprint in the leather. The other is filled with straw and has a "heat-hardened" piece of leather wrapped around the edge. According to archæologists, this "would easily draw blood if used in a slashing motion," and thus suggests to some that one glove was used for practice and the other for fighting (ibid.). Given the well-attested propensity for differential gloving on the hands of a single boxer, we believe it is possible that both gloves were used simultaneously in a fight by the same pugilist. Having one injurious glove and one more innocuous is hardly uncommon in ancient representations, including the fresco of the Boxing Boys at Akrotiri (Dioscurus and Dioscurus 2022c).

As in this most recent example, modern critics routinely attempt to assess—via the form of ancient boxing 'gloves'—how barbaric or humane their predecessors were. We find it more helpful to consider the functional primitives of boxing and how these are expressed

---

[402] We have argued that various references to the gruesome outcomes of epic boxing allude to a weaponized *cæstus.*, e.g., in the *Dionysiaca* (Section 2.6), though without describing the gauntlet in any detail.

[403] Etymologically-related words in English include 'scissor', 'excise', and 'decide'.

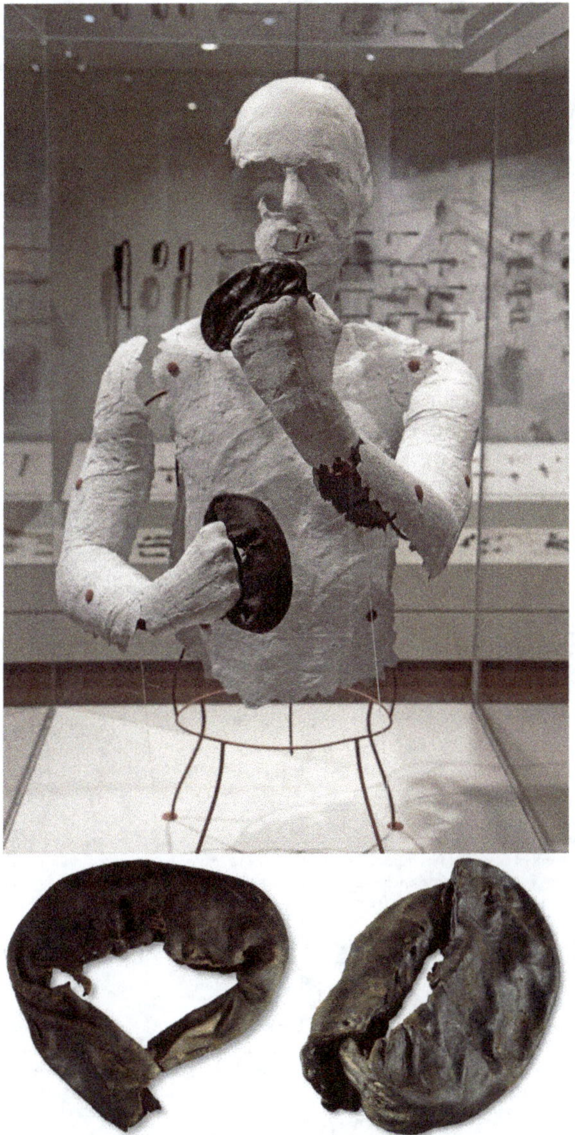

Figure 6: Vindolanda boxing cæstus (Vindolanda Trust). Dated c. AD 117–119.

in its material culture.[404] The primary termination condition for a boxing match is the unconsciousness of one fighter. Termination conditions such as submission, referee stoppage, injury, etc. are all secondary. This is why the knockout remains the *sine qua non* of the squared circle.[405] Because breaking a hand or wrist is a suboptimal way of terminating a boxing match, the hands must be reinforced. (This, of course, presupposes a rule set that allows a fighter to withdraw because of a broken hand, rather than be beaten into unconsciousness all the same.) The development of the Greek *himantes*, intended most likely to strengthen the hand against the force of its own blow, suggests that the Greeks did not wish to laureate a man merely because he had stronger bones than his adversary; he should, instead, be more skillful in his art. The binding of the hands, then, was one of the foremost æsthetic leaps in the history of boxing. With buttressed fists, the field was leveled for the demonstration of other skills.[406]

Similarly, the many faces of the Roman-era *cæstus* appeared in response to functional primitives. We believe these had to do with the perception of boxing as a sacrifice of the body, maybe even a form of ritual killing. Blood was required in and various were the means invented to procure it. The line between gauntlet and weapon became blurred. The Greeks tried the *himantes oxeis*, which tore and disfigured the face. The Lucanians, as we have seen (Dioscurus and Dioscurus 2023), experimented with a variety of gloving regimes, from the spiked to the claviform. Boxers in the Eastern Alps, including perhaps the Etruscans, wielded dumbbells. The purpose of all these was undoubtedly the same: to bleed an opponent dry while beating him unconscious.

The latest versions of the *cæstus* were intended not only to beat and bloody but to eviscerate. There can be no doubt that their construction was influenced heavily by gladiatorial weaponry. Was this boxing or swordplay? The question was perhaps irrelevant to spectators in the Late Antique world. Would the event be advertised as a *pugilum spectaculum* or as a gladiator fight? Perhaps it mattered little, as long as there was an effusion of blood and viscera.[407]

Our approach seeks to differentiate even the blunt Erycian *cæstus* pictured in Vergilian mosaics (Figures 24, 9) from the two-pronged device of later centuries (Figures 19, 18). Certainly, wearing one or the other would change the nature of the combat: to club or to pierce, to slash or to strike? Fighters were certainly trained in the appropriate tactics, though no

---

[404] The modern predisposition for this kind of analysis, we believe, is rooted in discussions from the nineteenth-century, when modern boxing gloves were first deployed. They were used to convince authorities and the viewing public that boxing was not dangerous. The same remains true in the twenty-first century, when the optics of the fight are arguably more important to the (economic) survival of sport boxing than the physical well-being of the combatants.

[405] The frequency and therefore the relevance of the KO is rapidly fading in the modern sport, however, where safety (or perhaps merely its illusion) seems an almost inexorable concern.

[406] Put another way, at some point the fist's susceptibility to fracture seems to have motivated the adoption of gloves to effectively "absorb and dissipate some of the punches' energy exchanged between boxers" (Chadli et al. 2018, p. 504). The bones of the face are harder than the bones of the fist and so heavily-padded boxing gloves (along with underlying bandages, gauze, and tape wrapped around the hands) naturally lead boxers to throw the heaviest punches possible at the head of an opponent, raising questions about the efficacy of modern sport boxing's precautionary measures.

[407] Critics of modern sport boxing have noted for decades that "a return to bare knuckles, or even mitts, would make the sport safer than it is with boxing gloves" (Anonymous 4 March 1995). Training gloves like the *episphairai* notwithstanding, ancient boxing handgear, which likely arose to buttress the fists of the striker, was not designed to protect the boxer being hit. If anything, boxing gauntlets were likely intended to increase the spilling of blood (as we see repeatedly in Italic and Roman boxing).

Figure 7: A first-century coin from Smyrna depicting a *cæstus*. The coin has been dated to the first century BC (private collection?).

records remain. It is unfortunate that Roman authors give us only one word for all these devices[408] when surely the boxers and their trainers knew what they were called and how to use them. We suspect a comprehensive oral tradition maintained for generations in the *palestræ* and *thermæ* of the empire.

A first-century BC coin from Smyrna (Fig 7) depicts a right hand (if the palm is down) bedecked in a device we might call a *cæstus*. Though the coin is eastern, the handgear is rather different from even the *himantes oxeis*. A thick strap wraps around the knuckles while two narrower straps cross on the back of the hand and attach at a cuff. The clearest innovation seems to be the perimetric rim around the hand, suggesting a plate may be attached on the underside. This reminds us of the Minoan boxing gauntlet, visible on the Boxer Rhyton (Dioscurus and Dioscurus 2022c). If it is a left hand (with palm up) then the thick strap would most likely be grasped by curled fingers and the plate would ride on the back of the hand, perhaps as in Figure 13. The *cæstus* depicted on the coin, however, lacks a toothed projection. As discussed in Section 3.1, the *cæstus* appeared on coins in Central Italy (Figures 4, 8) as early as the middle of the third century (Häberlin 1967).

Turning to a mysterious literary reference, the scholiast of the *Argonautica* 2.52–53 claims that the *himantes* described by Apollonius are in fact μύρηκες, a particularly nasty form of glove introduced as early as the fourth century BC. The name of the μύρηκες probably refers to 'ants' but we have no description of their construction. The 'ants' may be construed as lumps of lead sewn into the leather (cf. the Erycian *cæstus* of Vergil). Or perhaps being struck with the μύρηκες stung like an ant-bite.[409] The *cæstus* has been identified by one commentator as "the closest Roman equivalent of the μύρηκες" (Nelis 2001, p. 14)

Another kind of glove, the *flacculis* or *flocculis*, is mentioned by "Trebellius Pollio" in his *Life of Gallienus*.[410] It is perhaps the Latin translation of the soft *himantes*, or a boxing glove that incorporates a sheepskin (Borthwick 1964b). The date of the *Life* is disputed; it may have been composed as late as the fourth century AD. We believe the blood-absorbing

---

[408]We wryly note that English likewise contents itself with the term 'glove'—arguably even less specific—along with a handful of modifiers. Of course, the Anglophone world has not developed the wide variety of hand coverings employed in the ancient world.

[409]It is not necessary to think of the term μύρηκες as an example of gallows humor. Modern manufacturers of boxing gloves emblazon their wares with words like 'Sting' and 'Venum', presumably with no humorous intention.

[410]The age and authorship of the *Historia Augusta* is disputed, but it may have been written as late as the fourth century AD.

vellus 'sheepskin' that appears in Statius' boxing match (Section 3.4.2), is in fact a reference to the *flocculis*. The sheepskin sleeve is widely documented iconographically (e.g., Figures 2, 10). According to Junkelmann (2000, p. 80), the protection afforded by the padded sleeve allowed boxers to hold their bent arms "diagonally to shield the face or vertically to protect both the face and the top of the head. The boxer thus covered himself with his lower arm and not his fists."[411] The sleeve may have functioned for defense in a manner analogous to the modern boxing glove (particularly the heavier variety), which, due to its bulk, allows boxers to raise their hands to their face and cover up while throwing punches at their opponent from a close range.

Figure 8: Front of a third-century BC Umbrian coin from Tuder inscribed with the image of a right hand in a *cæstus* (compare Figure 4). The straps of the gauntlet are seen here crossing the back of the hand in an 'X' instead of a 'V'.

In *Fasti* (2.366–369), written around AD 8, Ovid describes the pastoral hours of the naked Romulus and Remus[412] as they disport themselves of the *cæstus* (ablative plural), javelin, and heavy stones:

> Romulus et frater pastoralisque iuventus
> solibus et campo corpora nuda dabant;
> cæstibus et iaculis et misso pondere saxi
> brachia per lusus experienda dabant:

The idyllic scene of boxing brothers at play suggests that the Romans did not view the *cæstus* as cruel implements of unmitigated horror—at least not in all events. It also points to the strong possibility that *cæstus* was the cover term for all boxing handgear in the Roman world.

Extremely round gloves, perhaps made to resemble the Greek *episphairai*, are worn by boxers in a floor mosaic at the National Bardo Museum in Tunis. One boxer, with a bruised eye and contorted nose, kneels while an effusion of blood spurts from his forehead. His

---

[411] Pace (Junkelmann 2000), modern boxers use much more than their fists to construct a guard. One of the greatest genetic endowments for a modern boxer are a short torso and long arms, which, bent at the elbows and raised to the face, can effectively cover the boxer from waist to brow. We do not believe that the padded sleeve necessarily implies a high guard.

[412] There is a discordant note here in the overtly Greek activity of Rome's founders.

opponent menaces him from the right with both hands raised as if to deliver further blows from above. The gloves are yellow with black lines, resembling the bodies of bumblebees. The dark bands may indicate metal ringing the glove. A cuff extends beyond the wrist. The mosaic is Roman, from around the third century AD.

A Gallo-Roman floor mosaic (Figure 24) found at Villelaure, France, dating to around the late second century AD, depicts the battle between Dares and Entellus found in the *Æneid* (Book 5, lines 362–484).[413] The boxers wear forearm-length *cæstus* that appear to be reinforced with metal at the knuckles.[414] One boxer strides forward, toward the viewer and away from his opponent. The other boxer moves away from his opponent and the viewer, while blood spurts from his forehead (J. Paul Getty Museum, 71.AH.106). A white bull kneels in the background.

A similar mosaic composition was discovered at Aix-en-Provence in the 1990s (Lavagne 1994). The image includes the sacrificed bull, here with a bloody muzzle.[415] The illustration of the *cæstus* suggests metal bands running around the cuff and the fist, as in Figure 24. Lavagne (1994, p. 211) describes the *cæstus* in this mosaic as "lead plates wrapped up in leather straps" (translation ours).[416] Tassles on the cuffs suggest ritual and recall the sartorial ornaments of Muay Thai boxing.

Another African representation of boxing comes from a fourth-century floor mosaic found near Gafsa (Roman Capsa) in modern Tunisia (Figure 10). The boxers wear armlength *cæstus* with blunt ends, similar to those in the Villelaure mosaic. The defensive technique is almost uncomfortably realistic: the boxer whose face we can see has awkwardly tipped his head back to avoid further blows, while bloods streams from his face to the ground. An official stoops down, to the right, holding a reed and gesturing with two outstretched fingers towards the battling pair, perhaps "to separate them" (Khanoussi 2006, p. 90). The larger mosaic contains a wide variety of athletic games, including *pankration*.[417] One critic argues, "Clearly, the pavement mosaic is a report on a spectacle of athletic and combat games that actually took place" (Khanoussi 2006, p. 91).

Note that the boxer's thumbs are outstretched in Figure 11. This suggests that the curved projection[418] was most likely held in place with a rod stretching between its two sides, grasped by the curled phalanges.[419] The toothed projection, which follows the line of the forearm,

---

[413] Though this is the most well-known, four other mosaics depicting the Vergilian boxing episode have been identified (Budrovich 2011). They all come from southern France and arguably suggest enthusiasm for pugilism and other arena spectacle in that region. The floor mosaic from the Rue des Magnans is illustrated in Figure 9.

[414] A metal cap for the knuckles, like the one pictured in the Villelaure mosaic, is housed in the Museum für Kunst und Gewerbe in Hamburg (no. 1997.356). Dated to the second or third century AD, the object fits snugly the four fingers curled in a fist; a transverse bar inside the cap allows it to be grasped (Junkelmann 2000, p. 78).

[415] Persistent bull sacrifice suggests Mithraic tauroctony, but more likely the equation runs the other way: bull sacrifice was ubiquitous in the ancient world as we have seen in these articles *passim*.

[416] *... plaquettes de plomb entourées de lanières de cuir ...*

[417] The *pankration* fighters appear to be bare-knuckle boxers. They brandish bare fists at one another without throwing kicks or otherwise displaying signs of pronograde combat, as opposed to another dueling pair that is probably wrestling. The artist had a good eye for combat: One of the wrestling figures, arched over his opponent's back, forces him to the ground with a wide grip on the back of his head.

[418] Poliakoff (1987a, p. 75) refers to "horseshoe shaped gloves" and exemplifies them in images that clearly depict what we refer to as 'dumbbells' (Dioscurus and Dioscurus 2023). We believe that the term 'horseshoe' is more aptly applied to the Roman *cæstus* seen in Figures 11 and 13; Poliakoff (op. cit, p. 78) gives a description of these, as well.

[419] This type of *cæstus* was evidently similar to the hippocrepiform or stapediform Okinawan *tekko*. Used as a form of fist-load weapon, the curved portion of the *tekko* wraps around the knuckles, though it does not shield the hand like the curved projection of the Roman *cæstus*.

Figure 9: Floor mosaic from *domus* of the Rue des Magnans, Aix-en-Provence. With plenty of blood, the mosaic synoptically depicts the fight between Dares and Entellus from Book 5 of the *Æneid*.

is attached by a cord extending to the cuff of the lambskin sleeve. Rather than securing the projection, this cord probably anchored the sleeve to hand, preventing it from riding up during the agon. The flat and curved projections were most likely made of metal and welded to one another. The Met *cæstus* (Figure 12) illustrates how the curved projection did not extend over the back of the hand—its edge at the back of the knuckles is clear. The marble fragment of a boxer's hand (found in a private collection in Switzerland) suggests a similar *cæstus* was constructed with an element covering the back of the hand and terminating in the toothed projection (Thuillier 2019, p. 502, Fig. 10). In this example, as well, the curved projection ends at the knuckles, suggesting it is a separate element held in the clenched fist. The element on the back of the hand appears to wrap around the thenar eminence of the thumb, suggesting that is was somehow secured there, or across the palm.

The flat, toothed projection seated on the back of the hand or knuckles was certainly an offensive weapon, but what was the purpose of the curved projection? This component may have been intended to shield the fingers from the attacks of an adversary, one who was probably accoutred in the same manner. One authority reasons that the curved projection or finger guard was most likely made of metal (Poliakoff 1987a, p. 78). If so, a boxer could easily throw a hook with the palm facing his opponent and lacerate him, leaving a bloody, meniscus-shaped wound. Indeed, if the edge of the curved projection were sharpened, the finger guard may have also served as an effective gouge, perhaps aimed at the eyes.

A second or early third-century AD mosaic from Patras, in Greece (Dunbabin 2015), presents us with a view of the Met *cæstus* in action (Figures 14, 15). The semi-cylindrical pro-

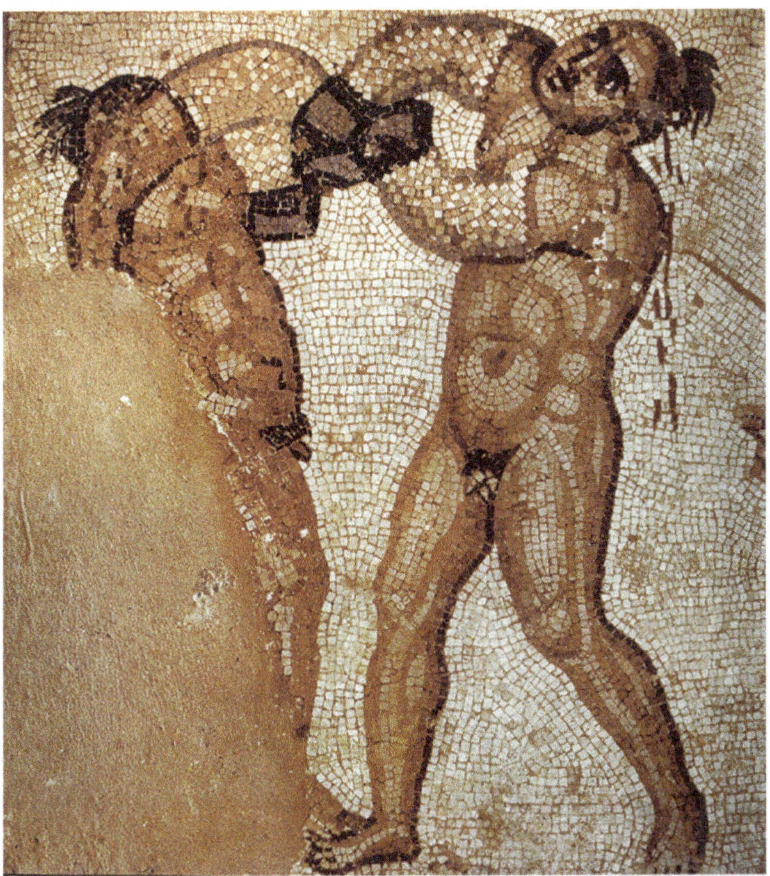

Figure 10: Boxers from floor mosaic found at Gafsa in modern Tunisia, dated to the fourth century AD.

Figure 11: Bronze half-figure of a boxer wearing a Roman *cæstus* and emerging from the calyx of a flower. Note the curved projection over the knuckles (the fingers are curled beneath them, forming a fist). The projections of the forearm, which may at first glance appear to be fingers, are in fact the toothed projections visible on the *cæstus* in Figure 12. Third century AD. National Museum, Athens, 7574.

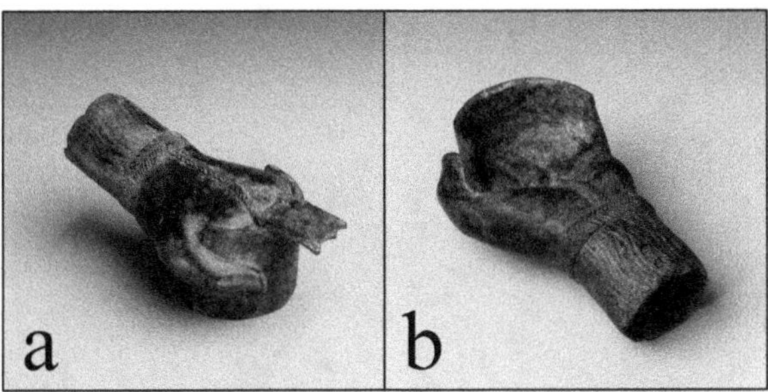

Figure 12: A bronze hand showing detail of a boxer's *cæstus* (a: pronate; b: supinate). A three-pointed projection extends from the knuckles while a semi-cylindrical strip (called a "coque" by Thuillier 2019) secured by the thumb curls around the knuckles and projects perpendicular to the palm / back of the hand. Metropolitan Museum of Art, Fifth Avenue, Accession Number 2001.129. Roman, 1st to 2nd century AD. A similar object is found in the Boston Museum of Fine Arts, Accession Number 1972.900.

tection is clearly visible, as are the pointed projections. The sleeve, doubtless influenced by the gladiatorial *manica*, reaches up over the biceps and the observer can see evidence of the laces holding it in place. The offensive fighter in each pair stretches his arms out and up, standing on tiptoe (a posture suggested frequently in epic accounts of boxing). An attack to the body seems almost comically possible in this stance. Perhaps it is true, as has often been repeated, that only blows to the head were allowed (Junkelmann 2000).

At the Baths of Caracalla, sculptural idealization (associated with the "glorification of the young male body") is juxtaposed with "very different contemporary references to the life of the *palæstra* in the athlete mosaics" (DeLaine 1997, pp. 78–79). The decoration was "designed to emphasize the palatial and almost heavenly splendor of the Baths and to allow the ordinary mortal to experience, however fleetingly and vicariously, the life of the rich and powerful" (DeLaine 1997, p. 84). The boxer depicted in Figure 16 was found on the floor of the west exhedra (Room 13W) attached to the west *palæstra* of the Baths. He is entirely naked with a partially erect or infibulated penis. He wears laced *cæstus* that reach up to his biceps; they terminate in two short spikes on the inner edge of the fist. He wears his hair in a *cirrus*.

Figure 17 illustrates a fragment of a mosaic floor (AD 300–350) found at Trier, in Germany. It depicts two naked boxers wearing spiked gauntlets. The spikes, which project from the knuckles of the index finger and auricularis, appear capable of producing devastating injury.[420] They were presumably held in place with a bar inside the *cæstus*, barely visible in the left hand of the boxer on the left. Each fighter has blood on his abdomen and legs. Boxing gloves with a similar form have been discovered on a relief from the Villa de Vareilles, in southern France, dated to the second half of the first century AD (Thuillier 2019, p. 502).

A pronged boxing glove is also visible on the left hand of the left-hand figure in a boxing scene from the second-century bath house of the Villa Selene, about three hours' walk

---

[420] This type of *cæstus* is also worn by boxers in a mosaic from Tusculum (Hirzel 1863, Gardiner 1910).

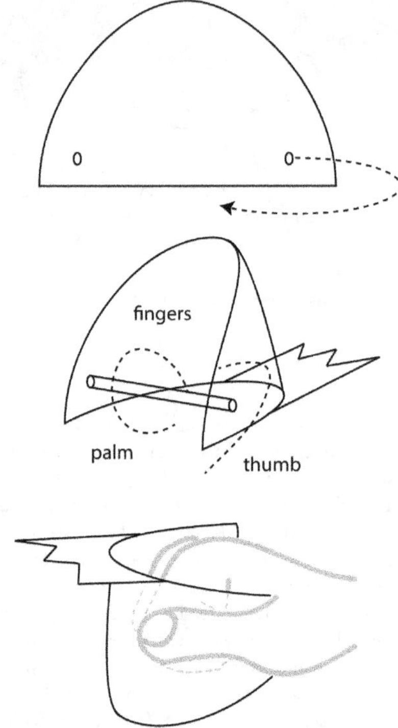

Figure 13: Schematic reconstruction of the Roman *cæstus* illustrated in Figures 11 and 12. The flat, toothed projection was undoubtedly an offensive weapon; it was attached by a cord (not shown here) to the sleeve (Figure 12). The curved, semi-circular plate most likely served to protect the fingers from blows delivered by an antagonist wearing a similar gauntlet. If sharpened, it might also have been an effective gouge.

Figure 14: Detail of mosaic from Patras, Greece (second or third century AD), Patras Archæological Museum.

Figure 15: Detail of mosaic from Patras, Greece (second or third century AD), Patras Archæological Museum.

Figure 16: Image of a boxer from the Baths of Caracalla (Room 13W), Rome (fourth century). The spikes on the boxer's gauntlet are unmistakably related to projections seen on other *cæstus* from this period, notably those at Lepcis Magna and Trier (Figures 18 and 17). The entire athlete mosaic is now housed in the Vatican Museum.

Figure 17: Bleeding boxers wearing spiked gauntlets. Mosaic floor found at Trier (Augusta Treverorum), ca. AD 300–350. There can be no doubt as to the lethal quality of these *cæstus*.

along the coast from Lepcis Magna in Libya. In the mosaic (Figure 18), a triumphant boxer extends his left *cæstus* across the right shoulder of his antagonist, whose downcast expression suggests his imminent defeat. The prongs of the winner's *cæstus* are visible in front of the downcast boxer's shoulder. Prongs are also faintly visible in the loser's *cæstus* as it crosses his chest. Compared to other depictions, blood is rather subtly portrayed—speckling the fighters' torsos and streaming from the nose and mouth of the loser. A table behind them is set with palm branches.

Boxers depicted on a second-century mosaic at the baths of Tarnaias (Massongex, Switzerland) seem to be outfitted with two different types of *cæstus* (Figure 19). The fighter on the left wears blunt, hammer-like gloves while the fighter on the right wears arm-length *cæstus*. The lead hand bears four spikes. The mosaic is somewhat naïve, so it is also possible they represent fingers. The boxers both wear loincloths in divergence from the Greek athletic tradition.

Boxers depicted in a third-century low relief found in the Villa de Vareilles, in southern France, suggest yet another variation on the *cæstus* (Figures 20, 21, 22). Here the sleeve, perhaps of sheepskin, arrives at nearly the shoulder on boxers naked but for a loincloth. The portion of the gauntlet reaching up to the elbow almost appears to be articulated armor. The fingers are thick, triangular projections of which there are three or four. Some of the boxers' hands are angled so that it appears they grasp a smooth object about the size of the palm.[421] We suspect these may be small weights, perhaps lumps of lead, held tightly in the fist. They would have served the same function as the East Alpine *hanteln*. The reinforced fingers of the glove would have prevented the fingers from being crushed by the extra impact of the blow. The reliefs, which are not associated with baths, evidently come from a funerary context (Thuillier 2019, p. 504).

---

[421] Thuillier (2019, p. 498) claims that it is semi-cylindrical and relates it to the "pads" posited by Lee (1997).

Figure 18: Boxer mosaic in Room 43 of the bath house at Villa Selene (second century AD), near Lepcis Magna, in Libya. The mosaic, which partially covers the interior of a dome, is dated to around the second century.

Figure 19: Second-century mosaic from the baths of Tarnaias (modern Massongex, Switzerland). The boxers wear loincloths, a departure from the Greek tradition.

Figure 20: Bearded boxer wearing a loincloth and arm-length *cæstus*, as depicted on a Gallo-Roman bas-relief at the Villa de Vareilles in what was then called Gallia Narbonensis, now southern France, dated AD 200–300.

Figure 21: Boxer depicted on a Gallo-Roman bas-relief at the Villa de Vareilles in what was then called Gallia Narbonensis, now southern France, dated AD 200–300.

Figure 22: Boxer depicted on a Gallo-Roman bas-relief at the Villa de Vareilles in what was then called Gallia Narbonensis, now southern France, dated AD 200–300.

Works of art like these evince the heuretic impulse of Roman and Romanized populations in developing new forms of pugilism, perhaps related to local fighting styles. The situla art reviewed earlier (Dioscurus and Dioscurus 2023) is suggestive of pre-Roman monomachy that involved hand-implements (*hanteln*) unknown to the Greeks. Rather than assume that the Romans spontaneously developed particularly violent forms of pugilism, we argue that Etruscan and Celtic bloodsport of the first millennium was an influential substrate of what was later regarded as (Roman) *pugilatus* (Dioscurus and Dioscurus 2023). Trier, for example, was originally inhabited by the Celtic Treveri. Can we be certain that the pronged *cæstus* featured in the Trier mosaic (Figure 17) were not developed under the influence of earlier Alpine boxing?

Jüthner believed that the Romans developed a metal *cæstus*, based on the Greek *himantes oxeis* (ὀξεῖς) for gladiatorial combat.[422] Lee (1997) questions this, arguing instead that this curious arm-length *cæstus* (see Figure 11) was fitted with an extended glove for the fingers and an extended pad in the palm.[423] Lee disagrees with the arguments, espoused by many, that Roman boxing was particularly violent and that gloves were "murderous". "The image of the bloodthirsty Roman," he concludes, "exerts a mythical allure that can prove all too seductive" (Lee 1997, 176). "The belief that the Romans used [such] gloves ... may say more

---

[422] The Greek (plural) adjective ὀξεῖς 'sharp', is directly related to *oxymoron* meaning 'sharp and dull'; and is cognate with the English noun *acid* via the Proto-Indo-European root *h_2ek-.

[423] It is easy to come to the same inference made by Lee based on visual inspection of such objects as a sarcophagus lid in the Museo Gregorio Profano, where the peculiar *cæstus* is visible exclusively in profile (Dunbabin 2015, Fig. 18, p. 209). However, based on our own inspection of many such artifacts where the observer is positioned at a variety of angles, we dispute the claim that the pad extends from the palm. What Lee calls a 'pad' is in fact a kind of finger-guard or even gouge that projects at a right angle from the knuckles. We schematize this curious type of *cæstus* in Figure 13.

about ourselves than the Romans" (ibid.).

Lee's *apologia* notwithstanding, the weight of evidence indeed suggests that in the Roman world, boxers were meant to do damage to one another in spectacular fashion, using the *cæstus*.[424] One question is whether the Roman version of pugilism differed significantly from that of other Bronze and Iron Age civilizations. While the curved projection in the curious *cæstus* may have been offensive and/or defensive in function, it is harder to claim that sharp projections from the knuckles were intended for anything other than disfigurement at best and disembowelment at worst (Figures 12, 17). Pugilistically-inclined Romans were naturally familiar with the story of the great Greek boxers Damoxenos and Kreugas (Dioscurus and Dioscurus 2023). Given the improbability of one fighter being able to disembowel his opponent in one blow using merely his fingers, a *cæstus* equipped with spikes could easily do the trick. By designing fighting gear that some critics find decadent or outlandishly brutal, perhaps the Romans were merely operationalizing and emulating the features of a legendary Greek boxing match.[425] One commentator notes that it is the "violation of the theatrical by the actual" or the "conflation" of the fictional and real world that provides the seductive "frisson to the experience of the spectators" (Bartsch 1994, p. 51). Is this really happening, the spectator asks himself? "Body-horror and violence are inherently alluring" to spectators who "play a role in the grisly spectacle" (McClellan 2019, p. 5).

We agree with Lee, of course, that it is unfair to indict Roman boxing as particularly algolagnistic, at least compared to its antecedents. Consider the *hanteln* grasped by the boxers of the Eastern Alps (Dioscurus and Dioscurus 2023), the superfluity of blood depicted in Etruscan frescoes, Greek boxing stories of disembowelment and death, and the evidence suggesting that even the Minoans used a form of sharp *cæstus* in the Bronze Age (Dioscurus and Dioscurus 2022b). In light of this evidence, why persist in claiming that the Romans degraded boxing? We offer an alternative: throughout the ancient Near East and the Mediterranean Basin, boxing was ubiquarian and focused on bloodshed. Modern boxing does not appear to share this preoccupation. However, we believe this has more to do with modern squeamishness over blood than it has to do with modern concern for the safety of boxers. Professional boxers are able to legally injure, cripple, and kill one another in almost every country.[426] Despite the presumed (and probably contraindicated) 'safety' of gloves and headgear, boxers routinely experience concussions; lacerations and other trauma to the

---

[424] Scholars remain remarkably squeamish on the issue, unable to accept the violence that was done in the Roman boxing 'ring', as if it could not, by definition, compare to the carnage of the gladiatorial arena. Take, for example, the projections on the *cæstus* in mosaics like the ones at Ostia (Figure 23). Dunbabin (2014, p. 712) contradicts Bohne (2011), who believes they represent fingers, but she still concludes, "it is not clear what material is meant," as if they might represent pipe cleaners. Junkelmann (2000, p. 78), who provides an elaborate characterization of the Roman boxing glove, ambiguously concludes that "the murderous character of the Roman *cæstus* should, I think, not be exaggerated." In our opinion, this is due to a lack of precision in the original sources for distinguishing the conventions of Greek and Roman boxing, coupled with the biases of generations who have focused their attention on the athletic, Greek variety of the sport.

[425] Such a spectacle would hardly be out of place in a culture capable of staging gruesome performances like the immolation of a condemned criminal in the guise of Hercules or the self-castration of another in the guise of Attis, *inter alia* (Coleman 1990, pp. 60–63). On recounting a public reënactment of Pasiphaë's sexual intercourse with a bull, Martial noted dryly, *accepit fabula prisca fidem* "seeing is believing" (*Lib. Spect.* 5.2). Audiences had a keen interest in witnessing the "actuality of what [was] being enacted" in the fatal charades of the amphitheater (Coleman 1990, p. 67).

[426] Most government bans on (modern, gloved) professional boxing have been short-lived: California (1914–1924); Cuba (1961–2013); Sweden (1970–2007); Norway (1982–2016). Iceland's 1956 ban is still in effect—the exception that proves the rule.

face including damage to the ears, nose, retinas, and eye sockets; broken ribs; and injuries to the hands, wrists, and elbows. Notwithstanding all this mayhem, it has been documented that boxers routinely "forsake ... their body in order to be involved in the sport" (Matthews 2021, p. 726). While the literal offering of spilt blood appears to be minimal (at present) in modern sport boxing, the offering of a broken body is still central. It is the brutality of boxing that defines it. Less visceral, violent boxing ceases to be boxing.[427] If Roman and Minoan boxing occupy one side on this spectrum of brutality, modern sport boxing occupies the other, with Greek boxing somewhere close to it.

The Greek emphasis on highly technical pugilism, including strong defense, would seem to produce a less spectacular show for an audience. As athletic boxing became a sort of participatory spectacle for the men engaged therein, it may have lost some of its prurient appeal to a mass audience. Gladiatorial boxing "corrected" for the technicality by explicitly reintroducing brutality. While the heavy sports in general were the most popular of the Greek athletic imports to Rome, wrestling and bare-fisted *pankration* were never as well represented as boxing (Dunbabin 2014, p. 711).

During the Republican period, "Greek athletes were occasionally brought into the city to perform in public spectacles. That often involved significant distortion of traditional Greek practice, for instance by presentation of Greek athletic contests in combination with gladiatorial combat" (König 2005, p. 216). This "distortion" may have been at the heart of the development of Roman *pugilatus* as something that differed considerably from Greek *pygmachia*. Still, there can be no question that "the heavy athletic disciplines [sc., boxing, wrestling, and *pankration*] appealed much more to Roman audiences of the Empire" than other athletic pursuits (Dunbabin 2015, p. 199).

Along with hunting, riding, swimming and drilling with military weapons, boxing was "held in high esteem" as a "simple, practical, military exercise" among the Romans (Yegül 2010, p. 121). However, athletic games "in the spirit of pure competition," were not to be found among a virtuous Roman's activities (ibid.). Despite opposition, Greek athletic practice was eventually "transformed and absorbed in its new form into the recreational program of the *thermae*" or large imperial bathing complexes. Exactly what form boxing took on at the Roman baths is unclear, but it likely involved strenuous sparring with soft gauntlets intended to obtund the blows. Representations of much more lethal bouts (Figures 16, 19, 23) were displayed prominently, however, as at the Baths of Neptune at Ostia (Newby 2002). Still, boxing, along with wrestling and *pankration*, was destined to compete with gladiatorial competition in the popular imagination, as evidenced, for example, by the permixtion of athletes and gladiators in the iconographic program of the Baths of Trajan, dedicated in AD 109 (Yegül 2010, p. 123).

In a territory as expansive as Rome's, with local customs of vastly divergent character, it should be no wonder if boxing developed distinctively according to the region in which fighters routinely squared off with one another. In his account of Caligula's life (*De Vita Caesarum, Caligula* 18), Suetonius tells us that the emperor greatly esteemed boxers (*pugil*) from Africa and Campania, presumably for their skill in the 'ring' (Thomson 1889).

---

[427] Efforts to minimize the brutality of boxing will merely make it unpopular, irrelevant, and imminently replaceable. Despite the actions of sanctioning bodies which 'own' sport boxing, humans will never stop valuing and operationalizing the raw brutality of formalized, man-to-man aggression. The resurgence, since 2016, of legal—and frequently gruesome—bare-knuckle boxing in the United States and the United Kingdom is a noteworthy example of this pugilistic atavism.

According to Plutarch (*Marcus Cato*, 20.4), Cato the Elder taught his son how to box in approximately 200 BC.[428] This indicates that the Romans preserved (or invented) some relatively wholesome version of the sport that a father could teach his son. This is a rare reference to boxing taking place in an ancient domestic setting, where children are encouraged to practice the sport.[429] Given Cato's objurgative attitude to Hellenization, it is possible that he taught his son a form of boxing that was native to Italy.

In the late first century AD, Tacitus fretted "that this new enthusiasm for boxing [would] distract young men from the proper activities suitable for them, namely warfare and military training," highlighting the difference between *arma* and *cæstus* (Newby 2005, p. 40).[430] The idea that Greek men were debilitated by the countless hours spent in the gymnasium and the *palæstra* was also mentioned in Lucan's *Civil War* (7.270–272). The Romans, Pliny the Younger lamented, would rather watch others fight then mix it up themselves (*Panegyric* 13.5). This storm of protest meant, of course, that boxing had in fact become popular at Rome (and perhaps too much on the spectatorial side). Writers would continue to produce the "standard Roman stereotypes about athletics—that it encourages degeneracy and pederasty, and replaces the proper training for warfare" (Newby 2005, p. 43). All the while, it is fairly clear that the Romans delighted "in athletic pursuits and spectacles" and that these even had "their place within childhood education and amusements," as suggested in Plutarch's history of Cato (ibid., p. 42). Seneca, in *Hercules* (1123–1125), associates the *palæstra* with boxing gloves, suggesting that the Romans understood boxing to be an activity integrated within the *palestræ*, perhaps better known as wrestling schools.

Figure 23: Detail of a mosaic featuring boxers with two-pronged *cæstus*. Ostia, Baths of Neptune, ca. AD 139.

Brown (2021, p. 450) suggests that Greeks and Romans collected and esteemed art with

---

[428] ἀλλὰ καὶ τῇ χειρὶ πὺξ παίειν (Perrin 1914).

[429] Another example may be found in the fresco of the Boxing Boys at Akrotiri (Dioscurus and Dioscurus 2022c).

[430] *Quid superesse, nisi ut corpora quoque nudent et caestus adsumant easque pugnas pro militia et armis meditentur?* (*Annals* 14.20).

depictions of combat sport because these permitted ordinary citizens "to relive excitement" and "to express allegiance," while making it possible for "sponsors to take credit" (Budrovich 2011). There are at least five floor mosaics in southern France that depict the boxing scene from the *Æneid*. They are all from the mid- to late second century AD. Each is an example of a synoptic narrative in which sequential events are presented in the same image "a single visual moment with contemporary resonances" (p. 8). The Æneidean boxing match and its characters seem to have had special relevance for Romans. There is a Pompeiian grafitto quoting the boxing scene: "Entelle heroum" O Entellus of heroes! It might have been intended to goad a local athlete or criticize an athlete's decline (Ferraro 1982). "[V]iewers of the boxer mosaics would have recognized associations between the religious nature of contemporary arena culture and the boxing scene's religious overtones" (Budrovich 2011, p. 39). According to the same author, the Vergilian boxing motif is notable, perhaps even unique, because "it combines two mental sets that rarely occur together in Roman visual culture: the heroic past and contemporary spectacle" (ibid., p. 48).

Figure 24: Gallo-Roman floor mosaic (from Villelaure, France) depicting the Æneidean boxing match between Entellus and Dares, along with the sacrificial bullock collapsing after a devastating blow to the head. Getty Museum, No. 71.AH.106, AD 175–200.

Attested in Statius' *Silvæ* (4 præf. 30–32) and Seneca's *Epistulæ Morales ad Lucilium* (80 1–2), *sphæromachia* is a poorly understood entertainment. By one interpretation, it was a kind of sham boxing. Contestants may have used the soft *sphairai* described in the *Laws* (8.830B) of Plato (Bury 1967–1968). According to one author, it was popular "for some six hundred years, at first privately in the Greek *palaistrai* and then later in Roman exhibition matches" where it serves "as at least one example of Roman taste for vigorous combat sport without bloodshed" (Scanlon 1986, p. 114). This activity may be what Pollio describes in the *Historia Augusta, Life of Gallienus* (8.3) as "not really boxing" (*non veritate pugillantes*).

The term *sphæromachia* literally means 'ball fight'.[431] Thus, it conceivably required pugilists to grip spherical weights, an activity arguably descended from East Alpine boxing (Dioscurus and Dioscurus 2023). This may offer an explanation for the mysterious smooth objects visible in the hands of boxers in a Gallo-Roman bas-relief (Figure 21). Spherical projections on the *cæstus* of two terracotta boxers (Figure 25) may be related as well.

Nudity in Roman boxing was not ubiquitous. According to one eminent scholar, "[T]he boxers depicted in Roman art wearing the dangerous *cæstus* are typically shown naked, following the practice of Greek, not Roman athletes. The fact that they are shown adhering to Hellenic practice strongly suggests that the Romans viewed this form of boxing as part of Greek athletics, rather than a variation on Roman arena contests, in which the gladiators wore armour and clothing" (Poliakoff 2021, p. 224). However, Roman boxers are occasionally depicted semi-nude (Figures 19, 20, 21, 22, and 25).

Mosaics portraying boxing at the Baths of Neptune at Ostia (Figure 23) function "as a prelude to the human activities nearby" (Newby 2005, p. 50). These mosaics include scenes of wrestling and weight-lifting in addition to pugilism. Such *tableaux* at the baths arguably promoted "an identification between the athletes shown on the ground and the bathers themselves" (ibid., pp. 50–51). In the second and early third centuries, at Rome, "The bathing public seems to have enjoyed the fantasy of seeing their own exercises as parallel to those of the athletic heroes of the current day, even if the competitors and victors in athletic festivals were still largely drawn from the eastern provinces" (Newby 2005, p. 273). The adoption of Greek-style festivals and training gathered gradually and reached a peak during the Severan period (193–235 AD; ibid.). "[W]hile traditional hostility to the Greek gymnasium had certainly weakened by the third century AD, the ideological values with which athletic success and education were invested in Greek culture never took root in Rome" (Newby 2005, p. 273). Roman baths integrated Greek athletics with the agrarian Italian custom of bathing in hot water, but the Romans still eyed "the Greek love for pure athletics ... with suspicion" (Yegül 2010, p. 120).

In a pair of well-preserved terracotta figures from the second or third century (British Museum, No. 1852,0401.1), the fighters' hands are wrapped in the *cæstus* with a ball-like projection on the knuckles (Figure 25). A sharp-edged object projects forward, held in place by the curled fingers. The ball-like projection may be welded to this object.

The boxers are noteworthy, too, for the fact that they are clothed. Though bare-chested, they wear a short garment from waist to upper thigh. The garment is belted and, most remarkably, bifurcated at the legs.[432] If our interpretation is accurate, this is the first attested pair of boxing trunks. There is, however, no evidence that the style caught on: boxers remained naked but for their *cæstus* throughout Late Antiquity. In addition, these boxers

---

[431] One modern translator of Plato regarded *sphæromachia* (σφαιρομαχέω) as a kind of hand ball contest like modern field hockey or polo (Bury 1967–1968).

[432] Closer inspection of the figures may reveal signs that the garment is layered: a short kilt covered by briefs (a *subligaculum*) that draw the kilt in at the thighs, causing it to resemble truncated drawers. A *subligaculum* of this type (sans kilt) is worn, for example, by two figures identified as Astacius and Iaculator on a gladiator mosaic excavated at Torrenova in Rome and held at the Galleria Borghese (third or fourth century AD, no inventory number).

appear to wear a codpiece beneath the garment. Unlike the drawers, which have no prior attestation in boxing so far as we are aware, a codpiece worn during a bout may date back to the Bronze Age, as suggested on the Minoan Boxer Rhyton (Dioscurus and Dioscurus 2022c).

Figure 25: Terracotta figures of boxers. The fighters wear *cæstus* with a ball-like projection on the knuckles and breeches that look remarkably like modern boxing trunks. First or second century BC, Italy (British Museum, No. 1852,0401.1).

Remijsen (2019, pp. 62–63) explains how *palæstræ*, one probable site of boxing training, functioned in the Hellenistic and Roman eras. Elites came to these locations to see and be seen, to participate in athletic competitions (particularly combat sports), and to have their children participate, as well.[433] The *palæstra* was not merely a wrestling school but a location where boxing and *pankration* were also practiced. The *palæstra* functioned as a space where ephebes could fight one another under adult supervision and where adults could continue their own martial praxis.[434]

---

[433]Junkelmann (2000, p. 76) notes that "members of the social élite who admired the ideals of Greek culture, including Greek athletics, did practice boxing and other sports, but as distinguished amateurs. To appear in public would have been degrading ..."

[434]An analogous institution is not evident in the modern West, since most gyms are neither particularly elitist nor do they incorporate combat sports to any considerable degree. Boxing or other martial arts gyms may be the closest

In Book 10 of the *Thebaid*, we learn that the boxer Alcidamas was successful in *palæstræ* as well as the dust of the Nemean Games (lines 498–499). The close connection between boxing and the *palæstra* is noteworthy here. Though the term is most often associated with 'wrestling' in English, as in Mozley (1928a), there is no other suggestion that Alcidamas was a wrestler and plenty of evidence that Statius identified him exclusively as a boxer, including this reference to the *palæstra* where boxing was routinely practiced. Dust, too, is usually associated with wrestling but here we must assume that it is also implicated in boxing.

Along with the Boxing Boys of Akrotiri (Dioscurus and Dioscurus 2022c), the Boxer at Rest[435] is without question the most celebrated and well-known representation of boxing from the ancient world (Figures 26, 27).[436] The boxer is striking and monumental, fixed as one of the most important representations of boxing, ancient or modern.

Contemporary art critic Saltz (2013) cited six features of the boxer ("brutal, brooding, beautiful, gigantic, ..., a kneaded muscular wrecked mountain") which arrest the viewer:

- Pose, "elemental" in its settled bulk. Perhaps the face is turned to focus his attention, or perhaps "he knows it might be unbearable to meet the gaze of something almost animal-like."
- Face, "[breathing] through his open mouth as if blood is caked in his nose." "His deformed cauliflower ears look like globules of flesh. His eyes and face are cut and bleeding."
- Blood, of copper inlay, and a bruise on right cheek. "Blood drips appear on his right side and arm."
- Genitals, scarred and infibulated so that no erection or ejaculation is possible ("typical for slaves and athletes of the time").
- Hands, "casual and changing but gentle."
- Foresight. "A ... breach opens between his world and ours."

To these observations we add the implied context of the figure in such a pose. The sculpture captures the moment of recovery seconds after a fight and before the accoutrements such as the *himantes* would be removed.[437] In keeping with the Greek practice of portraying events from daily life rather than only climactic scenes, the figure's poignant leisure impresses the viewer. A practicing boxer will appreciate the mirrored contemplation which takes place before the fight, when the wraps or *himantes* are bound on, and after the fight during the emotional comedown. Whether flush with victory or defeat, the seated boxer stoically accepts the judgment of the ring. He bears in his flesh the illuminated scars and blemishes that the sculptor chose also to capture, and we conclude that this is no idealization or avatar

---

analog to the ancient *palæstræ*, but little social capital accrues to those who frequent them, as it did to those who practiced boxing and other combatives at the Hellenistic and Roman *palæstræ*.

[435] Seated Boxer, Boxer of Quirinal, Boxer of Terme, etc.

[436] The statue was created during the early period of Roman ascendancy in the Italic peninsula, so we review its manifold significance here. For the Terme boxer, cf. Pollitt (1986, pp. 145–147). Williams (1945b) argued that the Terme Boxer and the Terme Ruler (Pollitt 1986, pp. 72–74) represented Castor and Amycus from an original triptych once complete with a statue of Polydeuces; Theocritus' poem would thus have drawn upon the original of these statues. More often, however, the Terme Ruler is considered to be the figure of a Hellenistic Prince, not one of the Dioscuri. The theory that casts the Seated Boxer as Amycus is not widely regarded. For example, Smith (1988, pp. 84–85) does not even mention it.

[437] Some have identified the boxer as pensive in defeat due to his pathos and reserve.

of boxing, but a real man in a real moment.[438] His pose is relaxed yet charged, feet not yet planted, the more-muscled back than chest of a practicing boxer, in sum a seated reflection of *contraposto*'s dynamism.

There can be no doubt that boxing at Rome, was in many ways a Greek cultural export. However, it stretches credulity to argue that Greek *pygmachia* was introduced to people on the Appenine peninsula who otherwise had no concept of fist fighting. Their native forms of personal combat must have influenced pugilism as it was practiced on Italian soil. The form of boxing that emerged was unique to Italy, and thence to the Roman world. Thus, Roman *pugilatus* had roots not only in Greece, but also in Etruria, the eastern Alps, and southern Italy (Dioscurus and Dioscurus 2023).[439]

We disagree with the notion that the Romans somehow corrupted pugilism, as is often claimed in popular accounts. The development of boxing in antiquity is typically presented to readers as a progression from the relatively wholesome to the debauched and sadistic. While there is considerable evidence of slaughter and bloodlust in Roman boxing, we have shown elsewhere that 'extreme' forms of the activity were normal long before the Romans started holding their spectacles, particularly on Crete (Dioscurus and Dioscurus 2022c), but also in the Alps and southern Italy (Section 4 in (Dioscurus and Dioscurus 2023). The Romans did not inherit from the Greeks a safe and wholesome passtime which they then proceeded to befoul. Instead, the evidence suggests that lethal forms of orthograde personal combat (without traditional weapons like swords or clubs) most likely developed independently in the culture of the Alps and was thence drawn into the orbit of Etruria. In central Italy, this boxing was incorporated into funerary ritual, perhaps due to the morbid outcome of most contests. Later influence from the Greeks seems to have positioned boxing, among the Romans, on the boundary (such as it is) between sport and ritual. Given the sanguinary nature of Etruscan and Alpine pugilism, not to mention the often overlooked violence of boxing among the Greeks, placing the burden of decadence on the Romans misses the larger point. To wit, people across cultures and time periods routinely accept, obscure, and sublimate the risks of violent injury and death so they can perpetuate the values inherent to ritualized personal orthograde and pronograde combat, including pugilism.

From a sympathetic contemporary perspective, the Romans merely have the misfortune of being the first culture to capture the life-and-death struggle of pugilism copiously and in vivid detail, in both art and literature. In other words, moderns judge them more harshly than their pugilistic predecessors because they left better written descriptions and far more excruciating images than their predecessors. That said, the Roman interest in the spectacular was fueled by the resources of empire to enable promoters and audiences to indulge exotic

---

[438] Thom Jones suggests that the boxer depicted is Theogenes (Jones 1991). More likely this will always be the Unknown Boxer.

[439] Some may argue that boxing in these regions was also introduced by the Greeks. The current archaeological record does not permit a simple solution to this question. We have argued that boxing was substantively different from Greek *pygmachia* in Italy and the eastern Alps—both in its equipment and cultural context—before the period of Roman ascendancy but not necessarily before Greek influence was felt (Dioscurus and Dioscurus 2023). To approach this latter issue, the Lucanian example may be instructive: How long would it take for a native group to adapt and apply a foreign practice like boxing to a cultural practice as important (and presumably conservative) as funerary ritual? We find it unlikely that the inclusion of Greek boxing in Italic funerals would have occurred quickly, if at all, and instead argue that boxing in Italy and the Eastern Alps pre-dated the Greeks. It may be possible to determine when Greek influence on Italic boxing became preponderant by examining (orientalizing) Etruscan depictions of pugilism, but we do not believe Greek boxing is represented in Lucanian depictions.

Figure 26: Bust of The Boxer at Rest. Note the inlaid copper details of blood.

Figure 27: The Boxer at Rest. Now housed at the Museo Nazionale Romano–Palazzo Massimo alle Terme in Rome. 330–50 BC.

Figure 28: The Boxer at Rest. The bronze as it was discovered on the slopes of the Quirinal Hill in 1885.

tastes in fighters (e.g., dwarves, which appear to have become something of an obsession at Rome) and innovations to the structure of the *cæstus* (though the Iron Age Alpine *hanteln* constitute a likely predecessor). In the Roman context, the influence of gladiatorial games on pugilism cannot be discounted, either (Section 3.6).

We conclude this section with a comment on Castor and Pollux, the semi-divine twins celebrated in the *Argonautica* and the *Idylls*. Pollux, of course, is routinely associated with boxing, but was he regarded as its patron in any religious sense? Was there an athletic or gladiatorial *cultus* associated with him? The Dioscuri were perhaps originally agonistic divinities of Tyrrhenia, numinous beings whose cult was related to boxing and hippic games, the most popular pastimes of the Etruscan elite (Thuillier 1985, p. 488–489). This tradition is likely related to a similar one in Sparta, where hand-to-hand fighting and equestrianism were regarded as vital aspects of warfare (Marroni 2019, p. 69). Still, Gartrell (2021) notes "that Pollux does not appear to have been celebrated as a boxer in Rome" despite ample qualifications as detailed in the *Argonautica* of Apollonius (Dioscurus and Dioscurus 2022d) as well as that of Valerius Flaccus (Section 3.3). After reviewing iconographic evidence (which rarely represents Pollux with a boxer's traits, outside scenes depicting his tangle with Amycus) and testimonia of ancient athletic guilds (Pollux is not mentioned), the author concludes that we are "unable to say definitively whether Pollux was worshipped as a boxer in Rome or not" (Gartrell 2021, p. 134).

We have written exhaustively about the role of Pollux/Polydeuces in his fight with Amycus in Dioscurus and Dioscurus (2022d) as well as Sections 2.1 and 3.3 of the present paper. Pollux appears as a boxer in a few more texts. Composing his *Fabulæ* around the time of Vergil, Hyginus refers to the fight between Amycus and Polydeuces (Herwagen 1535, p. 15). He writes that Amycus compels (*cogo*) anyone arriving in his kingdom to fight (*contendo*) with the *cæstus*.[440] Pollux did so, and killed (*interficio*) him.[441]

The *Orphic Argonautica*, a Greek poem written perhaps as late as the sixth century AD and translated into Latin in the eighteenth century, contains a brief rendering of the fight between Pollux and Amycus. The author refers to the 'bitterest boxing' (*pugilatus acerrimus*, ablative, with the deponent form of *experior* 'put to the test'). *Robustus Pollux* killed (*conficio*) his opponent, beating (*percutio*) his head with unyielding *cæstus* (*duris cæstibus*). Pollux' actions were 'like lightning' (*fulminis instar*).[442] It is hard to imagine that, with such a rich and varied literary tradition supporting Pollux' status as a pugilist, at least some of his adorants did not recognize his unique patronage over those who sought the utmost reward of daring in the Roman boxing 'ring'.

3.6 Boxing and gladiatorial combat

Unfortunately, a full understanding of Roman gladiatorial combat remains elusive, despite intense popular interest and many generations of study. A complete review of the literature

---

[440] The word is rendered *cæstis*, which does not conform to the fourth declension; it may be a corruption of the dative plural.

[441] *... Amycus Neptuni | Melies filius Bebryciæ rex. In huius regna qui uenerat, cæstis cogebat secum contendere, | deuictos perdebat. Hic cum Argonautas provocasset ad cæstus, Pollux cum eo contendit, & eum interfecit.*

[442] *Amycus Bebrycibus impiis imperitabat, qui Panomphæi Iouis legem non curans certamen hospitibus circumhabitantium hominum, quiscunque ad stabula sua et stabilem domum veniret, (660) proposuerat, pugilatu acerrimo vti fecum experirentur. Hunc igitur confecit robustus Pollux, percutiens subita vi (fulminis instar) caput duris cæstibus* (Estienne et al. 1764, p. 97).

on this topic lies beyond the scope of this paper. Here, we intend only to discuss the boundary between Roman *pugilatus* and gladiatorial spectacle. Fights between armed and armored gladiators, the most recognizable form of Roman agonistics, likely arose from a complex syncretism of cultural practices related to war, dueling, and human sacrifice. The Hellenized residents of Campania as well as their Etruscan neighbors are implicated in the development of the gory spectacle adopted and amplified by the Romans (Dioscurus and Dioscurus 2023). In the genetic sense, boxing and gladiatorial combat on the Appenine peninsula seem indissolubly linked. Even for those who argue that boxing was originally a Greek import, there can be no doubt that it was heavily influenced by gladiatorial competition over the course of Roman history.

On the origins of gladiatorial combat, Mouratidis (1996, p. 111) writes, "Scholars are still very uncomfortable with this subject and can give no real explanation ..." While ancient sources indicate that the Romans borrowed the gladiatorial games from the Etruscans, no ancient source avers that the Etruscans themselves invented them. Instead, graphic depictions of agonistic activities in different regions of Italy, from different time periods, are the primary sources of evidence in this doubtful controversy. According to some modern theories, the gladiatorial combats found their fullest pre-Roman expression in Campania, perhaps among the Samnites (Huergon 1970, p. 431). Today many scholars seem to agree that the direct precursors to Roman gladiator shows were indeed held in southern Italy, even if they did not originate there. This region remained a significant source of gladiators once the games had been adopted by the Romans.[443]

One theory posits that the Greeks who colonized Campania brought with them armed combat as a feature of their funeral games, though "[t]his suggestion is neither simple nor attractive" (Mouratidis 1996, p. 134).[444] The Etruscans, who competed and interacted with these Greeks in southern Italy, adopted and perhaps modified the practice. However, even Mouratidis admits that the cruel game of 'Phersu' was the Etruscan's own terrifying practice,[445] and that it was closely related to human sacrifice (pp. 126–128). Mouratidis (1996) points out the possibility that human sacrifice was a cultural export of Mycenæan Greece, as attested in Homer and a variety of visual depictions. The Etruscans were particularly captivated by Achilles' sacrifice of twelve Trojan prisoners at the funeral of Patroclus which "never ceased to haunt [their] imagination" (ibid., p. 132). Apart from the geographic and ethnic source of the games, Mouratidis (ibid., p. 132) opines on their functional genesis, as well:

> [T]hese bloody combats owe their origin to a funeral rite, an attenuation of
> the human sacrifice that in a number of early societies accompanied the death
> of important figures; for in gladiatorial fights the stronger or the abler of the
> contestants had a chance of survival ... [This] was regarded as a 'progressive'
> form of human sacrifice because instead of immolating captives on the tomb,
> they were made to combat each other in fro[n]t of it...[446]

In Rome, "gladiatorial combat, like sacrifice, was obviously a culturally sanctioned form

---

[443]Suetonius (*Caligula* 18) reports that Campania was also regarded as a source of highly skilled boxers into the first century AD (Thomson 1889).

[444]We suspect that this attitude is due to a traditional reluctance among classicists to descry in Greek civilization a penchant for bloodsport and ritual killing.

[445]Phersu appears to have involved placing a sack over a man's head and setting a vicious dog upon him.

[446]Compare, of course, the Amycus of the Valerian *Argonautica* (Section 3.3), an archetype of the barbarian at the edges of Greek civilization.

of violence. It was indeed related—or at any rate was understood by the Roman elite to be related—to human sacrifice, of which sources treat it as a substitute or development. It was originally associated with funeral ceremonies ..., and this association continued. Tertullian in the second century even suggests that the gladiatorial display originated in human sacrifice to the ghosts of the dead (*De Spec.* 12.1–3)" (Morgan 1998, p. 189). The important passage from Tertullian, as translated by Morgan (1998, p. 189), is as follows:

> The ancients thought that by this spectacle [sc., the *munus*] they were rendering a service to the dead, after they had modified it with a more civilized form of cruelty. For at one time, since it was believed that the souls of the dead were propitiated by human blood, they used to buy prisoners-of-war or slaves of low status and sacrifice them at funerals. Later they decided to conceal their impiety behind pleasure. So those they had procured were trained—to the point of learning how to be killed—in the weapons available and to the best of their ability and were then killed on the appointed day of the funeral at the tombs. In this way they found comfort for death in murder.[447]

The first gladiator matches took place at the Forum Boarium, associated with the Ara Maxima and with the fight between Hercules and Cacus (Morgan 1998, p. 187). When the gladiatorial games were first institutionalized by Augustus, the emperor seemed "to have recognized some kind of sacral dimension" in them (Morgan 1998, p. 189). They took place around the winter solstice and the vernal equinox. As for the gladiatorial *munus*, according to Morgan (1998), "there is a clear consensus in the sources that the *munus* had a ritualistic, and paradoxically life-*affirming* dimension for its audience" (original emphasis).

Gladiator bouts were marked by their own conventions, including some that may have descended from earlier Italic traditions. "[A] gladiatorial fight in Livy's day was typically preceded or opened by a distinct spectacle known as a *prolusio*. During this *prolusio*, the gladiators brandished their weapons with no intention to harm one another, performing (that is the best word for it) graceful movements, perhaps even with music and singing" (Carter 2008, p. 316). In a single combat described by Livy, one Gallic warrior even sticks out his tongue (ibid., p. 313). The relationship between the gladiatorial *prolusio* and the gestures of Etruscan boxers reminiscent of dancing (Dioscurus and Dioscurus 2023), is worthy of consideration.

There were explicitly religious overtones to the games, as one might well imagine in a recurring, public struggle between life and death. Gladiatorial games may have been related to the worship of Jupiter Latiaris, the protector of the ancient Latin League, or Nemesis, the goddess who enacts retribution against those who succumb to hubris—arrogance before the gods (Ville 1960).[448] When gladiators retired, they routinely "dedicated their weapons to Hercules" (Morgan 1998, p. 187).[449] A literary parallel is found in the Valerian *Argonautica*,

---

[447] *Officium autem mortuis hoc spectaculo facere se veteres arbitrabantur, posteaquam illud humaniore atrocitate temperaverunt. Nam olim, quoniam animas defunctorum humano sanguine propitiari creditum erat, captivos vel mali status servos mercati in exequiis immolabant. Postea placuit impietatem voluptate adumbrare. Itaque quos paraverant, armis quibus tunc et qualiter poterant eruditos, tantum ut occidi discerent, mox edicto die inferiarum apud tumulos erogabant. Ita mortem homicidiis consolabantur.*

[448] Ville in fact argues that this is not the case, though there are sources to this effect. The relation to Nemesis is suggested in Æneas' consolation to Dares regarding succumbing to the will of the gods (Section 3.1).

[449] For example Horace, *Ep.* 1.1.4–5, ... *Veianius armis | Herculis ad postem fixis latet abditus agro.*

where we are told that Amycus dedicated his gory *cæstus* to his father Neptune, depositing the gauntlets (called *arma*) on an altar (Section 3.3).

What was the relation between boxing and gladiatorial combat during the Roman era? How did the two competitions coexist and interact? Presumably, when Greek athletics were first (formally) introduced to Rome in the second century BC, Greek boxing was regarded with suspicion. Athletics were later promoted by philhellenic rulers like Nero and Domitian, but "without lasting success" (Junkelmann 2000, p. 75). Gladiator shows, by contrast, were by then considered distinctly Roman and had no trouble captivating the masses.

Köhne et al. (2000, pp. 75–80) argue that Greek boxing, once imported to Rome, was made more violent to suit Roman tastes, which had already become acclimated to gladiatorial combat.[450] While this may account for the subsumption of athletic boxing in Late Antiquity, it does not account entirely for the development of Roman boxing in the first place. Even if all forms of boxing were introduced to Iron Age Italy by the Greeks (which we doubt), then there are still several processes of cultural mediation (Alpine, Etruscan, and Lucanian) to account for. In any event, Italy appears to have been the ultimate site of development for a different kind of boxing, which we style 'gladiatorial'. Gladiatorial boxing, to hearken back to our tripartite division, partakes of ritual elements (sacrifice, i.e., the sacralization of death) and athletic elements (the celebration of life), but synthesizes them with entertainment.

From the iconographic record (e.g., Figures 16, 17, 19), we must infer that participation in the cruelest forms of Roman boxing was likely an "indirect death penalty" in the formulation of Coleman (1990, p. 56): "[O]ffenders were condemned to performances that might offer a chance of temporary survival, depending upon skill and luck, but would in the end usually prove fatal." This falls under Coleman's general rubric of "fatal charades" that were popular in the Roman arena during the first two centuries of the empire.

While "[t]he slaughter of animals and criminals in the arena tends to strike moderns as sadistic," to ancient Romans "these bloodthirsty displays were (like sacrifice) an acceptable, necessary form of killing" (Morgan 1998, p. 188). Gladiatorial boxing most likely fit into this *participation mystique*, as well. Indeed, "The arena was where Roman society dealt ... with the chaos represented by wild beasts and crime ... It was a symbol of an ordered world, the cosmos; it was the place where the civilized world confronted lawless nature" and the Romans found their own place within it (Wiedemann 1992, p. 179).[451] The lives of the victims bleeding out on the sand merited little, if any, consideration in the Roman mind: "The amphitheatre was where one went to witness and participate in ... the deaths of worthless and harmful persons" (Coleman 1990, p. 73). This callous disregard for life is perhaps one of the reasons the post-Enlightenment Westerner simply cannot resist the psychagogic magnetism of the Colosseum and the blood-bathed history it represents.

The increasingly fantastic *cæstus* of gladiatorial boxing seems related to the notion of *ludibrium*, a cruel degradation or an element of suspense. This was often added to Roman spectacles, e.g., Nero once had his victims clothed in animal skins before throwing them to dogs (Tacitus *Ann.* 15.44.4). The variation in the *cæstus* could thus be an example of Roman experimentation with *ludibrium*: which type of handgear would produce more lethal vio-

---

[450]Junkelmann (2000, p. 76) notes, "Damage to the head and face [in boxing] meant permanent disfigurement, which again helped to deprive boxing of the macabre eroticism of the gladiatorial contest."

[451]The modern Westerner still finds himself in the boxing ring. While spectatorship at the fights may have diminished over the past hundred years, boxing terminology and metaphor are still broadly integrated in colloquial English, for example.

lence? The changing form of the *cæstus* must have renewed public interest in boxing, just as the development of new gladiatorial types and their constant mixing and matching whetted the public appetite for *ludi* and *munera*.[452]

Teyssier (2009) has argued that the weapons and armor of gladiators were early derived form the military customs of various groups conquered by the Romans (e.g., the *samnis*, *gallus* and *thraex*). Later, other gladiator 'types' (e.g., the *crupellarius*, *laquearius*, and *dimachærus*) were invented based on a particular weapon or style of fighting with no obvious national origin. The distinction among classes of gladiators (from a modern perspective) is sometimes referred to as 'ethnic' versus 'technical'. In the same way a *gallus* or *thraex* was derived from the fighting traditions of conquered Gaul and Thrace, one might argue that the *pugil* was derived from conquered Greece. However, the *himantes* of the Greek boxer transformed into something rich and strange under Roman influence, including a sleeve reminiscent of the gladiatorial *manica* (Junkelmann 2000, p. 76). The Roman boxer was neither an 'ethnic' nor a 'technical' gladiator but a combination of the two. The primary reason for not including the *pugil* among gladiators is that he did not fight other gladiators: Boxers fought boxers whereas a *thraex* might fight a *laquearius*, *vel. simil.* The Romans must have perceived a distinction between a gladiator armed with a sword, dagger, or trident, and a *pugil* armed with a spiked glove. Though clearly a lethal weapon, the *cæstus* of the *pugil* was of a different quality than the *gladius*, perhaps because it was attached to the hand and arm.[453] Still, this did not prevent epic poets like Vergil from freely characterizing the *cæstus* as *arma* (Section 3.1).

By the early Christian era, gladiatorial competition throughout the empire waned (along with boxing; see below). The Church Fathers were not fans. Augustine wrote of his friend Alypius, who attended but resolved to keep his eyes closed during the *ludi*: "He drank up unawares the very Furies, was charmed by the barbarity of the combat, and became drunk on the pleasures of blood" (*Conf.* 6.13).[454] So powerful was the cruel *voluptas* of the games that it could corrupt the soul of even a devout person with his eyes shut tight. It is hard to imagine Augustine had a more favorable view of gladiatorial boxing.

3.7 The end of boxing in the Roman world

All fires burn out at last. The life of ancient boxing was roughly coterminous with classical antiquity—a period which boxing predated by more than a thousand years (Dioscurus and Dioscurus 2022b;c). In this section, we review some of the latest attestations of ancient boxing in the Roman world and offer explanations as to its widely-presumed disappearance from the historical record in around the fifth century AD.

As late as the third century, boxers were still celebrated for their athletic victories throughout the empire (Van Voorhis 2008). The boxers Piseas and Candidianus were memorialized

---

[452] Recent developments in western combat sports represent the same impulse, scaled down: promoters use boxing gloves of different weights and construction (cf. MMA gloves) to retain and increase spectatorship. A certain sense of novelty in the ring—a *frisson* of sanguineous expectation—is just as necessary to fill seats as it was twenty centuries ago.

[453] Reconstructing why the Romans did not think of the armed *pugil* as a gladiator is an exercise fraught with unknowns. We know of no ancient text in which an explicit comparison is made. Perhaps learned Roman authors could not separate gladiatorial boxing from its associations with Greek athletics, even though the Roman audience more generally perceived little, if any, difference, between these forms of bloodsport.

[454] *hauriebat furias et nesciebat et delectabatur scelere certaminis et cruenta voluptate inebriabatur.*

with two splendid statues placed at either end of the theater stage in Aphdrodisias, in Asia Minor (Newby 2005, p. 254ff.). These "honorific statues proclaim[ed] Aphrodisias' ability to continue to produce athletic victors" well into the first millennium. Though fragmentary (all the hands are lost), the boxers' arm-length *cæstus* can be seen reaching up towards the shoulder. The fighters wear the *cirrus vertice*, "a lock of hair high on the back of an otherwise shaven head" (ibid., p. 257).[455] This hairstyle was frequently associated with athletes in Late Antiquity (Figure 16).[456] One critic has pointed out that the *cæstus* are "carefully ornamented, covered with intricate patterning which suggests idealized presentation," perhaps indicating an ideological removal from "the sweat and untidiness of real-life combat" (König 2005, p. 123).

Figure 29: Detail of the Privatulus vase (once exhibited at the Staatliche Münzsammlung, Munich, no inv. number; present whereabouts unknown). This scene has been interpreted as a particularly late (sixth century) depiction of Greek pankratiasts, though the date is controversial. The expressive captions are written in vulgar Latin as if shouted by the crowd.

It has been argued that the scene on the Privatulus vase (Klose and Klein 2013),[457] once exhibited at the Staatliche Münzsammlung in Munich but with a presently unknown location, demonstrates how public attitudes towards boxing, wrestling, and *pankration* had changed during Late Antiquity, emphasizing the humiliation of the loser and the acrobatic nature of combat (Remijsen 2015). While intriguing, this view has not been widely adopted (Scanlon 2015, Dunbabin 2017).

One scene on the Privatulus vase depicts the eponymous victor duking it out with his opponent (Victorinus) while the latter assumes a defensive position, covering his face with

---

[455] The iconographic record does not support a shaven head for all pugilists who wore the *cirrus*. For example, mosaics in Roman Africa indicate a variety of fighters wearing the *cirrus* along with a full head of (tightly pulled-back) hair (Khanoussi 2006).

[456] "[T]he *cirrus* is not an exclusive attribute of athletes, for it [also] appears on representations of slaves, dancers, mimes, hunchbacks, and other grotesques" (Bartus 2016, p. 164).

[457] The vase is sometimes referred to as the Kovacs vase, based on the name of its (previous?) owner.

his hands. The caption, written in vulgar Latin,[458] includes an insult hurled by the canaille at Victorinus: CINEDE/QVIVIS/ADUC, "Get moving, catamite!"[459] Another vignette, perhaps depicting the climax of the bout, has the loser crouching at the feet of Privatulus, raising one finger in submission. The champ, reaching out to his fallen opponent, appears to obey the magnanimous throng, who exclaim, CADVCVS/ESTDA/LIMANU "He's down, give him a hand!" (Dunbabin 2017, p. 171). Elsewhere, we read the rather incomprehensible command OXILICERE PRIVATULUS, perhaps, "Go for it, Privatulus!"[460] The inscription QVIS-IBIFECIT/NONPLORET "Don't cry! You got yourself into this" accompanies a scene in which Privatulus lifts Victorinus from the ground by the hair and the buttocks while drawing the loser's fundament toward his groin.[461]

Figure 30: Detail of boxers from the Noheda Villa mosaic, Panel B. The mosaic, dated to the fourth century AD, was found in the ruins of a triple-apsed *triclinium* near Cuenca, Spain.

The fourth-century Noheda mosaic, discovered in central Spain, features two pairs of boxers (Valero Tévar 2013). Each figure is framed in a separate vaulted compartment but the members of each duo clearly interact with their partners. The boxers in Panel B (Figure 30) are thought to represent children or perhaps erotes because of their curly hair (Dunbabin 2017, p. 153, fn. 9). The left-hand gauntlet of the figure on the left fans out at the end, reminiscent of the Villelaure mosaic (Figure 24). The boxers in Panel E (not pictured) wear the *cirrus* hairstyle. Blood sprays from the head of one of the pugilists, and drips from his hand. The gloves of the boxers in Panel E appear to consist of strips wound around the fist. The loser's are dark, perhaps stained with blood. Both have some indication of a thumb.

Writing of a fourth-century statesman named Gallus,[462] Ammianus Marcellinus (14.7.3) notes his passion for boxing and provides one of the last contemporaneous references to the sport in the ancient world:

This also was a sign of his [sc., Gallus'] savage nature which was neither ob-

---

[458] According to Klose and Klein (2013, p. 144), the inscriptions on the vase "are written and formulated in a vulgar-colored Latin at the level of Proto-Romanic using the sparest syntax, so that there are problems for understanding and some commentary is required" (translation ours).

[459] Klose and Klein (2013, p. 145) have *Weichling, wer du auch seiest, tritt [gegen ihn]* "Weakling, whoever you be, stand [against him]!"

[460] Scanlon (2021, p. 71) translates the caption as "I, Privatulus, have been honored to be able [to win]."

[461] One commentator reads the image as an act of sodomy, with the hapless Victorinus in the pathic role (Scanlon 2021, p. 70).

[462] Constantius Gallus, designated cæsar, ruled from Antioch under the authority of the emperor Constantius II.

scure nor hidden, that he delighted in cruel sports [*ludicer*]; and sometimes in the Circus, absorbed in six or seven contests [*certamen*], he exulted in the sight of boxers [*pugil*] pounding [*concido*] each other to death and drenched [*perfundo*] with blood, as if he had made some great gain (Rolfe 1935–1940).[463]

Ammianus uses the verb *concido* to describe the activity of the boxers (*pugil*). The verb is from the same root as *cæstus*, viz., 'to cut'. Given that the boxers are bathed (*perfundo*) in blood, an alternative translation seems to be "cutting each other to pieces." This is further evidence that during Late Antiquity, the boundary between athletic boxing and fighting at arms had become increasingly obnubilate in the Roman *imaginaire*.

Boxing vanished from the historical record in around the fifth century AD; traditional, Greek-style athletic competitions were by then vanishingly rare. A few artifacts depicting boxing can be dated to the mid-fourth century or perhaps the early fifth, but no later (Dunbabin 2017, p. 151). Literary references to boxing also cease, snuffed out even before the last Olympic games were held at Antioch in the sixth century.

While it is still commonly claimed that the rulers of the Christianized Roman Empire banned boxing, this narrative has been revised (Remijsen 2015, Dunbabin 2017). Theodosius the Great is often cited as the doomsayer of ancient boxing, by virtue of having banned the Olympic games in AD 392/393. However, the games apparently continued, since his grandson Theodosius II took the trouble of banning them once more in 420/435. By the fifth century, the Roman emperors lacked "the power for or interest in managing contests across the empire"; neither is it clear that the games were any longer viewed as pagan festivities by the general public (Scanlon 2015, p. 84). Rather than attributing the end of the Olympics to Christian nomothesy, a sudden revulsion towards competitive violence and athletic nudity, or the by-then unpopular pagan associations of the games, a new generation of scholars now argues that socioeconomic changes were primarily responsible for their demise. Centralization of wealth in provincial capitals and hyper-inflation deprecated local athletic circuits. Games were staged less frequently and were less accessible to potential athletes. Roman spectacle, including gladiator matches and *venationes*, had a profound impact on popular tastes. Traditional Greek athletics were gradually supplanted by performances that may look to us more like the acts of a modern circus, complete with acrobats and pantomimes. Even the arena came to be known as the 'circus' with time.

As if gladiatorial fights were not strong enough competition, athletic wrestling, *pankration*, and boxing were perhaps displaced by a little-understood fighting sport called *pammachon*. Originally a synonym for *pankration*, by the third century AD *pammachon* was explicitly differentiated from the Greek activity. A late fourth-century athlete named Philoumenos was victorious in *pammachon*, in addition to the classical triumvirate of fighting sports (Remijsen 2010, p. 201). In a letter dated to the same century, a less pugnacious young man named Dios explains how, at an athletic event held in Egypt, he failed at *pankration* so decided to take up *pammachon* instead (ibid.). Unfortunately, very little is known about this Late Antique combat sport. Remijsen argues, without an abundance of evidence, that *pammachon* was more like modern professional wrestling, i.e., a kind of performed theatrical combat where the winners and losers were predetermined.

---

[463] *Erat autem diritatis eius hoc quoque indicium nec obscurum nec latens, quod ludicris cruentis delectabatur, et in circo sex vel septem aliquotiens deditus certaminibus, pugilum vicissim se concidentium, perfusorumque sanguine specie, ut lucratus ingentia, lætabatur.*

4 Conclusion

The Italic predilection for bloodletting made Greek boxing, with its focus on technique and defense, a lackluster affair to the Roman observer. The Romans transformed boxing into spectacle, eventually making of it a pastiche of Greek athletics and gladiatorial combat. They seem to have drawn on earlier models for such agonistic practice, including the bloody fights of the East Alpine boxers, the Etruscans, and the Lucanians. While Roman boxers still fought naked (a Greek trait, to be sure, though one known to pre-Roman Italy), they also wore spiked devices on their hands. Like the East Alpine *ročke*, these were intended to quickly dispatch an opponent in a fountain of blood—a feature celebrated, albeit obliquely, in Roman epic. The demise of boxing as an athletic practice in Late Antiquity was not so much a disappearance as a submersion in a far more popular and spectacular arms race that shared too many features with boxing to foster strong differentiation. Men striking each other with lightly-covered fists became men fracturing each others skulls with reinforced fists, and so forth. If the ontological boundary between these two activities is difficult for us to traduce, so, too, must it have been for the inhabitants of the Roman world.

Cato and Tacitus would have been satisfied when Roman arms finally came to supplant the ancient tradition of unarmed boxing, uninterrupted (but for the Bronze Age collapse) since the city-states of Sumer and culminating in the Greek athletic version which they found so deplorable. Vergil mingled the meanings of specific boxing handgear (i.e., the *cæstus*) and weapons (*arma*) more generally. For the *au courant*, swordplay reigned supreme, from the amphitheaters of Late Antiquity to the fencing schools of early modern Germany. It is this tradition of swords, and not of fists, that redounded to the peoples of Europe once Rome lay in ruin. Ancient pugilism awaited rediscovery in Britain—as exaptation of fencing rather than redivivus proper—but only after eleven centuries of stony sleep.

References

Gianfranco Agosti. Nonnus and late antique society. In Domenico Accorinti, editor, *Brill's Companion to Nonnus of Panopolis*, pages 644–668. Brill, Leiden, 2016.

Henricus Ludolfus Ahrens. *Bucolicorum Græcorum Theocriti, Bionis, Moschi Reliquiae, Accedentibus Incertorum Idylliis*. Teubner, Leipzig, 1887.

Anonymous. Hang up the boxing gloves. *The Economist*, 4 March 1995.

Theodoros Antoniadis. 'Boxing as a Stoic paradigm': A Philosophical reading of the fight between Amycus and Pollux in Valerius Flaccus' Argonautica (4.199–343) with a view to Seneca's De Ira. *Illinois Classical Studies*, 42:163–181, 2017.

Herbert Bannert and Nicole Kröll. Nonnus and the Homeric poems. In Domenico Accorinti, editor, *Brill's Companion to Nonnus of Panopolis*, pages 479–506. Brill, Leiden, 2016.

Shadi Bartsch. *Actors in the audience: Theatricality and Doublespeak from Nero to Hadrian*. Harvard University Press, Cambridge, MA, 1994.

Dávid Bartus. Two Roman bronze heads with cirrus from Brigetio. In Alessandra Giumlia-Mair and Carol C. Mattusch, editors, *Proceedings of the XVIIth International Congress on Ancient Bronzes, Izmir*, pages 163–168. Éditions Mergoil, Autun, 2016.

Neil W. Bernstein. Romanas veluti sævissima cum legiones tisiphone regesque movet: Valerius Flaccus' Argonautica and the Flavian Era. In Mark Heerink and Gesine Manuwald, editors, *Brill's Companion to Valerius Flaccus*, pages 154–169. Brill, Leiden, 2014.

Anke Bohne. *Bilder vom Sport. Untersuchungen zur Ikonographie römischer AthletenDarstellungen*. Weidmann, Hildesheim, 2011.

William S. Bonds. Two combats in the Thebaid. *Transactions of the American Philological Association*, 115:225–235, 1985.

E. Borthwick. The Gymnasium of Bromius: A note on Dionysius Chalcus, Fr.3. *The Journal of Hellenic Studies*, 84:49–53, 1964a.

E. K. Borthwick. A Note on boxing-gloves. *The Classical Review*, 14:142, 1964b.

Robert Brophy and Mary Brophy. Deaths in the Pan-Hellenic Games ii: All combative sports. *The American Journal of Philology*, 106:171–198, 1985.

Shelby Brown. Combat sports and gladiatorial combat in Greek and Roman private art. In Thomas Francis Scanlon and Alison Futrell, editors, *The Oxford Handbook of Sport and Spectacle in the Ancient World*, pages 439–454. Oxford University Press, Oxford, 2021.

Emma Buckley. Valerius Flaccus and Seneca's tragedies. In Mark Heerink and Gesine Manuwald, editors, *Brill's Companion to Valerius Flaccus*, pages 307–325. Brill, Leiden, 2014.

Nicole Elyse Budrovich. Receptions of spectacle: Virgil's Æneid and local identity in Gallo-Roman mosaics. Master's thesis, University of California, Berkeley, 2011.

R. G. Bury. *Plato. Plato in Twelve Volumes*, volume 10–11. Harvard University Press, Cambridge, MA, 1967–1968.

S. H. Butcher. *Demosthenes. Demosthenis. Orationes*. Clarendon Press, Oxford, 1903.

Francesco Cannizzaro. Games and war: Statius, Silius Italicus, and the failed heroic succession of Valerius Flaccus' Pollux. *Phoenix*, 74(3–4):281–299, 2020.

Michael Carter. Livy, Titus Manlius Torquatus and the gladiatorial 'prolusio'. *Rheinisches Museum Für Philologie*, 151(3/4):313–325, 2008.

Samir Chadli, Noureddine Ababou, Amina Ababou, and Nazim Ouadahi. Quantification of boxing gloves damping: Method and apparatus. *Measurement*, 129:504–517, 2018. doi: https://doi.org/10.1016/j.measurement.2018.07.036.

Matthew Chaldekas. The Ethnographic eye: Visual and verbal identification in Theocritus Idyll 22. *The Phœnix*, 74:15–35, 2020.

R. J. Cholmeley. *Idylls. Theocritus.* London, 1901.

Clifford Pease Clark. *Numerical Phraseology in Vergil.* PhD thesis, Princeton University, 1913.

K. M. Coleman. Fatal charades: Roman executions staged as mythological enactments. *The Journal of Roman Studies,* 80:44–73, 1990.

John Conington. *The Works of Virgil.* Whittaker and Co., London, 1876.

Robert Cowan. My family and other enemies: Argonautic antagonists and Valerian villains. In Mark Heerink and Gesine Manuwald, editors, *Brill's Companion to Valerius Flaccus,* pages 229–248. Brill, Leiden, 2014.

Nigel B. Crowther. The evidence for kicking in Greek boxing. *The American Journal of Philology,* 111:176–181, 1990.

Janet DeLaine. *The Baths of Caracalla: A Study in the design, construction, and econoics of large-scael building projects in imperial Rome.* Journal of Roman Archæology, Portsmouth, RI, 1997. Supplementary Series 25.

Alain Deremetz. Le combat du ceste d'Homere a Stace. In Françoise Bosman, Pierre Lambin, and Arnaud Waquet, editors, *Jeu et enjeu culturels du sport,* pages 53–64. Atlantica, Biarritz, 2011.

Alain Deremetz. Authorial poetics in Valerius Flaccus' Argonautica. In Mark Heerink and Gesine Manuwald, editors, *Brill's Companion to Valerius Flaccus,* pages 49–71. Brill, Leiden, 2014.

Henry B. Dewing. Argonautic associations of the Bosporus. *The Classical Journal,* 19(8): 469–483, 1924.

Jitse H. F. Dijkstra. The religious background of Nonnus. In Domenico Accorinti, editor, *Brill's Companion to Nonnus of Panopolis,* pages 75–88. Brill, Leiden, 2016.

Castor Dioscurus and Pollux Dioscurus. The development of boxing: Origins in biomechanics and social mechanics; The ancient world (Prehistory). *Scholia Pugillātōria,* 1: 1–22, 2022a.

Castor Dioscurus and Pollux Dioscurus. The development of boxing: The ancient world (Western Asia and Egypt). *Scholia Pugillātōria,* 1:23–71, 2022b.

Castor Dioscurus and Pollux Dioscurus. The development of boxing: The ancient world (The Ægean). *Scholia Pugillātōria,* 1:73–111, 2022c.

Castor Dioscurus and Pollux Dioscurus. The development of boxing: The ancient world (Classical Greece). *Scholia Pugillātōria,* 1:113–190, 2022d.

Castor Dioscurus and Pollux Dioscurus. The development of boxing: The ancient world (The Eastern Alps, Pre-Roman Italia, and Sardinia). *Scholia Pugillātōria,* 1:191–247, 2023.

John Dryden. *The Works of Virgil: containing his Pastorals, Georgics, and Æneis.* Jacob Tonson, London, 1697.

Katherine M. D. Dunbabin. Athletes represented in Roman mosaics and painting [review of Bohne 2011]. *Journal of Roman Archæology,* 27:710–716, 2014.

Katherine M. D. Dunbabin. The agonistic mosaic in the Villa of Lucius Verus and the Capitolia of Rome. *Journal of Roman Archæology,* 28:192–222, 2015.

Katherine M. D. Dunbabin. Athletes, acclamations, and imagery from the end of antiquity. *Journal of Roman Archæology,* 30:151–174, 2017.

Roger Dunkle. Games and transition: 'Æneid' 3 and 5. *The Classical World,* 98:157–178, 2005.

J. M. Edmonds. *The Greek Bucolic Poets.* Heinemann, London, 1912.

Henri Estienne, Andreas Christian Eschenbach, Johann Matthias Gesner, and Georg Christoph Hamberger. *Orpheōs hapanta: Orphei Argonavtica, Hymni libellvs De lapidibvs et fragmenta.* C. Fritsch, Leipzig, 1764.

Arthur Fairbanks. *Philostratus the Elder, Philostratus the Younger, Callistratus. Philostratus the Elder, Imagines. Philostratus the Younger, Imagines. Callistratus, Descriptions,* volume 256. Harvard University Press, Cambridge, MA, 1931.

H. R. Fairclough. *Virgil. Eclogues, Georgics, Aeneid,* volume 63–64 of *Loeb Classical Library.* Harvard University Press, Cambridge, MA, 1916.

H. R. Fairclough and Seldon L. Brown. *Virgil's Æneid: Books I-VI.* Benjamin H. Sanborn and Co., Chicago, IL, 1919.

Andrew Feldherr. Stepping out of the ring: Repetition and sacrifice in the boxing match in Æneid 5. In David Samuel Levine and Damien P. Nelis, editors, *Clio and the Poets: Augustan Poetry and the Traditions of Ancient Historiography,* pages 61–80. Brill, Leiden, 2002.

Salvatore Ferraro. *La presenza di Virgilio nei graffiti pompeiani.* Loffredo Editore, Naples, 1982.

Sylvie Franchet d'Espèrey. *Conflit, violence et non-violence dans la Thébaïde de Stace,* volume 60 of *Collection d'Études Anciennes.* Les Belles Lettres, Paris, 1999.

Elena Franchi. Die Herkunft der Phlegyer und der Dritte Heilige Krieg. *Hermes,* 141(4): 450–458, 2013.

Hélène Frangoulis. *Nonnos de Panopolis. Les Dionysiaques: Chant XXXVII,* volume 13. Les Belles Lettres, Paris, 1999.

Hélène Frangoulis. Nonnos transposant Homère: Étude du chant 37 des 'Dionysiaques' de Nonnos de Panopolis. *Revue De Philologie, De Littérature et d'Histoire Anciennes,* 69: 145–168, 1995.

E. Norman Gardiner. *Greek Athletic Sports and Festivals*. Macmillan and Co., London, 1910.

H. W. Garrod. Metrical stopgaps in Statius' Thebaid. *Journal of Philology*, 29:253–262, 1904.

Amber Gartrell. *The Cult of Castor and Pollux in Ancient Rome*. Cambridge University Press, Cambridge, 2021.

Camille Geisz. Narrative and digression in the Dionysiaca. In Domenico Accorinti, editor, *Brill's Companion to Nonnus of Panopolis*, pages 173–192. Brill, Leiden, 2016.

William H. Goodwin. *Plutarch. Plutarch's Morals*. Little, Brown, and Company, Boston, 1874.

Elliot J. Gorn. 'Gouge and bite, pull hair and scratch': The Social significance of fighting in the Southern backcountry. *American Historical Review*, 90:18–43, 1985.

Andrew Sydenham Farrar Gow. The Twenty-Second Idyll of Theocritus. *The Classical Review*, 56:11–18, 1942.

Andrew Sydenham Farrar Gow. *Theocritus II*. Cambridge University Press, Cambridge, 2 edition, 1952.

J. B. Greenough. *Vergil. Bucolics, Aeneid, and Georgics Of Vergil*. Ginn & Co., Boston, 1900.

Pierre Grimal. *La littérature latine*. Fayard, Paris, 1994.

Ernst Justus Häberlin. *Aes grave, das schwergeld Roms und mittelitaliens einschliesslich der ihm vorausgehenden rohbronzewährung*. Forni, Bologna, 1967.

Diran Hagopian. *Pollux' Faustkampf mit Amykos*. Braumüller, Vienna/Stuttgart, 1955.

J. B. Hall. Notes on Statius' 'Thebaid' Books 5 and 6. *Illinois Classical Studies*, 17:287–299, 1992.

P. Hardie. *The Epic Successors of Virgil: Studies in the dynamics of a tradition*. Cambridge University Press, Cambridge, 1993.

A. M. Harmon. *Lucian. Demonax*, volume 14 of *Loeb Classical Library*. Harvard University Press, Cambridge, MA, 1913.

Daniel E. Harris-McCoy. *Artemidorus' Oneirocritica: Text, Translation, and Commentary*. Oxford University Press, Oxford, 2012.

Elisabeth Hartmann. *Die trollvorstellungen in den sagen und märchen der skandinavischen völker*. W. Kohlhammer, Stuttgart, 1936.

Mark Heerink and Gesine Manuwald. Introduction. In Mark Heerink and Gesine Manuwald, editors, *Brill's Companion to Valerius Flaccus*, pages 1–6. Brill, Leiden, 2014.

James Henry. *Æneidea, or Critical, Exegetical and Æsthetical Remarks on the Æneis*. Ponsonby and Weldrick, Dublin, 1881. Vol. 3.

Johann Herwagen. *C. Iulii Hygini Augusti Liberti. Fabularum Liber (XVII)*. Johann Herwagen, Basel, 1535.

H. Hirzel. Musaico tuscolano. *Annali dell'Instituto di Corrispondenza, Archeologica*, 35: 397–412, 1863.

Jacques Huergon. *Recherches à l'histoire, la religion, et la civilisation de Capoue préromaine*. Éditions E. de Boccard, Paris, 1970.

Richard L. Hunter. *Theocritus and the Archæology of Greek Poetry*. Cambridge University Press, Cambridge, 1996.

Alan W. James and Kevin Hargreaves Lee. *A commentary on Quintus of Smyrna Posthomerica V*. Brill, Leiden, 2000.

Thom Jones. The Pugilist at rest. *The New Yorker*, 67(41):38–39, 1991.

M. Junkelmann. Greek athletics in Rome: Boxing, wrestling, and the pancration. In E. Köhne and C. Ewigleben, editors, *Gladiators and Cæsars*, pages 75–85. University of California Press, Berkeley, CA, 2000.

Julius Jüthner. *Philostratos über Gymnastik*. B. G. Teubner, Leipzig, 1909.

Julius Jüthner and Erwin Mehl. Pygme (pugilatus). In Konrat Ziegler, editor, *Paulys Realencyclopädie der classischen Altertumswissenschaft*, volume S9, pages 1306–1352. Alfred Druckenmüller Verlag, Stuttgart, 1962.

Carl Ludwig Kayser. *Philostratus the Lemnian (Philostratus Major)*, volume 2 of *Flavii Philostrati Opera*. B. G. Teubner, Leipzig, 1871.

Mustapha Khanoussi. Les spectacles des jeux athlétiques et de pugilat dans l'afrique romaine. *Mitteilungen des Deutschen Archäologischen Instituts, Römische Abteilung*, 98: 315–322, 1991.

Mustapha Khanoussi. Pugilist spectacles and athletic games in proconsular Africa. In Aïcha Ben Abed, editor, *Stories in Stone: Conserving Mosaics of Roman Africa*, pages 70–91. Getty Publications, Los Angeles, 2006.

D. Klose and T. Klein. Werbung für den Wettkampf in spätantiker Zeit: Die Bronzevase des Privatulus aus archäologischer und philologischer Sicht. In A. Gutsfeld and S. Lehmann, editors, *Der gymnische Agon in der Spätantike*, pages 143–150. Computus Druck, Gutenberg, 2013.

Eckart Köhne, Cornelia Ewigleben, and Ralph Jackson. *Gladiators and Cæsars: The Power of Spectacle in Ancient Rome*. University of California Press, Berkeley, CA, 2000.

Egil Kraggerud. Einige Namen in der Æneis. *Symbolæ Osloenses*, 36:30–39, 1960.

Otto Kramer. *C. Valeri Flacci Setini Balbi Argonauticon Libri Octo*. Teubner, Leipzig, 1913.

Mark Kriegel. *The Good Son: The Life of Ray "Boom Boom" Mancini*. Simon and Schuster, New York, 2013.

Donald G. Kyle. *Spectacles of Death in Ancient Rome*. Routledge, London, 1998.

Jason König. *Athletics and Literature in the Roman Empire*. Cambridge University Press, Cambridge, 2005.

Henri Lavagne. Le pavement de la rue des Magnans à Aix-en-Provence et la naissance des trames à 'décor multiple' dans la mosaïque gallo-romaine. *Gallia*, 51:202–215, 1994.

Hugh M. Lee. The Later Greek boxing glove and the 'Roman' cæstus: A centennial reevaluation of Jüthner's 'Über antike Turngeräthe'. *Nikephoros*, 10:161–178, 1997.

Léon Legras. *Étude sur la Thébaïde de Stace*. Société nouvelle de librairie et d'édition, Paris, 1905.

Matthew Leigh. Boxing and sacrifice: Apollonius, Vergil, and Valerius. *Harvard Studies in Classical Philology*, 105:117–155, 2010.

Roger Lesuer. *Stace. Thébaïde. Livres V–VIII*. Les Belles Lettres, Paris, 1991.

Gauthier Liberman. Lycophron, Alexandra. Collection des universités de France Série grecque by André Hurst. *Bryn Mawr Classical Review*, 3, 2009. Book review.

J. A. Lobell. Artifact. *Archæology*, 71(4):68, 2018.

Helen Lovatt. Mad about winning: Epic, war and madness in the games of Statius' Thebaid. *Materiali e Discussioni per l'analisi Dei Testi Classici*, 46:103–120, 2001.

Helen Lovatt. *Statius and Epic Games: Sport, Politics and Poetics in the Thebaid*. Cambridge University Press, Cambridge, 2005.

Calum Alasdair Maciver. *Quintus Smyrnæus' Posthomerica: Engaging Homer in late antiquity*. Brill, Leiden, 2012.

Elisa Marroni. *Il Culto dei Dioscuri in Italia: Caratteri e Significati*, volume 2. Edizioni ETS, Pisa, 2019.

John Masefield. *The Everlasting Mercy*. Sidgwick and Jackson, London, 1911.

Christopher R Matthews. 'The Fog soon clears': Bodily negotiations, embodied understandings, competent body action and 'brain injuries' in boxing. *International Review for the Sociology of Sport*, 56:719–738, 2021.

Anne Maugier-Sinha. Combattre ou s'incliner. Le combat de boxe comme métaphore de l'æmulatio dans les Argonautiques de Valerius Flaccus et la Thébaïde de Stace. *Mosaïque*, 3:87–108, 2010.

Nathan May. Amphion's worthless walls: Capaneus and the defeat of poetry in Statius' Thebaid. *Persephone*, 1:43–45, 2016.

Andrew M. McClellan. *Abused Bodies in Roman Epic*. Cambridge University Press, Cambridge, 2019.

Matthew M. McGowan. On the etymology and inflection of 'Dares' in Vergil's boxing match, 'Æneid' 5.362-484. *Classical Philology*, 97(1):80–88, 2002.

Charles McNelis. *Statius' Thebaid and the Poetics of Civil War*. Cambridge University Press, Cambridge, 2007.

Llewelyn Morgan. Assimilation and civil war: Hercules and Cacus. In Hans-Peter Stahl, editor, *Vergil's Æneid: Augustan Epic and Political Context*, pages 175–197. Duckworth, London, 1998.

Carroll Moulton. Theocritus and the Dioscuri. *Greek, Roman, and Byzantine Studies*, pages 41–47, 1973.

John Mouratidis. On the origin of the gladiatorial games. *Nikephoros*, 9:111–134, 1996.

John Henry Mozley. *Statius, P. Papinius. Thebaid, Achilleid*. William Heinemann, London, 1928a. 2 vols.

John Henry Mozley. *Valerius Flaccus. Argonautica*, volume 286 of *Loeb Classical Library*. William Heinemann, London, 1928b.

Gregory Nagy. Athletic contests in contexts of epic and other related archaic texts. In Thomas Francis Scanlon and Alison Futrell, editors, *The Oxford Handbook of Sport and Spectacle in the Ancient World*, pages 283–304. Oxford University Press, Oxford, 2021.

Damien Nelis. *Vergil's Æneid and the Argonautica of Apollonius Rhodius*, volume 39 of *ARCA Classical and Medieval Texts, Papers, and Monographs*. Francis Cairns, Cambridge, 2001.

Zahra Newby. Greek athletics as Roman spectacle: The Mosaics from Ostia and Rome. *Papers of the British School at Rome*, 70:177–203, 2002.

Zahra Newby. *Greek Athletics in the Roman World: Victory and Virtue*. Oxford University Press, Oxford, 2005.

W. R. Paton. *The Greek Anthology, Volume IV: Book 10: The Hortatory and Admonitory Epigrams. Book 11: The Convivial and Satirical Epigrams. Book 12: Strato's Musa Puerilis*, volume 85 of *Loeb Classical Library*. Harvard University Press, Cambridge, MA, 1918.

Bernadotte Perrin. *Plutarch. Plutarch's Lives*. Harvard University Press, Cambridge, MA, 1914.

Michael B. Poliakoff. Greek combat sport and the borders of athletics, violence, and civilization. In Thomas Francis Scanlon and Alison Futrell, editors, *The Oxford Handbook of Sport and Spectacle in the Ancient World*, pages 221–230. Oxford University Press, Oxford, 2021.

Michael Baron Poliakoff. *Studies in the Terminology of the Greek Combat Sports*. PhD thesis, University of Michigan, 1983.

Michael Baron Poliakoff. Entellus and Amycus: Vergil, 'Æn.' 5. 362–484. *Illinois Classical Studies*, 10(2):227–31, 1985.

Michael Baron Poliakoff. *Combat Sports in the Ancient World*. Yale University Press, New Haven, CT, 1987a.

Michael Baron Poliakoff. Melankomas, ἐκ κλίμακος, and Greek boxing. *The American Journal of Philology*, 108(3):511–518, 1987b.

J. J. Pollitt. *Art in the Hellenistic Age*. Cambridge University Press, Cambridge, 1986.

Heather L. Reid. Philostratus's 'Gymnasticus': The ethics of an athletic æsthetic. *Memoirs of the American Academy in Rome*, 61:77–90, 2016.

Sofie Remijsen. "Pammachon", a new sport. *The Bulletin of the American Society of Papyrologists*, 47:185–204, 2010.

Sofie Remijsen. *The End of Greek Athletics in Late Antiquity*. Cambridge University Press, Cambridge, 2015.

Sofie Remijsen. The fading allure of Greek athletics. In John Zilcosky and Marlo A. Burks, editors, *The Allure of Sports in Western Culture*. University of Toronto Press, Toronto, 2019.

Gérard-Jean Te Riele. Inscriptions conservées au musée d'olympie. *Bulletin de Correspondance Hellénique*, 88:169–195, 1964.

Rachel Sargent Robinson. *Sources for the History of Greek Athletics*. Self-published, Cincinnati, OH, 1955.

John C. Rolfe. *Ammianus Marcellinus. Rerum Gestarum*. Harvard University Press, Cambridge, 1935–1940.

W. H. D. Rouse. *Nonnus of Panopolis. Dionysiaca*. Harvard University Press, Cambridge, MA, 1940–1942. 3 vols.

Sarah Ruden. *The Aeneid, Vergil*. Yale University Press, New Haven, CT, 2008.

Jeffrey Rusten and Jason König. *Philostratus. Heroicus. Gymnasticus. Discourses 1 and 2*, volume 521 of *Loeb Classical Library*. Harvard University Press, Cambridge, MA, 2014.

Jerry Saltz. Behind the brilliance of the *boxer at rest*. *New York Magazine*, 46(2):12, 2013.

Rudolfo Savica, Mario Roberto Vaz Carneiro Filho, and Christopher J. Boes. Cleomedes of Astypalaea: A possible early sufferer of chronic traumatic encephalopathy. *Journal of Clinical Neuroscience*, 42:193–195, 2017.

Thomas F. Scanlon. Early Christians' embrace of the Greek athletic body. In Juan Ramón Carbó, editor, *Cuerpo y Espíritu: Deporte y Cristianismo en la Historia*, pages 53–78. Murcia, 2021.

Thomas Francis Scanlon. Boxing gloves and the games of Gallienus. *The American Journal of Philology*, 107:110–114, 1986.

Thomas Francis Scanlon. *Eros and Greek Athletics*. Oxford University Press, New York, 2002.

Thomas Francis Scanlon. Review essay: Satan's business or the people's choice: The Decline of athletics in in Late Antiquity. *The Ancient History Bulletin*, 29(1–2):80–90, 2015.

Tine Scheijnen. *Quintus of Smyrna's Posthomerica: A Study of Heroic Characterization and Heroism*. Brill, Leiden, 2018.

A. F. Scholfield. *Ælian. De Natura Animalium. On the Characteristics of Animals*. Loeb Classical Library. William Heinemann, London, 1958–1959.

Davide A. Secci. Ovid Met. 9.1–97: Through the eyes of Achelous. *Greece & Rome*, 56: 34–54, 2009.

Alexander Sens. A Beggarly boxer: Theocritus Idyll 22.134. *Harvard Studies in Classical Philology*, 96:123–126, 1994.

Alexander Sens. *Theocritus, Dioscuri (Idyll 22): Introduction, Text, and Commentary*, volume 114 of *Hypomnemata*. Vandenhoeck & Ruprecht, Göttingen, 1997.

D. R. Shackleton Bailey. *Statius. Thebaid, Volume I: Thebaid: Books 1–7*. Loeb Classical Library 207. Harvard University Press, Cambridge, MA, 2004.

Otto Skutsch. *The Annals of Quintus Ennius*. Oxford University Press, Oxford, 1985.

R. R. R. Smith. *Hellenistic Royal Portraits*. Oxford, Oxford University Press, 1988.

Eric Teyssier. *La mort en face: le dossier gladiateurs*. Actes Sud, Arles, 2009.

J. C. Thomas. *Boxing's Dirty Tricks and Outlaw Killer Punches*. Loompanics Unlimited, Port Townsend, WA, 1997.

R. F. Thomas. Two problems in Theocritus (Id. 5.49, 22.66). *Harvard Studies in Classical Philology*, 95:251–256, 1993.

Alexander Thomson. *Suetonius. The Lives of the Twelve Cæsars*. Gebbie, Philadelphia, 1889.

Jean-Paul Thuillier. *Les Jeux Athlétiques dans la Civilisation Étrusque*. École Française de Rome, Rome, 1985.

Jean-Paul Thuillier. Stace: Thébaïde 6, les jeux funèbres et les réalités sportives. *Nikephoros*, 9:151–167, 1996.

Jean-Paul Thuillier. Scène de boxe sur un bas-relief inédit de Gaule Narbonnaise: réflexions sur le ceste romain. *Journal of Roman Archaeology*, 32:495–504, 2019.

M. Valero Tévar. The late-antique villa at Noheda (Villar de Domingo García) near Cuenca and its mosaics. *Journal of Roman Archæology*, 26:307–330, 2013.

J. A. Van Voorhis. Two portrait statues of boxers and the culture of athletics in the 3rd c. AD. In C. Ratté and R. R. R. Smith, editors, *Aphrodisias Papers 4: New Research on the City and its Monuments*, pages 230–252. Journal of Roman Archæology, Portsmouth, RI, 2008. Supplement 70.

Berenice Verhelst. Minor characters in the Dionysiaca. In Domenico Accorinti, editor, *Brill's Companion to Nonnus of Panopolis*, pages 152–172. Brill, Leiden, 2016.

David Vessey. *Statius and the Thebaid*. Cambridge University Press, Cambridge, 2010.

Francis Vian. Μάρτυς chez Nonnos de Panopolis: étude de sémantique et de chronologie. *Revue des Études Grecques*, 110:143–160, 1997.

Francis Vian. Echoes and imitations of Apollonius Rhodius in late Greek epic. In Theodore D. Papanghelis and Antonios Rengakos, editors, *Brill's Companion to Apollonius Rhodius*, pages 387–411. Brill, Leiden, 2008. 2nd Ed.

G. Ville. Les jeux des gladiateurs dans l'Empire chrétien. *Mélanges de l'école française de Rome*, 72:273–335, 1960.

J. H. Vince. *Demosthenes. Demosthenes*. Harvard University Press, Cambridge, MA, 1930.

H. B. Walters, E. J. Forsdyke, and C. H. Smith. *Catalogue of Vases in the British Museum*. British Museum Publishing, London, 1893–1925. 3 vols.

Arthur S. Way. *Quintus Smyrnæus. The Fall of Troy*. G. P. Putnam's Sons, New York, 1913.

David West. The End and the meaning: *Æneid* 12.791–842. In Hans-Peter Stahl, editor, *Vergil's Æneid: Augustan Epic and Political Context*, pages 303–318. Duckworth, London, 1998.

Thomas E. J. Wiedemann. *Emperors and Gladiators*. Routledge, London, 1992.

Phyllis L. Williams. Note on the interpretation of the Ficoroni Cista. *American Journal of Archaeology*, 49(3):348–352, 1945a.

Phyllis L. Williams. Amykos and the dioskouroi. *American Journal of Archæology*, 49:330–347, 1945b.

R. D. Williams. *P. Vergili Maronis Æneidos Liber Quintus*. Clarendon Press, Oxford, 1960.

Robert Deryck Williams. *P. Vergili Maronis Aeneidos. Liber Quintus*. Oxford University Press, Oxford, 2015.

Theodore C. Williams. *The Æneid of Virgil*. Houghton Mifflin, Boston, MA, 1908.

Fikret Yegül. *Bathing in the Roman World*. Cambridge University Press, Cambridge, 2010.

John W. Zarker. The Hercules theme in the 'Æneid'. *Vergilius*, 18:34–48, 1972.

John Zilcosky. Wrestling, or the art of disentangling bodies. In John Zilcosky and Marlo A. Burks, editors, *The Allure of Sports in Western Culture*, pages 79–118. University of Toronto Press, Toronto, 2019.

Andrew Zissos. Spectacle and elite in the Argonautica of Valerius Flaccus. In A. J. Boyle and W. J. Dominik, editors, *Flavian Rome: Culture, Image, Text*, pages 659–684. Brill, Leiden, 2003.

Changelog

- ~2023.6.26 First public release.
- ~2023.7.8 Repagination in anticipation of printing.
- ~2023.10.04 Minor proofreading edits.